LAWS OF EVIDENCE

P9-DID-739

DELMAR CENGAGE Learning

Options.

Over 300 products in every area of the law: textbooks, online courses, CD-ROMs, reference books, companion websites, and more – helping you succeed in the classroom and on the job.

Support.

We offer unparalleled, practical support: robust instructor and student supplements to ensure the best learning experience, custom publishing to meet your unique needs, and other benefits such as Delmar Cengage Learning's Student Achievement Award. And our sales representatives are always ready to provide you with dependable service.

Feedback.

As always, we want to hear from you! Your feedback is our best resource for improving the quality of our products. Contact your sales representative or write us at the address below if you have any comments about our materials or if you have a product proposal.

Accounting and Financials for the Law Office • Administrative Law • Alternative Dispute Resolution • Bankruptcy Business Organizations/Corporations • Careers and Employment • Civil Litigation and Procedure • CLA Exam Preparation • Computer Applications in the Law Office • Constitutional Law • Contract Law • Court Reporting Criminal Law and Procedure • Document Preparation • Elder Law • Employment Law • Environmental Law • Ethics Evidence Law • Family Law • Health Care Law • Immigration Law • Intellectual Property • Internships Interviewing and Investigation • Introduction to Law • Introduction to Paralegalism • Juvenile Law • Law Office Management • Law Office Procedures • Legal Nurse Consulting • Legal Research, Writing, and Analysis • Legal Terminology • Legal Transcription • Media and Entertainment Law • Medical Malpractice Law Product Liability • Real Estate Law • Reference Materials • Social Security • Sports Law • Torts and Personal Injury Law • Wills, Trusts, and Estate Administration • Workers' Compensation Law

---

DELMAR CENGAGE Learning
5 Maxwell Drive
Clifton Park, New York 12065-2919

For additional information, find us online at:
www.cengage.com/delmar

LAWS OF EVIDENCE

Thomas Buckles, M.A., J.D.
Woodbury College

DELMAR
CENGAGE Learning™

Australia • Brazil • Japan • Korea • Mexico • Singapore • Spain • United Kingdom • United States

Laws of Evidence
Thomas Buckles

Business Unit Executive Director: Susan L. Simpfenderfer

Senior Acquisitions Editor: Joan M. Gill

Editorial Assistant: Lisa Flatley

Executive Production Manager: Wendy A. Troeger

Production Manager: Carolyn Miller

Production Editor: Betty L. Dickson

Executive Marketing Manager: Donna J. Lewis

Channel Manager: Wendy E. Mapstone

Cover Designer: Dutton and Sherman Design

© 2003 Delmar, Cengage Learning

ALL RIGHTS RESERVED. No part of this work covered by the copyright herein may be reproduced, transmitted, stored or used in any form or by any means graphic, electronic, or mechanical, including but not limited to photocopying, recording, scanning, digitizing, taping, Web distribution, information networks, or information storage and retrieval systems, except as permitted under Section 107 or 108 of the 1976 United States Copyright Act, without the prior written permission of the publisher.

For product information and technology assistance, contact us at **Cengage Learning Customer & Sales Support, 1-800-354-9706**

For permission to use material from this text or product, submit all requests online at **www.cengage.com/permissions**
Further permissions questions can be emailed to **permissionrequest@cengage.com**

Library of Congress Control Number: 2002031289

ISBN-13: 978-0-7668-0761-7

ISBN-10: 0-7668-0761-4

Delmar
Executive Woods
5 Maxwell Drive
Clifton Park, NY 12065
USA

Cengage Learning is a leading provider of customized learning solutions with office locations around the globe, including Singapore, the United Kingdom, Australia, Mexico, Brazil, and Japan. Locate your local office at **www.cengage.com/global**

Cengage Learning products are represented in Canada by Nelson Education, Ltd.

To learn more about Delmar, visit **www.cengage.com/delmar**

Purchase any of our products at your local bookstore or at our preferred online store **www.ichapters.com**

Notice to the Reader
Publisher does not warrant or guarantee any of the products described herein or perform any independent analysis in connection with any of the product information contained herein. Publisher does not assume, and expressly disclaims, any obligation to obtain and include information other than that provided to it by the manufacturer. The reader is expressly warned to consider and adopt all safety precautions that might be indicated by the activities described herein and to avoid all potential hazards. By following the instructions contained herein, the reader willingly assumes all risks in connection with such instructions. The publisher makes no representations or warranties of any kind, including but not limited to, the warranties of fitness for particular purpose or merchantability, nor are any such representations implied with respect to the material set forth herein, and the publisher takes no responsibility with respect to such material. The publisher shall not be liable for any special, consequential, or exemplary damages resulting, in whole or part, from the readers' use of, or reliance upon, this material.

Printed in the United States of America
5 6 7 8 9   15 14 13 12 11

FD313

This book is dedicated to Lou Buckles.
"Sunday's coming."

SUMMARY OF CONTENTS

CONTENTS

CHAPTER 4

CHALLENGES TO ADMISSIBILITY OF EVIDENCE   97

CHAPTER 13

EXCEPTIONS TO THE HEARSAY RULE 325

LIST OF EXHIBITS

LIST OF EVIDENTIARY CHECKLISTS

LIST OF CASES

PREFACE

Most law schools tend to prepare aspiring attorneys through the "case" method of study. In contrast, many undergraduate courses generally prepare other legal professionals, including those in paralegal fields who will be directly assisting the attorneys, and those in criminal justice who will be enforcing the laws, through an emphasis on "textbook" study. My purpose in writing this book is to combine these two methods, providing a readable text with interesting cases, a rich comparison of relevant federal and state rules, a wide variety of learning exhibits and features, and helpful evidentiary checklists. The mission of this book is to combine the principles of competency-based learning with the strengthening of essential skills necessary to effectively turn that learning into practice. It is designed for students in paralegal, criminal justice, pre-law, and legal studies; as well as those learners who just want to know more about the laws of evidence.

WHY STUDY EVIDENCE LAW?

Evidence law will teach you what can and cannot be admissible as evidence, and why. The most critical part of any legal action, civil or criminal, is the evidence presented to prove or disprove the facts at issue in the case. Not all evidence, however, is admissible at trial. Numerous laws and rules may exclude or limit evidence, even when that evidence may be important to the case. Success or failure depends on being able to recognize, gather, and present relevant, admissible evidence. Paralegals, investigators, criminal justice and legal personnel alike must all have an understanding of the laws of evidence and the rules they will have to follow in proving or disproving a case.

FEATURES OF THIS BOOK

This book is designed to provide a readable format, written to convey the "excitement" of the law. It is packed full of actual cases, evidentiary checklists, and exhibits to enhance reading and learning, bring the law "to life," and help the reader better understand evidence law and how it is used in the legal system. Chapters examine *what* the law is—providing clear definitions; *where* the law came from—exploring the rich history behind the law; *when* and *how* it is used today—comparing different laws and usage; *who* uses it—the players in the legal process; and *why*—including the public policy reasons behind the law, and how this public policy influences the gathering of evidence.

One of the many unique features of *Laws of Evidence* is the expansive use of interesting and relevant, real-life cases, many drawn from recent headlines. These cases are presented to help students better understand evidentiary rules by seeing how they are applied and analyzing the court's reasoning behind their decision. Another unique feature of *Laws of*

Evidence is the wealth of pedagogical features that emphasize the development and strengthening of essential skills necessary for students using evidence law, and allow for students to apply and practice what they learn.

Presented in a student-friendly, understandable format, each chapter will begin with an outline of what will be covered, along with an **Introduction** to the learning in that chapter. **Definitions** are provided along the margins throughout each chapter. At the end of every chapter, there will be a **Summary**, **Key Terms** section, and the **Web Sites** referred to or recommended.

Competency-Based Learning . . .
Practice-Based Education

This book incorporates both *competency-based learning* and *practice-based education* principles. Each chapter begins by identifying a set of measurable **Learning Outcomes**. These outcomes may be met by demonstrating the **Learning Outcomes and Practice Skills Checklist** at the end of the chapter. To support this learning throughout the book, there are a variety of examples, sample laws from other states, exhibits, and illustrations. To help facilitate an understanding of what is learned, there are thought-provoking questions, case problems, exercises, and practical, hands-on applications in each chapter. These features not only reinforce learning, but also serve to strengthen and help assess competencies and essential skills. Included in each chapter are:

- **Critical Thinking Questions**
- **Legal Analysis and Writing Problems**
- **Legal Research Using the Internet Applications**
- **You Be the Judge Exercises**
- **Advocacy and Communication Skills**
- **Practice Applications**

Critical Thinking Questions challenge students to examine, discuss, and reflect on the laws and legal concepts covered in their readings. *Legal Analysis and Writing* applications require students to apply what they have learned to a case problem using a legal analysis method or analyze a court opinion using a case briefing format. *Legal Research* is emphasized by integrating it with the use of *Internet* skills. Students are given a series of research assignments on the Internet, designed to not only develop their legal research, but their technology skills as well. As an added bonus, many of these assignments ask the student to research and compare his or her own state laws with those studied in the text, ensuring a more rounded understanding of the law, but also a knowledge of the considerable resources available to find out more. Each chapter includes *You Be the Judge* exercises that put the student in the role of the trial judge who has to rule on the admissibility of evidence. The student must then explain the ruling. At the end of every chapter is an *Advocacy and Communication Skills* assignment, calling for students to select a legal issue, then develop and present an oral persuasive argument advocating for one side or the other of the issue. Finally, each chapter has a *Practice Application* that strengthens the student's competencies and skills by requiring students to apply what they have learned in solving a case problem or preparing evidence for trial.

Don't Forget the Appendix

But wait, there's more! Don't forget to look through and use the materials in the Appendix. Here, you will not only find the **Federal Rules of Evidence**, but formats for all of the practical applications used throughout the book, including:

- **IRAC Method of Legal Analysis**
- **How to Brief a Legal Case**
- **Advocacy and Persuasive Arguments**
- **Thinking Law—Thinking Like a Lawyer**

ACKNOWLEDGMENTS

Anyone who works a full-time job and tries to tackle an additional major project, like writing a book (or raising children), can attest to the importance of family support. It is an understatement to say that I could not have written this book without the support and encouragement of my family. My wife, Lou, not only balanced her own job and college teaching, but was my "guardian" and best friend throughout this whole process—ensuring me the time to write without too many distractions. One of those distractions, my son, Cris, called or visited every night to offer motivating words of encouragement and to ask about my progress ("Are you done yet?"). I probably could have completed this book much sooner if he hadn't called so much . . . but I love him for it. My wonderful daughter-in-law, Bethany, should get a medal for her patience and ability to plan our family get-togethers around my writing schedule. A very special thank you goes to four little grand, no, GREAT kids! Thank you, Laura, Cristopher, Jacob, and Jessica, for your patience with me while I was working. I love you all and will try my best to make up for all I have missed with you over the past few months—especially the reading and sledding. Thanks to my sister-in-law, Maureen Currier, who worked on the original draft some years ago when I first began gathering material for an evidence course. It was her idea to turn this into a book. Here it is, Mo. Thanks to the paralegal students and all of the staff at Woodbury College in Montpelier, Vermont—one of the leaders in competency-based learning and putting learning into "action." Thanks also to the Community College of Vermont for allowing me time to complete this book.

I want to acknowledge acquisition editor Joan Gill and editorial assistant Lisa Flatley for their belief in this project, and especially for their patience in seeing it through. A special acknowledgment and thank you goes to editor Diane Colwyn for working with me during the months of revisions. She was always there to offer suggestions and encouragement. Without her helpful and motivating attitude, this book would never have been completed. Thanks to production editor Betty Dickson for guiding me through the production phase of this project, and a special thank you to Mary Jo Graham and Terry Routley of Carlisle Publishers Services for their keen eyes and excellent proofing of all my writing errors.

Finally, my appreciation goes to the following reviewers who braved the very "rough" first draft of this book, providing valuable comments and suggestions that were incorporated in this final version:

Elizabeth Church
Lake Superior State University

Allan Fork
El Camino College

Lisa Hunter
New York City Technical College

Judith M. Maloney
Long Island University/C. W. Post Legal Studies Institute

Brian J. McCully
Fresno City College

Gloria McPherson
Auburn University

Mike Rayboun
University of West Florida

Robert Reeback
Albuquerque Technical-Vocational Institute

Cases and Statutes

I would like to acknowledge and thank Delmar Group for allowing me to reprint portions of selected cases, statutes, and evidentiary rules from Westlaw statutes and evidentiary rules, the Delmar Reporters, and other Delmar sources, all reprinted with permission.

The new Connecticut rules notwithstanding, statutes and rules used were current as of this writing. However, as with any law, please check for changes before use.

Your Help is Appreciated

In this first edition, I have probably included too much information for some topics and not enough for others. I welcome your suggestions, requests, and comments on how I can continue to improve this book. You may contact me at buckles@sover.net

NATURE AND DEVELOPMENT OF EVIDENCE LAW

"Evidence is the basis of justice."

— *Jeremy Bentham, English Philosopher (1749–1832)*

"One cannot understand where a nation and its laws are, and where they are headed, without a good understanding of what has gone on before."

— *Savigny, Of the Vocation of Our Age for Legislation and Jurisprudence (1814)*

LEARNING OUTCOMES

In this chapter, you will learn about the following legal concepts:

- What Is Evidence?
- The Nature of Evidence Law
- Why We Have Evidence Law
- Where Evidence Law Comes From
- Development of Adversary System
- Development of Jury System
- Development of Common Laws of Evidence
- Development of Statutory Laws of Evidence
- Where Evidence Law is Found Today

INTRODUCTION

This chapter will examine the nature and development of evidence law. We will look at what evidence law is and why it is so important to our system of justice, both civil and criminal. We will learn how the presentation of evidence is essential to the search for truth in a legal proceeding. The trier of fact, usually the jury, must be able to hear and examine relevant evidence in order to render a just decision. However, a visitor to our courts may not understand why, if we are really searching for the truth, certain relevant evidence is excluded from trial. The jury may never get to see or know about this relevant evidence. How can this help in the "search for truth?" To answer this important question, it will also be necessary for us to look at where our evidence law came from and how it has developed over the years to the set of rules in use today. The famous Supreme Court jurist, Oliver Wendell Holmes, once said that the "life of the law has not been logic: it has been experience . . . . In order to know what it is, we must know what it has been, and what it tends to becomes."[1] In this chapter, we will examine what evidence law "has been and what it tends to become."

WHAT IS EVIDENCE?

Evidence
Anything that tends to prove or disprove a fact at issue in a legal action.

Evidence is anything that tends to prove or disprove a fact at issue in a legal action. It involves the offering of alleged proof through testimony or objects at court proceedings in order to persuade the trier of fact about an issue in dispute.

Over 200 years ago, Sir William Blackstone illustrated this definition, saying that evidence is "that which demonstrates, makes clear or ascertains the truth of the very fact or point in issue . . . on one side or other."[2] An 1889 state court decision held that "[t]he word evidence is applied to that which renders evident; and is defined to be any matter of fact, the effect, tendency, or design of which is to produce in the mind a persuasion, affirmative or disaffirmative, of the existence of some other matter of fact."[3] Modern state laws support these definitions. For example, California defines evidence as "testimony, writings, material objects, or other things presented to the senses that are offered to prove the existence or nonexistence of a

LEGAL ANALYSIS AND WRITING 1.1

Plaintiff is suing Defendant, claiming that Defendant intentionally drove through Plaintiff's property, causing damage. At trial, Plaintiff seeks to introduce evidence that Defendant had a prior conviction for reckless driving with property damage that was similar in nature to what happened to Plaintiff's property. Defendant's attorney says, "Objection, your honor. What defendant may have done before doesn't constitute evidence in *this* matter."

The following questions are based on the format shown in the Appendix for the *IRAC method of legal analysis.* Use this format, and the previous definition for *evidence,* as your rule to solve the above case problem:

1. What is the issue here?
2. What is the rule that covers this issue?
3. Analyze and apply the rule to the facts shown for this case in order to reach a conclusion.
4. State your conclusion.

fact."[4] Kansas defines it as the "means from which inferences may be drawn as a basis of proof in duly constituted judicial or fact-finding tribunals, and includes testimony in the form of opinion, and hearsay."[5]

Evidence can include almost anything submitted to the jury or trier of fact for consideration. It can be offered in many forms, from someone's own testimony to material objects, charts, photographs, recordings, documents, and other types of physical evidence.

THE NATURE OF EVIDENCE LAW

Evidence law is a body of rules that helps to govern conduct and determines what will be admissible in certain legal proceedings and trials. Evidence law developed from common law and can be found today in statutes, case law, and the Constitution. The study of evidence law can teach you what can and cannot be admitted at trial and why.

Evidence Law
Body of rules that helps to govern conduct and determines what will be admissible in certain legal proceedings and trials.

WHY WE HAVE EVIDENCE LAW

Evidence law developed in response to the common law evolution of the adversary system and the emergence of the jury. Rules were created to ensure efficiency and fairness in the adversary process while protecting the jury from prejudicial, unreliable, confusing, or irrelevant evidence. These rules of evidence promote the search for truth in a trial by determining what is relevant and admissible. In that search, courts have agreed that "the pertinent general principle, responding to the deepest needs of society, is that society is entitled to every man's evidence. As an underlying aim of judicial inquiry is ascertainable truth, everything rationally related to ascertaining the truth is presumptively admissible. Limitations are properly placed upon the operation of this general principle only to the very limited extent that permitting a refusal to testify or excluding relevant evidence has a public good transcending the normally predominant principle of utilizing all rational means for ascertaining truth."[6] Evidence law promotes the search for truth.

As the previous quote illustrates, the "underlying aim of judicial inquiry is ascertainable truth." The Georgia code emphasizes this with the statement that the "object of all legal investigation is the discovery of truth. The rules of evidence are framed with a view to this prominent end, seeking always for pure sources and the highest evidence."[7]

The Search for Truth Balanced with Public Policy

As we will examine more closely in later chapters, this search for truth must sometimes be balanced with public policy interests, which may limit the ascertainment of truth. Public policy interests include protecting the jury from prejudicial, misleading, or unreliable evidence; protecting certain societal relationships and confidential communications; and ensuring the smooth operation of justice by promoting efficient use of proceedings and excluding evidence which might cause confusion or a waste of time. In all of these cases evidence, even when relevant, might be excluded in order to "promote broader public interests in the observance of law and administration of justice."[8] Some examples of this include the exclusion of relevant evidence when it is found to be hearsay, prejudicial, or a privileged communication.

CRITICAL THINKING QUESTIONS 1.1

1. Should we have rules that exclude relevant evidence at trial, or should we allow any evidence, especially if one side to a dispute believes this information is important in presenting his or her case? Explain your reasons.

2. How can we balance public policy interests with the goal of determining the truth in a legal dispute?

YOU BE THE JUDGE 1.1

Jane is suing her doctor for malpractice in negligently performing an operation on her which caused further harm. Jane wants to introduce evidence at the trial that the doctor had malpractice insurance with a very high policy amount.

1. Does this constitute evidence in this matter?
2. Do you believe that it should be admitted? Explain your reasons.

Common Law
Case law; A uniform set of laws for a state or country based on court decisions.

Circuit Court
From "riding the circuit," a judge that travels around holding court sessions in different areas.

Precedent
A court decision that serves as a rule of law or standard to be looked at in deciding subsequent cases.

Stare Decisis
"Let the decision stand." A legal doctrine holding that a court should apply a principle which has already been decided to all later cases with similar facts.

WHERE EVIDENCE LAW COMES FROM

Although greatly shaped and influenced by many ancient laws, civilizations, and religions, our rules of evidence, like much of our law in the United States, stems from the English common law (see Exhibit 1.1).

Common Law of England

In A.D. 1066, William conquered England and then set out to end the fragmented feudal system by establishing a **common law** or uniform set of rules for the entire country. He created **circuit courts** and had his judges travel from county to county to hear and settle disputes. The judges wrote their important decisions in a yearbook called the *Curia Regis* and used these decisions as **precedents** to be followed in similar cases.

Common law was based on the decisions of judges and led to the principle of **stare decisis**, or "let the decision stand." This legal doctrine held that when a court has decided a case by applying a legal principle to a set of facts, courts should stick by that principle and apply it to all later cases with similar facts. This doctrine became the cornerstone of English and American legal systems.

CRITICAL THINKING QUESTIONS 1.2

1. Identify some major U.S. Supreme Court cases that have established legal precedents.
2. Explain the precedents that were established by these cases and whether they still remain as legal rules today.

Other Primary Legal Systems

Common law originated in England and affects approximately 30 percent of the world's population. It can be found in such countries as

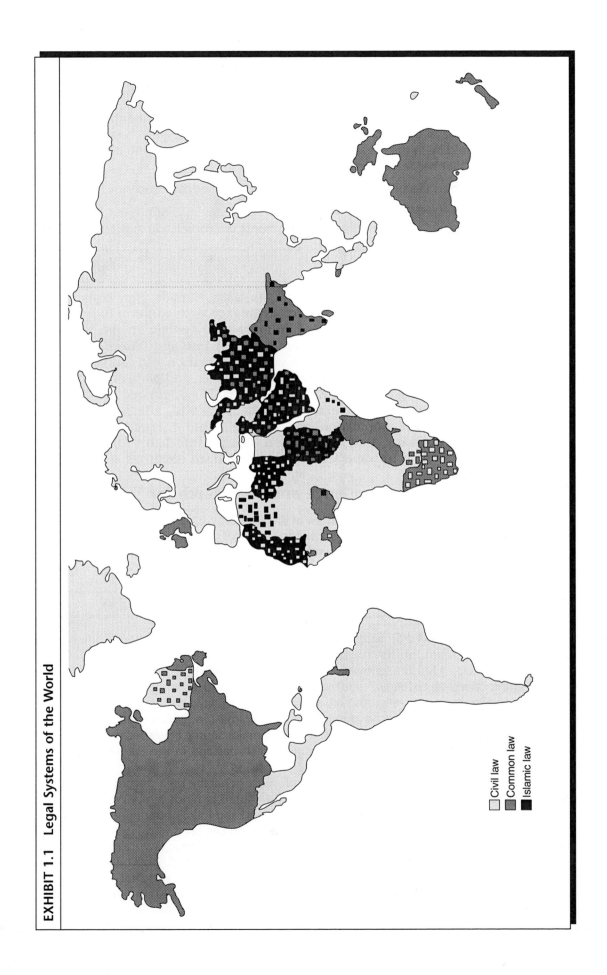

EXHIBIT 1.1 Legal Systems of the World

☐ Civil law
▨ Common law
■ Islamic law

5

LEGAL RESEARCH USING THE INTERNET SKILLS 1.1

Want to find out more about those famous Supreme Court cases you identified that established legal precedents? Check out one of the legal research web sites below and use their "Search" feature to find the case you are interested in. In the "Search" field, enter the case name or, if you do not know the case name, use "Keywords" that will search for the issues of interest to you.

FindLaw U.S. Supreme Court Decisions (http://www.findlaw.com/casecode/supreme.html)

U.S. Supreme Court (http://www.supremecourtus.gov/)

Supreme Court Collection of Cornell Law School (http://supct.law.cornell.edu/supct/)

Civil Law
World's leading legal system; based on Roman law and Napoleonic Code; relies on judge or magistrate to conduct an investigation, gather evidence, question witnesses, and determine facts.

Islamic Law
A legal system based on divine revelation as revealed by God to His Prophet Mohammed.

England, the United States, Australia, Canada, New Zealand, and various parts of the Far East, such as Singapore. In addition to the Common law, there are several other primary legal systems in the world today. (see Exhibit 1.1) Two of these are **Civil law** and **Islamic law.** Islamic law affects 20 percent of the world's population and can be found in over 40 countries, including Iran, Saudi Arabia, and parts of Africa, Afghanistan, and Pakistan. (see Exhibit 1.2) Civil law originated in France and Italy. It is the primary legal system in the world, affecting 50 percent of the world's population and can be found in such countries as France, Germany, Italy, Switzerland, Austria, and Latin American countries, as well as in some Arab and North African countries. (see Exhibit 1.3)

Laws of Evidence and the Search for Truth

As pointed out earlier, evidence involves the search for, and ascertainment of, truth through some form of legal proceeding or trial. Almost all societies have some type of laws or rules in place for this process. Years ago, Supreme

---

EXHIBIT 1.2   Islamic Legal System

Islamic law developed in the Middle East during the 7th century. It is based upon divine revelation, as revealed by God (called *Allah*), to His Prophet Mohammed (also spelled as Muhammad). Islam means "submission" and directs its Muslim followers to submit or surrender to God's will. Islamic law is known as *Shari'a*, meaning "the path to follow," and establishes a moral and legal code of conduct for Muslims. The *Shari'a* has sections to cover religious law, personal law, civil law, and criminal law. The *Koran* (or *Quran*), a book similar to the Bible, is the primary source of Islamic law, which contains the word of God as revealed by the Angel Gabriel to Mohammed. A second major source of Islamic law is the *Sunna*. This text contains the words and teachings of Mohammed. Each passage in the Sunna is referred to as a *Hadith* and explains the requirements of the Koran.

The judge in Islamic law is called a qadi. The qadi must generally be a devout male Muslim, held accountable to Allah in the performance of his duties. The Koran reminds him, "We have set thee as a viceroy in the earth, therefore, judge aright between mankind and follow not desire that it beguile thee away from the way of Allah." The qadi presides over legal proceedings and limits evidence to three types that are considered to possess a high degree of reliability in Islamic law: religious oaths, eyewitness testimony, and confessions. Testimony begins with the phrase *ashhadu* or "I bear witness," emphasizing that the witness is testifying as to matters he actually witnessed and that he is certain of the truthfulness of the evidence he will give. Contrary to the common law system where there are many exceptions, hearsay in Islamic legal proceedings is inadmissible in any form.

EXHIBIT 1.3   The Civil Law System

Civil law traces its roots to the Roman Empire and bases its system on written legal codes stemming originally from the *Corpus Juris Civilus* (Body of Civil Law) as published by the Roman Emperor, Justinian, around A.D. 528. This extensive set of laws was later used as the basis for the legal systems in France, Italy, Spain, and Germany. The civil law system, which was later modified by the Napoleonic Code of the early 1800s, looks to statutory or codified laws for legal proceedings and relies on a judge or magistrate to determine what evidence is admissible or inadmissible. Civil law is still followed today in France and throughout most of Europe, South America, and Quebec. In the United States, this system can still be found to some extent in Louisiana as a result of its French ancestry.

Court Justice Sutherland pointed out that "The fundamental basis upon which all rules of evidence must rest—if they are to rest upon reason—is their adaptation to the successful development of the truth. And, since experience is of all teachers the most dependable, and since experience also is a continuous process, it follows that a rule of evidence at one time thought necessary to the ascertainment of the truth should yield to the experience of a succeeding generation whenever that experience has clearly demonstrated the fallacy or unwisdom of the old rule."[9]

Throughout history, cultures have struggled to find the right methods and procedures in this ascertainment of truth.

Code of Hammurabi

One of the earliest known rules of formal law was established around 1750 B.C. by Hammurabi, the prince of Babylonia. Called the **Hammurabi Code**, it was believed to have been of divine origin, given to the prince by the gods with the mandate to "establish justice, . . . and to hold back the strong from oppressing the feeble." Written in stone, the laws were extremely comprehensive, covering every subject from civil law to criminal offenses and evidence.

Hammurabi Code
One of the earliest known sets of formal laws, established around 1750 B.C. by Hammurabi, prince of Babylonia.

In its attempt to ascertain the truth, this code established certain rules for the admissibility of evidence, as shown by the following translated excerpts:

2. If one brings an accusation against another, let the accused go to the river and leap into the river. If the accused sinks in the river his accuser shall take possession of his house. But if the river prove that the accused is not guilty, and he escape unhurt, then the accuser shall be put to death, while he who leaped into the river shall take possession of the house that had belonged to his accuser.
...
3. If one brings an accusation before the elders, and does not *prove* what he has charged, he shall, if it be a capital offense charged, be put to death.
...
9. If one loses an article, and finds it in the possession of another—if the person in whose possession the thing is found says, "A merchant sold it to me, I paid for it before witnesses," and if the owner of the thing says, "I will bring witnesses who know my property," then shall the purchaser bring the merchant who sold it to him, and the witnesses before whom he bought it, and the owner shall bring witnesses who can identify his property. The judge shall examine their testimony—both of the witnesses before whom the price was paid and of the witnesses who identify the lost article on oath. If the merchant is then proved to be a thief, he shall be put to death. The owner of the

lost article receives his property, and he who bought it receives the money he paid from the estate of the merchant.

10. If the purchaser does not bring the merchant and the witnesses before whom he bought the article, but its owner brings witnesses who identify it, then the buyer is the thief and shall be put to death, and the owner receives the lost article.[10]

CRITICAL THINKING QUESTIONS 1.3

1. What are the evidentiary features of the previous excerpts from the Code of Hammurabi?

2. One of the Code's laws (#196) stated: *If a man put out the eye of another man, his eye shall be put out.* Where else do we see the influence of this?

Trial by Ordeal

Trial by Ordeal
The earliest-known form of trial, where a defendant was cast into the holy river while tied down by rocks. Sinking usually meant guilt. Other variations of ordeal included being boiled in oil and burned at the stake.

As shown by the Hammurabi Code, most early searches for, and ascertainment of, truth in legal proceedings involved the belief that an all-powerful God could ultimately decide the evidence presented and whether someone was telling the truth, which would also determine the fate of the accused. In the belief that God would always take the side of the innocent, the accused or defendant would be tied and weighted down with rocks and thrown into the "holy river." Evidence and proof involving the issues of fact were shown by divine intervention. If the defendant was innocent, he or she would not sink and drown.

This was called **trial by ordeal**, and it lasted for several thousand years before finally ending in the early 13th century when the Church decided to use the inquisitorial method to conduct trials. (see Exhibit 1.4 for development of Civil and Common Law after this.)

EXHIBIT 1.4   How Civil Law and Common Law Developed

Around 1215, the Catholic Church decided that their priests could no longer sanction trial by ordeal. Instead, the Church went on in 1233 to authorize *Papal Inquisition* to deal with heresy. This practice by the Catholic Church, along with its reliance on principles of Canon and Roman civil law, influenced France and much of Europe and Latin America to develop the civil law for its legal system and the inquisitorial method as a trial procedure. This system relied on a central judge or magistrate to oversee the investigation of a legal dispute, to collect evidence, and to question witnesses. In these civil law systems, there was confidence that the judges were qualified to sift through what was relevant and what should be admissible as evidence. With its reliance on judges and on the codified principles of the civil law, this system did not make extensive use of juries and therefore had little need for formal rules of evidence.

However, when the Church and the rest of Europe were moving toward an inquisitorial method in the 13th century, England was beginning to adopt the *adversary system* and use a *jury* in its trial process. This was all part of the evolving common law system, which relied more on court decisions than written codes. Since the system was dependent on a lay jury who did not have legal training, rules were needed to help guide and protect both the jury and the legal process.

Today, the common law countries still rely on the adversary system and the jury. Although statutes and codes are used, court decisions are still relied upon to interpret the law and determine whether a law is constitutional. In civil law countries, juries are used and courts do some interpretation of laws, but the emphasis is still on the written codes and the reliance of a judge to obtain and weigh the evidence.

Trial by Battle

To supplement the trial by ordeal, the **trial by battle** was adopted in England in the 11th century. Again believing that God was on the innocent's side and would not let the guilty be victorious, determinations of truth and evidence in legal proceedings were decided by a contest or fight between the two opposing parties (the accused and the accuser, or the plaintiff and the defendant) called *contestants*. The victor was the innocent or prevailing party and won the case.

As this method evolved, the parties involved in a legal dispute were allowed to hire others to fight for them. These hired fighters were known as *champions* or *advocates*.

Trial by Battle
Legal disputes were resolved through a contest or fight between the opposing parties. The victor won the case.

CRITICAL THINKING QUESTIONS 1.4

1. Compare and contrast the civil law and common law systems.
2. What do you see as the strengths and weaknesses of each?

DEVELOPMENT OF THE ADVERSARY SYSTEM

As the trial by battle evolved, the only people actually doing battle were the hired champions or advocates, who would face off against each other in an adversarial contest. In the beginning of these contests, the victor was determined through an actual fight or battle, usually to the death of one of the adversaries. Later, these battles became more controlled by rules established by the judges to ensure a just competition. In these battles, the focus began to be on the rules and fairness of the *process*, and not just by whether one adversary won or lost.

The trial by battle led to what has become known as the **adversary system** of justice, with the belief that only *out of controlled battle would the truth emerge*. The adversary system, although much evolved by the emergence of the jury system and common law, is still at the center of the American legal process today.

Commenting on the importance of evidence law within the adversary system, the Supreme Court has stated that "We have elected to employ an adversary system . . . in which the parties contest all issues before a court of law. The need to develop all relevant facts in the adversary system is both fundamental and comprehensive. The ends of . . . justice would be defeated if judgments were to be founded on a partial or speculative presentation of the facts. The very integrity of the judicial system and public confidence in the system depend on full disclosure of all the facts, within the framework of the rules of evidence."[11]

Over the years, that "framework" of evidence rules became necessary to ensure the "control" in the "controlled battle" of the adversary system. With the judge as referee, rules of evidence developed to keep the adversarial process fair and orderly, which became even more important with the emergence of the jury system.

Adversary System
Parties to a legal dispute face off against each other and contest all issues before a court of law, under the legal maxim that *out of controlled battle would the truth emerge.*

Jury
A body of persons, usually 6 to 12, sworn to hear the facts of a case presented at trial.

Writ of Novel Disseisin
Administrative order issued by the king to dispossess a subject of property or to settle a dispute over land and taxes.

Writ
Written order by a court, instructing someone to either do or cease doing something.

DEVELOPMENT OF THE JURY SYSTEM

The **jury** system began to evolve in England in 1166, when Henry II issued the **Writ of Novel Disseisin**. This **writ**, or administrative order from the king, called for 12 knights to be sworn in as a jury to settle civil disputes over land and taxes. Criminal cases were still being settled at that time through trial by ordeal or battle. Early in the 13th century, when the Catholic Church stopped sanctioning the trial by battle, England looked to the same jury as was used under the *Novel Disseisin* to also hear criminal cases. Later in the 13th century, trial by jury became the standard in England for the ascertainment of truth in both civil and criminal proceedings.

Trial by Informed Jury

In the beginnings of the jury system, jurors were selected who had personal knowledge of the dispute or charges. Later, jury members were expected to conduct a separate inquiry and investigation on their own to determine the truth of the matters asserted. Today, part of this procedure has been incorporated into the **grand jury** system.

Trial by Oath Helpers

Part of the procedure for conducting an inquiry by the informed jury included a **wager of law**, which involved a witness (or one submitting proof of a matter) taking an oath as to its truth. Individuals were called as "oath helpers." These individuals would testify as to the reputation of the witness in the community for honesty. They did not testify about the facts at issue or the statement of the witness, but only to the witness' reputation for honesty. A form of this method is still used today to present evidence of reputation.

Trial by Uninformed, Impartial Jury

By the 16th century, a complete role-reversal for the jury had developed. By then, it was believed that the truth could be ascertained and a fair trial maintained only if the matters or issues in the case did not bias the jury. Jurors were selected from a cross-section of the community who would make their decision of fact based only on the evidence that was presented and what was heard from witnesses who testified under oath in their presence.

Jury Independence

In 1670, a case was decided which established the principle of *jury independence*. After being instructed by the judge to only regard evidence presented by the prosecution, a London jury went ahead and acquitted William Penn of unlawful assembly. The judge became so mad that he imprisoned the jury. On a **writ of habeas corpus**, the chief judge held that a jury was free to reach their own verdict based on the evidence and not be a "rubber stamp" of the prosecution or government. This case clearly established the independence of the jury to decide issues of fact, and reinforced the need for more structure in what evidence they would be allowed to hear and how that evidence would be treated.[12]

Grand Jury
A body of community members responsible for determining whether probable cause exists to bind an accused over for criminal prosecution.

Wager of Law
When a witness, or one submitting proof of a matter, takes an oath pledging its truth.

Writ of Habeas Corpus
Meaning "You have the body," this writ is used to order a person detaining another to produce the person detained and explain why that person is being detained.

CRITICAL THINKING QUESTIONS 1.5

1. What are the strengths and weaknesses of using the jury system to decide disputes?
2. Should we keep our jury system or have cases tried only before a judge? Explain your reasons.
3. Is it really possible to find an uninformed, unbiased jury? A jury of your peers?
4. Did O. J. Simpson have an uninformed jury? Timothy McVeigh?
5. What trials can you name that may not have been decided by an uninformed, unbiased jury?

DEVELOPMENT OF COMMON LAWS OF EVIDENCE

The Common law originated in England to establish, through court decisions, a uniform set of rules and laws. As this common law evolved, so did the use of the Adversary system as the means for contesting legal disputes. The jury system developed to help settle these legal contests. Together, these new systems influenced the development of Common laws of evidence.

Influence of Adversary and Jury Systems

The adversary and jury systems created a need for the establishment of guidelines and rules to assure their efficiency and fairness. The adversarial process was based on the concept that *out of a controlled battle emerged the truth*, but how would this "battle" be controlled? How far should these adversaries go and what evidence should they be allowed to present to prove their case? It had been decided that jurors had to be uninformed and impartial. However, this gave rise to fear and mistrust that these jurors, being unskilled in the law, would be unable to distinguish irrelevant, unreliable, or misleading evidence. This, in turn, could unduly influence their factfinding and verdict.

Rules Established for Guidelines and Procedures

As a result of these concerns, rules were developed to establish guidelines for proper trial and evidentiary procedure, and to exclude evidence that was improper. These rules were established through court decisions that became part of the common law. Some of the earliest examples of these rules were those developed to protect **privileged communications**. These privileges were recognized by the courts "to protect those interpersonal relationships which are highly valued by society and peculiarly vulnerable to deterioration should their necessary component of privacy be continually disregarded by courts of law."[13] Attorney-client privilege, for example, can be traced back to Roman law, and is the oldest form of evidentiary privilege known in the common law.

Privileged Communication
A confidential communication that is in the best interests of society to protect. An evidentiary privilege allows a witness to refuse to give testimony or the right to prevent someone else from testifying on the same matter.

Common Law Followed in America

The English common law of evidence was brought over and followed to a great extent in colonial America. However, American rules of evidence went much further than English law. There was growing mistrust of the influence of English government over American courts in the colonies. This resulted in the rapid development of common law rules in the 17th and 18th centuries to ensure that evidence presented to the jury was relevant and material, and not offered second-hand or as hearsay. After America won its independence and established a Constitution, the protections afforded individual rights resulted in even greater limitations on the use of evidence in American courts. Today, American rules of evidence are far more restrictive and exclusionary than those in England.

CRITICAL THINKING QUESTIONS 1.6

1. What other special "relationships" can you think of that have a level of confidentiality which should be protected through evidence law?
2. What aspect of these relationships are "highly valued by society and peculiarly vulnerable to deterioration should their necessary component of privacy be continually disregarded"?

3. Is there ever any justification for suspending the limitations and restrictions afforded by the rules of evidence (in the investigation or prosecution of the World Trade Center terrorist attacks, for example)?

DEVELOPMENT OF STATUTORY LAWS OF EVIDENCE

For hundreds of years, evidence laws were found only in the common law. Eventually, a need developed to have the multitude of complex common laws of evidence in an easy to find, uniform set of statutory rules. As a result, during the 1960s and 1970s, most states and the federal courts codified much of the common law evidence and developed a uniform set of evidence rules.

Part of Procedural Law

Substantive Law
Defines the law, providing elements and sanctions.

Procedural Law
Rules that set forth legal process and tell us how to enforce the law.

Laws, in general, are either **substantive law** or **procedural law**. That is, they either provide us with a definition and elements of a particular law or they provide us with rules to tell us how to enforce the law. Evidence law can be substantive in nature. For example, the substantive use of unreliable evidence is generally not admissible at trial. It can, however, be used to discredit a witness. We will see this concept more in later chapters. For the most part, evidence law is considered a part of procedural law. It provides us with rules, which instruct us in how to determine the admissibility and use of evidence in court proceedings. It also provides rules of conduct and procedures for all officers of the court, paralegals, and other legal and law enforcement personnel on how they should investigate, gather, and present evidence.

Need for Uniform Set of Rules

Statutory or legislated rules were developed in response to the numerous exceptions which arose under common law interpretations of evidentiary issues. As judges ruled more and more on the complexity of evidence laws, changing their interpretations and former rules, it became necessary to clarify these numerous exceptions and create a uniform set of statutory rules of evidence.

One of the early proponents for a uniform evidence code was the distinguished legal scholar, Dean Wigmore. In 1909, Dean Wigmore proposed a long and theoretical model for an evidence code that was often cited, but rarely adopted.[14] In 1945, a legal think tank, the American Law Institute, drafted a controversial *Model Code of Evidence* which was also lengthy, even more complex, and never adopted by any state. In 1953, the original Uniform Rules of Evidence were drafted by the National Conference of Commissioners on Uniform State Laws. It took some of the rules from the Model Code, but simplified them. The Uniform Rules were adopted in several states and later influenced the drafting of the Federal Rules. In 1965, California enacted a new evidence code based in part on the Uniform Rules. The California code also influenced the Federal Rules. In 1972, after years of study, the U.S. Supreme Court drafted the *Rules of Evidence for United States Courts*. In 1974, the Uniform Rules of Evidence were revised to reflect the newly proposed Federal Rules, and on July 1, 1975, Congress enacted the new Federal Rules of Evidence into law.

Why It Took So Long to Enact

These statutory rules of evidence developed far later than some of our other uniform rules (for example, torts or the Uniform Commercial Code). Like the making of most law, the answer to these delays lies in the competing interests and different opinions as to what a model code of evidence should look like. There is also a strong resistance among some states to adopt any uniform code that did not originate in their own jurisdiction. When the Supreme Court of Massachusetts rejected the Federal Rules, part of the reason they gave was that ". . . promulgation of rules of evidence would tend to restrict the development of common law principles. . . ." They went on to say that "the Federal Rules of Evidence . . . are, in some instances, less well adapted to the needs of modern trial practice than current Massachusetts law."[15]

LEGAL RESEARCH USING THE INTERNET SKILLS 1.2

1. Go on the Internet and research the Federal Rules of Evidence. See if you can find the notes by the House and Senate Judiciary Committees considering the original proposed rules in 1972. Look through them to ascertain why the rules were not enacted into law until 1974 and whether you find any comments or debate that might help us to understand why not all of the states adopted these Federal Rules.

[*Note:* If you get stuck and are unable to find these rules, see the list of web sites at the end of this chapter. Try to research and find the information on your own, first!]

WHERE EVIDENCE LAW IS FOUND TODAY

Evidence law today is primarily found in state and federal statutory rules. Case law is also an important source for learning how these rules have been interpreted or modified.

Statutory Law

Statutory law includes those laws passed by legislature and codified into rules and evidence codes.

Statutory Law
Laws passed by legislature.

Federal Rules of Evidence

Today, the **Federal Rules of Evidence**, enacted into law by Congress in 1975, are required throughout the federal court system. Although states are not bound by the Federal Rules, most states use these rules as a model for their own codes. Even states that do not completely use the Federal or Uniform Rules use them as standards and principles for their own opinions. The Federal Rules are provided for in Title 28 of the United States Code.

Federal Rules of Evidence
Statutory evidentiary rules used in all federal courts and as a model for most states.

Uniform Rules of Evidence

The **Uniform Rules of Evidence**, published by a National Conference of Commissioners on Uniform State Laws, were originally drafted several years before the Federal Rules and provided a framework which was later used in their development. After the Federal Rules were approved, the Uniform Rules were modified to model the Federal Rules. Today, the Uniform Rules have been adopted or used as a model in the majority of the states.

Uniform Rules of Evidence
Evidence code modeled after Federal Rules and published by the National Conference of Commissioners on Uniform State Laws.

State Evidentiary Rules or Codes

The majority of state evidence codes are based on the Federal or Uniform Rules. Other states, like California, have their own evidence code. As previously mentioned, California preceded and helped to influence the

Federal Rules. There are also a minority of states that still base their rules on common law. However, these states still look to the Federal and Uniform Rules as standards to consider in determining evidentiary issues.

Case Law

Case Law
Judge-made law based on court decisions; term is used today interchangeably with common law.

As described earlier, the rules of evidence evolved from the common law brought over to this country from England. Today, this body of law is more often called *"judge-made"* law or **case law**. Case law is still used if a particular evidentiary statute or issue needs to be clarified or interpreted by an appellate court. The court's decision may change the existing evidence rule or even establish new evidence law. If a statutory law is found by the court to violate a Constitutional provision, the court may overturn the statute.

Constitution

Constitutions contain some principles of law that place a limitation on evidence. For example, in the U.S. Constitution, the Fourth Amendment protects against unreasonable search and seizure. This protection has resulted in rules that exclude illegally obtained evidence from a criminal trial. The Fifth Amendment provides for a privilege against self-incrimination.

LEGAL RESEARCH USING THE INTERNET SKILLS 1.3

1. Use one of the following web sites to find out if your state has adopted the Uniform Rules of Evidence.

Uniform Rules of Evidence locator from LII, with a listing of states that have adopted the URE (http://www.law.cornell.edu/uniform/evidence.html)

Uniform Rules of Evidence (http://www.law.upenn.edu/bll/ulc/fnact99/ure88.htm)

Practice Tip 1.1

Researching Evidence Laws on the Internet
Want some help in finding and researching your state or federal evidence laws? Try visiting one of the following web sites:

Finding State Evidence Codes
An excellent resource for laws, court decisions, and legal resources of all kinds is the Legal Information Institute (LII), Cornell Law School.
(http://www.law.cornell.edu/states/listing.html)
FindLaw is another excellent legal resource for state and federal laws and cases.
(http://guide.lp.findlaw.com/casecode/)
ExpertPages.com, a directory of expert witnesses and consultants, offers a web site with links to many state rules of evidence.
(http://expertpages.com/state_rules_of_evidence.htm)

Finding Federal Rules of Evidence
Most web sites will refer you to the LII (Legal Information Institute) for their searchable copy of the Federal Rules of Evidence:
(http://www.law.cornell.edu/rules/fre/overview.html)
Another excellent resource is a web site created and maintained by Judge Richard Standridge, Circuit Court of Jackson County, Missouri.
(http://www.courtrules.org/fre.htm)

SUMMARY

Evidence is anything that tends to prove or disprove a fact at issue in a legal action. It involves the offering of alleged proof through testimony or objects at court proceedings in order to persuade the trier of fact about an issue in dispute. Evidence is essential to the search for and the ascertainment of truth in a legal dispute. Throughout history, societies have developed methods and procedures to help ensure fair and just legal proceedings in this search. In common law countries, these methods evolved into an adversary system where it is believed that out of a controlled battle, truth would emerge. The jury system also evolved to protect an individual's right to have evidence presented to, and decided by, a jury from his or her local community. To protect the jury from hearing information which might mislead them, to ensure that the proceedings were conducted in an efficient and just manner, and to protect public policy interests, rules of evidence were developed by the courts and promulgated in the form of common law. These common law rules were later codified and expanded into statutory provisions in most states. In 1975, after several years of study, the U.S. Supreme Court proposed and the Congress enacted the Federal Rules of Evidence. These rules became the model for the majority of the state evidence codes.

KEY TERMS

Adversary System	Hammurabi Code	Trial by Battle
Case Law	Islamic Law	Trial by Ordeal
Circuit Court	Jury	Uniform Rules of Evidence
Civil Law	Precedent	Wager of Law
Common Law	Privileged Communication	Writ
Evidence	Procedural Law	Writ of Habeas Corpus
Evidence Law	Stare Decisis	Writ of Novel Disseisin
Federal Rules of Evidence	Statutory Law	
Grand Jury	Substantive Law	

LEARNING OUTCOMES AND PRACTICE SKILLS CHECKLIST

☐ Learning Outcomes

After completing your reading, questions, and exercises, you should be able to demonstrate a better understanding of the learning concepts by answering the following questions:

1. Compare and contrast the different definitions of evidence presented in this chapter.
2. Distinguish between evidence and evidence law.
3. Explain why we have evidence law.
4. Assess why evidence is called a "search for truth" and, if so, why it must be balanced with public policy interests which may limit this search.
5. Describe where our evidence law came from.
6. Distinguish common law from civil law and Islamic law systems.
7. Discuss the importance of the adversary system and the emergence of the jury to the development of evidence law.
8. Identify the sources where the rules of evidence are found today.

9. Explain why statutory rules of evidence developed.
10. Describe the influence of the Federal Rules of Evidence on state codes.
11. Identify the sources where you would find evidence rules in your own state.

☐ Practice Skills

In addition to understanding the learning concepts, practice what you have learned through applications using critical thinking, legal analysis and writing, legal research, and advocacy skills, including:

Critical Thinking

1. Why do we need laws of evidence?
2. Why did it take so long to enact statutory rules of evidence?
3. Why do you think these statutory rules were enacted?
4. Why do the majority of state courts model their evidence codes after the Federal Rules?
5. Rules of evidence are still not consistently applied in state and federal courts. Would you change this? Why or why not?

Legal Analysis and Writing

1. What is the significance of the definitions for evidence discussed in this chapter?
2. How do these definitions influence the gathering of evidence?

Legal Research Using the Internet

1. Use one of the web sites identified in the *Practice Tips* to find the Federal Rules of Evidence. Research the notes by the advisory committees on the proposing of these rules and assess the comments and issues raised in their recommendations.
2. Use one of the web sites identified in the *Practice Tips* to find out whether your state rules of evidence are patterned after the Federal Rules.
3. Compare and contrast the Uniform Rules of Evidence with the Federal Rules.

PRACTICE APPLICATION 1.1

Find the rules of evidence for your state. Use your word processor's "Table" feature to prepare a table or chart with two columns. In one column, list the main sections of the evidence rules for your state. In the other column, list the sections of the Federal Rules. Use the rule numbers for each heading. Compare and contrast these sections.

1. Are your state rules similar to the Federal Rules?
2. If not, what are the primary differences?
3. If similar, do they both follow the same order?
4. Do the sections of each set of rules have similar topics or names?

Keep this chart and add to it as you learn the definition and elements of each rule. Continue to compare your state rules to the Federal Rules.

ADVOCACY AND COMMUNICATION SKILLS 1.1

Using the *Advocacy and Persuasive Arguments* format shown in the Appendix, select one of the following topics and inform your instructor whether you will argue for or against the issue. Then, prepare and deliver an oral persuasive argument:

1. Should we have rules that exclude evidence or should all evidence be allowed?
2. Should we keep the advocacy system?
3. Should we keep the jury system?

You will have 3 minutes to state your position and support it. After the other side presents his or her arguments, you will have an additional minute to rebut the position.

WEB SITES

CourtRules.org site, Circuit Court Judge Richard Standridge
http://www.courtrules.org/fre.htm
ExpertPages.com
http://expertpages.com/state_rules_of_evidence.htm
FindLaw
http://guide.lp.findlaw.com/casecode/
FindLaw U.S. Supreme Court Decisions
http://www.findlaw.com/casecode/supreme.html
Legal Information Institute (LII), Cornell Law School
http://www.law.cornell.edu/rules/fre/overview.html

http://www.law.cornell.edu/states/listing.html
Supreme Court Collection of Cornell Law School
http://supct.law.cornell.edu/supct/
Uniform Rules of Evidence
http://www.law.upenn.edu/bll/ulc/fnact99/ure88.htm
Uniform Rules of Evidence Locator from LII
http://www.law.cornell.edu/uniform/evidence.html
U.S. Supreme Court
http://www.supremecourtus.gov/

ENDNOTES

1. Oliver Wendell Holmes, *The Common Law*, 1909.
2. Sir William Blackstone, *Commentaries on the Laws of England* (1765).
3. *State v. Ward*, 61 Vt. 153 (1889).
4. *Cal. Evid. Code* §140.
5. *Kan. Stat.* §60-401. (a).
6. *Elkins v. United States*, 364 U.S. 206 (1960) (Frankfurter dissent).
7. *Ga. Code* Sec. 24-1-2.
8. *Upjohn Co. v. United States*, 449 U.S. 383 (1981).
9. *Funk v. United States*, 290 U.S. 371 (1933).
10. *The Code of Hammurabi*, Translated by L. W. King (1910).
11. *United States v. Nobles*, 422 U.S. 225 (1975).
12. *Bushel's Case*, 1670.
13. *Trammel v. United States*, 445 U.S. 40 (1980).
14. J. Wigmore, *Code of Evidence*, 1909.
15. *Judicial Court of Massachusetts*, 1982.

ROLE OF EVIDENCE LAW

"Affirmati Non Neganti Incumbit Probatio."

*—The burden of proof is upon him
who affirms—not on him who denies.*

LEARNING OUTCOMES

In this chapter, you will learn about the following legal concepts:

- How Public Policy Influences the Role of Evidence Law
- Goals and Purposes of Statutory Evidence Rules
- Role of Evidence Law in the Ascertainment of Truth
- Role of Evidence Law in Ensuring Fairness
- Role of Evidence Law in Promoting Efficiency
- Role of Evidence Law in Proving a Case

- Burden of Proof
- Standards or Degrees of Certainty in Burden of Proof
- Presumptions and Inferences
- Effect of a Presumption in a Civil Action
- Presumptions in Criminal Cases

Plaintiff
The party bringing a civil legal action.

Defendant
The party defending against a civil or criminal action.

Prosecutor
A government attorney who represents society in prosecuting a criminal action.

Social Policy
The influence of societal norms, values, traditions, and longer-term goals on the shaping of laws.

Public Policy
The influence of public opinion in the context of particular times and events on the shaping of laws.

In Absentia
A trial held when the defendant is not present.

INTRODUCTION

As discussed in the first chapter, our legal system employs an adversarial process, where it is believed that *out of a controlled battle or contest emerges truth*. This controlled contest is between two parties to a legal dispute—the **plaintiff**, or person bringing the legal action, and the **defendant**, the party defending against the action. In a criminal action, the plaintiff is the "state" or the "people," represented by a district or state's attorney, called a **prosecutor**.

The role of evidence law serves a three-fold purpose in this adversarial process. First and foremost, the goal of evidence law is to promote **social policy** and **public policy** for ensuring fairness and a just determination of the proceedings in the ascertainment of truth. Second, and within this context of fairness, evidence law provides a framework of guidelines and safeguards that protect the jury, and help to ensure an orderly, efficient legal process. Third, the role of evidence law is to ensure the "controlled" nature of the contest between adversarial parties by establishing rules and procedures for initiating and proving a legal action. It does this through rules and procedures for how evidence may be presented or challenged, who is responsible for presenting the evidence, and what evidence may be admissible or inadmissible. By doing this, it is also closely tied to other legal rules that determine how much proof must be presented in order to win the legal "contest."

HOW PUBLIC POLICY INFLUENCES THE ROLE OF EVIDENCE LAW

In the previous chapter, we learned how evidence law evolved in response to the development of the jury and adversary system. Growing social concerns and public sentiment about abuses in the new legal system influenced these responses. From trials held in secret (closed from the public) to defendants tried **in absentia**, events in England and America prior to America's independence led to public demands for more fairness in the legal process. In addition, the courts began to recognize the need to protect the jury from hearing unreliable evidence or from seeing certain tactics used by adversarial parties that resulted in needless delays and expense. The common law reflected these concerns by shaping the role of evidence rules to provide a framework for ensuring fairness throughout the trial process.

GOALS AND PURPOSES OF STATUTORY EVIDENCE RULES

When statutory rules of evidence began to be enacted, there was considerable discussion by the advisory committees about what the role of these new rules would be. For example, when Congress enacted the Federal Rules of Evidence in 1975, there were debates on the role and purposes of the new rules, even though most had been in existence in some form for years through the common law. Congress agreed on three overall purposes for the evidentiary rules, each influenced by public and social policy. Two overriding goals were also agreed upon. These were all stated in Rule 102, which provided for the "purpose and construction" of the evidentiary rules.[1] Utah, which adopted this federal rule, identified these purposes as ensuring fairness, eliminating unjustifiable expense and delay, and promoting growth and development of evidence law. The overriding goals of the rules were to ensure that truth was ascertained and that proceedings were justly determined (see Exhibit 2.1).[2]

EXHIBIT 2.1 Purpose of Rules of Evidence

Pennsylvania Rules of Evidence
Rule 102. Purpose and Construction.
These rules shall be construed to secure fairness in administration, elimination of unjustifiable expense and delay, and promotion of growth and development of the law of evidence to the end that the truth may be ascertained and proceedings justly determined.

ROLE OF EVIDENCE LAW IN THE ASCERTAINMENT OF TRUTH

As we noted in Chapter 1, the ascertainment of truth has always been a top goal in the development of evidence law. The U.S. Supreme Court stated that the "basic purpose of a trial is the determination of truth."[3] One famous Supreme Court justice, Felix Frankfurter, put it in a more eloquent manner when he wrote, "The pertinent general principle, responding to the deepest needs of society, is that society is entitled to every man's evidence. As an underlying aim of judicial inquiry is ascertainable truth, everything rationally related to ascertaining the truth is presumptively admissible. Limitations are properly placed upon the operation of this general principle only to the very limited extent that permitting a refusal to testify or excluding relevant evidence has a public good transcending the normally predominant principle of utilizing all rational means for ascertaining truth."[4] Many evidence codes included this principle when enacting statutory rules. For example, Congress included a provision stating that the rules of evidence "shall be construed . . . to the end that the truth may be ascertained and proceedings justly determined."[5]

In this search for the truth, the role of evidence is to provide proceedings that are "justly determined." To ensure this, a central purpose of the rules is to secure fairness.

ROLE OF EVIDENCE LAW IN ENSURING FAIRNESS

Although evidence is a search for truth, an important public policy is that this search be conducted in a fair manner. The U.S. Supreme Court addressed this by holding that the "law does not require that a defendant receive a perfect trial, only a fair one."[6] Many of the evidence rules are designed to provide safeguards to ensure this fairness. As a result, evidence may be excluded under the rules if obtained in an improper manner or if unreliable; or if it might prejudice or confuse the jury. Although there has been much controversy over the years about what constitutes a "fair" trial, this is one of the cornerstones of evidence law.

ROLE OF EVIDENCE LAW IN PROMOTING EFFICIENCY

Within the context of fairness, the role of evidence law is to promote efficiency by providing a framework of guidelines and safeguards that help to ensure an orderly, efficient legal process and serve to protect the jury. This can be seen through a number of evidentiary rules that exclude evidence that may tend to mislead or confuse the jury or waste time or expense. For example, evidence that does not pertain to the matter at issue may be excluded.[7] Evidence that is deemed unreliable due to its secondhand nature may be excluded.[8] Evidence will also be excluded if it may unfairly prejudice the jury, confuse the issues, cause a delay, or waste time.[9]

Judge as Referee and Filter

Evidence law places much of the responsibility for ensuring fairness and efficiency in the hands of the trial judge. The trial judge serves as a referee and a "filter," interpreting the evidence rules and deciding what evidence will be admissible and what evidence must be excluded. To protect the jury from hearing potentially prejudicial or unreliable evidence, rules exist to allow a judge to determine certain preliminary questions before the jury hears them. For example, a judge may hear and determine the admissibility of evidence or qualifications of a person to be a witness outside the hearing of the jury.[10] There are rules that allow a judge to hear arguments regarding the inadmissibility of evidence outside the hearing of the jury.[11] There is also a rule providing that the trial judge control the mode and order of interrogating witnesses and presenting evidence.[12] In all of these examples, the role of evidence law acts to allow the judge to serve as a "filter" to help ensure a fair, orderly, and efficient resolution of the legal dispute.

EVIDENTIARY CHECKLIST 2.1

Role of Evidence Law

☐   Promote social and public policies for ensuring fairness and a just determination of the proceedings in the ascertainment of truth.

☐   Within this context of fairness, provide a framework of guidelines and safeguards that protect the jury, and help to ensure an orderly, efficient legal process.

☐   Ensure the "controlled" nature of the contest between adversarial parties by establishing rules and procedures for proving a case.

CRITICAL THINKING QUESTIONS 2.1

1. Do you think that our adversarial system of resolving legal disputes through a controlled contest where evidence is obtained by one side and challenged by the other side works adequately? Why or why not?

2. What does Justice Frankfurter mean when he writes that "society is entitled to every man's evidence?" How do we balance this with the need for fairness?

3. How can we justify the goal of evidence as the ascertainment of truth when some important evidence may be excluded at trial because it is prejudicial, unreliable, confusing, or a waste of time?

4. What does the Court mean in their holding that the "law does not require that a defendant receive a perfect trial, only a fair one?" Give some examples of this.

5. Are we placing too much responsibility on the judge as "referee" and "filter" to ensure fairness and efficiency in our legal process? Explain your answer.

6. What safeguards do you think are in place or should be in place to make sure that the judge does his or her job in the above responsibilities?

ROLE OF EVIDENCE LAW IN PROVING A CASE

For the statutory rules, influenced by social and public policy, the role of evidence law is to provide a framework of rules and procedures to help govern and ensure a fair resolution of the legal dispute. However, to the parties involved in a legal action, the role of evidence is of a much more personal nature. To these parties, the role of evidence law serves to establish rules that determine what evidence may or may not be admissible as proof in a legal action. This is closely tied to related legal rules that determine what **burden of proof** is necessary to be successful in a legal action, and how this burden can be met.

Evidence versus Proof

Although often confused with each other, the terms evidence and proof have different meanings. Evidence involves the *means* by which some fact is offered to prove or disprove an issue in dispute, while proof is the *effect* that the evidence has on the trier of fact and the *conclusion* drawn from the evidence that has been submitted. Proof is inferred from the evidence submitted.

Evidence is classified by its types, forms, and functions, while proof is viewed in terms of its **onus probandi**, or "burden" of proving or establishing the requisite degree of belief in the mind of the trier of fact regarding the evidence submitted.

BURDEN OF PROOF

Burden of proof is the duty to meet a certain standard or establish the requisite degree of belief in the mind of the trier of fact regarding the evidence submitted. Under our adversary system, a party bringing a legal action has the burden of proving his or her case. This burden of proof actually involves two key elements: the **burden of production** and the **burden of persuasion**.

Burden of Production

The burden of production requires a party to a legal action to present enough evidence to support his or her contention or case regarding a matter at issue, which must be sufficient to avoid an adverse ruling by the Court. This is also known as the **burden of going forward**, where a party has the responsibility to introduce enough evidence to support his or her claim or action.

Prima Facie Case

In any legal action, the plaintiff has the burden of presenting a **prima facie** case. *Prima facie* translates to "at first sight" and means that, at first sight, all of the elements for a particular legal action have been established. For example, in a civil action for negligence, the plaintiff would have the burden of producing sufficient evidence to establish a negligent action. The elements required to establish a negligent action are: legal foreseeable duty, breach of duty, proximate cause, and injury.[13] If the plaintiff failed to establish each and every one of these elements, he or she would fail to meet the burden and the case could be dismissed or a verdict entered for the defendant.

Effect of Failing to Meet the Burden of Production

If the plaintiff's burden of production is met in a civil action, the defendant then might have the burden of producing evidence to rebut the evidence

Burden of Proof
The duty to meet a certain standard or establish the requisite degree of belief in the mind of the trier of fact regarding the evidence submitted.

Onus Probandi
Burden of proof.

Burden of Production
To introduce evidence on an issue sufficient enough to avoid an adverse ruling by the Court.

Burden of Persuasion
To present enough evidence to convince or persuade the trier of fact.

Burden of Going Forward
When a matter is at issue, a party must present evidence to address the issue.

Prima Facie
Translates to "at first sight" and means that, at first sight, all of the elements for a particular legal action have been established.

submitted or to introduce new evidence that establishes a defense or justification for the alleged action.

If the plaintiff fails to meet the burden of production or does not establish a prima facie case, the defendant may file a **motion for directed verdict** asking the judge to direct a verdict for the defendant because the plaintiff failed to meet his or her burden of production.

Motion for Directed Verdict
A request to the trial judge by a party to a legal action, asking the judge to direct a verdict for that party because the opposing party failed to meet his or her burden of production.

YOU BE THE JUDGE 2.1

Nancy Hung accidentally backed her car across the parking lot from a parking space, over a 6-inch curb, across a sidewalk, and through the wall of the Panda Chinese Restaurant in Huntsville, Alabama. Crystal Albert, a 10-year-old girl seated inside the restaurant, approximately 1 to 2 feet from the exterior wall and window, was struck by the car. When the car stopped, about one-half of the trunk was located inside the restaurant. Crystal died from injuries sustained from this accident. Hung had been a customer at the restaurant prior to the accident; she had not consumed any alcoholic beverages. Linda Albert, Crystal's mother, sued the Panda Restaurant, alleging negligence. Albert submits that they should have used concrete block rather than aluminum and glass "curtain wall construction" or should have erected guarding and barricades around the building. However, the premises were constructed in accordance with the Huntsville building code requirements.

The defendants claim that Crystal's death was caused by an intervening negligent act by Hung and that the defendants had no duty to protect Crystal from the type of harm that caused her injury, because the harm was not reasonably foreseeable. The defendants submit a motion asking the judge to dismiss the legal action or enter a directed verdict for the defendant on the grounds that the plaintiff failed to meet her burden of production to establish a prima facie case.

Would you grant the defendant's motion? Why or why not? Write a memo analyzing this issue with your conclusion and reasoning.

LEGAL RESEARCH USING THE INTERNET SKILLS 2.1

Find out how the Court ruled on the previous *You Be the Judge* problem by finding and reading the Alabama Supreme Court decision online! The citation for it is:

Albert v. Hsu, 602 So. 2d 895 (1992).

Practice Tip 2.1

Establishing a Prima Facie Case
When interviewing witnesses and investigating a cause of action in order to establish a prima facie case, always examine the definition of the legal action thoroughly beforehand. Break down the definition into the elements that will need to be established and proven. Ask questions and look for the facts that will establish each element and satisfy this proof. Be prepared to identify and collect evidence that will prove each and every element needed to establish the action.

EXHIBIT 2.2   Burden of Proof

Oregon Revised Statutes
Sec. 40.105 Rule 305.
Allocation of the burden of persuasion. A party has the burden of persuasion as to each fact the existence or nonexistence of which the law declares essential to the claim for relief or defense the party is asserting.

California Evidence Code
Sec. 520. The party claiming that a person is guilty of crime or wrongdoing has the burden of proof on that issue.
Sec. 521. The party claiming that a person did not exercise a requisite degree of care has the burden of proof on that issue.
Sec. 522. The party claiming that any person, including himself, is or was insane has the burden of proof on that issue.

Burden of Persuasion

The *burden of persuasion* is the responsibility of a party to convince the trier of fact of whatever degree of certainty is required for a judgment or verdict to be rendered. The burden of persuasion is what is commonly meant when the term *burden of proof* is discussed, and is generally not determined until the end of a trial or legal action, when a verdict has been reached (see Exhibit 2.2).

Reasonable Person Test

The legal test used to ascertain whether someone has met the burden of persuasion is called the **reasonable person test**. Sufficient admissible evidence must be submitted to allow a reasonable person to find that a fact exists or the burden has not been met.

Reasonable Person Test
Sufficient admissible evidence must be submitted to allow a reasonable person to find that a fact exists.

STANDARDS OR DEGREES OF CERTAINTY IN BURDENS OF PROOF

It is not necessary in the law to prove beyond *any* doubt to be successful in proving a case. The standard of proof will depend on the type of legal action. Each type of legal action has a specific standard or degree of certainty that must be proven in order to meet that particular burden of proof and persuasion. There are two primary standards or degrees of certainty for burdens of proof. *Beyond a reasonable doubt* is the standard required to convict a defendant in a criminal action. *Preponderance of evidence* is the standard required in a civil action. There is also a standard used for some issues in civil actions called *clear and convincing*. Finally, there are two standards used in criminal procedures, *reasonable suspicion* and *probable cause*.

Preponderance of the Evidence

Preponderance of Evidence is the standard or degree of certainty required as the burden of proof in civil cases. It is met when the trier of fact believes from the evidence that a fact is more probable than not. In its instructions to jurors in a civil case, the *Benchbook for U.S. District Court Judges* defines this standard of proof as follows:

"The plaintiff has the burden of proving his [her] case by what is called the preponderance of the evidence. That means the plaintiff has to produce "The

Preponderance of Evidence
Burden of proof in a civil action. The plaintiff must produce sufficient evidence to persuade the trier of fact that what the plaintiff claims is more likely true than not.

plaintiff has the burden of proving his [her] case by what is called the preponderance of the evidence. That means the plaintiff has to produce evidence which, considered in the light of all the facts, leads you to believe that what the plaintiff claims is more likely true than not. To put it differently, if you were to put the plaintiff's and the defendant's evidence on opposite sides of the scales, the plaintiff would have to make the scales tip somewhat on his [or her] side. If the plaintiff fails to meet this burden, the verdict must be for the defendant."[14]

Clear and Convincing Evidence

Clear and Convincing Evidence
Burden of proof in certain types of civil actions. Requires trier of fact to reasonably believe that there is a high probability that a fact is true.

Clear and convincing evidence is a standard of proof used in certain types of civil cases, including medical cases where the patient is making a decision to terminate life support, civil fraud cases, and some employment discrimination cases. This standard is higher than the *preponderance* burden in a normal civil action. Clear and convincing evidence requires the trier of fact to reasonably believe that there is a high probability that a fact is true. It is said to be *very probably true*.

One court defined clear and convincing evidence as "proof sufficient to persuade the trier of fact that the patient held a firm and settled commitment to the termination of life supports under the circumstances like those presented."[15] Another court defined it as evidence which "produces in the mind of the trier of fact a firm belief or conviction as to the truth of the allegations sought to be established, evidence so clear, direct and weighty and convincing as to enable [the factfinder] to come to a clear conviction, without hesitancy, of the truth of the precise facts in issue."[16]

Right to Die

In the following important case, the U.S. Supreme Court tackled a very controversial issue of whether a state may require a clear and convincing evidence standard in proceedings where parents sought to terminate artificial nutrition procedures for their daughter, Nancy Cruzan, the victim of a car accident which left her in a persistent vegetative state. Prior to the accident, Nancy had expressed her thoughts to a roommate that she would not wish to continue her life unless she could live at least halfway normally. If the life-sustaining procedures are terminated, Nancy will die. How would you rule on the parents' request?

CASE

Cruzan v. Director, Missouri Department of Health

497 U.S. 261 (1990).

Chief Justice Rehnquist delivered the opinion of the Court.

. . . .

On the night of January 11, 1983, Nancy Cruzan lost control of her car as she traveled down Elm Road in Jasper County, Missouri. The vehicle overturned, and Cruzan was discovered lying face down in a ditch without detectable respiratory or cardiac function. Paramedics were able to restore her breathing and heartbeat at the accident site, and she was transported to a hospital in an unconscious state. An attending neurosurgeon diagnosed her as having sustained probable cerebral contusions compounded by significant anoxia (lack of oxygen). The Missouri trial court in this case found that permanent brain damage generally results after 6 minutes in an anoxic state; it was estimated that Cruzan was deprived of oxygen from 12 to 14 minutes. She remained in a coma for approximately 3 weeks and then progressed to an unconscious state in which she was able to orally ingest some nutrition. In order to ease feeding and further the recovery, surgeons implanted a gastrostomy feeding and hydration tube in Cruzan with the consent of her then husband. Subsequent rehabilitative efforts proved unavailing. She now lies in a Missouri state hospital in what is commonly referred to as a persistent vegetative state: generally, a condition in which a person exhibits motor reflexes but evinces no indications of significant cognitive function. The State of Missouri is bearing the cost of her care. The State Supreme Court, adopting much of the trial court's findings, described Nancy Cruzan's medical condition as follows:

"... (1) Her respiration and circulation are not artificially maintained and are within the normal limits of a thirty-year-old female; (2) she is oblivious to her environment except for reflexive responses to sound and perhaps painful stimuli; (3) she suffered anoxia of the brain resulting in a massive enlargement of the ventricles filling with cerebrospinal fluid in the area where the brain has degenerated and [her] cerebral cortical atrophy is irreversible, permanent, progressive and ongoing; (4) her highest cognitive brain function is exhibited by her grimacing perhaps in recognition of ordinarily painful stimuli, indicating the experience of pain and apparent response to sound; (5) she is a spastic quadriplegic; (6) her four extremities are contracted with irreversible muscular and tendon damage to all extremities; (7) she has no cognitive or reflexive ability to swallow food or water to maintain her daily essential needs and ... she will never recover her ability to swallow sufficient to satisfy her needs. In sum, Nancy is diagnosed as in a persistent vegetative state. She is not dead. She is not terminally ill. Medical experts testified that she could live another thirty years."

. . . .

After it had become apparent that Nancy Cruzan had virtually no chance of regaining her mental faculties, her parents asked hospital employees to terminate the artificial nutrition and hydration procedures. All agree that such a removal would cause her death. The employees refused to honor the request without court approval. The parents then sought and received authorization from the state trial court for termination. The court found that a person in Nancy's condition had a fundamental right under the State and Federal Constitutions to refuse or direct the withdrawal of "death prolonging procedures." The court also found that Nancy's "expressed thoughts at age twenty-five in somewhat serious conversation with a housemate friend that if sick or injured she would not wish to continue her life unless she could live at least halfway normally suggests that given her present condition she would not wish to continue on with her nutrition and hydration."

The Supreme Court of Missouri reversed by a divided vote. The court recognized a right to refuse treatment embodied in the common-law doctrine of informed consent, but expressed skepticism about the application of that doctrine in the circumstances of this case.... The court found that Cruzan's statements to her roommate regarding her desire to live or die under certain conditions were "unreliable for the purpose of determining her intent," "and thus insufficient to support the co-guardians' claim to exercise substituted judgment on Nancy's behalf." It rejected the argument that Cruzan's parents were entitled to order the termination of her medical treatment, concluding that "no person can assume that choice for an incompetent in the absence of the formalities required under Missouri's Living Will statutes or the *clear and convincing, inherently reliable evidence absent here.*"

. . . .

Here, Missouri has in effect recognized that under certain circumstances a surrogate may act for the patient in electing to have hydration and nutrition withdrawn in such a way as to cause death, but it has established a *procedural safeguard* to assure that the action of the surrogate conforms as best it may to the wishes expressed by the patient while competent. Missouri requires that evidence of the incompetent's wishes as to the withdrawal of treatment be proved by *clear and convincing evidence.* The question, then, is whether the United States Constitution forbids the establishment of this procedural requirement by the State. We hold that it does not.

Whether or not Missouri's clear and convincing evidence requirement comports with the United States Constitution depends in part on what interests the State may properly seek to protect in this situation. Missouri relies on its interest in the protection and preservation of human life, and there can be no gainsaying this interest. As a general matter, the States—indeed, all civilized nations—demonstrate their commitment to life by treating homicide as a serious crime. Moreover, the majority of States in this country have laws imposing criminal penalties on one who assists another to commit suicide. We do not think a State is required to remain neutral in the face of an informed and voluntary decision by a physically able adult to starve to death. But in the context presented here, a State has more particular interests at stake. The choice between life and death is a deeply personal decision of obvious and overwhelming finality. We believe Missouri may legitimately seek to safeguard the personal element of this choice through the imposition of *heightened evidentiary requirements*. It cannot be disputed that the Due Process Clause protects an interest in life as well as an interest in refusing life-sustaining medical treatment. Not all incompetent patients will have loved ones available to serve as surrogate decisionmakers. And even where family members are present, "there will, of course, be some unfortunate situations in which family members will not act to protect a patient." A State is entitled to guard against potential abuses in such situations. Similarly, a State is entitled to consider that a judicial proceeding to make a determination regarding an incompetent's wishes may very well not be an adversarial one, with the added guarantee of accurate factfinding that the adversary process brings with it. Finally, we think a State may properly decline to make judgments about the "quality" of life that a particular individual may enjoy, and simply assert an unqualified interest in the preservation of human life to be weighed against the constitutionally protected interests of the individual.

In our view, Missouri has permissibly sought to advance these interests through the adoption of a *"clear and convincing" standard of proof* to govern such proceedings. "The function of a standard of proof, as that concept is embodied in the Due Process Clause and in the realm of factfinding, is to 'instruct the factfinder concerning the degree of confidence our society thinks he should have in the correctness of factual conclusions for a particular type of adjudication.'" We think it self-evident that the interests at stake in the instant proceedings are more substantial, both on an individual and societal level, than those involved in a run-of-the-mine civil dispute. But not only does the standard of proof reflect the importance of a particular adjudication, it also serves as "a societal judgment about how the risk of error should be distributed between the litigants." The more stringent the *burden of proof* a party must bear, the more that party bears the risk of an erroneous decision. We believe that Missouri may permissibly place an increased risk of an erroneous decision on those seeking to terminate an incompetent individual's life-sustaining treatment. An erroneous decision not to terminate results in a maintenance of the status quo; the possibility of subsequent developments

such as advancements in medical science, the discovery of new evidence regarding the patient's intent, changes in the law, or simply the unexpected death of the patient despite the administration of life-sustaining treatment at least create the potential that a wrong decision will eventually be corrected or its impact mitigated. An erroneous decision to withdraw life-sustaining treatment, however, is not susceptible of correction.

In sum, we conclude that a State may apply a clear and convincing evidence standard in proceedings where a guardian seeks to discontinue nutrition and hydration of a person diagnosed to be in a persistent vegetative state. The Supreme Court of Missouri held that in this case the testimony adduced at trial did not amount to clear and convincing proof of the patient's desire to have hydration and nutrition withdrawn. In so doing, it reversed a decision of the Missouri trial court which had found that the evidence "suggested" Nancy Cruzan would not have desired to continue such measures, but which had not adopted the standard of "clear and convincing evidence" enunciated by the Supreme Court. The testimony adduced at trial consisted primarily of Nancy Cruzan's statements made to a housemate about a year before her accident that she would not want to live should she face life as a "vegetable," and other observations to the same effect. The observations did not deal in terms with withdrawal of medical treatment or of hydration and nutrition. We cannot say that the Supreme Court of Missouri committed constitutional error in reaching the conclusion that it did.

The judgment of the Supreme Court of Missouri is Affirmed.

Justice Brennan, with whom Justice Marshall and Justice Blackmun join, dissenting.

"Medical technology has effectively created a twilight zone of suspended animation where death commences while life, in some form, continues. Some patients, however, want no part of a life sustained only by medical technology. Instead, they prefer a plan of medical treatment that allows nature to take its course and permits them to die with dignity." Nancy Cruzan has dwelt in that twilight zone for 6 years. She is oblivious to her surroundings and will remain so. Her body twitches only reflexively, without consciousness. The areas of her brain that once thought, felt, and experienced sensations have degenerated badly and are continuing to do so.

The cavities remaining are filling with cerebrospinal fluid. The "cerebral cortical atrophy is irreversible, permanent, progressive and ongoing." "Nancy will never interact meaningfully with her environment again. She will remain in a persistent vegetative state until her death." Because she cannot swallow, her nutrition and hydration are delivered through a tube surgically implanted in her stomach. A grown woman at the time of the accident, Nancy had previously expressed her wish to forgo continuing medical care under circumstances such as these. Her family and her friends are convinced that this is what she would want. A guardian ad litem appointed by the trial court is also convinced that this is what Nancy would want. Yet the Missouri Supreme Court, alone among state courts deciding such a question, has determined that an irreversibly vegetative patient will remain a passive prisoner of medical technology—for Nancy, perhaps for the next 30 years. Today the Court, while tentatively accepting that there is some degree of constitutionally protected liberty interest in avoiding unwanted medical treatment, including life-sustaining medical treatment such as artificial nutrition and hydration, affirms the decision of the Missouri Supreme Court. The majority opinion, as I read it, would affirm that decision on the ground that a State may require "clear and convincing" evidence of Nancy Cruzan's prior decision to forgo life-sustaining treatment under circumstances such as hers in order to ensure that her actual wishes are honored. Because I believe that Nancy Cruzan has a fundamental right to be free of unwanted artificial nutrition and hydration, which right is not outweighed by any interests of the State, and because I find that the improperly biased procedural obstacles imposed by the Missouri Supreme Court impermissibly burden that right, I respectfully dissent.

Nancy Cruzan is entitled to choose to die with dignity. . . .

LEGAL ANALYSIS AND WRITING 2.1

The following questions are based on the *How to Brief a Legal Case* format shown in the Appendix. Use this format to answer the following questions:

1. Summarize the facts in the previous case.
2. What is the legal issue?
3. What did the appellate court decide?
4. Why did the court decide this way?
5. Do you agree with the court's reasoning? Explain why or why not.

LEGAL RESEARCH USING THE INTERNET SKILLS 2.2

Find and read this important Supreme Court case online! Check out one of the legal research web sites below and use their "Search" feature to find this case. In the "Search" field, enter the cite or case name.

1. FindLaw U.S. Supreme Court Decisions (http://www.findlaw.com/casecode/supreme.html)
2. U.S. Supreme Court (http://www.supremecourtus.gov/)
3. Supreme Court Collection of Cornell Law School (http://supct.law.cornell.edu/supct/)

CRITICAL THINKING QUESTIONS 2.2

1. Should a plaintiff have to prove each and every element of legal action in order to win? Isn't it enough if most of the elements have been established?

2. What is meant by *burden of production* versus *burden of persuasion*? Give an example for each.

3. How would you go about explaining to the jury what *preponderance of the evidence* means?

4. How do the standards of proof influence the gathering of evidence?

5. Why did the Court in the *Cruzan* case take the side of the state against the wishes of the parents?

6. How would you respond to the minority opinion in *Cruzan* that "Nancy Cruzan is entitled to choose to die with dignity . . . ?"

Beyond a Reasonable Doubt

Beyond a Reasonable Doubt
Burden of proof in a criminal action. Requires the trier of fact to believe something to be "almost certainly true" and leaving no reasonable doubt.

Beyond a reasonable doubt is the standard for the burden of proof required to convict a defendant in a criminal action. This standard requires something to be "almost certainly true." Although the evidence does not have to be proved beyond any doubt, it must lead the trier of fact to an almost certainty of the truth of the facts asserted.

Landmark Supreme Court Case Establishing Standard

The following landmark U.S. Supreme Court decision first established "beyond a reasonable doubt" as a Constitutional requirement in criminal and juvenile cases in this country.

◆ Group #2 case #1

CASE

In re Winship
397 U.S. 358 (1970).

Justice Brennan delivered the opinion of the Court.

. . . This case presents the single, narrow question whether *proof beyond a reasonable doubt* is among the "essentials of due process and fair treatment" required during the adjudicatory stage when a juvenile is charged with an act which would constitute a crime if committed by an adult.

Section 712 of the New York Family Court Act defines a juvenile delinquent as "a person over seven and less than sixteen years of age who does any act which, if done by an adult, would constitute a crime." During a 1967 adjudicatory hearing . . . a judge in New York Family Court found that appellant, then a 12-year-old boy, had entered a locker and stolen $112 from a woman's pocketbook. The petition which charged appellant with delin-

quency alleged that his act, "if done by an adult, would constitute the crime or crimes of Larceny." The judge acknowledged that the proof might not establish guilt beyond a reasonable doubt, but rejected appellant's contention that such proof was required by the Fourteenth Amendment. The judge relied instead on . . . the New York Family Court Act which provides that "any determination . . . must be based on a *preponderance of the evidence*." During a subsequent dispositional hearing, appellant was ordered placed in a training school for an initial period of 18 months, subject to annual extensions of his commitment until his 18th birthday—6 years in appellant's case. The Appellate Division of the New York Supreme Court . . . affirmed without opinion. The New York Court of Appeals then affirmed. . . . We reverse.

The requirement that guilt of a criminal charge be established by proof beyond a reasonable doubt dates at least from our early years as a Nation. . . .

Although virtually unanimous adherence to the reasonable-doubt standard in common-law jurisdictions may not conclusively establish it as a requirement of due process, such adherence does "reflect a profound judgment about the way in which law should be enforced and justice administered." *Duncan v. Louisiana*, 391 U.S. 145, 155 (1968).

Mr. Justice Frankfurter stated that "it is the duty of the Government to establish. . . guilt beyond a reasonable doubt. This notion—basic in our law and rightly one of the boasts of a free society—is a requirement and a safeguard of due process of law in the historic, procedural content of 'due process.'" *Leland v. Oregon*, 343 U.S. 790 (1952) (dissenting opinion). . . .

Moreover, use of the reasonable-doubt standard is indispensable to command the respect and confidence of the community in applications of the criminal law. It is critical that the moral force of the criminal law not be diluted by a standard of proof that leaves people in doubt whether innocent men are being condemned. It is also important in our free society that every individual going about his ordinary affairs have confidence that his government cannot adjudge him guilty of a criminal offense without convincing a proper factfinder of his guilt with utmost certainty. Lest there remain any doubt about the constitutional stature of the reasonable-doubt standard, we explicitly hold that the Due Process Clause protects the accused against conviction except upon proof beyond a reasonable doubt of every fact necessary to constitute the crime with which he is charged.

. . . We therefore hold . . . that, where a 12-year-old child is charged with an act of stealing which renders him liable to confinement for as long as 6 years, then, as a matter of due process . . . the case against him must be proved beyond a reasonable doubt.

Reversed.

Justice Black, dissenting.

. . . The Court has never clearly held . . . that proof beyond a reasonable doubt is either expressly or impliedly commanded by any provision of the Constitution. The Bill of Rights, which in my view is made fully applicable to the States by the Fourteenth Amendment, does by express language provide for, among other things, a right to counsel in criminal trials, a right to indictment, and the right of a defendant to be informed of the nature of the charges against him. And in two places the Constitution provides for trial by jury, but nowhere in that document is there any statement that conviction of crime requires proof of guilt beyond a reasonable doubt. . . .

. . . .

I admit a strong, persuasive argument can be made for a standard of proof beyond a reasonable doubt in criminal cases—and the majority has made that argument well—but it is not for me as a judge to say for that reason that Congress or the States are without constitutional power to establish another standard that the Constitution does not otherwise forbid. It is quite true that proof beyond a reasonable doubt has long been required in federal criminal trials. It is also true that this requirement is almost universally found in the governing laws of the States. And as long as a particular jurisdiction requires proof beyond a reasonable doubt, then the Due Process Clause commands that every trial in that jurisdiction must adhere to that standard. But when, as here, a State through its duly constituted legislative branch decides to apply a different standard, then that standard, unless it is otherwise unconstitutional, must be applied to insure that persons are treated according to the "law of the land." The State of New York has made such a decision, and in my view nothing in the Due Process Clause invalidates it.

LEGAL ANALYSIS AND WRITING 2.2

The following questions are based on the *How to Brief a Legal Case* format shown in the Appendix. Use this format to answer the following questions:

1. Summarize the facts in the previous case.
2. What is the legal issue?
3. What did the appellate court decide?
4. Why did the court decide this way?
5. Do you agree with the court's reasoning? Explain why or why not.

LEGAL RESEARCH USING THE INTERNET SKILLS 2.3

Find and read this important Supreme Court case online! Check out one of the legal research web sites below and use their "Search" feature to find this case. In the "Search" field, enter the cite or case name.

1. FindLaw U.S. Supreme Court Decisions (http://www.findlaw.com/casecode/supreme.html)
2. U.S. Supreme Court (http://www.supremecourtus.gov/)
3. Supreme Court Collection of Cornell Law School (http://supct.law.cornell.edu/supct/)

What Is Reasonable Doubt?

There is no universal definition for reasonable doubt and, as a result, courts have long struggled to define it in a way to pass constitutional muster. One of the most famous definitions was an 1850 Massachusetts court decision that described reasonable doubt as a "term often used, probably pretty well understood, but not easily defined." The court went on to define it as "not a mere possible doubt" but one that "leaves the minds of jurors in that condition that they cannot say they feel an abiding conviction, to a moral certainty, of the truth of the charge."[17]

In an 1895 case, a trial court told the jury, "I will not undertake to define a reasonable doubt further than to say that a reasonable doubt is not an unreasonable doubt—that is to say, by a reasonable doubt you are not to understand that all doubt is to be excluded; it is impossible in the determination of these questions to be absolutely certain. You are required to decide the question submitted to you upon the strong probabilities of the case, and the probabilities must be so strong as, not to exclude all doubt or possibility of error, but as to exclude reasonable doubt."[18]

What Is Not Reasonable Doubt?

In the following 1990 Louisiana case, the jury was instructed that a reasonable doubt was "an actual substantial doubt," and that what was necessary to convict the defendant was a "moral certainty" of his guilt. The U.S. Supreme Court agreed to hear the case to decide whether "a reasonable juror could have interpreted the instruction to allow a finding of guilt based on a degree of proof below that required by the Due Process Clause."

group 3 case #1:

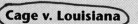

CASE

Cage v. Louisiana

498 U.S. 39 (1990).

Per Curiam

The motion of petitioner for leave to proceed in forma pauperis and the petition for a writ of certiorari are granted.

In state criminal trials, the Due Process Clause of the Fourteenth Amendment "protects the accused against conviction except upon proof beyond a reasonable doubt of every fact necessary to consti-

tute the crime with which he is charged." *In re Winship*, 397 U.S. 358 (1970). This reasonable-doubt standard "plays a vital role in the American scheme of criminal procedure." Among other things, "It is a prime instrument for reducing the risk of convictions resting on factual error." The issue before us is whether the reasonable doubt instruction in this case complied with *Winship*.

Petitioner was convicted in a Louisiana trial court of first-degree murder and was sentenced to death. He appealed to the Supreme Court of Louisiana, arguing, inter alia, that the reasonable-doubt instruction used in the guilt phase of his trial was constitutionally defective. The instruction provided in relevant part:

"If you entertain a reasonable doubt as to any fact or element necessary to constitute the defendant's guilt, it is your duty to give him the benefit of that doubt and return a verdict of not guilty. Even where the evidence demonstrates a probability of guilt, if it does not establish such guilt beyond a reasonable doubt, you must acquit the accused. This doubt, however, must be a reasonable one; that is one that is founded upon a real tangible substantial basis and not upon mere caprice and conjecture. It must be such doubt as would give rise to a grave uncertainty, raised in your mind by reasons of the unsatisfactory character of the evidence or lack thereof. A reasonable doubt is not a mere possible doubt. It is an actual substantial doubt. It is a doubt that a reasonable man can seriously entertain. What is required is not an absolute or mathematical certainty, but a moral certainty."

The Supreme Court of Louisiana rejected petitioner's argument. The court first observed that the use of the phrases "grave uncertainty" and "moral certainty" in the instruction, "if taken out of context, might overstate the requisite degree of uncertainty and confuse the jury." But "taking the charge as a whole," the court concluded that "reasonable persons of ordinary intelligence would understand the definition of 'reasonable doubt.'" It is our view, however, that the instruction at issue was contrary to the "beyond a reasonable doubt" requirement articulated in *Winship*.

In construing the instruction, we consider how reasonable jurors could have understood the charge as a whole. The charge did at one point instruct that to convict, guilt must be found beyond a reasonable doubt; but it then equated a reasonable doubt with a "grave uncertainty" and an "actual substantial doubt," and stated that what was required was a "moral certainty" that the defendant was guilty. It is plain to us that the words "substantial" and "grave," as they are commonly understood, suggest a higher degree of doubt than is required for acquittal under the reasonable-doubt standard. When those statements are then considered with the reference to "moral certainty," rather than evidentiary certainty, it becomes clear that a reasonable juror could have interpreted the instruction to allow a finding of guilt based on a degree of proof below that required by the Due Process Clause.

Accordingly, the judgment of the Supreme Court of Louisiana is reversed, and the case is remanded for further proceedings not inconsistent with this opinion.

LEGAL ANALYSIS AND WRITING 2.3

The following questions are based on the *How to Brief a Legal Case* format shown in the Appendix. Use this format to answer the following questions:

1. Summarize the facts in the previous case.
2. What is the legal issue?
3. What did the appellate court decide?
4. Why did the court decide this way?
5. Do you agree with the court's reasoning? Explain why or why not.

LEGAL RESEARCH USING THE INTERNET SKILLS 2.4

Find and read this important Supreme Court case online! Check out one of the legal research web sites below and use their "Search" feature to find this case. In the "Search" field, enter the cite or case name.

1. FindLaw U.S. Supreme Court Decisions (http://www.findlaw.com/casecode/supreme.html)
2. U.S. Supreme Court (http://www.supremecourtus.gov/)
3. Supreme Court Collection of Cornell Law School (http://supct.law.cornell.edu/supct/)

More Attempts to Define Reasonable Doubt

In the following two 1994 cases, the U.S. Supreme Court again tackles the question of what constitutes reasonable doubt. For the purposes of their decision, the Court has combined both cases.

CASE

Victor v. Nebraska
Sandoval v. California

511 U.S. 1 (1994).

Justice O'Connor delivered the opinion of the Court.

The government must prove beyond a reasonable doubt every element of a charged offense. *In re Winship*, 397 U.S. 358 (1970). Although this standard is an ancient and honored aspect of our criminal justice system, it defies easy explication. In these cases, we consider the constitutionality of two attempts to define "reasonable doubt."

I

The "beyond a reasonable doubt" standard is a requirement of due process, but the Constitution neither prohibits trial courts from defining reasonable doubt nor requires them to do so as a matter of course. Indeed, so long as the court instructs the jury on the necessity that the defendant's guilt be proven beyond a reasonable doubt, the Constitution does not require that any particular form of words be used in advising the jury of the government's burden of proof. Rather, "taken as a whole, the instructions [must] correctly conve[y] the concept of reasonable doubt to the jury." *Holland v. United States*, 348 U.S. 121 (1954).

In only one case have we held that a definition of reasonable doubt violated the Due Process Clause. *Cage v. Louisiana*, 498 U.S. 39 (1990). . . . In a subsequent case, we made clear that the proper inquiry is not whether the instruction "could have" been applied in unconstitutional manner, but whether there is a reasonable likelihood that the jury did so apply it. The constitutional question in the present cases, therefore, is whether there is a reasonable likelihood that the jury understood the instructions to allow conviction based on proof insufficient to meet the *Winship* standard. Although other courts have held that instructions similar to those given at petitioners' trials violate the Due Process Clause, both the Nebraska and the California Supreme Courts held that the instructions were constitutional. We granted certiorari, and now af-

firm both judgments.

II

On October 14, 1984, petitioner Sandoval shot three men, two of them fatally, in a gang-related incident in Los Angeles. About 2 weeks later, he entered the home of a man who had given information to the police about the murders and shot him dead; Sandoval then killed the man's wife because she had seen him murder her husband. Sandoval was convicted on four counts of first degree murder. . . . He was sentenced to death for murdering the woman and to life in prison without possibility of parole for the other three murders. The California Supreme Court affirmed the convictions and sentences.

The jury in Sandoval's case was given the following instruction on the government's burden of proof:

> "A defendant in a criminal action is presumed to be innocent until the contrary is proved, and, in case of a reasonable doubt whether his guilt is satisfactorily shown, he is entitled to a verdict of not guilty. This presumption places upon the State the burden of proving him guilty beyond a reasonable doubt. Reasonable doubt is defined as follows: it is not a mere possible doubt; because everything relating to human affairs, and depending on moral evidence, is open to some possible or imaginary doubt. It is that state of the case which, after the entire comparison and consideration of all the evidence, leaves the minds of the jurors in that condition that they cannot say they feel an abiding conviction, to a moral certainty, of the truth of the charge."

The California Supreme Court rejected Sandoval's claim that the instruction . . . violated the Due Process Clause.

The instruction given in Sandoval's case has its genesis in a charge given by Chief Justice Shaw of the Massachusetts Supreme Judicial Court more than a century ago:

> "[W]hat is reasonable doubt? It is a term often used, probably pretty well understood, but not easily defined. It is not mere possible doubt; because every thing relating to human affairs, and depending on moral evidence, is open to some pos-

sible or imaginary doubt. It is that state of the case, which, after the entire comparison and consideration of all the evidence, leaves the minds of jurors in that condition that they cannot say they feel an abiding conviction, to a moral certainty, of the truth of the charge. The burden of proof is upon the prosecutor. All the presumptions of law independent of evidence are in favor of innocence; and every person is presumed to be innocent until he is proved guilty. If upon such proof there is reasonable doubt remaining, the accused is entitled to the benefit of it by an acquittal. For it is not sufficient to establish a probability, though a strong one, arising from the doctrine of chances, that the fact charged is more likely to be true than the contrary; but the evidence must establish the truth of the fact to a reasonable and moral certainty; a certainty that convinces and directs the understanding, and satisfies the reason and judgment, of those who are bound to act conscientiously upon it. This we take to be proof beyond reasonable doubt." *Commonwealth v. Webster*, 59 Mass. 295 (1850).

The Webster charge is representative of the time when "American courts began applying [the 'beyond a reasonable doubt' standard] in its modern form in criminal cases." In *People v. Strong*, 30 Cal. 151 (1866), the California Supreme Court characterized the Webster instruction as "probably the most satisfactory definition ever given to the words 'reasonable doubt' in any case known to criminal jurisprudence." In *People v. Paulsell*, 115 Cal. 6 (1896), the court cautioned state trial judges against departing from that formulation. And in 1927, the state legislature adopted the bulk of the Webster instruction as a statutory definition of reasonable doubt. Indeed, the California Legislature has directed that the court may read to the jury section 1096 of this code, and no further instruction on the subject of the presumption of innocence or defining reasonable doubt need be given. The statutory instruction was given in Sandoval's case.

. . . .

Sandoval's primary objection is to the use of the phrases "moral evidence" and "moral certainty" in the instruction. As noted, this part of the charge was lifted verbatim from Chief Justice Shaw's Webster decision. . . .

. . .

We recognize that the phrase "moral evidence" is not a mainstay of the modern lexicon, though we do not think it means anything different today than it did in the 19th century. The few contemporary dictionaries that define moral evidence do so con-

sistently with its original meaning. Moreover, the instruction itself gives a definition of the phrase. The jury was told that "everything relating to human affairs, and depending on moral evidence, is open to some possible or imaginary doubt"—in other words, that absolute certainty is unattainable in matters relating to human affairs. Moral evidence, in this sentence, can only mean empirical evidence offered to prove such matters—the proof introduced at trial.

. . . .

These instructions correctly pointed the jurors' attention to the facts of the case before them, not (as Sandoval contends) the ethics or morality of Sandoval's criminal acts. Accordingly, we find the reference to moral evidence unproblematic.

We are somewhat more concerned with Sandoval's argument that the phrase "moral certainty" has lost its historical meaning, and that a modern jury would understand it to allow conviction on proof that does not meet the beyond a reasonable doubt standard. Words and phrases can change meaning over time: a passage generally understood in 1850 may be incomprehensible or confusing to a modern juror. And although some contemporary dictionaries contain definitions of moral certainty similar to the 19th century understanding of the phrase, we are willing to accept Sandoval's premise that "moral certainty," standing alone, might not be recognized by modern jurors as a synonym for "proof beyond a reasonable doubt." But it does not necessarily follow that the California instruction is unconstitutional.

Sandoval first argues that moral certainty would be understood by modern jurors to mean a standard of proof lower than beyond a reasonable doubt. In support of this proposition, Sandoval points to contemporary dictionaries that define moral certainty in terms of probability. But the beyond a reasonable doubt standard is, itself, probabilistic. [I]n a judicial proceeding in which there is a dispute about the facts of some earlier event, the factfinder cannot acquire unassailably accurate knowledge of what happened. Instead, all the factfinder can acquire is a belief of what probably happened. The problem is not that moral certainty may be understood in terms of probability, but that a jury might understand the phrase to mean something less than the very high level of probability required by the Constitution in criminal cases. Although, in this respect, moral certainty is ambiguous in the abstract, the rest of the instruction given in Sandoval's case lends content to the phrase. The jurors were told that they must have "an abiding conviction, to a moral certainty, of the truth of the charge." An instruction cast in terms of an abiding conviction as to guilt, without reference to moral certainty, correctly states the government's burden of proof.

. . . As used in this instruction, therefore, we are satisfied that the reference to moral certainty, in conjunction with the abiding conviction language, "impress[ed] upon the factfinder the need to reach a subjective state of near certitude of the guilt of the accused." *Jackson v. Virginia*, 443 U.S., at 315. Accordingly, we reject Sandoval's contention that the moral certainty element of the California instruction invited the jury to convict him on proof below that required by the Due Process Clause.

. . . .

We do not think it reasonably likely that the jury understood the words moral certainty either as suggesting a standard of proof lower than due process requires or as allowing conviction on factors other than the government's proof. At the same time, however, we do not condone the use of the phrase. As modern dictionary definitions of moral certainty attest, the common meaning of the phrase has changed since it was used in the Webster instruction, and it may continue to do so to the point that it conflicts with the *Winship* standard. Indeed, the definitions of reasonable doubt most widely used in the federal courts do not contain any reference to moral certainty. But we have no supervisory power over the state courts, and, in the context of the instructions as a whole, we cannot say that the use of the phrase rendered the instruction given in Sandoval's case unconstitutional.

III

On December 26, 1987, petitioner Victor went to the Omaha home of an 82-year-old woman for whom he occasionally did gardening work. Once inside, he beat her with a pipe and cut her throat with a knife, killing her. Victor was convicted of first degree murder. A three-judge panel found the statutory aggravating circumstances that Victor had previously been convicted of murder, and that the murder in this case was especially heinous, atrocious, and cruel. Finding none of the statutory mitigating circumstances, the panel sentenced Victor to death. The Nebraska Supreme Court affirmed the conviction and sentence. At Victor's trial, the judge instructed the jury that [t]he burden is always on the State to prove beyond a reasonable doubt all of the material elements of the crime charged, and this burden never shifts. The charge continued:

"'Reasonable doubt' is such a doubt as would cause a reasonable and prudent person, in one of the graver and more important transactions of life, to pause and hesitate before taking the represented facts as true and relying and acting thereon. It is such a doubt as will not permit you, after full, fair, and impartial consideration of all the evidence, to have an abiding conviction, to a moral certainty, of the guilt of the accused. At the same time, absolute or mathematical certainty is not required. You may be convinced of the truth of a fact beyond a reasonable doubt and yet be fully aware that possibly you may be mistaken. You may find an accused guilty upon the strong probabilities of the case, provided such probabilities are strong enough to exclude any doubt of his guilt that is reasonable. A reasonable doubt is an actual and substantial doubt arising from the evidence, from the facts or circumstances shown by the evidence, or from the lack of evidence on the part of the state, as distinguished from a doubt arising from mere possibility, from bare imagination, or from fanciful conjecture."

. . . .

Victor's primary argument is that equating a reasonable doubt with a "substantial doubt" overstated the degree of doubt necessary for acquittal. We agree that this construction is somewhat problematic. Any ambiguity, however, is removed by reading the phrase in the context of the sentence in which it appears: A reasonable doubt is an actual and substantial doubt . . . as distinguished from a doubt arising from mere possibility, from bare imagination, or from fanciful conjecture.

. . . .

Victor also challenges the "moral certainty" portion of the instruction. Though we reiterate that we do not countenance its use, the inclusion of the moral certainty phrase did not render the instruction given in Victor's case unconstitutional. . . .

IV

The Due Process Clause requires the government to prove a criminal defendant's guilt beyond a reasonable doubt, and trial courts must avoid defining reasonable doubt so as to lead the jury to convict on a lesser showing than due process requires. In these cases, however, we conclude that, "taken as a whole, the instructions correctly conveyed the concept of reasonable doubt to the jury." There is no reasonable likelihood that the jurors who determined petitioners' guilt applied the instructions in a way that violated the Constitution. The judgments in both cases are accordingly

Affirmed.

Justice Kennedy, concurring.

It was commendable for Chief Justice Shaw to pen an instruction that survived more than a century, but, as the Court makes clear, what once might have made sense to jurors has long since become archaic. In fact, some of the phrases here in question confuse far more than they clarify. Though the reference to "moral certainty" is not much better, California's use of "moral evidence" is the most troubling, and to me seems quite indefensible. The derivation of the phrase is explained in the Court's opinion, but, even with this help, the term is a puzzle. And for jurors who have not had the benefit of the Court's research, the words will do nothing but baffle. I agree that use of "moral evidence" in the California formulation is not fatal to the instruction here. I cannot understand, however, why such an unruly term should be used at all when jurors are asked to perform a task that can be of great difficulty even when instructions are altogether clear. The inclusion of words so malleable, because so obscure, might, in other circumstances, have put the whole instruction at risk. With this observation, I concur in full in the opinion of the Court.

. . . .

Justice Blackmun, with whom Justice Souter joins . . . concurring in part and dissenting in part.

In *Cage v. Louisiana*, 498 U.S. 39 (1990), this Court found a jury instruction defining reasonable doubt so obviously flawed that the resulting state court judgment deserved summary reversal. The majority today purports to uphold and follow *Cage*, but plainly falters in its application of that case. There is no meaningful difference between the jury instruction delivered at Victor's trial and the jury instruction issued in *Cage*, save the fact that the jury instruction in Victor's case did not contain the two words "grave uncertainty." But the mere absence of these two words can be of no help to the State, since there is other language in the instruction that is equally offensive to due process. I therefore dissent from the Court's opinion and judgment in *Victor v. Nebraska*.

I

Our democracy rests in no small part on our faith in the ability of the criminal justice system to separate those who are guilty from those who are not. This is a faith which springs fundamentally from the requirement that unless guilt is established beyond all reasonable doubt, the accused shall go free. It was not until 1970, however, in *In re Winship*, 397 U.S. 358, that the Court finally and explicitly held that the Due Process Clause protects the accused against conviction except upon proof beyond a reasonable doubt of every fact necessary to constitute the crime with which he is charged. . . . To be a meaningful safeguard, the reasonable doubt standard must have a tangible meaning that is capable of being understood by those who are required to apply it. It must be stated accurately and with the precision owed to those whose liberty or life is at risk. Because of the extraordinarily high stakes in criminal trials, [i]t is critical that the moral force of the criminal law not be diluted by a standard of proof that leaves people in doubt whether innocent men are being condemned. When reviewing a jury instruction that defines "reasonable doubt," it is necessary to consider the instruction as a whole, and to give the words their common and ordinary meaning. It is not sufficient for the jury instruction merely to be susceptible to an interpretation that is technically correct. The important question is whether there is a "reasonable likelihood" that the jury was misled or confused by the instruction, and therefore applied it in a way that violated the Constitution. Any jury instruction defining "reasonable doubt" that suggests an improperly high degree of doubt for acquittal or an improperly low degree of certainty for conviction offends due process.

. . . .

In my view, the predominance of potentially misleading language in Victor's instruction made it likely that the jury interpreted the phrase "substantial doubt" to mean that a "large" doubt, as opposed to a merely reasonable doubt, is required to acquit a defendant. . . . Considering the instruction in its entirety, it seems fairly obvious to me that the "strong probabilities" language increased the likelihood that the jury understood "substantial doubt" to mean "to a large degree."

. . . .

This confusing and misleading state of affairs leads me ineluctably to the conclusion that, in Victor's case, there exists a reasonable likelihood that the jury believed that a lesser burden of proof rested with the prosecution. . . . Where, as here, a jury instruction attempts but fails to convey with clarity and accuracy the meaning of reasonable doubt, the reviewing court should reverse the conviction and remand for a new trial.

LEGAL ANALYSIS AND WRITING 2.4

The following questions are based on the *How to Brief a Legal Case* format shown in the Appendix. Use this format to answer the following questions:

1. Summarize the facts in the previous case.
2. What is the legal issue?
3. What did the appellate court decide?
4. Why did the court decide this way?
5. Do you agree with the court's reasoning? Explain why or why not.

LEGAL RESEARCH USING THE INTERNET SKILLS 2.5

Find and read this important Supreme Court case online! Check out one of the legal research web sites below and use their "Search" feature to find this case. In the "Search" field, enter the cite or case name.

1. FindLaw U.S. Supreme Court Decisions (http://www.findlaw.com/casecode/supreme.html)
2. U.S. Supreme Court (http://www.supremecourtus.gov/)
3. Supreme Court Collection of Cornell Law School (http://supct.law.cornell.edu/supct/)

YOU BE THE JUDGE 2.2

In a criminal case, the defense requests the judge to issue the following instruction to the jury defining *reasonable doubt*:
"Reasonable doubt means that if you have any doubt as to the guilt of the defendant, you must return a not guilty verdict."
Would you allow this instruction? Why or why not?

Reasonable Suspicion
Standard of proof required for a law enforcement officer to stop and question a person, based on the officer's reasonable suspicion that the person has committed a crime, is committing a crime, or is about to commit a crime.

Probable Cause
Standard of proof required for search warrants and arrests in criminal actions. It requires that evidence be considered "more probable than not" in proving what is alleged.

Reasonable Suspicion

Reasonable suspicion is a term used in criminal law to justify a law enforcement officer's actions to stop and question a person based on suspicion that a person has committed a crime, is committing a crime, or is about to commit a crime. This type of certainty may be enough to justify an investigative stop, but would be less than the probable cause required to arrest. For example, suppose a police officer sees two people in a vehicle with its lights out and engine running, parked by a closed business late at night in a high crime rate area. The officer would have reason to stop and question the occupants of the vehicle, but, without more evidence, would lack legal cause to make an arrest.

PROBABLE CAUSE

Probable cause is more certain than reasonable suspicion. It is something that would be considered "more probable than not," and would include facts that would warrant a reasonable person to believe that a crime had been committed and that the accused had committed it.

CRITICAL THINKING QUESTIONS 2.3

1. How would you go about explaining to the jury what "reasonable doubt" is?

2. How do the standards of proof discussed in this section (i.e., probable cause, beyond a reasonable doubt) influence the gathering of evidence?

3. In a criminal case, how would you go about establishing "probable cause?"

4. In a criminal case, how would you go about establishing "reasonable suspicion" to justify the action of a police officer?

5. In an area with a high commercial burglary rate, a police officer questions a young man who is standing outside the rear entrance of a store that is not open. Would the officer have reasonable suspicion to question the young man at 2 A.M.? What about 2 P.M.? Explain the reasons for your conclusions.

6. What if this young man is observed by the officer to be inside of the closed store without permission. Would the officer then have probable cause to arrest the young man for burglary? Why or why not?

7. Without any other evidence, do you believe that the defendant could be convicted of burglary?

PRESUMPTIONS AND INFERENCES

The trier of fact generally has the responsibility to weigh all evidence presented and to decide what **inference** might be drawn from any facts presented. An inference is a deduction of fact that may logically be drawn from another fact. Sometimes, however, the law requires that an assumption of fact or conclusion be derived once that basic fact has been established. This is called a **presumption**. A presumption requires that the trier of fact accept the presumed fact unless evidence is offered by the opposing party to rebut the presumed fact. For example, in a civil action for negligent operation of a motor vehicle in Connecticut, if the operator is someone other than the owner of the motor vehicle, the operator is presumed to be an agent of the owner.[19] The trier of fact would be required to accept this unless evidence was then produced to prove that the vehicle was being operated without the owner's permission. A presumption is not evidence, but a legal finding that the jury is directed to make.

Presumptions are quite often the result of social and public policies (see Exhibit 2.3). For example, in most states, a marriage is presumed to be valid and a child born in lawful wedlock is presumed to be legitimate. These two presumptions facilitate social policy that promotes marriage and adequate protections for children. There is also a public policy interest in ensuring the support of the child if paternity is questioned.

Presumptions Can Be Conclusive or Rebuttable

Presumptions can be conclusive or rebuttable (see Exhibit 2.4). A **conclusive presumption** is one that cannot be contradicted and for which no evidence can be admitted to the contrary. These presumptions are really rules of law that maintain that proof of certain facts establishes specific legal rights or legal status. For example, jurors may hear evidence regarding the paternity of a child born to a married plaintiff who is

Inference
A deduction of fact that may logically be drawn from another fact.

Presumption
An assumption of fact that the law requires to be made from another fact.

Conclusive Presumption
A rule of law that proof of certain facts establishes a specific legal right or legal status. A conclusive presumption cannot be contradicted and no evidence can be admitted to the contrary.

EXHIBIT 2.3   Definitions of Presumptions

California Evidence Code

Sec. 600 (a). A presumption is an assumption of fact that the law requires to be made from another fact or group of facts found or otherwise established in the action. A presumption is not evidence.

Florida Statutes

Sec. 90.301 Presumption defined; inferences.

(1) For the purposes of this chapter, a presumption is an assumption of fact which the law makes from the existence of another fact or group of facts found or otherwise established.

Georgia Code

Sec. 24-4-20. Presumptions are either of law or of fact. Presumptions of law are conclusions and inferences which the law draws from given facts. Presumptions of fact are exclusively questions for the jury, to be decided by the ordinary test of human experience.

---

claiming that the defendant, who is not her husband, fathered the child. The jury may infer from the weight of the evidence and facts presented that the defendant is or is not the father. However, some states, like Oregon, have a rule that a child born in lawful wedlock is conclusively presumed legitimate.[20] If the above action was heard in one of these states, the jury would be directed to find that the child was fathered by the plaintiff's husband.

Examples of conclusive presumptions include:

1. A child born to a married woman is conclusively presumed legitimate if she was living with her husband at the time.
2. A child under the age of 7 is presumed at common law to be incapable of committing a crime.

Rebuttable Presumption

A presumption that the jury must make unless evidence to the contrary is introduced.

A **rebuttable presumption** is one that the jury must make unless evidence to the contrary is introduced. Most presumptions are rebuttable.

Examples of rebuttable presumptions include:

1. An accused is innocent until proven guilty.
2. A person intends the natural consequence of his or her actions.
3. A blood alcohol limit of .08 constitutes driving under the influence.
4. A person found dead did not commit suicide.
5. A letter that is properly addressed, stamped, and mailed will be delivered.

Prima Facie Evidence

In some states, a statute providing that a fact or group of facts is prima facie evidence of another fact establishes a presumption within the meaning of this rule (see Exhibit 2.5). This is not in the Federal Rules, but is included in many state rules of evidence. Its purpose is to allow statutes to make presumptions "prima facie" evidence of a fact. For example, the sale of an alcoholic beverage to a person exhibiting a liquor ID card may be prima facie evidence of the seller's compliance with the law on the sale of alcohol to minors.

Is There a Duty to Offer Evidence to Rebut a Presumption?

The following Vermont case looks at whether a defendant has a duty to rebut a presumption once it has been established.

EXHIBIT 2.4   Examples of Presumptions

California Evidence Code
Sec. 637. The things which a person possesses are presumed to be owned by him.
Sec. 638. A person who exercises acts of ownership over property is presumed to be the owner of it.
Sec. 641. A letter correctly addressed and properly mailed is presumed to have been received in the ordinary course of mail.
Sec. 663. A ceremonial marriage is presumed to be valid.
Sec. 665. A person is presumed to intend the ordinary consequences of his voluntary act.
Sec. 667. A person not heard from in five years is presumed to be dead.

Connecticut General Statute
Sec. 52-183. Presumption of agency in motor vehicle operation.
In any civil action brought against the owner of a motor vehicle to recover damages for the negligent or reckless operation of the motor vehicle, the operator, if he is other than the owner of the motor vehicle, shall be presumed to be the agent and servant of the owner of the motor vehicle and operating it in the course of his employment. The defendant shall have the burden of rebutting the presumption.

Missouri Revised Statute
Sec. 490-620. If any person who shall have resided in this state go from and do not return to this state for Five successive years, he shall be presumed to be dead in any case wherein his death shall come in question, unless proof be made that he was alive within that time.

EXHIBIT 2.5   Prima Facie Evidence and Presumptions

Vermont Rules of Evidence,
Rule 301 (b). Prima facie evidence. A statute providing that a fact or group of facts is prima facie evidence of another fact establishes a presumption within the meaning of this rule.

CASE

Larmay v. Vanetten

129 Vt. 368 (1971).
Supreme Court of Vermont.

Keyser, Justice.

This is an automobile passenger case brought to recover damages for injuries suffered by the plaintiff. The defendant denied liability and asserted the affirmative defenses of contributory negligence and assumption of the risk by the plaintiff. Trial was by jury. At the close of all of the evidence plaintiff moved for a directed verdict as to liability. The court granted the motion and submitted the case on the question of damages. The jury returned a verdict for the plaintiff to recover the sum of $5,500.00. The defendant appealed and claims (1) that the trial court erred in directing a verdict for the plaintiff and (2) that the verdict was excessive.

In considering the defendant's first ground of appeal we must take the evidence in the light most favorable to the defendant, she being the party against whom the motion was directed. The evidence thus viewed discloses the following factual situation relative to the defendant's liability.

The plaintiff was returning from work at about 7:30 P.M. on December 22, 1967, as a passenger in a Cadillac car owned and operated by a Mr. Goodrich northerly on Route 7 just south of Shelburne Village. The defendant was operating her Volvo automobile southerly at the same time and place. She was traveling behind a hay truck and in front of an automobile driven by a Mr. Pond. It was nearly dark and the cars had their lights on. Each vehicle was being operated at approximately 40–45 miles per hour. As the cars approached each other on the brow of a hill, the cars were in a near head-on collision which, according to the testimony, was caused by the defendant's car moving into the northbound lane in which the Goodrich car was traveling. The defendant concedes in her brief that her car traveled to her left into the northbound lane of traffic although she testified that she had no recollection of the facts surrounding the accident. The defendant was returning home from work after an office party and the last thing she recalled was that she was following behind a truck or tractor trailer through the village of Shelburne. The defendant's vehicle came to rest mostly in the northbound lane.

Mr. Pond testified that he pulled out in back of a Volvo on Route 7 in South Burlington and was following it and that the defendant's car was right behind a truck or tractor trailer. He said he noticed it tended to dart from one side of the road to the other, from the shoulder past the yellow line or center line and back to the shoulder again and it went like this all the way to Shelburne, at which point the accident took place. This evidence was uncontradicted.

The defendant contends that the mere presence of her vehicle in the opposite lane of traffic or the passage of her vehicle over the center line of the highway does not establish negligence on her part as a matter of law. By granting plaintiff's motion for a **directed verdict**, the court ruled that on the evidence the defendant was guilty of negligence as a **matter of law** in the operation of her automobile. *Beaucage v. Russell*, 127 Vt. 58. The burden of showing that the defendant was guilty of some negligent act or omission that proximately caused the accident was, of course, on the plaintiff. Under the rules of the road governing the conduct and operation of vehicles upon a public highway,

In 23 V.S.A. s 1032, it is provided:

> Operators of vehicles proceeding in opposite directions shall exercise due care and shall each keep to the right of the center of the highway so as to pass without interference.

The pertinent part of Section 1035 requires that

> an operator of a vehicle overtaking another vehicle proceeding in the same direction shall not pass to the left of the center of the highway unless the way ahead is clear of approaching traffic.

Section 1037 provides that

> a vehicle shall not pass another from the rear at the top of a hill or on a curve where the view ahead is in anyway obstructed. . . .

The rules of the road are safety statutes and proof of their violation, on the part of one charged with negligence, makes out a *prima facie* case of negligence against the offending operator. But this *presumption* of negligence is, of course, open to rebuttal. A true legal presumption is in the nature of evidence, and is to be weighed as such. Being a disputable presumption, *it shifts to the party against whom it operates the burden of evidence.* And the prima facie case would become the established case, if nothing further appears.

The presumption points out to the party on whom it lies the duty of going forward with evidence on the fact presumed. And when that party has produced evidence fairly and reasonably tending to show that the real fact is not as presumed, the office of the presumption is performed and disappears from the arena. We are not unmindful that safety rules are not hard and fast, nor absolute in application to all circumstances.

Thus, if the defendant desired to overcome the effect of the presumption it was her duty to present evidence to rebut it. She was accorded this opportunity but failed to exercise it. A diligent search of the record fails to disclose any evidence introduced by her in this respect. Her own testimony, of course, does not touch on the question of how and why the accident happened as it did. The defendant offered no countervailing evidence to the presumption or to explain her manner of operating her vehicle "darting from one side of the road to the other." If there was any such evidence it was not forthcoming and this left the presumption of negligence standing unchallenged.

The defendant claims the plaintiff, before he can have the benefit of the prima facie negligence doctrine, is required "to establish, through evidence, that it was an act of the defendant-operator which caused defendant's vehicle to cross the center line." This is not the law and, furthermore, the unchallenged testimony of Mr. Pond demonstrates with definite clarity that it was the act of the defendant which caused her car to be on the wrong side of the road.

The appellant calls attention to the testimony of Mr. Pond where he testified:

> "Well, we were heading—I was directly in back of the Volvo. We were heading up the hill out of Shelburne, and the Volvo was very close to the hay truck. It seemed it was almost under the hay truck, and then I just remember the Volvo darting out

into the northbound lane as if the car went out of control or it was a last minute decision to pass the hay truck, and at that time the Cadillac was right there and they just hit head on."

Later, he said: "I couldn't determine whether the Volvo was passing the hay truck. It was such a sudden move, it looked like it got out of control." The defendant contends that Mr. Pond's testimony clearly justifies a permissible inference that, for some reason, the defendant's vehicle became out of control before it ever left its proper lane of travel. A permissible inference must rest upon a logical deduction from established facts in order to provide a conclusion which the triers of fact may or may not find along with the other evidence in a case.

The defendant argues that since there was evidence allowing a reasonable inference of mechanical failure or dangerous road conditions, the court erred in granting plaintiff's motion for a directed verdict as to liability. First, there was no evidence of the existence of dangerous road condition but there was evidence that the weather was fair. Secondly, the testimony of Mr. Pond neither supports the argument nor the rationalization claimed for it. The evidence fails to establish the basic fact or facts which rise up to meet and counter the presumption of negligence.

Although we find no evidence in the record on which such an inference could be based, we must bear in mind that a presumption and an inference are not the same thing. A "presumption" is a deduction which the law requires a trier to make; an "inference" is a deduction which the trier may or may not make according to his own conclusions. A presumption is mandatory; an inference, permissible. At the close of evidence, the plaintiff, having established a violation of the safety statutes, made out a prima facie case of negligence against which no rebuttal evidence was produced fairly and reasonably tending to show that the real fact was not as presumed. Thus, the trial court properly granted plaintiff's motion on the question of liability.

The defendant cites cases relating to the doctrine of *res ipsa loquitur* which she claims is applicable because this case she asserts involves an unexplained accident. Concerning this claim we need only to point out that there are no basic facts in the record establishing the application of the doctrine. Affirmed.

LEGAL ANALYSIS AND WRITING 2.5

The following questions are based on the *How to Brief a Legal Case* format shown in the Appendix. Use this format to answer the following questions:

1. Summarize the facts in the previous case.
2. What is the legal issue?
3. What did the appellate court decide?
4. Why did the court decide this way?
5. How did the court apply a presumption in this case?

LEGAL RESEARCH USING THE INTERNET SKILLS 2.6

1. Use one of the following web sites to find out whether your state rules of evidence include any rule covering presumptions.

List of State Laws from Legal Information Institute of Cornell Law School
    (http://www.law.cornell.edu/ states/listing.html)

FindLaw (http://www.findlaw.com)

Federal Rules of Evidence: (http://www.law.cornell.edu/rules/fre/overview.html)

EFFECT OF A PRESUMPTION IN A CIVIL ACTION

Courts differ as to the effect that a presumption must be given in a civil action and the burden it imposes on the party opposing it. There are three different approaches taken by courts regarding this. One imposes only a burden of production or going forward with evidence to rebut the presumption. The second approach requires a more substantial burden of proof requirement. The third approach uses both the burden of production and the burden of proof.

When the Federal Rules were originally being proposed, the advisory committee for the Supreme Court recommended a rule that would require the more substantial burden of proof. The rationale was that a presumption would not carry sufficient weight if it could be rebutted simply by the burden of producing evidence instead of being made to prove the nonexistence of the presumed fact. Congress rejected this and adopted the burden of production approach, codified in Rule 301, which limits the effect of a presumption by requiring only a burden of going forward with evidence on the part of a party opposing a presumption.[21]

Burden of Production or "Bursting Bubble" Theory

Today, the federal courts and a majority of state courts still use the burden of production as the standard required to rebut a presumption (see Exhibit 2.6). Under this approach, the party opposing a presumption only needs to introduce evidence rebutting the presumed fact and this would then shift the burden back to the party who introduced the presumption. North Carolina reflects this approach in its definition of a presumption in a civil action. *North Carolina Rule of Evidence* 301 states that "a presumption imposes on the party against whom it is directed the burden of going forward with evidence to rebut or meet the presumption, but does not shift to such party the burden of proof in the sense of the risk of nonpersuasion, which remains throughout the trial upon the party on whom it was originally cast." This rule goes on to explain that the "burden of going forward is satisfied by the introduction of evidence sufficient to permit reasonable minds to conclude that the presumed fact does not exist. If the party against whom a presumption operates fails to meet the burden of producing evidence, the presumed fact shall be deemed proved, and the court shall instruct the jury accordingly."[22] The burden of production view is also known as the *"bursting bubble" theory* on the premise that once the burden has been met, the "bubble" created by the presumption bursts and no longer can be presumed.

Burden of Proof or Persuasion Theory

Some courts have followed the original recommendation of the advisory committee to the Federal Rules of Evidence that requires a higher burden for

---

EXHIBIT 2.6   Example of "Burden of Production" Approach to Presumptions

Ohio Rules of Evidence
Rule 301. Presumptions in General in Civil Actions.
In all civil actions and proceedings not otherwise provided for by statute . . . or by these rules, a presumption imposes on the party against whom it is directed the burden of going forward with evidence to rebut or meet the presumption, but does not shift to such party the burden of proof in the sense of the risk of non-persuasion, which remains throughout the trial upon the party on whom it was originally cast.

a party rebutting a presumption. This view was also adopted by the Uniform Rules of Evidence[23] and is known as the burden of proof theory. Under this approach, the party opposing a presumption has the burden of disproving the presumed fact. The burden of proof or persuasion is on the party opposing a presumed fact once the party offering the presumption has introduced evidence to support it. Oregon exemplifies this with their evidence rule requiring that, in civil actions, "a presumption imposes on the party against whom it is directed the burden of proving that the nonexistence of the presumed fact is more probable than its existence."[24] This view generally requires that the presumption be disproved by a preponderance of the evidence, the same standard used for civil actions.

Let's illustrate these two approaches with an example. In a civil action for misrepresentation, the defendant may claim that she mailed a letter to the plaintiff explaining the hidden costs in the plaintiff's recent purchase. If the plaintiff denies receiving the letter, the jury may infer from the evidence and facts presented whether or not the letter was mailed or received. Many states have a presumption like the one in the California Evidence Code, which states that a "letter correctly addressed and properly mailed is presumed to have been received in the ordinary course of mail."[25] In the above example, if the defendant can establish that the letter was properly mailed, a presumption would be created that the letter was, in fact, received by the plaintiff. The effect of a presumption is to then shift the burden back on the party opposing the presumption. Whether this burden is one of production or persuasion depends on the approach taken. Under the burden of production approach, the plaintiff could rebut the presumption by offering testimony that she did not receive the letter. Under the burden of proof approach (see Exhibit 2.7), the plaintiff, in order to rebut the presumption, would have to present sufficient evidence that would persuade the trier of fact by a preponderance that the letter was not mailed or that the plaintiff did not receive it (for example, a witness who testifies that she saw the defendant put the letter in her desk or a mailroom clerk who testifies that he checks all mail in for the plaintiff and had no record of receiving the letter in question).

EXHIBIT 2.7   Example of "Burden of Proof" Approach to Presumptions

Utah Rules of Evidence
Rule 301. Presumptions in general civil actions.
(a) Effect. In all civil actions and proceedings not otherwise provided for by statute or by these rules, a presumption imposes on the party against whom it is directed the burden of proving that the nonexistence of the presumed fact is more probable than its existence.

Combined Approach: Proof and Production Theory

Some states, like California and Florida, use a combined approach to dealing with presumptions. In these states, a presumption is either one requiring a burden of proof for the party opposing it, or a presumption requiring a burden of production on the party opposing it. The difference depends on whether the presumption is one that promotes a public policy concern or not. If it does, it requires a higher burden of proof. California gives an example of this through its definition that "a presumption affecting the burden of proof is a presumption established to implement some public policy other than to facilitate the determination of the particular action in which the presumption is applied, such as the policy in favor of establishment of a parent and child relationship, the validity of marriage, the stability of titles to property, or the security of those who entrust themselves or their property to the administration of others."[26]

California defines a presumption affecting the burden of producing evidence as "a presumption established to implement no public policy other than to facilitate the determination of the particular action in which the presumption is applied." (see Exhibit 2.8)[27]

Instructions to the Jury on Presumptions

The effect of a presumption on the trier of fact will only operate through an appropriate instruction by the trial judge. For example, if a party opposing a presumption has not met her burden of production, the court will direct the jury to find the existence of the presumed fact. As an example, in a civil action for negligence, the plaintiff offers evidence of a State-recognized presumption that the operator of a vehicle is the agent of the owner. If the defendant fails to meet her burden of rebutting this presumption, the court may issue the following instruction to the jury:

"The law presumes that, in a civil action for negligent operation of a motor vehicle, if the operator is other than the owner of the motor vehicle, the operator is presumed to be an agent of the owner. Since this evi-

---

EXHIBIT 2.8 Examples of States Using the Combined Approach to Presumptions

California Evidence Code

Sec. 603. A presumption affecting the burden of producing evidence is a presumption established to implement no public policy other than to facilitate the determination of the particular action in which the presumption is applied.

Sec. 604. The effect of a presumption affecting the burden of producing evidence is to require the trier of fact to assume the existence of the presumed fact unless and until evidence is introduced which would support a finding of its nonexistence, in which case the trier of fact shall determine the existence or nonexistence of the presumed fact from the evidence and without regard to the presumption.

Sec. 605. A presumption affecting the burden of proof is a presumption established to implement some public policy other than to facilitate the determination of the particular action in which the presumption is applied, such as the policy in favor of establishment of a parent and child relationship, the validity of marriage, the stability of titles to property, or the security of those who entrust themselves or their property to the administration of others.

Sec. 606. The effect of a presumption affecting the burden of proof is to impose upon the party against whom it operates the burden of proof as to the nonexistence of the presumed fact.

Florida Statutes

Sec. 90.302. Classification of rebuttable presumptions. Every rebuttable presumption is either:

(1) A presumption affecting the burden of producing evidence and requiring the trier of fact to assume the existence of the presumed fact, unless credible evidence sufficient to sustain a finding of the nonexistence of the presumed fact is introduced, in which event, the existence or nonexistence of the presumed fact shall be determined from the evidence without regard to the presumption; or

(2) A presumption affecting the burden of proof that imposes upon the party against whom it operates the burden of proof concerning the nonexistence of the presumed fact.

Sec. 90.303. Presumption affecting the burden of producing evidence defined.—In a civil action or proceeding, unless otherwise provided by statute, a presumption established primarily to facilitate the determination of the particular action in which the presumption is applied, rather than to implement public policy, is a presumption affecting the burden of producing evidence.

Sec. 90.304. Presumption affecting the burden of proof defined.—In civil actions, all rebuttable presumptions which are not defined in s.90.303 are presumptions affecting the burden of proof.

dence was presented by the plaintiff and not contested by the defendant in this matter, I instruct you to find that the operator of the vehicle was an agent of the owner."

If the burden of rebutting the presumption is one of proof and the defendant did offer evidence to rebut the presumption, the court may issue an instruction like the following:

"*If* you believe that the operator of the vehicle during the night of the accident in question was a person other than the owner of the vehicle, *then* you must find that the operator was acting as an agent of the owner, *unless* the defendant has proven by a preponderance of evidence that she, as the owner of the vehicle, did not give permission for anyone to use her vehicle that night."

CRITICAL THINKING QUESTIONS 2.4

1. What is the reasoning behind allowing presumptions in a civil action?
2. Assess the strengths and weaknesses of allowing these presumptions.
3. How do social or public policy concerns influence the creation of presumptions?
4. Why do we allow "conclusive" presumptions?
5. Assess the three approaches now taken by courts in requiring a party to meet a certain burden in order to rebut a presumption.
6. Which burden of proof do you think should be required of a party opposing a presumption? Why?

PRESUMPTIONS IN CRIMINAL CASES

The Federal Rules do not contain provisions for presumptions in criminal cases. However, many state rules do include such provisions. When a presumption operates against an accused in a criminal action, state courts generally allow, but do not require, the trier of fact to accept a presumed fact if the burden of proof has been met by the prosecution. However, a presumption does not shift to the accused the burden of either producing evidence or of persuading the trier of fact that the presumed fact does not exist. This burden of proof, beyond a reasonable doubt, in a criminal action remains with the prosecution throughout the trial.

A statute providing that a fact is prima facie evidence of another fact or of guilt usually establishes a presumption within the meaning of these rules. When a presumption operates against the accused, the court may not direct the jury to find the presumed fact against him. If a presumed fact establishes guilt or is an element of the offense, the court may submit the question of guilt or of the existence of the presumed fact to the jury, but only if a reasonable juror on the evidence as a whole, including the evidence of the basic fact, could find guilt or the presumed fact beyond a reasonable doubt. Oregon's evidence rule explains this, stating:

1. The judge is not authorized to direct the jury to find a presumed fact against the accused.
2. When the presumed fact establishes guilt or is an element of the offense or negates a defense, the judge may submit the question of guilt or the existence of the presumed fact to the jury only if:

   a) A reasonable juror on the evidence as a whole could find that the facts giving rise to the presumed fact have been established beyond a reasonable doubt; and

b) The presumed fact follows more likely than not from the facts giving rise to the presumed fact.[28]

When a presumption against an accused in a criminal action is submitted to the jury, the court will instruct the jury that if it finds the existence of the basic fact it may regard that fact as sufficient evidence of the presumed fact but is not required to do so (see Exhibit 2.9). For example, most states have a presumption that a blood alcohol content of .08 or greater constitutes intoxication for purposes of driving under the influence. If the jury hears evidence that a breath test administered to a defendant registered .09, that jury may presume that the defendant was intoxicated. However, they may hear additional evidence that convinces them otherwise—the breath test was operated improperly, the test results were inaccurate, and so on. If the presumed fact establishes guilt or is an element of the offense, or negatives a defense, the court will instruct the jury that its existence, on all the evidence, must be proved beyond a reasonable doubt (see Exhibit 2.10).

EXHIBIT 2.9   Presumptions in Criminal Cases

Wyoming Rules of Evidence
Rule 303.
(a) *Scope.* Except as otherwise provided by statute, in criminal cases, presumptions against an accused, recognized at common law or created by statute, including statutory provisions that certain facts are prima facie evidence of other facts or of guilt, are governed by this rule.
(b) *Submission to jury.* The court is not authorized to direct the jury to find a presumed fact against the accused. If a presumed fact establishes guilt or is an element of the offense or negatives a defense, the court may submit the question of guilt or of the existence of the presumed fact to the jury, but only if a reasonable juror on the evidence as a whole, including the evidence of the basic facts, could find guilt or the presumed fact beyond a reasonable doubt. If the presumed fact has a lesser effect, the question of its existence may be submitted to the jury provided the basic facts are supported by substantial evidence or are otherwise established, unless the court determines that a reasonable juror on the evidence as a whole could not find the existence of the presumed fact.
(c) *Instructing the jury.* Whenever the existence of a presumed fact against the accused is submitted to the jury, the court shall instruct the jury that it may regard the basic facts as sufficient evidence of the presumed fact but is not required to do so. In addition, if the presumed fact establishes guilt or is an element of the offense or negatives a defense, the court shall instruct the jury that its existence, on all the evidence, must be proved beyond a reasonable doubt.

EXHIBIT 2.10   Presumption of Innocence

In criminal law, under our system of criminal justice, there is a **presumption of innocence** for an accused or "innocent until proven guilty." The burden is therefore on the prosecutor to offer sufficient admissible evidence in order to prove the defendant guilty.

Presumption of Innocence
In a criminal case, an accused is presumed innocent until proven guilty.

Can Inference be Drawn by Possession?

In the following case, the U.S. Supreme Court decides what standard of proof is required to establish "a traditional common law inference deeply rooted in our law"—that an inference of guilty knowledge may be drawn from the fact of unexplained possession of stolen goods.

Group 2 Case # 2

CASE

Barnes v. United States

412 U.S. 837 (1973).

Justice Powell delivered the opinion of the Court.

Petitioner Barnes was convicted in United States District Court on . . . possessing United States Treasury checks stolen from the mails, knowing them to be stolen. . . . The trial court instructed the jury that ordinarily it would be justified in inferring from unexplained possession of recently stolen mail that the defendant possessed the mail with knowledge that it was stolen. We granted certiorari to consider whether this instruction comports with due process. The evidence at petitioner's trial established that on June 2, 1971, he opened a checking account using the pseudonym "Clarence Smith." On July 1, and July 3, 1971, the United States Disbursing Office at San Francisco mailed four Government checks in the amounts of $269.02, $154.70, $184, and $268.80 to Nettie Lewis, Albert Young, Arthur Salazar, and Mary Hernandez, respectively. On July 8, 1971, petitioner deposited these four checks into the "Smith" account. Each check bore the apparent endorsement of the payee and a second endorsement by "Clarence Smith." At petitioner's trial the four payees testified that they had never received, endorsed, or authorized endorsement of the checks. A Government handwriting expert testified that petitioner had made the "Clarence Smith" endorsement on all four checks and that he had signed the payees' names on the Lewis and Hernandez checks. Although petitioner did not take the stand, a postal inspector testified to certain statements made by petitioner at a post-arrest interview. Petitioner explained to the inspector that he received the checks in question from people who sold furniture for him door to door and that the checks had been signed in the payees' names when he received them. Petitioner further stated that he could not name or identify any of the salespeople. Nor could he substantiate the existence of any furniture orders because the salespeople allegedly wrote their orders on scratch paper that had not been retained. Petitioner admitted that he executed the Clarence Smith endorsements and deposited the checks but denied making the payees' endorsements.

The District Court instructed the jury that "possession of recently stolen property, if not satisfactorily explained, is ordinarily a circumstance from which you may reasonably draw the inference and find, in the light of the surrounding circumstances shown by the evidence in the case, that the person in possession knew the property had been stolen." The jury brought in guilty verdicts on all six counts, and the District Court sentenced petitioner to concurrent 3-year prison terms. The Court of Appeals for the Ninth Circuit affirmed, finding no lack of "rational connection" between unexplained possession of recently stolen property and knowledge that the property was stolen.

. . . .

I

We begin our consideration of the challenged jury instruction with a review of four recent decisions which have considered the validity under the Due Process Clause of criminal law presumptions and inferences. *Turner v. United States,* 396 U.S. 398 (1970); *Leary v. United States,* 395 U.S. 6 (1965); *United States v. Romano,* 382 U.S. 136 (1965); *United States v. Gainey,* 380 U.S. 63 (1965). In *United States v. Gainey,* the Court sustained the constitutionality of an instruction tracking a statute which authorized the jury to infer from defendant's unexplained presence at an illegal still that he was carrying on "the business of a distiller or rectifier without having given bond as required by law." Relying on the holding of *Tot v. United States,* 319 U.S. 463 (1943), that there must be a "rational connection between the fact proved and the ultimate fact presumed," the Court upheld the inference on the basis of the comprehensive nature of the "carrying on" offense and the common knowledge that illegal stills are secluded, secret operations. The following Term the Court determined, however, that presence at an illegal still could not support the inference that the defendant was in possession, custody, or control of the still, a narrower offense. "Presence is relevant and admissible evidence in a trial on a possession charge; but absent some showing of the defendant's function at the still, its connection with possession is too tenuous to permit a reasonable inference of guilt—'the inference of the one from proof of the other is arbitrary. . . .'" *United States v. Romano,* supra, at 141. Three and one-half years after *Romano,* the Court in *Leary v. United States* considered a challenge to a statutory inference that possession of marihuana, unless satisfactorily explained, was sufficient to prove that the defendant knew that the marihuana had been illegally imported into the United States. The Court concluded that in view of the significant possibility that any given marihuana was domestically grown and the improbability that a marihuana user would know whether his marihuana was of domestic or imported origin, the inference did not meet the standards set by *Tot, Gainey,* and *Romano.* Referring to these three cases, the *Leary* Court stated that an inference is "'irrational' or 'arbitrary,' and hence unconstitutional, unless it can at least be said with substantial assurance that the presumed fact is more likely than not to flow from the proved fact on which it is made to depend." In a footnote the Court stated that since the challenged inference failed to satisfy the more-likely-than-not standard, it did not have to "reach the question whether a criminal presumption which passes muster when so judged must also satisfy the criminal 'reasonable doubt' standard if proof of the crime charged or an essential element thereof depends upon its use."

Finally, in *Turner v. United States,* supra, decided the year following *Leary,* the Court considered the constitutionality of instructing the jury that it may infer from possession of heroin and cocaine that the defendant knew these drugs had been illegally imported. The Court noted that *Leary* reserved the question of whether the more-likely-than-not or the reasonable-doubt standard controlled in criminal cases, but it likewise found no need to resolve that question. It held that the inference with regard to heroin was valid judged by either standard. With regard to cocaine, the inference failed to satisfy even the more-likely-than-not standard.

The teaching of the foregoing cases is not altogether clear. To the extent that the "rational connection," "more likely than not," and "reasonable doubt" standards bear ambiguous relationships to one another, the ambiguity is traceable in large part to variations in language and focus rather than to differences of substance.

. . . What has been established by these cases, however, is at least this: that if a statutory inference submitted to the jury as sufficient to support conviction satisfies the reasonable-doubt standard (that is, the evidence necessary to invoke the inference is sufficient for a rational juror to find the inferred fact beyond a reasonable doubt) as well as the more-likely-than-not standard, then it clearly accords with due process.

In the present case we deal with a traditional common-law inference deeply rooted in our law. For centuries courts have instructed juries that an inference of guilty knowledge may be drawn from the fact of unexplained possession of stolen goods. . . . Early American cases consistently upheld instructions permitting conviction upon such an inference, and the courts of appeals on numerous occasions have approved instructions essentially identical to the instruction given in this case. This longstanding and consistent judicial approval of the instruction, reflecting accumulated common experience, provides strong indication that the instruction comports with due process.

. . . In the present case the challenged instruction only permitted the inference of guilt from unexplained possession of recently stolen property. The evidence established that petitioner possessed recently stolen Treasury checks payable to persons he did not know, and it provided no plausible explanation for such possession consistent with innocence. On the basis of this evidence alone common sense and experience tell us that petitioner must have known or been aware of the high probability that the checks were stolen. Such evidence was clearly sufficient to enable the jury to find beyond a reasonable doubt that petitioner knew the checks were stolen. Since the inference thus satisfies the reasonable-doubt standard, the most stringent standard the Court has applied in judging permissive criminal law inferences, we conclude that it satisfies the requirements of due process.

. . . .

Affirmed.

Standard of Proof for Inferences and Presumptions

The following U.S. Supreme Court case dealt with a car full of people and illegal weapons, where occupants were charged under a New York law that created a presumption of possession for anyone in the vehicle. At issue was what standard of proof had to be shown to establish the presumption, which depended on whether the presumption was permissive or mandatory.

LEGAL ANALYSIS AND WRITING 2.6

The following questions are based on the *How to Brief a Legal Case* format shown in the Appendix. Use this format to answer the following questions:

1. Summarize the facts in the previous case.
2. What is the legal issue?
3. What did the appellate court decide?
4. Why did the court decide this way?
5. Do you agree with the court's reasoning? Explain why or why not.

LEGAL RESEARCH USING THE INTERNET SKILLS 2.7

Find and read this important Supreme Court case online! Check out one of the legal research web sites below and use their "Search" feature to find this case. In the "Search" field, enter the cite or case name.

1. FindLaw U.S. Supreme Court Decisions (http://www.findlaw.com/casecode/supreme.html)
2. U.S. Supreme Court (http://www.supremecourtus.gov/)
3. Supreme Court Collection of Cornell Law School (http://supct.law.cornell.edu/supct/)

group 3 case # 2

CASE

Ulster County Court v. Allen
442 U.S. 140 (1979).

Justice Stevens delivered the opinion of the Court.

A New York statute provides that, with certain exceptions, the presence of a firearm in an automobile is presumptive evidence of its illegal possession by all persons then occupying the vehicle. . . .

Four persons, three adult males (respondents) and a 16-year-old girl (Jane Doe, who is not a respondent here), were jointly tried on charges that they possessed two loaded handguns, a loaded machinegun, and over a pound of heroin found in a Chevrolet in which they were riding when it was stopped for speeding on the New York Thruway shortly after noon on March 28, 1973. The two large-caliber handguns, which together with their ammunition weighed approximately 6 pounds, were seen through the window of the car by the investigating police officer. They were positioned crosswise in an open handbag on either the front floor or the front seat of the car on the passenger side where Jane Doe was sitting. Jane Doe admitted that the handbag was hers. The machinegun and the heroin were discovered in the trunk after the police pried it open. The car had been borrowed from the driver's brother earlier that day; the key to the trunk could not be found in the car or on the person of any of its occupants, although there was testimony that two of the occupants had placed something in the trunk before embarking in the borrowed car. The jury convicted all four of possession of the handguns and acquitted them of possession of the contents of the trunk.

Counsel for all four defendants objected to the introduction into evidence of the two handguns, the machinegun, and the drugs, arguing that the State had not adequately demonstrated a connection between their clients and the contraband. The trial court overruled the objection, relying on the presumption of possession created by the New York statute. Because that presumption does not apply if a weapon is found "upon the person" of one of the occupants of the car, the three male defendants also moved to dismiss the charges relating to the handguns on the ground that the guns were found on the person of Jane Doe. . . . The trial judge twice denied it, concluding that the applicability of the "upon the person" exception was a question of fact for the jury. At the close of the trial, the judge instructed the jurors that they were entitled to infer possession from the defendants' presence in the car. He did not make any reference to the "upon the person" exception in his explanation of the statutory presumption, nor did any of the defendants object to this omission or request alternative or additional instructions on the subject. . . .

. . . .

Inferences and presumptions are a staple of our adversary system of factfinding. It is often necessary for the trier of fact to determine the existence of an element of the crime—that is, an "ultimate" or "elemental" fact—from the existence of one or more "evidentiary" or "basic" facts. The value of these evidentiary devices, and their validity under the Due Process Clause, vary from case to case, however, depending on the strength of the connection between the particular basic and elemental facts involved and on the degree to which the device curtails the factfinder's freedom to assess the evidence independently. Nonetheless, in criminal cases, the ultimate test of any device's constitutional validity in a given case remains constant: the device must not undermine the factfinder's responsibility at trial, based on evidence adduced by the State, to find the ultimate facts beyond a reasonable doubt. See *In re Winship*, 397 U.S. 358.

The most common evidentiary device is the entirely permissive inference or presumption, which allows—but does not require—the trier of fact to infer the elemental fact from proof by the prosecutor of the basic one and which places no burden of any kind on the defendant. In that situation the basic fact may constitute prima facie evidence of the elemental fact. When reviewing this type of device, the Court has required the party challenging it to demonstrate its invalidity as applied to him. Because this permissive presumption leaves the trier of fact free to credit or reject the inference and does not shift the burden of proof, it affects the application of the "beyond a reasonable doubt" standard only if, under the facts of the case, there is no rational way the trier could make the connection permitted by the inference. For only in that situation is there any risk that an explanation of the permissible inference to a jury, or its use by a jury, has caused the presumptively rational factfinder to make an erroneous factual determination.

A mandatory presumption is a far more troublesome evidentiary device. For it may affect not only the strength of the "no reasonable doubt" burden but also the placement of that burden; it tells the trier that he or they must find the elemental fact upon proof of the basic fact, at least unless the defendant has come forward with some evidence to rebut the presumed connection between the two facts. In this situation, the Court has generally examined the presumption on its face to determine the extent to which the basic and elemental facts coincide. To the extent that the trier of fact is forced to abide by the presumption, and may not reject it based on an independent evaluation of the particular facts presented by the State, the analysis of the presumption's constitutional validity is logically divorced from those facts and based on the presumption's accuracy in the run of cases. It is for this reason that the Court has held it irrelevant in analyzing a mandatory presumption, but not in analyzing a purely permissive one, that there is ample evidence in the record other than the presumption to support a conviction.

Without determining whether the presumption in this case was mandatory, the Court of Appeals analyzed it on its face as if it were. In fact, it was not. . . . The trial judge's instructions make it clear that the presumption was merely a part of the prosecution's case, it gave rise to a permissive inference available only in certain circumstances, rather than a mandatory conclusion of possession, and that it could be ignored by the jury even if there was no affirmative proof offered by defendants in rebuttal. The judge explained that possession could be actual or constructive, but that constructive possession could not exist without the intent and ability to exercise control or dominion over the weapons. He also carefully instructed the jury that there is a mandatory presumption of innocence in favor of the defendants that controls unless it, as the exclusive trier of fact, is satisfied beyond a reasonable doubt that the defendants possessed the handguns in the manner described by the judge. In short, the instructions plainly directed the jury to consider all the circumstances tending to support or contradict the inference that all four occupants of the car had possession of the two loaded handguns and to decide the matter for itself without regard to how much evidence the defendants introduced.

. . . .

As applied to the facts of this case, the presumption of possession is entirely rational ... respondents were not "hitchhikers or other casual passengers," and the guns were neither "a few inches in length" nor "out of sight." The argument against possession by any of the respondents was predicated solely on the fact that the guns were in Jane Doe's pocketbook. ... Even if it was reasonable to conclude that she had placed the guns in her purse before the car was stopped by police, the facts strongly suggest that Jane Doe was not the only person able to exercise dominion over them. The two guns were too large to be concealed in her handbag. The bag was consequently open, and part of one of the guns was in plain view, within easy access of the driver of the car and even, perhaps, of the other two respondents who were riding in the rear seat. Moreover, it is highly improbable that the loaded guns belonged to Jane Doe or that she was solely responsible for their being in her purse. As a 16-year-old girl in the company of three adult men she was the least likely of the four to be carrying one, let alone two, heavy handguns. It is far more probable that she relied on the pocketknife found in her brassiere for any necessary self-protection. Under these circumstances, it was not unreasonable for her counsel to argue and for the jury to infer that when the car was halted for speeding, the other passengers in the car anticipated the risk of a search and attempted to conceal their weapons in a pocketbook in the front seat. The inference is surely more likely than the notion that these weapons were the sole property of the 16-year-old girl.

Under these circumstances, the jury would have been entirely reasonable in rejecting the suggestion—which, incidentally, defense counsel did not even advance in their closing arguments to the jury—that the handguns were in the sole possession of Jane Doe. Assuming that the jury did reject it, the case is tantamount to one in which the guns were lying on the floor or the seat of the car in the plain view of the three other occupants of the automobile. In such a case, it is surely rational to infer that each of the respondents was fully aware of the presence of the guns and had both the ability and the intent to exercise dominion and control over the weapons. The application of the statutory presumption in this case therefore comports with the standard laid down in *Tot v. United States*, 319 U.S., at 467, and restated in *Leary v. United States*, 395 U.S., at 36. For there is a "rational connection" between the basic facts that the prosecution proved and the ultimate fact presumed, and the latter is "more likely than not to flow from" the former.

Respondents argue, however, that the validity of the New York presumption must be judged by a "reasonable doubt" test rather than the "more likely than not" standard. ... Under the more stringent test, it is argued that a statutory presumption must be rejected unless the evidence necessary to invoke the inference is sufficient for a rational jury to find the inferred fact beyond a reasonable doubt. See *Barnes v. United States*, 412 U.S., at 842. Respondents' argument again overlooks the distinction between a permissive presumption on which the prosecution is entitled to rely as one not necessarily sufficient part of its proof and a mandatory presumption which the jury must accept even if it is the sole evidence of an element of the offense.

In the latter situation, since the prosecution bears the burden of establishing guilt, it may not rest its case entirely on a presumption unless the fact proved is sufficient to support the inference of guilt beyond a reasonable doubt. But in the former situation, the prosecution may rely on all of the evidence in the record to meet the reasonable-doubt standard. There is no more reason to require a permissive statutory presumption to meet a reasonable-doubt standard before it may be permitted to play any part in a trial than there is to require that degree of probative force for other relevant evidence before it may be admitted. As long as it is clear that the presumption is not the sole and sufficient basis for a finding of guilt, it need only satisfy the test described in *Leary*. The permissive presumption, as used in this case, satisfied the *Leary* test. And, as already noted, the New York Court of Appeals has concluded that the record as a whole was sufficient to establish guilt beyond a reasonable doubt. The judgment is reversed.

So ordered.

Justice Powell, with whom Justices Brennan, Stewart, and Marshall join, dissenting.

I am not in agreement . . . with the Court's conclusion that the presumption as charged to the jury in this case meets the constitutional requirements of due process as set forth in our prior decisions. On the contrary, an individual's mere presence in an automobile where there is a handgun does not even make it "more likely than not" that the individual possesses the weapon.

I

In the criminal law, presumptions are used to encourage the jury to find certain facts, with respect to which no direct evidence is presented, solely because other facts have been proved. See, e.g., *Barnes v. United States*, 412 U.S. 837 (1973). The purpose of such presumptions is plain: Like certain other jury instructions, they provide guidance for jurors' thinking in considering the evidence laid before them. Once in the juryroom, jurors necessarily draw inferences from the evidence—both direct and circumstantial. Through the use of presumptions, certain inferences are commended to the attention of jurors by legislatures or courts. Legitimate guidance of a jury's deliberations is an indispensable part of our criminal justice system. Nonetheless, the use of presumptions in criminal cases poses at least two distinct perils for defendants' constitutional rights. The Court accurately identifies the first of these as being the danger of interference with "the factfinder's responsibility at trial, based on evidence adduced by the State, to find the ultimate facts beyond a reasonable doubt." If the jury is instructed that it must infer some ultimate fact (that is, some element of the offense) from proof of other facts unless the defendant disproves the ultimate fact by a preponderance of the evidence, then the presumption shifts the burden of proof to the defendant concerning the element thus inferred.

But I do not agree with the Court's conclusion that the only constitutional difficulty with presumptions lies in the danger of lessening the burden of proof the prosecution must bear. As the Court notes, the presumptions thus far reviewed by the Court have not shifted the burden of persuasion, instead, they either have required only that the defendant produce some evidence to rebut the inference suggested by the prosecution's evidence, or merely have been suggestions to the jury that it would be sensible to draw certain conclusions on the basis of the evidence presented.

. . . .

[O]ur decisions uniformly have recognized that due process requires . . . that the truth of the inferred fact be more likely than not whenever the premise for the inference is true. Thus, to be constitutional a presumption must be at least more likely than not true.

II

In the present case, the jury was told:

"Our Penal Law also provides that the presence in an automobile of any machinegun or of any handgun or firearm which is loaded is presumptive evidence of their unlawful possession. In other words, [under] these presumptions or this latter presumption upon proof of the presence of the machinegun and the hand weapons, you may infer and draw a conclusion that such prohibited weapon was possessed by each of the defendants who occupied the automobile at the time when such instruments were found. The presumption or presumptions is effective only so long as there is no substantial evidence contradicting the conclusion flowing from the presumption, and the presumption is said to disappear when such contradictory evidence is adduced."

Undeniably, the presumption charged in this case encouraged the jury to draw a particular factual inference regardless of any other evidence presented: to infer that respondents possessed the weapons found in the automobile "upon proof of the presence of the machinegun and the hand weapon" and proof that respondents "occupied the automobile at the time such instruments were found." I believe that the presumption thus charged was unconstitutional because it did not fairly reflect what common sense and experience tell us about passengers in automobiles and the possession of handguns. People present in automobiles where there are weapons simply are not "more likely than not" the possessors of those weapons.

Under New York law, "to possess" is "to . . . have physical possession or . . . exercise dominion or control. . . ." Plainly, the mere presence of an individual in an automobile—without more—does not indicate that he exercises "dominion or control over" everything within it. . . .

In sum, it seems to me that the Court today ignores the teaching of our prior decisions. By speculating about what the jury may have done with the factual inference thrust upon it, the Court in effect assumes away the inference altogether, constructing a rule that permits the use of any inference—no matter how irrational in itself—provided that otherwise there is sufficient evidence in the record to support a finding of guilt. Applying this novel analysis to the present case, the Court upholds the use of a presumption that it makes no effort to defend in isolation. In substance, the Court—applying an unarticulated harmless-error standard—simply finds that the respondents were guilty as charged. They may well have been, but rather than acknowledging this rationale, the Court seems to have made new law with respect to presumptions that could seriously jeopardize a defendant's right to a fair trial.

Accordingly, I dissent.

LEGAL ANALYSIS AND WRITING 2.7

The following questions are based on the *How to Brief a Legal Case* format shown in the Appendix. Use this format to answer the following questions:

1. Summarize the facts in the previous case.
2. What is the legal issue?
3. What did the appellate court decide?
4. Why did the court decide this way?
5. Do you agree with the court's reasoning? Explain why or why not.

LEGAL RESEARCH USING THE INTERNET SKILLS 2.8

Find and read this important Supreme Court case online! Check out one of the legal research web sites below and use their "Search" feature to find this case. In the "Search" field, enter the cite or case name.

1. FindLaw U.S. Supreme Court Decisions (http://www.findlaw.com/casecode/supreme.html)
2. U.S. Supreme Court (http://www.supremecourtus.gov/)
3. Supreme Court Collection of Cornell Law School (http://supct.law.cornell.edu/supct/)

CRITICAL THINKING QUESTIONS 2.5

1. What is the reasoning behind allowing presumptions in a criminal action?
2. What safeguards are in place to ensure that a defendant in a criminal action is not convicted on a presumption alone?
3. How would you distinguish the holdings of the *Barnes* decision from that in *Ulster County*?
4. How did the majority opinion in *Ulster County* use the holding in *Barnes* to support their decision?
5. How did the dissenting opinion in *Ulster County* use the holding in *Barnes* to support their decision?

SUMMARY

The role of evidence law serves a three-fold purpose in our legal process: to promote social and public policies for ensuring fairness and a just determination of the proceedings in the ascertainment of truth; to provide a framework of guidelines and safeguards that protect the jury, and help to ensure an orderly, efficient legal process; and to ensure the "controlled" nature of the contest between adversarial parties by establishing rules and procedures for proving a legal action. The U.S. Supreme Court addressed the overriding goal of fairness by holding that the "law does not require that a defendant receive a perfect trial, only a fair one." Many of the evidence rules are designed to provide safeguards to ensure this fairness. Evidence law places much of the responsibility for ensuring fairness and efficiency in the hands of the trial judge. The trial judge serves as a referee and a "filter," interpreting the evidence rules and deciding what evidence will be admissible and what evidence must be excluded.

Although the role of evidence greatly affects the proving of a case, *evidence* and *proof* have different meanings. Evidence involves the *means* by which some fact is offered to prove or disprove an issue in dispute, while proof is the *effect* that the evidence has on the trier of fact and the *conclusion* drawn from the evidence that has been submitted. *Burden of proof* is the duty to meet a certain standard or establish the requisite degree of belief in the mind of the trier of fact regarding the evidence submitted. Under our adversary system, a party bringing a legal action has the burden of proving his or her case. This burden of proof actually involves two key elements: the *burden of production* and the *burden of persuasion*. Each type of legal action has a specific standard or degree of certainty that must be proven in order to meet that particular burden of proof and persuasion. *Beyond a reasonable doubt* is the standard required to convict a defendant in a criminal action. This standard requires something to be "almost certainly true." *Preponderance of evidence* is the standard required in a civil action. It is met when the trier of fact believes from the evidence that a fact is more probable than not. There is also a standard called *clear and convincing* used in certain types of civil cases. This standard is higher than the *preponderance* burden and is said to be *very probably true*.

An inference is a deduction of fact that may logically be drawn from another fact. Sometimes, however, the law requires that an assumption of fact or conclusion be made from another fact once that basic fact has been established. This is called a *presumption*. A presumption requires that the trier of fact accept the presumed fact unless evidence is offered by the opposing party to rebut the presumed fact. Presumptions are quite often the result of social and public policies. Presumptions can be conclusive or rebuttable. A conclusive presumption is one that cannot be contradicted and for which no evidence can be admitted to the contrary. A rebuttable presumption is one that the jury must make unless evidence to the contrary is introduced. Most presumptions are rebuttable. Courts differ as to the effect that a presumption must be given in a civil action and the burden it imposes on the party opposing it. There are three different approaches taken by courts regarding this. One imposes only a *burden of production* or *going forward* with evidence to rebut the presumption. The second approach requires a more substantial *burden of proof* requirement. The third approach uses both the burden of production and the burden of proof. When a presumption operates against an accused in a criminal action, state courts generally allow, but do not require, the trier of fact to accept a presumed fact if the burden of proof has been met by the prosecution. However, a presumption in a criminal case does not shift to the accused the burden of either producing evidence or of persuading the trier of fact that the presumed fact does not exist. This burden of proof, *beyond a reasonable doubt*, in a criminal action remains with the prosecution throughout the trial.

KEY TERMS

Beyond a Reasonable Doubt	In Absentia	Prima Facie
Burden of Going Forward	Inference	Probable Cause
Burden of Persuasion	Motion for Directed Verdict	Prosecutor
Burden of Production	Onus Probandi	Public Policy
Burden of Proof	Plaintiff	Reasonable Person Test
Clear and Convincing Evidence	Preponderance of Evidence	Reasonable Suspicion
Conclusive Presumption	Presumption	Rebuttable Presumption
Defendant	Presumption of Innocence	Social Policy

☐ Learning Outcomes

After completing your reading, questions, and exercises, you should be able to demonstrate a better understanding of the learning concepts by answering the following questions:

1. Explain the role of evidence rules in the legal process.
2. Describe how public and social policy influences the role of evidence rules.
3. Identify the purposes of the evidence rules influenced by this public policy.
4. Define the term "prima facie" and discuss the importance of this concept in establishing a case.
5. Define "burden of proof" and identify the two elements that make up this burden.
6. Explain what the following terms mean and how each is used. Give an example for each.
   a."Burden of production"
   b."Burden of persuasion"
   c."Beyond a reasonable doubt"
   d."Preponderance of evidence"
7. Compare and contrast the burden of proof in a criminal action with the burden required in a civil action.
8. Distinguish between "preponderance of evidence" and the "clear and convincing evidence" standard.
9. Compare and contrast "reasonable suspicion" with "probable cause." Explain when each might be used.
10. Define "presumption" and discuss its importance in the role of evidence.
11. Distinguish between rebuttable and conclusive presumptions. Give examples for each.
12. Compare and contrast the approaches (burden of proof, production, and combined) taken by different courts in the effect of a presumption on an opposing party.
13. Explain the difference between the use of a presumption in a civil case and the use of a presumption in a criminal case.

☐ Practice Skills

In addition to understanding the learning concepts, practice what you have learned through applications using critical thinking, legal analysis and writing, legal research, and advocacy skills, including:

Critical Thinking

1. Why are the primary purposes of the evidence rules to ensure fairness, eliminate unjustifiable expense and delay, and promote growth and development of the law of evidence to the ends that the truth be ascertained and proceedings justly determined?
2. Are these goals really compatible? Why or why not?
3. How can we balance these goals in a way that ensures fairness yet ascertains the truth?
4. Why do we have rules to govern the proving of a case and to determine what burden of proof is required in different circumstances?
5. Do you believe that these rules provide adequate safeguards for the parties to a legal action?

6. What public policy issues or considerations do you think might be behind these rules?
7. If it were up to you, would you keep these rules as they are, delete them, narrow them, or expand them? Explain your reasoning.
8. How do these rules influence the gathering of evidence or preparing of witnesses?

Legal Analysis and Writing

Analyze the following rules and cases by summarizing their holdings, explaining their significance, and assessing any issue that might arise in their application.

1. Rule 301.
2. Rule 303 (Presumptions in a criminal action).
3. *Cruzan v. Missouri Department of Health.*
4. *In re Winship.*
5. *Cage v. Louisiana.*
6. *Victor v. Nebraska.*
7. *Barnes v. United States.*
8. *Ulster County v. Allen.*

Legal Research Using the Internet

1. Find the annotated Federal Rules of Evidence on the Internet and assess the comments made in the proposing of the rules covered in this chapter.
2. Find your state's rules of evidence regarding relevance exceptions and concepts covered in this chapter. Compare and contrast with the federal and/or modern rules, and some of the state rules listed in this chapter.
3. Find out if your state appellate court posts its case decisions on the Internet. If so, find a case that illustrates an issue or rule discussed in this chapter. If your state decisions are not on the Internet, go instead to the web site for the U.S. Circuit Court of Appeals in your circuit, or search the U.S. Supreme Court decisions.

PRACTICE APPLICATION 2.1

The U.S. Supreme Court has held that the "criminal trial of an incompetent defendant violates due process" and has stated that a defendant may not be put to trial unless he "has sufficient present ability to consult with his lawyer with a reasonable degree of rational understanding . . . [and] a rational as well as factual understanding of the proceedings against him." The standard of proof established by the Court to determine whether a defendant is incompetent to stand trial is preponderance of the evidence. The following is the order and rationale of a trial judge in an Oklahoma criminal case, finding a defendant competent to stand trial:

"Well, I think I've used the expression . . . in the past that normal is like us. Anybody that's not like us is not normal, so I don't think normal is a proper definition that we are to use with incompetence. My shirtsleeve opinion of Mr. Cooper is that he's not normal. Now, to say he's not competent is something else. . . . But you know, all things considered, I suppose it's possible for a client to be in such a predicament that he can't help his defense and still not be incompetent. I suppose that's a possibility, too. . . . I'm going to say that I don't believe he has carried the burden by clear and convincing evidence of his incompetency and I'm going to say we're going to go to trial."

Should this trial judge's decision be overturned on appeal? Why or why not? Use the format shown in the Appendix for the *IRAC Method of Legal Analysis* and the readings, rules, and cases discussed in this chapter to analyze this question. Write a short memo giving your analysis, reasoning, and conclusions.

LEGAL RESEARCH USING THE INTERNET SKILLS 2.9

Find out how the Court ruled in the previous *Practice Application* problem by finding and reading the U.S. Supreme Court decision online! The citation for it is:
Cooper v. Oklahoma, 517 U.S. 348 (1996).

ADVOCACY AND COMMUNICATION SKILLS 2.1

Using the previous *Practice Application* case problem, form two teams, representing the prosecution and defense.

1. Each team will prepare a definition of the burdens of proof (preponderance of evidence, clear and convincing, and beyond a reasonable doubt) that will be addressed in this case and that you would like the judge to include in his or her final instructions to the jury. Your team may use the definitions provided in this chapter as a guide only; the final definition must be in the team's own words.

2. Each team will prepare and present an oral argument of the issue in this case problem: whether the trial judge's decision constitutes reversible error. Each team will have 5 minutes for their argument and an additional 3 minutes, after the opposing team has presented their argument, for rebuttal.

WEB SITES

Federal Rules of Evidence
http://www.law.cornell.edu/rules/fre/overview.html
FindLaw
http://www.findlaw.com
FindLaw
http://guide.lp.findlaw.com/casecode/
FindLaw U.S. Supreme Court Decisions
http://www.findlaw.com/casecode/supreme.html
List of State Laws from Legal Information Institute of Cornell Law School
http://www.law.cornell.edu/states/listing.html

National Center for State Courts—State and Federal Court Web Sites
http://www.ncsconline.org/D_kis/info_court_web_sites.html#state
Supreme Court Collection of Cornell Law School
http://supct.law.cornell.edu/supct/
U.S. Courts Site with Links to All Circuit Courts of Appeal
http://www.uscourts.gov/links.html
U.S. Supreme Court
http://www.supremecourtus.gov/

ENDNOTES

1. *Fed. R. Evid.* 102.

2. See *Utah R. Evid.* 102.

3. *Tehan v. Shott*, 382 U.S. 406 (1966).

4. *Elkins v. United States*, 364 U.S. 206 (1960) (Frankfurter dissent).

5. See *Fed. R. Evid.* 102.

6. *Michigan v. Tucker*, 417 U.S. 433 (1974).

7. See, for example, Fed. R. Evid. 402, Irrelevant Evidence Inadmissible.

8. See, for example, Fed. R. Evid. 802, Hearsay Rule.

9. See, for example, Fed. R. Evid. 403, Exclusion of Relevant Evidence on Grounds of Prejudice, Confusion, or Waste of Time.

10. See, for example, Fed. R. Evid. 104, Preliminary Questions.

11. See, for example, Fed. R. Evid. 103 (c), Rulings on Evidence, Hearing of Jury.

12. See Rule 611, Mode and Order of Interrogation and Presentation.

13. *John R. Cowley & Bros., Inc. v. Brown*, 569 So.2d 375 (Ala. 1990).

14. Federal Judicial Center, *Benchbook for U.S. District Court Judges* (March 2000).

15. *In re Westchester County Medical Center on behalf of O'Connor*, 72 N.Y. 2d 517 (1988).

16. *In re Jobes*, 108 N.J., at 407.

17. *Commonwealth v. Webster*, 59 Mass. 295 (1850).

18. *Dunbar v. United States*, 156 U.S. 185 (1895).

19. *Conn. Gen. Stat.* Sec. 52-183.

20. *Or. Rev. Stat.* Sec. 40.135 Rule 311 (v). Presumptions.

21. *Fed. R. Evid.* 301.

22. *N. C. R. Evid.* 301.

23. See *Uniform Rules of Evidence*, Rule 301.

24. *Or. Rev. State* Sec. 40.120 Rule 308.

25. *Cal. Evid. Code,* Sec. 641.

26. *Cal. Evid. Code,* Sec. 605.

27. *Cal. Evid. Code,* Sec. 603.

28. *Or. Rev. Stat.* Sec. 40.125 Rule 309. Presumptions in Criminal Proceedings.

GATHERING AND PRESENTING EVIDENCE AT TRIAL

*"To gather facts, prepare a case,
Always heed this vow—
Ask the Who and What and Why
And Where and When and How."*

—*Thomas Buckles*

"Evidence is like a gourmet meal. It's all in the presentation."

—*Anon. Trial Lawyer/Chef*

LEARNING OUTCOMES

In this chapter, you will learn about the following legal concepts:

- How Evidence Law Influences the Information-Gathering Process
- Types of Evidence
- Forms of Evidence
- Exculpatory Evidence
- Judicial Notice
- Stipulations

- Gathering Evidence to Establish a Case
- Gathering Evidence to Prove a Case
- Preparing Evidence and Exhibits for Trial
- Presenting Evidence at Trial
- Identification and Authentication
- What Is Not Evidence?
- Making the Record

INTRODUCTION

In the last chapter, we looked at the role of Evidence Law and how it serves to ensure fairness and just proceedings in the search for truth, as well as providing rules and guidelines for proving a case. In this chapter, we will look at the types and forms of evidence needed to establish and prove a case, and how to gather and present this evidence at trial.

HOW EVIDENCE LAW INFLUENCES THE INFORMATION-GATHERING PROCESS

Evidence law influences the information-gathering process. Laws affect every aspect of how information is obtained and presented through evidence in the trial process. As we learned in the previous chapter, there are laws that establish how much evidence is necessary to constitute a legal action and how much evidence is required to prove a case. The gathering of information and evidence must be focused on establishing the elements to a legal action and meeting the burden in proving that action at trial. As we will see in later chapters, there are rules that govern the admissibility of any evidence gathered. These rules also determine which evidence will not be admissible. For example, information will be excluded as evidence when it does not pertain to the matter at issue. Even when it is important to the matter at issue, information may be excluded if it is unreliable, confusing, or prejudicial. Information will not be admissible as evidence if it violates some public policy that protects a special relationship or communication, like an attorney and client, or husband and wife. We will be examining these rules in detail throughout this text. The importance at this point is in understanding that evidence law and rules form a framework that guide what information should be gathered and how that information must be obtained.

TYPES OF EVIDENCE

To effectively gather evidence to be presented at trial, we need to first understand what constitutes evidence and what needs to be looked for in obtaining information. We know that evidence is defined as something that tends to prove or disprove a fact or matter at issue. Evidence is classified by type and form. There are two basic types of evidence, **direct evidence** and **circumstantial evidence.**

Direct Evidence

Direct evidence proves a disputed fact *directly* through the testimony of a witness who saw or heard the dispute at issue. An eyewitness is the best and most common example of direct evidence. Direct evidence relies on the senses and perception of the eyewitness and does not require any intervening or indirect fact to be proven first. There are no inferences that need to be drawn from direct evidence. For example, if Mary witnessed the defendant stab Paul with a knife, and Mary testifies as to what she saw, this would be direct evidence.

Circumstantial Evidence

Circumstantial evidence proves a disputed fact indirectly by first proving another fact. From this other fact an **inference** may be drawn as to the original disputed fact. We have often heard it said on television, "You can't prove anything! All you have is *circumstantial* evidence!" In reality, most cases are proven with circumstantial evidence. This type of evidence can be

Direct Evidence
Evidence that proves a disputed fact directly, through an eyewitness, for example.

Circumstantial Evidence
Proves a disputed fact indirectly by first proving another fact. From this other fact an inference may be drawn as to the original disputed fact.

Inference
A deduction of fact that may logically be drawn from another fact.

much more credible than eyewitness testimony. For example, suppose Mary hears a commotion in the next room. She hears someone yell, "Help, he's stabbing me!" Mary opens the door to the room and sees the defendant standing over Paul holding a bloody knife in his hand. There is no one else seen in the room.

This would be an example of circumstantial evidence. There is no direct evidence that could be offered to prove that Mary actually saw the defendant stab Paul, but from what Mary heard and saw, there can be an inference drawn as to this fact. If the defendant's fingerprints were found on the bloody knife, this would be another example of circumstantial evidence. Other examples of circumstantial evidence in this case might include matching the blood on the knife to that of the victim, finding the victim's bloodstains on the clothing of the defendant, and evidence of prior threats made to the victim by the defendant. By offering Mary's testimony, along with the other circumstantial evidence, a trier of fact might *infer* that the defendant stabbed Paul.

EVIDENTIARY CHECKLIST 3.1

	Types of Evidence	Example
☐	Direct	Eyewitness
☐	Circumstantial	Fingerprint

FORMS OF EVIDENCE

In addition to the two basic types of evidence, there are four basic forms of evidence: testimonial, physical, documentary, and demonstrative.

Testimonial Evidence

Testimonial evidence is oral or "spoken" evidence presented by witnesses who come into court to give their testimony under oath. This is the most common form of evidence and it is also used as a foundation for or to explain most of the other forms of evidence. For example, if you have a violent assault that has occurred, you may have a victim or other people who actually witnessed the assault. You may also have people who heard the commotion and saw the defendant run from the scene. These people would all be called as witnesses to *testify* as to what they saw or heard.

In addition to these witnesses, you might have crime scene evidence— bloody clothing, fingerprints, or the weapon used—that helps to prove the crime or link the defendant to it. To be admitted as legal evidence, these objects must be documented through the *testimony* of a witness who can verify that the evidence was taken from the crime scene or explain the significance of the item.

Testimonial Evidence
Oral or "spoken" evidence presented by witnesses who come into court to give their testimony under oath.

Physical Evidence

Physical evidence, also called *real* or *tangible* evidence, is something that can be tangibly perceived by the trier of fact. This form of evidence includes objects or materials that can be seen, touched, felt, and identified by their own nature. Because of this, physical evidence is considered more reliable than other forms of evidence and is often said to "speak for itself" in its impact as evidence. Examples of physical evidence in criminal actions

Physical Evidence
Something that can be tangibly perceived; objects or materials that can be seen, touched, or felt.

would include the weapon used in a violent crime, fingerprints or blood-stains found at a crime scene, a stolen item, or illegal drugs. Examples of physical evidence in civil actions might include a surgical object found in a patient after an operation, a faulty instrument panel in an aircraft accident, or a punctured tire.

Documentary Evidence

Documentary Evidence
A writing or record, including letters, typewriting, wills, contracts, deeds, notes, printings, pictures, sketches, or recordings.

Documentary evidence is sometimes called "writings" and consists of letters, typewriting, wills, contracts, deeds, notes, printings, pictures, sketches, recordings, and similar materials. Like physical evidence, a proper foundation must be presented through a witness who can testify as to the document's authenticity.

Demonstrative Evidence

Demonstrative Evidence
Evidence that "demonstrates," illustrates, or recreates evidence that has already been presented.

Demonstrative evidence "demonstrates," illustrates, or recreates evidence that has already been presented. A sketch, diagram, or photograph of an accident, crime scene, or injuries sustained in a liability lawsuit would be examples of this illustrative evidence. Other examples would include displays, mock-ups, and skeletons used to explain or illustrate other evidence.

EVIDENTIARY CHECKLIST 3.2

Forms of Evidence	Example
☐ Testimonial	Witness
☐ Physical	Fingerprint
☐ Documentary	Will or Contract
☐ Demonstrative	Diagram of Accident Scene

EVIDENTIARY CHECKLIST 3.3
TYPES AND FORMS OF EVIDENCE

Types of Evidence	Forms of Evidence
☐ Direct	☐ Testimonial
☐ Circumstantial	☐ Physical
	☐ Documentary
	☐ Demonstrative

CRITICAL THINKING QUESTIONS 3.1

1. How does evidence law influence the gathering of evidence? Give examples.
2. How does public policy influence the gathering of evidence? Give examples.
3. Which type of evidence would you prefer to have in proving a case, direct or circumstantial? Explain your answer.
4. Why do we classify evidence as to types and forms?
5. What do you think would be the strengths and weaknesses in using the different forms of evidence? Give an example of each.

EXCULPATORY EVIDENCE

When gathering information to establish or prove a legal action, evidence may be found that tends to clear a party of blame or guilt. This is called **exculpatory evidence.** This term is primarily used in criminal actions, although it may be used in civil actions. For example, an **exculpatory clause** in a contract might clear a party of an otherwise harmful act or hold a party harmless from default. However, it is mainly applicable to criminal actions, where the law requires the prosecution to reveal any exculpatory evidence gathered to the defense. A violation of this may result in what is known as a **Brady Motion,** named after a 1963 Supreme Court case that held the "suppression by the prosecution of evidence favorable to an accused upon request violates due process where the evidence is material either to guilt or to punishment, irrespective of the good faith or bad faith of the prosecution."[1]

This becomes especially important to the defense while gathering evidence in a criminal action. However, it can be even more important for the law enforcement and prosecution investigators. Since the Brady decision, other Supreme Court cases have held that the duty to disclose exculpatory evidence is applicable even though there has been no request by the accused.[2] The Court has further held that the rule encompasses evidence "known only to police investigators and not to the prosecutor."[3] Finally, the Court has held that a "prosecutor has a duty to learn of any favorable evidence known to the others acting on the government's behalf in this case, including the police."[4]

Exculpatory Evidence
Evidence that tends to clear a party of blame or guilt.

Exculpatory Clause
A portion of a writing or contract that clears a party of an otherwise harmful act or holds a party harmless from default.

Brady Motion
A motion to dismiss a case because evidence favorable to the accused has been suppressed by the State, either willfully or inadvertently, resulting in prejudice to the defendant.

What Is Required to Prove a Brady Violation?

A Brady Motion is a request for a judge to dismiss a case because evidence favorable to the accused has been suppressed by the State, either willfully or inadvertently, resulting in prejudice to the defendant. The following is a **syllabus** of a 1999 U.S. Supreme Court decision that identifies the three elements that must be established in order to prove a Brady violation.

Syllabus
A summary of a court's opinion which covers each primary point of law decided.

CASE

Strickler v. Greene, Warden

No. 98-5864 (1999).

The Commonwealth of Virginia charged petitioner with capital murder and related crimes. Because an open file policy gave petitioner access to all of the evidence in the prosecutor's files, petitioner's counsel did not file a pretrial motion for discovery of possible exculpatory evidence. At the trial, Anne Stoltzfus gave detailed eyewitness testimony about the crimes and petitioner's role as one of the perpetrators. The prosecutor failed to disclose exculpatory materials in the police files, consisting of notes taken by a detective during interviews with Stoltzfus, and letters written by Stoltzfus to the detective, that cast serious doubt on significant por-

tions of her testimony. The jury found petitioner guilty, and he was sentenced to death. The Virginia Supreme Court affirmed.

In subsequent state habeas corpus proceedings, petitioner advanced an ineffective assistance of counsel claim based, in part, on trial counsel's failure to file a motion under *Brady v. Maryland*, 373 U.S. 83, for disclosure of all exculpatory evidence known to the prosecution or in its possession. In response, the Commonwealth asserted that such a motion was unnecessary because of the prosecutor's open file policy. The trial court denied relief. The Virginia Supreme Court affirmed. Petitioner then filed a federal habeas petition and was granted access to the exculpatory Stoltzfus materials for the first time.

The District Court vacated petitioner's capital murder conviction and death sentence on the grounds that the Commonwealth had failed to disclose those materials and that petitioner had not, in consequence, received a fair trial. The Fourth Circuit reversed because petitioner had procedurally defaulted his Brady claim by not raising it at his trial or in the state collateral proceedings. In addition, the Fourth Circuit concluded that the claim was, in any event, without merit.

Held: Although petitioner has demonstrated cause for failing to raise a Brady claim, Virginia did not violate Brady and its progeny by failing to disclose exculpatory evidence to petitioner.

(a) There are three essential components of a true Brady violation: the evidence at issue must be favorable to the accused, either because it is exculpatory, or because it is impeaching; that evidence must have been suppressed by the State, either willfully or inadvertently; and prejudice must have ensued. The record in this case unquestionably establishes two of those components. The contrast between (a) the terrifying incident that Stoltzfus confidently described in her testimony and (b) her initial statement to the detective that the incident seemed a trivial episode suffices to establish the impeaching character of the undisclosed documents. Moreover, with respect to some of those documents, there is no dispute that they were known to the Commonwealth but not disclosed to trial counsel. It is the third component—whether petitioner has established the necessary prejudice—that is the most difficult element of the claimed Brady violation here. Because petitioner acknowledges that his Brady claim is procedurally defaulted, this Court must first decide whether that default is excused by an adequate showing of cause and prejudice. In this case, cause and prejudice parallel two of the three components of the alleged Brady violation itself. The suppression of the Stoltzfus documents constitutes one of the causes for the failure to assert a Brady claim in the state courts, and unless those documents were "material" for Brady purposes, their suppression did not give rise to sufficient prejudice to overcome the procedural default.

(b) Petitioner has established cause for failing to raise a Brady claim prior to federal habeas because (a) the prosecution withheld exculpatory evidence; (b) petitioner reasonably relied on the prosecution's open file policy as fulfilling the prosecution's duty to disclose such evidence; and (c) the Commonwealth confirmed petitioner's reliance on the open file policy by asserting during state habeas proceedings that petitioner had already received everything known to the government. This Court need not decide whether any one or two of the foregoing factors would be sufficient to constitute cause, since the combination of all three surely suffices.

(c) However, in order to obtain relief, petitioner must convince this Court that there is a reasonable probability that his conviction or sentence would have been different had the suppressed documents been disclosed to the defense. The adjective is important. The question is not whether the defendant would more likely than not have received a different verdict with the suppressed evidence, but whether in its absence he received a fair trial, understood as a trial resulting in a verdict worthy of confidence. *Kyles v. Whitley*, 514 U.S. 419. Here, other evidence in the record provides strong support for the conclusion that petitioner would have been convicted of capital murder and sentenced to death, even if Stoltzfus had been severely impeached or her testimony excluded entirely. Notwithstanding the obvious significance of that testimony, therefore, petitioner cannot show prejudice sufficient to excuse his procedural default. Affirmed.

LEGAL ANALYSIS AND WRITING 3.1

The following questions are based on the *How to Brief a Legal Case* format shown in the Appendix. Use this format to answer the following questions:

1. Summarize the facts in the previous case.
2. What is the legal issue?
3. What did the Court decide?
4. Why did the Court decide this way?
5. What did the Court identify as the elements required to show a Brady violation?

LEGAL RESEARCH USING THE INTERNET SKILLS 3.1

Find and read the full text of this Supreme Court case online! Check out one of the legal research web sites below and use their "Search" feature to find this case. In the "Search" field, enter the cite or case name.

1. FindLaw U.S. Supreme Court Decisions (http://www.findlaw.com/casecode/supreme.html)
2. U.S. Supreme Court (http://www.supremecourtus.gov/)
3. Supreme Court Collection of Cornell Law School (http://supct.law.cornell.edu/supct/)

CRITICAL THINKING QUESTIONS 3.2

1. What is exculpatory evidence and what safeguards are in place to ensure that this information is provided to the defense?
2. Why did the court deny the Brady Motion in the Strickler decision?

JUDICIAL NOTICE

When a certain fact is commonly known in the community or capable of accurate and ready determination, a trial judge may recognize and accept it as true at trial. This may be done without any of the previous forms of evidence being introduced and without further proof. This is called **judicial notice** (see Exhibit 3.1). An 1897 court described its effect in saying, "Judicial notice takes the place of proof, and is of equal force. As a means of establishing facts, it is therefore superior to evidence. In its appropriate field, it displaces evidence, since as it stands for proof, it fulfills the object which evidence is designed to fulfill and makes evidence unnecessary."[5]

Judicial notice is not a form of evidence, but serves to save time by accepting well-known and commonly accepted facts. Judicial notice can be done through the request of one of the parties to the action or through the judge's own decision. Judicial notice governs only adjudicative facts—the facts of the case.

Utah is representative of the evidentiary rules for judicial notice. Taking Federal Rule 201 verbatim, Utah sets forth two initial requirements

Judicial Notice
When a judge recognizes and accepts a certain fact that is commonly known in the community or capable of accurate and ready determination.

EXHIBIT 3.1   Examples of Judicial Notice

Connecticut General Statute
   Sec. 52-163. Judicial notice of special acts, regulations of state and municipal agencies and municipal ordinances. The court shall take judicial notice of: (1) Private or special acts of this state, (2) regulations of any agency of this state, as defined in section 4–166, (3) ordinances of any town, city or borough of this state, and (4) regulations of any board, commission, council, committee or other agency of any town, city or borough of this state.

Missouri Revised Statutes
   Sec. 490.700. The courts of this state shall take judicial notice, without proof, of the population of all cities in this state according to the last enumeration of the inhabitants thereof, state, federal or municipal, made under or pursuant to any law of this state or of the United States.
   Sec. 490.080. Every court of this state shall take judicial notice of the common law and statutes of every state, territory and other jurisdiction of the United States.

for the kind of facts that can be judicially noticed. First, it requires that a judicially noticed fact must not be subject to any reasonable dispute. Second, a judicially noticed fact must be restricted to matters of common knowledge generally known within the territorial jurisdiction of the trial court or easily determined from accuracy sources.[6] As one Utah court stated, "A court is presumed to know what every man of ordinary intelligence must know about such things."[7] Examples of facts that can be judicially noticed include the laws of a state, the world being round, Sunday follows Saturday, location of a particular street, and so on.

The rationale behind judicial notice is that by recognizing and accepting certain facts that are commonly known in the community or capable of accurate and ready determination, the court will save time and expense in the trial, ensuring a more efficient and effective process.

When Judicial Notice is Discretionary or Mandatory

A court may take judicial notice whether requested by one of the parties or not. The court must take judicial notice if requested by either side in an action and the court is supplied with the necessary information (see Exhibit 3.2). Judicial notice may be taken at any stage of the proceeding.

Effect of Judicial Notice

The effect of judicial notice being taken is different in civil and criminal actions. In a civil action, the court must instruct the jury to accept as conclusive any fact judicially noticed. In a criminal case, the court would instruct the jury that it may, but is not required to, accept as conclusive any fact judicially noticed.

EXHIBIT 3.2   Judicial Notice

Texas Rules of Evidence
   Rule 201(a) Scope of Rule. This rule governs only judicial notice of adjudicative facts.
   (b) Kinds of Facts. A judicially noticed fact must be one not subject to reasonable dispute in that it is either (1) generally known within the territorial jurisdiction of the trial court or (2) capable of accurate and ready determination by resort to sources whose accuracy cannot reasonably be questioned.
   (c) When Discretionary. A court may take judicial notice, whether requested or not.
   (d) When Mandatory. A court shall take judicial notice if requested by a party and supplied with the necessary information.
   (e) Opportunity to Be Heard. A party is entitled upon timely request to an opportunity to be heard as to the propriety of taking judicial notice and the tenor of the matter noticed. In the absence of prior notification, the request may be made after judicial notice has been taken.
   (f) Time of Taking Notice. Judicial notice may be taken at any stage of the proceeding.
   (g) Instructing Jury. In civil cases, the court shall instruct the jury to accept as conclusive any fact judicially noticed. In criminal cases, the court shall instruct the jury that it may, but is not required to, accept as conclusive any fact judicially noticed.

Stipulation
An agreement between parties to a legal action, where one party admits to or agrees not to contest the offering of a certain fact, relieving the other party from the burden of proving it.

STIPULATIONS

Another legal device to save time at trial is a **stipulation.** A stipulation is an agreement between the parties to a legal action, where one party admits to or agrees not to contest the offering of a certain fact, relieving the other party from the burden of going forward to prove the fact. A stipulation prevents the agreeing party from contesting the evidence later.

EVIDENTIARY CHECKLIST 3.4

Elements Required for Judicial Notice

For judicial notice to be taken, the following elements must be established:

☐   The fact to be judicially noticed must be one not subject to reasonable dispute.

☐   The fact must be either generally known within the territorial jurisdiction of the trial court, or

☐   Capable of accurate and ready determination by resort to sources whose accuracy cannot reasonably be questioned.

Why Would Anyone Stipulate to Anything at Trial?

Stipulation can be a strategic tool, used to prevent the jury from hearing certain facts, like the results of a test or the qualifications of an expert witness. For example, during a foundation being established for the testimony of an expert witness, a medical expert, the opposing party states: "Your honor, at this time we would like to stipulate to the background and experience of the witness."

By stipulating before any information is provided, the party would be able to keep the jury from finding out more about the extensive qualifications and experience of the witness. However, the side offering the witness may not agree to the stipulation. In that case, it may turn on the judge's decision as to whether the stipulation would be accepted.

CRITICAL THINKING QUESTIONS 3.3

1. When may a judge take judicial notice?
2. What is the reasoning behind allowing judicial notice of certain facts rather than requiring a party to prove the fact?
3. Give some examples of what would constitute judicial notice of facts.
4. What effect do you think social or public policy has on the development of judicial notice rules?
5. Why do we allow stipulations?
6. Why would anyone stipulate to anything in a trial?
7. In what specific types of cases might the admission of stipulations be important?

GATHERING EVIDENCE TO ESTABLISH A CASE

The importance of the quote at the beginning of this chapter cannot be overstated. Who, what, when, where, why, and how must be at the core of any methodical approach to gathering evidence. There is an old trial adage that you should never ask a witness a question at trial that you don't already know the answer to. The key here is thorough and detailed *preparation*. Failure to be prepared is a recipe for losing a case. Remember the O. J. Simpson murder trial where a prosecutor asked the defendant to try on the "bloody" leather glove? How many of us who have ever worn a leather glove know how difficult it is to put on after getting wet or cold? It shrinks a little and can take quite a while to push your hand through and stretch it back into place. A simple test with a similar pair of gloves before trial would have revealed this. Instead, the prosecution watched helplessly as the defendant struggled to fit his hand into that glove. As a result of this failure to adequately prepare on the part of the prosecution, the defense seized the opportunity, imploring the jury in closing arguments that "if the glove does not fit, you must acquit!" The jury did just that.

Cause of Action
The basis for a lawsuit.

There are two primary goals in gathering evidence: to determine whether a **cause of action** exists or not, and, if so, to prove or disprove the case. There are subgoals as well. One of the most important is gathering enough evidence to convince your opponent to settle the case before trial. This is especially important because 95 percent of all cases are settled before trial.

LEGAL RESEARCH USING THE INTERNET 3.2

Check out information and statistics about case filings and disposition at these web sites:

1. Federal Judicial Center (http://www.fjc.gov/)
2. National Center for State Courts (http://www.ncsconline.org/)
3. U.S. Courts (http://www.uscourts.gov/)

Determining Cause of Action

When gathering information to establish whether or not there is a cause of action, the role of evidence is to piece together what happened to the plaintiff or victim and ascertain whether sufficient evidence exists to support a case. If so, what is the cause of action? To determine this, we need to look at the definition and elements of the law involved. Laws have definitions that can be broken down into the elements needed to establish them. To prove a case, each element of the law that was broken or legal harm alleged must be proven. This is called establishing a *prima facie* case. As we discussed in the previous chapter, prima facie translates to "at first sight" and means that at first sight, all of the elements for a particular legal action have been established.

Establishing a Prima Facie Case

A prima facie case is one in which all of the elements of a particular legal action must be established in order to prove the case. For example, in the last chapter a *You Be the Judge* problem presented the case of a woman who backed her car through the back window of a Chinese restaurant, killing a 10-year-old child inside of the restaurant. The mother of the child brought a civil action for negligence against the owners of the restaurant, alleging that the restaurant failed to prevent her daughter's death by not installing appropriate concrete barriers in front of the windows.[8] To establish a prima facie cause of action for negligence, a plaintiff must prove that the defendant had a legal and foreseeable duty, that the defendant breached this duty, and that this breach caused the harm to the plaintiff. The law requires each and every element to be established in order to show a prima facie case. At trial, these elements will need to be established in a manner that meets the burden of proof required to prove a particular case. In a civil action, the burden of proof is a preponderance of evidence.

YOU BE THE JUDGE 3.1

A police officer pulls a driver over for suspicion of drunk driving and administers a breath test that registers 2.0. Anything over .08 is presumed by law to constitute intoxication for purposes of drunk driving violations. The officer testifies that she witnessed the defendant driving a vehicle in an erratic manner before she made the traffic stop. When she approached the defendant, she detected the odor of alcohol about the defendant's breath and the defendant spoke in a slurred manner of speech. The defendant also failed a field sobriety test given before the breath test was administered. The defendant was arrested and charged with drunk driving. Drunk driving is defined by law as "Any person who operates a vehicle while intoxicated or under the influence of alcohol." No one else testifies at the trial to the validity of the breath-testing procedures or the meaning of the results of the breath test. Defendant files a motion to dismiss for lack of a prima facie case.

Would you grant the defendant's motion? Why or why not? Write a memo analyzing this issue with your conclusion and reasoning.

Sources of Evidence

Where can evidence be found? The type of legal action will guide and determine what evidence is sought after and collected, and where it might be found. Whether it is civil or criminal will also have a bearing on how evidence is collected. For example, in criminal law, the Fourth Amendment prohibits unreasonable search and seizure by government agents. If police obtain evidence in an unreasonable manner, it can be excluded from trial. In a civil case, however, there is no Fourth Amendment protection. Depending on whether it is a civil or criminal action will help to guide the search for evidence.

Most evidence will be found and gathered through extensive interviewing of the plaintiff or victim, and the witnesses to the incident under investigation. Through these interviews, facts must be gathered and verified, and a plan developed for other evidence needed. Essential to most cases is a need to find and examine reports and records involved in the matter. These may be private and public records. Examples include police records and accident reports, hospital and medical records, insurance documents, contracts, wills, court records, business records and accounts, school records, and credit bureau records.

It is also important to check relevant statutes, administrative regulations, and case law to not only define the legal action, but to check how this action has been handled or interpreted by government agencies or the courts. In addition, these sources are essential to finding out if any law or regulation exists that might affect the case. For example, in the previous negligence case, one of the most important sources of evidence would be local building codes and inspection records to see if a barrier was required for the restaurant or whether the building was built to code. Government records would also be valuable to find out if the defendant restaurant had any reported prior safety violations.

Once a cause of action has been determined and established, a formal legal complaint may be initiated and preparations started to collect evidence and plan for the proving of the case. It is also at this stage prior to trial that attempts are generally made to settle or resolve the case out of court.

> ## *Practice Tip 3.1*
>
> **Think Ahead!**
>
> *When gathering evidence, be sure to think ahead to the ultimate goal. What will be admissible at trial? How will the opposing side challenge our evidence and what additional evidence do we need to find in order to overcome that challenge? The majority of cases are settled without going to trial, but the reason for most of these settlements is due to the feeling by one side or the other that their evidence is insufficient to win at trial.*

GATHERING EVIDENCE TO PROVE A CASE

After establishing that a cause of action exists to proceed with a case, the second and perhaps most important role of gathering evidence is to prove the case. In proving the case, the focus will be on the planning, preparation, and organization of witnesses and evidence to be presented at trial. Here we would look at what additional evidence needs to be gathered in order to prove our case at trial. As evidence is gathered and compiled, the strength of the case needs to be assessed. What is the weight and credibility of witnesses and evidence? Finally, there is a need to anticipate the evidentiary challenges that might be offered by the opposing side and develop a plan to overcome these challenges so that all evidence will be admitted.

Evidence is intended to be used at trial in a civil or criminal action to persuade the trier of fact, usually the jury, of the guilt or innocence, liability or not, of the defendant. Although evidence can be obtained at any time before or during trial, it is usually obtained during the pretrial processes known as *investigation* or **discovery.**

Obtaining Evidence in the Investigation Stage

For the plaintiff's legal team, obtaining evidence begins in the investigation stage through interviews with the plaintiff. The interview should seek to determine what happened, where, who was involved, when, how, and why. It should ascertain what information the plaintiff has already collected and how this evidence and information can be utilized in order to establish a prima facie case. Establishing a prima facie case is key to the building of a successful case. For example, if a breach of contract were alleged, evidence must prove that a valid contract existed, with a valid offer, acceptance, consideration, and legal capacity. Investigation would include interviews with the plaintiff, witnesses, and any party who could help to prove or disprove any of the facts at issue. The investigation also seeks to uncover documents and evidence that may be relevant to proving or disproving the facts at issue.

Discovery

In the investigation process, there is a formal stage in the litigation process for obtaining, reviewing, and examining evidence. This stage is called *discovery*, where both sides to a legal action attempt to learn more about their opponent's case and evidence in order to help them better prepare for trial. Discovery of information and evidence can be obtained through three legal devices: **deposition, interrogatories,** and **production of documents.**

Discovery
A pretrial device where parties to a legal action attempt to learn more about their opponent's case and evidence.

Deposition
A discovery device where information about a legal action is gathered by questioning witnesses or parties outside of the courtroom, but under oath and with a court reporter present to record the testimony.

Interrogatories
A series of written questions, answered under oath, sent to a witness or party by an opposing party, to help facilitate the gathering of information and evidence in preparation for a case.

Production of Documents
A discovery device requesting certain written records and documentary evidence.

Deposition

A *deposition* is a pretrial discovery device where witnesses or parties to a lawsuit are questioned outside of the courtroom, but under oath and with a court reporter present to record the sworn testimony. This is generally limited to civil lawsuits, although a few states allow depositions to be taken in criminal actions.[9] In a deposition, witnesses or parties can be called by either side's attorneys and questioned by both sides. This questioning usually takes place at one of the attorney's offices, with a court reporter present to record the testimony given. The purpose of a deposition is to gather information about a case. It can also provide a type of rehearsal for the trial, giving each side an opportunity to observe a witness or party firsthand and assess their demeanor, testimony, and credibility.

Interrogatories

The next type of discovery device is the *interrogatories*. This is a series of written questions, answered under oath, which are sent through the mail to a witness or party by an opposing party. These questions are designed to help facilitate the gathering of information and evidence, such as dates, times, locations, names of those involved, or witnesses. For example, in a civil action for negligence stemming from an auto accident, interrogatories might ask about a party's driving record and license, or whether his license has ever been revoked or suspended. The interrogatories might ask where he was going to or coming from prior to the accident, whether he had consumed alcohol or drugs, or had any prior accidents.

Practice Tip 3.2

Preparing Interrogatories

Most state and federal statutes have sample or "form" sets of interrogatories that can be used to supplement your own. When preparing interrogatory questions, be sure to think about what the cause of action is, what elements will need to be proven, and what evidence will be offered by the opposing side. For example, in a civil action for harm caused by an accident where the driver had been drinking, the following questions should be included:

Q: How much alcohol did you have to drink that evening?

Q: What type of alcoholic beverage did you drink?

Q: What time did you consume this alcohol?

Q: Where did you drink this alcohol?

Q: Who was present when you were drinking?

Q: How long were you at this location?

Q: Have you ever been stopped for drunk driving?

Q: Have you ever been arrested for drunk driving?

Q: Have you ever been convicted of drunk driving?

These would only make up a portion of the questions needed. Interrogatories should include a thorough set of questions designed to help establish the elements of a legal action, as well as to obtain background and supporting evidence that will help prove the action at trial. The questions should include some that are designed to check veracity by rephrasing a question and asking it again with different wording. Questions should also be designed to elicit new information and leads for further investigation or verification.

Motion to Compel
A formal request for a trial judge to order the production of documents or other evidence.

Subpoena Duces Tecum
An order of a court, at the request of a party to a legal action, requiring another party to produce certain documents or records.

Due Process
Constitutional protections extended to the accused in a criminal action.

Exclusionary Rule
A legal rule, established by case law, that prohibits the admission of illegally obtained evidence in a criminal action.

Production of Documents

The third type of discovery is the request for the *production of documents* or evidence. This is usually done through a **motion to compel,** where the court orders the production, or a **Subpoena Duces Tecum,** where the court orders someone to bring the documents or evidence in. Requests for production can be important in obtaining documents and evidence such as medical and bank records, statements, phone bills, and business records.

Special Considerations for Criminal Actions

Evidence is obtained in the investigation stage of a criminal action in much the same way as for civil cases: interviewing the victim (this is the plaintiff in civil actions), witnesses, and all other parties who might have relevant information regarding the crime. The criminal action, however, carries very special limitations. This is part of the **due process** requirements for the criminal justice system.

Central to these constitutional limitations is the Fourth Amendment. The Fourth Amendment provides protection against unreasonable search or seizure by government agents and law enforcement officers who then attempt to use that evidence in a criminal prosecution. In interpreting these limitations, the U.S. Supreme Court has created the **Exclusionary Rule** that prohibits the admission of evidence obtained illegally or in violation of the Fourth Amendment. Another constitutional protection is covered in the Fifth Amendment, which limits how police can interrogate suspects and defendants in criminal prosecutions in order to obtain evidence in the form of their admission or confession.

The discovery process is also different for criminal than it is for civil actions. In criminal actions, the discovery process favors the defendant. A defendant in a criminal action may obtain most any report, document, or evidence that the prosecution possesses for the case, but the prosecution is limited in what they might examine or receive from the defense. The prosecution is generally entitled to view the defense lists for expert witnesses expected to be called, and for alibi witnesses. However, the defense does not have to disclose, as a general rule, other evidence and witnesses on their behalf.

PREPARING EVIDENCE AND EXHIBITS FOR TRIAL

As described earlier, there are four forms of evidence: testimonial, physical, documentary, and demonstrative. Of these, witness testimony will be the primary source of evidence at trial. Evidence is usually presented in the order that the legal action took place. Sometimes, in order for one witness to testify, another person must first testify to establish the qualification of the witness to testify about a particular matter. For example, a police officer will testify that she administered a breath test in the proper manner to a drunk driving suspect. To show that the police officer was properly trained and certified in how to administer the breath test, the officer will need to either establish this on the stand or another witness (the training instructor, for example) will need to testify. Similarly, when a witness testifies to properly administering the test, another witness may have to be called to explain what the test results mean. This all underscores the need to properly plan and organize the list of witnesses in a manner to present the most effective case.

The same principle applies to exhibits. An **exhibit** is an item offered in evidence that is properly marked for later identification. Aside from testimonial evidence, the other forms of evidence will generally require that they be presented in the form of an exhibit. For example, physical evidence in the form of a fingerprint, the weapon of a crime, or tool will all need to be marked and identified as evidentiary exhibits (Plaintiff's Exhibit A, for example).

Again, the need for proper planning of these exhibits is most important. Exhibits need to be organized so that they support witness testimony and are introduced at the right point in the trial. The key throughout this planning is to employ the Boy Scout motto to "be prepared." Plan, gather, verify, plan more, organize, and manage all witnesses and evidence.

Exhibit
An item offered in evidence that is properly marked for later identification.

Practice Tip 3.3

Checklist for Organizing and Managing Evidence Exhibits

- ☐ What is the evidence?
- ☐ Who found or collected it?
- ☐ Who can identify it in court?
- ☐ How can it be identified?
- ☐ Where was it found or collected?
- ☐ Why would it be in this location?
- ☐ What were the circumstances around finding it?
- ☐ Was there anything unusual or out of place?
- ☐ Was it photographed at this scene?
- ☐ If so, by whom and in what capacity?
- ☐ Did it require any examination or analysis by a lab?
- ☐ If so, what lab, what results, and who did the analysis?
- ☐ What does this evidence tend to prove or disprove?
- ☐ What legal citations or authorities can be used to support this evidence?
- ☐ Where in the trial should this evidence be presented?
- ☐ What challenges are anticipated to its introduction?
- ☐ What evidence and legal citations can be used to overcome these challenges?
- ☐ What offer of proof can be presented?
- ☐ What exhibit number will be assigned to the evidence?

CRITICAL THINKING QUESTIONS 3.4

1. Why do we require that each and every element of a legal action be proven?
2. When you have an element such as "foreseeability" or "with the intent to . . . " how would you go about proving this?
3. If most cases are settled before trial, why are we so concerned about gathering evidence to prove a case at trial?
4. Why are the "5 w's" and the "h" (who, what, when, where, why, and how) so important in gathering evidence?
5. How are the discovery devices used to gather evidence?
6. What is the reasoning behind the need for effective organization of evidence exhibits before trial?

PRESENTING EVIDENCE AT TRIAL

Evidence at trial is usually introduced through the testimony of a witness. Testimonial evidence is also required in order to identify and authenticate other forms of evidence presented, whether physical, documentary, or demonstrative.

Testimonial Evidence

Direct Examination
Initial questioning of a witness by the party that called the witness to the stand.

Object
To challenge evidence or testimony introduced at trial.

Cross-Examine
Questioning of a witness by the opposing party on matters within the scope of the direct examination, usually to discredit the testimony of the witness or to develop facts that may help the cross-examiner's case.

Testimonial evidence is introduced by calling a specific witness to the stand, swearing the witness in, and asking questions of him or her called **direct examination.** An example of this process might be:

Plaintiff:	Your Honor, we call Mr. John Jones to the stand.
Court:	Mr. Jones, do you swear or affirm to tell the truth, the whole truth, and nothing but the truth?
Witness:	I do.
Court:	Plaintiff may begin.
Plaintiff:	Thank you, your Honor. Mr. Jones, where were you during the evening of March 5th of this year?

While direct examination is going on, the other side has an opportunity to **object** to the questions asked or to the witness's answers, and, afterward, will have the opportunity to **cross-examine** the witness in order to clarify answers given or attempt to discredit the witness.

Unless an opinion is allowed, testimony is limited to the witness's personal knowledge of the matter before the court (see Exhibit 3.3). This is generally accomplished by having the witness testify to what he or she saw or heard.

EXHIBIT 3.3   Witness May Only Testify to Personal Knowledge

New Jersey Rules of Evidence
Rule 602. Lack of Personal Knowledge.
   Except as otherwise provided by Rule 703 (bases of opinion testimony by experts), a witness may not testify to a matter unless evidence is introduced sufficient to support a finding that the witness has personal knowledge of the matter. Evidence to prove personal knowledge may, but need not, consist of the testimony of the witness himself.

Laying a Foundation

Laying a Foundation
Presenting evidence that sets the groundwork for other evidence, and authenticating and identifying the evidence.

In order to be admitted, evidence must be properly offered to the trier of fact. Often, this will first require an explanation of how the witness came to be in the place where some event was witnessed, or how an item of evidence was obtained, maintained, or tested. This process is called **laying a foundation.** For example, to have a witness testify that she saw the defendant's car run a red light and hit the plaintiff, you must first show that the witness was in a position to see this event at the time and location of the accident in dispute.

Physical, Documentary, and Demonstrative Evidence

For physical, documentary, demonstrative, and scientific evidence, there are additional requirements for laying a proper foundation (see

---

EXHIBIT 3.4   Steps for Laying a Foundation

There are certain steps for laying a foundation to introduce physical, documentary, or certain demonstrative evidence into court. Here is an example of one procedure:

Step 1   Have the proposed piece of evidence marked as an exhibit for identification (e.g., *Plaintiff's Exhibit #1 in Identification*).

Step 2   Identify and authenticate the exhibit by having a witness testify that it is what it purports to be, that it is relevant to the disputed issues, and that its condition has not substantially changed.

Step 3   Offer the proposed evidence to opposing counsel for inspection. At this point, opposing counsel may state any objections to the admissibility of the proposed evidence.

Step 4   The court will rule on the admissibility.

Step 5   Once admitted as evidence, the exhibit will be named *Plaintiff's Exhibit #1 in Evidence* and it may be viewed and examined by the jury.

Exhibit 3.4). These forms of evidence must also be properly identified and authenticated. It must also be shown that the custody and integrity of the evidence was maintained.

IDENTIFICATION AND AUTHENTICATION

There are two requirements to laying a proper foundation for the introduction of this evidence: **identification** and **authentication** (see Exhibit 3.5). According to Wyoming Rule 901, which reflects the majority trend, these requirements are satisfied "by evidence sufficient to support a finding that the matter in question is what its proponent claims."[10] Identification is satisfied by having a witness testify that she recognizes the object in question and can identify it. Authentication can be done through the witness testifying to the object's authenticity, that it is what it purports to be, or, in the case of demonstrative evidence like photographs or diagrams, that it is a true and accurate representation of the scene where it was obtained.

Identification
Part of laying a foundation, where a witness testifies that she can recognize a piece of evidence and identify it.

Authentication
Part of laying a foundation, where a witness testifies that evidence is what it purports to be.

EXHIBIT 3.5   Requirement of Identification or Authentication

Tennessee Rules of Evidence
    Rule 901(a). General provision. The requirement of authentication or identification as a condition precedent to admissibility is satisfied by evidence sufficient to support a finding that the matter in question is what its proponent claims.

Who Determines When Evidence of Authentication Is Sufficient?

In the following Iowa case, defendant argues that photographs of him posing next to marijuana plants should not have been admitted into evidence because no competent evidence established the time at which or place where the pictures had been taken. The appellate court decides who makes this determination.

CASE

United States v. Englebrecht

917 F.2d 376 (8th Cir. 1990).

Appeal from the United States District Court for the Northern District of Iowa.

Heaney, Senior Circuit Judge.

Eugene Englebrecht appeals from his conviction of . . . manufacturing and possession of marijuana with intent to distribute . . . and five counts of laundering monetary instruments. . . . Englebrecht . . . argues that the district court erroneously admitted into evidence photographs of Englebrecht posing by marijuana plants. . . . After considering each of Englebrecht's claims, we affirm the district court's decision.

. . .

Englebrecht . . . contends that photographs of him posing next to marijuana plants should not have been admitted into evidence. . . . According to Englebrecht, no competent evidence established the time at which or place where the pictures had been taken. Federal Rule of Evidence 901 governs this claim, stating that the "requirement of authentication . . . is satisfied by evidence sufficient to support a finding that the matter in question is what its proponent claims." Fed. R. Evid. 901(a). Evaluating the sufficiency of a showing of a photograph's authenticity rests with the trial court's discretion, and its determination will not be overturned absent a clear abuse of discretion. We find no such abuse here.

At trial, the government claimed that the photographs in question showed Englebrecht standing in his marijuana crop sometime in 1988, the time during which the conspiracy was alleged to have occurred. The only facts in dispute were the time and place at which the photos were taken. The photos were found during the search of Englebrecht's home on the day of his arrest. One of Englebrecht's drug customers testified that Englebrecht had shown him the photos and boasted that the marijuana crop pictured belonged to Englebrecht. A detective testified that the background in the photographs matched an area of the farm next to the one on which Englebrecht lived. Another of Englebrecht's customers testified that Englebrecht told him that the marijuana in the pictures was grown in 1988, and that 1988 was the only year during which Englebrecht grew marijuana. This testimony adequately establishes that the photographs picture what the government claims. See *United States v. Blackwell*, 694 F.2d 1325 (1982) (circumstantial evidence made photographs seized from defendant's hotel room admissible even though no witness could testify as to when, where, or by what process they were taken, or whether they fairly and accurately depicted any particular scene on any particular date); *United States v. Kandiel*, 865 F.2d 967 (8th Cir. 1989) (tape recordings found in defendant's possession were admissible without showing of origin, method, or time of recording since contents of the tapes made references to people, places, and activities that were corroborative of other testimony in the record).

. . .

Pursuant to the above conclusions, we affirm the district court's decision.

EVIDENTIARY CHECKLIST 3.5

Elements Required for Identification

☐ Witness must be able to recognize the evidence in question.
☐ Witness must be able to identify the evidence in question.

Conditional Relevance
An admissibility standard when presenting certain evidence, when the relevancy of that evidence depends upon the fulfillment of a condition of fact.

Conditional Relevance

The rule requiring authentication or identification is one of **conditional relevance**; that is, evidence is not **relevant** unless it is first what the proponent purports it to be. Evidentiary Rule 104(b) provides the framework for this admissibility standard. As provided in North Carolina's Rule 104(b), when the relevancy of evidence depends first upon the fulfillment of a con-

---

EVIDENTIARY CHECKLIST 3.6

Elements Required for Authentication

☐ Evidence must be sufficient to support a finding that the matter in question is what it purports to be or what its proponent claims it is, or, in the case of Demonstrative Evidence:

☐ The demonstrative evidence must be a true and accurate representation of the scene it depicts or where it was obtained.

---

dition of fact (see Exhibit 3.6), like proper identification and authentication, the court shall admit it upon the introduction of evidence sufficient to support a finding of the fulfillment of the condition.[11] In other words, the party introducing the evidence must first offer a foundation from which the trier of fact could reasonably find that the evidence is what the proponent says it is. Once this is done, relevance has been satisfied and the witness may testify about the evidence.

Relevant
Evidence is relevant when it tends to prove or disprove a fact in issue.

EXHIBIT 3.6   Relevancy Conditioned on Fact

Pennsylvania Rules of Evidence
   Rule 104(b). When the relevancy of evidence depends upon the fulfillment of a condition of fact, the court shall admit it upon, or subject to, the introduction of evidence sufficient to support a finding of the fulfillment of the condition.

Examples of Identification or Authentication

The evidence rules provide specific examples of how evidence can be identified or authenticated. Some of these include:

Testimony of witness with knowledge.   One of the most common ways to authenticate evidence is to call a witness who has personal knowledge of the evidence and can testify that the evidence is what it is claimed to be. A police officer who discovered a piece of evidence at the crime scene and marked the evidence or bag for identification is an example of this. Another example is someone who witnessed the signing of a contract.

Nonexpert opinion on handwriting.   A lay witness, or nonexpert, can give an opinion as to the genuineness of handwriting as long as it is based upon familiarity with the handwriting that was not acquired for purposes of the litigation.

Comparison by trier or expert witness.   Sometimes, items of physical evidence can be authenticated by being compared with other specimens of evidence that have already been authenticated. This is usually done by an expert witness, who compares and authenticates such things as fingerprints, blood, hair, fibers, and DNA. An expert witness is used whenever scientific knowledge is needed to make an authentication or comparison of specimens. A comparison can also be done by the trier of fact, especially if it is something that may not require sophisticated scientific knowledge, like handwriting samples, or comparing shoes or knives.

Distinctive characteristics and the like. The distinctive characteristics of an item of evidence may be sufficient to authenticate it. Appearance, contents, substance, internal patterns, or other distinctive characteristics, taken in conjunction with circumstances, may all be looked at in making this determination. A registered receipt is an example.

Voice identification. Identification of a voice, whether heard firsthand or through mechanical or electronic transmission or recording, may be made by a witness who is familiar with the voice. The witness may base his or her opinion on hearing the voice at any time under circumstances connecting it with the alleged speaker.

Telephone conversations. Telephone conversations may be authenticated by offering evidence that a call was made to the number assigned at the time by the telephone company to a particular person or business. In the case of a person, circumstances, including self-identification, must be shown that the person answering was the one called. In the case of a business, it must be shown that the call was made to a place of business and the conversation related to business reasonably transacted over the telephone.

Public records or reports. Evidence that is in the form of a public record is authenticated by having the custodian of these records testify.

Ancient documents or data compilation. Authentication can be made by showing that the evidence is an ancient document. This is done by establishing that a document is in such condition as to create no suspicion concerning its authenticity, is in a place where it, if authentic, would likely be, and has been in existence 20 years or more at the time it is offered.

Process or system. Authentication may be sufficient by introducing evidence which describes a process or system used to produce a result and which shows that the process or system produces an accurate result. A Breathalyzer machine used to test for alcohol in the bloodstream is an example of this. Medical diagnostic equipment, such as X-Rays and cat-scans, are other examples. To authenticate this evidence, it may first be necessary to introduce evidence that the machine was in working order and is accurate in its results.

Methods provided by statute or rule. The evidence rules allow any method of authentication or identification if provided by law.

Self-Authentication

Some records and documents are considered so trustworthy that there is no requirement that outside evidence be introduced as to their authenticity. The document itself is sufficient. We call this evidence **self-authenticating.** Most public records are examples of this. Additional examples include certified copies of public records, official government publications, newspapers and periodicals, documents executed by a notary public, and commercial papers.

Self-Authenticating
When the presenting of a document itself is sufficient to establish authentication, without any need for outside evidence.

Effect of Identification and Authentication Requirement

The effect of an authentication and identification requirement is to provide a standard to ensure that evidence presented at trial is genuine (that it is what the party presenting it says it is). Simply because evidence has been authenticated does not mean that it will be found credible or reliable by the trier of fact. Authentication only establishes that the evidence has been shown to be what it purports to be. The opposing side may still offer evidence to counter the authentication.

Problems arise when the authentication involves more complex issues, such as how certain scientific evidence is collected or tested, or whether some items can be authenticated, like computer-generated documents and images, tape recordings, and videotapes. Another problem with authentication deals with how the legal integrity of evidence has been maintained until trial—called the *chain of custody*.

Chain of Custody

The **chain of custody** is the means for verifying the authenticity and **legal integrity of evidence** by establishing where the evidence has been and who handled it prior to trial. Also called the *chain of evidence*, this area of evidence law establishes the criteria for maintaining this integrity and the procedure for establishing and verifying its identity at trial. An investigator in a criminal case, for example, may testify that a weapon in question is the same weapon that was taken from a crime scene. She may identify and authenticate the evidence from initials that she had marked on the weapon or from the serial number that she had noted. After establishing this identity and authentication, the investigator will be asked to verify that the evidence has been kept safe, without tampering, prior to bringing it to trial. Any person who had contact with the evidence must also be accounted for.

Chain of Custody
Means for verifying the authenticity and integrity of evidence by establishing where the evidence has been and who handled it prior to trial.

Legal Integrity of Evidence
The principle that evidence must not be tampered with, altered, substituted, or falsified.

A Chain Is Only as Strong as its Weakest Link

A general rule holds that there should be as few persons as possible that have custody of evidence and those who do must be identifiable or explained in foundation. Because a chain is only as strong as its weakest link, the chain of custody may be broken or vulnerable to attack if the evidence has been damaged, tampered with, or found to be missing during any period of time which cannot be accounted for. The following Indiana case helped to establish the rule where "evidence has passed out of the possession of the original receiver and into the possession of others, a chain of possession must be established to avoid any claim of substitution, tampering, or mistake, and failure to submit such proof may result in the exclusion of the evidence or testimony as to its characteristics."

Group #2 Case #3

CASE

Graham v. State of Indiana
253 Ind. 525 (1970).
Supreme Court of Indiana.

Hunter, Chief Justice.

Appellant, Anthony Graham, was charged by indictment in two counts with possession and sale of heroin, a narcotic drug in violation of the Indi-

ana Narcotic Act. . . . Trial was had . . . and appellant was found not guilty as to count one relating to the sale of narcotics, and guilty as to count two relating to the possession of same. . . .

The arguments set forth in the memorandum accompanying appellant's motion for a new trial may be summarized as follows: (a) there is insufficient evidence to support the conviction of possession of narcotics, to-wit: heroin, because there was at least one unexplained break in the chain of custody of the seized narcotic which precluded a finding that the white powder substance allegedly received by a "buyer" from appellant was in fact the same white powder found to contain heroin in the police laboratory . . . .

The chain of evidence method of identification is a widely recognized concept in both criminal and civil law. In most cases it is not possible to establish the identity of an exhibit in question by a single witness. The exhibit has usually passed through several hands before being analyzed or examined or before being produced in court. Certainly this is the case here. The record indicates that, from the time of the alleged "buy" until the trial, the exhibit was handled by at least eight different property clerks who either received or released it from the police property room. In addition it was handled by at least three police officers at different times during the same period. Under such circumstances as these it is necessary to establish a complete chain of evidence tracing the possession of the exact and original exhibit to the final custodian. If one link of the chain is entirely missing, the exhibit cannot be introduced or made the basis for the testimony or the report of an expert or officer. If the testimony of the state's expert witnesses as to the narcotic content of the white powder is sought to be offered at trial, then the state should be prepared to establish a "chain of evidence" by either producing police custody records showing the same or by testimony of witnesses. This is not a new rule in Indiana but rather a shorthand recognition of the well-established *evidentiary requirement* that a *foundation must be laid* connecting the evidence with the defendant before it is admissible at the trial. The danger of tampering, loss, or mistake with respect to an exhibit is greatest where the exhibit is small and is one which has physical characteristics fungible in nature and similar in form to substances familiar to people in their daily lives. The white powder in this case could have been heroin, or it could have been, for example, baking powder, powdered sugar, or even powdered milk. The burden on the state in seeking to admit such evidence is clear. Unless the state can show, by producing records or testimony, the continuous whereabouts of the exhibit at least between the time it came into their possession until it was laboratory tested to determine its composition, testimony of the state as to the laboratory's findings is inadmissible.

Turning to the case at bar we find that the exhibit in question was deposited in the usual manner in the police custody room on the afternoon of November 22, 1966, within two hours after the "buy." The police property room records reflected receipt of same and no challenge to the evidence is made by appellant up to that point. However, on the next day, November 23, 1966, the record reveals that a Sergeant Elmore from the crime laboratory removed the exhibit from the police property room and that it was not returned until 6 days later when it was brought back by a Lieutenant Sullivan. The exhibit's whereabouts or disposition during this period was neither ascertainable from police records nor explained by any state's witnesses. Neither Sergeant Elmore nor Lieutenant Sullivan testified at the trial. What happened to the Juicy Fruit gum wrapper and its contents between November 23 and November 29 was not testimonially established. It would appear to be unreasonable and unrealistic to argue that the unaccounted for absence of a police exhibit of this nature for 6 days and 6 nights is not a complete break in the chain of evidence.

Not until February 21, 1967, did the chemical examination take place which formed the basis for the expert testimony of the state's laboratory witness and the basis for the conviction. The fact that the chewing gum wrapper was identifiable as that acquired from appellant at the drugstore cannot cure the defective evidentiary chain of custody which preceded the laboratory experiments. Appellant was not convicted for possession of a chewing gum wrapper.

We think that the facts in this case insofar as they relate to the custody of the alleged heroin compel us to conclude that the evidence of the laboratory findings should have been excluded. The added burden imposed upon the prosecution by this holding is not great. Had the state produced either Sergeant Gilmore or Lt. Sullivan to account for the exhibit's whereabouts during the 6-day period, or to explain any discrepancies in the police department's custody records, there likely would have been no grounds to challenge the continuity of custody. Ordinarily where the chain of evidence is challenged, production of the record books of the police custody room will suffice. The fact that an out-of-the-ordinary procedure was followed or that oral testimony was required to explain errors in the written police records would go to the weight rather than the admissibility of the evidence.

We believe the rule announced here can be summarized as follows: whereas in the case of seized or purchased narcotics, the object offered in evidence has passed out of the possession of the original receiver and into the possession of others, a chain of possession must be established to avoid any claim of substitution, tampering, or mistake, and failure to submit such proof may result in the exclusion of the evidence or testimony as to its characteristics. Where such evidence or testimony is improperly introduced and is prejudicial to the party against whom it is directed, then the judgment of the trial court should be reversed.

LEGAL ANALYSIS AND WRITING 3.2

The following questions are based on the *How to Brief a Legal Case* format shown in the Appendix. Use this format to answer the following questions:

1. Summarize the facts in the previous case.
2. What is the legal issue?
3. What did the appellate court decide?
4. Why did the court decide this way?
5. Do you agree with the court's reasoning? Explain why or why not.

Degree of Proof Depends on the Nature of Evidence Presented

In the following New Mexico case, the court held that "the degree of proof needed to establish an uninterrupted chain of custody depends upon the nature of the evidence at issue." It then set forth guidelines for determining these factors.

group #3 case 3

CASE

United States v. Clonts

966 F.2d 1366 (10th Cir. 1992).
Appeal from the United States District Court for the District of New Mexico.

Anderson, Circuit Judge.

Defendant-Appellant, Charles Edward Clonts, was convicted by a jury of conspiracy to distribute less than 50 kilograms of marijuana in violation of 21 U.S.C. 846, and 18 U.S.C. 2, and possession with intent to distribute less than 50 kilograms of marijuana in violation of 21 U.S.C. 841(a)(1) and 841(b)(1)(D). On appeal Defendant argues that, because of an alleged defect in the chain of custody of the marijuana, there was insufficient evidence to sustain his conviction. . . . Because we find no merit in Defendant's contentions, we affirm.

Facts

Testimony at trial established that in June, 1990, Defendant was introduced to Mr. Jimmy Searles, a special agent with the United States Customs Service who was working undercover investigating narcotics violations. After subsequent meetings and conversations with Agent Searles, Defendant eventually asked Agent Searles to "front" him 25 pounds of marijuana, which the agent agreed to do. Defendant told Agent Searles that a friend of his was a pilot who would fly him to Tucson where the marijuana would be sold. Agent Searles ultimately agreed to front Defendant one hundred pounds of marijuana, filling three large suitcases. When asked if he could handle that much in a Cessna 150, Defendant replied, "Oh, we can handle that. That's no problem." When Agent Searles and a fellow agent met Defendant at the Las

Cruces airport to transfer the marijuana, Defendant was asked whether he was "ready to do it." He indicated that he was. He and the two agents each took one of the suitcases from the trunk of the agents' car and carried them to the plane. When the three men reached the plane, Defendant placed all three suitcases in the plane's back compartment. After the two agents left, other agents from the Customs Service surrounded the plane and arrested Defendant.

Chain of Custody

On appeal, Defendant argues that the testimony concerning the chain of custody of the marijuana and the analysis of the evidence was insufficient to sustain a guilty verdict. He points out that no marijuana was introduced at trial, that the three empty suitcases which were introduced at trial had not been marked as evidence and were only identified visually by the government's witness as being the ones involved in the transaction, that the marijuana bricks had not been marked as evidence, either before or after they were removed from the suitcases, and that the only identification of marijuana during the trial came when Agent Searles testified that upon smelling the suitcases he concluded that they had contained "some pretty good quantity of marijuana." Additionally, Defendant complains that each individual package was not tested to verify that it was marijuana, and that, while Defendant stipulated that the substance sent to the United States Customs Service Laboratory in New Orleans by case agent Bart Skelton was marijuana, there was no proof that the substance analyzed by the lab actually came from the suitcases.

The degree of proof needed to establish an uninterrupted chain of custody depends upon the nature of the evidence at issue. If the evidence is unique, readily identifiable and resistant to change, the foundation for admission need only be testimony that the evidence is what it purports to be. Alternatively, if the evidence is open to alteration or tampering, or is not readily identifiable, the trial court requires a more elaborate chain of custody to establish that the evidence has not been tampered with or altered. Because the marijuana here is not unique or resistant to alteration, a sufficient chain of custody is required to support its admission. Once admitted, however, whatever deficiencies remain in the chain of custody go to the weight of the evidence, not its admissibility. "The jury evaluates the defects and, based on its evaluation, may accept or disregard the evidence."

In this case, Mr. Bart Skelton, the case agent, testified that he took custody of the suitcases on July 13, 1990, the day of Defendant's arrest. They were delivered to him by the agent who had confiscated the suitcases at the time of the arrest, and who identified them at trial as the ones pertaining to this case. The suitcases were admitted into evidence without objection. Agent Skelton further testified that he inspected the contents of the suitcases when he received them on July 13 and that he weighed and sampled the marijuana located inside 2 days later. That same day, he shipped several samples to the New Orleans lab. After this testimony, the following stipulation was read to the jury:

1. The substance delivered to the United States Customs Service Laboratory by Special Agent Bart Skelton for testing was found to be marijuana.

2. The marijuana weighed less than 50 kilograms.

3. Marijuana is a schedule I controlled substance.

4. This stipulation may be read during the course of the trial and may be admitted as an exhibit.

Defendant now argues that this stipulation merely concedes that the substance analyzed at the lab was marijuana, but that there was no proof that the substance from the suitcases was that actually analyzed by the lab or that the substance eventually analyzed by the lab was even related to his case. He contends that the direct evidence, even when bolstered by the stipulation, is insufficient to sustain his conviction. We disagree.

The stipulation was signed by the Defendant, his attorney, and the attorney for the government. Because the marijuana was the subject of the charges against Defendant, it is safe to infer that, at the time the stipulation was signed, all parties were describing the relevant marijuana. Defendant's chain of custody argument appears to us as an afterthought which is logically unsupportable, given the fact of a stipulation, executed in preparation for trial, with no caveat or exception made for a chain of custody issue.

. . . Given the fact of the stipulation and the direct evidence regarding the chain of custody of the marijuana, we cannot say that the district court abused its discretion in finding it improbable that the evidence had been materially altered and in admitting testimony regarding it into evidence.

. . . .

The judgment of the District Court for the District of New Mexico is affirmed.

LEGAL ANALYSIS AND WRITING 3.3

The following questions are based on the *How to Brief a Legal Case* format shown in the Appendix. Use this format to answer the following questions:

1. Summarize the facts in the previous case.
2. What is the legal issue?
3. What did the appellate court decide?
4. Why did the court decide this way?
5. Do you agree with the court's reasoning? Explain why or why not.

LEGAL RESEARCH USING THE INTERNET SKILLS 3.3

Try to find this case or another one with a similar issue online! Check out one of the legal research web sites below, go to the federal circuit for this court decision, and use their "Search" feature to find this case or another case that refers to it. In the "Search" field, enter the cite or case name. If you have access to Westlaw or Lexis, try to find this case using one of these legal search sites.

1. U.S. Courts Site with Links to All Circuit Courts of Appeal (http://www.uscourts.gov/links.html)
2. National Center for State Courts—State and Federal Court Web Sites (http://www.ncsconline.org/D_kis/info_court_web_sites.html)
3. FindLaw (http://guide.lp.findlaw.com/casecode/)

Will a "Missing Link" Break the Chain?

Is "precision in developing the 'chain of custody'" an iron-clad requirement? The following case addresses this issue.

CASE

United States v. Howard-Arias

679 F.2d 363 (4th Cir. 1982).

The appellant, Edmundo Howard-Arias, was convicted after a jury trial of possession of marijuana on the high seas with intent to distribute it and of possession with intent to import it into the United States under 21 U.S.C. ss 955a(a) and 955a(d). His appeal challenges certain evidentiary rulings, procedures used during the sentencing phase of his trial, and his multiple convictions and sentences, contending that they violate the double jeopardy clause of the Fifth Amendment. Finding no merit to his arguments, we affirm.

The appellant's claims regarding the admission of certain evidence need not long detain us. His first argument is that the government failed to establish a continuous "chain of custody" for the marijuana from the time of its seizure on the seas off the Virginia coast until its introduction at trial. It is conceded that one of the DEA agents involved in the transfer and testing of the bales and samples drawn from them did not testify at trial. The Coast Guard officer who seized and tested the marijuana, the officer to whom he surrendered it, the DEA custodian at Norfolk, and the DEA chemist all appeared as witnesses. The special agent who received the marijuana from the Coast Guard for transit to the DEA in Norfolk did not.

The "chain of custody" rule is but a variation of the principle that real evidence must be authenticated prior to its admission into evidence. The purpose of this threshold requirement is to establish that the item to be introduced (i.e., marijuana) is what it purports to be (i.e., marijuana seized from the "Don Frank"). Therefore, the ultimate question is whether the authentication testimony was sufficiently complete so as to convince the court that it is improbable that the original item had been exchanged with another or otherwise tampered with.

Contrary to the appellant's assertion, precision in developing the "chain of custody" is not an iron-clad requirement, and the fact of a "missing link does not prevent the admission of real evidence, so long as there is sufficient proof that the evidence is what it purports to be and has not been altered in any material aspect." *United States v. Jackson*, 649 F.2d 967 (3d Cir.)(1981). Resolution of this question rests with the sound discretion of the trial judge, and we cannot say that he abused that discretion in this case. . . . Affirmed.

LEGAL ANALYSIS AND WRITING 3.4

The following questions are based on the *How to Brief a Legal Case* format shown in the Appendix. Use this format to answer the following questions:

1. Summarize the facts in the previous case.
2. What is the legal issue?
3. What did the appellate court decide?
4. Why did the court decide this way?
5. Do you agree with the court's reasoning? Explain why or why not.

LEGAL RESEARCH USING THE INTERNET SKILLS 3.4

Try to find a case online that deals with a chain of custody issue. Check out one of the legal research web sites below, go to the federal circuit for this court decision, and use their "Search" feature to find this case or another case that refers to it. In the "Search" field, enter the cite or case name. If you have access to Westlaw or Lexis, try to find this case using one of these legal search sites.

1. U.S. Courts Site with Links to All Circuit Courts of Appeal (http://www.uscourts.gov/links.html)
2. National Center for State Courts—State and Federal Court Web Sites (http://www.ncsconline.org/ D_kis/info_court_web_sites.html)
3. FindLaw (http://guide.lp.findlaw.com/casecode/)

Best Evidence or Original Document Rule

The *best evidence* or *original document rule* holds that where the content of a writing, recording, or photograph is in issue, the original must be produced.[12] The rules define writings as anything that consists of letters, words, or numbers, including computer-generated or electronic recordings, or any other form of data compilation (see Exhibit 3.7). Photographs include still photographs, X-Ray films, videotapes, and motion pictures. An "original" of a writing or recording is the record itself. An "original" of a photograph includes the negative or any print from it. If data are stored in a computer or similar device, any printout or other output readable by sight, shown to reflect the data accurately, is an "original."[13]

EXHIBIT 3.7   Best Evidence or Original Document Rule

Wyoming Rules of Evidence
Rule 1002. Requirement of original.
   To prove the content of a writing, recording, or photograph, the original writing, recording, or photograph is required, except as otherwise provided in these rules or by statute.

Many courts believe that this rule has been misunderstood by parties in gathering and presenting evidence, and that modern society has narrowed the purpose of the rule. One noted New York court decision stated:

> "The 'oft-mentioned and much misunderstood' *best evidence rule* simply requires the production of an original writing where its contents are in dispute and sought to be proven. At its genesis, the rule was primarily designed to guard against 'mistakes in copying or transcribing the original writing.' Given the technological advancements in copying, in modern day practice the rule serves mainly to protect against fraud, perjury and 'inaccuracies which derive from faulty memory.'
>
> Under a long-recognized exception to the best evidence rule, secondary evidence of the contents of an unproduced original may be admitted upon threshold factual findings by the trial court that the proponent of the substitute has sufficiently explained the unavailability of the primary evidence and has not procured its loss or destruction in bad faith. Loss may be established upon a showing of a diligent search in the location where the document was last known to have been kept, and through the testimony of the person who last had custody of the original. Indeed, the more important the document to the resolution of the ultimate issue in the case, 'the stricter becomes the requirement of the evidentiary foundation [establishing loss] for the admission of secondary evidence.' In other words, the court should give careful consideration to the possible motivation for the non-production of the original in determining whether the foundational proof of loss was sufficient."[14]

Admissibility of Duplicates

Since the reason for an original document or best evidence rule is to ensure that the evidence introduced is authentic, the evidence rules do permit a duplicate to be admissible. This will be allowed to the same extent as an original unless a genuine question is raised as to the authenticity of the original, or under circumstances where it would be unfair to admit the duplicate in lieu of the original.[15]

When Originals Are Not Required

Oregon reflects the evidence rule for when an original is not required. According to the Oregon rule, an original is not required, and other evidence of the contents of a writing, recording, or photograph is admissible if the original has been lost or destroyed, or it is not obtainable by any judicial process, or the other side will not produce it.[16] Extremely lengthy or "voluminous" writings or recordings that cannot conveniently be examined in court may be presented in the form of a chart or summary.[17] If this is done, the originals or duplicates shall be made available for examination or copying by the opposite party and may have to be produced in court. In order to offer a summary, a proper foundation must first be introduced for the admission of the original writings. When the originals have been authenticated, then another foundation must be offered to authenticate the summary. If the original would not be admissible, the summary cannot be admitted.

Functions of the Court and Jury

When admissibility under these rules depends upon the fulfillment of a condition of fact, the question of whether the condition has been fulfilled is ordinarily for the court to determine in accordance with the provisions of Rule 104. For example, if there is an issue raised about whether a duplicate can be admitted or whether other evidence can be admitted if the original has been lost or destroyed, then the court must make this decision after first determining about the original. However, when an issue is raised whether the asserted writing ever existed, or whether the evidence presented at the trial is the original, the issue is for the trier of fact to determine as in the case of other issues of fact.

Jim Bakker and the PTL

The following North Carolina case deals with the televangelist, Jim Bakker, and his fund-raising activities, which resulted in Bakker's conviction for fraud. One of the issues in this case was whether over two hundred hours of PTL broadcasts could be summarized for use at trial.

CASE

United States v. Bakker

925 F.2d 728 (4th Cir. 1991).

Appeal from the United States District Court for the Western District of North Carolina, at Charlotte.

Wilkinson, Circuit Judge.

This appeal stems from the trial and sentencing of a well-known televangelist, James O. Bakker. Bakker raises numerous challenges to his conviction for fraud and conspiracy. We affirm his conviction. . . .

I.

In 1974, James Bakker formed a corporation known as the PTL. PTL stands for "Praise the Lord" and "People that Love." The PTL's activities soon expanded from their initial focus on televised religious broadcasting. For example, in the late 1970s PTL began construction on "Heritage USA," described by PTL officials as a Christian retreat center for families. The concept of the center became increasingly ambitious. In 1983, Bakker announced plans to enlarge the center by adding a vacation park, "Heritage Village," that would include the 500-room Grand Hotel. Between 1984 and 1986, appellant announced further proposals to expand the Village by constructing the Towers Hotel, 50 bunkhouses, and several additional facilities.

Bakker planned to finance these projects by selling lifetime partnerships. He offered 11 different partnership programs ranging in cost from $500 to $10,000. Eight of the partnerships promised bene-

fits that included annual lodging in one of the Heritage Village facilities. In January 1984, appellant began using the mail to solicit lifetime partners. Also, from February 1984 through May 1987, Bakker used broadcasts carried on the PTL Television Network and various commercial affiliates to solicit lifetime partners. Many of these partners drew on meager incomes to purchase Heritage Village lodging benefits. Appellant raised at least $158 million through the sale of approximately 153,000 partnerships with lodging benefits.

Bakker promised television viewers that he would limit the sale of partnerships to ensure that each partner would be able to use the facilities annually. Appellant, however, oversold the partnerships. He promised, for instance, to limit the sale of Grand Hotel partnerships to 25,000 but actually sold 66,683. In addition, Bakker used relatively few of the funds solicited from the partners to construct promised facilities. In fact, of the proposed Heritage Village facilities, only the Grand Hotel and one bunkhouse were actually completed. Instead, Bakker used partnership funds to pay operating expenses of the PTL and to support a lavish lifestyle. This extravagant living included gold-plated fixtures and a $570 shower curtain in his bathroom, transportation in private jets and limousines, an air-conditioned treehouse for his children and an air-conditioned doghouse for his pets. This combination of overselling partnerships and diverting partnership proceeds meant that the overwhelming majority of the partners never received the lodging benefits Bakker promised them.

In response to these activities, a grand jury on December 5, 1988 indicted Bakker on 8 counts of mail fraud in violation of 18 U.S.C. §1341, 15 counts of wire fraud in violation of 18 U.S.C. §1343, and 1 count of conspiracy in violation of 18 U.S.C. §371. Bakker's trial began on August 28, 1989 and lasted 5 weeks. The jury found him guilty on all 24 counts. The court sentenced him to 45 years imprisonment and fined him $500,000. Bakker now appeals his conviction and sentence.

. . . .

Bakker . . . contends that the trial court abused its discretion in two evidentiary rulings. In one, the trial court admitted into evidence videotapes which the government claimed summarized Bakker's efforts during PTL broadcasts to solicit lifetime partners. In the other ruling, the court prevented Bakker from introducing two charts which purported to summarize the construction and availability of facilities at Heritage Village. In our view, the trial court did not abuse its discretion in making either of these rulings.

1.

As part of the government's case, an F.B.I. agent testified that he reviewed over two hundred hours of PTL broadcasts that had aired from February 1984 to April 1987 and edited them into 11 composite tapes. These tapes, which allegedly showed Bakker's attempts during the broadcasts to solicit funds for Heritage Village, were admitted into evidence. Bakker objects both to the procedure by which the trial court admitted the tapes into evidence and to the substance of the tapes themselves.

Bakker contends that before the composite tapes could come into evidence, the original broadcast tapes on which the composites were based first had to be introduced into evidence under Fed. R. Evid. 1006. Bakker's argument, however, attempts to graft onto Rule 1006 a requirement that is at odds with the Rule's purpose and plain meaning. The purpose of Rule 1006 is to provide a practicable means of summarizing voluminous information. Fed. R. Evid. 1006 Advisory Committee's Note. This purpose was well served in this case since viewing all of the original broadcast tapes would have taken over 200 hours of the court's and jury's time. The language of the Rule also does not require that the original voluminous material be in-

troduced into evidence; rather it simply requires that the material be made available to the other party. It is undisputed that Bakker's counsel had access to the original broadcast tapes at least 6 months prior to trial. Requiring the government to formally introduce the underlying tapes into evidence would have served no useful purpose.

The cases Bakker relies on in arguing that the originals must be introduced are inapposite. These cases deal with situations where a party is attempting to use a chart or other device to summarize information that has already been introduced into evidence. In these circumstances, the device used to summarize is merely an aid to the factfinder's understanding, not evidence itself. By contrast under Rule 1006, the summary of voluminous information is itself the evidence to be examined by the factfinder. Thus, no need exists to introduce the underlying voluminous material into evidence. Bakker also argues that the substance of the composite tapes was unrepresentative of his broadcasts. Bakker's objection is misplaced because it goes to the weight to be accorded to the composite tapes, not to their admissibility. Once the court properly determined that the tapes were admissible, Bakker had ample opportunity to demonstrate to the jury the proper weight that it should attach to the composites. For instance, Bakker played for the jury the tapes of three of his broadcasts in their entirety in an attempt to show that the composites were unrepresentative. In sum, it can hardly be claimed that Bakker was prejudiced by the admission of the composite tapes.

Bakker also contends that the trial court abused its discretion by denying his motions to have his chart summaries admitted into evidence. These charts purported to summarize the lodging facilities available to lifetime partners. The court sustained the government's initial objection to the charts being admitted into evidence, though the court did allow Bakker to testify about the charts' contents and to use them to refresh his recollection. After Bakker had finished testifying, his counsel renewed his motion to admit the chart summaries, but the court again denied the motion.

Our prior discussion of the distinction between the types of devices used to summarize information is also relevant here. Bakker's charts did not purport to summarize voluminous records; rather they allegedly summarized information already introduced into evidence. The governing standard then is that "summary charts may be admitted if they are based upon and fairly represent competent evidence already before the jury." *United States v. Porter*, 821 F.2d at 975. The problem for Bakker is that the government objected at trial that his charts did not fairly represent the evidence already before the jury, and the court sustained these objections. Bakker then stated that his "memory" served as additional supporting evidence for the charts. The trial court was right to conclude that a party's memory is no substitute for "evidence already before the jury."

The government demonstrated at least two ways in which the charts unfairly represented the evidence. First, the charts showed that PTL condo-miniums were available to house lifetime partners. Yet, Bakker conceded that partners were not informed that the condominiums were available and that they were actually not used to house partners. Second, the charts showed that prospective partners were notified that they might have to accept campsites in lieu of hotel rooms. In fact, Bakker admitted that he did not so notify prospective partners. Based on this information, we believe the court properly exercised its discretion in excluding chart "summaries" that could easily have misled the jury.

. . . .

We conclude, therefore, that Bakker's trial was free of reversible error. . . .

LEGAL ANALYSIS AND WRITING 3.5

The following questions are based on the *How to Brief a Legal Case* format shown in the Appendix. Use this format to answer the following questions:

1. Summarize the facts in the previous case.
2. What is the legal issue?
3. What did the appellate court decide?
4. Why did the court decide this way?
5. Do you agree with the court's reasoning? Explain why or why not.

LEGAL RESEARCH USING THE INTERNET SKILLS 3.5

Try to find this case or another one that deals with a similar issue online! Check out one of the legal research web sites below, go to the federal circuit for this court decision, and use their "Search" feature to find this case or another case that refers to it. In the "Search" field, enter the cite or case name. If you have access to Westlaw or Lexis, try to find this case using one of these legal search sites.

1. U.S. Courts Site with Links to all Circuit Courts of Appeal (http://www.uscourts.gov/links.html)
2. National Center for State Courts—State and Federal Court Web Sites (http://www.ncsconline.org/D_kis/info_court_web_sites.html)
3. FindLaw (http://guide.lp.findlaw.com/casecode/)

WHAT IS NOT EVIDENCE?

In presenting evidence at trial, it is also important to know what is not considered evidence. In its recommendations for instructing the jury, the *Benchbook for U.S. District Court Judges* lists what is not evidence at trial. This list includes statements, questions, and arguments by lawyers; objections to questions; testimony that the court excluded or admonished the jury to disregard; and anything that may have been seen or heard outside of the courtroom.[18]

CRITICAL THINKING QUESTIONS 3.5

1. Why do we have rules that require a foundation to be shown before evidence is presented and testified about?
2. What public policy reasons do you think are behind these rules?
3. Why are we concerned about the chain of custody for certain evidence presented at trial?
4. What safeguards are in place to ensure the legal integrity of evidence and do you think these safeguards are adequate? Explain your reason.
5. What is the reasoning behind the best evidence or original document requirement?
6. Do you think that this requirement is still important today with our reliance on copies for most of our transactions and records?

MAKING THE RECORD

Because of the adversarial nature of trials, there are always winners and losers. The possibility of losing requires that the parties involved protect their opportunity to appeal if they believe that there were errors that occurred at the trial which caused or contributed to their loss. Therefore, every legal team has to work on two levels during a trial: to win the case, and to **"make the record"** of everything that occurs at the trial in case they do lose and have to appeal. To *make the record* means to ensure that a properly maintained **record** of case documents and a thorough **transcript** of the trial proceedings is kept.

Appellate Court Decides Errors of Law, Not Facts

If the case is appealed from the decision at the trial level, the appellate level court does not decide any factual issues that were raised at trial. The appellate court can only decide if there were prejudicial errors of law that occurred during the trial that deprives a party of a fair trial. Therefore, it is important for trial counsel to ensure that they carefully build and preserve a record of the trial proceedings which may include anything that pertains to their objections of decisions by the trial judge or which may constitute an error of law upon appeal.

What Is in the Record?

The *record* of a trial is made up of all the papers, pleadings, complaints, motions, briefs, orders, jury instructions, and the like that go into a lawsuit or court proceeding. One of the most important parts to the record is the official *transcript* of the trial.

Importance of Making the Record

This transcript is the formal record of what was said and done at trial, including any "on-the-record" conversations or offers of proof. The transcript is recorded by the court reporter as it actually happens. For this

Make the Record
Ensuring that a properly maintained **record** of case documents and a thorough **transcript** of the trial proceedings is kept.

Record
Papers, pleadings, complaints, motions, briefs, orders, jury instructions, and the like that go into a lawsuit or court proceeding.

Transcript
Formal record, taken by a court reporter, of what is said and done at trial, including any "on-the-record" conversations or offers of proof.

reason, it becomes important for the legal teams involved to ensure that every word is recorded by the court reporter as if they were dictating the material to a personal secretary, and that gestures and certain body movements are explained.

Example: "Let the record show that the witness has pointed to the defendant."

Example: "Let the record show the witness has responded to this question by nodding his head in the affirmative."

CRITICAL THINKING QUESTIONS 3.6

1. What is meant by the role of evidence in "making the record?"
2. What is the "record" and what is it made up of?
3. How does one go about "making the record" or ensuring that a record is made? Give examples.
4. Why are we so concerned about making the record and who is this record being made for?
5. Why is the responsibility for making the record largely on the part of the parties? Why isn't the regular court transcript sufficient enough to rely on?

SUMMARY

Laws affect every aspect of how information is obtained and presented through evidence in the trial process. There are laws that establish how much evidence is necessary to constitute a legal action and how much evidence is required to prove a case. The gathering of information and evidence must be focused on establishing the elements to a legal action and meeting the burden in proving that action at trial. To do this, we must first understand how evidence is classified. Evidence is classified by type and form. There are two basic types of evidence: direct evidence and circumstantial evidence. Direct evidence proves a disputed fact directly through the testimony of a witness who saw or heard the dispute at issue. Circumstantial evidence proves a disputed fact indirectly by first proving another fact. In addition to the two basic types of evidence, there are four basic forms of evidence: testimonial, physical, documentary, and demonstrative. Testimonial evidence is "spoken" evidence presented by witnesses who come into court to give their testimony under oath. Physical evidence is something that can be tangibly perceived by the trier of fact. Documentary evidence consists of writings, pictures, and recordings. Demonstrative evidence "demonstrates" or illustrates evidence that has already been presented. Although not a form of evidence, certain facts commonly known in the community or capable of accurate and ready determination may be accepted as true at trial. This is called judicial notice and is used to save time in both the need for gathering and presenting evidence.

There are two primary goals in gathering evidence: to determine whether a cause of action exists or not, and, if so, to prove or disprove the case. The type of legal action will guide and determine what evidence is sought after and collected, and where it might be found. In proving the case, the focus will be on the planning, preparation, and organization of witnesses and evidence to be presented at trial. Evidence at trial is usually introduced through the testimony of a witness. Testimonial evidence is introduced by calling a specific witness to the stand, swearing the witness in, and asking questions of him or her. In order to be admitted, evidence must be properly presented to the trier of fact. Often, this will first require an explanation of how the witness came to be in the place where some event was witnessed, or how an item of evidence was obtained, maintained, or tested. This process is called laying a foundation. There are two requirements to laying a proper foundation for the introduction of this evidence: identification and authentication. These requirements are satisfied "by evidence sufficient to support a finding that the matter in question is what its proponent claims." A means for verifying where the evidence has been and who handled it prior to trial is called the chain of custody. Related to foundation and authentication is the best evidence or original document rule that requires an original to be produced at trial when the evidence being presented is a writing, recording, or photograph.

When presenting evidence at trial, legal teams work on two levels: to win the case, and to "make the record" of everything that occurs at the trial in case they lose and have to appeal. To *make the record* means to ensure that a properly maintained record of case documents and a thorough transcript of the trial proceedings is kept.

KEY TERMS

Authentication	Due Process	Object
Brady Motion	Exclusionary Rule	Physical Evidence
Cause of Action	Exculpatory Clause	Production of Documents
Chain of Custody	Exculpatory Evidence	Record
Circumstantial Evidence	Exhibit	Relevant
Conditional Relevance	Identification	Self-Authenticating
Cross-Examine	Inference	Stipulation
Demonstrative Evidence	Interrogatories	Subpoena Duces Tecum
Deposition	Judicial Notice	Syllabus
Direct Evidence	Laying a Foundation	Testimonial Evidence
Direct Examination	Legal Integrity of Evidence	Transcript
Discovery	Make the Record	
Documentary Evidence	Motion to Compel	

LEARNING OUTCOMES AND PRACTICE SKILLS CHECKLIST

☐ Learning Outcomes

After completing your reading, questions, and exercises, you should be able to demonstrate a better understanding of the learning concepts by answering the following questions:

1. Explain how evidence law influences the gathering of evidence. Give examples.
2. Distinguish between *direct* and *circumstantial* evidence. Give examples of each.
3. Identify, define, and give examples of each form of evidence.
4. Define *exculpatory* evidence and explain what it pertains to.
5. Describe what a *Brady Motion* is, when it is used, and what elements must be proven to establish a Brady violation.
6. Explain what *judicial notice* means and when it is used. Give examples.

7. Identify the elements that must be established for *judicial notice* to be taken.
8. Discuss what a *stipulation* is and when it is used.
9. What are the two primary goals in gathering evidence?
10. Define *prima facie* and explain what is meant by establishing a prima facie case. Give an example.
11. Name sources where evidence can be found and gathered.
12. Explain what *discovery* is and when it is used.
13. Identify and describe the three discovery devices. Give examples for each.
14. How is evidence presented at trial? Give examples.
15. Explain what is meant by *laying a foundation*.
16. Distinguish the terms *identification* and *authentication*, and describe how they are used in the presentation of evidence.
17. Identify the elements required to establish that evidence has been identified and authenticated.
18. Distinguish *chain of custody* from the *legal integrity of evidence*.
19. Explain how *chain of custody* can be established and why it is important in presenting evidence.
20. Assess the *best evidence* or original document rule, defining the terms and explaining their significance in presenting evidence.
21. Explain what is meant by *making the record* and why this is important in the role of evidence.
22. Describe some of the steps to ensure that the "record" is adequately made.

□ Practice Skills

In addition to understanding the learning concepts, practice what you have learned through applications using critical thinking, legal analysis and writing, legal research, and advocacy skills, including:

Critical Thinking

1. Why do we have rules to govern the gathering and proving of a case?
2. Do you believe that these rules provide adequate safeguards for the parties to a legal action?
3. How do the primary purposes of the evidence rules to ensure fairness and eliminate unjustifiable expense and delay affect the gathering and presentation of evidence?
4. In gathering and presenting evidence, how can we balance these primary purposes of evidence rules in a way that ensures fairness yet ascertains the truth?
5. What public policy issues or considerations do you think might be behind these rules?
6. If it were up to you, would you keep these rules as they are, delete them, narrow them, or expand them? Explain your reasoning.
7. How do these rules influence the gathering of evidence or preparing of witnesses?

Legal Analysis and Writing

Analyze the following rules and cases by summarizing their holdings, explaining their significance, and assessing any issue that might arise in their application.
1. Rule 104(b).
2. Rule 201.
3. Rule 901.

4. Rule 1002.
5. *Strickler v. Greene.*
6. *Graham v. Indiana.*
7. *United States v. Howard-Arias.*
8. *United States v. Bakker.*

Legal Research Using the Internet

1. Find the annotated Federal Rules of Evidence on the Internet and assess the comments made in the proposing of the rules covered in this chapter.
2. Find your state's rules of evidence regarding relevant exceptions and concepts covered in this chapter. Compare and contrast with the federal and/or modern rules, and some of the state rules listed in this chapter.
3. Find out if your state appellate court posts their case decisions on the Internet. If so, find a case that illustrates an issue or rule discussed in this chapter. If your state decisions are not on the Internet, go instead to the web site for the U.S. Circuit Court of Appeals in your circuit, or search the U.S. Supreme Court decisions.

PRACTICE APPLICATION 3.1

Plaintiff applied for a life insurance policy with defendant, a life insurance company, and was accepted on a "conditional receipt," subject to passing a medical exam to verify that plaintiff was an "acceptable health risk" for purposes of coverage. Because defendant's underwriters believed that claimant's medical history raised some concerns about a potential heart condition that might have disqualified him from the coverage he sought, defendant requested that plaintiff complete a physical examination and have an X-Ray taken. This was done on March 20. The X-Ray was sent to defendant's radiologist for analysis. The radiologist concluded in a written report which lies at the core of this dispute that plaintiff had an enlarged heart. On April 9, plaintiff died from a cause unrelated to a heart condition. Since defendant had yet to finally accept or reject claimant's application for insurance at the time of his death, defendant insurer rejected his application, and returned the premium paid. Plaintiff's wife sued to recover the insurance proceeds. Defendant disclaimed liability on the ground that the plaintiff had an enlarged heart at the time of his application which rendered him an unacceptable risk and thus uninsurable. During discovery and trial, defendant could not locate the X-Ray taken. In place of the X-Ray, defendant sought to introduce the radiologist's testimony and his written report to establish that plaintiff's X-Ray would have revealed an enlarged heart.

Defense counsel contends that an X-Ray is a writing subject to the best evidence rule, and because the X-Ray is missing and presumed lost—a fact defendant is ready to attempt to prove—defendant should have been permitted to establish the contents of that lost writing by any competent secondary evidence. Plaintiff moves to preclude the evidence, arguing that the best evidence rule requires the X-Ray be presented and sets up an absolute bar to the admission of secondary evidence in the form of the radiologist's testimony in the absence of the original X-Ray.

How would you decide this? Use the format shown in the Appendix for the *IRAC Method of Legal Analysis* and the readings, rules, and cases discussed in this chapter to analyze this question. Write a short memo giving your analysis, reasoning, and conclusions.

LEGAL RESEARCH USING THE INTERNET SKILLS 3.6

Find out how the Court ruled on the previous *Practice Application* problem by trying to find and read this New York decision online! The citation for it is:

Schozer v. William Penn Life Insurance Company of New York, 84 N.Y.2d 639 (1994)

ADVOCACY AND COMMUNICATION SKILLS 3.1

Using the previous *Practice Application* case problem, form two teams, representing the prosecution and defense.

1. Each team will prepare and present an oral argument of the issue in this case problem: whether the radiologist's testimony should be allowed or whether the X-Ray is required to be presented under the best evidence rule. Each team will have 5 minutes for their argument and an additional 3 minutes, after the opposing team has presented their argument, for rebuttal.

WEB SITES

Federal Judicial Center
http://www.fjc.gov/
FindLaw
http://guide.lp.findlaw.com/casecode/
FindLaw U.S. Supreme Court Decisions
http://www.findlaw.com/casecode/supreme.html
National Center for State Courts
http://www.ncsconline.org/
National Center for State Courts—State and Federal Court Web Sites
http://www.ncsconline.org/D_kis/info_court_web_ sites.html# state

Supreme Court Collection of Cornell Law School
http://supct.law.cornell.edu/supct/
U.S. Courts
http://www.uscourts.gov/
U.S. Courts Site with Links to All Circuit Courts of Appeal
http://www.uscourts.gov/links.html
U.S. Supreme Court
http://www.supremecourtus.gov/

ENDNOTES

1. *Brady v. Maryland*, 373 U.S. 83 (1963).
2. *United States v. Agurs*, 427 U.S. 97 (1976).
3. *Kyles v. Whitley*, 514 U.S. 419 (1995).
4. Ibid.
5. *State v. Maine*, 69 Conn. 123 (1897).
6. Utah R. Evid. 201.
7. *Little Cottonwood Water Co. v. Kimball*, 76 Utah 243 (1930).
8. *Albert v. Hsu*, 602 So.2d 895 (1992).
9. See *Vermont Rules of Criminal Procedure*.
10. Wyo. R. Evid. 901.
11. See N. C. R. Evid. 104(b).
12. See Fed. R. Evid. Rule 1002.
13. See, for example, Or. Rev. Stat. Sec. 40.550 Rule 1001.
14. *Schozer v. William Penn Life Insurance Company of New York*, 84 N.Y.2d 639 (1994).
15. Fed. R. Evid. 1003.
16. Or. Rev. Stat. Sec. 40.565 Rule 1004.
17. See, for example, Vt. R. Evid. 1006.
18. Federal Judicial Center, *Benchbook for U.S. District Court Judges* (March, 2000, Rev.).

CHALLENGES TO ADMISSIBILITY OF EVIDENCE

"When you have no basis for argument, abuse the plaintiff."

—*Cicero*

"The point appears here in its virgin state, wearing all its maiden blushes, and is therefore out of place."

—*Bleckley, Judge, Cleveland v. Chambliss, 64 Ga. 352 (1879)*

LEARNING OUTCOMES

In this chapter, you will learn about the following legal concepts:

- Challenges to Admissibility of Evidence
- Pretrial Challenges
- Challenges During Trial
- Challenges After Trial
- Plain Error

INTRODUCTION

All information that tends to prove or disprove something in issue is evidence. However, not all evidence is allowed at trial. Evidence that would be allowed at trial is called **admissible.** If not allowed or suppressed from trial, the evidence is referred to as **inadmissible.** For example, Joan, if called as a witness, would testify to the following: "Marge told me that she saw Sam steal the ring." Although this testimony may be true and relevant to the issue of whether Sam stole the ring, it could be objected to as unreliable **hearsay** and ruled inadmissible. This chapter will examine how evidence is challenged and excluded from use at trial.

CHALLENGES TO ADMISSIBILITY OF EVIDENCE

Evidence is central to the proving or disproving of a case. Trying to keep evidence from being admitted, or limiting how it is admitted, can be done by raising evidentiary challenges. Parties can raise these challenges either before trial in the form of a **pretrial motion,** during trial in the form of an **objection** or **motion to strike,** or after trial in the form of an **appeal.** There are two primary purposes behind evidentiary challenges: to keep the jury from hearing certain evidence, and to preserve any error committed on the record for appeal.

PRETRIAL CHALLENGES

Objections over evidence should be presented before trial, whenever possible. These pretrial objections may come in the form of a **motion to exclude** or **suppress** certain evidence, or a **motion in limine,** which asks the court to rule on an evidentiary issue before it goes before the jury. A motion in limine may also be made during trial.

Motion to Suppress

A motion to suppress evidence is used in pretrial hearings for criminal actions. It is usually based on Fourth Amendment protections against unreasonable search and seizure, Fifth Amendment limitations on self-incrimination, and Fifth and Fourteenth Amendment safeguards for **due process.** A motion to suppress is asking the judge to exclude certain evidence that was obtained improperly, even though that evidence may be relevant and highly incriminating.

Motion to Exclude

A motion to exclude functions much the same as one to suppress, except that it usually is based on the exclusionary rules of evidence, such as privilege, hearsay, relevance, prior bad acts, and evidence that might be prejudicial to the factfinder. A motion to exclude can be used in both civil and criminal actions.

Motion in Limine

A motion in limine is similar to a motion to exclude. It is one of the most common forms of motions to exclude evidence. It can be filed either before trial or during trial, and allows a trial court to rule on the admissibility of evidence before the evidence is offered. It is often used during trial in an effort to avoid raising excessive objections before the jury. The effective use

---

Admissible
Evidence that would be allowed at trial.

Inadmissible
Evidence that would not be allowed at trial.

Hearsay
A statement made out-of-court and offered in court as evidence. Hearsay is generally secondhand information ("I was told . . . ") and considered more unreliable than a witness testifying in court to firsthand knowledge.

Pretrial Motion
An official request made of the judge prior to a trial, with an opportunity for the opposing party to challenge the request. A pretrial motion usually asks the court to order the admission or exclusion of certain evidence.

Objection
A challenge to the admissibility of evidence, usually done as, or just before, evidence is offered.

Motion to Strike
An objection to a statement made by a witness with a request to the judge to have the statement stricken from the trial record.

Appeal
A formal request made of a higher court to review the findings of a lower court for error.

Motion to Exclude
A request made by a party to a legal action asking the judge to prevent certain evidence from being admitted at trial because it violates a law or rule of evidence.

of a motion in limine can help move a trial along while ensuring that fair decisions are made about what evidence will be admitted. However, some judges are reluctant to rule on evidence before seeing how it will be offered in the context of the trial. When a judge rules on a motion in limine, the ruling serves to also preserve the issue for appeal, without the need for an additional objection at trial.

CRITICAL THINKING QUESTIONS 4.1

1. Why would we encourage the use of pretrial motions to challenge evidence before trial?

2. What are some of the strengths and weaknesses of challenging evidence before trial?

3. Why do you think the motion in limine is so important in challenging evidence?

CHALLENGES DURING TRIAL

As previously mentioned, there are three methods for challenging evidence during trial. If filed during a trial, a *motion in limine* is usually filed in the early stages. *Objections* to evidence or to questions asked of witnesses are raised throughout the trial. *Motions to strike* are typically raised when a party needs to challenge and have the jury disregard an objectionable answer given by a witness.

Motion in Limine

As previously discussed, a motion in limine is a formal request made by a party to a legal action asking the judge to prevent certain evidence from being admitted at trial. This motion may be made before or during trial. If it is made during trial, the arguments on the motion are heard without the jury present.

Often during a trial, a motion in limine cannot be used. A party may not want to tip the opponent to potential evidence being offered. Usually, an evidentiary challenge is over the form of the question asked by the opposing side in examining a witness. Admissibility of evidence is then challenged in the form of an *objection* before the witness has answered the question or a *motion to strike* after the witness has answered the question.

Objections

An *objection* is a challenge made to the admissibility of evidence during the trial. An objection is raised when evidence is offered that the objecting party believes should be excluded under some legal grounds. The objection is the method for keeping the evidence out. Objections can be to substance or form. An objection may also be raised for an answer given by a witness that is *non-responsive*.

Objections to Substance

An **objection to substance** is a challenge of the substantive evidence being offered or to the answer being called for in a question to a witness. For example, a party that objects to a document being offered without a proper foundation is challenging the evidence itself. When a witness is

Motion to Suppress
Similar to *motion to exclude*, with its primary use in criminal actions and generally based on constitutional grounds.

Motion in Limine
Similar to *motion to exclude*, except that it may be raised either before or during trial.

Due Process
Fundamental principle in a criminal action holding that a person has a right to reasonable notice of a charge against him, and an opportunity to be heard in his defense, which includes the right to call witnesses on his behalf and to confront those witnesses against him.

Objection to Substance
When an opposing party challenges the substantive evidence being offered or the answer being called for in a question to a witness.

being questioned on the stand, an objection to substance, or substantive objection, is challenging the answer called for by the question. These types of objections are grounded on a specific rule of evidence or other exclusionary law. An example of this is hearsay (see Exhibit 4.1). Hearsay is an out-of-court statement, other than one made by the declarant, offered to prove the truth of the matter being asserted. Hearsay is specifically excluded by the evidence rules.[1] An objection raised to a question that calls for a hearsay answer is an objection to substance:

Q: What did your neighbor tell you that she heard that day?
D: Objection, calls for hearsay.
Ct: Sustained.

Here, the objection has resulted in the testimony being excluded.

EXHIBIT 4.1   Hearsay Rule

New Jersey Rules of Evidence
Rule 802. Hearsay is not admissible except as provided by these rules or by other law.

Beyond the Scope
Questioning of a witness that goes beyond what was covered in the previous line of questions.

Another example of an objection to substance is when a question asked of a witness during cross-examination goes beyond what was covered during direct examination (see Exhibit 4.2). This is called a **beyond the scope** objection. Evidence rules limit cross-examination to the subject matter of the direct examination and matters affecting the credibility of the witness.[2] A question that attempts to go beyond this may raise an objection. For example, on direct examination, a witness is asked about and testifies to events that took place on a particular date. During cross-examination, the witness is asked about a different date not brought up during the direct exam. This would be the basis for a *beyond the scope* objection. The purpose behind this objection is to prevent the introduction of new evidence under the pretense of cross-examination. The cross-examiner will have an opportunity to offer new evidence when she presents her case.

EXHIBIT 4.2   Scope of Cross-Examination

Oregon Revised Statutes
Sec. 40.370 Rule 611 (2).
    Cross-examination should be limited to the subject matter of the direct examination and matters affecting the credibility of the witness. The court may, in the exercise of discretion, permit inquiry into additional matters as if on direct examination.

Texas Rules of Evidence
Rule 611 (b). Scope of Cross-Examination.
    A witness may be cross-examined on any matter relevant to any issue in the case, including credibility.

Grounds for Objections to Substance

In addition to hearsay and beyond the scope, other grounds for substantive objections include relevance, privileges, insufficient foundation, best evidence, character evidence, impermissible opinion, privileged communication, and evidence or questioning about a sexual assault victim's prior sexual behavior. These terms and concepts will be defined and are the subject of discussion in later chapters. For now, however, it is important to note that any violation of a rule of evidence or other law could be grounds for objection. An objection to the *substance* of a question or answer can lead to this evidence not being allowed (see Exhibit 4.3).

EXHIBIT 4.3   Grounds for Objections to Substance

An *objection to substance* may be based on any exclusionary rule of evidence or other law. In addition to hearsay and beyond the scope discussed previously, here are some other of the more common examples of these objections:

Best or Original Evidence Rule

Whenever a document, recording, or photograph is being offered into evidence, the original is generally required. Failure to produce an original may result in an objection under the *original or best evidence rule*.[3]

   Example: "Objection, your Honor. This violates the *original evidence* requirement of Rule 1002. Counsel is attempting to offer a copy of a newspaper that is intended to prove authorship of a letter to the editor."

Incompetent

This objection is broadly based on rules that exclude evidence that is not from a reliable source. One such evidentiary rule requires a witness to have *personal knowledge* about a matter the witness is testifying about. If a witness does not have personal knowledge of the matter, the witness may not testify.[4] The *incompetent* objection may also be raised if a witness has a problem recalling or communicating an event,[5] or does not understand or accept the duty to testify truthfully.[6] Evidence that is illegally obtained or lacks a proper foundation may also be incompetent.

   Example: "Objection. This witness is incompetent under Rule 602 to testify concerning this matter. She does not have personal knowledge."

Irrelevant

Evidence must be relevant. Relevant evidence is evidence having any tendency in reason to prove any material fact.[7] Evidence must be relevant or it is excluded under evidence rules.

   Example: "Objection, your Honor. Irrelevant under Rule 402. What happened to plaintiff's car 2 weeks after the accident has no relevance to this matter. It doesn't prove or disprove anything at issue here."

   Relevance objections may also be raised over the improper offering of character evidence,[8] prior bad acts,[9] reputation,[10] or habit evidence.[11]

Lacks Foundation

Also used as an *incompetent* objection, this objection is based on evidentiary rules requiring proper identification and authentication of evidence before it can be admitted. For example, before a witness can testify to what he saw or heard, a foundation must be laid to show that the witness was in a position to see or hear the event that he is testifying to. Physical evidence must have a proper foundation established before it can be admitted.

   Example: "Objection, your Honor. Lacks foundation. Counsel has not shown that this witness took these photographs or that they accurately represent this scene."

Opinion

A lay witness may only testify to what he or she perceived (i.e. what he saw, felt, heard, smelled, or tasted). Courts will, however, sometimes allow a lay witness to offer an opinion if limited to those reasonably based on the perceptions of the witness and helpful to a better understanding of the witness's testimony or determination of a fact at issue.[12] For example: "She acted angry." "He acted drunk." Generally, opinion evidence is excluded under the same evidence rules that govern the competence of witnesses.

   Example: "I object, your Honor. This question calls for an inadmissible opinion on the part of the witness under Rule 701. The witness is not qualified to give an opinion as to the cause of this accident."

(Continued)

EXHIBIT 4.3   Grounds for Objections to Substance *Continued*

Privileged Communication

Some confidential communications are protected by law and cannot be a part of witness testimony.[13] Attorney–client, husband–wife, doctor–patient, and clergy–penitent are examples.

   Example: "Objection. This question calls for witness to disclose privileged communication between physician and patient in violation of Rule 503. I claim this privilege on behalf of the defendant."

Prejudicial

An important evidentiary rule excludes evidence on the grounds of prejudice, confusion, or waste of time.[14] The test for this is when the evidence's probative value is substantially outweighed by the danger of unfair prejudice, confusion of issues, or misleading of jury. If this occurs, an objection may be raised and the evidence, even when relevant, is excluded.

   Example: "Objection, your Honor. Rule 403. There has been no evidence offered about defendant's drinking and it is not relevant to this matter. Asking this witness about it would substantially prejudice the jury."

Objections to Form

Objection to Form
When an opposing party challenges the form of a question asked of a witness.

An **objection to form** is challenging the form of the question—the manner in which a question is worded or asked. If a question is worded in a way to confuse, harass, or unduly embarrass a witness, it may be objected to. Similarly, a question that leads a witness to a particular answer, or requires the witness to speculate or make assumptions, will trigger an objection. For example, a question may be asked of a witness that is worded in a way to suggest the answer to the witness. This would be a leading question.

Q: Ms. Jones, didn't the defendant stop at that red light?
D: Objection, leading the witness.
Ct: Sustained.

Because these objections challenge how a question is worded, rewording or rephrasing the question may overcome the challenge:

Q: Ms. Jones, didn't the defendant stop at that red light?
D: Objection, leading the witness.
Ct: Sustained.
Q: I'll rephrase, your Honor. Ms. Jones, describe what the defendant did at that red light.
A: She stopped.

The objection here was overcome by a simple rephrasing of the question, which allowed the witness an opportunity to answer the question in a more direct way for the jury.

   An objection is generally made by stating, "Objection, your Honor . . . " and stating the grounds for the objection. "Objection, your Honor. Calls for a conclusion."

Grounds for Objections to Form

Although objections to the form of a question may not rely on any specific exclusionary law, they are generally grounded in two evidentiary rules. One rule, commonly codified as Rule 611(a), requires a trial court to govern the questioning of witnesses and the presenting of evidence so that witnesses are not harassed or unduly embarrassed, and time is not wasted (see Exhibit 4.4).[15]

Another rule, Rule 403, excludes evidence that may confuse, prejudice, or mislead the jury (see Exhibit 4.5). This rule also excludes evidence that causes undue delay or needless presentation of cumulative evidence.[16]

EXHIBIT 4.4   Court Controls Questioning of Witnesses

Kentucky Rules of Evidence
Rule 611(a). Control by court. The court shall exercise reasonable control over the mode and order of interrogating witnesses and presenting evidence so as to:
   (1) Make the interrogation and presentation effective for the ascertainment of the truth;
   (2) Avoid needless consumption of time; and
   (3) Protect witnesses from harassment or undue embarrassment.

EXHIBIT 4.5   Exclusion of Prejudicial or Misleading Evidence

Wyoming Rules of Evidence
Rule 403. Exclusion of relevant evidence on grounds of prejudice, confusion, or waste of time. Although relevant, evidence may be excluded if its probative value is substantially outweighed by the danger of unfair prejudice, confusion of the issues, or misleading the jury, or by considerations of undue delay, waste of time, or needless presentation of cumulative evidence.

Leading Questions

Leading questions are ones which suggest the answer to the witness (see Exhibit 4.6). Many believe that any question that has an apostrophe in it—couldn't, wouldn't, didn't—should be objected to or at least considered suspect (see Exhibit 4.7). Generally, leading questions are not allowed on direct examination, but are on cross-examination; for example, if you were to ask a witness on direct examination, "On that Saturday night, you saw the defendant running from that house, didn't you?" This would tend to suggest to the witness an answer and would be grounds for objection (see Exhibit 4.8).

Leading Questions
Questions that contain or suggest the answer to a witness.

Sometimes leading questions are permitted in order to deal with preliminary matters which are not in issue. An example of a leading question that would be allowed is, "You are a detective with the police department, are you not?"

EXHIBIT 4.6   Leading Questions

North Carolina Rules of Evidence
Rule 611(c). Leading questions. Leading questions should not be used on the direct examination of a witness except as may be necessary to develop his testimony. Ordinarily leading questions should be permitted on cross-examination. When a party calls a hostile witness, an adverse party, or a witness identified with an adverse party, interrogation may be by leading questions.

EXHIBIT 4.7   Example of Leading Question

Plaintiff Q:	Was he holding his head when he got out of the car?
Defense:	Objection, your Honor. Leading the witness.
Court:	Sustained.

EXHIBIT 4.8   Grounds for Form Objections

Objections to form challenge the manner or wording of a question asked of a witness. These objections may not be based on any specific rule of evidence, but are grounded in the general rules discussed protecting against prejudice, confusion, or waste of time. An objection to form may be raised by simply stating the grounds. "Objection, your Honor. Argumentative." Some of the objections to form include:

Argumentative

Argumentative questions are designed to persuade the jury as to some fact rather than to gain new information. One form of an argumentative question is when the witness is asked only to agree to conclusions drawn by the question of counsel.

Examples: "You're not telling the truth, are you?"

"How can you remember that number when you can't even remember your own phone number?"

Asked and Answered

This question is designed to emphasize to the jury an answer that has already been given.

Example: "Tell us again how many times the defendant struck the victim."

Assumes Facts Not in Evidence

This question assumes facts to be true which have not yet been proven in court.

Examples: "Was this report similar to the others made by the victim?"

"When did you stop beating your wife?"

Note, however, that there may be exceptions to this when dealing with expert witnesses.

Calls for Conclusion

Witnesses should only testify to facts and matters within their personal knowledge. Conclusions are to be left to the province of the jury. When a witness is asked why something happened or is asked to draw a conclusion from a set of facts, it raises the objection *calls for a conclusion*.

Example: "Why did he stop when he saw her?"

Compound Question

A compound question is one that contains two or more questions within it.

Example: "Did you, or did anyone else, return his call that day?"

Confusing

A question that is worded in an unclear manner may be objected to as *confusing*.

Example: "Did you go to work today or eat your lunch?"

Conjecture or Speculation

A lay witness is only allowed to testify on matters based on his or her own perception. He or she may not speculate or give opinions on facts outside this area unless qualified as experts.

Example: "Is it possible that there were other contracts?"

Cumulative

This objection asks the judge to prevent wasting the jury's time with a needless presentation of cumulative evidence.

Example: In a civil defamation action, calling numerous witnesses who will all testify that they heard the defendant call the plaintiff a thief.

Narrative

Narrative answers can prevent the opposing side from having a reasonable opportunity to make a timely objection. If a witness were asked to recount everything that happened on a particular day, it would allow for a series of rambling and irrelevant answers. For this reason, most questioning is in the form of specific questions that usually call for yes or no answers, or a brief, concise answer that is limited to one specific area.

Example: "Tell the jury everything you did that afternoon."

Speculative

A question that asks a witness to guess or speculate on an answer, this may be permitted for reasonable areas of speculation based on the witness's own perception and common experience, like someone's age or whether a person acted angry. However, a question would be speculative if it called for any opinion or conjecture by the witness that was outside of the witness's perception or asked the witness for conjecture or to guess about something.

Example: "Is it possible that she entered this room by mistake?"

Practice Tip 4.1

Avoiding Objections

You can avoid some challenges by preparing questions to ask a witness that do not trigger an objection. For example, instead of asking "What did you tell him?" ask "What did you say?"

Non-Responsive Answer

Sometimes, a witness will volunteer an answer that goes beyond the scope of the question asked or was not called for in the question. When this happens, the questioner may object to her own witness's answer and request that the answer be stricken as non-responsive. If it violates any of the previously noted objections, those grounds may also be given. For example, a witness is asked if she saw anyone coming out of the store as she entered it. The witness answers, "Yes, I saw the defendant and he was carrying a knife and a black bag." This answer goes beyond the scope of the question asked and would be objected to as non-responsive.

Rulings on Admissibility

As part of the adversary process, it is the responsibility of the party challenging the evidence to raise any objection. The trial judge, as an impartial referee, rules on an objection once it has been raised and is responsible for determining the admissibility of any evidence. The judge is not supposed to initiate any objection. If no objection is raised and the evidence is not challenged, it may be admitted.

CRITICAL THINKING QUESTIONS 4.2

1. Why do we allow so many grounds for objecting to evidence?
2. What are some reasons for allowing these objections?
3. Why do we allow objections that can be met by simply rephrasing the question?
4. Why do we use short questions and answers as our format for questioning witnesses? Why don't we just allow the witness to tell his or her story without interruption?
5. What other objections can you think of that would be relevant to challenging the admissibility of evidence?

Motion to Strike

A *motion to strike* is a form of objection to evidence *after* it has already been made and where there was no reasonable opportunity to object to it before it was admitted. Often, it is a case of a proper question being asked, but the witness giving an improper answer. The following examples illustrate this:

Q: After you heard the car horn, what happened next?
A: Joe told me that he saw the red car run into the tree.
D: Move to strike witness's answer, your Honor. Hearsay.

Since this may constitute impermissible hearsay, an objection would be made. However, because the witness already said it, the objection would be in the form of a motion to have the response stricken from the record.

A motion to strike is asking that the witness's answer be stricken from the trial record. It really is not removed from the official trial record. The purpose of the motion is to have the jury instructed by the judge to disregard the answer, and so that the answer could not be used later as evidence. This is accomplished by an accompanying request to the judge. An example of this might be:

Q: Did you see the defendant leave the theater?
A: Yes, he ran out holding a knife. I think he had just used it on Mr. Smith.
D: Move to strike that answer, your Honor. Impermissible speculation. I request that the jury be instructed to disregard the answer made by the witness.
Court: Jury is instructed to disregard the answer given by the witness.

The problem with this is that the jury has already heard the answer. Will they really disregard it? If the witness's answer was prejudicial to a party's case, an additional motion may be introduced by that party asking for a **mistrial.** This is usually based on the grounds that the harm done by the witness's answer was substantially prejudicial to the party and cannot be undone without a new trial. The trial court will rarely grant a motion for a mistrial.

Objections and Motions to Strike are either SUSTAINED or OVERRULED

If an objection is **sustained** by the trial judge, the evidence objected to is excluded, and a witness is not allowed to answer the question objected to. If the objection is **overruled,** the evidence is allowed to be admitted, and the witness is allowed to answer the question asked. Failure to object or motion to strike testimony already given is considered a waiver of future grounds for appeal.

Waiver

The motion to strike must be made immediately after the objected to testimony is offered or it constitutes a **waiver** for future grounds of appeal. A waiver prevents the party from bringing the issue back up on appeal.

Practice Tip 4.2

Motion to Strike

Here is a format to use in a motion to strike that covers the jury instruction: "Your Honor, I move that the answer given by this witness be stricken as__[state grounds], and that the jury be instructed to disregard the answer."

Timely and Specific

An objection or motion to strike must be **timely and specific** (see Exhibit 4.9). It must be timely made in order to **make the record** and establish a basis for a later appeal, if overruled. Timely requires that it be made when the challenged evidence is being offered. It must be specific as to the form and grounds for objection.

Mistrial
A mistrial can be found by the trial judge when a prejudicial error occurs during trial causing harm that the judge does not believe can be undone without a new trial.

Sustained
To decide for or affirm. When a judge sustains an objection, the evidence objected to is excluded.

Overruled
To decide against or disallow. When a judge overrules an objection, the evidence objected to is allowed.

Waiver
Relinquish or forego a right or privilege.

Timely and Specific
An objection must be made prior to or when the challenged evidence is being offered. It must be specific as to the form and grounds for the objection.

Make the Record
Making the record means entering something in the transcript or official documents compiled in a trial so that the appellate court will be able to see it in case of an appeal. The "record" consists of all of these documents.

Purposes Served by Timely Objections

A timely objection serves several purposes. At the trial level, it serves to exclude evidence if the judge sustains it. It also is made part of the permanent trial "record" to provide the basis for appeal, if overruled by the judge. Because the trial judge is seen as an "umpire" between the two adversarial parties, the judge has no obligation to raise objections.

EXHIBIT 4.9   Rulings on Evidence—Timely and Specific

Tennessee Rules of Evidence
Rule 103(a). Effect of Erroneous Ruling.
  Error may not be predicated upon a ruling which admits or excludes evidence unless a substantial right of the party is affected, and
  (1) Objection. In case the ruling is one admitting evidence, a timely objection or motion to strike appears of record, stating the specific ground of objection if the specific ground was not apparent from the context.

EVIDENTIARY CHECKLIST 4.1

Objections at Trial

Objections to Evidence
- ☐ Evidence is offered or question is asked of witness.
- ☐ Opposing party objects to evidence or question, stating grounds for objection.
- ☐ Judge either sustains or overrules objection.
- ☐ If objection sustained, party offering evidence may make offer of proof if evidence is being excluded or rephrase question if objection is to the form of the question.
- ☐ If objection overruled, evidence may be admitted.

What Constitutes "Timely" When a Witness Answer Is Unexpected?

In the following case, the witness gives an unexpected answer and several minutes elapse before the defense offers an objection.

Group 2 Case #4

CASE

Government of the Virgin Islands v. Archibald
987 F.2d 180 (3d Cir. 1993).
[Archibald was convicted of three counts of rape on a 14-year-old girl, Latoya Chinnery. Latoya had admitted to her mother, Ursula Williams, that she had engaged in sexual intercourse with Archibald on three separate occasions. According to Latoya, Archibald would attract her attention at night by throwing rocks at her screen or by knocking on the window. She would let Archibald in through a screen door and have intercourse with him. Archibald would then leave the house. Latoya admitted that she liked Archibald and knew that he was her sister Tasha's boyfriend. At trial, the mother testified that she knew Archibald because he was a neighbor and because he had fathered the child of her daughter Tasha. She further testified

that, at the time of trial, Tasha was 15 years of age and the child was 6 months old. Williams' testimony thus revealed that Archibald had engaged in sexual intercourse with Tasha when she was 13 or 14 years old. Under Virgin Islands law, such intercourse constitutes third degree rape. Archibald asserts that evidence of his prior criminal act should have been excluded. . . . Archibald argues that the evidence of his sexual relations with Tasha was not probative of any material issue in the case other than to show that he had a propensity to engage in intercourse with underage females. The government . . . suggests that Archibald waived his right to challenge admission of the evidence by failing to make a timely objection. . . .]

COWEN, Circuit Judge.

. . . .

A.

The government suggests that Archibald failed to preserve his . . . objection by not objecting immediately after Williams testified that Archibald fathered Tasha's child. At trial, Williams testified as follows:

Q: How do you happen to know Alan Archibald?
A: He is a neighbor of mine and he has a child with my daughter Tasha Chinnery.
Q: How old is the child?
A: The baby?
Q: Yes.
A: He is 6 months.
Q: How old is Tasha?
A: 15.

Immediately following this response, the government requested a sidebar conference. Acknowledging that it had just elicited evidence of a prior crime, the government asked the court to instruct the jury that the evidence was offered only to show how the witness knew Archibald. During the ensuing colloquy, counsel for Archibald objected to the admission of the testimony. . . . The district court disregarded the objection . . . and allowed the government to continue examining Williams.

Fed. R. Evid. 103(a)(1) requires a party to make a "timely objection." The requirement of a timely objection promotes judicial economy by enhancing the trial court's ability to remedy the asserted error. If a party fails to object in a timely fashion, the objection is waived and we will review the admission of evidence only for plain error.

The appropriate time to raise an objection is as soon as the party knows or reasonably should know of the grounds for objection, unless postponement is desirable for a special reason and not unfair to the opposition. . . . Occasionally, however, a question that is unobjectionable elicits an objectionable reply, or previously admitted testimony becomes objectionable only in the light of subsequent testimony. In such circumstances, the grounds for objection are not known until after the objectionable testimony is given, and an "after-objection" may be interposed when the grounds become apparent. In the context of the present case, counsel for Archibald reasonably could not have anticipated that Williams would offer evidence of a prior crime in response to the government's question, "How do you happen to know Alan Archibald?" The government implicitly concedes as much by alleging that Williams' testimony was offered "inadvertently." Accordingly, the first time that the grounds for objection became apparent was after Williams responded to the question. At this point, the damage to Archibald already had been done, and defense counsel's rather brief postponement of his objection neither prejudiced the government nor in any way impaired the court's ability to remedy the asserted error. Because the delay was minimal and caused no demonstrable prejudice, Archibald's objection was timely.

♦

LEGAL ANALYSIS AND WRITING 4.1

The following questions are based on the *How to Brief a Legal Case* format shown in the Appendix. Use this format to answer the following questions:

1. Summarize the facts in the previous case.
2. What is the legal issue?
3. What did the appellate court decide?
4. Why did the court decide this way?
5. Do you agree with the court's reasoning? Explain why or why not.

LEGAL RESEARCH USING THE INTERNET SKILLS 4.1

Try to find this case or another one that refers to it online! Check out one of the legal research web sites below, go to the federal circuit for this court decision, and use their "Search" feature to find this case or another case that refers to it. In the "Search" field, enter the cite or case name. If you have access to Westlaw or Lexis, try to find this case using one of these legal search sites.

1. U.S. Courts Site with Links to All Circuit Courts of Appeal (http://www.uscourts.gov/links.html)
2. National Center for State Courts—State and Federal Court Web Sites (http://www.ncsconline.org/ D_kis/info_court_web_sites.html)
3. FindLaw (http://guide.lp.findlaw.com/casecode/)

Failure to Object

Where no objection is offered, evidence of any type may be received. Failure to object or a motion to strike testimony already given is also considered a waiver of future grounds for appeal.

Speak Now or Forever Hold Your Objection . . .

In the following case, the defense objects to the government introducing evidence using a "drug courier profile." Unfortunately, the objection at trial is based on different grounds than used in the subsequent appeal. Will the appellate court still accept it? If not, will they still find there was sufficient error to overturn the trial court's decision?

group 3-case 4

CASE

United States v. Gomez-Norena

908 F.2d 497 (9th Cir. 1990).

[Jaime Gomez was convicted of possession of cocaine with intent to distribute. At the Los Angeles airport, Customs Inspector Espinoza, using an official "drug courier profile," questioned a disembarking passenger, Jaime Gomez. He discovered that Gomez had "begun his trip from the reputed drug capital, Medellin, Colombia. Second, Gomez had paid for his ticket with cash. Third, Gomez had an Australian visa and would be in the United States only for the three hours before his flight to Sydney. Fourth, the 23-year-old Gomez was a newcomer to international travel. Fifth, Gomez had checked only one piece of baggage." Inspector Espinoza told other customs inspectors to "watch out for Mr. Gomez" because he fit the drug courier profile. Gomez was subsequently searched by the other customs inspectors and two plastic bags containing cocaine were found hidden in the side of Gomez's suitcase. A jury convicted Gomez for pos-

sessing cocaine with intent to distribute. . . . Gomez argues on appeal that the district court improperly admitted testimony regarding the drug courier profile. . . .]

Hall, Circuit Judge.

. . . .

II

Gomez first challenges the admissibility of Inspector Espinoza's testimony concerning his statements to the other customs inspectors that Gomez fit the drug courier profile. Because the objections raised at trial are relevant to our standard of review, we reproduce the testimony in full:

Prosecutor:	What did you tell Inspector Zito or Inspector Little or any of the others about. . . .
Defense:	Objection. Calling for hearsay.
Prosecutor:	Your Honor.
The Court:	Ladies and gentlemen. I permit this, which the law says I can, but only on the question of what was in

the inspectors'—those ones he told whatever he told to—mind at the time they carried on their activities. Now it is hearsay, the defendant wasn't there, but we do permit hearsay to be passed from one law enforcement officer to another, and this is appropriate, so the objection is overruled. With that instruction that you can consider only as to what the inspectors had in their mind when, and if, anything further happened in the presence of the defendant. With that instruction, objection overruled.

Prosecutor: Inspector Espinoza, what did you say to the other inspectors about the defendant?

Espinoza: I instructed the inspectors to watch out for Mr. Gomez.

Prosecutor: Did you give them any particulars?

Espinoza: Yes, I did. I told them that in the past that we've intercepted cocaine couriers with the same. . . .

Defense: Objection, your Honor. Move to strike. Rule 404(b) objection.

The Court: Same ruling. Overruled. Let's have a continuing objection. Continue. Overruled.

Prosecutor: Thank you, your Honor. I would appreciate it.

The Court: My instruction to the Jury, which I gave you, is to only determine what the inspectors who may have had further contact with the defendant, and we'll see about that. Otherwise, I'll strike it. But only with respect to what they had in their mind when they had further contact with the defendant. I'm talking about the people Espinoza talked to. All right? Got it? With that instruction, objection overruled.

Prosecutor: What did you tell them, Inspector?

Espinoza: I told them to look out after Mr. Gomez, because in the past we've had the same type of narcotics couriers with the same M.O. that Mr. Gomez had: Cash ticket, in transit, in transit without a [United States] visa, to Australia,

with one or more pieces of checked luggage.

Prosecutor: You said "M.O."; what did you mean by that?

Espinoza: The same—his profile, same cash ticket.

The Court: M.O. Modus Operandi?

Espinoza: Yes.

The Court: That's what he asked you.

Prosecutor: What did you mean when you said with the same M.O.?

Espinoza: Well, in the past we've had the same type of narcotics carriers coming from Colombia.

Prosecutor: Going in transit to Australia?

Espinoza: Yeah.

A

Gomez's central claim on appeal is that Espinoza's testimony regarding the drug courier profile was unfairly prejudicial and thus inadmissible under Federal Rule of Evidence 403. However, he has not properly preserved that claim for review. As the transcript indicates, Gomez objected on two grounds: (1) inadmissible hearsay, see Fed. R. Evid. 802, and (2) improper character evidence, see Fed. R. Evid. 404(b). A party challenging the admission of evidence must timely object and state the specific grounds for his objection. Fed. R. Evid. 103(a)(1). This rule serves to ensure that "the nature of the error [is] called to the attention of the judge, so as to alert him to the proper course of action and enable opposing counsel to take corrective measures." Advisory Committee's Note to Rule 103(a), 56 F.R.D. 183 (1972).

Thus, a party fails to preserve an evidentiary issue for appeal not only by failing to make a specific objection, but also by making the wrong specific objection. An objection overruled, therefore, naming a ground which is untenable, cannot be availed of because there was another and tenable ground which might have been named but was not. Because Gomez failed to make a Rule 403 objection below, we review the admission of the drug courier profile testimony for plain error. A plain error is a highly prejudicial error affecting substantial rights.

B

Courts are keenly aware of the dangers of admitting testimony concerning the drug courier profile. For example, the Eighth Circuit has held that such testimony may never be introduced as substantive evidence of guilt. . . . However, this case does not implicate those concerns. Here the government introduced Inspector Espinoza's testimony not to prove that Gomez was guilty, but to provide the jury with a full and accurate portrayal of the events as they unfolded on that Friday afternoon. Indeed, the district judge twice cautioned the jury that it could consider Espinoza's testimony only as background material. We agree with the Eleventh Circuit that admitting the use of drug courier profile testimony for this limited purpose greatly reduces the potential for unfair prejudice and thus cannot amount to plain error.

IV

In sum, we hold that the district court did not commit plain error by admitting the drug courier profile testimony for the limited purpose of providing the jury with background information.

For these reasons, the judgment of the district court is AFFIRMED.

LEGAL ANALYSIS AND WRITING 4.2

The following questions are based on the *How to Brief a Legal Case* format shown in the Appendix. Use this format to answer the following questions:

1. Summarize the facts in the previous case.
2. What is the legal issue?
3. What did the appellate court decide?
4. Why did the court decide this way?
5. Do you agree with the court's reasoning? Explain why or why not.

LEGAL RESEARCH USING THE INTERNET SKILLS 4.2

Try to find this case or another one that refers to it online! Check out one of the legal research web sites below, go to the federal circuit for this court decision, and use their "Search" feature to find this case or another case that refers to it. In the "Search" field, enter the cite or case name. If you have access to Westlaw or Lexis, try to find this case using one of these legal search sites.

1. U.S. Courts Site with Links to All Circuit Courts of Appeal (http://www.uscourts.gov/links.html)
2. National Center for State Courts—State and Federal Court Web Sites (http://www.ncsconline.org/D_kis/info_courts_web_sites.html)
3. FindLaw (http://guide.lp.findlaw.com/casecode/)

Offer of Proof

Parties seeking to admit evidence that has been objected to and excluded by the court will usually make an **offer of proof.** An offer of proof is when the party having the evidence excluded offers an explanation to the trial judge as to why the evidence is important and admissible (see Exhibit 4.10). This must be done out of the hearing of the jury.[17] An offer of proof may be presented by a statement explaining to the trial judge what the answer of the witness would have been and what this testimony or evidence would tend to prove. For example, "Your Honor, if the witness were

Offer of Proof
A party having evidence excluded offers an explanation to the trial judge as to why the evidence is important and admissible.

permitted to answer the question, she would have testified that. . . . We contend that this would show. . . ." An offer of proof may also be presented through the continued examination of a witness. In this method, the court allows a party to ask the questions objected to in order to establish, for the offer of proof, what answer the witness would have given. Again, this is done outside of the hearing of the jury.

There are two purposes behind the offer of proof requirement. The first purpose is to allow the trial judge to make an informed evidentiary ruling. An offer of proof explains to the trial judge the reasoning behind asking a particular question of a witness or attempting to admit a particular item of evidence. The second purpose is to "create a clear record that an appellate court can review to determine whether there was reversible error in excluding the testimony."[18] Generally, an offer of proof is needed in order to preserve an objection for the record. On appeal, the offer of proof in the record provides the appellate court with more detail to help determine whether the trial court committed reversible error by excluding the evidence.

Because the offer of proof is made part of the official record of the trial, it is an important strategy tool. It makes a last effort to try and persuade the trial judge of the relevance of the evidence. It also notes why this evidence is admissible in case the trial judge excludes it and the case goes up on appeal.

EXHIBIT 4.10   Rulings on Evidence—Offer of Proof

Pennsylvania Rules of Evidence
Rule 103. Rulings on Evidence.
   (a) Effect of Erroneous Ruling. Error may not be predicated upon a ruling which admits or excludes evidence unless:
   Offer of Proof. In case the ruling is one excluding evidence, the substance of the evidence was made known to the court by offer or by motion in limine or was apparent from the context within which the evidence was offered.

Practice Tip 4.3

Format for Offer of Proof
Here's a format to use in an offer of proof:
"Your Honor, if the witness were permitted to answer the question, she would have testified that _____ [summarize what witness would have testified to]. We contend that this would show _____ [summarize what the testimony of the witness would have tended to prove that was material to the case]."

Offer of Proof Contemplates Contemporaneity

In the following case, the court looks at when an offer of proof is needed, and finds that the rule "contemplates some contemporaneity between the trial judge's knowledge about the proposed evidence and the evidentiary ruling to allow a proper decision at the time the evidence is offered."

CASE

Polys v. Trans-Colorado Airlines, Inc.

941 F.2d 1404. (10th Cir. 1991).

Appeal from the United States District Court for the District of Colorado.

Anderson, Circuit Judge.

Plaintiffs, David L. Polys and Marcia Polys, appeal a judgment in favor of the defendant, Trans-Colorado Airlines, Inc., in the Polyses' personal injury suit against Trans-Colorado. We affirm.

On January 14, 1984, Trans-Colorado Flight 216, which originated in Albuquerque, New Mexico, landed at the Durango, Colorado airport, skidded to the left, and stopped abruptly upon impact with a snowbank. David Polys was one of four passengers aboard that plane. Approximately 2 years later, the Polyses filed a personal injury action against Trans-Colorado Airlines, Inc. David Polys claimed that the "aircraft landing incident caused a closed head injury to him which produced disabling psychological and psychiatric effects." Mrs. Polys joined the action claiming a loss of consortium. Trans-Colorado admitted negligence in the operation of the aircraft, but denied causation and damages. After a bench trial, the United States District Court for the District of Colorado held for the defendants, finding that the Polyses had "failed to prove that the conduct of the defendant's agents on January 14, 1984, caused any injury to David Polys."

. . . .

I.

The Polyses argue that the district court erred in excluding the deposition testimonies of two expert witnesses, Dr. Schultz and Dr. Daven. We disagree because the Polyses failed to preserve the issue for appeal by making an offer of proof and the court's ruling did not amount to plain error. Federal Rule of Evidence 103(a) states in pertinent part:

> Error may not be predicated upon a ruling which admits or excludes evidence unless a substantial right of the party is affected, and
>
> . . . .
>
> (2) Offer of proof. In case the ruling is one excluding evidence, the substance of the evidence was made known to the court by offer or was apparent from the context within which questions were asked.

The first purpose of the offer of proof requirement is to allow the trial judge to make an informed evidentiary ruling. The plain language of Federal Rule of Evidence 103(a)(2) requires that the judge be informed contemporaneously with the proponent's attempt to admit the evidence. This will be accomplished if the substance and purpose of the evidence are apparent to the judge from the context in which it is offered, or an offer of proof either precedes or immediately follows the ruling so that the trial judge can reconsider. To satisfy the rule, we have previously stated that "merely telling the court the content of . . . proposed testimony" is not an offer of proof. Rather . . . the proponent must explain what it expects to show and "the grounds for which the party believes the evidence to be admissible . . . so that the trial court is on notice of the purpose for which the evidence is offered while there is still time to remedy the situation."

The second purpose for the offer of proof is to create a clear record that an appellate court can review to "determine whether there was reversible error in excluding the testimony." *New Mexico Sav. & Loan Assoc. v. United States Fidelity and Guar. Co.,* 454 F.2d 328 (10th Cir. 1972). Once we find that a party, either in fact or substance, made an offer of proof of excluded evidence, then a trial judge's "decision to admit or exclude evidence 'will not be reversed by this court absent a clear abuse of discretion.'" *Big Horn Coal Co. v. Commonwealth Edison Co.,* 852 F.2d 1259 (10th Cir. 1988). This is especially true with respect to deposition testimony.

Under this standard of review, we strongly defer to the trial court. The review is generally setting specific, looking at whether the district court correctly weighed appropriate factors. Even if the trial judge abused his or her discretion in making a decision to exclude evidence, we will overlook the error as harmless unless a party's substantial right was affected. On the other hand, if the complaining party failed to meet the offer of proof standard, we can reverse only if there was plain error affecting a party's substantial rights. Fed. R. Evid. 103(d). Although the plain error doctrine applies to both criminal and civil cases, with respect to the latter, "the 'plain error' exception . . . has been limited to errors which seriously affect 'the fairness, integrity or public reputation of judicial proceedings.'" *McEwen v. City of Norman, Okla.,* 926 F.2d 1539 (10th Cir. 1991). The "miscarriage of justice" must be "patently plainly erroneous and prejudicial." *Aspen Highlands Skiing Corp. v. Aspen Skiing Co.,* 738 F.2d 1509 (10th Cir. 1984).

The Polyses' counsel made no formal offer of proof when the district court sustained Trans-Colorado's objection to the admission of both Dr. Daven's and Dr. Schultz's deposition testimonies. Following the exclusion of Dr. Daven's testimony, counsel responded "Thank you, Judge. The next witness we would call . . . ." The next witness was to be Dr. Schultz. Polyses' counsel submitted his deposition testimony for admission. Although their counsel briefly explained that the first will-call witness was out of the country and the second was out of the district, both over 100 miles away, he did not explain the substance or purpose of the experts' testimonies. In response to the sustained objection, Polyses' counsel merely called the next witness.

Furthermore, the context in which the deposition evidence was offered, following the Polyses' first witness, revealed nothing about the substance or purpose of the testimonies. The Polyses argue, nonetheless, that they met the Rule 103(a)(2) requirement because "in the course of proceedings, the district court was made aware of the nature and substance of the excluded testimony." To support this argument, the Polyses cite four times during the trial when Dr. Daven or Dr. Schultz were discussed. When the doctors' names came up one and two days later, however, the plaintiffs' counsel made no effort to argue for admittance of the deposition testimony and they never explained what its contribution would have been. The plaintiffs appear to believe that if the significance of excluded evidence becomes apparent later, a trial judge sua sponte must reconsider its earlier evidentiary ruling. The plaintiffs misunderstand the offer of proof requirement. First, eliciting through later testimony the substance of previously excluded evidence, without more in the way of explanation or proffer to the court, satisfies neither the plain language of, nor the purpose for, Rule 103(a)(2). As we stated, the Rule contemplates some contemporaneity between the trial judge's knowledge about the proposed evidence and the evidentiary ruling to allow a proper decision at the time the evidence is offered. Even considering, hypothetically, that counsel had requested admission of the excluded deposition testimonies later in the proceedings when other witnesses testified about these doctors, the testimony in question was not sufficient to apprise the district court of the substance and purpose of the excluded testimony and would not have satisfied the second purpose of the rule—to create a clear record for us to review the trial court's decision. Therefore, because the Polyses have not preserved the issue for appeal, we can not review the district court's decision to exclude the deposition testimonies for abuse of discretion. Consequently, we do not reach the harmless error question. Instead, we examine the record for plain error.

We note that it is difficult to find plain error in cases like this because "failure to comply with normal requirements of offers of proof is likely to produce a record which simply does not disclose the plain error." Fed. R. Evid. 103(d) Advisory Committee's Note. On the facts before us, however, we can not say exclusion of the deposition testimonies was plain error comprising an exceptional case of prejudice or unfairness.

. . .

In sum, absent offers of proof, we can not review the district court's ruling that excluded Doctors Daven's and Schultz's deposition testimonies for abuse of discretion. In addition, we hold that that ruling was not plain error. It was not error and, even if it was, it did not affect a substantial right of the Polyses. Therefore, we will not reverse the district court.

In accordance with the foregoing, we AFFIRM the district court order.

LEGAL ANALYSIS AND WRITING 4.3

The following questions are based on the *How to Brief a Legal Case* format shown in the Appendix. Use this format to answer the following questions:

1. Summarize the facts in the previous case.
2. What is the legal issue?
3. What did the appellate court decide?
4. Why did the court decide this way?
5. Do you agree with the court's reasoning? Explain why or why not.

LEGAL RESEARCH USING THE INTERNET SKILLS 4.3

Try to find this case or another one that refers to it online! Check out one of the legal research web sites below, go to the federal circuit for this court decision, and use their "Search" feature to find this case or another case that refers to it. In the "Search" field, enter the cite or case name. If you have access to Westlaw or Lexis, try to find this case using one of these legal search sites.

1. U.S. Courts Site with Links to All Circuit Courts of Appeal (http://www.uscourts.gov/links.html)
2. National Center for State Courts—State and Federal Court Web Sites (http://www.ncsconline.org/D_kis/_info_court_web_sites.html)
3. FindLaw (http://guide.lp.findlaw.com/casecode/)

Trial Court May Add to Offer of Proof

To provide more information about an offer of proof, the trial court may add other statements that show the character of the evidence offered, the form in which it was offered, the objection made, or the ruling thereon. Examples of other statements may be those made during arguments over the offer of proof, or statements made during a **sidebar** conference. The court may also direct the making of an offer in question and answer form.

Sidebar
A conference between the judge and attorneys usually held in front or to the side of judge's bench and out of hearing from the jury.

Keeping Offers of Proof Out of the Hearing of Jury

Rule 103(c) provides that in jury cases, the trial court will conduct the proceedings to the extent practicable, so as to prevent inadmissible evidence from being suggested to the jury by any means (see Exhibit of 4.11). Specifically, the rule lists the making of statements regarding evidence or offers of proof, or asking questions in the hearing of the jury.

EXHIBIT 4.11   Rulings on Evidence—Hearing of Jury

Ohio Rules of Evidence
Rule 103(C). Hearing of jury.
    In jury cases, proceedings shall be conducted, to the extent practicable, so as to prevent inadmissible evidence from being suggested to the jury by any means, such as making statements or offers of proof or asking questions in the hearing of the jury.

Practice Tip 4.4

Preparing for Offer of Proof
Here's a tip for ensuring that an offer of proof is made whenever any of your evidence is excluded:
When preparing evidence exhibits and questions for witness testimony prior to trial, write up a brief offer of proof for each in case any is objected to and excluded. Doing this in advance will better prepare your legal team in understanding the nature and importance of the evidence being offered, and in ensuring a timely response if excluded.

CHALLENGES AFTER TRIAL

After a trial has ended, many states allow a party to file a motion asking the trial court to reconsider its verdict or judgment. This may be based on an argument that certain evidence was improperly admitted. Most of the time, these motions are denied and the verdict or judgment stands. A final challenge would then be in the form of an appeal.

Appeal

An appeal is a formal petition in writing to an appellate court requesting that it review the findings of a trial court for error. It is filed by one of the parties to the legal action heard in the trial court. Upon appeal, an appellate court will review the trial judge's rulings and instructions regarding evidence presented. In order for an appellate court to review errors pertaining to the admission or exclusion of evidence at the trial court, the following conditions need to be met:

1. A timely objection was made at the trial court.
2. The objection at trial was specific.
3. The objection is not being raised on appeal for the first time.

Courts have long held that objections and challenges over evidence should first ". . . be addressed to the discretion of the trial court. This is because the trial court, which has observed the entire trial and the demeanor of the attorneys, can better gauge the impact of the allegedly prejudicial language than an appellate court reviewing a cold record. Moreover, an objection permits the court to take corrective action where appropriate. But where a defendant has not objected to allegedly improper language, the trial court is deprived of an opportunity to correct and we are deprived of the trial court's views on the question."[19] The Supreme Court stated this in a 1936 decision, "The verdict of a jury will not ordinarily be set aside for error not brought to the attention of the trial court. This practice is founded upon considerations of fairness to the court and to the parties and of the public interest in bringing litigation to an end after fair opportunity has been afforded to present all issues of law and fact."[20] "Failure to enforce defense counsel's obligation to object to mistakes at trial would have the unsalutary effect of encouraging attorneys to remain silent about some fault on the part of the trial court . . . and so, without giving it a chance to correct the situation, arm themselves with ground for reversal if the verdict should go against them."[21]

Basis for Appeal—Error of Law

Harmless Error
A properly objected to mistake made during trial that is found by an appellate court not to affect substantial rights and therefore does not constitute grounds for reversal.

Prejudicial Error
A properly objected to mistake made during trial that is found by an appellate court to affect substantial rights constituting grounds for reversal.

The appellate court will only look at errors of law made by the trial court. They will not decide factual issues raised during the trial. There are two types of error of law that could be found by the appellate court when a timely and specific objection was made at trial: **harmless error** and **prejudicial error**. Harmless error is error that has been properly objected to (i.e., timely and specific) at trial, but on appeal is not found to affect any substantial rights and has a minimal effect on the verdict. Harmless error does not constitute grounds for reversal. Prejudicial error has also been properly objected to at trial, and on appeal, has been found to affect substantial rights or have a substantial influence on the verdict. Prejudicial error constitutes grounds for reversal (see Exhibit 4.12).

As stated in the Evidence Rules, the key to determining whether an error is harmless or prejudicial is if it affected a "substantial right."[22] In trying to figure out what this meant and how it could be used to determine a "harmless error," one court said,

> "Rule 103(a) indicates that courts of appeals should not reverse on the basis of erroneous evidentiary rulings unless a party's 'substantial right' is affected. This question is not susceptible to mechanical analysis. However, we have stated repeatedly that an error is harmless if the court is sure, after reviewing the entire record, that the error did not influence the jury or had but a very slight effect on its verdict."[23]

EVIDENTIARY CHECKLIST 4.2

Appellate Review of Trial Court Checklist

☐   Timely objection was made at trial.

☐   Objection at trial was specific.

☐   Objection is not being raised on appeal for the first time (unless plain error is found).

EXHIBIT 4.12   What Constitutes Reversible Error

Ohio Rules of Evidence
Rule 103. Rulings on Evidence.
    (1) Evidential error is not presumed to be prejudicial. Error may not be predicated upon a ruling which admits or excludes evidence unless a substantial right of the party is affected. . . .

Florida Statute.
    Sec. 90.104 (1). A court may predicate error, set aside or reverse a judgment, or grant a new trial on the basis of admitted or excluded evidence when a substantial right of the party is adversely affected. . . .

When "Close" Is Good Enough

In the following Puerto Rico case, the court deals with whether failure to identify the precise evidentiary rule when stating grounds for an objection is close enough to satisfy the "specific" requirement.

CASE

Bonilla v. Yamaha Motors Corp.
955 F.2d 150 (1st Cir. 1992).
Appeal from the United States District Court for the District of Puerto Rico.

Brown, Senior Circuit Judge.

Jorge Bonilla brought this product liability action against Yamaha Motors Corporation to recover for injuries he incurred in a motorcycle accident.

Bonilla alleged that a design defect in the braking mechanism of Yamaha's FJ1100 motorcycle caused his accident. After a 9-day jury trial, the jury found that a design defect did exist, but that this defect was not the proximate cause of Bonilla's accident. Bonilla now appeals the judgment based on this verdict, asserting that the court erred by 1) permitting the defense to introduce evidence of Bonilla's prior and subsequent speeding tickets. . . .

The Crash

On June 22, 1985, Jorge Bonilla was driving his 1984 Yamaha FJ1100 motorcycle on Road 187 in Isla Verde, Puerto Rico, at a speed of approximately 50 or 60 miles per hour. As Bonilla attempted to negotiate a wide right turn, he lost control of the bike and crashed into a metal guardrail which divided the road. Bonilla testified that his brakes completely failed and ultimately caused his accident. At trial, Bonilla developed the theory that the motorcycle's braking system overheated and experienced vapor lock, resulting in complete failure due to frequent braking in heavy stop-and-go traffic. Yamaha, however, refuted Bonilla's claim that the accident was caused by brake failure, and undertook to show that Bonilla's speeding was the sole reason for the crash. Yamaha's evidence warranted the potential inference that Bonilla was driving at an excessive speed, in traffic that was not heavy, and on a defect-free, well-lighted road.

(1) The Speeding Tickets

What this case begins and ends with is the trial court's admission of evidence of Bonilla's prior and subsequent speeding offenses. On cross-examination, Yamaha confronted Bonilla with a certified copy of his driving and offense record, which showed that Bonilla was fined for excessive speed in September, 1981, approximately 4 years prior to his accident, and again in April, 1987, about 2 years after his accident. The following exchange occurred on the first day of trial, June 5, 1990:

MR. UBARRI [Yamaha's counsel]:	Isn't it true, Mr. Bonilla, that prior to the occurrence of this accident you have been fined for speeding?
MR. CALDERON [Bonilla's counsel]:	Objection.
THE COURT:	Overruled.
A:	I don't recall.
MR. UBARRI [Yamaha's counsel]:	Mr. Bonilla, isn't it a fact thateven after the occurrence of this accident you had been fined for speeding?
A:	No.
MR. CALDERON [Bonilla's counsel]:	I object again for relevancy.
THE COURT: (sidebar discussion)	Noted.
THE COURT:	Ask your question.
MR. UBARRI [Yamaha's counsel]:	Yes, Mr. Bonilla, isn't the document that I have shown you a certification from the Department of Transportation and Public Works pertaining to your record as a driver?
A:	Yes, sir.
MR. UBARRI [Yamaha's counsel]:	Isn't it also a fact, Mr. Bonilla, that according to this official certification issued by the Department of Transportation of Puerto Rico you were fined for excessive speed on two occasions? One prior to the accident and another one after the accident?
A:	Yes, sir.

During the sidebar, and again over Bonilla's objections, the trial court made clear its reasons for allowing the questioning:

> "I will overrule the objection as to the speeding because if he is denying that, I think that is proper grounds for impeachment. . . . I will also allow you to confront him with the certification, specifically and limited to those two violations, 1981 and 1987 for excessive speeds. . . . He has denied ever having been fined for speeding. This is impeachment material to his denials."

In addition to the colloquy that took place before the jury, apparently the trial court admitted on the second day of trial, June 6, 1990, Bonilla's certified driving record. Bonilla urges successfully that the trial court erred by permitting the oral testimony and admitting the documentary evidence concerning his speeding offenses. He contends that this evidence must have led the jury to the verdict conclusion that speeding, not the design defect, caused his accident.

(a) The Test for Error

Under Fed. Rule Evid. 103(a), this court must review a challenged evidentiary decision to determine whether (1) a substantial right of the party is affected, and (2) whether a timely objection or motion to strike appears of record, stating the specific ground of objection if the specific ground was not apparent from the context.

(b) Timely and Specific Objection

We deal initially with 103(a)'s second requirement that the objection be both timely and specific. The above exchange indicates that during cross-examination, Bonilla objected to Yamaha's questions regarding Bonilla's speeding primarily on . . . Rule 403 undue prejudice grounds.

Similarly, Bonilla timely objected to the admission of his driving record on the limited basis that this evidence was highly prejudicial. All of these objections were made clear by Bonilla's later request . . . which asked that the jury be instructed that evidence of prior or subsequent bad acts cannot be considered to determine that the plaintiff acted in conformity with such acts on the instant occasion, specifically citing Fed. Rule Evid. 404(b). Yamaha counters that because Bonilla did not mouth the words of Rule 404(b) or refer to it specifically by number at the time the evidence first came in, any later objection under this rule was ineffectual. In a nutshell, Yamaha argues that Bonilla's specific invocation of 404(b) in his request for a Special Instruction to the Jury came too late.

We recognize at the outset the well-established rule that an objection to the admission of evidence must be timely made by the party opposing the admission, or error is waived. But as this court has stated before, Rules 403 and 404(b) go hand in glove, since 404(b) "describes a particular form of evidence that might create the 'unfair prejudice' anticipated under Fed. R. Evid. 403." *U.S. v. Currier, 836 F.2d 11 at 17* (1st Cir. 1987). We conclude that, under the circumstances of this case, Bonilla's objections were sufficiently timely and specific to warrant review of the admission of Bonilla's speeding offenses under Rule 404(b).

. . . .

(d) Harmful Error

Under Rule 103(a), wrongful admissions must affect a substantial right in order to constitute reversible error. When evidence is charged to have been improperly admitted, any error is more likely to be found harmful, and thus reversible, where the evidence is substantively important, inflammatory, repeated, emphasized, or unfairly self-serving. Without a doubt, the admission of evidence concerning Bonilla's speeding offenses was substantively important, inflammatory, and highly prejudicial. Although the jury decided that the braking system on the FJ1100 motorcycle was defectively designed, it declined to find that this was the proximate cause of Bonilla's crash. After a close examination of the record, we are forced to conclude that evidence of Bonilla's speeding, both before and after the accident, may very well have tipped the scale against Bonilla and in Yamaha's favor, on its theory that speed, not design, was the author of Bonilla's injuries. If this evidence proved anything, it proved that a person who has twice been caught speeding is likely to have been speeding at the time in question, a connection which legal policy and Rule 404(b) strictly forbid. Because the error was not harmless, we must reverse and remand for a new trial.

LEGAL ANALYSIS AND WRITING 4.4

The following questions are based on the *How to Brief a Legal Case* format shown in the Appendix. Use this format to answer the following questions:

1. Summarize the facts in the previous case.

2. What is the legal issue?

3. What did the appellate court decide?

4. Why did the court decide this way?

5. Do you agree with the court's reasoning? Explain why or why not.

LEGAL RESEARCH USING THE INTERNET SKILLS 4.4

Try to find this case or another one that refers to it online! Check out one of the legal research web sites below, go to the federal circuit for this court decision, and use their "Search" feature to find this case or another case that refers to it. In the "Search" field, enter the cite or case name. If you have access to Westlaw or Lexis, try to find this case using one of these legal search sites.

1. U.S. Courts Site with Links to All Circuit Courts of Appeal (http://www.uscourts.gov/links.html)
2. National Center for State Courts—State and Federal Court Web Sites (http://www.ncsconline.org/D_kis/info_court_web_sites.html#federal)
3. FindLaw (http://guide.lp.findlaw.com/casecode/)

YOU BE THE JUDGE 4.1

Fahy was convicted in a Connecticut State Court of willfully injuring a public building by painting swastikas on a synagogue. At his trial, a can of paint and a paint brush were admitted into evidence over his objection. The paint and brush had been obtained by means of an illegal search and seizure by police. On appeal, Fahy argues that this evidence contributed to his conviction and the fact that it was illegally obtained constitutes prejudicial error. The prosecution counters that there was sufficient evidence on which Fahy could have been convicted without the evidence complained of, and therefore the admission of the evidence only constituted harmless error.

How would you rule? Harmless or prejudicial error? Explain your reasons.

LEGAL RESEARCH USING THE INTERNET SKILLS 4.5

Find out how the court ruled on the above *You Be the Judge* problem, and why, by reading the Supreme Court decision online! The citation for it is:
Fahy v. Connecticut, 375 U.S. 85 (1963).

Check out one of the legal research web sites below and use their "Search" feature to find this case. In the "Search" field, enter the cite or case name.

1. FindLaw U.S. Supreme Court Decisions (http://www.findlaw.com/casecode/supreme.html)
2. U.S. Supreme Court (http://www.supremecourtus.gov/)
3. Supreme Court Collection of Cornell Law School (http://supct.law.cornell.edu/supct/)

PLAIN ERROR

Plain Error
A mistake that was not properly objected to at trial, but on appeal is found to affect substantial rights in such a fundamental way that it would cause a party to be deprived of a fair trial if not rectified.

If a timely and specific objection was not made at trial, an appellate court will not review any issues pertaining to the admitting or excluding of evidence unless **plain error** can be found (see Exhibit 4.13). Plain error is a mistake that was not properly objected to at trial, but on appeal is found to affect substantial rights in such a fundamental way that it would cause a party to be deprived of a fair trial if not rectified. An example of plain error is when an improperly obtained confession is admitted into evidence and used against a defendant in a criminal trial.

Plain error is grounded in the Evidence Rules. Ohio Rule 103(D), for example, states that "Nothing in this rule precludes taking notice of plain errors affecting substantial rights although they were not brought to the attention of the court."[24] The legal concept of plain error can be traced back in the common law over a hundred years. An 1896 Supreme Court case held that even though a proper question was not raised on appeal, "if a plain error was committed in a matter so absolutely vital to defendants, we feel ourselves at liberty to correct it."[25]

EXHIBIT 4.13   Plain Error

Alaska Rules of Evidence
Rule 103(d). Plain error.
    Nothing in this rule precludes taking notice of plain errors affecting substantial rights although they were not brought to the attention of the court.

Florida Statute
    Sec. 90.104(3). Nothing in this section shall preclude a court from taking notice of fundamental errors affecting substantial rights, even though such errors were not brought to the attention of the trial judge.

Plain Error Doctrine

The **plain error doctrine** stems in part from the previous evidence rule and in part from case law. It holds that appellate courts may, of their own motion, take notice of fundamental errors affecting substantial rights, even when they were not properly objected to at trial. A 1936 Supreme Court case is credited with establishing this doctrine when it ruled that " . . . in exceptional circumstances, especially in criminal cases, appellate courts, in the public interest, may, of their own motion, notice errors to which no exception has been taken, if the errors are obvious, or if they otherwise seriously affect the fairness, integrity, or public reputation of judicial proceedings."[26] Courts have since interpreted this, and the subsequent evidence rule pertaining to plain error, as requiring a fundamental error that, unless rectified, would deprive a party of a fair trial.

As one reasoned, "Because attorneys should not profit from a failure to object, reversal is warranted, in the absence of an objection, only where necessary to prevent a miscarriage of justice or a gross violation of a party's constitutional rights . . . plain error will be found only if the argument is so egregious that there is no room for doubt as to its prejudicial effect and this Court is convinced that affirmance would result in a miscarriage of justice."[27] Another court stated that the "plain error rule is not a run-of-the-mill remedy. The intention of the rule is to serve the ends of justice; therefore it is invoked only in exceptional circumstances."[28]

Plain Error Doctrine
Appellate courts may, of their own motion, notice errors to which no exception has been taken, if the errors are obvious, or if they otherwise seriously affect the fairness, integrity, or public reputation of judicial proceedings.

EVIDENTIARY CHECKLIST 4.3

Appellate Court Checklist for Reversible Error

If timely and specific objection is made at trial:

☐ **Harmless Error:**   When no substantial rights have been involved; No basis for appellate court reversal.

(Continued)

> Continued
>
> **OR**
>
> ☐ **Prejudicial Error:** When substantial rights have been involved; Basis for appellate court reversal.
>
> If NO timely and specific objection is made at trial:
>
> ☐ **Plain Error:** Appellate court can only overturn the trial court decision if an error affects substantial rights in such a fundamental way that it would cause a party to be deprived of a fair trial if not rectified.

Supreme Court Case that Set the Standard

Although the concept of plain error can be traced farther back, the following 1936 Supreme Court case is credited with establishing a "plain error doctrine," even though it did not identify it as such. See if you can point out the phrase that does this.

Group #2 Case #5

CASE

United States v. Atkinson

297 U.S. 157 (1936).

Mr. Justice Stone delivered the opinion of the Court.

This case was brought here on certiorari, to review a determination of the Court of Appeals for the Fifth Circuit. . . . The challenged holding is that there is statutory authority for including in contracts of United States government insurance covering death or total permanent disability a provision that "the permanent loss of hearing of both ears . . . shall be deemed to be total disability." The case was tried in the District Court to a jury which rendered a verdict for the plaintiff, respondent here. Judgment in his favor was affirmed by the Circuit Court of Appeals for the Fifth Circuit . . . .

The government, by its assignment of errors here, assails, as it did in the court below, the correctness of this ruling, but examination of the record discloses that no such objection was presented to the trial court. In consequence the government is precluded from raising the question on appeal.

The trial judge instructed the jury that respondent might recover either on the theory that his loss of hearing constituted in fact a permanent disability preventing his pursuit of any substantially gainful occupation, or that his loss of hearing of both ears, if permanent, was a permanent disability as defined by the policy. The jury was thus left free to return a verdict for respondent if it found that he had suffered permanent loss of hearing of both ears, regardless of its effect upon his ability to earn his livelihood. The government failed to question the correctness of these instructions either by exception or request to charge, and its motion for a directed verdict was upon other grounds not now material.

The verdict of a jury will not ordinarily be set aside for error not brought to the attention of the trial court. This practice is founded upon considerations of fairness to the court and to the parties and of the public interest in bringing litigation to an end after fair opportunity has been afforded to present all issues of law and fact. . . . In exceptional circumstances, especially in criminal cases, appellate courts, in the public interest, may, of their own motion, notice errors to which no exception has been taken, if the errors are obvious, or if they otherwise seriously affect the fairness, integrity, or public reputation of judicial proceedings. But no such case is presented here. The judgment must be affirmed for the reason that the error assigned was not made the subject of appropriate exception or request to charge upon the trial. Affirmed.

LEGAL ANALYSIS AND WRITING 4.5

The following questions are based on the *How to Brief a Legal Case* format shown in the Appendix. Use this format to answer the following questions:

1. What is the legal issue in the previous case?
2. What did the Supreme Court decide?
3. Why did the Court decide this way?
4. What is the standard established in this decision that is still used for determining plain error?

LEGAL RESEARCH USING THE INTERNET SKILLS 4.6

Find and read this historically important Supreme Court case online! Check out one of the legal research web sites below and use their "Search" feature to find this case. In the "Search" field, enter the cite or case name.

1. FindLaw U.S. Supreme Court Decisions (http://www.findlaw.com/casecode/supreme.html)
2. U.S. Supreme Court (http://www.supremecourtus.gov/)
3. Supreme Court Collection of Cornell Law School (http://supct.law.cornell.edu/supct/)

CRITICAL THINKING QUESTIONS 4.3

1. What is the difference between an objection and a motion to strike?
2. What is the reasoning behind requiring objections to be timely and specific?
3. Why do we make an exception when there is plain error?
4. What is an example of plain error, and what can be done in collecting evidence or preparing witnesses to prevent this?
5. Why do we set a standard of substantial or prejudicial error in overturning a trial court decision? Why not any error?

YOU BE THE JUDGE 4.2

Frady was convicted of first-degree murder and sentenced to life imprisonment. Nineteen years after his conviction, Frady files a motion seeking to vacate his sentence because of erroneous instructions given by the judge to the jury at his trial. Frady claims that these instructions erroneously instructed on the meaning of malice, an element of murder, and that this error eliminated any possibility of a manslaughter verdict. At trial, Frady did not object to the instructions, nor did he raise the issue on his original appeal 19 years ago. The government argues that because Frady did not object at the trial or afterward on appeal, there is no basis for his motion 19 years later. Frady claims that plain error can be found by an appellate court regardless of whether an objection was made at trial and no matter how long ago the trial took place.

Do you agree with the government or Frady? How would you rule on Frady's motion? Explain your answer.

LEGAL RESEARCH USING THE INTERNET SKILLS 4.7

Find out how the court ruled on the previous *You Be the Judge* problem, and why, by reading the Supreme Court decision online! The citation for it is:

United States v. Frady, 456 U.S. 152 (1982).

Check out one of the legal research web sites below and use their "Search" feature to find this case. In the "Search" field, enter the cite or case name.

1. FindLaw U.S. Supreme Court Decisions (http://www.findlaw.com/casecode/supreme.html)
2. U.S. Supreme Court (http://www.supremecourtus.gov/)
3. Supreme Court Collection of Cornell Law School (http://supct.law.cornell.edu/supct/)

SUMMARY

The admissibility of evidence may be challenged either before trial in the form of a pretrial motion, during trial in the form of an objection or motion to strike, or after trial in the form of an appeal. There are two primary purposes behind evidentiary challenges: to keep the jury from hearing certain evidence, and to preserve any error committed on the record for appeal. Pretrial objections may come in the form of a motion to exclude or suppress certain evidence, or a motion in limine, which asks the court to rule on an evidentiary issue before it goes before the jury. A motion in limine may also be made during trial. During a trial, an evidentiary challenge is over the form or substance of a question asked by the opposing side in examining a witness. Admissibility of evidence is then challenged in the form of an *objection* before the witness has answered the question or a *motion to strike* after the witness has answered the question. An objection is raised when evidence is offered that the objecting party believes should be excluded under some legal grounds. Objections can be to substance or form. An objection to *substance* is a challenge of the substantive evidence being offered or to the answer being called for in a question to a witness. These types of objections are grounded on a specific rule of evidence or other exclusionary law. An objection to *form* is challenging the form of the question—the manner in which a question is worded or asked. If a question is worded in a way to confuse, harass, or unduly embarrass a witness, it may be objected to. Similarly, a question that leads a witness to a particular answer, or requires the witness to speculate or make assumptions, will trigger an objection.

An objection must be timely and specific. Timely requires that it be made when the challenged evidence is being offered. It must be specific as to the form and grounds for objection. Where no objection is offered, evidence of any type may be received. A *motion to strike* is a form of objection to evidence *after* it has already been made and where there was no reasonable opportunity to object to it before it was admitted. Most generally, a motion to strike occurs when a witness is asked a question on the stand and answers it before opposing counsel has had a reasonable opportunity to object to the question itself. If an objection or motion to strike is sustained by the trial judge, the evidence objected to is excluded. If it is overruled, the evidence is admitted. Failure to object or move to strike is considered a waiver of future grounds for appeal. Parties seeking to admit evidence that has been objected to and excluded by the court will usually make an offer of proof. The purpose of this is to explain to the trial judge and to state "for the record" his or her purpose in asking a particular question of a witness or attempting to admit a particular item of evidence. Generally, an offer of proof is needed in order to preserve an objection for the record. On appeal, the offer of proof in the record provides the appellate court with more detail to help determine whether the trial court committed reversible error by excluding the evidence.

In order for an appellate court to reverse or remand a case, it must be shown that an error of law was made by the trial judge in admitting or excluding evidence and that a timely and specific objection was made at trial. There are three types of error that might occur at the trial level and which may be found in an appellate review: harmless error, prejudicial error, and plain error. Harmless error is error that has been properly objected to at trial, but on appeal is not found to affect any substantial rights. Prejudicial error has also been properly objected to at trial, and on appeal, has been found to affect substantial rights that constitute grounds for reversal. Plain error is error that was not properly objected to at trial, but on appeal is found so fundamental that it would cause a party to be deprived of a fair trial if not rectified.

KEY TERMS

Admissible	Mistrial	Overruled
Appeal	Motion in Limine	Plain Error
Beyond the Scope	Motion to Exclude	Plain Error Doctrine
Due Process	Motion to Strike	Prejudicial Error
Harmless Error	Motion to Suppress	Pretrial Motion
Hearsay	Objection	Sidebar
Inadmissible	Objection to Form	Sustained
Leading Question	Objection to Substance	Timely and Specific
Make the Record	Offer of Proof	Waiver

LEARNING OUTCOMES AND PRACTICE SKILLS CHECKLIST

☐ Learning Outcomes

After completing your reading, questions, and exercises, you should be able to demonstrate a better understanding of the learning concepts by answering the following questions:

1. Compare and contrast a *motion to suppress* and *motion in limine*.
2. Distinguish between *objections to substance* and *objections to form*.
3. Explain what an objection to substance is and give examples of when it would be used and the grounds for using it.
4. Describe what an objection to form is and give examples of when it would be used and the grounds for using it.
5. Define the following objections and identify the Evidence Rule that the objection is based on, if any. Give an example of how the objection might be used.

   a) Leading question
   b) Beyond the scope
   c) Irrelevant
   d) Prejudicial
   e) Argumentative
   f) Calls for conclusion

g) Speculation

h) Non-responsive answer

6. Explain what is meant by rephrasing a question to overcome an objection. Give an example.
7. Discuss the process for raising an objection in court, including the possible rulings by the judge.
8. Explain what an offer of proof is and the purposes behind it.
9. Identify and explain the two elements needed for an objection to be reviewed by an appellate court.
10. Explain what the appellate court is limited to in reviewing the record of a trial.
11. Distinguish between harmless error and prejudicial error. Give examples of each.
12. Distinguish between prejudicial error and plain error.
13. Define plain error and give an example.

☐ Practice Skills

In addition to understanding the learning concepts, practice what you have learned through applications using critical thinking, legal analysis and writing, legal research, and advocacy skills, including:

Critical Thinking

1. Why do courts allow the variety of objections described in this chapter?
2. Do you believe that the objections discussed in this chapter provide adequate safeguards?
3. What public policy issues or considerations do you think might be behind allowing the use of these objections?
4. If it were up to you, would you keep these objections as they are, delete them, narrow them, or expand them? Explain your reasoning.
5. How do these rules influence the gathering of evidence or preparing of witnesses?

Legal Analysis and Writing

Analyze the following rules and cases by summarizing their holdings, explaining their significance, and assessing any issue that might arise in their application.

1. Rule 103(a).
2. Rule 103(a)(1).
3. Rule 103(a)(2).
4. Rule 103(b).
5. Rule 103(d).
6. *Government of the Virgin Islands v. Archibald.*
7. *Polys v. Trans-Colorado Airlines, Inc.*
8. *United States v. Atkinson.*

Legal Research Using the Internet

1. Find the annotated Federal Rules of Evidence on the Internet and assess the comments made in the proposing of the rules covered in this chapter.
2. Find your state's rules of evidence regarding objections, offers of proof, and reversible error covered in this chapter. Compare and contrast with

the federal and/or modern rules, and some of the state rules listed in this chapter.

3. Find out if your state appellate court posts their case decisions on the Internet. If so, find a case that illustrates an issue or rule discussed in this chapter. If your state decisions are not on the Internet, go instead to the web site for the U.S. Circuit Court of Appeals in your circuit, or search the U.S. Supreme Court decisions.

PRACTICE APPLICATION 4.1

Plaintiff is suing defendant (store owner) for negligence in not sanding the store's parking lot after an ice storm. Plaintiff slipped and fell in the parking lot, breaking her leg. The following questions were asked of a witness (who worked at the store) on direct examination by plaintiff's attorney:

1. "Did you see the plaintiff in the parking lot and did you see her fall down?"
2. "Was the parking lot covered with ice?"
3. "From where you were standing, did it look like the parking lot had been sanded?"
4. "Is there any doubt in your mind that plaintiff's injury was caused by falling on the ice?"
5. "Did a co-worker tell you that she heard your employer say that he was not going to pay to have the parking lot sanded and that the customers could all fall down as far as he was concerned?"
6. "You were supposed to have sanded that parking lot, weren't you?"

On behalf of the defense: for each of the above questions, name the objection you would raise, if any, and your grounds for raising the objection.

ADVOCACY AND COMMUNICATION SKILLS 4.1

1. Form teams from small groups of no more than 3–4 each, with the instructor to serve as judge. Rephrase each of the above *Practice Application* questions in a way that the question might be admissible.
2. Conduct an examination of a witness, asking the original question and, after an objection by the opposing team, the rephrased question. The opposing team should be prepared to object to the rephrased question using appropriate grounds.
3. If the judge sustains any objection, orally deliver an offer of proof.

PRACTICE APPLICATION 4.2

In the previous *Practice Application*, the following questions were properly objected to at trial, but the judge overruled the objection and allowed the witness to answer:

1. "Did you see the plaintiff in the parking lot and did you see her fall down?"
   Witness answer: "Yes. She slipped on the ice out there and fell."
2. "Was the parking lot covered with ice?"
   Witness answer: "Yes."
3. "From where you were standing, did it look like the parking lot had been sanded?"
   Witness answer: "No, it didn't look like it had been sanded all day."

The following questions were not objected to at trial, and the witness answered:

4. "Is there any doubt in your mind that plaintiff's injury was caused by falling on the ice?"
   Witness answer: "Nope."
5. "Did a co-worker tell you that she heard your employer say that he was not going to pay to have the parking lot sanded and that the customers could all fall down as far as he was concerned?"
   Witness answer: "Yes."
6. "You were supposed to have sanded that parking lot, weren't you?"
   Witness answer: "Well, someone should have."

Use the format shown in the Appendix for the *IRAC Method of Legal Analysis* and the readings, rules, and cases discussed in this chapter to analyze the above case problems and determine whether any of the above constitutes error on appeal. If so, what type of error and is it reversible? Write a memo giving your analysis, reasoning, and conclusions.

WEB SITES

Federal Rules of Evidence
http://www.law.cornell.edu/rules/fre/overview.html
FindLaw
http://www.findlaw.com
FindLaw
http://guide.lp.findlaw.com/casecode/
FindLaw U.S. Supreme Court Decisions
http://www.findlaw.com/casecode/supreme.html
List of State Laws from Legal Information Institute of Cornell Law School
http://www.law.cornell.edu/states/listing.html

National Center for State Courts—State and Federal Court Web Sites
http://www.ncsconline.org/D_kis/info_court_web_site s. html#state
Supreme Court Collection of Cornell Law School
http://supct.law.cornell.edu/supct/
U.S. Courts Site with Links to All Circuit Courts of Appeal
(http://www.uscourts.gov/links.html)
U.S. Supreme Court
(http://www.supremecourtus.gov/)

ENDNOTES

1. Fed. R. Evid. 802.
2. Colo. R. Evid. 611(b).
3. See, for example, Fed. R. Evid. 1002.
4. Miss. R. Evid. 602.
5. See, for example, Ohio R. Evid. 601, or Wash Rev. Code RCW 5.60.020.
6. Md. R. Evid. 5-603. Oath or affirmation.
7. Kan. Stat. Sec. 60-401(b).
8. Fed. R. Evid. 404(a).
9. Fed. R. Evid. 404(b).
10. Fed. R. Evid. 405.
11. Fed. R. Evid. 406.
12. See, for example, Cal. Evid. Code Sec. 800.
13. See, for example, Conn. Gen. Stat. Sec. 52-146c, or Georgia Code, Section 24-9-21.
14. See, for example, Alaska R. Evid. 403.
15. See, for example, Fed. R. Evid. 611(a). Mode and Order of Interrogation and Presentation.
16. See, for example, Wyo. R. Evid. 403. Exclusion of Relevant Evidence on Grounds of Prejudice, Confusion, or Waste of Time.
17. See, for example, Fed. R. Evid. 103(c).
18. *Polys v. Trans-Colorado Airlines, Inc.*, 941 F.2d 1404 (10th Cir. 1991).
19. *State v. Francis*, 151 Vt. 296 (1989).
20. *United States v. Atkinson*, 297 U.S. 157 (1936).
21. *State v. Ross*, 152 Vt. 462 (1979).
22. See, for example, Fed. R. Evid. 103(a).
23. *Pregeant v. Pan Am. World Airways, Inc.*, 762 F.2d 1245, 1249 (5th Cir. 1985).
24. Ohio R. Evid. 103(D).
25. *Wiborg v. United States*, 163 U.S. 632 (1896).
26. *United States v. Atkinson*, 297 U.S. 157 (1936).
27. *State v. Cohen*, No. 87-329 (Vt. 1991).
28. *United States v. DiBenedetto*, 542 F.2d 490 (1976).

RELEVANCY

"Evidence which tends to establish some fact material to the case, or which tends to make a fact at issue more or less probable, is relevant."

—*Commonwealth v. Scott, 480 Pa. 50 (1978)*

LEARNING OUTCOMES

In this chapter, you will learn about the following legal concepts:

- Common Law Requirement: Relevant and Material

- Modern Requirement for Admissibility: Relevancy

- Logical and Legal Relevance

- Exclusion of Relevant Evidence on Grounds of Prejudice

- Exclusion of Relevant Evidence on Grounds of Confusion or Waste of Time

INTRODUCTION

In the previous chapter, we looked at how the admissibility of evidence can be challenged through a variety of motions and objections. One of those objections was for *relevance*, whether the evidence offered has a bearing on or pertains to a matter at issue in the case. In this chapter, we will examine this basic requirement for admissibility in more detail. We will also look at rules that allow for excluding relevant evidence when it is too prejudicial to the trier of fact.

COMMON LAW REQUIREMENT: RELEVANT AND MATERIAL

Relevant
Evidence is relevant when it tends to prove or disprove a fact in issue.

Material
Evidence being offered must have a bearing on or relate to the issue in dispute.

One of the oldest requirements for the admissibility of evidence is whether it is **relevant** and **material** to the matters for which it is being offered. Evidence is relevant when it tends to prove or disprove a fact in issue. Evidence is material when it has a bearing on or relates to the issue in dispute. At common law, evidence had to be both relevant and material to be admissible in court. It had to tend to prove or disprove a fact for which it was being offered, and it had to be material to the fact at issue. Each was a separate concept. The fact that a criminal defendant possessed a firearm may be relevant to an assault case where numerous threats were made, but it may not be material if the assault was done with a knife. In a trial for damages in an auto accident case, the fact that the defendant had been drinking might be relevant to the defendant's state of mind before the accident and material to proving liability for the accident. However, if the defendant had already admitted liability for the accident, the drinking may not be material to the remaining issues of the nature and scope of injuries.

MODERN REQUIREMENT FOR ADMISSIBILITY: RELEVANCY

Relevancy
A basic requirement for the admissibility of evidence is that it tends to prove or disprove a fact in issue.

Under the modern rules, the concept of materiality has been merged into the threshold requirement of **relevancy.** The term *relevant* remains and the term *material* is no longer used separately. This is shown in the modern definition of relevant evidence. Tennessee's definition states that "relevant evidence" means "evidence having any tendency to make the existence of any fact that is of consequence to the determination of the action more probable or less probable than it would be without the evidence."[1] As can be seen by this definition, the concepts of relevance and materiality have been merged. Relevance is shown in the words "having any tendency to make the existence of any fact . . . more probable or less probable than it would be without the evidence." Materiality is shown by the words "any fact that is of consequence to the determination of the action." To be relevant, evidence must have a tendency to prove or disprove a material fact in issue.

What is Relevancy?

Probative
Tends to prove something.

Evidence is relevant when it tends to prove or disprove a fact in issue (see Exhibit 5.1). In order to satisfy the relevance requirement, evidence must be **probative;** that is, it must *tend* to prove something. However, it does not *have* to actually prove anything. It must simply tend to be more probable than not in proving or disproving something at issue in a case. As a Pennsylvania court noted, "Evidence which tends to establish some fact material to the case, or which tends to make a fact at issue more or less probable, is relevant."[2]

EXHIBIT 5.1   Comparing Definitions of "Relevant Evidence"

Ohio Rules of Evidence
Rule 401. "Relevant evidence" means evidence having any tendency to make the existence of any fact that is of consequence to the determination of the action more probable or less probable than it would be without the evidence.

Florida Statutes
Sec. 90.401. Relevant evidence is evidence tending to prove or disprove a material fact.

Georgia Code
Sec. 24–2–1. Evidence must relate to the questions being tried by the jury and bear upon them either directly or indirectly. Irrelevant matter should be excluded.

Even the slightest tendency is sufficient. If we are trying to prove that the defendant forged a document using a red pen, the fact that the defendant owned a red pen does not, standing alone, prove that this same red pen was used in the forgery or that the defendant actually forged the document. It may, however, be relevant because it tends to shed some light on and add another piece to the puzzle of who forged the document.

Standard of Probability

The test here is the **standard of probability:** Is it more probable than it would be without the evidence? If so, the standard has been met and the evidence is deemed relevant. More probable than not is a fairly low standard and, when in doubt, courts tend to admit evidence as relevant.

Standard of Probability
Evidence is relevant if what it tends to show would be more probable than it would be without the evidence.

Doctrine of the Scintilla Rule

Some courts look to the **Doctrine of the Scintilla Rule.** This rule holds that, "where there is any evidence, however slight, tending to support a material issue, the case must go to the jury as the exclusive judges of the weight of the evidence, although the judge may be of the opinion that the weight of the evidence is insufficient to support the issue. Accordingly, it has been often written that, although the testimony may be highly improbable, the court should submit the case to the jury."[3]

Doctrine of Scintilla Rule
Where there is any evidence, however slight, tending to support a material issue, it must be left up to the jury to decide.

EVIDENTIARY CHECKLIST 5.1

Test for Relevance
- ☐   Evidence must relate to a fact of consequence to the determination of the action.
- ☐   Evidence must have a tendency to make the existence of this fact more or less probable than it would be without the evidence.

Is Evidence Relevant When it Exceeds the Scope of the Matter at Issue?

The question before the court in the following sex discrimination case questions relevance, where the plaintiff seeks to introduce evidence that she was asked by a supervisor to have sexual relations. This would be relevant in a sexual harasssment case, but is it also relevant and admissible in a sex discrimination case?

group 3: case 5

CASE

Rutherford v. Harris County, Texas

United States Court of Appeals for the Fifth Circuit. No. 98-20623 (1999).
Appeal from the United States District Court for the Southern District of Texas.

Fitzwater, District Judge.

A county deputy constable who contended she had been passed over for promotion and subjected to adverse employment actions based on her sex sued her employer for discriminating against her in violation of Title VII of the Civil Rights Act of 1964. A jury found in her favor and the district court awarded damages, front pay, back pay, prejudgment interest, attorney's fees, and injunctive relief. The employer's appeal presents questions concerning the sufficiency of the evidence and the propriety of various evidentiary rulings. . . .

. . . Harris County complains that the district court abused its discretion by permitting Rutherford to introduce evidence that Sgt. Wells had asked her to have sexual relations with him. It argues that in Rutherford's Equal Employment Opportunity Commission (EEOC) charge, and in her affidavit in support of her separate EEOC retaliation charge, she referred to sex discrimination, not sexual harassment. Harris County points out that the district court granted summary judgment before trial because Rutherford had not exhausted her administrative remedies with respect to any sexual harassment claims. It maintains that the court abused its discretion in overruling its objection because the evidence exceeded the scope of Rutherford's EEOC charges and was irrelevant in a case where the sexual harassment claim had been dismissed before trial. Harris County argues that the court's ruling prejudiced it severely.

The district court did not abuse its discretion in allowing Rutherford to offer proof that Sgt. Wells had asked her to have sexual relations with him. Evidence concerning a claim that is not on trial because it exceeds the scope of the plaintiff's EEOC charge does not automatically lose its relevance or probative

value to a claim that remains. Cf. *United Air Lines, Inc. v. Evans*, 431 U.S. 553, 558 (1977) (holding that untimely charges may still constitute relevant background evidence in a proceeding in which current practice is at issue).

. . . .

Evidence is relevant if it has any tendency to make the existence of any fact of consequence to the determination of the action more probable or less probable than it would be without the evidence. Fed. R. Evid. 401. Rutherford introduced proof of Sgt. Wells' conduct in order to prove discriminatory intent. At a minimum, the evidence was relevant to Rutherford's attempt to refute Harris County's contention that it opted not to promote her to the full-time deputy position because she had made numerous, severe errors in accident reports. Rutherford sought to demonstrate that Corporal Hartley began closely scrutinizing and heavily criticizing her work only after his superior—Sgt. Wells—requested unsuccessfully that Rutherford have sexual relations with him. Moreover, in January 1995, before being rebuffed, Sgt. Wells gave Rutherford high marks concerning her written work. In September 1995, after she had spurned Sgt. Wells' overtures, Corporal Hartley downgraded her severely. The district court did not abuse its discretion in admitting this evidence.

. . . .

Second, when we view this evidence in the context of the entire record, as we must, and assess it as it relates to Rutherford's failure to promote claim, which is the only relevant context in light of our ruling that Harris County is entitled to a new trial of the disparate treatment claim, we are unable to say that the ruling excluding the evidence caused Harris County substantial prejudice. The focus of the promotion claim was Rutherford's proof that she was more qualified than was Green and that Harris County's articulated reasons for not promoting her were pretextual. We decline to reverse the verdict based on the district court's evidentiary rulings.

LEGAL ANALYSIS AND WRITING 5.1

The following questions are based on the *How to Brief a Legal Case* format shown in the Appendix. Use this format to answer the following questions:

1. Summarize the facts in the previous case.
2. What is the legal issue?
3. What did the appellate court decide?
4. Why did the court decide this way?
5. Do you agree with the court's reasoning? Explain why or why not.

LEGAL RESEARCH USING THE INTERNET SKILLS 5.1

Try to find this case or another one that refers to it online! Check out one of the legal research web sites below, go to the federal circuit for this court decision, and use their "Search" feature to find this case or another case that refers to it. In the "Search" field, enter the cite or case name. If you have access to Westlaw or Lexis, try to find this case using one of these legal search sites.

1. U.S. Courts Site with Links to all Circuit Courts of Appeal (http://www.uscourts.gov/links.html)
2. National Center for State Courts—State and Federal Court Web Sites (http://www.ncsconline.org/D_kis/info_court_web_sites.html#federal)
3. FindLaw (http://guide.lp.findlaw.com/casecode/)

What's in a Prison Gang Name?

In the following case, the Supreme Court looks at whether identifying a defendant as a member of a prison gang is relevant use of character evidence or "mere abstract beliefs" that are irrelevant.

CASE

Dawson v. Delaware

503 U.S. 159 (1992).

Chief Justice Rehnquist delivered the opinion of the Court.

The question presented in this case is whether the First and Fourteenth Amendments prohibit the introduction in a capital sentencing proceeding of the fact that the defendant was a member of an organization called the Aryan Brotherhood, where the evidence has no relevance to the issues being decided in the proceeding. We hold that they do. Shortly after midnight on December 1, 1986, petitioner David Dawson and three other inmates escaped from the Delaware Correctional Center near Smyrna, Delaware. Dawson stole a car and headed south, while the other three inmates stole another car and drove north. Early that morning, Dawson burglarized a house near Kenton, Delaware, stealing a motorcycle jacket, several pocket watches, and containers of loose change. He then proceeded to the home of Richard and Madeline Kisner, located about half a mile from the burglary site. Mrs. Kisner was alone in the house, preparing to leave for work. Dawson brutally murdered Mrs. Kisner, stole the Kisners' car and some money, and fled further south.

He reappeared later that evening at [a bar] in Milford, Delaware, wearing a motorcycle jacket that was too big for him. While at the bar, Dawson introduced himself to Patty Dennis, and told her that his name was "Abaddon," which he said meant "one of Satan's disciples." Dawson was subsequently asked to leave the bar. Later that evening, a Delaware state police officer responded to a call to investigate a one-car accident. The car involved in the accident had been stolen from a location near the . . . bar, and had been driven into a ditch, but the driver had left the scene. The police began a house-to-house search for Dawson, and found him at 5:25 the next morning, on the floor of a Cadillac parked about three-tenths of a mile from the accident site.

A jury convicted Dawson of first-degree murder, possession of a deadly weapon during the commission of a felony, and various other crimes. The trial court then conducted a penalty hearing before the jury to determine whether Dawson should be sentenced to death for the first-degree murder conviction. The prosecution gave notice that it intended to introduce (1) expert testimony regarding the origin and nature of the Aryan Brotherhood, as well as the fact that Dawson had the words "Aryan Brotherhood" tattooed on the back of his right hand, (2) testimony that Dawson referred to himself as "Abaddon" and had the name "Abaddon" tattooed in red letters across his stomach, and (3) photographs of multiple swastika tattoos on Dawson's back and a picture of a swastika he had painted on the wall of his prison cell. Dawson argued that this evidence was inflammatory and irrelevant, and that its admission would violate his rights under the First and Fourteenth Amendments.

Before the penalty phase began, the parties agreed to a stipulation regarding the Aryan Brotherhood evidence. The stipulation provided: "The Aryan Brotherhood refers to a white racist prison gang that began in the 1960s in California in response to other gangs of racial minorities. Separate gangs calling themselves the Aryan Brotherhood now exist in many state prisons including Delaware."

In return for Dawson's agreement to the stipulation, the prosecution agreed not to call any expert witnesses to testify about the Aryan Brotherhood . . . . At the penalty hearing, the prosecution read the stipulation to the jury and introduced evidence that Dawson had tattooed the words "Aryan Brotherhood" on his hand. The trial judge permitted the prosecution to present the evidence related to the name "Abaddon" as well, but excluded all of the swastika evidence. In addition, the prosecution submitted proof of Dawson's lengthy criminal record. Dawson, in turn, presented mitigating evidence based on the testimony of two family members and on the fact that he had earned good time

credits in prison for enrolling in various drug and alcohol programs. The jury found three statutory aggravating circumstances, each making Dawson eligible for the death penalty under Delaware law; it determined (1) that the murder was committed by an escaped prisoner, (2) that the murder was committed during the commission of a burglary, and (3) that the murder was committed for pecuniary gain. The jury further concluded that the aggravating evidence outweighed the mitigating evidence, and recommended that Dawson be sentenced to death. The trial court, bound by that recommendation, imposed the death penalty.

The Supreme Court of Delaware affirmed the convictions and the death sentence. The court rejected Dawson's claim that the evidence concerning the Aryan Brotherhood and his use of the name "Abaddon" should have been excluded from the penalty hearing. It observed that, having found at least one statutory aggravating factor, the jury was "required to make an individualized determination of whether Dawson should be executed or incarcerated for life, based upon Dawson's character, his record and the circumstances of the crime," and that it was desirable for the jury to have as much information before it as possible when making that decision. The court acknowledged that the Constitution would prohibit the consideration of certain irrelevant factors during the sentencing process, but stated that "punishing a person for expressing his views or for associating with certain people is substantially different from allowing . . . evidence of [the defendant's] character [to be considered] where that character is a relevant inquiry." Because the evidence relating to the Aryan Brotherhood and the name "Abaddon" properly focused the jury's attention on Dawson's character, and did not appeal to the jury's prejudices concerning race, religion, or political affiliation, the court upheld its introduction during the penalty phase. We granted certiorari, 499 U.S. 946 (1991), to consider whether the admission of this evidence was constitutional error. We hold that its admission in this case was error, and so reverse.

We have held that the First Amendment protects an individual's right to join groups and associate with others holding similar beliefs. Because his right to associate with the Aryan Brotherhood is constitutionally protected, Dawson argues, admission of evidence related to that association at his penalty hearing violated his constitutional rights. . . . We think this submission is, in the light of our decided cases, too broad. [Prior] cases emphasize that "the sentencing authority has always been free to consider a wide range of relevant material." *Payne v. Tennessee*, 501 U.S. 808 (1991) ("[A] judge may appropriately conduct an inquiry broad in scope, largely unlimited either as to the kind of information he may consider, or the source from which it may come"); *Williams v. New York*, 337 U.S. 241 (1949). We have previously upheld the consideration, in a capital sentencing proceeding, of evidence of racial intolerance and subversive advocacy where such evidence was relevant to the issues involved.

In *Barclay v. Florida*, 463 U.S. 939 (1983), for example, we held that a sentencing judge in a capital case might properly take into consideration "the elements of racial hatred" in Barclay's crime as well as "Barclay's desire to start a race war." One year later, in *United States v. Abel*, 469 U.S. 45 (1984), we held that the Government could impeach a defense witness by showing that both the defendant and the witness were members of the Aryan Brotherhood, and that members were sworn to lie on behalf of each other. We held the evidence admissible to show bias, even assuming that membership in the organization was among the associational freedoms protected by the First Amendment. Though *Abel* did not involve a capital sentencing proceeding, its logic is perfectly applicable to such a proceeding. We therefore conclude that the Constitution does not erect a per se barrier to the admission of evidence concerning one's beliefs and associations at sentencing simply because those beliefs and associations are protected by the First Amendment.

Although we cannot accept Dawson's broad submission, we nevertheless agree with him that, in this case, the receipt into evidence of the stipulation regarding his membership in the Aryan Brotherhood was constitutional error. Before the penalty hearing, the prosecution claimed that its expert witness would show that the Aryan Brotherhood is a white racist prison gang that is associated with drugs and violent escape attempts at prisons, and that advocates the murder of fellow inmates. If credible and otherwise admissible evidence to that effect had been presented, we would have a much different case. But, after reaching an agreement with Dawson, the prosecution limited its proof regarding the Aryan Brotherhood to the stipulation. The brief stipulation proved only that an Aryan Brotherhood prison gang originated in California in the 1960s, that it entertains white racist beliefs,

and that a separate gang in the Delaware prison system calls itself the Aryan Brotherhood. We conclude that the narrowness of the stipulation left the Aryan Brotherhood evidence totally without relevance to Dawson's sentencing proceeding.

. . . .

Because the prosecution did not prove that the Aryan Brotherhood had committed any unlawful or violent acts, or had even endorsed such acts, the Aryan Brotherhood evidence was also not relevant to help prove any aggravating circumstance. In many cases, for example, associational evidence might serve a legitimate purpose in showing that a defendant represents a future danger to society. A defendant's membership in an organization that endorses the killing of any identifiable group, for example, might be relevant to a jury's inquiry into whether the defendant will be dangerous in the future. Other evidence concerning a defendant's associations might be relevant in proving other aggravating circumstances. But the inference which the jury was invited to draw in this case tended to prove nothing more than the abstract beliefs of the Delaware chapter. Delaware counters that even these abstract beliefs constitute a portion of Dawson's "character," and thus are admissible in their own right under Delaware law.

Whatever label is given to the evidence presented, however, we conclude that Dawson's First Amendment rights were violated by the admission of the Aryan Brotherhood evidence in this case, because the evidence proved nothing more than Dawson's abstract beliefs. Cf. *Texas v. Johnson*, 491 U.S. 397(1989) ("[T]he government may not prohibit the expression of an idea simply because society finds the idea itself offensive or disagreeable"). Delaware might have avoided this problem if it had presented evidence showing more than mere abstract beliefs on Dawson's part, but, on the present record, one is left with the feeling that the Aryan Brotherhood evidence was employed simply because the jury would find these beliefs morally reprehensible. Because Delaware failed to do more, we cannot find the evidence was properly admitted as relevant character evidence.

. . . .

For the foregoing reasons, we vacate the judgment of the Supreme Court of Delaware, and remand for further proceedings not inconsistent with this opinion.

It is so ordered.

LEGAL ANALYSIS AND WRITING 5.2

The following questions are based on the *How to Brief a Legal Case* format shown in the Appendix. Use this format to answer the following questions:

1. Summarize the facts in the previous case.
2. What is the legal issue?
3. What did the appellate court decide?
4. Why did the court decide this way?
5. Do you agree with the court's reasoning? Explain why or why not.

LEGAL RESEARCH USING THE INTERNET SKILLS 5.2

Find and read this Supreme Court case online! Check out one of the legal research web sites below and use their "Search" feature to find this case. In the "Search" field, enter the cite or case name.

1. FindLaw U.S. Supreme Court Decisions (http://www.findlaw.com/casecode/supreme.html)
2. U.S. Supreme Court (http://www.supremecourtus.gov/)
3. Supreme Court Collection of Cornell Law School (http://supct.law.cornell.edu/supct/)

CRITICAL THINKING QUESTIONS 5.1

1. In the definition of relevance, what does it mean that evidence must have a tendency to make the existence of a fact more or less probable than it would be without the evidence?
2. How would this be established?
3. In the *Rutherford* case, how did the court find relevance when the evidence referred to sex discrimination, and not the sexual harassment that the plaintiff was complaining of?
4. Why did the Court in the *Dawson* case decide that the Aryan evidence was not relevant and what should the prosecution have done to ensure that it was relevant?

LOGICAL AND LEGAL RELEVANCE

Logical Relevance
When evidence tends to prove or disprove a fact in issue.

Legal Relevance
Even when relevant, evidence is not admissible if it violates any other evidence rule or law.

The concept of relevance includes **logical relevance** and **legal relevance,** both of which are necessary in order for evidence to be admissible. Logical relevance is established if evidence tends to prove or disprove a fact in issue. The evidence must logically pertain to the case and tend to prove or disprove something related to the determination of the case. This is really the normal definition of relevance. Legal relevance, however, pertains to the legal admissibility of relevant evidence. Legal relevance requires that evidence not violate any other evidence rule or law. For example, there are evidentiary rules that exclude hearsay or prejudicial evidence, even when relevant to a case.

Practice Tip 5.1

Logical and Legal Relevance
Remember that evidence needs to satisfy both logical and legal relevance. It must tend to prove or disprove a fact in issue, but, even so it will not be admissible if it violates any other evidence rule or law.

Relevant Evidence Is Generally Admissible—Irrelevant Evidence Is Inadmissible

A fundamental rule of evidence is that relevant evidence is admissible and evidence that is not relevant is not admissible (see Exhibit 5.2).[4] This rule makes it clear that, unless otherwise limited or prohibited, all relevant evidence is admissible. However, the concept of *legal relevance* is also found within this rule and modifies this principle by setting out the sources which may result in relevant evidence being excluded. There may be constitutional provisions, statutes, or other laws that even provide for the exclusion of relevant evidence. The Constitution, for example, may limit or exclude evidence seized in violation of the Fourth Amendment protection against unreasonable search or a confession obtained in violation of the Fifth Amendment protection against self-incrimination. The Rules of Evidence themselves provide exclusions against the admission of certain evidence, even when relevant. Examples of this may include evidence that wastes time, is confusing, or is prejudicial. Other examples include hearsay, privileged communications, and exclusions of evidence that does not meet the best or original evidence rule.

EXHIBIT 5.2   Relevant Evidence Generally Admissible—Irrelevant Evidence Inadmissible

Texas Rules of Evidence
Rule 402. All relevant evidence is admissible, except as otherwise provided by Constitution, by statute, by these rules, or by other rules prescribed pursuant to statutory authority. Evidence which is not relevant is inadmissible.

YOU BE THE JUDGE 5.1

In a civil action for negligence, plaintiff alleges that defendant caused a car accident by talking on a cell phone and not paying attention to traffic. Plaintiff wants to introduce evidence that defendant had a prior conviction for drunk driving.
    Would you allow this evidence? Why or why not?

EXCLUSION OF RELEVANT EVIDENCE ON GROUNDS OF PREJUDICE

Even when relevant, evidence may still be excluded if its probative value is substantially outweighed by the danger of unfair prejudice to the trier of fact. This can present a difficult decision for the trial judge, who must rule on what constitutes prejudice. Evidence is generally presented in a case to try and persuade or influence the trier of fact. This evidence, if relevant to the matter at issue, will often have an adverse and prejudicial effect on an opponent's case. The key, then, is whether the prejudice is *unfair*. Evidence would not be unfairly prejudicial unless "its primary purpose or effect is to appeal to a jury's sympathies or to provoke horror or a desire to punish."[5] An example of this would be the introduction of gruesome photos in a negligence case involving an accident. The Supreme Court addressed this concept further in a criminal case, defining unfair prejudice as evidence that "speaks to the capacity of some concededly relevant evidence to lure the factfinder into declaring guilt on a ground different from proof specific to the offense charged. . . . "[6] An example of this might be evidence of prior bad acts or crimes committed by a defendant. This evidence might be relevant to prove that the defendant had a history of committing similar crimes, but this fact might also unfairly prejudice the jury into believing that if the defendant did it once, he or she would do it again.

CRITICAL THINKING QUESTIONS 5.2

1. What is the difference between logical and legal relevance?
2. What would be some examples of legal relevance?
3. How do you think public policy has influenced the relevant evidence exclusions, such as prejudicial, wasting time, and confusing the jury?
4. When a goal of presenting evidence is to prejudice and destroy the opponent's case, how can a court determine when evidence must be excluded as too prejudicial?
5. What would constitute wasting of time or confusing the jury? Give examples.

YOU BE THE JUDGE 5.2

Defendant is on trial for treason in being an "American Taliban"—one who traveled to Afghanistan, joined the Taliban, and took up arms against American soldiers. The prosecution wants to introduce photographs and film of the attacks against the World Trade Center towers, even though the defendant has not been charged in connection with these acts. The defense objects to these photographs and film as irrelevant and prejudicial.

Would you allow this evidence? Why or why not?

EXCLUSION OF RELEVANT EVIDENCE ON GROUNDS OF CONFUSION, OR WASTE OF TIME

Relevant evidence may also be excluded if it causes a confusion of the issues, misleads the jury, or results in undue delay, waste of time, or needless presentation of cumulative evidence (see Exhibit 5.3). A common example is when one side to an action wants to call numerous witnesses to the stand to testify to the same thing. For example, each witness will testify that he or she saw the defendant's car in a particular location, or each witness heard defendant threaten the plaintiff. This evidence may be relevant, but the court may limit the number of witnesses who can be called to testify. To allow too many witnesses to provide the very same testimony could be unnecessarily repetitive and not only waste time, but confuse the jury about the importance of so many witnesses testifying about the same thing.

EXHIBIT 5.3   Exclusion of Relevant Evidence on Grounds of Prejudice, Confusion, or Waste of Time

Wyoming Rules of Evidence
Rule 403. Although relevant, evidence may be excluded if its probative value is substantially outweighed by the danger of unfair prejudice, confusion of the issues, or misleading the jury, or by considerations of undue delay, waste of time, or needless presentation of cumulative evidence.

Balancing Test

Most courts have adopted a **balancing test** where the probative value of evidence is weighed against the prejudicial effect that allowing the evidence might produce. The court looks at whether the danger of prejudice is "unfair" and whether it "substantially" outweighs the relevance. Unfair prejudice might unduly influence or cause a jury or factfinder to reach an emotional decision, rather than one based on logic and the evidence.

Balancing Test
Weighs probative value of evidence against its prejudicial effect.

EVIDENTIARY CHECKLIST 5.2

Balancing Test
☐   Probative Value _____ Prejudicial Effect on Jury
                            ^

What Constitutes "Prejudicial?"

In the following Supreme Court case, the issue is whether it constitutes prejudice when a trial court "spurns" a defendant's offer to concede to a prior conviction. In this case, the defendant wanted to stipulate to a prior conviction in general rather than have the prosecution produce the full record of the prior conviction, including the name and nature of the offense.

CASE

Johnny Lynn Old Chief v. United States
519 U.S. 172 (1997).
[Johnny Old Chief was charged with assault with a dangerous weapon and for violation of 18 U.S.C. 922(g)(1) which makes it unlawful for anyone "who has been convicted in any court, of a crime punishable by imprisonment for a term exceeding one year" to "possess . . . any firearm." This prior conviction was for an assault causing serious bodily injury. To avoid having this prior conviction revealed to the jury, the defendant offered to stipulate to the fact of the prior conviction in exchange for the prosecution not offering any evidence regarding the prior conviction other than

to say that defendant had "been convicted of a crime punishable by imprisonment exceeding one (1) year." The prosecutor refused to join in a stipulation, insisting on the prosecution's right to prove the case his own way, and the District Court agreed, ruling orally that, "If he doesn't want to stipulate, he doesn't have to." At trial, over renewed objection, the prosecution introduced evidence of Old Chief's prior conviction, which disclosed that on December 18, 1988, he "did knowingly and unlawfully assault" an individual resulting in serious bodily injury, for which Old Chief was sentenced to five years' imprisonment. After hearing the evidence, the jury found Old

Chief guilty on all counts, and he appealed, arguing the offer to stipulate to the fact of the prior conviction rendered evidence of the name and nature of the offense inadmissible under Rule 403 of the Federal Rules of Evidence, the danger being that unfair prejudice from that evidence would substantially outweigh its probative value.]

Justice Souter delivered the opinion of the Court.

Subject to certain limitations, 18 U.S.C. 922(g)(1) prohibits possession of a firearm by anyone with a prior felony conviction, which the Government can prove by introducing a record of judgment or similar evidence identifying the previous offense. Fearing prejudice if the jury learns the nature of the earlier crime, defendants sometimes seek to avoid such an informative disclosure by offering to concede the fact of the prior conviction. The issue here is whether a district court abuses its discretion if it spurns such an offer and admits the full record of a prior judgment, when the name or nature of the prior offense raises the risk of a verdict tainted by improper considerations, and when the purpose of the evidence is solely to prove the element of prior conviction. We hold that it does.

. . . .

As a threshold matter, there is Old Chief's erroneous argument that the name of his prior offense as contained in the record of conviction is irrelevant to the prior-conviction element, and for that reason inadmissible under Rule 402 of the Federal Rules of Evidence. Rule 401 defines relevant evidence as having "any tendency to make the existence of any fact that is of consequence to the determination of the action more probable or less probable than it would be without the evidence." To be sure, the fact that Old Chief's prior conviction was for assault resulting in serious bodily injury rather than, say, for theft was not itself an ultimate fact, as if the statute had specifically required proof of injurious assault. But its demonstration was a step on one evidentiary route to the ultimate fact, since it served to place Old Chief within a particular subclass of offenders for whom firearms possession is outlawed by 922(g)(1). A documentary record of the conviction for that named offense was thus relevant evidence in making Old Chief's 922(g)(1) status more probable than it would have been without the evidence.

. . . .

The principal issue is the scope of a trial judge's discretion under Rule 403, which authorizes exclusion of relevant evidence when its "probative value is substantially outweighed by the danger of unfair prejudice, confusion of the issues, or misleading the jury, or by considerations of undue delay, waste of time, or needless presentation of cumulative evidence." Old Chief relies on the danger of unfair prejudice.

. . . .

The term "unfair prejudice," as to a criminal defendant, speaks to the capacity of some concededly relevant evidence to lure the factfinder into declaring guilt on a ground different from proof specific to the offense charged. . . . Such improper grounds certainly include the one that Old Chief points to here: generalizing a defendant's earlier bad act into bad character and taking that as raising the odds that he did the later bad act now charged (or, worse, as calling for preventive conviction even if he should happen to be innocent momentarily). As then-Judge Breyer put it, "Although . . . 'propensity evidence' is relevant, the risk that a jury will convict for crimes other than those charged—or that, uncertain of guilt, it will convict anyway because a bad person deserves punishment—creates a prejudicial effect that outweighs ordinary relevance." *United States v. Moccia*, 681 F.2d 61 (CA1 1982). . . .

Rule of Evidence 404(b) reflects this common-law tradition by addressing propensity reasoning directly: "Evidence of other crimes, wrongs, or acts is not admissible to prove the character of a person in order to show action in conformity therewith." There is, accordingly, no question that propensity would be an "improper basis" for conviction and that evidence of a prior conviction is subject to analysis under Rule 403 for relative probative value and for prejudicial risk of misuse as propensity evidence.

. . . .

In dealing with the specific problem raised by 922(g)(1) and its prior-conviction element, there can be no question that evidence of the name or nature of the prior offense generally carries a risk of unfair prejudice to the defendant. That risk will vary from case to case, for the reasons already given, but will be substantial whenever the official record offered by the Government would be arresting enough to lure a juror into a sequence of bad character reasoning. Where a prior conviction was for a gun crime or one similar to other charges in a pending case the risk of unfair prejudice would be especially obvious, and Old Chief sensibly worried that the prejudicial effect of his prior assault conviction, significant enough with respect to the current gun charges alone, would take on added weight from the related assault charge against him.

. . . .

The District Court was . . . presented with alternative, relevant, admissible evidence of the prior conviction by Old Chief's offer to stipulate. Old Chief's proffered admission would, in fact, have been not merely relevant but seemingly conclusive evidence of the element. . . . As a consequence, although the name of the prior offense may have been technically relevant, it addressed no detail in the definition of the prior-conviction element that would not have been covered by the stipulation or admission. Logic, then, seems to side with Old Chief.

. . . .

For purposes of the Rule 403 weighing of the probative against the prejudicial, the functions of the competing evidence are distinguishable only by the risk inherent in the one and wholly absent from the other. In this case, as in any other in which the prior conviction is for an offense likely to support conviction on some improper ground, the only reasonable conclusion was that the risk of unfair prejudice did substantially outweigh the discounted probative value of the record of conviction, and it was an abuse of discretion to admit the record when an admission was available . . . .

The judgment is reversed, and the case is remanded to the Ninth Circuit for further proceedings consistent with this opinion.

Dissent: Justice O'Connor, with whom the Chief Justice, Justice Scalia, and Justice Thomas join, dissenting.

The Court today announces a rule that misapplies Federal Rule of Evidence 403 and upsets, without explanation, longstanding precedent regarding criminal prosecutions. I do not agree that the Government's introduction of evidence that reveals the name and basic nature of a defendant's prior felony conviction in a prosecution brought under 18 U.S.C. 922(g)(1) "unfairly" prejudices the defendant within the meaning of Rule 403. Nor do I agree with the Court's newly minted rule that

a defendant charged with violating 922(g)(1) can force the Government to accept his concession to the prior conviction element of that offense, thereby precluding the Government from offering evidence on this point. I therefore dissent.

I

Rule 403 provides that a district court may exclude relevant evidence if, among other things, "its probative value is substantially outweighed by the danger of unfair prejudice." Certainly, Rule 403 does not permit the court to exclude the Government's evidence simply because it may hurt the defendant. As a threshold matter, evidence is excludable only if it is "unfairly" prejudicial, in that it has "an undue tendency to suggest decision on an improper basis." Advisory Committee's Note on Fed. Rule Evid. 403, 28 U.S.C. App., p. 860. . . . Perhaps petitioner's case was damaged when the jury discovered that he previously had committed a felony and heard the name of his crime. But I cannot agree with the Court that it was unfairly prejudicial for the Government to establish an essential element of its case against petitioner with direct proof of his prior conviction.

The structure of 922(g)(1) itself shows that Congress envisioned jurors' learning the name and basic nature of the defendant's prior offense. . . . Section 922(g)(1) does not merely prohibit the possession of firearms by "felons," nor does it apply to all prior felony convictions. . . . Within the meaning of 922(g)(1), . . . "a crime" is not an abstract or metaphysical concept. Rather, the Government must prove that the defendant committed a particular crime. . . .

Even more fundamentally, in our system of justice, a person is not simply convicted of "a crime" or "a felony." Rather, he is found guilty of a specified offense, almost always because he violated a specific statutory prohibition. For example, in the words of the order that the Government offered to prove petitioner's prior conviction in this case, petitioner "did knowingly and unlawfully assault Rory Dean Fenner, said assault resulting in serious bodily injury. . . . " That a variety of crimes would have satisfied the prior conviction element of the 922(g)(1) offense does not detract from the fact that petitioner committed a specific offense. The name and basic nature of petitioner's crime are inseparable from the fact of his earlier conviction and were therefore admissible to prove petitioner's guilt.

. . . .

The principle is illustrated by the evidence that was admitted at petitioner's trial to prove the other element of the 922(g)(1) offense—possession of a "firearm." The Government submitted evidence showing that petitioner possessed a 9mm semiautomatic pistol. Although petitioner's possession of any number of weapons would have satisfied the requirements of 922(g)(1), obviously the Government was entitled to prove with specific evidence that petitioner possessed the weapon he did. In the same vein, consider a murder case. Surely the Government can submit proof establishing the victim's identity, even though, strictly speaking, the jury has no "need" to know the victim's name, and even though the victim might be a particularly well loved public figure. The same logic should govern proof of the prior conviction element of the 922(g)(1) offense. That is, the Government ought to be able to prove, with specific evidence, that petitioner committed a crime that came within 922(g)(1)'s coverage.

The Court never explains precisely why it constitutes "unfair" prejudice for the Government to directly prove an essential element of the 922(g)(1) offense with evidence that reveals the name or basic nature of the defendant's prior conviction. It simply notes that such evidence may lead a jury to conclude that the defendant has a propensity to commit crime, thereby raising the odds that the jury would find that he committed the crime with which he is currently charged. With a nod to the part of Rule 404(b) that says "evidence of other crimes, wrongs, or acts is not admissible to prove the character of a person in order to show action in conformity therewith," the Court writes:

> "There is, accordingly, no question that propensity would be an 'improper basis' for conviction and that evidence of a prior conviction is subject to analysis under Rule 403 for relative probative value and for prejudicial risk of misuse as propensity evidence."

A few pages later, it leaps to the conclusion that there can be "no question that evidence of the name or nature of the prior offense generally carries a risk of unfair prejudice to the defendant."

Yes, to be sure, Rule 404(b) provides that "evidence of other crimes, wrongs, or acts is not admissible to prove the character of a person in order to show action in conformity therewith." But Rule 404(b) does not end there. It expressly contemplates the admission of evidence of prior crimes for other purposes, "such as proof of motive, opportunity, intent, preparation, plan, knowledge, identity, or absence of mistake or accident." The list is plainly not exhaustive, and where, as here, a prior conviction is an element of the charged offense, neither Rule 404(b) nor Rule 403 can bar its admission. The reason is simple: In a prosecution brought under 922(g)(1), the Government does not submit evidence of a past crime to prove the defendant's bad character or to "show action in conformity therewith." It tenders the evidence as direct proof of a necessary element of the offense with which it has charged the defendant. To say, as the Court does, that it "unfairly" prejudices the defendant for the Government to establish its 922(g)(1) case with evidence showing that, in fact, the defendant did commit a prior offense misreads the Rules of Evidence and defies common sense.

. . . .

The Court manufactures a new rule that, in a 922(g)(1) case, a defendant can force the Government to accept his admission to the prior felony conviction element of the offense, thereby precluding the Government from offering evidence to directly prove a necessary element of its case. I cannot agree that it "unfairly" prejudices a defendant for the Government to prove his prior conviction with evidence that reveals the name or basic nature of his past crime. Like it or not, Congress chose to make a defendant's prior criminal conviction one of the two elements of the 922(g)(1) offense. Moreover, crimes have names; a defendant is not convicted of some indeterminate, unspecified "crime." Nor do I think that Federal Rule of Evidence 403 can be read to obviate the well accepted principle, grounded in both the Constitution and in our precedent, that the Government may not be forced to accept a defendant's concession to an element of a charged offense as proof of that element. I respectfully dissent.

◆

The following questions are based on the *How to Brief a Legal Case* format shown in the Appendix. Use this format to answer the following questions:

1. Summarize the facts in the previous case.
2. What is the legal issue?
3. What did the appellate court decide?
4. Why did the court decide this way?
5. Do you agree with the court's reasoning? Explain why or why not.

Find and read this Supreme Court case online! Check out one of the legal research web sites below and use their "Search" feature to find this case. In the "Search" field, enter the cite or case name.

1. FindLaw U.S. Supreme Court Decisions (http://www.findlaw.com/casecode/supreme.html)
2. U.S. Supreme Court (http://www.supremecourtus.gov/)
3. Supreme Court Collection of Cornell Law School (http://supct.law.cornell.edu/supct/)

Is There Mathematical Relevance?

The following case is often used in law schools to show how evidence of mathematical probability can be taken to extremes, especially when not backed up by proper foundation or relevance. This California Supreme Court decision looks at whether a "trial by mathematics" can result in the prejudicial stacking of the "odds" against a defendant.

Group 2 Case #6

CASE

People v. Collins

Supreme Court of California.

68 Cal. 2d 319 (1968).

Sullivan, J.

We deal here with the novel question whether evidence of mathematical probability has been properly introduced and used by the prosecution in a criminal case. While we discern no inherent incompatibility between the disciplines of law and mathematics and intend no general disapproval or disparagement of the latter as an auxiliary in the factfinding processes of the former, we cannot uphold the technique employed in the instant case. As we explain in detail, infra, the testimony as to

mathematical probability infected the case with fatal error and distorted the jury's traditional role of determining guilt or innocence according to long-settled rules. Mathematics, a veritable sorcerer in our computerized society, while assisting the trier of fact in the search for truth, must not cast a spell over him. We conclude that on the record before us defendant should not have had his guilt determined by the odds and that he is entitled to a new trial. We reverse the judgment.

A jury found defendant Malcolm Ricardo Collins and his wife defendant Janet Louise Collins guilty of second degree robbery. Malcolm appeals from the judgment of conviction. Janet has not appealed.

On June 18, 1964, about 11:30 A.M. Mrs. Juanita Brooks, who had been shopping, was walking home along an alley in the San Pedro area of the City of Los Angeles. She was pulling behind her a wicker basket carryall containing groceries and had her purse on top of the packages. She was using a cane. As she stooped down to pick up an empty carton, she was suddenly pushed to the ground by a person whom she neither saw nor heard approach. She was stunned by the fall and felt some pain. She managed to look up and saw a young woman running from the scene. According to Mrs. Brooks the latter appeared to weigh about 145 pounds, was wearing "something dark," and had hair "between a dark blond and a light blond," but lighter than the color of defendant Janet Collins' hair as it appeared at trial. Immediately after the incident, Mrs. Brooks discovered that her purse, containing between $35 and $40, was missing.

About the same time as the robbery, John Bass, who lived on the street at the end of the alley, was in front of his house watering his lawn. His attention was attracted by "a lot of crying and screaming" coming from the alley. As he looked in that direction, he saw a woman run out of the alley and enter a yellow automobile parked across the street from him. He was unable to give the make of the car. The car started off immediately and pulled wide around another parked vehicle so that in the narrow street it passed within 6 feet of Bass. The latter then saw that it was being driven by a male Negro, wearing a mustache and beard. At the trial Bass identified defendant as the driver of the yellow automobile. However, an attempt was made to impeach his identification by his admission that at the preliminary hearing he testified to an uncertain identification at the police lineup shortly after the attack on Mrs. Brooks, when defendant was beardless.

In his testimony Bass described the woman who ran from the alley as a Caucasian, slightly over 5 feet tall, of ordinary build, with her hair in a dark blonde ponytail, and wearing dark clothing. He further testified that her ponytail was "just like" one which Janet had in a police photograph taken on June 22, 1964.

. . . .

At the 7-day trial the prosecution experienced some difficulty in establishing the identities of the perpetrators of the crime. The victim could not identify Janet and had never seen the defendant. The identification by the witness Bass, who observed the girl run out of the alley and get into the automobile, was incomplete as to Janet and may have been weakened as to defendant. There was also evidence, introduced by the defense, that Janet had worn light-colored clothing on the day in question, but both the victim and Bass testified that the girl they observed had worn dark clothing.

In an apparent attempt to bolster the identifications, the prosecutor called an instructor of mathematics at a state college. Through this witness he sought to establish that, assuming the robbery was committed by a Caucasian woman with a blond ponytail who left the scene accompanied by a Negro with a beard and mustache, there was an overwhelming probability that the crime was committed by any couple answering such distinctive characteristics. The witness testified, in substance, to the "product rule," which states that the probability of the joint occurrence of a number of mutually independent events is equal to the product of the individual probabilities that each of the events will occur. Without presenting any statistical evidence whatsoever in support of the probabilities for the factors selected, the prosecutor then proceeded to have the witness assume probability factors for the various characteristics which he deemed to be shared by the guilty couple and all other couples answering to such distinctive characteristics.

[NOTE: In the example employed for illustrative purposes at the trial, the probability of rolling one die and coming up with a "2" is 1/6; that is, any one of the six faces of a die has one chance in six of landing face up on any particular roll. The probability of rolling two "2s" in succession is 1/6 X 1/6, or 1/36; that is, on only one occasion out of 36 double rolls (or the roll of two dice) will the selected number land face up on each roll or die. . . . Although the prosecutor insisted that the factors he used were only for illustrative purposes—to demonstrate how the probability of the occurrence of mutually independent factors affected the probability that they would occur together—he nevertheless attempted to use factors which he personally related to the distinctive characteristics of defendants. In his argument to the jury he invited the jurors to apply their own factors, and asked defense counsel to suggest what the latter would deem as reasonable. The prosecutor himself proposed the individual probabilities set out in the table below. Although the transcript of the examination of the mathematics instructor and the information volunteered by the prosecutor at that time create some uncertainty as to precisely which of the characteristics the prosecutor assigned to the individual probabilities, he restated in his argument to the jury that they should be as follows:

Characteristic	Individual Probability
A. Partly yellow automobile	1/10
B. Man with mustache	1/4
C. Girl with ponytail	1/10
D. Girl with blonde hair	1/3
E. Negro man with beard	1/10
F. Interracial couple in car	1/1,000

In his brief on appeal defendant agrees that the foregoing appeared on a table presented in the trial court.]

Applying the product rule to his own factors the prosecutor arrived at a probability that there was but one chance in 12 million that any couple possessed the distinctive characteristics of the defendants. Accordingly, under this theory, it was to be inferred that there could be but one chance in 12 million that defendants were innocent and that another equally distinctive couple actually committed the robbery. Expanding on what he had thus purported to suggest as a hypothesis, the prosecutor offered the completely unfounded and improper testimonial assertion that, in his opinion, the factors he had assigned were "conservative estimates" and that, in reality, "the chances of anyone else besides these defendants being there, . . . having every similarity, . . . is something like one in a billion."

Objections were timely made to the mathematician's testimony on the grounds that it was *immaterial*, that it invaded the province of the jury, and that it was based on unfounded assumptions. The objections were "temporarily overruled" and the evidence admitted subject to a motion to strike. When that motion was made at the conclusion of the direct examination, the court denied it, stating that the testimony had been received only for the "purpose of illustrating the mathematical probabilities of various matters, the possibilities for them occurring or re-occurring."

. . . As we shall explain, the prosecution's introduction and use of mathematical probability statistics injected two fundamental prejudicial errors into the case: (1) The testimony itself lacked an adequate foundation both in evidence and in statistical theory; and (2) the testimony and the manner in which the prosecution used it distracted the jury from its proper and requisite function of weighing the evidence on the issue of guilt, encouraged the jurors to rely upon an engaging but *logically irrelevant* expert demonstration, foreclosed the possibility of an effective defense by an attorney apparently unschooled in mathematical refinements, and placed the jurors and defense counsel at a disadvantage in sifting relevant fact from inapplicable theory.

We initially consider the defects in the testimony itself. As we have indicated, the specific technique presented through the mathematician's testimony and advanced by the prosecutor to measure the probabilities in question suffered from two basic and pervasive defects—an inadequate evidentiary foundation and an inadequate proof of statistical independence. First, as to the foundational requirement, we find the record devoid of any evidence relating to any of the six individual probability factors used by the prosecutor and ascribed by him to the six characteristics as we have set them out. . . . To put it another way, the prosecution produced no evidence whatsoever showing, or from which it could be in any way inferred, that only one out of every ten cars which might have been at the scene of the robbery was partly yellow, that only one out of every four men who might have been there wore a mustache, that only one out of every ten girls who might have been there wore a ponytail, or that any of the other individual probability factors listed were even roughly accurate.

The bare, inescapable fact is that the prosecution made no attempt to offer any such evidence. Instead, through leading questions having perfunctorily elicited from the witness the response that the latter could not assign a probability factor for the characteristics involved, the prosecutor himself suggested what the various probabilities should be and these became the basis of the witness's testimony. It is a curious circumstance of this adventure in proof that the prosecutor not only made his own assertions of these factors in the hope that they were "conservative" but also in later argument to the jury invited the jurors to substitute their "estimates" should they wish to do so. We can hardly conceive of a more fatal gap in the prosecution's scheme of proof. A foundation for the admissibility of the witness's testimony was never even attempted to be laid, let alone established. His testimony was neither made to rest on his own testimonial knowledge nor presented by proper hypothetical questions based upon valid data in the record. . . .

But, as we have indicated, there was another glaring defect in the prosecution's technique, namely an inadequate proof of the statistical independence of the six factors. No proof was presented that the characteristics selected were mutually independent, even though the witness himself acknowledged that such condition was essential to the proper application of the "product rule" or "multiplication rule." To the extent that the traits or characteristics were not mutually independent (e.g., Negroes with beards and men with mustaches obviously represent overlapping categories), the "product rule" would inevitably yield a wholly erroneous and exaggerated result even if all of the individual components had been determined with precision.

In the instant case, therefore, because of the aforementioned two defects—the inadequate evidentiary foundation and the inadequate proof of statistical independence—the technique employed by the prosecutor could only lead to wild conjecture without demonstrated relevancy to the issues presented. It acquired no redeeming quality from the prosecutor's statement that it was being used only "for illustrative purposes" since, as we shall point out, the prosecutor's subsequent utilization of the mathematical testimony was not confined within such limits.

We now turn to the second fundamental error caused by the probability testimony. Quite apart from our foregoing objections to the specific technique employed by the prosecution to estimate the probability in question, we think that the entire enterprise upon which the prosecution embarked, and which was directed to the objective of measuring the likelihood of a random couple possessing the characteristics allegedly distinguishing the robbers, was gravely misguided. At best, it might yield an estimate as to how infrequently bearded Negroes drive yellow cars in the company of blonde females with ponytails.

The prosecution's approach, however, could furnish the jury with absolutely no guidance on the crucial issue: Of the admittedly few such couples, which one, if any, was guilty of committing this robbery? Probability theory necessarily remains silent on that question, since no mathematical equation can prove beyond a reasonable doubt (1) that the guilty couple in fact possessed the characteristics described by the People's witnesses, or even (2) that only one couple possessing those distinctive characteristics could be found in the entire Los Angeles area.

As to the first inherent failing we observe that the prosecution's theory of probability rested on the assumption that the witnesses called by the People had conclusively established that the guilty couple possessed the precise characteristics relied upon by the prosecution. But no mathematical formula could ever establish beyond a reasonable doubt that the prosecution's witnesses correctly observed and accurately described the distinctive features which were employed to link defendants to the crime. Conceivably, for example, the guilty couple might have included a light-skinned Negress with bleached hair rather than a Caucasian blonde; or the driver of the car might have been wearing a false beard as a disguise; or the prosecution's witnesses might simply have been unreliable.

The foregoing risks of error permeate the prosecution's circumstantial case. Traditionally, the jury weighs such risks in evaluating the credibility and probative value of trial testimony, but the likelihood of human error or of falsification obviously cannot be quantified; that likelihood must therefore be excluded from any effort to assign a number to the probability of guilt or innocence. Confronted with an equation which purports to yield a numerical index of probable guilt, few juries could resist the temptation to accord disproportionate weight to that index; only an exceptional juror, and indeed only a defense attorney schooled in mathematics, could successfully keep in mind the fact that the probability computed by the prosecution can represent, at best, the likelihood that a random couple would share the characteristics testified to by the People's witnesses—not necessarily the characteristics of the actually guilty couple.

As to the second inherent failing in the prosecution's approach, even assuming that the first failing could be discounted, the most a mathematical computation could ever yield would be a measure of the probability that a random couple would possess the distinctive features in question. In the present case, for example, the prosecution attempted to compute the probability that a random couple would include a bearded Negro, a blonde girl with a ponytail, and a partly yellow car; the prosecution urged that this probability was no more than one in 12 million. Even accepting this conclusion as arithmetically accurate, however, one still could not conclude that the Collinses were probably the guilty couple. On the contrary . . . the prosecution's figures actually imply a likelihood of over 40 percent that the Collinses could be "duplicated" by at least one other couple who might equally have committed the San Pedro robbery. Urging that the Collinses be convicted on the basis of evidence which logically establishes no more than this seems as indefensible as arguing for the conviction of X on the ground that a witness saw either X or X's twin commit the crime.

Again, few defense attorneys, and certainly few jurors, could be expected to comprehend this basic flaw in the prosecution's analysis. Conceivably even the prosecutor erroneously believed that his equation established a high probability that no other bearded Negro in the Los Angeles area drove a yellow car accompanied by a ponytailed blonde. In any event, although his technique could demonstrate no such thing, he solemnly told the jury that he had supplied mathematical proof of guilt.

Sensing the novelty of that notion, the prosecutor told the jurors that the traditional idea of proof beyond a reasonable doubt represented "the most hackneyed, stereotyped, trite, misunderstood concept in criminal law." He sought to reconcile the jury to the risk that, under his "new math" approach to criminal jurisprudence, "on some rare occasion . . . an innocent person may be convicted." "Without taking that risk," the prosecution continued, "life would be intolerable . . . because . . . there would be immunity for the Collinses, for people who chose not to be employed to go down and push old ladies down and take their money and be immune because how could we ever be sure they are the ones who did it?"

In essence this argument of the prosecutor was calculated to persuade the jury to convict defendants whether or not they were convinced of their guilt to a moral certainty and beyond a reasonable doubt. Undoubtedly the jurors were unduly impressed by the mystique of the mathematical demonstration but were unable to assess its *relevancy* or value. Although we make no appraisal of the proper applications of mathematical techniques in the proof of facts . . . we have strong feelings that such applications, particularly in a criminal case, must be critically examined in view of the substantial unfairness to a defendant which may result from ill-conceived techniques with which the trier of fact is not technically equipped to cope. We feel that the technique employed in the case before us falls into the latter category.

We conclude that the court erred in admitting over defendant's objection the evidence pertaining to the mathematical theory of probability and in denying defendant's motion to strike such evidence. . . . [W]e think that under the circumstances the "trial by mathematics" so distorted the role of the jury and so disadvantaged counsel for the defense, as to constitute in itself a miscarriage of justice. . . . The judgment against defendant must therefore be reversed . . . .

LEGAL ANALYSIS AND WRITING 5.4

1. Summarize the facts and holding in the previous case.
2. Do you agree with the court's reasoning? Explain why or why not.
3. What is the significance of the holding in this case?

CRITICAL THINKING QUESTIONS 5.3

1. In the *Old Chief* case, why did the prosecution reject the defendant's offer of stipulation? What made the evidence of the defendant's prior conviction unfairly prejudicial?
2. In the *People v. Collins*, why did the court believe that evidence of mathematical probability had not been properly introduced and used by the prosecution?
3. What could the prosecution do, if anything, to bolster the admissibility of this evidence?

SUMMARY

One of the oldest requirements for the admissibility of evidence is whether it is relevant and material to the matters for which it is being offered. Evidence is relevant when it tends to prove or disprove a fact in issue. Evidence is material when it has a bearing on or relates to the issue in dispute. At common law, evidence had to be both relevant and material to be admissible in court. Under the modern rules, the concept of materiality has been merged into the threshold requirement of relevancy. Today, "relevant evidence" means evidence having any tendency to make the existence of any fact that is of consequence to the determination of the action more probable or less probable than it would be without the evidence. Evidence is relevant when it tends to prove or disprove a fact in issue. In order to satisfy the relevance requirement, evidence must be probative; that is, it must *tend* to prove something. The test here is the *standard of probability*. Is it more probable than it would be without the evidence? If so, the standard has been met and the evidence is deemed relevant.

The concept of relevance includes *logical relevance* and *legal relevance*, both of which are necessary in order for evidence to be admissible. Logical relevance is established if evidence tends to prove or disprove a fact in issue. Legal relevance, however, pertains to the legal admissibility of relevant evidence. Legal relevance requires that evidence not violate any other evidence rule or law. A fundamental rule of evidence is that relevant evidence is admissible and evidence that is not relevant is not admissible. However, the concept of *legal relevance* modifies this principle by setting out the sources which may result in relevant evidence being excluded. There may be constitutional provisions, statutes, or other laws that provide for the exclusion of even relevant evidence.

Even when relevant, evidence may still be excluded if its probative value is substantially outweighed by the danger of unfair prejudice to the trier of fact. Relevant evidence may also be excluded if it causes a confusion of the issues, misleads the jury, or results in undue delay, waste of time, or needless presentation of cumulative evidence.

KEY TERMS

Balancing Test	Logical Relevance	Relevancy
Doctrine of Scintilla Rule	Material	Relevant
Legal Relevance	Probative	Standard of Probability

LEARNING OUTCOMES AND PRACTICE SKILLS CHECKLIST

☐ Learning Outcomes

After completing your reading, questions, and exercises, you should be able to demonstrate a better understanding of the learning concepts by answering the following questions:

1. Define relevancy and distinguish it from materiality.
2. Describe how the concept of materiality is covered under the modern rules.
3. Distinguish between logical and legal relevance.
4. Explain the rule that excludes relevant evidence when it is prejudicial and the reasoning behind the rule. Give an example.
5. Describe what is meant by "confusing the jury, wasting time, or cumulative evidence." Give examples of each.

☐ Practice Skills

In addition to understanding the learning concepts, practice what you have learned through applications using critical thinking, legal analysis and writing, legal research, and advocacy skills, including:

Critical Thinking

1. Why do we have the exceptions to the rule described in this chapter that all relevant evidence is admissible?
2. Do you believe that the current exceptions discussed in this chapter provide adequate safeguards?
3. What public policy issues or considerations do you think might be behind these rules?
4. If it were up to you, would you keep these exceptions as they are, delete them, narrow them, or expand them? Explain your reasoning.
5. How do these rules influence the gathering of evidence or preparing of witnesses?

Legal Analysis and Writing

Analyze the following rules and cases by summarizing their holdings, explaining their significance, and assessing any issue that might arise in their application.

1. Rule 401.
2. Rule 402.
3. Rule 403.
4. *Johnny Lynn Old Chief v. United States.*
5. *People v. Collins.*

Legal Research Using the Internet

1. Find the annotated Federal Rules of Evidence on the Internet and assess the comments made in the proposing of the rules covered in this chapter.
2. Find your state's rules of evidence regarding relevance exceptions and concepts covered in this chapter. Compare and contrast with the federal and/or modern rules, and some of the state rules listed in this chapter.
3. Find out if your state appellate court posts their case decisions on the Internet. If so, find a case that illustrates an issue or rule discussed in this chapter. If your state decisions are not on the Internet, go instead to the web site for the U.S. Circuit Court of Appeals in your circuit, or search the U.S. Supreme Court decisions.

PRACTICE APPLICATION 5.1

Defendant was prosecuted for the murder of his wife, even though neither the victim's body nor a murder weapon was ever recovered, and there were no witnesses to the crime. At trial, prosecution wants to introduce the following evidence:

1. A computer disk that had been found in defendant's desk. On that disk was a file named "murder," which appeared to be a 26-step guide to carrying out a murder.
2. A witness who will testify that defendant purchased a .25 caliber pistol 2 days before the victim disappeared.
3. A witness who will testify that defendant told him that the best way to kill someone else was to shoot him behind the ear.

4. A witness who will testify that defendant asked him how he could remove bloodstains from concrete.
5. A witness who will testify that defendant once told her that she should not "be surprised if 6 months down the road . . . you hear that Shirley is dead, . . . because I am going to kill her."
6. A witness who will testify that defendant told her that there might be bodies hidden in mine shafts in Pennsylvania, and that "if he wanted to get rid of [his wife], nobody would ever see her again."

Defense objects to this evidence, claiming that it is irrelevant and more prejudicial than probative.

Use the format shown in the Appendix for the *IRAC Method of Legal Analysis* and the readings, rules, and cases discussed in this chapter to analyze and determine whether the evidence in each example can be admitted. Write a memo giving your analysis, reasoning, and conclusions.

LEGAL RESEARCH USING THE INTERNET SKILLS 5.4

Find out how the court ruled on the previous *Practice Application* problem by finding and reading the court opinion online. The citation for it is:
United States v. Russell, 971 F.2d 1098 (1992).

ADVOCACY AND COMMUNICATION SKILLS 5.1

From small groups of no more than 3–4 each, form teams for prosecution, defense, and judges. Using the previous *Practice Application* problem, the prosecution and defense teams should each prepare oral arguments in support of, or an objection to, each of the pieces of evidence on the grounds of relevance or prejudice.

Each piece of evidence or witness testimony is to be argued separately. The defense will begin by presenting their argument as to why the evidence is irrelevant or prejudicial. After the defense has delivered their argument in support of their objections to the evidence, the prosecution will present their argument as to why the evidence is relevant and not prejudicial. The judges will then rule on whether the evidence or testimony will be allowed. Use a different team member for each argument.

You Be the Judge 5.3

In a criminal trial for kidnapping, the victim identified the defendant as her kidnapper and testified that she remembered seeing a "panther" tattoo on the defendant's arm. To support this testimony, the prosecution wants to introduce an upper-body photograph of the defendant depicting a "panther tattoo" on an arm and "devil tattoos and a massive jagged scar" on the upper body. The defense objects to this photograph as irrelevant and prejudicial.

Would you allow this evidence? Why or why not?

LEGAL RESEARCH USING THE INTERNET SKILLS 5.5

Find out how the court ruled on the previous *You Be The Judge* problem by finding and reading the court opinion online. The citation for it is:
United States v. Weeks, 919 F.2d 248 (5th Cir. 1990).

WEB SITES

Federal Rules of Evidence
http://www.law.cornell.edu/rules/fre/overview.html
FindLaw
http://www.findlaw.com
FindLaw
http://guide.lp.findlaw.com/casecode/
FindLaw U.S. Supreme Court Decisions
http://www.findlaw.com/casecode/supreme.html
List of State Laws from Legal Information Institute of Cornell Law School
http://www.law.cornell.edu/states/listing.html

National Center for State Courts—State and Federal Court Web Sites
http://www.ncsconline.org/D_kis/info_court_web_sites.html#state
Supreme Court Collection of Cornell Law School
http://supct.law.cornell.edu/supct/
U.S. Courts Site with Links to All Circuit Courts of Appeal
http://www.uscourts.gov/links.html
U.S. Supreme Court
http://www.supremecourtus.gov/

ENDNOTES

1. Tenn. R. Evid. 401.
2. *Commonwealth v. Scott*, 480 Pa. 50 (1978).
3. *Globe Indemnity Co. v. Davies*, 47 S.W.2d 990.
4. See *Federal Rule of Evidence*, Rule 402.
5. *State v. Jones*, No. 92-521 (Vt. Sup. Ct, 1993).
6. *Johnny Lynn Old Chief v. United States*, 519 U.S. 172 (1997).

CHARACTER EVIDENCE

"Character is habit long continued."

—*Plutarch*

LEARNING OUTCOMES

In this chapter, you will learn about the following legal concepts:

- Character Evidence
- Evidence of Prior Bad Acts and Other Crimes
- Habit and Routine Practice
- Subsequent Remedial Measures
- Inadmissibility of Pleas
- Victim's Past Sexual Behavior
- Evidence of Similar Crimes in Sexual Assault Cases

INTRODUCTION

In the previous chapter, we looked at the concept of relevancy, one of the oldest requirements for the admissibility of evidence. We saw how this concept includes *logical relevance* and *legal relevance*, both of which are necessary in order for evidence to be admissible. Logical relevance is established if evidence tends to prove or disprove a fact in issue. Legal relevance requires that evidence not violate any other evidence rule or law. Part of the evidentiary rules covering legal relevance is whether a person's character traits, reputation, or prior conduct can be admitted into evidence. This chapter will examine these issues, comparing when this evidence may be admitted and when it may not be admitted.

CHARACTER EVIDENCE

Character Evidence
Personal qualities and traits that describe a person and how he or she would act under a particular set of circumstances.

Character evidence involves evidence of personal qualities and traits that describe a person's nature and how he or she would act under a particular set of circumstances. For example, a person might be described by others as "quiet and gentle" or "loud and mean;" "never in trouble" or "always in trouble;" "honest" or "dishonest."

General Rule

The general rule is that evidence of a person's character or trait of character is not admissible to prove conduct on a particular occasion.

Exceptions to the General Rule

There are several exceptions to the general rule that character evidence is not admissible to prove conduct on a particular occasion or to prove that someone acted in conformity with a character trait.

Character of the Accused

In a criminal case, evidence of the defendant's character is admissible when offered by the accused, or by the prosecution to rebut the testimony offered by the accused (see Exhibit 6.1). For example, in a "hockey rink" manslaughter case, the defendant took his son to the boy's hockey practice. The defendant got into an argument with another father about too much "roughhousing" by the boys on the ice. The two men began to push each other, and the defendant, who was much bigger than the other man, knocked the smaller man down and repeatedly hit the man, causing his death. At his trial for manslaughter, the defense put on witnesses who characterized the defendant as a "gentle giant" and not an aggressor. The prosecution rebutted this testimony through witnesses who testified to the aggressive actions and violence of the defendant toward the victim.

Character of the Victim

Evidence offered by an accused about the character of the victim may be allowed if it is relevant to the matter at issue and is not unduly prejudicial. (for example, evidence about the character of the victim as an aggressor or bully to bolster a self-defense plea by the defendant). In the previous "hockey rink" example, the defense introduced witnesses who testified that the victim started the fight and that the defendant was defending himself.

EXHIBIT 6.1   Character Evidence Not Admissible to Prove Conduct

North Carolina Rules of Evidence
Rule 404(a). Character Evidence Generally. Evidence of a person's character or a trait of his character is not admissible for the purpose of proving that he acted in conformity therewith on a particular occasion, except:

(1) Character of Accused. Evidence of a pertinent trait of his character offered by an accused, or by the prosecution to rebut the same;

(2) Character of Victim. Evidence of a pertinent trait of character of the victim of the crime offered by an accused, or by the prosecution to rebut the same, or evidence of a character trait of peacefulness of the victim offered by the prosecution in a homicide case to rebut evidence that the victim was the first aggressor;

(3) Character of Witness. Evidence of the character of a witness, as provided in Rules 607, 608, and 609.

Character evidence may also be used by the prosecution to rebut the testimony offered by the defendant. For example, the prosecution may offer evidence of the victim's peaceful character in order to rebut evidence by the defendant that the victim was the first aggressor. In the "hockey rink" case, the prosecution called witnesses who described how the defendant threw the first punch and later refused to stop beating the victim despite pleas from several of the witnesses. [The defendant was convicted of involuntary manslaughter.]

Character of the Witness

Whether criminal or civil, evidence about the character of a witness may also be admitted for impeachment purposes. This is generally provided for in the rules pertaining to the impeachment of witnesses, and evidence of character and conduct of witnesses.[1] Generally, these rules hold that the credibility of a witness may be attacked or supported by evidence in the form of opinion or reputation. However, the admissibility of this character evidence is subject to certain limitations, including:

> The evidence may refer only to character for truthfulness or untruthfulness, and evidence of truthful character is admissible only after the character of the witness for truthfulness has been attacked by opinion or reputation evidence.[2]

EVIDENTIARY CHECKLIST 6.1

Character Evidence

General Rule: Not admissible to prove conduct.

Exceptions:

☐   Evidence of pertinent trait of character offered by accused, or by the prosecution to rebut the same.

☐   Evidence of pertinent trait of character of the victim of a crime offered by an accused, or by the prosecution to rebut the same, or evidence of a character trait of peacefulness of the victim offered by the prosecution in a homicide case to rebut evidence that the victim was the first aggressor.

☐   Evidence of the character of a witness, as provided in Rules 607, 608, and 609.

When Character is an Essential Element

When character or trait of character is the ultimate issue in a case or an essential element of a charge, claim, or defense, proof may be made of *specific instances* of that person's conduct (see Exhibit 6.2). An example of this is when an employee sues her employer for defamation, claiming that the employer slandered her by accusing her of theft in front of other employees. Because the plaintiff's character for honesty is an essential element of the claim, evidence of specific instances of plaintiff's conduct for honesty may be introduced.

Another example might be the defense of insanity offered in a criminal case. Because the sanity of the defendant is an essential element of the defense to the crime charged, evidence of the defendant's character or conduct would be admissible when it was relevant to the sanity issue. In one case, a defendant was charged with accosting a victim at gunpoint, then kidnapping and sexually assaulting the victim. The defense offered was insanity, with the defendant claiming to have suffered from post-traumatic stress disorder. He also claimed amnesia about the charges as a result of unconscious flashbacks which caused the defendant to believe that he was in Vietnam. To rebut this testimony, prosecutors introduced testimony about a prior crime committed by the defendant where he told a psychiatrist that he had met with a student to collect a drug debt, then blacked out from drugs, but police records showed that he had never met the student before, had accosted her at gunpoint, and had sexually assaulted and kidnapped her. The court admitted this testimony over the defendant's objection that it was not admissible to prove the conduct and that any relevance to sanity was "substantially outweighed by the danger of unfair prejudice." The defendant was convicted and appealed, but the appellate court found that this testimony was admissible because it was offered to rebut a pertinent trait of character which had been offered by the accused. The court stated:

> Because defendant put his sanity in issue, his prior conduct relevant to sanity was admissible when offered by the state. . . . As is often the case when insanity is at issue, the acts charged are conceded and the history of behavior relevant to the central issue depicts defendant in a devastating way. Jurors may react to such evidence in opposite ways—favoring a conclusion that defendant was insane "because a sane person would not do such things" or disfavoring the defense because such a person is viewed as too dangerous to benefit from the defense. Regardless of the potential reactions, withholding information about defendant's behavioral history undercuts the integrity of the jury's fact-finding function. Raising the insanity defense is radical legal surgery. The risks are great, but the evidence must not be so truncated that the verdict becomes uninformed.[3]

EXHIBIT 6.2   Specific Instances of Conduct When Character Is an Essential Element

Tennessee Rules of Evidence
Rule 405. Methods of Proving Character.

(b) Specific Instances of Conduct. In cases in which character or a trait of character of a person is an essential element of a charge, claim, or defense, proof may also be made of specific instances of that person's conduct.

Threatening the President Is No Laughing Matter

Can a prosecutor comment to the jury about a defendant's in-court behavior in laughing over evidence that he threatened the life of the President? Is the prosecutor's comment relevant for the purpose of showing that the defendant was of bad character because he considered the charges of threatening the life of the President to be a joke? The following case addresses these issues.

group 3: case 6

CASE

United States v. Schuler

813 F.2d 978 (9th Cir. 1987).

Boochever, Circuit Judge.

Scott Schuler appeals his conviction for threatening the life of the President of the United States in violation of 18 U.S.C. 871 (1982). At issue is whether, in closing argument, a prosecutor's reference to a non-testifying defendant's in-court behavior and demeanor . . . constitute error. We find that it was reversible error to allow comment on the defendant's off-the-stand behavior. . . .

I. FACTS

. . . Schuler was arrested for attempting to shoplift in the Bullock's Department Store in Indio, California. Security agents took Schuler to the store offices to await police. After reaching the store offices, Schuler began a tirade of name calling, racial slurs, and assorted vulgar comments. His tirade continued when the Riverside County Sheriff arrived and as Schuler was escorted from the department store to the police car. When he arrived at the police station and was being taken from the police car, Schuler told the arresting officer that when the President came to town, he would get him. On the basis of this remark Schuler was charged with violating 18 U.S.C. 871.

At trial the defense asserted that Schuler's remark was merely an expression of anger directed at the law enforcement officers, not a serious threat to the President, and therefore, did not constitute a violation of 18 U.S.C. 871. The jury announced that they were unable to reach a verdict, and the trial resulted in a mistrial. At a second trial, the same witnesses were called and the evidence was primarily the same. In closing argument, the prosecutor stated:

> While Mr. Schuler was being interrogated by the two security agents, Schuler made a number of racial comments about the number of people he was going to kill, a number of sexual comments. I noticed a number of you were looking at Mr. Schuler while that testimony was coming in and a number of you saw him laugh and saw him laugh as they were repeated.

Defense counsel immediately objected and the district court overruled the objection, instructing the jury that the prosecutor's argument was proper. . . . The jury found Schuler guilty.

II. ANALYSIS

. . . .

The prosecutor's comment in closing argument on Schuler's laughter during testimony about the threats Schuler made presents procedural and substantive questions. The procedural difficulty derives from the fact that there is nothing in the record indicating that the laughter did occur, although Schuler nowhere objects that it did not. It is very difficult for an appellate court to review an issue that is not grounded in the record. If counsel considers such an outbreak to be significant, he or she should ask the trial court to have it included in the record.

Assuming that the laughter did occur, we are faced with the substantive issue whether the failure to exclude the prosecutor's reference to Schuler's courtroom behavior constituted reversible error. This issue involves several facets, including whether such remarks (1) introduce character evidence solely to prove guilt. . . .

Federal Rule of Evidence 404(a) prohibits the introduction of evidence of the character of the accused solely to prove guilt. The prosecutor's remarks in effect did this by suggesting to the jury that Schuler's laughter was relevant apparently for the purpose of showing that he was of bad character because he considered the charges of threatening the life of the President to be a joke. The district court's comments in overruling Schuler's objections reinforced that suggestion. The jury may, also, have inferred that Schuler was, at the time of trial, of such a mental state that the President's life would be seriously jeopardized if Schuler were acquitted and allowed back on the streets. While the offense of threatening the life of the President requires proof of a "knowing and willful" act, 18 U.S.C. § 871, and to that extent involves proof of Schuler's mental state, his laughter at trial could not have any relevancy for that purpose. His courtroom behavior off the witness stand was legally irrelevant to the question of his guilt of the crime charged.

The District of Columbia Circuit, when faced with a similar situation, reversed the conviction based in part on the prosecutor's reference to the defendant's courtroom behavior and the district court's refusal to instruct the jury that such behavior must not be considered. *United States v. Wright*, 160 U.S. App. D.C. 57 (D.C. Cir. 1973).

The court stated:

> Unless and until the accused puts his character at issue by giving evidence of his good character or by taking the stand and raising an issue as to his credibility, the prosecutor is forbidden to introduce evidence of the bad character of the accused simply to prove that he is a bad man likely to engage in criminal conduct. . . .

This basic principle cannot be circumvented by allowing the prosecutor to comment on the character of the accused as evidenced by his courtroom behavior. That the jury witnesses the courtroom behavior in any event does not make it proper for the prosecutor to tell them, with the court's approval, that they may consider it as evidence of guilt.

. . . .

Because the prosecutor's comments could have influenced the jury's guilty verdict, the comments were not harmless beyond a reasonable doubt. While we do not take the charged offense lightly, we find it necessary to reverse.

Reversed.

LEGAL ANALYSIS AND WRITING 6.1

The following questions are based on the *How to Brief a Legal Case* format shown in the Appendix. Use this format to answer the following questions:

1. Summarize the facts in the previous case.

2. What is the legal issue?

3. What did the appellate court decide?

4. Why did the court decide this way?

5. Do you agree with the court's reasoning? Explain why or why not.

LEGAL RESEARCH USING THE INTERNET SKILLS 6.1

Try to find this case or another one that refers to it online! Check out one of the legal research web sites below, go to the federal circuit for this court decision, and use their "Search" feature to find this case or another case that refers to it. In the "Search" field, enter the cite or case name. If you have access to Westlaw or Lexis, try to find this case using one of these legal search sites.

1. U.S. Courts Site with Links to All Circuit Courts of Appeal (http://www.uscourts.gov/links.html)

2. National Center for State Courts—State and Federal Court Web Sites (http://www.ncsconline.org/D_kis/info_court_web_sites.html#federal)

3. FindLaw (http://guide.lp.findlaw.com/casecode/)

CRITICAL THINKING QUESTIONS 6.1

1. What is the reasoning behind the general rule that evidence of a person's character or trait of character is not admissible to prove conduct on a particular occasion?
2. Why is a defendant in a criminal action allowed to introduce evidence of the character of the victim?
3. Do you think this rule should be changed? Why or why not?
4. Give some examples of when character would be the ultimate issue.

EVIDENCE OF PRIOR BAD ACTS AND OTHER CRIMES

Wyoming Rule of Evidence 404(b) is typical of the modern rules in holding that evidence of other crimes is not admissible to prove character in order to prove that someone acted in conformity therewith (see Exhibit 6.3). This rule operates to exclude evidence of prior acts that are similar to the charged crime, if the evidence is introduced for the purpose of showing a general propensity to commit the acts in question. For example, we cannot offer evidence that defendant had been convicted of burglary or rape in order to show that the defendant had a propensity to commit these types of crime (i.e., if he did it once, he'd do it again).

The dangers of prejudice and confusion outweigh the probative value of such evidence, if it is offered only for that purpose. There are, however, exceptions to this general rule.

EXHIBIT 6.3   Character Evidence to Prove Other Crimes or Prior Bad Acts

Wyoming Rules of Evidence
Rule 404(b). Other Crimes, Wrongs, or Acts.
    Evidence of other crimes, wrongs, or acts is not admissible to prove the character of a person in order to show that he acted in conformity therewith. It may, however, be admissible for other purposes, such as proof of motive, opportunity, intent, preparation, plan, knowledge, identity, or absence of mistake or accident.

When Evidence of Other Crimes Is Admissible to Prove Character

Although evidence of other crimes and prior bad acts is not admissible to prove someone's inherent character, it may be used to show other purposes, such as proof of motive, opportunity, or means. Evidence may also be admissible to prove intent, knowledge, modus operandi (M.O.), preparation, plan, knowledge, identity, or absence of mistake or accident.

When prior bad act evidence is offered to show identity, the test for relevance can require a higher standard. The prior acts must be so distinctive, in effect, to constitute the defendant's signature. Although the prior acts of the accused and the charged acts do not have to be identical, they must possess common features that make it highly likely that the unknown perpetrator and the accused are the same person. Whereas a few common features that are unique may be sufficient, a larger number of them, less remarkable, taken together, may also have significant probative value.[4] For example, in several cases, evidence of past sexual assaults were used to show the defendant's identity, where the defendant attacked the victims in a similar way. The courts concluded that evidence of the defendant's prior sexual assault of the prior victims were similar enough to be probative on the issue of identity.[5]

Still May Be Excluded as Prejudicial

Even when found to be relevant under Rule 404(b) or a similar rule, evidence of prior bad acts may still be excluded under Rule 403, if its prejudicial effect outweighs its probative value. A defendant may argue that admission of this evidence would provoke or prejudice the jury to punish because of what the defendant did before and not what was proven in the current action.

In trying to balance these concerns, courts have agreed that virtually all evidence offered by the prosecution in a criminal case is prejudicial to some degree against the accused, so the courts will exclude under Rule 403 only if it is *unfairly* prejudicial to a defendant. Evidence is unfairly prejudicial if its primary purpose or effect is to appeal to a jury's sympathies, arouse its sense of horror, or provoke its instinct to punish.[6]

When Evidence of Other Crimes Is Offered

When evidence of "other" crimes is offered, does it have to be proven? The following Supreme Court case deals with this issue in a prosecution for possession of stolen videocassette tapes where evidence of stolen televisions is offered without proof that the televisions were stolen.

CASE

Huddleston v. United States

485 U.S. 681 (1988).

[Huddleston was charged with selling stolen goods and possession of stolen property. A shipment of 32,000 Memorex videocassette tapes valued at $4.53 per tape was stolen from an Overnight Express yard in Illinois sometime between April 11 and 15. On April 17, Huddleston contacted the manager of a rent-to-own store in Michigan and offered to sell a large number of Memorex tapes for $2.75 to $3 per tape. A total of 5,000 tapes were sold. There was no dispute that the tapes which petitioner sold were stolen; the only material issue at trial was whether petitioner knew they were stolen. The District Court allowed the Government to introduce evidence of "similar acts" under Rule 404(b), concluding that such evidence had "clear relevance as to [petitioner's knowledge]." The first piece of similar act evidence offered by the Government was the testimony of a record store owner who testified that Huddleston sold him new 12" black and white televisions for $28 apiece. The second piece of similar act evidence was the testimony of an undercover FBI agent posing as a buyer for an appliance store who testified that Huddleston offered to sell him a large quantity of Amana appliances—28 refrigerators, 2 ranges, and 40 icemakers for $8,000. It was determined that the appliances had a value of approximately $20,000 and were part of a shipment that had been stolen. Huddleston testified that he had no knowledge that any of the goods were stolen. The District Court instructed the jury that the similar acts evidence was to be used only to establish Huddleston's knowledge, and not to prove his character. The jury convicted on the possession count only and Huddleston appeals, arguing that the similar acts evidence for the televisions was prejudicial since the prosecution failed to prove that the televisions were stolen. The Court of Appeals for the Sixth Circuit affirmed the conviction, noting that "the evidence concerning the televisions was admitted for a proper purpose and that the probative value of this evidence was not outweighed by its potential prejudicial effect."]

Chief Justice Rehnquist delivered the opinion for a unanimous Court.

Federal Rule of Evidence 404(b) provides:

"Other crimes, wrongs, or acts.—Evidence of other crimes, wrongs, or acts is not admissible to prove the character of a person in order to show action in conformity therewith. It may, however, be admissible for other purposes, such as proof of motive, opportunity, intent, preparation, plan, knowledge, identity, or absence of mistake or accident."

This case presents the question whether the district court must itself make a preliminary finding that the Government has proved the "other act" by a preponderance of the evidence before it submits the evidence to the jury. We hold that it need not do so.

. . . .

Federal Rule of Evidence 404(b)—which applies in both civil and criminal cases—generally prohibits the introduction of evidence of extrinsic acts that might adversely reflect on the actor's character, unless that evidence bears upon a relevant issue in the case such as motive, opportunity, or knowledge. Extrinsic acts evidence may be critical to the establishment of the truth as to a disputed issue, especially when that issue involves the actor's state of mind and the only means of ascertaining that mental state is by drawing inferences from conduct. The actor in the instant case was a criminal defendant, and the act in question was "similar" to the one with which he was charged. Our use of these terms is not meant to suggest that our analysis is limited to such circumstances.

Before this Court, petitioner argues that the District Court erred in admitting . . . testimony as to petitioner's sale of the televisions. The threshold inquiry a court must make before admitting similar acts evidence under Rule 404(b) is whether that evidence is probative of a material issue other than character. The Government's theory of relevance was that the televisions were stolen, and proof that petitioner had engaged in a series of sales of stolen merchandise from the same suspicious source would be strong evidence that he was aware that each of these items, including the Memorex tapes, was stolen. As such, the sale of the televisions was a "similar act" only if the televisions were stolen. Petitioner acknowledges that this evidence was admitted for the proper purpose of showing his knowledge that the Memorex tapes were stolen. He asserts, however, that the evidence should not have been admitted because the Government failed to prove to the District Court that the televisions were in fact stolen.

Petitioner argues from the premise that evidence of similar acts has a grave potential for causing improper prejudice. For instance, the jury may choose to punish the defendant for the similar rather than the charged act, or the jury may infer that the defendant is an evil person inclined to violate the law. Because of this danger, petitioner maintains, the jury ought not to be exposed to similar act evidence until the trial court has heard the evidence and made a determination under Federal Rule of Evidence 104(a) that the defendant committed the similar act. Rule 104(a) provides that "[p]reliminary questions concerning the qualification of a person to be a witness, the existence of a privilege, or the admissibility of evidence shall be determined by the court, subject to the provisions of subdivision (b)." According to petitioner, the trial court must make this preliminary finding by at least a preponderance of the evidence.

We reject petitioner's position, for it is inconsistent with the structure of the Rules of Evidence and with the plain language of Rule 404(b). Article IV of the Rules of Evidence deals with the relevancy of evidence. Rules 401 and 402 establish the broad principle that relevant evidence—evidence that makes the existence of any fact at issue more or less probable—is admissible unless the Rules provide otherwise. Rule 403 allows the trial judge to exclude relevant evidence if, among other things, "its probative value is substantially outweighed by the danger of unfair prejudice." Rules 404 through 412 address specific types of evidence that have generated problems. Generally, these latter Rules do not flatly prohibit the introduction of such evidence but instead limit the purpose for which it may be introduced. Rule 404(b), for example, protects against the introduction of extrinsic act evidence when that evidence is offered solely to prove character. The text contains no intimation, however, that any preliminary showing is necessary before such evidence may be introduced for a proper purpose. If offered for such a proper purpose, the evidence is subject only to general strictures limiting admissibility such as Rules 402 and 403.

. . . .

We conclude that a preliminary finding by the court that the Government has proved the act by a preponderance of the evidence is not called for under Rule 104(a). This is not to say, however, that the Government may parade past the jury a litany of potentially prejudicial similar acts that have been established or connected to the defendant only by unsubstantiated innuendo. Evidence is admissible under Rule 404(b) only if it is relevant . . . . In the Rule 404(b) context, similar act evidence is relevant only if the jury can reasonably conclude that the act occurred and that the defendant was the actor. In the instant case, the evidence that petitioner was selling the televisions was relevant under the Government's theory only if the jury could reasonably find that the televisions were stolen.

. . . .

In assessing whether the evidence was sufficient to support a finding that the televisions were stolen, the court here was required to consider not only the direct evidence on that point—the low price of the televisions, the large quantity offered for sale, and petitioner's inability to produce a bill of sale—but also the evidence concerning petitioner's involvement in the sales of other stolen merchandise . . . , such as the Memorex tapes and the Amana appliances. Given this evidence, the jury reasonably could have concluded that the televisions were stolen, and the trial court therefore properly allowed the evidence to go to the jury.

We share petitioner's concern that unduly prejudicial evidence might be introduced under Rule 404(b). We think, however, that the protection against such unfair prejudice emanates not from a requirement of a preliminary finding by the trial court, but rather from four other sources: first, from the requirement of Rule 404(b) that the evidence be offered for a proper purpose; second, from the relevancy requirement of Rule 402—as enforced through Rule 104(b); third, from the assessment the trial court must make under Rule 403 to determine whether the probative value of the similar acts evidence is substantially outweighed by its potential for unfair prejudice, and fourth, from Federal Rule of Evidence 105, which provides that the trial court shall, upon request, instruct the jury that the similar acts evidence is to be considered only for the proper purpose for which it was admitted.

Affirmed.

LEGAL ANALYSIS AND WRITING 6.2

The following questions are based on the *How to Brief a Legal Case* format shown in the Appendix. Use this format to answer the following questions:

1. Summarize the facts in the previous case.
2. What is the legal issue?
3. What did the appellate court decide?
4. Why did the court decide this way?
5. Do you agree with the court's reasoning? Explain why or why not.

LEGAL RESEARCH USING THE INTERNET SKILLS 6.2

Find and read this Supreme Court case online! Check out one of the legal research web sites below and use their "Search" feature to find this case. In the "Search" field, enter the cite or case name.

1. FindLaw U.S. Supreme Court Decisions (http://www.findlaw.com/casecode/supreme.html)
2. U.S. Supreme Court (http://www.supremecourtus.gov/)
3. Supreme Court Collection of Cornell Law School (http://supct.law.cornell.edu/supct/)

EVIDENTIARY CHECKLIST 6.2

Evidence of Other Crimes or Prior Bad Acts

General Rule: Not admissible to prove character of a person to show that the person acted in conformity with the character trait

Exceptions: Admissible to prove

☐ Motive or opportunity
☐ Intent, preparation, plan, or knowledge
☐ Identity
☐ Absence of mistake or accident

Are Prior Speeding Tickets Admissible?

In the following North Carolina case, the court decides whether evidence of prior speeding tickets may be admitted in an auto accident trial to show "intent, preparation, plan or motive to race or speed on the day in question."

CASE

Sparks v. Gilley Trucking Co.

992 F.2d 50 (4th Cir. 1993).

Appeal from the United States District Court for the Western District of North Carolina, at Asheville.

Niemeyer, Circuit Judge.

The principal issue presented in this appeal is whether evidence of prior speeding tickets may be admitted under Federal Rule of Evidence 404(b) to prove negligence in an automobile tort case. We hold that in the circumstances of this case it was prejudicial error for the district court to have admitted such evidence, and we therefore vacate the judgment and remand the case for a new trial.

I

Late on a June afternoon in 1987, Milton E. Sparks was driving up a mountain near the North Carolina–Tennessee border in his red Corvette when a logging truck came down the mountain in the opposite direction. After the vehicles passed by each other, Sparks lost control of his car, hit a tree, and sustained serious personal injuries. Sparks sued Gilley Trucking Company, the owner of the logging truck, alleging negligence, and Gilley Trucking filed a defense contending that Sparks' own negligence contributed to the accident. At trial Sparks testified that the truck was traveling in the middle of the road and that, in trying to avoid a collision, he ran off the road and hit a tree. The driver of the truck testified to different facts, stating that Sparks was driving at an excessive rate of speed in the middle of the road and lost control when he swerved to avoid hitting the truck.

To advance its theory that Sparks was speeding and, indeed, racing at the time of the accident, Gilley Trucking was allowed to introduce, over Sparks' objection, evidence that Sparks had been convicted of speeding on several prior occasions. Relying on Federal Rule of Evidence 404(b), the district court admitted the evidence "to show intent, preparation, plan or motive to race or speed on the day in question." This evidence formed a principal part of Gilley Trucking's defense that on the day of the accident Sparks was contributorily negligent. Gilley Trucking also presented testimony of the investigating police officer who estimated Sparks' rate of speed immediately before the accident at 70 m.p.h.

The jury found that negligence of both drivers contributed to the accident and, as required by North Carolina law, rendered judgment for the defendant trucking company. On appeal Sparks contends that the district court erred in admitting both the evidence of prior speeding tickets and the expert testimony.

II

The principal issue turns on whether the fact that Sparks was convicted of speeding on prior occasions had a "tendency to make the existence of any fact that is of consequence to the determination of the action more probable or less probable than it would be without the evidence." Fed. R. Evid. 401. The analysis begins with the recognition that Federal Rule of Evidence 404(a) provides that "evidence of a person's character or a trait of character" is not admissible to prove that a person acted in conformity with that character or trait on a particular occasion. Attempting to prove conduct by showing a character trait is too general and unreliable a method, and therefore it is excluded under the same principle as is reflected in Rule 403—any probative value is "substantially outweighed by the danger of unfair prejudice." Accordingly, Rule 404(b) provides that evidence of prior "crimes, wrongs or acts" may be admitted to prove a relevant fact except when it is offered solely "to prove the character of a person in order to show action in conformity therewith." Rule 404(b) is thus a rule of inclusion that permits the admission of prior acts if probative to an aspect of the case and not offered merely to establish a character trait which would encompass the type of conduct in question.

Thus, when intent to commit a crime is at issue, we have regularly permitted the admission of prior acts to prove that element. A criminal defendant, for example, cannot deny knowledge of drug trafficking or an intent to traffic in drugs and at the same time preclude the admission of the government's evidence of prior occasions when he willingly trafficked in drugs. We have held repeatedly that when intent to commit an act is an element of a crime, prior activity showing a willingness to commit that act may be probative. The Supreme Court pointed out in *Huddleston v. United States*, 485 U.S. 681

(1988), the importance that prior act evidence may have in deciding a disputed issue, "especially when that issue involves the actor's state of mind and the only means of ascertaining that mental state is by drawing inferences from conduct." Thus when evidence of prior acts is probative of a fact material to the case, Rule 404(b) permits its admission even when it may tend also to show a character trait. To protect against the danger of prejudice the court should give a limiting instruction under Rule 105 if one is requested and must, in any event, weigh the prejudicial effect under Rule 403.

In a common law negligence case, however, the issue is generally not the defendant's state of mind. Rather the factfinder must determine whether the defendant was acting as a reasonable person would have acted in similar circumstances. In this case Gilley Trucking was attempting to prove that Sparks was speeding or racing at the time of the accident and therefore driving in a negligent manner that contributed to the resulting accident. Yet proof of negligence does not require a showing of intent or plan, the stated purposes for which the prior speeding tickets were admitted by the district court. Moreover, prior acts of speeding alone do not establish intent because a speeding violation does not depend on intent. A speeding ticket may be issued regardless of the defendant's state of mind. Indeed, accidental or inadvertent speeding may result in the issuance of a speeding ticket.

If Gilley Trucking was attempting to show that Sparks was racing at the time of the accident, it took upon itself the unnecessary burden of showing that Sparks was speeding intentionally to show that he was driving negligently. While an intentional act does require proof of a state of mind, for which prior acts may be admissible, a showing of prior acts of speeding without more is still not relevant to establishing this state of mind. Gilley Trucking made no effort to show that any prior speeding was deliberate or was in any way related to racing. Indeed, Sparks' explanations tend to suggest that the conduct resulted more from inadvertence. For example, he said, "As far as I know every speeding ticket I've ever had has been out on interstate road traveling back and forth to and from jobs."

Nor did Gilley Trucking present any foundation for the theory that the prior tickets revealed a "plan" or a "motive" to race on the day of the accident, and none of the evidence about the tickets discloses preparation to speed or race on that day. The relatively extensive evidence of the several prior speeding tickets in this case tended to show at most a trait about Sparks, that he tended to speed, and to suggest that because he speeded on prior occasions, he was speeding at the time of the accident. This purpose for using the prior acts evidence, however, is the one specifically prohibited by Rule 404, as we have already observed, and the evidence should not have been admitted.

While it was error to have admitted evidence of the prior speeding tickets in the circumstances of this case, a new trial is warranted only if admission of the evidence was not harmless error. In the circumstances of this case we do not find the error harmless. When the speeding tickets are excluded, the evidence presents close factual issues. Sparks

and the Gilley Trucking driver testified to different versions of the events leading to the accident. There was conflicting testimony and physical evidence of Sparks' speed. Against the backdrop of this stand-off, the jury heard detailed evidence about several prior occasions when Sparks was convicted of speeding, and this evidence thus became an important aspect of Gilley Trucking's presentation to the jury. We cannot determine that the evidence did not adversely affect the outcome of the case. Accordingly, we conclude that a new trial is necessary in this case.

. . . .

Reversed and Remanded.

CRITICAL THINKING QUESTIONS 6.2

1. What is the reasoning behind the rule excluding evidence of other crimes or prior bad acts?

2. How can you reconcile the probative value of allowing evidence of other crimes to prove motive or identity with the prejudicial effect of this evidence?

3. In the *Huddleston* case, what four sources did the Court say that the protection against unfair prejudice emanates from?

4. What did the court in *Sparks v. Gilley Trucking* say that the evidence of speeding tickets unfairly suggests?

YOU BE THE JUDGE 6.1

A mother leaves her two young children, ages 4 and 6, home alone late at night for over 3 hours while she goes to a bar. In a criminal action for child neglect, the prosecutor wants to introduce evidence that the mother had been previously convicted for child abuse in the beating of another child who was removed from her custody 9 years ago.
Would you allow this evidence? Why or why not?

Methods of Proving Character

In any case where evidence of character is allowed, proof may be made by testimony as to **reputation** in the community or by testimony in the form of an **opinion** (see Exhibit 6.4). On cross-examination, questions may be asked about specific instances of conduct. However, in cross-examining a character witness, inquiry into specific instances of conduct is permissible only to determine whether the witness has heard about the instance, and if so, whether it has affected the witness's opinion of the defendant's character. The evidence is admissible only to impeach the testimony of the character witness, not to show that the defendant has a propensity or character to engage in the type of misconduct for which she is on trial.

Reputation
How a person's character is generally viewed or estimated by others in that person's community.

Opinion
A judgment or conclusion made by a witness based on the witness's own personal knowledge or perception.

EXHIBIT 6.4   Methods of Proving Character

Idaho Rules of Evidence
Rule 405. (a) Reputation or Opinion. In all cases in which evidence of character or a trait of character of a person is admissible, proof may be made by testimony as to reputation or by testimony in the form of an opinion. On cross-examination, inquiry is allowable into relevant specific instances of conduct.

(b) Specific Instances of Conduct. In cases in which character or a trait of character of a person is an essential element of a charge, claim, or defense, proof may also be made of specific instances of the person's conduct.

Massachusetts General Laws
Chapter 233: Section 21A. Evidence of reputation. Evidence of the reputation of a person in a group with the members of which he has habitually associated in his work or business shall be admissible to the same extent and subject to the same limitations as is evidence of such reputation in a community in which he has resided.

Practice Tip 6.1

Reputation Evidence

Here is an example of questions that might be asked to qualify and prepare a witness in laying a foundation to admit reputation evidence:

1. *How do you know the defendant?*
2. *How long have you known the defendant?*
3. *How long have you lived in the defendant's community?*
4. *What have you heard of defendant's reputation in the community?*
5. *From whom have you heard this?*
6. *How many people have you heard this from?*
7. *Have you heard anything negative about the defendant?*
8. *If so, what have you heard?*

Character as Synonym for Reputation

In the following classic case, the Supreme Court examines the issues surrounding the admissibility of reputation evidence, finding that "[w]hat commonly is called 'character evidence' is only such when 'character' is employed as a synonym for 'reputation.'" This case decision has been widely quoted and cited in discussions about character and reputation evidence.

Group 2 Case #7

CASE

Michelson v. United States
335 U.S. 469 (1948).

Justice Jackson delivered the opinion of the Court.

In 1947 petitioner Michelson was convicted of bribing a federal revenue agent. The Government proved a large payment by accused to the agent for the purpose of influencing his official action. The defendant, as a witness on his own behalf, admitted passing the money but claimed it was done in response to the agent's demands, threats, solicitations, and inducements that amounted to entrapment. It is enough for our purposes to say that determination of the issue turned on whether the jury should believe the agent or the accused.

On direct examination of defendant, his own counsel brought out that, in 1927, he had been convicted of a misdemeanor having to do with trading in counterfeit watch dials. On cross-examination it appeared that in 1930, in executing an application for a license to deal in second-hand jewelry, he answered "No" to the question whether he had theretofore been arrested or summoned for any offense. Defendant called five witnesses to prove that he enjoyed a good reputation. Two of them testified that their acquaintance with him extended over a period of about 30 years and the others said they had known him at least half that long. A typical examination in chief was as follows:

Q: Do you know the defendant Michelson?
A: Yes.
Q: How long do you know Mr. Michelson?
A: About 30 years.
Q: Do you know other people who know him?
A: Yes.
Q: Have you had occasion to discuss his reputation for honesty? You have talked to others?
A: Yes.
Q: And what is his reputation?
A: Very good.

These are representative of answers by three witnesses; two others replied, in substance, that they never had heard anything against Michelson. On cross-examination, four of the witnesses were asked, in substance, this question: "Did you ever hear that Mr. Michelson on March 4, 1927, was convicted of a violation of the trademark law in New York City in regard to watches?" This referred to the 20-year-old conviction about which defendant himself had testified on direct examination. Two of them had heard of it and two had not. To four of these witnesses the prosecution also addressed the question the allowance of which, over defendant's objection, is claimed to be reversible error: "Did you ever hear that on October 11th, 1920, the defendant, Solomon Michelson, was arrested for receiving stolen goods?" None of the witnesses appears to have heard of this. The trial court asked counsel for the prosecution, out of presence of the jury, "Is it a fact according to the best information in your possession that Michelson was arrested for receiving stolen goods?" Counsel replied that it was, and to support his good faith exhibited a paper record which defendant's counsel did not challenge. The judge also on three occasions warned the jury, in terms that are not criticized, of the limited purpose for which this evidence was received.

Defendant–petitioner challenges the right of the prosecution so to cross-examine his character witnesses. The Court of Appeals held that it was permissible . . . . Serious and responsible criticism has been aimed, however, not alone at the detail now questioned by the Court of Appeals but at common-law doctrine on the whole subject of proof of reputation or character. It would not be possible to appraise the usefulness and propriety of this cross-examination without consideration of the unique practice concerning character testimony, of which such cross-examination is a minor part. Courts that follow the common-law tradition almost unanimously have come to disallow resort by the prosecution to any kind of evidence of a defendant's evil character to establish a probability of his guilt. Not that the law invests the defendant with a presumption of good character, but it simply closes the whole matter of character, disposition, and reputation on the prosecution's case-in-chief. The State may not show defendant's prior trouble with the law, specific criminal acts, or ill name among his neighbors, even though such facts might logically be persuasive that he is by propensity a probable perpetrator of the crime. The inquiry is not rejected because character is irrelevant; on the contrary, it is said to weigh too much with the jury and to so overpersuade them as to prejudge one with a bad general record and deny him a fair opportunity to defend against a particular charge. The overriding policy of excluding such evidence, despite its admitted probative value, is the practical experience that its disallowance tends to prevent confusion of issues, unfair surprise, and undue prejudice.

But this line of inquiry firmly denied to the State is opened to the defendant because character is relevant in resolving probabilities of guilt. He may introduce affirmative testimony that the general estimate of his character is so favorable that the jury may infer that he would not be likely to commit the offense charged. This privilege is sometimes valuable to a defendant for this Court has held that such testimony alone, in some circumstances, may be enough to raise a reasonable doubt of guilt and that in the federal courts a jury in a proper case should be so instructed. When the defendant elects to initiate a character inquiry, another anomalous rule comes into play. Not only is he permitted to call witnesses to testify from hearsay, but indeed such a witness is not allowed to base his testimony on anything but hearsay. What commonly is called "character evidence" is only such when "character" is employed as a synonym for "reputation." The witness may not testify about defendant's specific acts or courses of conduct or his possession of a particular disposition or of benign mental and moral traits; nor can he testify that his own acquaintance, observation, and knowledge of defendant leads to his own independent opinion that defendant possesses a good general or specific character, inconsistent with commission of acts charged. The witness is, however, allowed to summarize what he has heard in the community, although much of it may have been said by persons less qualified to judge than himself. The evidence which the law permits is not as to the personality of defendant but only as to the shadow his daily life has cast in his neighborhood. This has been well described in a different connection as "the slow growth of months and years, the resultant picture of forgotten incidents, passing events, habitual and daily conduct, presumably honest because disinterested, and safer to be trusted because prone to suspect. It is for that reason that such general repute is permitted to be proven. It sums up a multitude of trivial details. It compacts into the brief phrase of a verdict the teaching of many incidents and the conduct of years. It is the average intelligence drawing its conclusion."

While courts have recognized logical grounds for criticism of this type of opinion-based-on-hearsay testimony, it is said to be justified by "overwhelming considerations of practical convenience" in avoiding innumerable collateral issues which, if it were attempted to prove character by direct testimony, would complicate and confuse the trial, distract the minds of jurymen, and befog the chief issues in the litigation. Another paradox in this branch of the law of evidence is that the delicate and responsible task of compacting reputation hearsay into the "brief phrase of a verdict" is one of the few instances in which conclusions are accepted from a witness on a subject in which he is not an expert. However, the witness must qualify to give an opinion by showing such acquaintance with the defendant, the community in which he has lived, and the circles in which he has moved, as to speak with authority of the terms in which generally he is regarded. To require affirmative knowledge of the reputation may seem inconsistent with the latitude given to the witness to testify when all he can say of the reputation is that he has "heard nothing against defendant." This is permitted upon assumption that, if no ill is reported of one, his reputation must be good. But this answer is accepted only from a witness whose knowledge of defendant's habitat and surroundings is intimate enough so that his failure to hear of any relevant ill repute is an assurance that no ugly rumors were about.

Thus the law extends helpful but illogical options to a defendant. Experience taught a necessity that they be counterweighted with equally illogical conditions to keep the advantage from becoming an unfair and unreasonable one. The price a defendant must pay for attempting to prove his good name is to throw open the entire subject which the law has kept closed for his benefit and to make himself vulnerable where the law otherwise shields him. The prosecution may pursue the inquiry with contradictory witnesses to show that damaging rumors, whether or not well-grounded, were afloat—for it is not the man that he is, but the name that he has which is put in issue. Another hazard is that his own witness is subject to cross-examination as to the contents and extent of the hearsay on which he bases his conclusions, and he may be required to disclose rumors and reports that are current even if they do not affect his own conclusion. It may test the sufficiency of his knowledge by asking what stories were circulating concerning events, such as one's arrest, about which people normally comment and speculate. Thus, while the law gives defendant the option to show as a fact that his reputation reflects a life and habit incompatible with commission of the offense charged, it subjects his proof to tests of credibility designed to prevent him from profiting by a mere parade of partisans. To thus digress from evidence as to the offense to hear a contest as to the standing of the accused, at its best opens a tricky line of inquiry as to a shapeless and elusive subject matter. At its worst it opens a veritable Pandora's box of irresponsible gossip, innuendo, and smear. In the frontier phase of our law's development, calling friends to vouch for defendant's good character, and its counterpart—calling the rivals and enemies of a witness to impeach him by testifying that his reputation for veracity was so bad that he was unworthy of belief on his oath—were favorite and frequent ways of converting an individual litigation into a community contest and a trial into a spectacle. Growth of urban conditions, where one may never know or hear the name of his next-door neighbor, have tended to limit the use of these techniques and to deprive them of weight with juries. The popularity of both procedures has subsided, but courts of last resort have sought to overcome danger that the true issues will be obscured and confused by investing the trial court with discretion to limit the number of such witnesses and to control cross-examination. Both propriety and abuse of hearsay reputation testimony, on both sides, depend on numerous and subtle considerations, difficult to detect or appraise from a cold record, and therefore rarely and only on clear showing of prejudicial abuse of discretion will Courts of Appeals disturb rulings of trial courts on this subject.

Wide discretion is accompanied by heavy responsibility on trial courts to protect the practice from any misuse. . . . The question permitted by the trial court, however, involves several features that may be worthy of comment. Its form invited hearsay; it asked about an arrest, not a conviction, and for an offense not closely similar to the one on trial; and it concerned an occurrence many years past. Since the whole inquiry, as we have pointed out, is calculated to ascertain the general talk of people about defendant, rather than the witness's own knowledge of him, the form of inquiry, "Have you heard?" has general approval, and "Do you know?" is not allowed.

A character witness may be cross-examined as to an arrest whether or not it culminated in a conviction, according to the overwhelming weight of authority. This rule is sometimes confused with that which prohibits cross-examination to credibility by asking a witness whether he himself has been arrested. Arrest without more does not, in law any more than in reason, impeach the integrity or impair the credibility of a witness. It happens to the innocent as well as the guilty. Only a conviction, therefore, may be inquired about to undermine the trustworthiness of a witness.

. . . .

The inquiry as to an arrest is permissible also because the prosecution has a right to test the qualifications of the witness to bespeak the community opinion. If one never heard the speculations and rumors in which even one's friends indulge upon his arrest, the jury may doubt whether he is capable of giving any very reliable conclusions as to his reputation. . . .

The good character which the defendant had sought to establish was broader than the crime charged and included the traits of "honesty and truthfulness" and "being a law-abiding citizen." Possession of these characteristics would seem as incompatible with offering a bribe to a revenue agent as with receiving stolen goods. The crimes may be unlike, but both alike proceed from the same defects of character which the witnesses said this defendant was reputed not to exhibit. It is not only by comparison with the crime on trial but by comparison with the reputation asserted that a court may judge whether the prior arrest should be made subject of inquiry. By this test the inquiry was permissible. It was proper cross-examination because reports of his arrest for receiving stolen goods, if admitted, would tend to weaken the assertion that he was known as an honest and law-abiding citizen. The cross-examination may take in as much ground as the testimony it is designed to verify. To hold otherwise would give defendant the benefit of testimony that he was honest and law-abiding in reputation when such might not be the fact . . . .

The judgment is

Affirmed.

LEGAL ANALYSIS AND WRITING 6.3

The following questions are based on the *How to Brief a Legal Case* format shown in the Appendix. Use this format to answer the following questions:

1. Summarize the facts in the previous case.
2. What is the legal issue?
3. What did the appellate court decide?
4. Why did the court decide this way?
5. Do you agree with the court's reasoning? Explain why or why not.

LEGAL RESEARCH USING THE INTERNET SKILLS 6.3

Find and read this important Supreme Court case online! Check out one of the legal research web sites below and use their "Search" feature to find this case. In the "Search" field, enter the cite or case name.

1. FindLaw U.S. Supreme Court Decisions (http://www.findlaw.com/casecode/supreme.html)
2. U.S. Supreme Court (http://www.supremecourtus.gov/)
3. Supreme Court Collection of Cornell Law School (http://supct.law.cornell.edu/supct/)

CRITICAL THINKING QUESTIONS 6.3

1. What is the reasoning behind the allowing of reputation evidence to prove character?
2. In our modern society, do we actually know our neighbors well enough to testify to their reputation in the community?
3. How can the courts ensure that reputation evidence is trustworthy?
4. What did the *Michelson* court say about reputation and character evidence?

HABIT AND ROUTINE PRACTICE

Habit
A person's customary practice or pattern of behavior when repeatedly engaging in particular actions or situations.

Routine Practice
A regular course of conduct of a group of persons or an organization in response to repeated specific situations.

A **habit** is a person's customary practice or pattern of behavior when repeatedly engaging in particular actions or situations. Virginia defines a habit as "a person's regular response to repeated specific situations."[7] **Routine practice** is defined as "a regular course of conduct of a group of persons or an organization in response to repeated specific situations."[8] Virginia's Code of Evidence regarding habit or routine practice is reflective of the modern rules (see Exhibit 6.5). It holds that evidence of the habit of a person or of the routine practice of an organization, whether corroborated or not, is relevant to prove that the conduct of a person on a particular occasion was in conformity with that habit or routine practice.[9]

Habit is relevant and generally admissible because it demonstrates a higher level of trustworthiness inherent in its routine. People who develop habits tend to stick with them in repeated situations. For example, an individual may have a habit of putting on a seat belt every time that person gets into a vehicle, taking a particular route in driving to and from work, or stopping at a store each day to pick up a paper. Although it may be rebutted, this evidence is still relevant to show that a person acted in conformity with that person's general habit or routine. For a business or organization, this level of "routine practice" is even more trustworthy. There are several evidentiary rules that allow for routine business practices and records.

In considering habit or routine practice evidence, courts generally look for non-volitional activity that occurs on a reflexive and regular basis. Courts require that a regular practice of meeting a particular kind of situation with a specific type of response must be demonstrated.[10] Some courts have emphasized that it is this non-volitional nature of habit evidence that makes it relevant and probative. Activity that requires conscious and volitional thought and decision making would probably not be considered as habit.

EXHIBIT 6.5   Habit and Routine Practice

Idaho Rules of Evidence
Rule 406. Evidence of the habit of a person or of the routine practice of an organization, whether corroborated or not and regardless of the presence of eyewitnesses, is relevant to prove that the conduct of the person or organization on a particular occasion was in conformity with the habit or routine practice.

SUBSEQUENT REMEDIAL MEASURES

Utah represents the modern rules regarding **subsequent remedial measures** that might be taken to ensure that a problem is fixed (see Exhibit 6.6). Their Rule 407 holds that when measures are taken after an event which, if taken previously, would have prevented or made the event less likely to occur, evidence of the subsequent measures is not admissible to prove negligence or culpable conduct in connection with the event.[11] This rule is founded on public policy to encourage the repair or fixing of an unsafe condition so that it doesn't happen again. For example, if a company makes repairs or improves a safety feature after an accident, those repairs or improvements will not be admissible against the company to prove that the company caused the accident or was negligent at the time of the accident. To qualify for this exclusion, there must be some "remedial measure" taken. In one case, for example, a company investigated the cause of a fire involving one of their products. A subsequent report on the cause of this fire was found to be admissible by the court because it did not constitute a remedial "measure."[12]

Subsequent Remedial Measures
Measures taken after an event to repair or ensure that an unsafe condition does not happen again.

EXHIBIT 6.6   Subsequent Remedial Measures

Uniform Rules of Evidence
Rule 407. Whenever, after an event, measures are taken which, if taken previously, would have made the event less likely to occur, evidence of the subsequent measures is not admissible to prove negligence or culpable conduct in connection with the event. This rule does not require the exclusion of evidence of subsequent measures when offered for another purpose, such as proving ownership, control, or feasibility of precautionary measures, if controverted, or impeachment.

INADMISSIBILITY OF PLEAS

To promote the open discussion and negotiation of plea agreements, most evidence laws contain a rule like Rule 410 of the Wyoming Rules of Evidence (see Exhibit 6.7). Under Rule 410, evidence of the following is not admissible against a defendant who made the plea or was a participant in the plea discussions:

1. Evidence of a plea of guilty which was later withdrawn
2. An admission to a criminal charge, later withdrawn
3. A plea of nolo contendere
4. An offer to plead to the crime charged or any other crime, or of statements made in connection with any of the foregoing withdrawn pleas or offers[13]

Nolo Contendere
"No Contest." A plea that carries the same punishment as a guilty plea, but where defendant neither admits nor denies the crime.

These statements would not be admissible in a civil or criminal action, case, or proceeding against the person who made the plea or offer. One of the most common examples of how this rule is used is found in cases where a defendant in a criminal action pleads **nolo contendere** or "no contest" so that the defendant's plea cannot be used in a subsequent civil action. For example, a defendant pleads *no contest* to a drunk driving causing injury prosecution. In a subsequent civil action for personal injury, this plea cannot be used as evidence of defendant's negligence.

The U.S. Supreme Court has, however, held that plea negotiations and agreements under Rule 410 can be waived by a defendant. In a 1995 decision, the Court held that "the plea-statement Rules expressly contemplate a degree of party control that is consonant with the background presumption of waivability" and that Rule 410 creates "a privilege of the defendant . . . like other evidentiary privileges, this one may be waived or varied at the defendant's request."[14]

EXHIBIT 6.7   Inadmissibility of Pleas

Wyoming Rules of Evidence
Rule 410. Withdrawn Pleas and Offers.

Evidence of a plea of guilty, later withdrawn, or admission of the charge, later withdrawn, or of a plea of nolo contendere, or of an offer so to plead to the crime charged or any other crime, or of statements made in connection with any of the foregoing withdrawn pleas or offers, is not admissible in any civil or criminal action, case, or proceeding against the person who made the plea or offer.

VICTIM'S PAST SEXUAL BEHAVIOR

For many years, the victim in rape and sexual assault cases was subjected to harsh and often accusatory cross-examination at trial. The focus of such a trial often became the prior sexual behavior or predisposition of the victim, rather than on the alleged crime by the defendant. As a result of this offensive treatment of victims, a series of **rape shield laws** were passed in the 1970s (see Exhibit 6.8). These laws were designed to protect the privacy of victims of sexual assaults when they testify in court from a degrading cross-examination into intimate details of their private lives. The laws were also designed to prevent the wasting of time on what many courts called irrelevant and distractive evidence.

Rape Shield Laws
Laws designed to protect the privacy of victims of sexual assaults when they testify in court.

EXHIBIT 6.8   Example of Rape Shield Law

Pennsylvania Rape Shield Law
18 Pa.C.S.A. § 3104. Evidence of Victim's Sexual Conduct.

(a) General Rule.—Evidence of specific instances of the alleged victim's past sexual conduct, opinion evidence of the alleged victim's past sexual conduct, and reputation evidence of the alleged victim's past sexual conduct shall not be admissible in prosecutions under this chapter except evidence of the alleged victim's past sexual conduct with the defendant where consent of the alleged victim is at issue and such evidence is otherwise admissible pursuant to the rules of evidence.

Federal Rule

The rape shield laws were codified in the evidence rules of several states in the late 1970s. Congress added this to the Federal Rules of Evidence in 1978 with the adoption of Rule 412. Under Rule 412, in any civil or criminal proceeding involving alleged sexual misconduct, evidence offered to prove that a victim engaged in other sexual behavior or evidence offered to prove any alleged victim's sexual predisposition is not admissible. There are exceptions to this rule, however. In a criminal case, the following evidence is admissible, if otherwise admissible under these rules:

1. Evidence of specific instances of sexual behavior by the alleged victim offered to prove that a person other than the accused was the source of semen, injury, or other physical evidence;

2. Evidence of specific instances of sexual behavior by the alleged victim with respect to the person accused of the sexual misconduct offered by the accused to prove consent or by the prosecution; and

3. Evidence the exclusion of which would violate the constitutional rights of the defendant.

In a civil case, evidence offered to prove the sexual behavior or sexual predisposition of any alleged victim is admissible if it is otherwise admissible under these rules and its probative value substantially outweighs the danger of harm to any victim and of unfair prejudice to any party. Evidence of an alleged victim's reputation is admissible only if it has been placed in controversy by the alleged victim.[15]

Procedure to Determine Admissibility

A party intending to offer evidence under one of these exceptions must file a written motion before trial specifically describing the evidence and stating the purpose for which it is offered unless the court, for good cause, requires a different time for filing or permits filing during trial; and serve the motion on all parties and notify the alleged victim or, when appropriate, the alleged victim's guardian or representative.

Before admitting evidence under this rule the court must conduct a hearing in camera and afford the victim and parties a right to attend and be heard. The motion, related papers, and the record of the hearing must be sealed and remain under seal unless the court orders otherwise.[16]

EVIDENCE OF SIMILAR CRIMES IN SEXUAL ASSAULT CASES

In 1995, Federal Rules were developed by Congress to admit evidence of similar past crimes in sexual assault and child molestation cases, both criminal and civil (see Exhibit 6.9). The first of these, Rule 413, provided for evidence of similar offenses when a defendant is accused of a sexual assault in a criminal action. Rule 414 followed, substituting "child molestation" for sexual assault. Finally, Rule 415 extended this to civil cases for evidence of either sexual assault or child molestation.

These Federal Rules have not yet been adopted by most states.

EXHIBIT 6.9   Federal Rules of Evidence: Similar Crimes in Sexual Assault Cases

Rule 413. Evidence of Similar Crimes in Sexual Assault Cases.

(a) In a criminal case in which the defendant is accused of an offense of sexual assault, evidence of the defendant's commission of another offense or offenses of sexual assault is admissible, and may be considered for its bearing on any matter to which it is relevant.

(b) In a case in which the Government intends to offer evidence under this rule, the attorney for the Government shall disclose the evidence to the defendant, including statements of witnesses or a summary of the substance of any testimony that is expected to be offered, at least fifteen days before the scheduled date of trial or at such later time as the court may allow for good cause.

(c) This rule shall not be construed to limit the admission or consideration of evidence under any other rule.

(d) For purposes of this rule and Rule 415, "offense of sexual assaults" means a crime under Federal law or the law of a State. . . .

Rule 414. Evidence of Similar Crimes in Child Molestation Cases.

(a) In a criminal case in which the defendant is accused of an offense of child molestation, evidence of the defendant's commission of another offense or offenses of child molestation is admissible, and may be considered for its bearing on any matter to which it is relevant.

(b) In a case in which the Government intends to offer evidence under this rule, the attorney for the Government shall disclose the evidence to the defendant, including statements of witnesses or a summary of the substance of any testimony that is expected to be offered, at least fifteen days before the scheduled date of trial or at such later time as the court may allow for good cause.

(c) This rule shall not be construed to limit the admission or consideration of evidence under any other rule.

(d) For purposes of this rule and Rule 415, "child" means a person below the age of fourteen, and "offense of child molestation" means a crime under Federal law or the law of a State. . . .

Rule 415. Evidence of Similar Acts in Civil Cases Concerning Sexual Assault or Child Molestation.

(a) In a civil case in which a claim for damages or other relief is predicated on a party's alleged commission of conduct constituting an offense of sexual assault or child molestation, evidence of that party's commission of another offense or offenses of sexual assault or child molestation is admissible and may be considered as provided in Rule 413 and Rule 414 of these Rules.

(b) A party who intends to offer evidence under this Rule shall disclose the evidence to the party against whom it will be offered, including statements of witnesses or a summary of the substance of any testimony that is expected to be offered, at least fifteen days before the scheduled date of trial or at such later time as the court may allow for good cause.

(c) This rule shall not be construed to limit the admission or consideration of evidence under any other rule.

CRITICAL THINKING QUESTIONS 6.4

1. Why do we allow habit evidence?
2. Why do we exclude evidence of subsequent remedial measures to prove negligence?
3. A plea of nolo contendere carries the same weight as a guilty plea as far as punishment. Why then would we not allow it as evidence in a subsequent action?
4. How do we balance the need to protect victims of sexual assault from degrading and intrusive cross-examination as provided for in the rape shield laws with the right of a defendant to effective confrontation and right to a fair defense?
5. How can we provide adequate safeguards for a defendant when we allow evidence of similar crimes in sexual assault and child molestation cases?

LEGAL RESEARCH USING THE INTERNET SKILLS 6.4

Use one of the following web sites to find out whether your state rules of evidence include any of the above newer Federal Rules.

List of State Laws from Legal Information Institute of Cornell Law School (http://www.law.cornell.edu/states/listing.html)

FindLaw (http://www.findlaw.com)

Federal Rules of Evidence (http://www.law.cornell.edu/rules/fre/overview.html)

SUMMARY

Evidence of a person's character or trait of character is generally not admissible to prove conduct on a particular occasion. When character or trait of character is the ultimate issue in a case or an essential element of a charge, claim, or defense, proof may be made of *specific instances* of that person's conduct. Evidence of other crimes is generally not admissible to prove character in order to prove that someone acted in conformity therewith. However, it may be used to show other purposes, such as proof of motive, opportunity, or means. Evidence may also be admissible to prove intent, knowledge, modus operandi, preparation, plan, knowledge, identity, or absence of mistake or accident. Even when found to be, evidence of prior bad acts may still be excluded under Rule 403, if its prejudicial effect outweighs its probative value. In any case where evidence of character is allowed, proof may be made by testimony as to reputation in the community or by testimony in the form of an opinion. Evidence of the habit of a person or of the routine practice of an organization, whether corroborated or not, is relevant to prove that the conduct of a person on a particular occasion was in conformity with that habit or routine practice.

To promote the open discussion and negotiation of plea agreements, evidence of a guilty plea which was later withdrawn, a plea of nolo contendere, or an offer or negotiation to plead is not admissible against a defendant who made the plea or was a participant in the plea discussions.

The rape shield laws were codified in the evidence rules of several states in the late 1970s. Congress added this to the Federal Rules of Evidence in 1978 with the adoption of Rule 412. Under Rule 412, in any civil or criminal proceeding involving alleged sexual misconduct, evidence offered to prove that a victim engaged in other sexual behavior or evidence offered to prove any alleged victim's sexual predisposition is not admissible. In 1995, Federal Rules were developed by Congress to admit evidence of similar past crimes in sexual assault and child molestation cases, both criminal and civil. The first of these, Rule 413, provided for evidence of similar offenses when a defendant is accused of a sexual assault in a criminal action. Rule 414 followed, substituting "child molestation" for sexual assault. Finally, Rule 415 extended this to civil cases for evidence of either sexual assault or child molestation. These Federal Rules have not yet been adopted by most states.

KEY TERMS

Character Evidence

Habit

Nolo Contendere

Opinion

Rape Shield Laws

Reputation

Routine Practice

Subsequent Remedial Measures

LEARNING OUTCOMES AND PRACTICE SKILLS CHECKLIST

☐ Learning Outcomes

After completing your reading, questions, and exercises, you should be able to demonstrate a better understanding of the learning concepts by answering the following questions:

1. Discuss the general rule for admitting character evidence and the exceptions to this rule.
2. Explain when prior bad acts or other crimes can and cannot be admitted as evidence to prove character.
3. Identify and discuss the methods for proving character.
4. Explain whether character evidence may be admitted when character is an ultimate issue or an essential element of a charge or defense. Give an example.
5. Distinguish between habit and character evidence.
6. Explain when habit evidence can be admitted. Give an example.
7. Describe the reasoning behind admitting evidence of subsequent remedial measures. Give an example.
8. Identify some of the newer evidence rules that protect victims of sexual assault and allow for the admission of evidence in sexual assault or related cases. Discuss whether these rules have been accepted in state courts.

☐ Practice Skills

In addition to understanding the learning concepts, practice what you have learned through applications using critical thinking, legal analysis and writing, legal research, and advocacy skills, including:

Critical Thinking

1. Why do we have the rules excluding character evidence and the exceptions to these rules described in this chapter?
2. Do you believe that the current rules and exceptions discussed in this chapter provide adequate safeguards?
3. What public policy issues or considerations do you think might be behind these rules?
4. If it were up to you, would you keep these exceptions as they are, delete them, narrow them, or expand them? Explain your reasoning.
5. How do these rules influence the gathering of evidence or preparing of witnesses?

Legal Analysis and Writing

Analyze the following rules and cases by summarizing their holdings, explaining their significance, and assessing any issue that might arise in their application.

1. Rule 404(a) and (b).
2. Rule 405(a) and (b).
3. Rule 406.
4. Rule 407.
5. Rule 410.
6. *Huddleston v. United States.*
7. *Michelson v. United States.*

Legal Research Using the Internet

1. Find the annotated Federal Rules of Evidence on the Internet and assess the comments made in the proposing of the rules covered in this chapter.
2. Find your state's rules of evidence regarding relevance exceptions and concepts covered in this chapter. Compare and contrast with the federal and/or modern rules, and some of the state rules listed in this chapter.
3. Find out if your state appellate court posts their case decisions on the Internet. If so, find a case that illustrates an issue or rule discussed in this chapter. If your state decisions are not on the Internet, go instead to the web site for the U.S. Circuit Court of Appeals in your circuit, or search the U.S. Supreme Court decisions.

PRACTICE APPLICATION 6.1

In the "hockey rink" manslaughter case, defendant took his son to the boy's hockey practice. The defendant got into an argument with another father about too much "roughhousing" by the boys on the ice. The two men began to argue. The other man, who was much smaller than the defendant, pushed the defendant and called him a name. The defendant knocked the smaller man down, kicked him several times, and repeatedly slammed the man's head against the floor, causing the man's death. The defendant was charged with manslaughter.

1. At the trial, the prosecution wants to introduce evidence that the defendant had been arrested 15 years ago of domestic violence against a previous spouse. In that case, the spouse had called the defendant a name and the defendant reacted by knocking the spouse down, kicking her several times, and repeatedly slamming her head against the floor.

2. The defense has pled self-defense and when they present their case, they want to introduce character evidence that portrays the defendant as a "gentle giant" with a peaceful reputation and not an aggressor.
3. The prosecution wants to rebut this evidence with a witness who will testify that she pleaded with defendant to stop beating the victim at the hockey rink.
4. The prosecution also wants to rebut this evidence with a witness who will testify that the defendant had a reputation for being loud and had a habit of yelling at hockey games.

Use the format shown in the Appendix for the *IRAC Method of Legal Analysis* and the readings, rules, and cases discussed in this chapter to analyze the above case problems and determine whether the evidence in each example can be admitted. Write a memo giving your analysis, reasoning, and conclusions.

ADVOCACY AND COMMUNICATION SKILLS 6.1

Form plaintiff and defense teams from small groups of no more than 3–4 each. Using the previous example about the "hockey rink" manslaughter case, the defense team should prepare and ask questions of a defense witness that pertain to the reputation of a defendant. The plaintiff team may then cross-examine. After direct and cross-examination has ended, the plaintiff team may present and ask questions of a rebuttal witness. The defense may then cross-examine this witness. During each line of questioning, the opposing team should be prepared to object, if needed, using objections from earlier readings. Use a different team member for each examination:
1. Plaintiff team will conduct a direct exam of no more than 5 minutes.
2. Defense team will conduct a cross-exam of no more than 5 minutes.

YOU BE THE JUDGE 6.2

Defendant was charged with child molestation on his stepdaughter, including several incidents when defendant would enter her bedroom at night and attempt to touch her "in a way [she] didn't like." Once, the victim awoke to find the defendant touching her breasts. She asked defendant what he was doing, and he replied he was covering her with a blanket. At trial, prosecutors want to call the victim's sister as a witness. The sister would testify that when she was 10 or 11 years of age, she awoke on three occasions to find the defendant beside her bed, touching her breasts and vaginal area. When she asked defendant what he was doing, he said he was "straightening up the covers."
Would you allow this evidence? Why or why not?

LEGAL RESEARCH USING THE INTERNET SKILLS 6.5

Find out how the court ruled on the above *You Be the Judge* problem by finding and reading the California Supreme Court decision online! The citation for it is:
   People v. Ewoldt, 7 Cal. 4th 380 (1994).

WEB SITES

Federal Rules of Evidence
(http://www.law.cornell.edu/rules/fre/overview.html)
FindLaw
(http://www.findlaw.com)
FindLaw
(http://guide.lp.findlaw.com/casecode/)
FindLaw U.S. Supreme Court Decisions
(http://www.findlaw.com/casecode/supreme.html)
List of State Laws from Legal Information Institute of Cornell Law School
(http://www.law.cornell.edu/states/listing.html)

National Center for State Courts—State and Federal Court Web Sites
(http://www.ncsconline.org/D_kis/info_court_web_sites.html#federal)
Supreme Court Collection of Cornell Law School
(http://supct.law.cornell.edu/supct/)
U.S. Courts Site with Links to all Circuit Courts of Appeal
(http://www.uscourts.gov/links.html)
U.S. Supreme Court
(http://www.supremecourtus.gov/)

ENDNOTES

1. For example, see Rules 607–609.
2. See Fed. R. Evid. 608.
3. *State v. Percy*, 158 Vt. 410 (1992).
4. *United States v. Myers*, 550 F.2d 1036 (5th Cir. 1977).
5. See *State v. Shedrick*, 59 Ohio St. 3d 146 (1991) and *State v. White*, 101 N.C. App. 593 (1991).
6. *State v. Jones*, 160 Vt. 440 (1993).
7. Va. Code § 8.01–397.1. B. Habit and Routine Practice Defined.
8. Ibid.
9. Ibid.
10. See, for example, *Frase v. Henry*, 444 F.2d 1228 (10th Cir. 1971).
11. *Utah Rules of Evidence*, Rule 407. Subsequent Remedial Measures.
12. See *Prentiss & Carlisle v. Koehring-Waterous*, 972 F.2d 6 (1st Cir. 1992).
13. See *Wyoming Rules of Evidence*, Rule 410.
14. *United States v. Mezzanatto*, 115 S. Ct. 797 (1995).
15. See Fed. R. Evid. 412.
16. Fed. R. Evid. 412(c).

WITNESSES AND COMPETENCY

"One eye witness is worth more than ten who tell what they have heard."
—*Plautus, 184 B.C.*

LEARNING OUTCOMES

In this chapter, you will learn about the following legal concepts:

- Role of Witnesses in the Legal Process
- Where Witness Laws Came From
- Witnesses and Due Process
- Witnesses and Competency

- Elements of Competency
- Competency of Children as Witnesses
- Competency of Judge or Juror as Witnesses

Witness
A person who testifies at trial, generally from firsthand knowledge about a fact at issue.

Competency
Legal fitness to testify as a witness.

INTRODUCTION

In this chapter, we will examine the role of the **witness** in the trial process and focus on the **competency** required to be a witness. What is a witness and why are witnesses so essential to the trial process? Should we exclude anyone from being a witness? Are children competent to be witnesses? What about convicted criminals? The mentally ill? Do we still require a religious oath before allowing a witness to testify? What factors do we need to consider in determining the competency of a witness? We will explore these questions and determine what qualifies a witness to testify.

ROLE OF WITNESSES IN THE LEGAL PROCESS

Witnesses are central to the introduction of evidence and the proving of a case at trial. We look to witnesses to provide evidence in the form of testimony to help the triers of fact better ascertain the truth. This testimony must be from firsthand, personal knowledge. Witnesses are also called to lay a foundation for other evidence being offered, to identify and authenticate this evidence, and even to offer their opinions as to how this evidence was obtained or what it means.

What Is A Witness?

A witness is a person who can give a firsthand account of something from personal knowledge. In a legal proceeding, the witness does this by being called to the stand, taking an oath, and testifying to firsthand perception (i.e., what he saw, heard, felt, smelled, or tasted).

WHERE WITNESS LAWS CAME FROM

Laws governing witnesses can be traced back hundreds of years to early England, when restrictions were placed on who could testify and limitations were set on the scope of testimony. Among those who could not testify were felons, atheists, children, and spouses. Going back to the laws of the Roman Empire, there were restrictions on slaves being called as witnesses against their masters, or lawyers as witnesses against a client.

WITNESSES AND DUE PROCESS

Due Process
Fundamental principle in a criminal action, holding that a person has a right to reasonable notice of a charge against him, and an opportunity to be heard in his defense, which includes the right to call witnesses on his behalf and to confront those witnesses against him.

In criminal trials, the right to present witnesses on our own behalf and the right to confront witnesses against us is at the heart of **due process**. Mr. Justice Black, writing for the Supreme Court in 1948, identified these rights as among the minimum essentials of a fair trial:

> A person's right to reasonable notice of a charge against him, and an opportunity to be heard in his defense—a right to his day in court—are basic in our system of jurisprudence; and these rights include, as a minimum, a right to examine the witnesses against him, to offer testimony, and to be represented by counsel.[1]

Several years later, the Court emphasized this, saying:

> The right to offer the testimony of witnesses, and to compel their attendance, if necessary, is in plain terms the right to present a defense, the right to present the defendant's version of the facts as well as the prosecution's to the jury so it may decide where the truth lies. Just as an accused has the right to confront the prosecution's witnesses for the purpose of challenging their testimony, he has the right to present his own witnesses to establish a defense. This right is a fundamental element of due process of law.[2]

CRITICAL THINKING QUESTIONS 7.1

1. Why do we need witnesses?
2. Could we not speed up the trial process and still achieve the same goals by having the judge or attorneys read written statements or summaries from witnesses?
3. What are the strengths and weaknesses of allowing witnesses?
4. Why do we consider it a fundamental principle of due process to allow for witnesses in criminal trials?

WITNESSES AND COMPETENCY

The basic requirement for a witness to be able to testify is *competency*. Competency is the legal fitness or capacity of a witness to testify.

Common Law

At common law, many different types of witnesses were considered legally incompetent to testify. Interested parties to actions could not testify because their interest in the outcome of the case might tend to influence their testimony. Spouses could not testify against one another because of the potential disruption to the marital relationship. Children could not testify because it was thought that they lacked the **legal capacity** to understand the duty to tell the truth. Felons could not testify because of their loss of civil rights. Witnesses were not deemed competent if they did not believe in God or refused to take an oath.

Legal Capacity
Legally fit or qualified.

Modern Rule

Although some of the common law rules still exist in varied form, the modern rule today is that all witnesses are competent except as provided by another rule of evidence or statute (see Exhibit 7.1). The effect of this is to leave most grounds of competency to the trier of fact as questions of credibility.

EXHIBIT 7.1   Examples of Modern Rules for Witness Competency

Federal Rules of Evidence
Rule 601. General Rule of Competency.
   Every person is competent to be a witness except as otherwise provided in these rules. However, in civil actions and proceedings, with respect to an element of a claim or defense as to which State law supplies the rule of decision, the competency of a witness shall be determined in accordance with State law.

California Evidence Code
Sec. 700. Except as otherwise provided by statute, every person, irrespective of age, is qualified to be a witness and no person is disqualified to testify to any matter.

LEGAL RESEARCH USING THE INTERNET SKILLS 7.1

Use one of the following web sites to find out whether your state rules of evidence pertaining to witness competency are patterned after the Federal Rules.

List of State Laws from Legal Information Institute of Cornell Law School (http://www.law.cornell.edu/states/listing.html)

FindLaw (http://www.findlaw.com)

Federal Rules of Evidence (http://www.law.cornell.edu/rules/fre/overview.html)

ELEMENTS OF COMPETENCY

Witness competency is assessed through the determination of three key elements: *personal knowledge*, understanding the *duty to tell the truth*, and *capacity for communication* (being capable of communicating or expressing herself to the judge and jury).

1. Personal Knowledge

Personal Knowledge
A witness must be able to testify from a firsthand perception of having seen, heard, felt, touched, or smelled something.

To help ensure reliability in the factfinding process, a witness must have **personal knowledge** about the matter being testified to, as opposed to a mere opinion (see Exhibit 7.2). A Mississippi Rule, for example, states that a "witness may not testify to a matter unless evidence is introduced sufficient to support a finding that the witness has personal knowledge of the matter."[3] Personal knowledge involves *perception* and *recollection*. A witness must be testifying about an event that the witness perceived through one of her senses (sight, hearing, and so on). It must be firsthand knowledge, and not what she has heard from others. She must also be able to recollect it. Evidence to prove personal knowledge usually comes from the witness's own testimony (see Exhibit 7.3).

EXHIBIT 7.2   Lack of Personal Knowledge

Pennsylvania Rules of Evidence
Rule 602.

A witness may not testify to a matter unless evidence is introduced sufficient to support a finding that the witness has personal knowledge of the matter. Evidence to prove personal knowledge may, but need not, consist of the witness's own testimony. This Rule is subject to the provisions of Rule 703, relating to opinion testimony by expert witnesses.

EXHIBIT 7.3   Example of Testimony Lacking Personal Knowledge

Defense: You don't know whether the defendant had access to the computer network?
Witness: No, I was told that she did not have access.
Defense: You don't have personal knowledge of whether she did?
Witness: No, only what I was told by my supervisor.
Defense: I move to strike the last answer. It's based on what witness was told by others, not based on her personal knowledge or based on anything within this witness's ability to speak from her personal knowledge.

CRITICAL THINKING QUESTIONS 7.2

1. Why do we have rules that limit witness testimony to personal knowledge?
2. Do you think this rule is a good one? Explain why or why not.
3. What public policy issues, if any, are behind this rule?
4. How does this rule influence the gathering of evidence or preparing of witnesses?
5. If you were preparing a witness for trial, what factors would you need to consider to comply with this rule?

LEGAL ANALYSIS AND WRITING 7.1

Plaintiff wants to call a witness to the stand in a civil case involving injury that resulted from defendant's alleged drunk driving. The witness was standing in a crowd of people when defendant's vehicle jumped the curb and struck several bystanders. Although the witness did not see defendant driving the vehicle, she was in the middle of the crowd when rescue workers pulled defendant out of the vehicle. The witness will testify that she smelled the odor of alcoholic beverage in the air at that time. She will further testify that prior to the defendant being pulled out of the vehicle, she did not smell any alcohol.

Defense challenges the competency of the witness to testify from personal knowledge. What is the result? Use the format shown in the Appendix for the *IRAC Method of Legal Analysis* to solve the above case problem.

2. Duty to Tell the Truth

A witness must be capable of understanding the **duty to tell the truth** and take an oath or affirmation to this effect. Historically, this oath required a religious basis and a witness generally had to swear before God with a hand on the Bible. Modern rules recognize the need for more diversity in the types of witnesses who testify and require only an "oath or affirmation in a form calculated to awaken the witness's conscience and impress the witness's mind with the duty" to tell the truth.[4] The judge must be satisfied that the witness understands this obligation (see Exhibit 7.4). The modern rule really serves as a notice to the witness that failure to tell the truth may result in perjury charges.

Duty to Tell the Truth
Legal obligation of witness to testify truthfully under penalty of perjury.

EXHIBIT 7.4   Examples of State Rules Requiring Oath or Affirmation

Texas Rules of Evidence
Rule 603. Oath or Affirmation.
    Before testifying, every witness shall be required to declare that the witness will testify truthfully, by oath or affirmation administered in a form calculated to awaken the witness' conscience and impress the witness' mind with the duty to do so.

(Continued)

EXHIBIT 7.4   Examples of State Rules Requiring Oath or Affirmation   *Continued*

New Jersey Rules of Evidence
Rule 603. Oath or Affirmation.
   Before testifying a witness shall be required to take an oath or make an affirmation or declaration to tell the truth under the penalty provided by law. No witness may be barred from testifying because of religious belief or lack of such belief.

Can "Truth" Be Replaced with "Fully Integrated Honesty?"

In the following Nevada case, the court decides whether there is any required form of oath that needs to be taken for a witness at trial (see Exhibit 7.5). In this trial for tax evasion, the defendant wants an alternative oath that replaces the word "truth" with the phrase "fully integrated Honesty."

CASE

United States v. Ward
973 F.2d 730 (9th Cir. 1992).
Appeal from the United States District Court for the District of Nevada.

Fletcher, Circuit Judge.

... On March 29, 1990, a grand jury indicted Ward on three counts each of tax evasion and failure to file income tax returns. Ward chose to represent himself at trial. On July 9, 1990, Ward filed a "Motion to Challenge the Oath," which proposed an alternative oath that replaced the word "truth" with the phrase "fully integrated Honesty." The oath would read, "Do you affirm to speak with fully integrated Honesty, only with fully integrated Honesty and nothing but fully integrated Honesty?" For reasons we will not attempt to explain, Ward believed that honesty is superior to truth. Magistrate Lawrence R. Leavitt ruled ... that "the oath or affirmation which has been administered in courts of law throughout the United States to millions of witnesses for hundreds of years should not be required to give way to the defendant's idiosyncratic distinctions between truth and honesty."

... A three-day trial commenced on February 11, 1991. Ward made a lengthy opening statement and actively cross-examined government witnesses. At a sidebar during the second day of trial, Ward offered to take both the standard oath and his oath. The prosecutor was amenable to the compromise, but the district court refused to allow it. "This is an oath that has been used for a very

long time," the district court said, "and I'm not going to establish a precedent where someone can come in and require the court to address that matter differently." At the close of the government's case on the third day of trial, Ward asked once again to testify under his oath. The judge again refused, saying, "The oath has been used for a very long time. ... That's the oath that will be administered." Ward did not testify and presented no witnesses. The jury convicted Ward of all counts after an hour's deliberation. Ward now appeals. He argues that the district court's insistence on an oath that violated his beliefs abridged his First Amendment right to free exercise of religion and his Fifth Amendment right to testify in his own defense.

DISCUSSION

... To begin with, there is no constitutionally or statutorily required form of oath. Federal Rule of Evidence 603 requires only that a witness "declare that the witness will testify truthfully, by oath or affirmation administered in a form calculated to awaken the witness's conscience and impress the witness's mind with the duty to do so." The advisory committee notes to Rule 603 explain that "the rule is designed to afford the flexibility required in dealing with religious adults, atheists, conscientious objectors, mental defectives, and children. Affirmation is simply a solemn undertaking to tell the truth; no special verbal formula is required." ... [I]t cannot matter what words or ceremonies are used in imposing the oath, provided he recognizes them as binding by his belief.

. . . All the district judge need do is to make inquiry as to what form of oath or affirmation would not offend defendant's religious beliefs but would give rise to a duty to speak the truth.

Neither the magistrate nor the district court cited to any . . . authorities, relying instead on their perception that the standard oath had not changed "for hundreds of years." While oaths including the familiar "truth, whole truth, and nothing but the truth" formulation date back at least to the seventeenth century, the principle that the form of the oath must be crafted in a way that is meaningful to the witness also predates our constitution. In *Omichund v. Barker*, 1 Atk. 22 (1744), Lord Chief Judge Willes wrote, "It would be absurd for [a non-Christian witness] to swear according to the Christian oath, which he does not believe; and therefore, out of necessity, he must be allowed to swear according to his own notion of an oath." See also *Atcheson v. Everitt*, 1 Cowper 382 (1776) ("As the purpose of [the oath] is to bind his conscience, every man of every religion should be bound by that form which he himself thinks will bind his own conscience most").

This case has an odd twist in that the defendant offered to take the traditional oath if he could also take his own. His own oath superimposed on the traditional one would have taken nothing away from the commitment to tell the truth under penalties of perjury and, indeed, in the defendant's mind imposed upon him a higher duty. Under these circumstances the district court clearly abused its discretion in refusing the oath and preventing the defendant's testimony. Reversed and Remanded.

Poole, Circuit Judge, dissenting.

. . . I believe that Ward's objection to the oath ordinarily required of witnesses by Fed. R. Evid. 603 amounts to nothing more than a philosophical predilection. Ward does not tell us how his concerns about the misuse of the word "truth" affects his ability to cope with the pressures and challenges of his daily life. He does not enlighten us as to how habitual application of the term "honesty" provides him spiritual growth, relates to his understanding of life's purpose and meaning, or guides his daily routine. He does tell us that "honesty" means that all of the world's problems will disappear because then we will all know people are not lying, but I fail to see how this prediction satisfies the requirement that Ward's preference for a particular word be as important, or even as relevant, as religion is in the lives of many people.

Even were I to give Ward the benefit of the doubt and ascribe religious significance to his "ultimate concern" with the merits of the word "honesty," I would still decline to require the district court to accommodate his objection. . . . Ward's proposed alternative oath does not contain an acknowledgement of the duty to speak truthfully and does not ensure that the defendant is aware of the cost of dishonesty. The majority's accommodation of Ward's "purely secular philosophical concerns" will result not in protection of a valuable Constitutional right but in numerous wasteful and time-consuming attacks on the oath mandated as a means of guaranteeing truth and of expediting the administration of justice. I dissent.

LEGAL ANALYSIS AND WRITING 7.2

The following questions are based on the *How to Brief a Legal Case* format shown in the Appendix. Use this format to answer the following questions:

1. Summarize the facts in the previous case.

2. What is the legal issue?

3. How did the appellate court decide?

4. Why did the court decide this way?

5. Do you agree with the court's reasoning? Explain why or why not.

EXHIBIT 7.5   Forms of Oath or Affirmation

Florida Evidence Code
Sec. 90.605. Oath or Affirmation of Witness. (1) Before testifying, each witness shall declare that he or she will testify truthfully, by taking an oath or affirmation in substantially the following form: "Do you swear or affirm that the evidence you are about to give will be the truth, the whole truth, and nothing but the truth?" The witness's answer shall be noted in the record.

Maryland Rules
Rule 1-303. Form of Oath. (a) *Generally.* . . . [W]henever an oral oath is required by rule or law, the person making oath shall solemnly swear or affirm under the penalties of perjury that the responses given and statements made will be the whole truth and nothing but the truth.

---

3. Capable of Communicating

Capable of Communicating
A witness must be able to express himself and communicate so as to be reasonably understood by the judge or jury.

A witness must be **capable of communicating** or expressing himself so as to be reasonably understood by the judge or jury (see Exhibit 7.6). The New Jersey Rules regard a witness competent unless "incapable of expression concerning the matter so as to be understood."[5] This capacity of communication may be done directly or through an interpreter. If an interpreter is used, the interpreter is subject to the rules of evidence relating to qualification as an expert and the administration of an oath or affirmation to make a true translation. The interpreter must demonstrate an ability to interpret accurately, effectively, and impartially.

EXHIBIT 7.6   Examples of State Rules Defining Incompetency

Kentucky Rules of Evidence
Rule 601. Competency.

> (b) Minimal Qualifications. A person is disqualified to testify as a witness if the trial court determines that he:

> (1) Lacked the capacity to perceive accurately the matters about which he proposes to testify;

> (2) Lacks the capacity to recollect facts;

> (3) Lacks the capacity to express himself so as to be understood, either directly or through an interpreter; or

> (4) Lacks the capacity to understand the obligation of a witness to tell the truth.

New Jersey Rules of Evidence
Rule 601. General Rule of Competency.

Every person is competent to be a witness unless (a) the judge finds that the proposed witness is incapable of expression concerning the matter so as to be understood by the judge and jury either directly or through interpretation, or (b) the proposed witness is incapable of understanding the duty of a witness to tell the truth, or (c) except as otherwise provided by these rules or by law.

Pennsylvania Rules of Evidence
Rule 601. Competency.

> (b) Disqualification for Specific Defects. A person is incompetent to testify if the Court finds that because of a mental condition or immaturity the person: (1) is, or was, at any relevant time, incapable of perceiving accurately; (2) is unable to express himself or herself so as to be understood either directly or through an interpreter; (3) has an impaired memory; or (4) does not sufficiently understand the duty to tell the truth.

(Continued)

EXHIBIT 7.6   Examples of State Rules Defining Incompetency   *Continued*

Revised Code of Washington
Sec. 5.60.050. Who Are Incompetent. The following persons shall not be competent to testify:

> (1) Those who are of unsound mind, or intoxicated at the time of their production for examination, and
>
> (2) Those who appear incapable of receiving just impressions of the facts, respecting which they are examined, or of relating them truly.

EVIDENTIARY CHECKLIST 7.1

Elements of Witness Competency

Witness competency is assessed through the determination of three key elements:

☐   A witness must have *personal knowledge* about the matter being testified to.

☐   A witness must be capable of understanding the *duty to tell the truth* and take an oath or affirmation to this effect.

☐   A witness must be capable of *communicating* or expressing herself so as to be reasonably understood by the judge or jury.

CRITICAL THINKING QUESTIONS 7.3

1. What public policy issues, if any, are behind the competency rules?
2. How do these rules influence the gathering of evidence or preparing of witnesses?
3. If you were preparing a witness for trial, what factors would you need to consider to comply with these rules?
4. If your opponent was planning to call a witness who had a diagnosed mental condition, what steps would you take to help your legal team exclude or attack the admissibility or credibility of the evidence?

YOU BE THE JUDGE 7.1

Defendant challenges plaintiff's calling of a witness who has been diagnosed with multiple personality disorders.

1. Would you let this witness testify? Why or why not?
2. What factors would you need to consider in order to make this decision?

LEGAL RESEARCH USING THE INTERNET SKILLS 7.2

Use the Internet to find and report on a case decision from your state appellate court (or, if your state does not provide these on the Internet, go to the federal court of appeals for your circuit) that illustrates an issue dealing with the competency of a witness.

> ### Practice Tip 7.1
>
> Here is a checklist to help ensure that your witness is competent to testify:
> ☐   Does your witness have personal knowledge of the matters about which she is testifying?
> ☐   Can your witness accurately perceive the matters about which she is testifying?
> ☐   Can your witness recollect facts?
> ☐   Can your witness express herself so as to be understood, either directly or through an interpreter?
> ☐   Does your witness understand the duty to tell the truth?

COMPETENCY OF CHILDREN AS WITNESSES

Throughout early common law, most children were not considered competent to testify, especially those under the age of 7. From the ages of 7 to 14, there was a presumption of incompetence, which could be rebutted with evidence. These early common law standards were changed by a major Supreme Court decision in 1895. In *Wheeler v. United States*, the court addressed the issue of what age determined witness competency.

CASE

Wheeler v. United States

159 U.S. 523 (1895) .

Justice Brewer delivered the opinion of the Court.

On January 2, 1895, George L. Wheeler was by the circuit court of the United States for the Eastern district of Texas adjudged guilty of the crime of murder, and sentenced to be hanged; whereupon he sued out this writ of error.

The . . . objection is to action of the court in permitting the son of the deceased to testify. The homicide took place on June 12, 1894, and this boy was five years old on the 5th of July following. The case was tried on December 21, at which time he was nearly five and a half years of age. The boy, in reply to questions put to him on his voir dire, said, among other things, that he knew the difference between the truth and a lie; that if he told a

lie, the bad man would get him; and that he was going to tell the truth. When further asked what they would do with him in court if he told a lie, he replied that they would put him in jail. He also said that his mother had told him that morning to "tell no lie," and, in response to a question as to what the clerk said to him when he held up his hand, he answered, "Don't you tell no story."

. . .[T]here is no precise age which determines the question of competency. This depends on the capacity and intelligence of the child, his appreciation of the difference between truth and falsehood, as well as of his duty to tell the former. The decision of this question rests primarily with the trial judge, who sees the proposed witness, notices his manner, his apparent possession or lack of intelligence, and may resort to any examination which will tend to disclose his capacity and intelligence, as well as his understanding of the obligations of an oath. . . . So far as can be judged from the not very extended examination which is found in the record, the boy was intelligent, understood the difference between truth and falsehood, and the consequences of telling the latter, and also what was required by the oath which he had taken. . . .

We think that, under the circumstances of this case, the disclosures on the voir dire were sufficient to authorize the decision that the witness was competent, and therefore there was no error in admitting his testimony. These being the only questions in the record, the judgment must be affirmed.

LEGAL ANALYSIS AND WRITING 7.3

The following questions are based on the *How to Brief a Legal Case* format shown in the Appendix. Use this format to answer the following questions:

1. Summarize the facts in the previous case.

2. What is the legal issue?

3. How did the appellate court decide?

4. Why did the court decide this way?

5. Do you agree with the court's reasoning? Explain why or why not.

LEGAL RESEARCH USING THE INTERNET SKILLS 7.3

Find and read the *Wheeler* case online! Check out one of the legal research web sites below and use their "Search" feature to find this case. In the "Search" field, enter the case name.

1. FindLaw U.S. Supreme Court Decisions (http://www.findlaw.com/casecode/supreme.html)

2. U.S. Supreme Court (http://www.supremecourtus.gov/)

3. Supreme Court Collection of Cornell Law School (http://supct.law.cornell.edu/supct/)

Effect of *Wheeler* Decision

The effect of this major case decision was to change the common law for the next hundred years. *Wheeler* held that there is no precise age which determines the question of witness competency. To establish this, a court needs to consider the "capacity and intelligence of the child, his appreciation of the difference between truth and falsehood, as well as of his duty to tell the former." The question of competency was left for the trial judge.

Modern Rules

Today, although age may be a factor in determining competency in many courts (see Exhibit 7.7) it is not the decisive factor. Most states and all federal courts allow a child to testify as long as the child can show the personal knowledge, understand the duty to tell the truth, and be able to communicate his or her testimony in some reasonable manner to the trier of fact.

The following 1996 federal case out of New Mexico shows the modern federal trend in allowing children to testify.

CASE

United States v. Allen J.

127 F. 3d 1292 (10th Cir.,1997).

Appeal from the United States District Court for the District of New Mexico.

[Allen J. was adjudicated a juvenile delinquent in the United States District Court for the District of New Mexico, after the court found that he had committed Aggravated Sexual Abuse in violation of 18 U.S.C. §§ 2241(a) and 2246(2)(A) by knowingly using force to engage in a sex act with a juvenile. The case was in federal court because the incident took place within the Navajo Nation Indian Reservation in New Mexico. The district court placed Allen J. on probation until he reached the age of 21 and required, among other things, completion of sex offender and substance abuse treatment at a youth facility.]

The only issue Allen J. raises on appeal is whether the trial court erred in finding the victim competent to testify. . . . The competency of witnesses to testify in federal criminal trials is governed by Fed. R. Evid. 601. Rule 601 establishes a presumption "[e]very person is competent to be a witness." Fed. R. Evid. 601. This means there is no minimum or baseline mental capacity requirements witnesses must demonstrate before testifying. Indeed, the drafters of Rule 601 considered mental capacity not to be a question of competence, but to be a question "particularly suited to the [trier of fact] as one of weight and credibility." In addition to the general presumption of competency found in Rule 601, there is a specific statutory presumption children are competent to testify . . . . A court may only conduct a competency examination of a child witness upon submission of a written motion by a party offering compelling proof of incompetency. Even if this hurdle is met and a competency examination is held, the purpose of the examination is only to determine if the child is capable of "understanding and answering simple questions." 18 U.S.C. § 3509(c)(8). . . .

Prior to trial, Allen J. filed a motion challenging the victim's competence to testify and requesting a competency examination. In the motion, he offered as proof of incompetency two documents indicating "the possibility that [the victim] may suffer from Fetal Alcohol Syndrome or Fetal Alcohol Exposure" and "mild retardation and learning disabilities." The district court judge. . .

did not find any compelling reason to hold a competency examination based on the information contained in Allen J.'s motion. The court reasoned even if the 13-year-old victim had a minor learning disability, she would be at least as capable of testifying as much younger children who had testified in previous cases before the court. . . .

[T]he Wheeler test this court has relied upon for years no longer completely states the applicable standard for determining the competency of a child witness, although it may inform any examinations taking place . . . and may help explain the type of evidence necessary to demonstrate a compelling reason for such an examination. We agree with the district court's conclusion that the evidence offered by Allen J. in his Motion to Examine Child Witness for Competence did not constitute a "compelling reason" to hold a competency examination. . . . The evidence offered by Allen J. did not begin to show the victim had such severe problems she could not "understand and answer simple questions" or "underst[and] the difference between truth and falsehood, and the consequences of falsehood, and what was required by the oath."

When the victim was called to testify, the court asked her a series of questions seeking to confirm she understood the importance of the oath. These questions included: "Do you understand what it is to tell the truth?" and "Do you know the difference between the truth and a lie?" The victim did not respond to the judge's questioning. The court then asked the prosecutor to try questioning the witness. The prosecutor began with simple questions ("[W]hat is your last name?", "How old are you?", and "Where do you live?"), which the victim answered. After about 30 questions along these lines, almost all of which the victim was able to answer correctly, the prosecutor shifted to questions relating to the difference between the truth and lies. Among other questions, the prosecutor asked the victim if she understood she had promised to tell the truth in court, to which the victim responded affirmatively. After this series of questions, which established the victim knew the difference between a truth and a lie, knew she was to tell the truth in court, and knew she would be punished if she told a lie, the court directed the prosecutor to proceed to the heart of her case. Defense counsel objected repeatedly throughout this process and throughout the remainder of the victim's testimony. Allen J. essentially bases his appeal on several instances in the victim's testimony where she had difficulty answering questions. The victim did not respond to the trial judge's questioning. She gave wrong answers to some of counsel's questions (e.g., she said she was 11, when she was 13), and she gave nonsensical answers to others (e.g., she answered "true" to the question "Is it good or bad to tell a lie?"). In addition, she apparently paused for long periods of time before answering some questions. Any inconsistencies in the victim's story or problems with her testimony, however, raise questions of credibility, not competence. Allen J.'s argument boils down to an attack on credibility couched in terms of competence. This court has rejected similar arguments before. The credibility of a witness is a question to be determined by the trier of fact, not this court. Over one hundred years ago, the Supreme Court held it was proper for a 5-year-old to give critical testimony in a capital case. *Wheeler*, 159 U.S. at 524. Since that time, the trend in the law has been to grant trial courts even greater leeway in deciding if a witness is competent to testify.

We find nothing in the record demonstrating the district court abused its discretion in permitting the victim in this case to testify. The decision of the district court is, therefore, Affirmed.

LEGAL ANALYSIS AND WRITING 7.4

The following questions are based on the *How to Brief a Legal Case* format shown in the Appendix. Use this format to answer the following questions:

1. Summarize the facts in the previous case.
2. What is the legal issue?
3. How did the appellate court decide?
4. Why did the court decide this way?
5. Do you agree with the court's reasoning? Explain why or why not.

LEGAL RESEARCH USING THE INTERNET SKILLS 7.4

Try to find and read the *Allen* case online! Check out one of the legal research web sites below and use their "Search" feature to find this case. In the "Search" field, enter the cite or case name.

1. U.S. Courts Site with Links to All Circuit Courts of Appeal (http://www.uscourts.gov/links.html)
2. National Center for State Courts—State and Federal Court Web Sites (http://www.ncsconline.org/D_kis/info_court_web_sites.html#federal)
3. FindLaw (http://guide.lp.findlaw.com/casecode/)

Statements of Child Victims

A problem occurs when a child victim, as in an abuse case, is too young to understand the duty to tell the truth or to appreciate the consequences of an oath, but has made **hearsay** statements which are being testified to by a different and competent witness. In this case, even though the child's testimony may have been incompetent on the stand, it is still generally admissible when testified to as a hearsay rule exception by a competent witness. Most courts reason that since the child is not testifying, there is no

Hearsay
A statement made out-of-court and offered in court as evidence to prove the truth of the assertion made in the statement.

issue as to competency. Also, since most of the hearsay exceptions in these cases fall under some type of present sense or excited utterances, the statements made by the child are viewed as trustworthy.

In a 1990 decision, the U.S. Supreme Court rejected defendant's argument that a hearsay statement by a child was inadmissible under the **Confrontation Clause** if the child would have been found incompetent to testify. The Court held that "a per se rule of exclusion would not only frustrate the truth-seeking purpose of the Confrontation Clause, but would also hinder States in their own enlightened development of the law of evidence." This decision found that a declarant's incompetence would not automatically exclude admission of her out-of-court statement under a hearsay exception.[6]

Confrontation Clause
In a criminal proceeding, the defendant's Sixth Amendment right "to be confronted with the witnesses against him. . . ."

EXHIBIT 7.7   Some States Still Limit Competency for Children as Witnesses

Ohio Rules of Evidence
Rule 601. General Rule of Competency. Every person is competent to be a witness except:

(A) Those of unsound mind, and children under ten years of age, who appear incapable of receiving just impressions of the facts and transactions respecting which they are examined, or of relating them truly.

Texas Rules of Evidence
Rule 601. Competency and Incompetency of Witnesses.

(a) General Rule. Every person is competent to be a witness except as otherwise provided in these rules. The following witnesses shall be incompetent to testify in any proceeding subject to these rules:

(2) Children. Children or other persons who, after being examined by the court, appear not to possess sufficient intellect to relate transactions with respect to which they are interrogated.

Balancing Probative Value versus Unfair Prejudice

Even when competent, a witness may not be allowed to testify when the probative value of his testimony is substantially outweighed by the risk of unfair prejudice, consumption of time, or confusion to the jury.[7]

COMPETENCY OF JUDGE OR JUROR AS WITNESS

Although common law permitted it, the general rule today is that a presiding judge cannot testify at the trial for which she is presiding (see Exhibit 7.8). A judge should be viewed as impartial and it is believed that any testimony by the judge might unduly influence the jury, as well as the parties.

Members of a jury cannot testify at the trial for which they are sitting (see Exhibit 7.9). Even if an inquiry arises into the validity of a verdict or indictment, a juror cannot testify as to any matter or statement occurring during the course of the jury's deliberations. Neither can a juror testify to the effect of anything from the trial on any juror's mind or emotions that might have influenced a juror. However, a juror may testify on the question whether extraneous prejudicial information was improperly brought to the jury's attention or whether any outside influence was improperly brought to bear upon any juror.

EXHIBIT 7.8   Example of Rules Prohibiting Judge as Witness

Kentucky Rules of Evidence
Rule 605. Competency of Judge as Witness.
   The judge presiding at the trial may not testify in that trial as a witness. No objection need be made in order to preserve the point.

Is a Judge's Law Clerk Competent to Testify as a Witness?

In the following "slip and fall" case, the judge's law clerk visited the scene where plaintiff fell and was later allowed to testify to what he saw. The appellate court had to decide the propriety of this testimony.

CASE

Kennedy v. Great Atlantic and Pacific Tea Co.

551 F.2d 593 (5th Cir. 1977).

[Plaintiff was an elderly man who walked into the rear entrance of an A&P store during a heavy rain. Just inside the entrance, plaintiff slipped and broke his hip. Plaintiff sued the store for negligence, claiming that his slip and fall was due to a wet floor. The first trial ended in a mistrial. Prior to the second trial, the judge's law clerk visited the store during a heavy rain, looked inside, and saw a puddle of water on the floor where the plaintiff had fallen. The law clerk was later allowed to testify to what he saw. The jury subsequently awarded judgment in favor of the plaintiff and the defense appealed.]

. . . .

Counsel adequately challenges the propriety of permitting the . . . testimony by pointing to the serious threat to the ability of the jury to receive with proper degree of impartiality the testimony of the actions of the trial judge's law clerk who . . .

went out and had a private view of the premises . . . and was now presented as a witness to facts which greatly favored plaintiff.

. . . It is impossible to believe that the jury must not have attached some special significance to this testimony of the judge's law clerk. . . . [T]he jury must have thought that for the judge's law clerk to take the trouble to go out and see the property to satisfy himself about this one fact, it must have some special importance. . . . What was the jury to think about this young man's injecting himself into the controversy after having heard the case being tried in the court in which he was playing a significant part?

In addition, there was the imprimatur of character, credibility, and reliability that was automatically implied as coming from the court itself when the trial judge introduced the witness as his present law clerk.

The judgment is REVERSED and the case is REMANDED. . . .

LEGAL ANALYSIS AND WRITING 7.5

The following questions are based on the *How to Brief a Legal Case* format shown in the Appendix. Use this format to answer the following questions:

1. Summarize the facts in the previous case.

2. What is the legal issue?

3. What did the appellate court decide?

4. Why did the court decide this way?

5. Do you agree with the court's reasoning? Explain why or why not.

CRITICAL THINKING QUESTIONS 7.4

1. The evidence rules say that a presiding judge may not testify in that trial as a witness. Why do you think that the appellate court decided that the testimony of the judge's law clerk was also improper?
2. What do you think was the actual legal rule or basis for the appellate court's decision?
3. Would it make a difference if the law clerk had happened by the store prior to knowing anything about the legal case?

EXHIBIT 7.9   Example of Rule Prohibiting Juror as Witness

Ohio Rules of Evidence
Rule 606. Competency of Juror as Witness.

(A) At the Trial. A member of the jury may not testify as a witness before that jury in the trial of the case in which he is sitting as a juror. If he is called so to testify, the opposing party shall be afforded an opportunity to object out of the presence of the jury.

(B) Inquiry into Validity of Verdict or Indictment. Upon an inquiry into the validity of a verdict or indictment, a juror may not testify as to any matter or statement occurring during the course of the jury's deliberations or to the effect of anything upon his or any other juror's mind or emotions as influencing him to assent to or dissent from the verdict or indictment or concerning his mental processes in connection therewith. A juror may testify on the question whether extraneous prejudicial information was improperly brought to the jury's attention or whether any outside influence was improperly brought to bear on any juror, only after some outside evidence of that act or event has been presented. However a juror may testify without the presentation of any outside evidence concerning any threat, any bribe, any attempted threat or bribe, or any improprieties of any officer of the court. His affidavit or evidence of any statement by him concerning a matter about which he would be precluded from testifying will not be received for these purposes.

SUMMARY

In trials, we look to witnesses to provide evidence in the form of testimony to help the triers of fact better ascertain the truth. The witness does this by being called to the stand, taking an oath, and testifying to firsthand perception (i.e., what she saw, heard, felt, smelled, or tasted). Laws governing witnesses can be traced back hundreds of years to early England, when restrictions were placed on who could testify and limitations on the scope of their testimony. The basic requirement for a witness to be able to testify is competency. Competency is the legal fitness or capacity of a witness to testify. Among those who could not testify at common law were felons, atheists, children, and spouses. The modern rule today is that all witnesses are competent except as provided by some other rule of evidence or statute. These other rules typically assess witness competency through the determination of three key elements: personal knowledge, understanding the duty to tell the truth, and being capable of communicating or expressing himself to the judge and jury. To help ensure reliability in the factfinding process, a witness must have personal knowledge about the matter being testified to, as opposed to a mere opinion. A witness must be capable of understanding the duty to tell the truth and take an oath or affirmation to this effect. A witness must be capable of communicating or expressing herself so as to be reasonably understood by the judge or jury. This capacity of communication may be done directly or through an interpreter.

The general rule is that a presiding judge cannot testify at the trial for which he is presiding. A judge should be viewed as impartial and it is believed that any testimony by the judge might unduly influence the jury, as well as the parties. Members of a jury cannot testify at the trial for which they are sitting. Other than these rules declaring that judges and jurors are incompetent to be witnesses, most grounds of competency are left to the trier of fact as questions of credibility.

KEY TERMS

Capable of Communicating	Due Process	Legal Capacity
Competency	Duty to Tell the Truth	Personal Knowledge
Confrontation Clause	Hearsay	Witness

LEARNING OUTCOMES AND PRACTICE SKILLS CHECKLIST

☐ Learning Outcomes

After completing your reading, questions, and exercises, you should be able to demonstrate a better understanding of the learning concepts by answering the following questions:

1. Discuss the relationship between witnesses and due process.
2. Define witness competency.
3. Identify the types of witnesses that were deemed incompetent to testify at common law.
4. Explain the modern rule regarding competency of witnesses, how it differs from the common law rule, and why you think these rules have changed.
5. Identify the three key elements for determining witness credibility.
6. Distinguish *personal knowledge* as one of these elements and discuss the reasoning behind the rule requiring this for determining witness credibility.
7. Assess the change in the oath or affirmation requirement from its historical basis to the modern rule and discuss the reason for this change.
8. Describe the *capacity for communication* element in determining witness credibility and give examples of how different state rules have interpreted this requirement.
9. Explain the rule pertaining to a judge or juror as witness, and the reasoning behind this rule.

☐ Practice Skills

In addition to understanding the learning concepts, practice what you have learned through applications using critical thinking, legal analysis and writing, legal research, and advocacy skills, including:

Critical Thinking

1. What witnesses were considered incompetent to testify under the common law and why?
2. Under modern rules, who is competent to testify?

3. Why do you think the rules have changed in regard to the competency of witnesses? In your answer, include any public policy interests that might be involved.
4. Do you agree with these changes? Why or why not?
5. What safeguards are provided today to ensure the competency of witnesses?
6. If it were up to you, would you keep these rules as they are, delete them, narrow them, or expand them? Explain your reasoning.
7. How do these rules influence the gathering of evidence or preparing of witnesses?

Legal Analysis and Writing

Analyze the following rules and cases by summarizing their holdings, explaining their significance, and assessing any issue that might arise in their application.

1. Rule 601.
2. Rule 602.
3. Rule 603.
4. Rule 605.
5. Rule 606.
6. *United States v. Ward.*
7. *Wheeler v. United States.*
8. *United States v. Allen J.*
9. *Kennedy v. Great Atlantic and Pacific Tea Co.*

Legal Research Using the Internet

1. Find the Federal Rules of Evidence on the Internet and assess the notes and comments made in the proposing of the rules covered in this chapter.
2. Find your state's rules of evidence regarding the rules and concepts covered in this chapter. Compare and contrast with the federal and/or modern rules, and some of the other state rules listed in this chapter.
3. Find out if your state appellate court posts their case decisions on the Internet. If so, find a case that illustrates an issue or rule discussed in this chapter. If your state decisions are not on the Internet, go instead to the web site for the U.S. Circuit Court of Appeals in your circuit, or search the U.S. Supreme Court decisions.

PRACTICE APPLICATION 7.1

Tanner was convicted of a felony. Before sentencing, his defense attorneys received a telephone call from one of the trial jurors who said that several members of the jury had consumed alcohol and taken drugs at various times throughout the trial. Tanner sought to introduce evidence of jury misconduct and show that the jury was not competent to reach a verdict. Defense attorneys filed a motion to interview these jurors, and to hold an evidentiary hearing at which the jurors would be witnesses. The trial court denied these motions, saying that they were barred by Rule 606(b). Tanner appeals, claiming that failure to allow evidence of jury misconduct violated his right to a trial by a competent jury.

1. Was the trial correct in denying these motions? Why or why not?
2. What factors would you need to consider in order to make this decision?

Use the format shown in the Appendix for the *IRAC Method of Legal Analysis* and the readings, rules, and cases discussed in this chapter to analyze this question. Write a short memo giving your analysis, reasoning, and conclusions.

LEGAL RESEARCH USING THE INTERNET SKILLS 7.5

Find out the answer to the above problem by finding and reading the *Tanner* case online! The citation for it is:

Tanner v. United States, 483 U.S. 107 (1987).

Check out one of the legal research web sites below and use their "Search" feature to find this case. In the "Search" field, enter the cite or case name.

1. FindLaw U.S. Supreme Court Decisions (http://www.findlaw.com/casecode/supreme.html)
2. U.S. Supreme Court (http://www.supremecourtus.gov/)
3. Supreme Court Collection of Cornell Law School (http://supct.law.cornell.edu/supct/)

For extra credit, complete a case brief of this case.

ADVOCACY AND COMMUNICATION SKILLS 7.1

Form plaintiff and defense teams from small groups of no more than 3–4 each. Choose one of the following fact situations, prepare, and present an oral argument in support of why this testimony should or should not be admitted. Each side will have 3 minutes for their argument and 1 minute for rebuttal.

1. Plaintiff wants to call a 5-year-old child as a witness in a negligence case involving an auto accident.
2. Defendant wants to testify but refuses to take an oath, offering to say the following instead: "I do not recognize the jurisdiction of this court or the present laws of this state, but I am a truthful person."

WEB SITES

Federal Rules of Evidence
http://www.law.cornell.edu/rules/fre/overview.html
FindLaw
http://www.findlaw.com
FindLaw State and Federal Circuit Court Locator
http://guide.lp.findlaw.com/casecode/
FindLaw U.S. Supreme Court Decisions
http://www.findlaw.com/casecode/supreme.html
List of State Laws from Legal Information Institute of Cornell Law School
http://www.law.cornell.edu/states/listing.html

National Center for State Courts—State and Federal Court Web Sites
http://www.ncsconline.org/D_kis/info_court_web_sites.html#federal
Supreme Court Collection of Cornell Law School
http://supct.law.cornell.edu/supct/
U.S. Courts Site with Links to All Circuit Courts of Appeal
http://www.uscourts.gov/links.html
U.S. Supreme Court Decisions
http://www.supremecourtus.gov/

ENDNOTES

1. *In re Oliver*, 333 U.S. 257 (1948).
2. *Washington v. Texas*, 388 U.S. 14 (1967).
3. M.R.E. 602. Lack of Personal Knowledge.
4. Texas Rules of Evidence, Rule 603. Oath or Affirmation.
5. N.J.R.E. 601.
6. *Idaho v. Wright*, 497 U.S. 805.
7. Fed. R. Evid. 403.

WITNESS EXAMINATION AND CREDIBILITY

"Cross-examination is the principal means by which the believability of a witness and the truth of his testimony are tested."

—*Davis v. Alaska, 415 U.S. 308 (1974)*

LEARNING OUTCOMES

In this chapter, you will learn about the following legal concepts:

- Examination of Witnesses
- "Mode and Order" of Questioning Witnesses
- How Witnesses Are Examined on the Stand
- Witness Examination and Credibility
- Ensuring Witness Credibility
- Witness Preparation
- Direct Examination

- Rehabilitation of Witness
- Forgetful Witness
- Examining Witness Concerning Prior Statement
- Cross-Examination
- Interrogation of Witnesses by the Court
- Religious Beliefs or Opinions
- Exclusion of Witnesses

INTRODUCTION

In the last chapter, we explored the role of witness competency. We looked at the factors we need to consider in determining whether a witness is legally qualified to testify. When a witness does testify, what methods do we use to question the witness? How do we ensure that the witness will testify in an honest and reliable manner? This chapter will delve into these questions, assessing the issues involved in examining witnesses on the stand, with the focus on witness preparation and witness credibility.

EXAMINATION OF WITNESSES

As we have seen in earlier chapters, evidence is presented primarily through the calling and examination of witnesses at trial. Witnesses are essential to helping the trier of fact ascertain the truth in a matter. Not only does their testimony establish facts that help to prove or disprove a case, but witnesses provide key testimony that supports, authenticates, and provides a foundation for other forms of evidence. Because of their importance to a trial, rules were developed to govern the questioning of witnesses.

"MODE AND ORDER" OF QUESTIONING WITNESSES

One of the first rules developed allowed the trial court control over the "mode and order" of questioning witnesses and the presenting of evidence (see Exhibit 8.1). As the Ohio rules reflect, this was done in order that the questioning and presentation effectively ascertains the truth while avoiding "needless consumption of time," and protecting witnesses from "harassment or undue embarrassment."[1] California rules also provide for this, but contain a slightly different wording that the court exercises reasonable control over the interrogation of a witness "so as to make such interrogation as rapid, as distinct, and as effective for the ascertainment of the truth. . . ."[2]

EXHIBIT 8.1   Mode and Order of Interrogation and Presentation

Texas Rules of Evidence
Rule 611(a) Control by Court. The court shall exercise reasonable control over the mode and order of interrogating witnesses and presenting evidence so as to (1) make the interrogation and presentation effective for the ascertainment of the truth, (2) avoid needless consumption of time, and (3) protect witnesses from harassment or undue embarrassment.

Direct Examination
Initial questioning of a witness by the party that called the witness to the stand.

Cross-Examination
Questioning of a witness by the opposing party on matters within the scope of the direct examination, usually to discredit the testimony of the witness or to develop facts that may help the cross-examiner's case.

HOW WITNESSES ARE EXAMINED ON THE STAND

The party bringing the legal action—the plaintiff in a civil case or prosecution in a criminal case—has the responsibility of first calling witnesses and presenting evidence. The initial questioning of a witness by the plaintiff or party calling the witness to the stand is called **direct examination**. During this examination, the defense may object to a question asked or ask the court to strike an answer that violates an evidentiary rule. When the direct examination has been completed, the defense will have the opportunity for **cross-examination** of the witness in order to clarify answers given or attempt to discredit the witness. After a witness has been cross-examined by the opposing party, the original party that called the witness to the stand may question the witness again to clarify facts brought out during the cross. This questioning is called a **redirect examination**. After redirect, the opposing party may conduct a **recross-examination**, but is limited to facts brought out on the redirect. Examination of a witness will usually be ended after a recross.

Upon the resting of the plaintiff's case, when the plaintiff has submitted all evidence and called witnesses, the defense then has an opportunity to call witnesses and present evidence. This time, the defense will be able to conduct a direct examination of defense witnesses, and the plaintiff may cross-examine these witnesses.

WITNESS EXAMINATION AND CREDIBILITY

As we saw in the last chapter, a witness must be competent to testify. The modern rule is to presume that all witnesses are competent. Once a witness begins to testify and is examined through questioning by each party, the emphasis shifts from competency to **credibility**; how believable that witness will be to the trier of fact. For the party calling the witness, the strategy now becomes one of making the witness appear trustworthy and worthy of belief. For the opposing party, the strategy will be to challenge or cast doubts upon the believability or credibility of the witness.

ENSURING WITNESS CREDIBILITY

There are several methods used to help ensure witness credibility on the stand (see Exhibit 8.2). Among the most common are:

1. Testify in Person

Other than certain exceptions for hearsay, witnesses are expected to testify in person. This allows the trier of fact to watch the witness's demeanor, confidence, and body language as he testifies, to help in the assessment of reliability and credibility. It is the trier of fact who will determine the credibility of a particular witness and how much weight to assign that witness's evidence or testimony.

2. Oath or Affirmation

As mentioned earlier, every witness is required to take an oath or affirmation before testifying. The oath or affirmation must be "in a form calculated to awaken the witness's conscience and impress the witness's mind with the duty" . . . to tell the truth.

3. Subject to Perjury if Untruthful

In conjunction with the oath or affirmation, witnesses may be subject to criminal perjury charges or contempt of court for testifying untruthfully on the stand.

4. Personal Knowledge

We have discussed personal knowledge as an element of witness competency. It is also a method of ensuring credibility by limiting testimony to matters within the firsthand perceptions of the witness. In doing so, it is believed that a witness will be less susceptible to exaggeration or commenting on matters outside of her own perceptions and memory.

Redirect Examination
After a witness has been cross-examined by the opposing party, the original party that called the witness to the stand may conduct a reexamination.

Recross-Examination
After redirect examination, another round of questioning a witness by the opposing party on matters within the scope of the redirect examination.

Credibility
Believability and trustworthiness of a witness.

5. Testimony Must Be Relevant

In addition to testifying from firsthand knowledge, witness testimony must also be relevant; it must have a bearing on and tend to prove or disprove a matter at issue in the trial. To keep testimony focused on relevant information, attorneys tend to ask short, limiting questions of "who, what, when, where, and how."

6. Subject to Cross-Examination

Perhaps one of the most powerful safeguards against untruthfulness by witnesses is the right of the opposing party to confront that witness and to cross-examine him or her. This confrontation and cross-examination will not only question what the witness perceived and can remember and communicate, but may also attack the very character and credibility of the witness.

EXHIBIT 8.2   Examples of Rules to Determine Credibility

California Evidence Code

Sec. 780. Except as otherwise provided by statute, the court or jury may consider in determining the credibility of a witness any matter that has any tendency in reason to prove or disprove the truthfulness of his testimony at the hearing, including but not limited to any of the following:

(a) His demeanor while testifying and the manner in which he testifies.

(b) The character of his testimony.

(c) The extent of his capacity to perceive, to recollect, or to communicate any matter about which he testifies.

(d) The extent of his opportunity to perceive any matter about which he testifies.

(e) His character for honesty or veracity or their opposites.

(f) The existence or nonexistence of a bias, interest, or other motive.

(g) A statement previously made by him that is consistent with his testimony at the hearing.

(h) A statement made by him that is inconsistent with any part of his testimony at the hearing.

(i) The existence or nonexistence of any fact testified to by him.

(j) His attitude toward the action in which he testifies or toward the giving of testimony.

(k) His admission of untruthfulness.

Florida Evidence Code

Sec. 90.608. Any party, including the party calling the witness, may attack the credibility of a witness by:

(1) Introducing statements of the witness which are inconsistent with the witness's present testimony.

(2) Showing that the witness is biased.

(3) Attacking the character of the witness in accordance with the provisions of s. 90.609 or s. 90.610.

(4) Showing a defect of capacity, ability, or opportunity in the witness to observe, remember, or recount the matters about which the witness testified.

(5) Proof by other witnesses that material facts are not as testified to by the witness being impeached.

EVIDENTIARY CHECKLIST 8.1

Factors to Ensure Witness Credibility

- ☐ Witnesses testify in person
- ☐ Oath or affirmation
- ☐ Subject to perjury if untruthful
- ☐ Personal knowledge
- ☐ Testimony must be relevant
- ☐ Subject to cross-examination

Exceptions to General Rule That Testimony Must Be Given in Court

Although, as a general rule, witnesses are expected to provide their testimony in court at the trial, there are exceptions when the witness is unavailable for trial. Acceptable reasons for unavailability include:

1. Death
2. Physical disability
3. Mental incapacity
4. Some child victims of abuse
5. Refusal to testify on the part of witnesses
6. Witness who has moved away or left the jurisdiction

In the case that a witness is unavailable for trial, a deposition or prior court testimony of the witness may be offered instead. To be admitted as an exception, there must be a showing that the deposition or prior testimony was made under oath and that the opposing side had an opportunity to cross-examine the witness at the time the testimony was given.

CRITICAL THINKING QUESTIONS 8.1

1. What changes would you make to the way witnesses are examined on the stand? Explain your reasons.
2. How can we reconcile Rule 611's provision protecting witnesses from "harassment or undue embarrassment" with the fact that courts allow the credibility of a witness to be attacked on the stand?
3. Do you think that the factors to ensure credibility discussed in this section provide adequate safeguards? Why or why not?

WITNESS PREPARATION

To help ensure that the witness and testimony given is credible, proper pretrial preparation of the witness should be conducted by the party calling that witness. Like the proverbial "location, location, location" as the three main points in starting a business, "no surprises, no surprises, no surprises" can sum up witness planning and preparation.

Interview

One of the most important steps in this preparation is to conduct a thorough interview of the prospective witness. The first area of questioning is to determine what the witness saw or heard, what the witness remembers, and what that witness can testify to. Structure the interview and questioning to cover all of the factors that ensure credibility. Ask specific questions that confirm these factors from different perspectives. Can the witness testify from firsthand knowledge? Did the witness perceive the events to be testified about in an accurate manner? How good are the observation powers of the witness? How good is the memory of the witness? Ask questions that will help to test this, especially surrounding the event in question and the testimony to be given. For example, ask questions about the time of day, weather conditions, how far away the witness was standing or sitting, or other factors that might limit the ability of the witness to have firsthand knowledge. How old is the witness? Does the witness have any physical or emotional limitation? What is the witness's eyesight or hearing condition, and does the witness wear glasses or a hearing aid, or have any other limitation that might affect what will be testified about? What was the witness doing immediately before and after the event? Can the witness accurately recall and describe the events?

Another line of questioning should follow up on the competency of the witness to testify. Is there an age problem? Any question of mental incompetence or intoxication? Does the witness understand the duty to tell the truth?

Investigation

Another step in ensuring witness credibility is to conduct a thorough witness and fact investigation. Find out how credible the witness is and whether there is anything in the statements or background of the witness that might affect his or her credibility on the stand. Did the facts occur as the witness stated? What other evidence or witnesses corroborate this witness? Are there any inconsistencies in the statement of the witness, either by itself or when compared to other witness statements? Any gaps? How does the witness react when asked about this? Does the witness tend to exaggerate or be hiding anything? Does the witness have any interest or potential bias in regard to the case or outcome? What will the demeanor of this witness be on the witness stand? Does the witness appear to be honest and trustworthy? Does the witness have any prior arrests or convictions, or anything that might result in impeachment? What is the reputation of the witness in the community for truthfulness?

Preparing the Witness

Finally, witnesses need to be adequately prepared for the trial. Witnesses should be helped to understand what will be asked on the stand and what the trial process will involve. Where will the witness sit, what questions will be asked, and who will be present during questioning? What will the other side ask about? Walking a witness through the steps of the trial and his testimony will not only relieve the anxiety of the witness, but help to boost his confidence by removing much of the fear of the unknown for the witness.

Practice Tip 8.1

Witness Preparation Checklists

To help ensure a successful witness examination, develop your own set of witness preparation checklists, using some of the following tips:

Witness Competency

The key here is to determine what the witness saw or heard, what the witness remembers, and what that witness can testify to, as well as uncover any competency issues that might prevent the witness from testifying or discredit the testimony. Questions that might be asked for this include:

☐   Can the witness testify from firsthand knowledge?

☐   Did the witness perceive the events to be testified about in an accurate manner?

☐   How good are the observation powers of the witness?

☐   How good is the memory of the witness?

☐   Can the witness recall events accurately and communicate these facts?

☐   How old is the witness?

☐   What day and time did events occur?

☐   What were the weather conditions?

☐   What was the witness doing immediately before and after the event?

☐   How far away was the witness standing or sitting?

☐   What was the witness's eyesight or hearing condition?

☐   Does the witness wear glasses or a hearing aid?

☐   Does the witness have any physical or emotional limitation?

☐   Any question of mental incompetence or intoxication?

☐   Does the witness have any other limitation that might affect what will be testified about?

☐   Are there other factors that might limit the ability of the witness to have or testify to firsthand knowledge?

☐   Does the witness understand the duty to tell the truth?

Witness Credibility

Another step in preparing a witness is to ascertain whether there is anything in the statements or background of the witness that might affect his or her credibility on the stand. Questions that are helpful in this regard include:

☐   Did the facts occur as the witness stated?

☐   What other evidence or witnesses corroborate this witness?

☐   Are there any inconsistencies in the statement of the witness, either by itself or when compared to other witness statements?

☐   Any gaps in witness's statement?

☐   How does the witness react when asked about this?

☐   Does the witness tend to exaggerate or be hiding anything?

☐   What will the demeanor of this witness be on the witness stand?

CRITICAL THINKING QUESTIONS 8.2

1. What do you think is the most important reason for preparing a witness before trial?

2. What conflicts or issues might arise from preparing a witness as to the questions asked on the stand?

(Continued)

CRITICAL THINKING QUESTIONS 8.2 *Continued*

3. What other questions could you ask to test the ability of your witness to remember and communicate events that will be testified to on the stand?

4. What should you do if you discover that your witness is being untruthful?

DIRECT EXAMINATION

When the trial begins and the witness is called for direct examination, there are usually three elements to this form of questioning. First, the witness is identified through an introduction. This may be accomplished by asking where the witness lives or works. Next, a foundation is provided showing the connection of the witness and the evidence the witness will provide in the matter at issue. Finally, the witness testifies about her knowledge of the matter at issue through a series of short questions designed to elicit specific responses that are relevant to the case. Direct examination is usually carried out so that the witness tells a story in a chronological manner. To help ensure that the testimony stays focused and relevant, it is generally limited to open-ended questions preceded by who, where, when, what, or how: "Where were you on the night of March 2nd, at 10 P.M.?" "What did you see at that time?" An example of this process might be:

Plaintiff: Your Honor, at this time, we call Mr. Jay Smith to the stand.
Court: Mr. Smith, raise your right hand. Do you swear or affirm to tell the truth, the whole truth, and nothing but the truth?
Witness: I do, your Honor.
Court: Plaintiff may begin.
Plaintiff: Thank you, your Honor. Mr. Smith, where do you work?
Witness: I work at Downtown Minimart.
Plaintiff: How long have you worked there?
Witness: I've worked there for 5 years.
Plaintiff: Were you working there at 10 P.M. on the evening of March 2nd this year?
Witness: Yes, I was.
Plaintiff: Would you tell the jury what happened at that time?

Leading Questions

Leading Question
Question that contains or suggests the answer to a witness.

Leading questions are those that contain or suggest the answer to a witness (see Exhibit 8.3 to Exhibit 8.5). For example, "You were involved in a shooting on March 2nd, were you not?" is leading. "Did anything happen to you on March 2nd?" is not. Leading questions are generally not permitted during direct examination, because it may provide an unfair advantage to the party presenting his case. However, leading questions are allowed during cross-examination. The modern rules allow a trial judge to permit leading questions on direct examination, but limit their use. One limitation is to permit only those leading questions on direct examination that "may be necessary to develop the witness's testimony."[3] This is usually done to save time, as when a witness is led through an initial identification process:

Q: Ms. Jones, you are a detective with the city police department, are you not?

A: Yes, I am.

Q: And, on March 2nd of this year, were you on duty at the police department?

A: Yes, I was.

Q: And, while on duty, did you receive a call for assistance from Officer Smith?

A: Yes, I did.

Questions to develop the witness's testimony or lay a foundation are not leading. For example:

Q: Were you in the Downtown Minimart on March 2nd?

A: Yes, I was.

Q: Did something happen there at 10 P.M.?

A: Yes, it did.

Q: Did you see what happened?

A: Yes.

Q: What happened?

These questions are allowed because they help to lay a foundation to show that the witness had personal knowledge of the events that are being testified about.

A court may also allow leading questions on direct examination if the witness being called to the stand is identified as a hostile witness or adverse party. Examples of hostile witnesses include friends, relatives, neighbors, or co-workers of the other party in the legal action. The reasoning behind allowing the use of leading questions is that a hostile witness may not respond fairly or may be reluctant to respond fully to the open-ended questions normally used in direct examination. If this happens, the questioning can become more like a cross-examination, where the use of leading questions are typically used.

EXHIBIT 8.3   Example of a Leading Question

Plaintiff Q:	Would it be fair to say that during the course of –
Defense:	Object to leading, your Honor.
Court:	Sustained.
Plaintiff Q:	I'll rephrase. During the course of your survey, did you speak to Mr. Jones?

EXHIBIT 8.4   Mode and Order of Interrogation and Presentation

North Carolina Rules of Evidence
Rule 611.(c) Leading Questions. Leading questions should not be used on the direct examination of a witness except as may be necessary to develop his testimony. Ordinarily leading questions should be permitted on cross-examination. When a party calls a hostile witness, an adverse party, or a witness identified with an adverse party, interrogation may be by leading questions.

EXHIBIT 8.5   Leading Questions

California Evidence Code
Sec. 767(a). Except under special circumstances where the interests of justice otherwise require:

(1) A leading question may not be asked of a witness on direct or redirect examination.

(2) A leading question may be asked of a witness on cross-examination or recross-examination.

LEGAL ANALYSIS AND WRITING 8.1

Plaintiff calls witness to the stand, but during direct examination the witness becomes embarrassed and reluctant to fully answer the questions. Plaintiff asks the permission of the court to treat the witness as hostile and use leading questions. Defense objects.

Use the format shown in the Appendix for the *IRAC Method of Legal Analysis,* and Rule 611(c) (previously shown) to solve this case problem.

LEGAL RESEARCH USING THE INTERNET SKILLS 8.1

1. Use one of the following web sites to find out whether your state rules of evidence are patterned after the Federal Rules or the Uniform Rules.

   List of State Laws from Legal Information Institute of Cornell Law School (http://www.law.cornell.edu/states/listing.html)

   FindLaw (http://www.findlaw.com)

   Federal Rules of Evidence (http://www.law.cornell.edu/rules/fre/overview.html)

Rehabilitation of Witness

Rehabilitation
Restoring the credibility of a witness after his or her credibility has been attacked on the stand.

After the direct examination of a witness has been completed, the opposing party may cross-examine the witness. If this cross-examination has attacked the credibility of the witness or left confusing or unanswered questions, the party originally calling the witness to the stand may conduct a redirect examination. During this redirect, the witness may be asked to clarify any new information brought out during cross-examination, or to explain or repudiate any damaging information. Restoring the credibility of the witness after his or her credibility has been attacked on the stand is called **rehabilitation**. An example of the form this question might take during redirect is: "Mr. Jones, what did you mean when you said. . . ?" Rehabilitation might also include the introduction of other witnesses or evidence to restore credibility.

FORGETFUL WITNESS

If a witness is forgetful and cannot remember a matter or event when asked on the stand, there are two ways to obtain that information and have it admitted as evidence.

Present Memory Refreshed

In questioning a witness who is unable to remember something asked on the stand, it is permissible to jog or "refresh" the memory of that witness by letting the witness refer to a writing or object (her notes, a report, shopping list) (see Exhibit 8.6). After the witness's memory has been refreshed, the witness must then testify to the event without reading from or looking at the thing used to jog her memory. The witness must then be able to testify independent of and without relying further on the writing. This is often called **present memory refreshed**. The key here is that the writing only serves to jog the memory of the witness and that the witness can then testify independently of the writing.

When a writing is used to refresh memory, the trial court may allow the opposing party to have the writing produced at the hearing.[4] The opposing party may inspect the writing, cross-examine the witness about it, and even introduce into evidence those portions that relate to the testimony of the witness.

Present Memory Refreshed
When witness is permitted to refer to his or her writing or notes in order to jog memory.

Past Recollection Recorded

If the witness still has no independent recollection after attempting to "refresh" his memory, the witness will not be permitted to testify about the matter from his personal knowledge. However, the document or writing used to attempt to refresh the witness's memory may be admissible by itself and, if admitted, the witness may be asked to read the document to the jury. This is called **past recollection recorded.** The document will not be shown to the jury unless the opposing party offers it. The evidence is in the reading of the document.

Past Recollection Recorded
When witness is unable to refresh memory by reviewing notes or writing, witness may not testify, but the document may be read into evidence.

EXHIBIT 8.6   Writing Used to Refresh Memory

Colorado Rules of Evidence
Rule 612. If a witness uses a writing to refresh his memory for the purpose of testifying, either

  (1) while testifying, or

  (2) before testifying,

if the court in its discretion determines it is necessary in the interests of justice, an adverse party is entitled to have the writing produced at the hearing, to inspect it, to cross-examine the witness thereon, and to introduce in evidence those portions which relate to the testimony of the witness. If it is claimed that the writing contains matters not related to the subject matter of the testimony the court shall examine the writing in camera, excise any portions not so related, and order delivery of the remainder to the party entitled thereto. . .

EXAMINING WITNESS CONCERNING PRIOR STATEMENT

In examining a witness concerning a prior statement made by the witness, whether written or not, the statement need not be shown nor its contents disclosed to the witness at that time, but on request the same must be shown or disclosed to opposing counsel.

Extrinsic Evidence of Prior Inconsistent Statement of Witness

Extrinsic Evidence
Evidence obtained from outside the courtroom. An example of extrinsic evidence might be an employment application that a witness had falsified.

Extrinsic evidence of a prior inconsistent statement by a witness is not admissible unless the witness is afforded an opportunity to explain or deny the same and the opposite party is afforded an opportunity to interrogate the witness thereon, or the interests of justice otherwise require (see Exhibit 8.7). This provision does not apply to admissions of a party-opponent as defined in Rule 801(d)(2).

EXHIBIT 8.7   Extrinsic Evidence of Prior Inconsistent Statement of Witness

Mississippi Rules of Evidence
Rule 613(b). Extrinsic evidence of a prior inconsistent statement by a witness is not admissible unless the witness is afforded an opportunity to explain or deny the same and the opposite party is afforded an opportunity to interrogate him thereon, or the interests of justice otherwise require. This provision does not apply to admissions of a party-opponent as defined in Rule 801(d)(2).

CRITICAL THINKING QUESTIONS 8.3

1. How "open-ended" should questions asked on direct examination be? What would be wrong with asking a witness to tell us all she remembers about an evening or event in question?
2. What are the strengths and weaknesses of using leading questions?
3. Why would a party call a hostile or adverse witness to the stand?
4. Do you think it is ethical to call a hostile witness with the intention of asking leading questions that might embarrass the witness but bring out important information for your side? Why or why not?
5. How far can one go in jogging the memory of a witness? There is the story of the attorney who took off his sock and had the witness smell it to jog the witness's memory about being in the gym. Would this be acceptable? Explain your reasons.

CROSS-EXAMINATION

After one side completes the direct examination of their witness, the opposing side may conduct a cross-examination. A cross-examination involves the questioning of a witness by the opposing party on matters within the scope of the direct examination. This is usually accomplished to discredit the testimony of the witness or to develop facts that may bolster the cross-examiner's case.

Purpose of Cross-Examination

The purpose of the cross-examination is to ask questions of the witness which are designed to assess the truth, reliability, and trustworthiness of his testimony and the credibility of the witness. One of the primary purposes of the cross-examination is to discredit the witness. In an Alaska case, the U.S. Supreme Court stated that, "Cross-examination is the principal means by which the believability of a witness and the truth of his testimony are tested. Subject always to the broad discretion of a trial judge to preclude repetitive and unduly harassing interrogation, the cross-examiner is not only permitted to delve into the witness's story to test the witness's perceptions and memory, but the cross-examiner has traditionally been allowed to impeach, i.e., discredit, the witness."[5]

A secondary, but equally important purpose is to elicit facts from the witness which might support or bolster the cross-examiner's case. An example of this is an eyewitness who admits that the defendant accused of a crime looks similar to several other individuals.

Scope of Cross-Examination

The scope of the cross-examination extends only to the subject matter of the direct examination or to matters affecting the credibility of the witness (see Exhibit 8.8). For example, if a witness testified on direct examination that she was with the defendant on a particular day, it might be beyond the scope of the direct for the cross-examination to ask the witness about a different day. However, this rule allows the court discretion in permitting "inquiry into additional matters as if on direct examination."[6]

EXHIBIT 8.8   Mode and Order of Interrogation and Presentation

Federal Rules of Evidence
Rule 611(b) Scope of Cross-Examination. Cross-examination should be limited to the subject matter of the direct examination and matters affecting the credibility of the witness. The court may, in the exercise of discretion, permit inquiry into additional matters as if on direct examination.

(c) Leading Questions. Leading questions should not be used on the direct examination of a witness except as may be necessary to develop the witness's testimony. Ordinarily leading questions should be permitted on cross-examination. When a party calls a hostile witness, an adverse party, or a witness identified with an adverse party, interrogation may be by leading questions.

"Artful" Cross-Examination

The following Fourth Circuit case out of Virginia illustrates an improper and what the court calls an "egregious example of 'artful' cross-examination."

CASE

United States v. Hall
989 F.2d 711 (4th Cir. 1993).
Appeal from the United States District Court for the Western District of Virginia, at Big Stone Gap.

Hall, Circuit Judge.

Hall was convicted of conspiracy to distribute cocaine. Because Hall was improperly cross-examined, we reverse his convictions and remand for a new trial.

I.

. . . Following his arrest, his wife allegedly provided inculpatory information to the government. According to a "summary" of a "Regional Narcotics Task Force Debrief," Mrs. Hall told Special Assistant United States Attorney Tim McAfee that she had witnessed Hall and others using cocaine. Additionally, she revealed the content of several conversations in which she and her husband discussed his drug use and his inevitable indictment. Before trial, Mrs. Hall signed an affidavit indicating that she would assert her marital privilege against being compelled to testify against her husband. The government did not attempt to call Mrs. Hall as a witness. However, during the cross-examination of the defendant, the prosecutor stated that he possessed a statement made by Mrs. Hall. The prosecutor then held the "statement" in his hand and read portions of it during the cross-examination.

. . .

Q: Mr. Hall, isn't it true that your wife caught you using cocaine as early as 1987?
A: No, she didn't.
Q: In the kitchen, didn't she?

. . .

Q: She caught you using cocaine on the kitchen table, and you kicked her out of the house?

Hall's counsel objected to all questions concerning Mrs. Hall as lacking a foundation, as being outside the scope of the direct, and because Mrs. Hall had not testified. Prosecutor McAfee then stated, in the jury's presence, "I have a foundation for it. I have a three page statement from Ms. Hall." The district court overruled Hall's objection and McAfee continued to question Hall about Mrs. Hall's "statement":

Q: In fact, isn't it also true, Mr. Hall, that you even brought your wife with you for a cocaine deal?

. . . .

Q: In fact, after Debbie Greer got busted, you were so concerned about that and what Debbie Greer was going to say about her relationship with you that you shared that concern and concerns with your wife, Tammie Hall?

Hall's objections were overruled. McAfee then continued to ask Hall about other statements that he had made to his wife. . . .

This case presents an egregious example of "artful" cross-examination. McAfee repeatedly told the jury that he possessed a statement given by the defendant's wife. He then proceeded to read the statement to the jury under the guise of cross-examining Hall. In effect, the government gained extremely damaging inculpatory testimony that could not have been introduced into evidence. The government's use of Mrs. Hall's unauthenticated statement violated Fed. R. Evid.

Rule 802 ("Hearsay is not admissible except as provided by these rules. . ."), both Mr. and Mrs. Hall's spousal privileges, and introduced testimony of a witness who could not be cross-examined as required by the Confrontation Clause.

B. Curative instruction.

After the close of the evidence, the court offered the following curative instruction:

During [cross examination] the Government Counsel asked the defendant if he made certain statements to his wife, and the defendant denied making such statements. The jury is instructed that if no evidence has been shown that such statements were made by the defendant, the jury shall make no such inference that such statements were made simply because the questions were asked, and shall disregard any and all questions asked relating to statements allegedly made to Tammie Hall, the wife of the defendant.

The normal presumption is that the jury will follow a curative instruction. However, this presumption cannot apply when the curative instruction fails by its own terms to address the error. . . .

Because the instruction failed to address the jury's exposure to prejudicial statements that could not have been introduced into evidence, it failed to cure the error introduced by McAfee's wrongful cross-examination. . . . First, the impermissible aspects of the cross-examination did not concern subsidiary matters, but, rather, the essence of the prosecution's case: whether Hall had possessed and distributed cocaine. Second, the cross-examination was of the defendant himself. This factor distinguishes this case from others where less consequential witnesses were improperly cross-examined. Third, this was not a single isolated incident: McAfee repeatedly asked Hall impermissible questions. . . .

. . . .

The role of the federal prosecutor is not to seek a conviction at any cost. Instead, as a representative of the United States, the prosecutor's interest in a criminal prosecution is not that it shall win a case, but that justice shall be done. . . . It is as much [the prosecutor's] duty to refrain from improper methods calculated to produce a wrongful conviction as it is to use every legitimate means to bring about a just one.

. . . .

Hall's convictions are reversed, and the case is remanded for a new trial.

The following questions are based on the *How to Brief a Legal Case* format shown in the Appendix. Use this format to answer the following questions:

1. Summarize the facts in the previous case.
2. What is the legal issue?
3. How did the appellate court decide?
4. Why did the court decide this way?
5. Do you agree with the court's reasoning? Explain why or why not.

Try to find and read this case online! Check out one of the legal research web sites below, go to the federal circuit for this court decision, and use their "Search" feature to find this case. In the "Search" field, enter the cite or case name. If you have access to Westlaw or Lexis, try to find this case using one of these legal search sites.

1. U.S. Courts Site with Links to All Circuit Courts of Appeal (http://www.uscourts.gov/links.html)
2. National Center for State Courts—State and Federal Court Web Sites (http://www.ncsconline.org/D_kis/info_court_web_sites.html#federal)
3. FindLaw (http://guide.lp.findlaw.com/casecode/)

Is Address of Witness Beyond the Scope of Cross-Examination?

Does asking a witness where he lives go beyond the scope of a proper cross-examination? In this Supreme Court case, the trial judge refused to allow it, calling it "immaterial and not proper cross-examination."

CASE

Alford v. United States

282 U.S. 687 (1931).

[Alford was tried in the District Court for Southern California of using the mails to defraud. During trial, the prosecution called Mr. Bradley, a former employee of Alford, to the witness stand. On direct examination, Bradley gave damaging testimony regarding the defendant. Upon cross-examination, the following questions seeking to elicit the witness's place of residence were excluded on the government's objection that they were immaterial and not proper cross-examination.

Q: by Defense: Where do you live, Mr. Bradley?

Prosecution: That is objected to as immaterial and not proper cross-examination.

Court: I cannot see the materiality.

Defense: Why, I think the jury has a perfect right to know who the witness is, where he lives and what his business is, and we have the right to elicit that on cross-examination. I may say that this is the first witness the Government has called that they have not elicited the address from.

Court: I will sustain the objection.

Q: by Defense: What is your business, Mr. Bradley?

A: My profession is an accountant, public accountant.

Q: What is your occupation now?

A: I am not doing anything at the present time on account of this case.

Q: On account of this case?

A: Yes.

Q: Do you live in Los Angeles?

Prosecution: That is objected to as immaterial and invading the Court's ruling.

Court: I have ruled on that question.

Defense: I will temporarily pass on to something else. I would like leave to submit authorities on my right to develop that on cross-examination. I haven't them with me.

Court: All right. . . .

The jury were thereupon excused by the court . . . after which the following proceedings were had relative to the materiality of the testimony, as to the residence and place thereof of Mr. Bradley.

Court: In what particular do you think that evidence is material?

Defense: I think it is material for this purpose, first, not only on the general grounds I urged in asking the question, but on the additional grounds that I have been informed and caused to believe that this witness himself is now in the custody of the Federal authorities.

Prosecution: You mean Mr. Bradley? You mean by the Federal authorities here?

Defense: I don't know by what authorities, but that is my impression, that he is here in the custody of the Federal authorities. If that is so, I have a right to show that for the purpose of showing whatever bias or prejudice he may have.

Court: No; I don't think so. If you can prove he has ever been convicted of a felony, that is a different thing.

Defense: I realize that is the rule. I may impeach him if he has been convicted of a felony.

Court: No. You may prove that fact as going to his credibility, but you can't merely show that he is detained or in charge of somebody. Everybody is presumed to be innocent until proven guilty.

Defense: It is a violent presumption sometimes, I know.

Court: Your defendant is certainly to be given the benefit of that presumption.

Defense: I have no doubt of that.

Court: If that is all you have, I will have to stand on the ruling. . . .

Defense: I would like, if the Court please, our exception noted to the Court's ruling made yesterday after the jury retired to the effect that we could not inquire as to the present address and residence of the witness.

Court: Very well.

Alford was subsequently convicted and appealed, claiming error by the trial judge in not allowing the cross-examination. The Court of Appeals upheld the trial court, saying: "A witness is not on trial and has no means of protecting himself. Here it was evident that the counsel for the appellant desired to discredit the witness, without, so far as is shown, in any way connecting the expected answer with a matter on trial." The U.S. Supreme Court granted certiorari.]

Justice Stone delivered the opinion of the Court.

Cross-examination of a witness is a matter of right. Its permissible purposes, among others, are that the witness may be identified with his community so that independent testimony may be sought and offered of his reputation for veracity in his own neighborhood, that the jury may interpret his testimony in the light reflected upon it by knowledge of his environment, and that facts may be brought out tending to discredit the witness by showing that his testimony in chief was untrue or biased. Counsel often cannot know in advance what pertinent facts may be elicited on cross-examination. For that reason it is necessarily exploratory; and the rule that the examiner must indicate the purpose of his inquiry does not, in general, apply. It is the essence of a fair trial that reasonable latitude be given the cross-examiner, even though he is unable to state to the court what fact a reasonable cross-examination might develop. Prejudice ensues from a denial of the opportunity to place the witness in his proper setting and put the weight of his testimony and his credibility to a test, without which the jury cannot fairly appraise them. To say that prejudice can be established only by showing that the cross-examination, if pursued, would necessarily have brought out facts tending to discredit the testimony in chief, is to deny a substantial right and withdraw one of the safeguards essential to a fair trial. . . .

The question, "Where do you live?" was not only an appropriate preliminary to the cross-examination of the witness, but on its face . . . was an essential step in identifying the witness with his environment, to which cross-examination may always be directed. But counsel for the defense went further, and in the ensuing colloquy with the court urged, as an additional reason why the question should be allowed, not a substitute reason, as the court below assumed, that he was informed that the witness was then in court in custody of the federal authorities, and that that fact could be brought out on cross-examination to show whatever bias or prejudice the witness might have. The

purpose obviously was not, as the trial court seemed to think, to discredit the witness by showing that he was charged with crime, but to show by such facts as proper cross-examination might develop, that his testimony was biased because given under promise or expectation of immunity, or under the coercive effect of his detention by officers of the United States, which was conducting the present prosecution. . . .

The extent of cross-examination with respect to an appropriate subject of inquiry is within the sound discretion of the trial court. It may exercise a reasonable judgment in determining when the subject is exhausted. But no obligation is imposed on the court, such as that suggested below, to protect a witness from being discredited on cross-examination, short of an attempted invasion of his constitutional protection from self incrimination, properly invoked. There is a duty to protect him from questions which go beyond the bonds of proper cross-examination merely to harass, annoy or humiliate him. But no such case is presented here. The trial court cut off in limine all inquiry on a subject with respect to which the defense was entitled to a reasonable cross-examination. This was an abuse of discretion and prejudicial error.

Reversed.

LEGAL ANALYSIS AND WRITING 8.3

The following questions are based on the *How to Brief a Legal Case* format shown in the Appendix. Use this format to answer the following questions:

1. Summarize the facts in the previous case.

2. What is the legal issue?

3. What did the appellate court decide?

4. Why did the court decide this way?

5. Do you agree with the court's reasoning? Explain why or why not.

LEGAL RESEARCH USING THE INTERNET SKILLS 8.3

Find and read this Supreme Court case online! Check out one of the legal research web sites below and use their "Search" feature to find this case. In the "Search" field, enter the cite or case name.

1. FindLaw U.S. Supreme Court Decisions (http://www.findlaw.com/casecode/supreme.html)

2. U.S. Supreme Court (http://www.supremecourt.us.gov/)

3. Supreme Court Collection of Cornell Law School (http://supct.law.cornell.edu/supct/)

YOU BE THE JUDGE 8.1

In a civil action for employment discrimination based on age, plaintiff is questioned on direct examination about his work record and the steps which led up to his being fired from his job. On cross-examination, defense asks plaintiff, "How many times have you been fired before?" Plaintiff objects that this question goes beyond the scope of direct. Would you allow this question? Why or why not?

INTERROGATION OF WITNESSES BY THE COURT

The court may call a witness to the stand or question a witness who is on the stand. Mississippi's Evidence Rule 614 is an example of the modern rule governing this, stating that "The court may, on its own motion or at the suggestion of a party, call witnesses, and all parties are entitled to cross-examine witnesses thus called."[7] If the court does this, all parties are entitled to cross-examine the witness. Examples of when judicial questioning might be appropriate is when a witness is nervous or reluctant to testify, or just confused about a line of questioning. The danger of judicial intervention or questioning is that the jury might view the judge's actions as advocating for one of the parties.

RELIGIOUS BELIEFS OR OPINIONS

Religious beliefs or opinions are not admissible to attack credibility. The Colorado rule exemplifies most states and the federal courts in saying that "evidence of the beliefs or opinions of a witness on matters of religion is not admissible for the purpose of showing that by reason of their nature the witness's credibility is impaired or enhanced."[8] However, when the religious belief of a witness is relevant to issues other than credibility, such as knowledge of specific religious practices, then this evidence may be admissible.

CRITICAL THINKING QUESTIONS 8.4

1. Why do we limit the scope of a cross-examination to the subject matter inquired about in the direct examination?
2. Which do you think is more important on cross-examination: eliciting information from a witness that will support your case, or discrediting the witness? Explain your reasons.
3. Where do you think the court in the *Hall* case "drew the line" in determining how far the prosecution could go in cross-examining the defendant?
4. In the *Alford* case, the Court held that asking a witness where he lived was an appropriate question in cross-examination. Can you think of any examples today where a witness would not be required to divulge her address on the stand?
5. What are the strengths and weaknesses of the court being allowed to call a witness to the stand or question a witness who is on the stand?

EXCLUSION OF WITNESSES

When requested by one of the parties, the court may order that witnesses are excluded so that they cannot hear the testimony of other witnesses (see Exhibit 8.9). The reasoning behind this rule is to protect the factfinding process from collusion or influence of witnesses if allowed to listen to testimony before being called to the stand. Some parties may not be excluded. Parties to the legal action may not be excluded because their exclusion would raise issues of due process. A party who is not a natural person may have a representative present. A person authorized by statute to be present cannot be excluded.[9] Finally, the court will not exclude a person whose presence is shown by a party to be essential to the presentation of the party's cause. Examples of these last two might include a key person who helped the party during litigation, like a police officer, or an expert witness who needs to hear testimony of witnesses in order to provide an opinion in later testimony.

EXHIBIT 8.9   Example of Rule for Exclusion of Witnesses

Kentucky Rules of Evidence
Rule 615. Exclusion of Witnesses. At the request of a party the court shall order witnesses excluded so that they cannot hear the testimony of other witnesses and it may make the order on its own motion. This rule does not authorize exclusion of:

(1) A party who is a natural person;

(2) An officer or employee of a party which is not a natural person designated as its representative by its attorney; or

(3) A person whose presence is shown by a party to be essential to the presentation of the party's cause.

CRITICAL THINKING QUESTIONS 8.5

1. What are the reasons for allowing the exclusion of witnesses?
2. Which witnesses may be excluded?
3. Do you think this rule is a good one? Explain why or why not.

SUMMARY

In a trial, evidence is presented primarily through the calling and examination of witnesses. The court controls the "mode and order" of questioning witnesses and the presenting of evidence. When requested by one of the parties, the court may order that witnesses are excluded so that they cannot hear the testimony of other witnesses. The initial questioning of a witness by the party that called the witness to the stand is called *direct examination*. Direct examination is usually carried out so that the witness tells a story in a chronological manner. If a witness is forgetful and cannot remember a matter or event when asked on the stand, the witness may be permitted to refer to writing or notes in order to jog his or her memory. After one side completes the direct examination of their witness, the opposing side may conduct a *cross-examination*. A cross-examination involves the questioning of a witness by the opposing party on matters within the scope of the direct examination. This is usually accomplished to discredit the testimony of the witness or to develop facts that may bolster the cross-examiner's case. If the credibility of the witness has been attacked, the party originally calling the witness may conduct a *redirect examination* to attempt to restore credibility. This is called *rehabilitation*.

For the party calling a witness, credibility can be strengthened through proper preparation of the witness before trial. Witnesses should be helped to understand what will be asked on the stand and what the trial process will involve. Walking a witness through the steps of the trial and her testimony will not only relieve the anxiety of the witness, but help to boost her confidence by removing much of the fear of the unknown for the witness.

KEY TERMS

Credibility	Leading Question	Redirect Examination
Cross-Examination	Past Recollection Recorded	Rehabilitation
Direct Examination	Present Memory Refreshed	
Extrinsic Evidence	Recross-Examination	

LEARNING OUTCOMES AND PRACTICE SKILLS CHECKLIST

☐ Learning Outcomes

After completing your reading, questions, and exercises, you should be able to demonstrate a better understanding of the learning concepts by answering the following questions:

1. Identify the forms of examination used to question witnesses on the stand.
2. Explain who controls the mode and order of questioning witnesses, and why.
3. Compare and contrast direct examination with cross-examination, discussing their use in the questioning of witnesses, including purpose and scope.
4. Describe some steps that can be taken to prepare a witness for examination on the stand.
5. Describe the methods allowed when a forgetful witness cannot remember a matter or event when asked on the stand.
6. Distinguish redirect from direct examination.
7. Define rehabilitation as it pertains to witnesses, and discuss how it is used.
8. Explain what a leading question is and when it may be used.
9. Assess when and why leading questions may be used on direct and cross-examinations.

10. Define credibility and identify the methods used to ensure witness credibility.
11. Discuss the issues involved in admitting extrinsic evidence of a prior inconsistent statement by a witness.
12. Explain whether the trial judge may call a witness to the stand or question a witness who is on the stand, and what issues might result from this practice.
13. Describe what the rule for exclusion of witnesses pertains to and the reasoning behind it.

☐ Practice Skills

In addition to understanding the learning concepts, practice what you have learned through applications using critical thinking, legal analysis and writing, legal research, and advocacy skills, including:

Critical Thinking

1. Why do we have rules that govern the examination of witnesses?
2. Do you believe that the current rules provide adequate safeguards for this process?
3. What public policy issues or considerations do you think might be behind these rules?
4. If it were up to you, would you keep the rules governing examination of witnesses as they are, delete them, narrow them, or expand them? Explain your reasoning.
5. How do these rules influence the gathering of evidence or preparing of witnesses?

Legal Analysis and Writing

Analyze the following rules and cases by summarizing their holdings, explaining their significance, and assessing any issue that might arise in their application.

1. Rule 611(a).
2. Rule 611(b).
3. Rule 611(c).
4. Rule 614.
5. Rule 615.
6. *Alford v. United States.*

Legal Research Using the Internet

1. Find the annotated Federal Rules of Evidence on the Internet and see if any comments were made in the proposing of the rules covered in this chapter.
2. Find your state's rules of evidence regarding the examination of witnesses and concepts covered in this chapter. Compare and contrast with the federal and/or modern rules, and some of the state rules listed in this chapter.
3. Find out if your state appellate court posts their case decisions on the Internet. If so, find a case that illustrates an issue or rule discussed in this chapter. If your state decisions are not on the Internet, go instead to the web site for the U.S. Circuit Court of Appeals in your circuit, or search the U.S. Supreme Court decisions.

ADVOCACY AND COMMUNICATION SKILLS 8.1

Facts:

Plaintiff's witness will testify that she works with defendant at a company that builds and paints furniture. After working the night shift, witness and defendant stopped at a bar for a few drinks. Defendant offered witness a ride home and on the way, witness felt that defendant drove at an excessive speed. When plaintiff's car, which was in front of defendant, braked suddenly, defendant could not stop in time and rear-ended plaintiff's vehicle, causing injury to plaintiff.

Directions:

Form teams from small groups of no more than 3–4 each. Prepare a set of questions to ask the above witness and conduct a direct, cross, redirect, or recross-examination of the witness. During each line of questioning, the opposing team should be prepared to object, if needed, using objections from earlier readings. Use a different team member for each examination:

1. Plaintiff team will conduct a direct exam of no more than 5 minutes.
2. Defense team will conduct a cross-exam of no more than 5 minutes.
3. Plaintiff team will have 3 minutes to redirect.
4. Defense team will have 3 minutes to recross.

PRACTICE APPLICATION 8.1

In the above *Advocacy* problem, the witness is asked by the defense how many drinks she had on the evening in question. The witness replies that she cannot remember and the defense wants to refresh the witness's memory by showing her a copy of the police accident report taken that evening where the witness had told the investigating officer that she had drank "four or five" glasses of wine. Plaintiff objects, arguing that the witness's memory cannot be refreshed if she says that she cannot remember a fact.

Use the format shown in the Appendix for the *IRAC Method of Legal Analysis* and the readings, rules, and cases discussed in this chapter to analyze the above problem and determine whether the defense may refresh witness's memory by showing her the police report. Write a memo giving your analysis, reasoning, and conclusions.

WEB SITES

Alabama Judicial System On–Line
http://www.judicial.state.al.us/
Federal Rules of Evidence
http://www.law.cornell.edu/rules/fre/overview.html
FindLaw
http://www.findlaw.com
FindLaw
http://guide.lp.findlaw.com/casecode/
FindLaw U.S. Supreme Court Decisions
http://www.findlaw.com/casecode/supreme.html
Guide to State Rules of Evidence
http://expertpages.com/state_rules_of_evidence.htm
List of State Laws from Legal Information Institute of Cornell Law School
http://www.law.cornell.edu/states/listing.html

National Center for State Courts—State and Federal Court Web Sites
http://www.ncsconline.org/D_kis/info_court_web_sites.html#federal
Supreme Court Collection of Cornell Law School
http://supct.law.cornell.edu/supct/
U.S. Courts Site with Links to All Circuit Courts of Appeal
http://www.uscourts.gov/links.html
U.S. Supreme Court
http://www.supremecourtus.gov/

ENDNOTES

1. Ohio Evid. R. 611(a). Mode and Order of Interrogation and Presentation. Control by court.
2. Cal. Evid. Code Section 765(a).
3. Fed. R. Evid. 611(c). Leading Questions.
4. Fed. R. Evid. 612. Writing Used to Refresh Memory.
5. *Davis v. Alaska*, 415 U.S. 308 (1974).
6. Fed. R. Evid. 611(b). Scope of Cross-Examination.
7. M.R.E. 614. Calling and Interrogation of Witnesses by Court.
8. *Colorado Rules of Evidence*, Rule 610. Religious Beliefs or Opinions.
9. Fed. R. Evid. 615, Amended Dec. 1, 1998.

CHAPTER 9

IMPEACHMENT OF WITNESSES

"We better know there is a fire whence we see much smoke rising than we could know it by one or two witnesses swearing to it. The witnesses may commit perjury, but the smoke cannot."

—Abraham Lincoln, 1864

LEARNING OUTCOMES

In this chapter, you will learn about the following legal concepts:

- Impeachment of Witnesses
- Who May Impeach?
- Impeachment by Bias
- Impeachment by Evidence of Character
- Opinion and Reputation Evidence
- Specific Instances of Conduct

- Use of Character Evidence Today
- Impeachment by Conviction of Crime
- Crimes Involving Dishonesty
- Criminal Defendant as Witness
- No Comment Rule

INTRODUCTION

We have learned that in order to testify at trial, a witness must be competent (that is, legally capable of testifying). When a witness does begin to testify and is examined through questioning by each party, the emphasis becomes one of credibility; how believable that witness will be to the trier of fact. In this chapter, we will assess the methods utilized for the **impeachment**, or attacking, of the credibility of a witness. We will look at who may impeach and how this is done, including impeachment by bias, character, and conviction of crime.

IMPEACHMENT OF WITNESSES

Impeachment is a form of attacking the credibility of a witness in order to convince the jury that the testimony given is not truthful or that the witness is unreliable. There are a variety of methods for impeaching a witness and different state rules will emphasize these various methods.

Georgia rules, for example, include methods where a witness may be impeached by disproving the facts testified to by him, contradictory statements, or by evidence as to his general bad character.[1] In Florida, the credibility of a witness may be impeached by introducing statements of the witness which are inconsistent with the witness's present testimony; showing that the witness is biased; attacking the character of the witness; showing a defect of capacity, ability, or opportunity in the witness to observe, remember, or recount the matters about which the witness testified; or by proof by other witnesses that material facts are not as testified to by the witness being impeached.[2]

The various rules do have a common framework. They provide for impeachment by attacking competence and credibility. Competence may be impeached by showing that the witness has a problem in testifying from personal knowledge, or the ability to perceive an event, remember, or communicate what was perceived. Credibility may be impeached by showing bias, prejudice, or an interest in the outcome of the case that might have influenced the testimony of the witness. Credibility may also be impeached by attacking the untruthful character of the witness, bad reputation, certain prior convictions of the witness, or contradictory or inconsistent statements made by the witness.

WHO MAY IMPEACH?

At common law, a party calling a witness could not attack the credibility of that witness. This was called the **voucher rule**, where the party calling the witness "vouched" for that witness's credibility. The modern rules changed that, providing that any party may attack the credibility of a witness, including the party calling the witness (see Exhibit 9.1).[3] However, a witness may not be called for the sole reason of impeaching him. For example, a prosecutor in a criminal action may not call a hostile witness just to have the opportunity to introduce hearsay evidence that might help the prosecution's case. Of course, if the prosecution called the witness in good faith and the witness subsequently turned hostile, then the prosecution may use impeachment.

Why Impeach Your Own Witness?

There may be several reasons for a party to want to impeach the party's own witness. One reason might be damaging information about a witness

Impeachment
Attacking the credibility of a witness in order to convince the jury that the testimony given is not truthful or that the witness is unreliable.

Voucher Rule
Old common law rule that the party calling a witness "vouched" for that witness's credibility. Replaced in most states by modern rule that allows credibility of a witness to be attacked by any party.

EXHIBIT 9.1   Modern Rule for Who May Impeach

Pennsylvania Rules of Evidence
Rule 607. Impeachment of Witness.
   (a) Who May Impeach. The credibility of any witness may be attacked by any party, including the party calling the witness.

---

that a party wants the trier of fact to learn before the other side has a chance to introduce it. An example of this might be a prior conviction. The party calling the witness may decide that it would be a better strategy of damage control and to show the jury that they are "not hiding anything."

Another example of wanting to impeach one's own witness is when the witness may be reluctant to testify or hostile to the party calling the witness. An example of a hostile witness may be the calling of a gang member to testify in a case against another member of the gang, or the calling of a witness to testify against her friend or a member of her family. In the following case, the prosecution called the girlfriend of a man accused of murder. The girlfriend did not want to testify against the defendant and the prosecutor offered evidence to impeach the witness.

CASE

Burgin v. State

747 So.2d 916 (1999).
Court of Criminal Appeals of Alabama.

Cobb, Judge.

Ricky Burgin appeals from his conviction of capital murder, see § 13A-5-(a)(10), Ala.Code 1975. . . . This appeal follows. We affirm.

In his only assignment of error, Burgin argues that the trial court erred in allowing the prosecution to impeach its own witness and then to offer the impeachment evidence as substantive evidence. Specifically, Burgin argues that the prosecutor was improperly allowed to call as a witness Pearlie Reed, Burgin's girlfriend and the mother of his child, knowing that she was a hostile witness and that she would refuse to testify. Burgin argues that Reed was called as a prosecution witness so that the prosecutor could introduce as impeachment evidence a prior statement of Reed's in which she recounted a confession Burgin had made to her. Rule 607, Ala. R. Evid., states, "The credibility of a witness may be attacked by any party, including the party calling the witness."

"[Rule] 607 allows the government to impeach its own witness. However, 'the government must not

knowingly elicit testimony from a witness in order to impeach him with otherwise inadmissible testimony'." *United States v. Gomez-Gallardo,* 915 F.2d 553 (9th Cir.1990). Impeachment is improper when employed as a guise to present substantive evidence to the jury that would be otherwise inadmissible. A determination must be made as to whether the government examined the witness for the primary purpose of placing before the jury substantive evidence which is otherwise inadmissible. "It would be an abuse of the rule. . . for the prosecution to call a witness that it [knows will] not give it useful evidence, just so it [can] introduce hearsay evidence against the defendant in the hope that the jury would miss the subtle distinction between impeachment and substantive evidence. . . . " *United States v. Webster,* 734 F.2d 1191 (7th Cir.1984). However, a prosecutor may call a witness it knows may be hostile, and it may impeach that witness's credibility. Surprise is not a necessary prerequisite to impeaching one's own witness under Rule 607. *United States v. Palacios,* 556 F.2d 1359 (5th Cir.1977). . . . A prosecutor's decision to call such a witness is subject to a good-faith standard, and it is "always open for the defendant to argue that the probative value of the evidence offered to impeach the witness is clearly outweighed by the prejudicial impact it might have on the jury, because the jury would have difficulty confining use of the evidence to impeachment." *United States v. Webster*, 734 F.2d at 1193. In the case before us, the prosecutor called Pearlie Reed and, after some preliminary questions, the following occurred:

Q [Prosecutor]:	At some point in time, Pearlie, during the course of your relationship with [Burgin], and after the incident that occurred in August 1995, did Ricky tell you about that incident? Not easy to do, is it?
THE COURT:	You need to answer the question, please, ma'am.
Q:	Did Ricky tell you about that incident?
A:	Yes.
Q:	Speak up.
A:	Yes.
Q:	What did he tell you about it?
A:	I can't do it.
Q:	You can't do what? You can't do what?
A:	I don't want to.
Q:	You don't want to testify against him?
A:	No.
Q:	Did Ricky—you will have to answer these questions. Let me ask you this: Do you remember in April of 1996 going to the police and telling the police what happened?
A:	Yes.
Q:	Or what you knew about the incident? Do you remember doing that?
A:	Yes.
Q:	And did you tell—I withdraw that. Did you—tell the ladies and gentlemen of the jury what Ricky Burgin told you he did or had to do with this incident. Did he tell you he was there?
THE COURT:	Don't lead the witness, please. Answer the question, please, ma'am.
A:	Yes.
Q:	Yes, what?
THE COURT:	Ask her a direct question. Ask her what he said, if anything.
Q:	Pearlie, what did Ricky say, if anything?
A:	I don't want to testify.

At this point, the trial court instructed Ms. Reed that she had to answer the questions. When she still refused, the jury was excused and the trial judge again instructed Ms. Reed about her obligations as a witness to answer the questions. When Ms. Reed expressed a desire to invoke her Fifth Amendment rights, the trial court explained to her that, as a witness, she had no liberty interests at stake and that she could not refuse to answer questions on that basis. He then explained to her that she could be held in contempt and incarcerated if she continued to refuse to answer questions .... Back in front of the jury, she was again asked if she had a conversation with Burgin about his involvement in the murders. Ms. Reed responded, "No." At that point, over the objections of defense counsel on the ground that the prosecutor was impeaching his own witness, the prosecutor began to question Ms. Reed about the particulars of a statement she had made to police investigators. In that statement she told them that Burgin had told her that he and his codefendants had robbed and killed Fred Williams and Sharon Mixon. Ms. Reed acknowledged that she had voluntarily approached police investigators and had made the statement, but she testified that she had lied and was making parts of it up because she had gotten mad at Burgin, and that other portions of her statement came from "what I had heard" from persons other than Burgin.

During the prosecutor's closing argument, he began to argue as substantive facts the information from Pearlie Reed's statement to the police. When defense counsel objected, the trial court repeatedly sustained the objections, noting that Ms. Reed's statement to the police was not "substantive evidence of the truth of the matter." During the trial judge's instructions to the jury, he said: "During the course of the trial all of these attorneys had the opportunity to ask questions in your presence and to argue their case to you and it's probably apparent to you that they don't agree what the facts are in this case. Perhaps, they don't agree on inferences that you should draw. And that's understandable. But their job is to help you find the truth. And if you find that any argument made by either side is not supported by the evidence as you recall it, then disregard that because the assertions of counsel are not evidence." Shortly thereafter, the trial judge instructed: "There was a witness asked about a statement made out of court but [she] now denies the truthfulness of it. That evidence is admissible for your consideration as you evaluate the testimony of that witness, but it is not admissible as substantive evidence of the matters now denied."

Burgin argues that the prosecutor called Pearlie Reed, knowing she was a hostile witness, as a subterfuge to get before the jury evidence of her statement, which would otherwise be inadmissible hearsay. We do not agree. The record reflects that, while Reed was certainly a reluctant witness who made it clear that she did not want to testify against her boyfriend, she originally answered the prosecutor's questions and, indeed, told the jury that Burgin had related to her that he was present at the murders. It was only after being given an ultimatum by the trial judge—either to answer the prosecutor's questions or to face incarceration—that Ms. Reed changed her story and denied that Burgin had told her about the murders. At that point, the prosecutor was permitted by Rule 607 to question Ms. Reed's credibility by pointing out that she had related to the police a detailed version of the murders that she claimed Burgin had confessed to her. We note that Ms. Reed did not deny telling the police that Burgin had confessed to her his involvement in the murders, but she claimed she had lied to the police because she was mad at Burgin. Because Ms. Reed first told the jury that Burgin had told her he was present at the murder scene, and then completely changed her story, her credibility became an issue, requiring the prosecutor to impeach his own witness. Finally, even though the prosecutor tried to argue as substantive evidence of Burgin's guilt the facts he elicited during his impeachment of Ms. Reed, the trial court repeatedly sustained objections to that argument and later gave the jury proper limiting instructions regarding that specific impeachment evidence. A proper limiting instruction is deemed to cure the effects of a prejudicial remark made before a jury. For the foregoing reasons, we hold that the trial court did not err when it allowed the prosecutor to impeach Ms. Reed with a prior inconsistent statement. . . .

Affirmed.

LEGAL ANALYSIS AND WRITING 9.1

The following questions are based on the *How to Brief a Legal Case* format shown in the Appendix. Use this format to answer the following questions:

1. Summarize the facts in the previous case.

2. What is the legal issue?

3. What did the appellate court decide?

4. Why did the court decide this way?

5. Do you agree with the court's reasoning? Explain why or why not.

LEGAL RESEARCH USING THE INTERNET SKILLS 9.1

The Burgin appeal was heard by the Alabama Court of Criminal Appeals. Is this the highest appellate court in Alabama? Find out by logging onto the Alabama Judicial System On-Line or by finding it through one of the other following sites:

1. Alabama Judicial System On-Line (http://www.judicial.state.al.us/)

2. National Center for State Courts—State and Federal Court Web Sites (http://www.ncsconline.org/ D_kis/info_court_web_sites.html#federal)

3. FindLaw (http://guide.lp.findlaw.com/casecode/)

> ## CRITICAL THINKING QUESTIONS 9.1
>
> 1. What is impeachment?
> 2. Why do we need evidentiary rules that govern impeachment?
> 3. What public policy issues, if any, do you think are behind these rules?
> 4. Why did the rules change regarding who may impeach?
> 5. Do you agree with these changes? Why or why not?

IMPEACHMENT BY BIAS

Witness Bias
Prejudice, special interest, or some motive that may influence a witness's testimony.

Witness bias is prejudice, special interest, or some motive that may influence a witness's testimony. Impeachment by bias is not specifically listed in many of the state rules or the Federal Rules of Evidence. It is, however, permissible in most states and in the federal courts. Some states have codified this. Florida, for example, has a rule stating that the credibility of a witness may be impeached by showing that the witness is biased.[4] Ohio has a rule that allows "bias, prejudice, interest, or any motive to misrepresent" to impeach a witness either by examination of the witness or by extrinsic evidence (see Exhibit 9.2).[5] The majority of courts rely on case decisions, such as the following important Supreme Court case, to allow bias as a permissible and established basis of impeachment under the Rules.

Group 2 Case #9

◆

CASE

United States v. Abel
469 U.S. 45 (1984).

Justice Rehnquist delivered the opinion for a unanimous Court.

[Abel and two cohorts were indicted for robbing a bank. The cohorts pled guilty, but Abel went to trial. One of the cohorts, Ehle, agreed to testify against Abel. Abel countered Ehle's testimony with that of a witness, Mills, who was not a participant in the robbery but was friendly with respondent and with Ehle, and had spent time with both in prison. Mills testified that after the robbery Ehle had admitted to Mills that Ehle intended to implicate Abel falsely, in order to receive favorable treatment from the Government. The prosecutor in turn attempted to discredit Mills' testimony by calling Ehle back to the stand and eliciting from Ehle the fact that Abel, Mills, and Ehle were all members of the "Aryan Brotherhood," a secret prison gang that required its members always to deny the existence of the organization and to commit perjury, theft, and murder on each member's behalf.

Defense counsel objected to Ehle's proffered rebuttal testimony as too prejudicial to respondent. The District Court held that the probative value of Ehle's rebuttal testimony outweighed its prejudicial effect. The jury convicted respondent.]

We hold that the evidence showing Mills' and respondent's membership in the prison gang was sufficiently probative of Mills' possible bias towards respondent to warrant its admission into evidence. Thus it was within the District Court's discretion to admit Ehle's testimony. . . .

. . . [T]he Rules do not by their terms deal with impeachment for "bias," although they do expressly treat impeachment by character evidence and conduct, Rule 608, by evidence of conviction of a crime, Rule 609, and by showing of religious beliefs or opinion, Rule 610. . . . This Court had held in *Alford v. United States*, 282 U.S. 687 (1931), that a trial court must allow some cross-examination of a witness to show bias. Our decision in *Davis v. Alaska*, 415 U.S. 308 (1974), holds that the Confrontation Clause of the Sixth Amendment requires a defendant to have some opportunity to show bias on the part of a prosecution witness. With this state of unanimity confronting the drafters of the Federal Rules of Evidence, we think it unlikely that they intended to scuttle entirely the evidentiary availability of cross-examination for bias.

[C]ommentators, without mentioning the omission, treat bias as a permissible and established basis of impeachment under the Rules. We think this conclusion is obviously correct. Rule 401 defines as "relevant evidence" evidence having any tendency to make the existence of any fact that is of consequence to the determination of the action more probable or less probable than it would be without the evidence. Rule 402 provides that all relevant evidence is admissible. . . . A successful showing of bias on the part of a witness would have a tendency to make the facts to which he testified less probable in the eyes of the jury than it would be without such testimony. The correctness of the conclusion that the Rules contemplate impeachment by showing of bias is confirmed by. . . the provisions allowing any party to attack credibility in Rule 607, and allowing cross-examination on "matters affecting the credibility of the witness" in Rule 611(b). The Courts of Appeals have upheld use of extrinsic evidence to show bias both before and after the adoption of the Federal Rules of Evidence.

We think the lesson to be drawn from all of this is that it is permissible to impeach a witness by showing his bias under the Federal Rules of Evidence just as it was permissible to do so before their adoption. . . .

Ehle's testimony about the prison gang certainly made the existence of Mills' bias towards respondent more probable. Thus it was relevant to support that inference. Bias is a term used in the "common law of evidence" to describe the relationship between a party and a witness which might lead the witness to slant, unconsciously or otherwise, his testimony in favor of or against a party. Bias may be induced by a witness's like, dislike, or fear of a party, or by the witness's self-interest. Proof of bias is almost always relevant because the jury, as finder of fact and weigher of credibility, has historically been entitled to assess all evidence which might bear on the accuracy and truth of a witness's testimony. The "common law of evidence" allowed the showing of bias by extrinsic evidence, while requiring the cross-examiner to "take the answer of the witness" with

respect to less favored forms of impeachment. Mills' and respondent's membership in the Aryan Brotherhood supported the inference that Mills' testimony was slanted or perhaps fabricated in respondent's favor. A witness's and a party's common membership in an organization, even without proof that the witness or party has personally adopted its tenets, is certainly probative of bias.

Respondent makes an . . . argument based on Rule 608(b). That Rule allows a cross-examiner to impeach a witness by asking him about specific instances of past conduct, other than crimes covered by Rule 609, which are probative of his veracity or "character for truthfulness or untruthfulness." The Rule limits the inquiry to cross-examination of the witness, however, and prohibits the cross-examiner from introducing extrinsic evidence of the witness's past conduct. Respondent claims that the prosecutor cross-examined Mills about the gang not to show bias but to offer Mills' membership in the gang as past conduct bearing on his veracity. This was error under Rule 608(b), respondent contends, because the mere fact of Mills' membership, without more, was not sufficiently probative of Mills' character for truthfulness. Respondent cites a second error under the same Rule, contending that Ehle's rebuttal testimony concerning the gang was extrinsic evidence offered to impugn Mills' veracity, and extrinsic evidence is barred by Rule 608(b).

. . . It seems clear to us that the proffered testimony with respect to Mills' membership in the Aryan Brotherhood sufficed to show potential bias in favor of respondent; because of the tenets of the organization described, it might also impeach his veracity directly. But there is no rule of evidence which provides that testimony admissible for one purpose and inadmissible for another purpose is thereby rendered inadmissible; quite the contrary is the case. It would be a strange rule of law which held that relevant, competent evidence which tended to show bias on the part of a witness was nonetheless inadmissible because it also tended to show that the witness was a liar. We intimate no view as to whether the evidence of Mills' membership in an organization having the tenets ascribed to the Aryan Brotherhood would be a specific instance of Mills' conduct which could not be proved against him by extrinsic evidence except as otherwise provided in Rule 608(b). It was enough that such evidence could properly be found admissible to show bias.

The following questions are based on the *How to Brief a Legal Case* format shown in the Appendix. Use this format to answer the following questions:

1. Summarize the facts in the previous case.
2. What is the legal issue?
3. What did the appellate court decide?
4. Why did the court decide this way?
5. Do you agree with the court's reasoning? Explain why or why not.

Find and read this Supreme Court case online! Check out one of the legal research web sites below and use their "Search" feature to find this case. In the "Search" field, enter the cite or case name.

1. FindLaw U.S. Supreme Court Decisions (http://www.findlaw.com/casecode/supreme.html)
2. U.S. Supreme Court (http://www.supremecourtus.gov/)
3. Supreme Court Collection of Cornell Law School (http://supct.law.cornell.edu/supct/)

EXHIBIT 9.2   Example of Newer Rule for Impeachment by Bias or Contradiction

Ohio Rules of Evidence
Rule 616. Bias of Witness.
In addition to other methods, a witness may be impeached by any of the following methods:

(A) Bias. Bias, prejudice, interest, or any motive to misrepresent may be shown to impeach the witness either by examination of the witness or by extrinsic evidence.

(B) Sensory or Mental Defect. A defect of capacity, ability, or opportunity to observe, remember, or relate may be shown to impeach the witness either by examination of the witness or by extrinsic evidence.

(C) Specific Contradiction. Facts contradicting a witness's testimony may be shown for the purpose of impeaching the witness's testimony. . . .

CRITICAL THINKING QUESTIONS 9.2

1. What type of bias is necessary for impeachment purposes?
2. How would you go about establishing and impeaching a witness for bias? Give examples.
3. How do rules allowing evidence of bias to impeach influence the gathering of evidence or preparing of witnesses?

IMPEACHMENT BY EVIDENCE OF CHARACTER

One of the two primary methods for impeachment covered by both common law and modern rules is by **evidence of character**. When used to describe a witness, character includes those personal qualities and traits pertaining to truthfulness. Subject to limitations, evidence of character may be used to impeach the credibility of a witness. In an earlier chapter on relevancy, we learned of the rule that excludes any evidence of a person's character for the purpose of proving that the person acted in conformity to that character trait on a specific occasion.[6] One of the exceptions noted in this rule, however, is for impeachment purposes. When using evidence of character to impeach, there are two forms allowed under the modern rules: Opinion and Reputation Evidence, and Specific Instances of Conduct.

Evidence of Character
When used to describe a witness, character includes those personal qualities and traits pertaining to truthfulness. Evidence of character would be facts or information used to attack or support a witness's qualities for truthfulness.

OPINION AND REPUTATION EVIDENCE

Opinion and reputation evidence is one of the two impeachment forms using the evidence of character (see Exhibit 9.3). Texas Rule 608(a) is representative of the modern rules regarding the use of opinion and reputation evidence to impeach. The rule states that the credibility of a witness may be attacked or supported by evidence in the form of opinion or reputation, but subject to two limitations. First, the evidence may refer only to character for truthfulness or untruthfulness. Second, evidence of truthful character is admissible only after the character of the witness for truthfulness has been attacked by opinion or reputation evidence or otherwise.[7]

This rule points out that witness credibility may be attacked, but that evidence of good character, or **bolstering evidence**, may not be used by a party until the character of that party's witness has been attacked. Bolstering evidence is evidence used to support or fortify a case or witness.

Opinion and Reputation Evidence
Evidence used to attack or support a witness's character for truthfulness.

Bolstering Evidence
Evidence used to support or fortify a case or witness.

EXHIBIT 9.3   Example of Evidence of Reputation Rule

Massachusetts General Laws
Chapter 233: Section 21A. Evidence of Reputation.
Evidence of the reputation of a person in a group with the members of which he has habitually associated in his work or business shall be admissible to the same extent and subject to the same limitations as is evidence of such reputation in a community in which he has resided.

SPECIFIC INSTANCES OF CONDUCT

Specific instances of conduct are the second impeachment form using the evidence of character. Specific instances of conduct may be used to impeach a witness, but only under limiting conditions (see Exhibit 9.4 and Exhibit 9.5). North Carolina Evidence Rule 608(b) is similar to the modern rules that deal with using conduct to impeach. This rule provides that specific instances of the conduct of a witness, for the purpose of attacking or supporting his credibility, other than conviction of crime as provided in Rule 609, may not be proved by extrinsic evidence. This means that if a witness denies the specific conduct asked about, it may not be proved by other evidence. The rule does provide, however, that these specific instances of conduct may be inquired into on cross-examination. Allowing this form of inquiry is at the discretion of the court, and will be permitted only if the conduct is probative of truthfulness or untruthfulness (see Exhibit 9.6). If allowed, the inquiry will be limited to conduct concerning the character of the witness for truthfulness or untruthfulness, or concerning the character for truthfulness or untruthfulness of another witness as to whose character the witness being cross-examined has testified.[8]

EVIDENTIARY CHECKLIST 9.1

Elements Needed to Impeach Character of Witness

☐ Opinion and reputation evidence may refer only to character for truthfulness or untruthfulness.

☐ Evidence of truthful character is admissible only after the character of the witness for truthfulness has been attacked by opinion or reputation evidence or otherwise.

☐ Specific instances of the conduct of a witness may be inquired into on cross-examination but only concerning character for truthfulness or untruthfulness, and may not be proved by extrinsic evidence.

EXHIBIT 9.4   Example of Modern Rule for Impeaching Character of Witness

Mississippi Rules of Evidence
Rule 608. Evidence of Character and Conduct of Witness.

(a) Opinion and Reputation Evidence of Character. The credibility of a witness may be attacked or supported by evidence in the form of opinion or reputation, but subject to these limitations:

   (1) the evidence may refer only to character for truthfulness or untruthfulness, and

   (2) evidence of truthful character is admissible only after the character of the witness for truthfulness has been attacked by opinion or reputation evidence or otherwise.

(b) Specific Instances of Conduct. Specific instances of the conduct of a witness, for the purpose of attacking or supporting his credibility, other than conviction of crime as provided in Rule 609, may not be proved by extrinsic evidence. They may, however, in the discretion of the court, if probative of truthfulness or untruthfulness, be inquired into on cross-examination of the witness (1) concerning his character for truthfulness or untruthfulness, or (2) concerning the character for truthfulness or untruthfulness of another witness as to which character the witness being cross-examined has testified.

EXHIBIT 9.5   Other Rules for Impeaching Character of Witness

Georgia Code
Sec. 24-9-84. Proof of Bad character. A witness may be impeached by evidence as to his general bad character. The impeaching witness should first be questioned as to his knowledge of the general character of the witness, next as to what that character is, and lastly he may be asked if from that character he would believe him on his oath. The witness may be sustained by similar proof of character.

(Continued)

EXHIBIT 9.5   Other Rules for Impeaching Character of Witness *Continued*

The particular transactions or the opinions of single individuals shall not be inquired of on either side, except upon cross-examination in seeking for the extent and foundation of the witness's knowledge.

Kentucky Rules of Evidence
Rule 608. Evidence of Character.

Opinion and Reputation Evidence of Character. The credibility of a witness may be attacked or supported by evidence in the form of opinion or reputation, but subject to the limitation that the evidence may refer only to general reputation in the community.

Massachusetts General Laws
Chapter 233: Section 23. Impeachment of Party's Own Witness.

The party who produces a witness shall not impeach his credit by evidence of bad character, but may contradict him by other evidence, and may also prove that he has made at other times statements inconsistent with his present testimony; but before proof of such inconsistent statements is given, the circumstances thereof sufficient to designate the particular occasion shall be mentioned to the witness, and he shall be asked if he has made such statements, and, if so, shall be allowed to explain them.

EXHIBIT 9.6   Evidence of Bad Character Required Before Good Character Admitted

---

California Evidence Code
Sec. 790. Evidence of the good character of a witness is inadmissible to support his credibility unless evidence of his bad character has been admitted for the purpose of attacking his credibility.

USE OF CHARACTER EVIDENCE TODAY

In a 1948 case, the Supreme Court discussed the importance of character evidence and its use in modern society. This case was reported in our earlier chapter on relevance. However, the importance of what the court said to our present discussion on the use of character evidence requires its repeating:

. . . What commonly is called "character evidence" is only such when "character" is employed as a synonym for "reputation." The witness may not testify about defendant's specific acts or courses of conduct or his possession of a particular disposition or of benign mental and moral traits; nor can he testify that his own acquaintance, observation, and knowledge of defendant leads to his own independent opinion that defendant possesses a good general or specific character, inconsistent with commission of facts charged. The witness is, however, allowed to summarize what he has heard in the community, although much of it may have been said by persons less qualified to judge than himself. The evidence which the law permits is not as to the personality of defendant but only as to the shadow his daily life has cast in his neighborhood.

. . . However, the witness must qualify to give an opinion by showing such acquaintance with the defendant, the community in which he has lived and the circles in which he has moved, as to speak with authority of the terms in which generally he is regarded. To require affirmative knowledge of the reputation may seem inconsistent with the latitude given to the witness to testify when all he can say of the reputation is that he has "heard nothing against defendant." This is permitted upon assumption that, if no ill is reported of one, his reputation must be good. But this answer is accepted only from a witness whose knowledge of defendant's habitat and surroundings is intimate enough so that his failure to hear of any relevant ill repute is an assurance that no ugly rumors were about. . . .

... The price a defendant must pay for attempting to prove his good name is to throw open the entire subject which the law has kept closed for his benefit and to make himself vulnerable where the law otherwise shields him. The prosecution may pursue the inquiry with contradictory witnesses to show that damaging rumors, whether or not well-grounded, were afloat—for it is not the man that he is, but the name that he has which is put in issue. Another hazard is that his own witness is subject to cross-examination as to the contents and extent of the hearsay on which he bases his conclusions, and he may be required to disclose rumors and reports that are current even if they do not affect his own conclusion. It may test the sufficiency of his knowledge by asking what stories were circulating concerning events, such as one's arrest, about which people normally comment and speculate. Thus, while the law gives defendant the option to show as a fact that his reputation reflects a life and habit incompatible with commission of the offense charged, it subjects his proof to tests of credibility designed to prevent him from profiting by a mere parade of partisans.

... In the frontier phase of our law's development, calling friends to vouch for defendant's good character, and its counterpart—calling the rivals and enemies of a witness to impeach him by testifying that his reputation for veracity was so bad that he was unworthy of belief on his oath—were favorite and frequent ways of converting an individual litigation into a community contest and a trial into a spectacle. Growth of urban conditions, where one may never know or hear the name of his next-door neighbor, have tended to limit the use of these techniques and to deprive them of weight with juries. The popularity of both procedures has subsided, but courts of last resort have sought to overcome danger that the true issues will be obscured and confused by investing the trial court with discretion to limit the number of such witnesses and to control cross-examination. Both propriety and abuse of hearsay reputation testimony, on both sides, depend on numerous and subtle considerations, difficult to detect or appraise from a cold record, and therefore rarely and only on clear showing of prejudicial abuse of discretion will Courts of Appeals disturb rulings of trial courts on this subject.[9]

CRITICAL THINKING QUESTIONS 9.3

1. Why should the character of a witness matter as long as that witness is competent to testify?
2. In today's fast-paced, urban society, do we really know one another well enough to testify about someone's reputation in the community?
3. What type of foundation should be shown to present this reputation and character evidence?
4. Why is evidence of truthful character admissible only after the character of the witness for truthfulness has been attacked?
5. Why do we allow specific instances of the conduct of a witness to be inquired into only on cross-examination and not allow proof by extrinsic evidence?

IMPEACHMENT BY CONVICTION OF CRIME

The second primary method of impeachment covered by both common law and modern rules is by evidence of a conviction of crime. Washington Evidence Rule 609 is representative of the modern rule regarding this method of impeachment. The Washington rule states that for the purpose of attacking the credibility of a witness in a criminal or civil case, evidence that the witness has been convicted of a crime shall be admitted if elicited from the witness or established by public record during examination of the witness. The crime must be one that was punishable by death or imprisonment in excess of 1 year under the law under which the witness was convicted.[10] For most states, this would constitute a **felony** conviction.[11] This modern rule is a carryover from the common law skepticism of felons as competent witnesses. The rule allows the jury to decide how the prior conviction will affect the credibility of the witness.

Felony
A crime punishable by death or imprisonment in excess of 1 year.

Probative Value Must Outweigh Prejudicial Effect

In order for evidence of a conviction to be admitted, the court must also determine that the probative value of admitting this evidence outweighs the prejudice to the party against whom the evidence is offered. This refers to the key rule of evidence, Rule 403, which excludes even relevant evidence on grounds of prejudice, confusion, or waste of time.[12]

CRIMES INVOLVING DISHONESTY

If the witness has been convicted of a crime that involved dishonesty or false statement, the rules say that it *shall* be admitted *regardless of the punishment*.[13] There is no Rule 403 balancing requirement for admitting this type of evidence.

Time Limit

Although a few jurisdictions differ, most state rules and the Federal Rules have set a 10-year time limit for admitting any evidence of convictions.[14] This time limit runs from the date of the conviction or of the release of the witness from the confinement imposed for that conviction, whichever is the later date. If a conviction is over 10 years old, it will not be admitted unless the court determines, "in the interests of justice, that the probative value of the conviction supported by specific facts and circumstances substantially outweighs its prejudicial effect."[15]

However, evidence of a conviction more than 10 years old is not admissible unless the proponent gives to the adverse party sufficient advance written notice of intent to use such evidence to provide the adverse party with a fair opportunity to contest the use of such evidence (see Exhibit 9.7 and Exhibit 9.8).[16]

Other Limitations

There are generally three other limitations to the modern rules for admitting evidence of a conviction. First, evidence of a conviction is not admissible if the conviction has been the subject of a **pardon**, or other equivalent procedure based on a finding of either the innocence or rehabilitation of the person convicted.[17] Second, evidence of a **juvenile adjudication** is generally not admissible. In a criminal case, however, some courts may allow evidence of a juvenile adjudication of a witness other than the accused if conviction of the offense would be admissible to attack the credibility of an adult and the court is satisfied that admission in evidence is necessary for a fair determination of the issue of guilt or innocence.[18] Finally, the pendency of an appeal does not render evidence of a conviction inadmissible. Evidence of the pendency of an appeal is admissible.[19]

Pardon
Official forgiveness or exemption from the penalties or punishment of criminal conviction, usually given by governor or president.

Juvenile Adjudication
A final determination in a juvenile delinquency proceeding, similar to a verdict in an adult prosecution.

EVIDENTIARY CHECKLIST 9.2

Elements Needed to Impeach for Conviction of Crime

1. **Crimes Involving Dishonesty**
   - ☐ Did the crime involve dishonesty or false statement?

2. **All Other Crimes**
   - ☐ Was conviction for the crime punishable by death or imprisonment in excess of 1 year?
   - ☐ If so, does the probative value of admitting this evidence outweigh the prejudice to the party against whom the evidence is offered?

For Either of the Above
   - ☐ Has a period of more than 10 years elapsed since the date of the conviction or of the release of the witness from the confinement imposed for that conviction, whichever is the later date? If so, it may not be admitted unless its probative value substantially outweighs prejudicial effect.
   - ☐ Has the conviction been the subject of a pardon, annulment, or certificate of rehabilitation? If so, it cannot be admitted.
   - ☐ Was the conviction a juvenile adjudication? If so, it may not be admitted unless the offense would be admissible to attack the credibility of an adult and the court is satisfied that admission in evidence is necessary for a fair determination of the issue of guilt or innocence.

EXHIBIT 9.7   Modern Rule for Impeachment by Evidence of Conviction of Crime

Washington Rules of Evidence
Rule 609. Impeachment by Evidence of Conviction of Crime.

(a) General Rule. For the purpose of attacking the credibility of a witness in a criminal or civil case, evidence that the witness has been convicted of a crime shall be admitted if elicited from the witness or established by public record during examination of the witness but only if the crime (1) was punishable by death or imprisonment in excess of 1 year under the law under which the witness was convicted, and the court determines that the probative value of admitting this evidence outweighs the prejudice to the party against whom the evidence is offered, or (2) involved dishonesty or false statement, regardless of the punishment.

(b) Time Limit. Evidence of a conviction under this rule is not admissible if a period of more than 10 years has elapsed since the date of the conviction or of the release of the witness from the confinement imposed for that conviction, whichever is the later date, unless the court determines, in the interests of justice, that the probative value of the conviction supported by specific facts and circumstances substantially outweighs its prejudicial effect. However, evidence of a conviction more than 10 years old as calculated herein, is not admissible unless the proponent gives to the adverse party sufficient advance written notice of intent to use such evidence to provide the adverse party with a fair opportunity to contest the use of such evidence.

(Continued)

EXHIBIT 9.7   Modern Rule for Impeachment by Evidence of Conviction of Crime   *Continued*

(c) Effect of Pardon, Annulment, or Certificate of Rehabilitation. Evidence of a conviction is not admissible under this rule if (1) the conviction has been the subject of a pardon, annulment, certificate of rehabilitation, or other equivalent procedure based on a finding of the rehabilitation of the person convicted, and that person has not been convicted of a subsequent crime which was punishable by death or imprisonment in excess of 1 year, or (2) the conviction has been the subject of a pardon, annulment, or other equivalent procedure based on a finding of innocence.

(d) Juvenile Adjudications. Evidence of juvenile adjudications is generally not admissible under this rule. The court may, however, in a criminal case allow evidence of a finding of guilt in a juvenile offense proceeding of a witness other than the accused if conviction of the offense would be admissible to attack the credibility of an adult and the court is satisfied that admission in evidence is necessary for a fair determination of the issue of guilt or innocence.

(e) Pendency of Appeal. The pendency of an appeal therefrom does not render evidence of a conviction inadmissible. Evidence of the pendency of an appeal is admissible.

EXHIBIT 9.8   Other Rules for Impeachment by Evidence of Conviction of Crime

Maryland Rules
Rule 5-609. Impeachment by Evidence of Conviction of Crime.

(a) *Generally.*—For the purpose of attacking the credibility of a witness, evidence that the witness has been convicted of a crime shall be admitted if elicited from the witness or established by public record during examination of the witness, but only if (1) the crime was an infamous crime or other crime relevant to the witness's credibility and (2) the court determines that the probative value of admitting this evidence outweighs the danger of unfair prejudice to the witness or the objecting party.

New Jersey Rules of Evidence
Rule 609. Impeachment by Evidence of Conviction of Crime.

For the purpose of affecting the credibility of any witness, the witness's conviction of a crime shall be admitted unless excluded by the judge as remote or for other causes. Such conviction may be proved by examination, production of the record thereof, or by other competent evidence.

You Be the Judge 9.1

Defense seeks to impeach plaintiff's witness by offering evidence of two prior juvenile adjudications, one for disorderly conduct and the other for filing a false report: bomb scare.
Would you admit this? Why or why not?

LEGAL RESEARCH USING THE INTERNET SKILLS 9.3

Find your state evidence rules on the Internet and see if your state has a rule that allows evidence of juvenile adjudications to impeach.

Practice Tip 9.1

Witness Preparation Checklist

To help ensure a successful witness examination, develop your own set of witness preparation checklists, using some of the following tips:

Witness Impeachment

☐   *Does the witness have any interest or potential bias in regard to the case or outcome?*

☐   *Does the witness appear to be honest and trustworthy?*

☐   *Does the witness have any prior arrests or convictions, or anything that might result in impeachment?*

☐   *What is the reputation of the witness in the community for truthfulness?*

CRIMINAL DEFENDANT AS WITNESS

In a criminal trial, a defendant may appear as a witness in her own behalf, or that defendant may choose to exercise her constitutional right to remain silent, under the Fifth Amendment. If a defendant does voluntarily testify, then that defendant "waives" her privilege against self-incrimination and subjects herself to cross-examination and impeachment.

In the following Supreme Court case, the defendant, who was prosecuted for smuggling illegal drugs, took the stand and testified in her own defense, denying any knowledge of the drug smuggling. Because she knew that the government planned to admit evidence of the defendant's prior felony conviction to impeach her credibility, the defendant tried to lessen the impact of this before the trier of fact by admitting on direct examination to her prior conviction. She later challenges the admission of this prior conviction.

CASE

Ohler v. United States

United States Supreme Court.

529 U.S. 753 (2000).

Chief Justice Rehnquist delivered the opinion of the Court.

Petitioner, Maria Ohler, was arrested and charged with importation of marijuana and possession of marijuana with the intent to distribute. The District Court granted the Government's motion in limine seeking to admit evidence of her prior felony conviction as impeachment evidence under Federal Rule of Evidence 609(a)(1). Ohler testified at trial and admitted on direct examina-tion that she had been convicted of possession of methamphetamine in 1993. The jury convicted her of both counts, and the Court of Appeals for the Ninth Circuit affirmed. We agree with the Court of Appeals that Ohler may not challenge the in limine ruling of the District Court on appeal.

Maria Ohler drove a van from Mexico to California in July 1997. As she passed through the San Ysidro Port of Entry, a customs inspector noticed that someone had tampered with one of the van's interior panels. Inspectors searched the van and discovered approximately 81 pounds of marijuana. Ohler was arrested and charged with importation of marijuana and possession of marijuana with the intent to distribute. Before trial, the Government filed motions in limine seeking to admit Ohler's prior felony conviction as character evidence under Federal Rule of Evidence 404(b) and as impeachment evidence under Rule 609(a)(1). The District Court denied the motion to admit the conviction as character evidence, but reserved ruling on whether the conviction could be used for impeachment purposes. On the first day of trial, the District Court ruled that if Ohler testified, evidence of her prior conviction would be admissible under Rule 609(a)(1). She testified in her own defense, denying any knowledge of the marijuana. She also admitted on direct examination that she had been convicted of possession of methamphetamine in 1993. The jury found Ohler guilty of both counts, and she was sentenced to 30 months in prison and 3 years' supervised release.

On appeal, Ohler challenged the District Court's in limine ruling allowing the Government to use her prior conviction for impeachment purposes. The Court of Appeals for the Ninth Circuit affirmed, holding that Ohler waived her objection by introducing evidence of the conviction during her direct examination. . . . We affirm.

Generally, a party introducing evidence cannot complain on appeal that the evidence was erroneously admitted. Ohler argues . . . that if a defendant is forced to wait for evidence of the conviction to be introduced on cross-examination, the jury will believe that the defendant is less credible because she was trying to conceal the conviction. The Government disputes that the defendant is unduly disadvantaged by waiting for the prosecution to introduce the conviction on cross-examination. First, the Government argues that it is debatable whether jurors actually perceive a defendant to be more credible if she introduces a conviction herself. Second, even if jurors do consider the defendant more credible, the Government suggests that it is an unwarranted advantage because the jury does not realize that the defendant disclosed the conviction only after failing to persuade the court to exclude it.

Whatever the merits of these contentions, they tend to obscure the fact that both the Government and the defendant in a criminal trial must make choices as the trial progresses. For example, the defendant must decide whether or not to take the stand in her own behalf. If she has an innocent or mitigating explanation for

evidence that might otherwise incriminate, acquittal may be more likely if she takes the stand. Here, for example, petitioner testified that she had no knowledge of the marijuana discovered in the van, that the van had been taken to Mexico without her permission, and that she had gone there simply to retrieve the van. But once the defendant testifies, she is subject to cross-examination, including impeachment by prior convictions, and the decision to take the stand may prove damaging instead of helpful. A defendant has a further choice to make if she decides to testify, notwithstanding a prior conviction. The defendant must choose whether to introduce the conviction on direct examination and remove the sting or to take her chances with the prosecutor's possible elicitation of the conviction on cross-examination.

The Government, too, in a case such as this, must make a choice. If the defendant testifies, it must choose whether or not to impeach her by use of her prior conviction. Here the trial judge had indicated he would allow its use, but the Government still had to consider whether its use might be deemed reversible error on appeal. This choice is often based on the Government's appraisal of the apparent effect of the defendant's testimony. If she has offered a plausible, innocent explanation of the evidence against her, it will be inclined to use the prior conviction; if not, it may decide not to risk possible reversal on appeal from its use.

Due to the structure of trial, the Government has one inherent advantage in these competing trial strategies. Cross-examination comes after direct examination, and therefore the Government need not make its choice until the defendant has elected whether or not to take the stand in her own behalf and after the Government has heard the defendant testify.

Petitioner's submission would deny to the Government its usual right to decide, after she testifies, whether or not to use her prior conviction against her. She seeks to short-circuit that decisional process by offering the conviction herself (and thereby removing the sting) and still preserve its admission as a claim of error on appeal.

. . . .

Finally, Ohler argues that applying this rule to her situation unconstitutionally burdens her right to testify. She relies on *Rock v. Arkansas*, 483 U.S. 44 (1987), where we held that a prohibition of hypnotically refreshed testimony interfered with the defendant's right to testify. But here the rule in question does not prevent Ohler from taking the stand and presenting any admissible testimony which she chooses. She is of course subject to cross-examination and subject to impeachment by the use of a prior conviction. In a sense, the use of these tactics by the Government may deter a defendant from taking the stand. But, as we said in *McGautha v. California*, 402 U.S. 183 (1971):

It has long been held that a defendant who takes the stand in his own behalf cannot then claim the privilege against cross-examination on matters reasonably related to the subject matter of his direct examination. . . . It is also generally recognized that a defendant who takes the stand in his own behalf may be impeached by proof of prior convictions or the like. . . . Again, it is not thought inconsistent with the enlightened administration of criminal justice to require the defendant to weigh such pros and cons in deciding whether to testify.

For these reasons, we conclude that a defendant who preemptively introduces evidence of a prior conviction on direct examination may not on appeal claim that the admission of such evidence was error.

The judgment of the Court of Appeals for the Ninth Circuit is therefore affirmed.

LEGAL ANALYSIS AND WRITING 9.3

The following questions are based on the *How to Brief a Legal Case* format shown in the Appendix. Use this format to answer the following questions:

1. Summarize the facts in the previous case.
2. What is the legal issue?
3. How did the appellate court decide?
4. Why did the court decide this way?
5. Do you agree with the court's reasoning? Explain why or why not.

LEGAL RESEARCH USING THE INTERNET SKILLS 9.4

Find and read this Supreme Court case online! Check out one of the legal research web sites below and use their "Search" feature to find this case. In the "Search" field, enter the case name or citation.

1. FindLaw U.S. Supreme Court Decisions (http://www.findlaw.com/casecode/supreme.html)
2. U.S. Supreme Court (http://www.supremecourtus.gov/)
3. Supreme Court Collection of Cornell Law School (http://supct.law.cornell.edu/supct/)

CRITICAL THINKING QUESTIONS 9.4

1. Why do we allow evidence of a felony conviction or crime involving dishonesty to impeach a witness's credibility?
2. Wouldn't a criminal conviction tend to prejudice a jury against any witness?

(Continued)

> ### CRITICAL THINKING QUESTIONS 9.4   *Continued*
>
> 3. How do the rules governing impeachment influence the gathering of evidence or preparing of witnesses?
> 4. If you were preparing evidence for trial, what factors would you need to consider in order to comply with these rules?
> 5. If your opponent was planning to call a witness who had a juvenile adjudication or conviction over 10 years old, what steps would you take to help your legal team attack the credibility of the evidence?

Does Impeachment Extend to Allowing Evidence Not Otherwise Admissible?

The following landmark Supreme Court case shows the prosecution attempt to introduce a statement—which had been made by the defendant and deemed inadmissible as prosecution evidence—to impeach the defendant's credibility after the defendant testifies in his own defense.

CASE

Harris v. New York
401 U.S. 222 (1971).

Chief Justice Burger delivered the opinion of the Court.

We granted the writ in this case to consider petitioner's claim that a statement made by him to police under circumstances rendering it inadmissible to establish the prosecution's case in chief under *Miranda v. Arizona* may not be used to impeach his credibility. The State of New York charged petitioner in a two-count indictment with twice selling heroin to an undercover police officer . . . . Petitioner took the stand in his own defense. He admitted knowing the undercover police officer but denied a sale on January 4, 1966. He admitted making a sale of contents of a glassine bag to the officer on January 6 but claimed it was baking powder and part of a scheme to defraud the purchaser. On cross-examination petitioner was asked seriatim whether he had made specified statements to the police immediately following his arrest on January 7—statements that partially contradicted petitioner's direct testimony at trial. In response to the cross-examination, petitioner testified that he could not remember virtually any of the questions or answers recited by the prosecutor. At the request of petitioner's counsel the written statement from which the prosecutor had read questions and answers in his impeaching process was placed in the record for possible use on appeal; the statement was not shown to the jury. The trial judge instructed the jury that the statements attributed to petitioner by the prosecution could be considered only in passing on petitioner's credibility and not as evidence of guilt. In closing summations both counsel argued the substance of the impeaching statements. The jury then found petitioner guilty on the second count of the indictment.

At trial the prosecution made no effort in its case in chief to use the statements allegedly made by petitioner, conceding that they were inadmissible under *Miranda v. Arizona*, 384 U.S. 436 (1966). The transcript of the interrogation used in the impeachment, but not given to the jury, shows that no warning of a right to appointed counsel was given before questions were put to petitioner when he was taken into custody. Petitioner makes no claim that the statements made to the police were coerced or involuntary.

. . . *Miranda* barred the prosecution from making its case with statements of an accused made while in custody prior to having or effectively waiving counsel. It does not follow from *Miranda* that evidence inadmissible against an accused in the prosecution's case in chief is barred for all purposes, provided of course that the trustworthiness of the evidence satisfies legal standards.

... Petitioner's testimony in his own behalf concerning the events of January 7 contrasted sharply with what he told the police shortly after his arrest. The impeachment process here undoubtedly provided valuable aid to the jury in assessing petitioner's credibility, and the benefits of this process should not be lost, in our view, because of the speculative possibility that impermissible police conduct will be encouraged thereby. Assuming that the exclusionary rule has a deterrent effect on proscribed police conduct, sufficient deterrence flows when the evidence in question is made unavailable to the prosecution in its case in chief.

Every criminal defendant is privileged to testify in his own defense, or to refuse to do so. But that privilege cannot be construed to include the right to commit perjury. Having voluntarily taken the stand, petitioner was under an obligation to speak truthfully and accurately, and the prosecution here did no more than utilize the traditional truth-testing devices of the adversary process. Had inconsistent statements been made by the accused to some third person, it could hardly be contended that the conflict could not be laid before the jury by way of cross-examination and impeachment. The shield provided by Miranda cannot be perverted into a license to use perjury by way of a defense, free from the risk of confrontation with prior inconsistent utterances. We hold, therefore, that petitioner's credibility was appropriately impeached by use of his earlier conflicting statements.

Affirmed.

LEGAL ANALYSIS AND WRITING 9.4

The following questions are based on the *How to Brief a Legal Case* format shown in the Appendix. Use this format to answer the following questions:

1. Summarize the facts in the previous case.

2. What is the legal issue?

3. What did the appellate court decide?

4. Why did the court decide this way?

5. Do you agree with the court's reasoning? Explain why or why not.

LEGAL RESEARCH USING THE INTERNET SKILLS 9.5

Find and read this Supreme Court case online! Check out one of the legal research web sites below and use their "Search" feature to find this case. In the "Search" field, enter the cite or case name.

1. FindLaw U.S. Supreme Court Decisions (http://www.findlaw.com/casecode/supreme.html)

2. U.S. Supreme Court (http://www.supremecourtus.gov/)

3. Supreme Court Collection of Cornell Law School (http://supct.law.cornell.edu/supct/)

NO COMMENT RULE

If a defendant in a criminal action chooses not to become a witness as an exercise of his constitutional right to remain silent, the prosecutor cannot subsequently comment on the failure of the defendant to take the stand in his own behalf.

But, what about the use of prearrest silence to impeach a defendant in a criminal action? The following Supreme Court case dealt with an individual who stabbed a man and did not contact authorities for 2 weeks. The prosecutor commented on this prearrest silence in closing remarks to the jury at the defendant's trial for murder.

CASE

Jenkins v. Anderson
447 U.S. 231 (1980).

Justice Powell delivered the opinion of the Court.

The question in this case is whether the use of pre-arrest silence to impeach a defendant's credibility violates . . . the Fifth . . . Amendment to the Constitution.

I

On August 13, 1974, the petitioner stabbed and killed Doyle Redding. The petitioner was not apprehended until he turned himself in to governmental authorities about 2 weeks later. At his state trial for first-degree murder, the petitioner contended that the killing was in self-defense. . . . During the cross-examination, the prosecutor questioned the petitioner about his actions after the stabbing:

Q: And I suppose you waited for the Police to tell them what happened?

A: No, I didn't.

Q: You didn't?

A: No.

Q: I see. And how long was it after this day that you were arrested, or that you were taken into custody?

(After some discussion of the date on which petitioner surrendered, the prosecutor continued:)

Q: When was the first time that you reported the things that you have told us in Court today to anybody?

A: Two days after it happened.

Q: And who did you report it to?

A: To my probation officer.

Q: Well, apart from him?

A: No one.

Q: Who?

A: No one but my—

Q: (Interposing) Did you ever go to a Police Officer or to anyone else?

A: No, I didn't.

Q: As a matter of fact, it was two weeks later, wasn't it?

A: Yes.

In closing argument to the jury, the prosecutor again referred to the petitioner's prearrest silence. The prosecutor noted that petitioner had "waited two weeks, according to the testimony—at least two weeks before he did anything about surrendering himself or reporting [the stabbing] to anybody.". . . The petitioner was convicted of manslaughter and sentenced to 10 to 15 years' imprisonment in state prison. The Michigan Court of Appeals affirmed the conviction, and the Michigan Supreme Court denied leave to appeal. The petitioner then sought a writ of habeas corpus from the Federal District Court for the Eastern District of Michigan, contending that his constitutional rights were violated when the prosecutor questioned him concerning prearrest silence. A Federal Magistrate concluded that the petition for habeas corpus relief should be denied. The District Court adopted the Magistrate's recommendation. The United States Court of Appeals for the Sixth Circuit affirmed. This Court granted a writ of certiorari. We now affirm.

II

At trial the prosecutor attempted to impeach the petitioner's credibility by suggesting that the petitioner would have spoken out if he had killed in self-defense. The petitioner contends that the prosecutor's actions violated the Fifth Amendment as applied to the States through the Fourteenth Amendment. The Fifth Amendment guarantees an accused the right to remain silent during his criminal trial, and prevents the prosecution from commenting on the silence of a defendant who asserts the right. In this case, of course, the petitioner did not remain silent throughout the criminal proceedings. Instead, he voluntarily took the witness stand in his own defense. This Court's decision in *Raffel v. United States*, 271 U.S. 494 (1926), recognized that the Fifth Amendment is not violated when a defendant who testifies in his own defense is impeached with his prior silence. The defendant in Raffel was tried twice. At the first trial, a Government agent testified that Raffel earlier had made an inculpatory statement. The defendant did not testify. After the first trial ended in deadlock the agent repeated his testimony at the second trial, and Raffel took the stand to deny making such a statement. Cross-examination revealed that Raffel had not testified at the first trial. The Court held that inquiry into prior silence was proper because "[t]he immunity from giving testimony is one which the defendant may waive by offering himself as a witness. . . . When he takes the stand in his own behalf, he does so as any other witness, and within the limits of the appropriate rules he may be cross-examined. . . ." Thus, the Raffel Court concluded that the defendant was "subject to cross-examination impeaching his credibility just like any other witness."

. . . Attempted impeachment on cross-examination of a defendant, the practice at issue here, may enhance the reliability of the criminal process. Use of such impeachment on cross-examination allows prosecutors to test the credibility of witnesses by asking them to explain prior inconsistent statements and acts. A defendant may decide not to take the witness stand because of the risk of cross-examination. But this is a choice of litigation tactics. Once a defendant decides to testify, "[t]he interests of the other party and regard for the function of courts of justice to ascertain the truth become relevant, and prevail in the balance of considerations determining the scope and limits of the privilege against self-incrimination." *Brown v. United States*, 356 U.S. 148, 156 (1958). Thus, impeachment follows the defendant's own decision to cast aside his cloak of silence and advances the truth-finding function of the criminal trial. We conclude that the Fifth Amendment is not violated by the use of prearrest silence to impeach a criminal defendant's credibility. . . .

IV

Our decision today does not force any state court to allow impeachment through the use of prearrest silence. Each jurisdiction remains free to formulate evidentiary rules defining the situations in which silence is viewed as more probative than prejudicial. We merely conclude that the use of prearrest silence to impeach a defendant's credibility does not violate the Constitution. The judgment of the Court of Appeals is Affirmed.

LEGAL ANALYSIS AND WRITING 9.5

The following questions are based on the *How to Brief a Legal Case* format shown in the Appendix. Use this format to answer the following questions:

1. Summarize the facts in the previous case.
2. What is the legal issue?
3. What did the appellate court decide?
4. Why did the court decide this way?
5. Do you agree with the court's reasoning? Explain why or why not.

LEGAL RESEARCH USING THE INTERNET SKILLS 9.6

Find and read this Supreme Court case online! Check out one of the legal research web sites below and use their "Search" feature to find this case. In the "Search" field, enter the cite or case name.

1. FindLaw U.S. Supreme Court Decisions (http://www.findlaw.com/casecode/supreme.html)
2. U.S. Supreme Court (http://www.supremecourtus.gov/)
3. Supreme Court Collection of Cornell Law School (http://supct.law.cornell.edu/supct/)

SUMMARY

Impeachment is a form of attacking the credibility of a witness in order to convince the jury that the testimony given is not truthful or that the witness is unreliable. Any party may attack the credibility of a witness, including the party calling the witness. Credibility may generally be impeached in one of three ways: bias, character, or conviction of a crime. Impeachment by bias or an interest in the outcome of the case is especially relevant to show that it might have influenced the testimony of the witness. Impeachment by attacking the untruthful character of the witness or bad reputation is allowed, but only after the character of the witness for truthfulness has first been attacked. Specific instances of conduct may be used to impeach a witness, but may not be proved by extrinsic evidence. Impeachment by evidence of a conviction of crime is generally allowed for crimes that were punishable by death or imprisonment in excess of 1 year. In most states, for evidence of a conviction to be admitted, the court must also determine that the probative value of admitting this evidence outweighs the prejudice to the party against whom the evidence is offered. Although a few jurisdictions differ, most state rules and the Federal Rules have set a 10-year time limit for admitting any evidence of convictions.

In a criminal trial, a defendant may appear as a witness in his own behalf or that defendant may choose to exercise his constitutional right to remain silent, under the Fifth Amendment. If a defendant does voluntarily testify, then that defendant "waives" his privilege against self-incrimination and subjects himself to cross-examination and impeachment.

KEY TERMS

Bolstering Evidence	Juvenile Adjudication	Voucher Rule
Evidence of Character	Opinion and Reputation	Witness Bias
Felony	Evidence	
Impeachment	Pardon	

LEARNING OUTCOMES AND PRACTICE SKILLS CHECKLIST

☐ Learning Outcomes

After completing your reading, questions, and exercises, you should be able to demonstrate a better understanding of the learning concepts by answering the following questions:

1. Define impeachment.
2. Distinguish between the common law and modern rule for who may impeach.
3. Describe when a party would want to impeach the party's own witness.
4. Identify the different methods of impeachment.
5. Discuss impeachment by bias, including what it is, and when and why it is used.
6. Explain the different types of impeachment by evidence of character.
7. Discuss when attacking the untruthful character of the witness or bad reputation is allowed.
8. Compare and contrast how impeachment by evidence of character and specific instances of conduct are proven.
9. Explain what impeachment by evidence of a conviction of crime is.
10. Identify the limiting factors for allowing evidence of a conviction of crime.
11. Explain the significance of a defendant in a criminal trial being a witness in his own behalf and what effect this has in any attempt to impeach his testimony.

☐ Practice Skills

In addition to understanding the learning concepts, practice what you have learned through applications using critical thinking, legal analysis and writing, legal research, and advocacy skills, including:

Critical Thinking

1. What are the strengths and weaknesses of allowing impeachment?
2. How can we ensure adequate safeguards for this process?
3. Do you believe that the current rules provide these safeguards? Why or why not?
4. What public policy issues or considerations do you think might be behind these rules?
5. If it were up to you, would you keep the rules governing impeachment of witnesses as they are, delete them, narrow them, or expand them? Explain your reasoning.
6. How do the impeachment rules influence the gathering of evidence or preparing of witnesses?

Legal Analysis and Writing

Analyze the following rules and cases by summarizing their holdings, explaining their significance, and assessing any issue that might arise in their application.

1. Rule 607.
2. Rule 608.
3. Rule 609.
4. *Burgin v. State.*
5. *United States v. Abel.*
6. *Ohler v. United States.*
7. *Harris v. New York.*
8. *Jenkins v. Anderson.*

Legal Research Using the Internet

1. Find the annotated Federal Rules of Evidence on the Internet and assess the comments made in the proposing of the rules covered in this chapter.
2. Find your state's rules of evidence regarding relevance exceptions and concepts covered in this chapter. Compare and contrast with the federal and/or modern rules, and some of the state rules listed in this chapter.
3. Find out if your state appellate court posts their case decisions on the Internet. If so, find a case that illustrates an issue or rule discussed in this chapter. If your state decisions are not on the Internet, go instead to the web site for the U.S. Circuit Court of Appeals in your circuit, or search the U.S. Supreme Court decisions.

PRACTICE APPLICATION 9.1

After defendant testifies in a civil breach of contract case:

1. Defense wants to call a witness to testify that defendant has an impeccable reputation for truthfulness.
2. Plaintiff wants to call a witness to testify that defendant has a reputation for untruthfulness.

3. Plaintiff wants to introduce evidence in the form of previous employment applications of defendant to show that defendant lied on these applications.
4. Plaintiff wants to introduce evidence that defendant had been convicted of robbery 15 years ago, and had been released from prison 10 years ago.
5. Plaintiff wants to introduce evidence that defendant had juvenile adjudications for fraud.

Use the format shown in the Appendix for the *IRAC Method of Legal Analysis* and the evidentiary rules discussed in this chapter to analyze the above case problems and determine whether the evidence in each example can be admitted. Using the IRAC method, write a memo to your legal team giving your analysis and conclusions.

ADVOCACY AND COMMUNICATION SKILLS 9.1

Facts:

In a criminal prosecution for involuntary manslaughter, defendant, who is claiming self-defense, takes the stand to testify. Plaintiff wants to introduce the following evidence to impeach defendant:

1. Defendant was arrested, but not convicted for assault 2 years ago.
2. Defendant was civilly audited and charged with penalties for filing a false income tax return 3 years ago.
3. Defendant had a conviction for child molestation 5 years ago.
4. Defendant had a conviction for felonious assault 12 years ago.

Directions:

Form plaintiff and defense teams from small groups of no more than 3–4 each. Prepare a set of questions to ask the above witness and conduct a direct, cross, redirect, or recross-examination of the witness. During each line of questioning, the opposing team should be prepared to object, if needed, using objections from earlier readings. Use a different team member for each examination.

1. Plaintiff team will conduct a direct exam of no more than 5 minutes.
2. Defense team will conduct a cross-exam of no more than 5 minutes.
3. Plaintiff team will have 3 minutes to redirect.
4. Defense team will have 3 minutes to recross.

WEB SITES

Alabama Judicial System On-Line
http://www.judicial.state.al.us/

FindLaw
http://guide.lp.findlaw.com/casecode/

FindLaw U.S. Supreme Court Decisions
http://www.findlaw.com/casecode/supreme.html

Guide to State Rules of Evidence
http://expertpages.com/state_rules_of_evidence.htm

National Center for State Courts—State and Federal Court Web Sites
http://www.ncsconline.org/D_kis/info_court_web_sites.html#federal

Supreme Court Collection of Cornell Law School
http://supct.law.cornell.edu/supct/

U.S. Courts Site with Links to All Circuit Courts of Appeal
http://www.uscourts.gov/links.html

U.S. Supreme Court
http://www.supremecourtus.gov/

ENDNOTES

1. Ga. Code, Sections 24-9-82, 24-9-83, and 24-9-84.
2. Fla Evid. Code, Sec. 90.608 Who may impeach.
3. Fed. R. Evid. 607.
4. Fla Evid. Code, Sec. 90.608.
5. Ohio Evid. R. 616. Bias of Witness.
6. Fed. R. Evid. 404(a) Character Evidence Not Admissible to Prove Conduct.
7. Texas Rules of Evidence, Rule 608. Evidence of Character and Conduct of Witness.
8. North Carolina Rules of Evidence, Rule 608. Evidence of character and conduct of witness.
9. *Michelson v. United States*, 335 U.S. 469 (1948).
10. Washington ER 609(a)(1). Impeachment by Evidence of Conviction of Crime.
11. In a few states, like Vermont, a felony is a crime punishable by incarceration of more than two years. In these states, the rule would say "by a felony conviction . . .".
12. See, for example, Colorado Rules of Evidence, Rule 403. Exclusion of Relevant Evidence on Grounds of Prejudice, Confusion, or Waste of Time.
13. See, for example, Mississippi Rule 609(a)(2).
14. However, see states like Massachusetts with a 5 year limit, and Maryland with a 15 year limit, others with no limit.
15. Idaho Rules of Evidence, Rule 609(b). Time Limit.
16. Ohio Evid. R. 609(b). Time Limit.
17. Kentucky Rules of Evidence, K.R.E. 609(c) Effect of pardon, annulment, or certificate of rehabilitation.
18. Mississippi Rules of Evidence, M.R.E. 609(d). Juvenile Adjudications.
19. See Fla. Evid. Code, Sec. 90-610(2) or Pennsylvania Rules of Evidence, Rule 609(e).

OPINIONS AND EXPERT TESTIMONY

"The line between opinion and fact is at best only one of degree."

—*Judge Learned Hand,*
Central R.R. v. Monahan (1926)

LEARNING OUTCOMES

In this chapter, you will learn about the following legal concepts:

- What Is Opinion Testimony?
- Why We Allow Opinion Testimony
- Opinion Testimony by Lay Witnesses
- When Opinion Testimony by Lay Witnesses Can Be Admitted
- What Lay Witnesses Can Testify To

- Opinion Testimony by Expert Witnesses
- When Opinion Testimony by Expert Witnesses Can Be Admitted
- Bases of Opinion Testimony by Experts
- Opinion on Ultimate Issue
- Court Appointed Experts

INTRODUCTION

We have examined the laws of evidence pertaining to the use of witnesses at trial. We have looked at some of the issues involved and identified the objections that might be raised. Several of these objections—"calls for a conclusion" or "assuming facts not in evidence"—may go to the qualifications of a witness to state an opinion. What is an opinion and when can a witness give his or her opinion? For example, if you were called to the witness stand, what could you give an opinion on? When would the court allow you to give an opinion? Could you give an opinion on the general state of your health or how you feel on a particular day? How about someone else's health? Could you list a set of physical symptoms that you might be experiencing in regard to your health? Given those symptoms, could you give an opinion as to what disease or condition might explain the symptoms? The answers to these questions will depend on whether you are a lay witness or an expert witness. In this chapter, you will examine the differences between a lay and expert witness, look at what opinion evidence is, and when it can be given.

WHAT IS OPINION TESTIMONY?

Opinion
Judgment or conclusion made based on impressions, perceptions, or (in the case of experts) special skills and knowledge.

An **opinion** is a judgment or conclusion we make based on our impressions, perceptions, or (in the case of experts) special skills and knowledge. **Opinion testimony** is when a witness offers this judgment or conclusion in the form of her view about what certain impressions or evidence means.

Opinion Testimony
When a witness offers judgment or conclusion in the form of her view about what certain evidence means.

WHY WE ALLOW OPINION TESTIMONY

As we learned earlier, the general rule is that a witness cannot testify to a matter unless that witness has personal knowledge of the matter. The reason for this rule is to help ensure the reliability of information presented to the trier of fact by requiring witnesses to testify only to what the witnesses actually saw or heard (as well as other senses). Opinions are used during trials, but they are monitored by the court to ensure that they do not usurp the jury's function of deciding the facts. Courts are mindful that a witness's opinion may supplant factual statements drawn from a witness's personal knowledge from which the jury could draw its own conclusions. However, opinion testimony can also be helpful to the factfinding process. Courts have long recognized the place of opinion testimony by both lay and expert witnesses to help juries better understand the evidence.

CRITICAL THINKING QUESTIONS 10.1

1. What is an opinion and why do we have evidentiary rules that govern their admissibility?
2. Are there any public policy interests or reasons for these rules?
3. Do we need these rules? Explain why or why not.
4. Where do we or should we draw the line between facts and opinion?

OPINION TESTIMONY BY LAY WITNESSES

Lay Witness
An ordinary (non-expert) witness with no special training or expertise in the matter testified about who is providing testimony from personal knowledge.

A **lay witness** is an ordinary witness who must testify from personal knowledge about a matter at issue. A lay witness is a non-expert with no special training or expertise in the matter testified about. At common law, the general rule was that lay witnesses were prohibited from giving opinions. A Nebraska court explained the reasoning behind this rule: "Opinion testimony in its broadest sense encroaches upon the province of the jury to determine for themselves the ultimate facts of the case."[1]

Courts, however, have long recognized that it is a fine line separating the stating of facts and the stating of an opinion. Often during testimony, it is difficult for a witness to express a series of factual observations without including opinion. For example, how do you testify to a person's age or demeanor without expressing an opinion?

In a 1926 court decision, Judge Learned Hand criticized the common law rule prohibiting opinions, saying that "the exclusion of opinion evidence has been carried beyond reason in this country, and . . . it would be a large advance if courts were to admit it with freedom. The line between opinion and fact is at best only one of degree. . . . It is a good rule . . . to reproduce the scene as it was, and so to correct the personal equations of the witnesses. But one must be careful not to miss the forest for the trees, as generally happens, unless much latitude is allowed."[2]

Over the years, courts relaxed their limits on opinion testimony by lay witnesses. Courts reasoned that opinions based on the perception of the witness were less complicated for the jury than opinions based on expert knowledge. If these lay opinions were helpful to understanding a fact in issue, the courts allowed them. As one court stated, "Unlike expert opinion, where the opinion is the product of applying special skill in some art, trade, or profession acquired apart from the case, lay opinion expresses a conclusion drawn from observations in circumstances where it is impractical, if possible at all, to recount the observed 'factual' components of the opinion. The common illustrations are an expression of a lay observer of a car's speed or a person's expression or emotional state. Because these opinions draw upon the facts in the case itself, they are more easily confronted than are expert opinion, whose source is often extraneous to the case at trial. As such, receipt of lay opinions is much less likely to be prejudicial, especially where its role is cumulative and is not essential to the sufficiency of the evidence. . . ."[3]

WHEN OPINION TESTIMONY BY LAY WITNESSES CAN BE ADMITTED

These changes in the common law were later carried out in statutes, both state and federal. Most courts today use Rule 701 of the Federal Rules of Evidence, or something similar, as a standard for admitting opinion testimony by a lay witness. This rule provides that lay witnesses may give testimony in the form of opinions when the opinion is "rationally based on the perception of the witness, helpful to a clear understanding of the witness's testimony or the determination of a fact in issue, and not based on scientific, technical, or other specialized knowledge."[4]

Test for Allowing Lay Opinion Testimony

Modern statutes generally allow the admission of lay opinions when two elements are met. The first element is the requirement of *firsthand knowledge*, where the opinion is based on personal knowledge or observation of the witness. The second element is that the opinion must be *helpful to the jury* in better understanding the issues (see Exhibit 10.1). This provides more latitude for a witness who would otherwise have difficulty expressing his perceptions in a factual sequence. Recognizing that there is often a thin line between fact and opinion, the rule was designed to allow non-experts to express opinions "that are in reality only a shorthand statement of fact."[5]

EVIDENTIARY CHECKLIST 10.1

When Opinion Testimony by Lay Witnesses Can Be Admitted

- ☐ When rationally based on the perception of the witness
- ☐ When helpful to a clear understanding of the witness's testimony or the determination of a fact in issue
- ☐ When not based on scientific, technical, or other specialized knowledge

---

WHAT LAY WITNESSES CAN TESTIFY TO

Lay witnesses are usually called to testify about statements of fact regarding what they have seen or heard, but they may also give opinions about common things which are based upon their perceptions (for example, that the defendant was upset, angry, or drunk; the value of their property; and so on). A Kentucky case, for example, allowed lay opinion about demeanor or conduct. A witness testified that the defendant had "just a kind of strange look in his eyes." Another witness was permitted to say the defendant gave him an "intense look."[6]

Lay witnesses may also qualify as "expert" witnesses on certain topics. Police officers routinely testify about accident scenes, but may also qualify as experts in regard to giving an opinion about the speed of vehicles or skid marks.

EXHIBIT 10.1   Comparison of Evidentiary Rules for Opinion Testimony by Lay Witnesses

Federal Rules of Evidence
Rule 701. Opinion Testimony by Lay Witnesses.
    If the witness is not testifying as an expert, the witness's testimony in the form of opinions or inferences is limited to those opinions or inferences which are (a) rationally based on the perception of the witness and (b) helpful to a clear understanding of the witness's testimony or the determination of a fact in issue, and (c) not based on scientific, technical, or other specialized knowledge within the scope of Rule 702.

California Evidence Code
Section 800. If a witness is not testifying as an expert, his testimony in the form of an opinion is limited to such an opinion as is permitted by law, including but not limited to an opinion that is:

(a) Rationally based on the perception of the witness; and

(b) Helpful to a clear understanding of his testimony.

Florida Evidence Code
Section 90.701. Opinion Testimony of Lay Witnesses. If a witness is not testifying as an expert, the witness's testimony about what he or she perceived may be in the form of inference and opinion when:

(Continued)

EXHIBIT 10.1   Comparison of Evidentiary Rules for Opinion Testimony by Lay Witnesses *Continued*

(1) The witness cannot readily, and with equal accuracy and adequacy, communicate what he or she has perceived to the trier of fact without testifying in terms of inferences or opinions and the witness's use of inferences or opinions will not mislead the trier of fact to the prejudice of the objecting party; and

(2) The opinions and inferences do not require a special knowledge, skill, experience, or training.

Georgia Code
Section 24-9-65. Where the question under examination, and to be decided by the jury, shall be one of opinion, any witness may swear to his opinion or belief, giving his reasons therefor. If the issue shall be as to the existence of a fact, the opinions of witnesses shall be generally inadmissible.

LEGAL ANALYSIS AND WRITING 10.1

In a lawsuit over an injury allegedly caused by defendant's drunk driving, plaintiff proffers a lay witness who will testify that she works with defendant and has seen the defendant come in to work on several occasions, in her opinion, "hung over."

The following questions are based on the format shown in the Appendix for the *IRAC Method of Legal Analysis*. Use this format, and Federal Rule 701 as your guide, to solve the above case problem:

1. What is the issue here?
2. What is the rule that covers this issue?
3. Apply the rule to the facts shown for this case and analyze in order to reach a conclusion.
4. State your conclusion.

LEGAL RESEARCH USING THE INTERNET SKILLS 10.1

Use one of the following web sites to find out whether your state rules of evidence pertaining to opinion testimony are patterned after the Federal Rules.

1. List of State Laws from Legal Information Institute of Cornell Law School (http://www.law.cornell.edu/states/listing.html)
2. FindLaw (http://www.findlaw.com)
3. Federal Rules of Evidence (http://www.law.cornell.edu/rules/fre/overview.html)

Can a Lay Witness Give an Opinion as to Age?

The following case illustrates the problem when witnesses were asked to describe why they thought a young woman was over 16 years of age, but the witnesses were not allowed to give an opinion as to how old they thought she was. How do you testify to "facts" that support a conclusion about a person's age?

The defendant in the case, Yazzie, was convicted of statutory rape, based on the following statute:

18 U.S.C. 2243. Sexual Abuse of a Minor or Ward.

(a) Of a Minor.—Whoever, in the special maritime and territorial jurisdiction of the United States or in a Federal prison, knowingly engages in a sexual act with another person who—
(1) has attained the age of 12 years but has not attained the age of 16 years; and
(2) is at least 4 years younger than the person so engaging; or attempts to do so, shall be fined under this title, imprisoned not more than 15 years, or both.
. . .
(c) Defenses.—(1) In a prosecution under subsection (a) of this section, it is a defense, which the defendant must establish by a preponderance of the evidence, that the defendant reasonably believed that the other person had attained the age of 16 years.
(d) State of Mind Proof Requirement.—In a prosecution under subsection (a) of this section, the Government need not prove that the defendant knew—
(1) the age of the other person engaging in the sexual act; or
(2) that the requisite age difference existed between the persons so engaging.

At the time of the alleged crime, the defendant was 20 years of age (one month from his 21st birthday), and the victim was 15 and a half years of age.

CASE

United States v. Yazzie

976 F.2d 1252 (9th Cir. 1992).

Reinhardt, Circuit Judge.

Johnny Yazzie, Jr., appeals his conviction for sexual abuse of a minor (statutory rape) . . . .

Yazzie's sole defense to the statutory rape charge was an affirmative defense permitted under 18 U.S.C. § 2243(c): that at the time of the incident, he reasonably believed that the minor, who was then fifteen-and-a-half years old, was at least sixteen. . . . To establish the reasonableness of his belief, he testified that at the time of the incident, the minor smoked cigarettes, drove a car, used makeup, and looked "mature" enough to be at least sixteen.

. . . To further establish the reasonableness of his belief, Yazzie called several witnesses who offered to testify that as of the date of the alleged sexual abuse, their observations caused them to believe the minor to be between sixteen and twenty years old. The district court excluded this testimony, ruling that defense witnesses were permitted to testify to their perceptions of the minor's physical appearance and behavior at the time of the incident but were barred from stating their opinion

that the minor was at least sixteen years of age. The reason for the ruling, the court explained, was that a witness's belief as to the minor's age was "subjective and has nothing to do with what [Yazzie] might have believed."

In accordance with the district court's ruling, Yazzie's witnesses did not testify as to their beliefs regarding the minor's age. Instead, three of Yazzie's witnesses confirmed his claim that the minor smoked cigarettes on the night in question; two testified that they had seen her drive a car before the alleged sexual abuse took place; and two testified that she wore makeup at the time of the incident. Further, three witnesses testified that the minor appeared sexually mature at the time of the alleged sexual abuse. One stated that the minor "was tall and . . . appeared to be a lady . . . a lady like she was full, how do you say, she was fully developed," and that "she was mainly filled out, she was very tall." Another testified that the minor's body shape made her look "like an older person." A third stated that the minor "was well into her womanhood, well developed . . . [and] had her curves and . . . was into her maturity." In addition, one witness testified that the minor drank beer on the night of the incident.

. . .

II.

Fed. R. Evid. 701 permits a lay witness to give opinion testimony as long as the opinion is "(a) rationally based on the perception of the witness and (b) helpful to a clear understanding of the witness's testimony or the determination of a fact in issue." Fed. R. Evid. 701. The admissibility of lay opinion testimony under Rule 701 is "committed to the sound discretion of the trial judge and his decision will be overturned only if it constitutes a 'clear abuse of discretion.'" *United States v. Burnette,* 698 F.2d 1038 (9th Cir. 1983). We understand Rule 701 to mean that opinions of non-experts may be admitted where the facts could not otherwise be adequately presented or described to the jury in such a way as to enable the jury to form an opinion or reach an intelligent conclusion. If it is impossible or difficult to reproduce the data observed by the witnesses, or the facts are difficult of explanation, or complex, or are of a combination of circumstances and appearances which cannot be adequately described and presented with the force and clearness as they appeared to the witness, the witness may state his impressions and opinions based upon what he observed. It is a means of conveying to the jury what the witness has seen or heard.

Here, the opinion testimony not only meets the requirements of sub-part (a) of Rule 701, but of both the alternative sub-parts of (b). The testimony helps in the understanding of the witnesses' descriptive testimony and in determining a critical fact at issue—whether it was reasonable for Yazzie to believe that the minor was sixteen or older.

In the case before us, the jurors could not themselves assess how old the minor looked at the time of the incident: by the time of the trial, the minor was almost seventeen years old, and her appearance was undoubtedly substantially different than it had been on the night in question, a year and a half earlier. Thus, the jurors were wholly dependent on the testimony of witnesses. Yet the witnesses were permitted to testify only to the minor's describable features and behavior. Their testimony was no substitute for a clear and unequivocal statement of their opinions. It did not tell the jury that these witnesses believed the minor to be at least sixteen years old at the time of the incident.

Our finding that the trial judge erred in not admitting the opinions of Yazzie's witnesses as to the minor's age is supported by all of the considerations that underlie Rule 701's authorization of the use of lay opinion testimony. First, it is difficult to distinguish a fifteen-and-a-half-year-old from a sixteen-year-old, and it is still more difficult to put into words why one believes that a person is one age and not the other. There is a certain intangible element involved in one's conclusions on such a question. We form an opinion of a person's age from "a combination of circumstances and appearances which cannot be adequately described and presented with the force and clearness as they appear" to us. Mannerisms and facial features are notoriously difficult to describe accurately, and one's reasons for concluding that a person is a particular age are both too complex and too indefinable to set out fully.

In addition, a witness may not know, let alone be able to report precisely, what factors induced his or her conclusion. In such a case, the fact that the witness reached the conclusion is the important part of the testimony, not the largely undeterminable or inexplicable reasons that prompted the conclusion. Furthermore, age is a matter on which everyone has an opinion. Knowingly or unknowingly, we all form conclusions about people's ages every day. It is therefore particularly appropriate for a lay witness to express an opinion on the subject.

Here, the witnesses' opinions were especially appropriate for another reason. The issue was whether the defendant held an opinion and if so whether that opinion was reasonable. It is relevant that others having a similar opportunity to observe the minor formed an opinion as to her age that was similar to the opinion the defendant claimed to have formed. Their testimony goes both to Yazzie's credibility and to the reasonableness of his belief. The district court's decision deprived the jury of the most direct evidence available as to the age that the minor reasonably appeared to be on the night of the incident. Thus, the judge's ruling constituted a clear abuse of discretion.

. . . While it is true that each side may find persons willing to offer opinions helpful to it, the jury is perfectly capable of weighing the veracity and bias of the witnesses. Here, the jury was deprived of that opportunity. It was compelled to resolve the crucial issue in the case before it on the basis of far less direct evidence than could have been provided. Because the evidence supporting the statutory rape charge was inconclusive and the excluded testimony was of considerable importance, we cannot say that a rational jury more probably than not would have convicted the defendant had the testimony not been excluded. We therefore conclude that the error was not harmless and that Yazzie's conviction must be Reversed.

◆

What the Yazzie Case Illustrates

This case illustrates how witnesses' opinions can be helpful to a jury, especially where the "facts" to which the witness would otherwise have to testify are difficult to articulate. The Yazzie Court found that an opinion by a lay witness can be an effective means of "conveying to the jury what the witness has seen or heard." By limiting this opinion testimony, the trial court "deprived the jury of the most direct evidence available as to the age that the minor reasonably appeared to be on the night of the incident" and "constituted a clear abuse of discretion."

LEGAL ANALYSIS AND WRITING 10.2

The following questions are based on the *How to Brief a Legal Case* format shown in the Appendix. Use this format to answer the following questions:

1. Summarize the facts in the previous case.
2. What is the legal issue?
3. What did the appellate court decide?
4. Why did the court decide this way?
5. Do you agree with the court's reasoning? Explain why or why not.

LEGAL RESEARCH USING THE INTERNET SKILLS 10.2

Try to find and read the Yazzie case online! Check out one of the legal research web sites below and use their "Search" feature to find this case. In the "Search" field, enter the cite or case name.

1. U.S. Courts Site with Links to All Circuit Courts of Appeal (http://www.uscourts.gov/links.html)
2. National Center for State Courts—State and Federal Court Web Sites (http://www.ncsconline.org/D_kis/info_court_web_sites.html#federal)
3. FindLaw (http://guide.lp.findlaw.com/casecode/)

CRITICAL THINKING QUESTIONS 10.2

1. Can we really testify to a set of facts based on personal knowledge without giving an opinion?
2. Select a classmate who has sat next to you during this course (or a neighbor, or friend). What can you describe about that person—his or her age, mannerisms, interests, job, goals, clothing worn, family life? Are your descriptions based on personal, firsthand knowledge (i.e., what you saw or heard) or based on opinion?
3. In what types of cases in various areas of law would the opinion of a lay witness be important? Be specific in naming the type of case, area of law, and why the opinion might be important. (For example, in a negligence case under tort law, an opinion as to whether the defendant appeared intoxicated shortly before an auto accident.)
4. When would allowing a lay witness to give an opinion intrude upon the "province of the jury?"

YOU BE THE JUDGE 10.1

Plaintiff asks lay witness to give her opinion, based on what she saw and heard, as to the mental condition of defendant on a particular day. Defendant objects, saying this calls for a medical opinion which is beyond the knowledge of a lay witness.

1. Do you believe this opinion should be admitted? Why or why not? Explain your reasons.

Practice Tip 10.1

To help determine that a potential lay witness will be able to give an opinion, use the following checklist:

- [ ] *Is the opinion based on the personal knowledge or observation of the witness?*
- [ ] *Will the opinion be helpful to the jury in better understanding the issues?*
- [ ] *Is the opinion based on scientific, technical, or other specialized knowledge? (If so, the witness may need to be qualified as an expert.)*

OPINION TESTIMONY BY EXPERT WITNESSES

An **expert witness** is one who is qualified beyond the lay witness by special knowledge, skills, experience, training, and/or education. An expert witness can testify to and give opinions on matters which are outside of the knowledge of the average person, and that require special experience or knowledge of witnesses skilled in that particular science, art, or trade. These opinions can be based on firsthand observation, like a psychiatrist who examined one of the parties, or it can be based on a hypothetical question put to the expert, based on her training and expertise (see Exhibit 10.2). A lay witness may qualify as an "expert" witness on certain topics. For example, a police officer may qualify as an expert when testifying about an accident scene or gang behavior.

Expert Witness
A witness qualified by specialized skills or knowledge whose testimony or opinion can assist the trier of fact to better understand evidence in issue.

EXHIBIT 10.2   Actual Testimony by Expert Witness

Attorney:	Doctor, how many autopsies have you performed on dead people?
Expert Witness:	All of my autopsies have been on dead people.

WHEN OPINION TESTIMONY BY EXPERT WITNESSES CAN BE ADMITTED

Most evidence codes reflect Wyoming Rule 702 in providing that when "scientific, technical, or other specialized knowledge will assist the trier of fact to understand the evidence or to determine a fact in issue, a witness qualified as an expert may testify thereto in the form of an opinion or otherwise, if the testimony is based upon sufficient facts or data, the testimony is the product of reliable principles and methods, and the witness has applied the principles and methods reliably to the facts of the case."[7] Expert testimony in the form of opinions are generally based on firsthand observation or some type of specialized or scientific testing by the witness, like a psychiatrist who examined the defendant, or a forensic scientist who analyzed an item of evidence (see Exhibit 10.3).

The Federal Rules were amended just prior to 2001 to follow the standard established in 1993 by *Daubert v. Merrell Dow Pharmaceuticals*.[8] The effects of this case will be discussed in the next chapter. The rule change, however, added a provision at the end of the above rule that expert testimony had to be based upon sufficient facts or data, the product of reliable principles and methods, and the expert witness had to apply the principles and methods reliably to the facts of the case.[9] These new additions to Federal Rule 702 have not yet been adopted by most of the states.

EVIDENTIARY CHECKLIST 10.2

When Opinion Testimony by Expert Witness Can Be Admitted

- ☐ When scientific, technical, or other specialized knowledge will assist the trier of fact to understand the evidence or to determine a fact in issue
- ☐ When a witness is qualified as an expert by knowledge, skill, experience, training, or education

And, under the Federal Rules, if:

- ☐ Testimony is based upon sufficient facts or data
- ☐ Testimony is the product of reliable principles and methods
- ☐ Expert witness has applied the principles and methods reliably to the facts of the case

---

EXHIBIT 10.3   Comparison of Evidentiary Rules for Opinion Testimony by Expert Witnesses

Federal Rules of Evidence

Rule 702. Testimony by Experts.

If scientific, technical, or other specialized knowledge will assist the trier of fact to understand the evidence or to determine a fact in issue, a witness qualified as an expert by knowledge, skill, experience, training, or education, may testify thereto in the form of an opinion or otherwise, if (1) the testimony is based upon sufficient facts or data, (2) the testimony is the product of reliable principles and methods, and (3) the witness has applied the principles and methods reliably to the facts of the case.

Florida Evidence Code

Section 90.702. Testimony by Experts. If scientific, technical, or other specialized knowledge will assist the trier of fact in understanding the evidence or in determining a fact in issue, a witness qualified as an expert by knowledge, skill, experience, training, or education may testify about it in the form of an opinion; however, the opinion is admissible only if it can be applied to evidence at trial.

California Evidence Code

Section 801. If a witness is testifying as an expert, his testimony in the form of an opinion is limited to such an opinion as is:

(a) Related to a subject that is sufficiently beyond common experience that the opinion of an expert would assist the trier of fact; and

(Continued)

EXHIBIT 10.3   Comparison of Evidentiary Rules for Opinion Testimony by Expert Witnesses
Continued

(b) Based on matter (including his special knowledge, skill, experience, training, and education) perceived by or personally known to the witness or made known to him at or before the hearing, whether or not admissible, that is of a type that reasonably may be relied upon by an expert in forming an opinion upon the subject to which his testimony relates, unless an expert is precluded by law from using such matter as a basis for his opinion.

Ohio Rules of Evidence
Rule 702. Testimony by Experts.
A witness may testify as an expert if all of the following apply:

(A) The witness' testimony either relates to matters beyond the knowledge or experience possessed by lay persons or dispels a misconception common among lay persons;

(B) The witness is qualified as an expert by specialized knowledge, skill, experience, training, or education regarding the subject matter of the testimony;

(C) The witness' testimony is based on reliable scientific, technical, or other specialized information. To the extent that the testimony reports the result of a procedure, test, or experiment, the testimony is reliable only if all of the following apply:

(1) The theory upon which the procedure, test, or experiment is based is objectively verifiable or is validly derived from widely accepted knowledge, facts, or principles;

(2) The design of the procedure, test, or experiment reliably implements the theory;

(3) The particular procedure, test, or experiment was conducted in a way that will yield an accurate result.

Practice Tip 10.2

To help determine whether a potential witness will meet the standards imposed by **Daubert v. Merrell Dow Pharmaceuticals**, use the following checklist:

☐　Does your witness qualify as an expert by knowledge, skill, experience, training, or education?

☐　Will his or her testimony be based upon sufficient facts or data to be able to assist the trier of fact to understand the evidence or to determine a fact in issue?

☐　Will his or her testimony be the product of reliable principles and methods?

☐　Has your witness applied these principles and methods reliably to the facts of this case?

BASES OF OPINION TESTIMONY BY EXPERTS

At common law, experts were limited in their opinions to information obtained from firsthand observations, examination, and testing. Today, the "otherwise" mentioned in the modern rules might include an answer based on a hypothetical question put to the expert witness based on information obtained by the expert outside of the courtroom, or based on the expert's specialized training or knowledge (see Exhibit 10.4). For example, at common law, a psychiatrist had to testify based on her own examination or observation. Modernly, this expert could testify based on information that is not admissible at trial (interviews with other people, for example) or reliance on acceptable theories.

Another rule goes further in allowing that the facts or data that the expert bases an opinion upon may be known to the expert either at or before the trial. It also provides that these facts or data do not have to be admitted into evidence at trial if "of a type reasonably relied upon by experts in the particular field" which would form opinions or inferences about the subject at issue.[10]

EXHIBIT 10.4   Example of Rule for Bases of Opinion Testimony by Experts

Texas Rules of Evidence
Rule 703. The facts or data in the particular case upon which an expert bases an opinion or inference may be those perceived by, reviewed by, or made known to the expert at or before the hearing. If of a type reasonably relied upon by experts in the particular field in forming opinions or inferences upon the subject, the facts or data need not be admissible in evidence.

Federal Rules of Evidence
Rule 703. The facts or data in the particular case upon which an expert bases an opinion or inference may be those perceived by or made known to the expert at or before the hearing. If of a type reasonably relied upon by experts in the particular field in forming opinions or inferences upon the subject, the facts or data need not be admissible in evidence in order for the opinion or inference to be admitted. Facts or data that are otherwise inadmissible shall not be disclosed to the jury by the proponent of the opinion or inference unless the court determines that their probative value in assisting the jury to evaluate the expert's opinion substantially outweighs their prejudicial effect.

Expert Witnesses and the Patty Hearst Trial

When the Symbionese Liberation Army kidnapped publishing magnate William Randolph Hearst's granddaughter, Patty Hearst, it created a national manhunt for the victim and terrorists. When it was later discovered that Patty had participated in a bank robbery as an accomplice to the other terrorists, it shocked the nation. At her trial, Ms. Hearst alleged that she had been brainwashed by the terrorists and was the victim of duress in being forced to participate in the robbery. To bolster this defense, her attorneys offered expert witnesses who would testify to the defendant's mental state at the time of the crime. The prosecution objected, arguing that this testimony would go to the ultimate issue of intent, which was irrelevant to the charge and not admissible under federal law.

CASE

United States v. Hearst
412 F. Supp. 889 (N.D. Cal. 1976).
Memorandum and Order Denying Plaintiff's Motions to Bar Defendants Proffered Psychiatric Testimony and Motion to Strike Expert Testimony.

Carter, Chief Judge.

The Government has filed extensive points and authorities in support of its motion to bar the introduction of testimony by expert witnesses on the defendant's mental state at the time of the bank robbery for which she is now on trial. While the Court has no quarrel with the basic tenet of the decisions cited, it does not find them applicable to the case at hand.

In large part, the Government's argument is that since in this Circuit the crime of bank robbery, as defined in the applicable federal statute, 18 U.S.C. § 2113(a), has been held not to require proof of a specific, but only a general, intent . . . expert testimony offered to show that the defendant acted with a reduced mental capacity is irrelevant to any triable issue and therefore inadmissible. Without disputing the soundness of the premise on which this argument rests, the Court will simply point out that in this case the expert testimony is not being offered to prove diminished capacity sufficient to negate specific intent.

As the Court understands the purpose of psychiatric expert testimony offered here by the defense, it is to explain the effects kidnapping, prolonged incarceration, and psychological and physical abuse may have had on the defendant's mental state at the time of the robbery, insofar as such mental state is relevant to the asserted defense of coercion or duress. The jury, of course, are free to accept or reject the defendant's own account of her experiences with her captors. If they choose, however, to believe her testimony, then they may be served by the testimony of the experts called by both sides in determining whether or not the defendant was coerced into committing the offenses charged in the indictment.

It is a settled principle of law that "[t]he trial judge has broad discretion in the matter of the admission or exclusion of expert evidence, and his action is to be sustained unless manifestly erroneous." *Salem v. United States Lines Co.*, 370 U.S. 31 (1962). The standard to be applied in the exercise of this discretion is clearly stated in *United States v. Brown*, 501 F.2d 146 (9th Cir. 1974):

> If the Court in its discretion, which may not be disturbed absent clear abuse, is convinced that the expert may materially assist the jury beyond their common experience as amplified by argument of counsel, the expert should be allowed to testify.

Moreover, the federal courts have announced in numerous decisions that even where an expert's opinion touches the ultimate issue which the jury must decide, "it is admissible so long as it relates to matters within the witness's special competence and skill and not to matters of common knowledge and observation." *Riley v. United States*, 96 U.S. App. D.C. 258 (1955).

The ultimate issue in this case is, of course, the defendant's intent at the time of the offense. While the Court is mindful that the Ninth Circuit has generally upheld trial court decisions rejecting psychiatric testimony offered to prove a defendant's mental state where insanity has not been interposed as a defense, it is equally aware of its discretionary authority to allow such testimony where it can be of assistance to the jury in understanding a matter of importance that is beyond the pale of common experience. The Court is of the opinion that the peculiar question to which the experts here will address themselves whether the defendant's initial status as a kidnap victim and the subsequent treatment of her by her captors could have deprived her of the requisite general intent to commit the offense charged is not only relevant to the asserted defense of coercion but also beyond the common experience of most jurors and within the special competence of the experts. The jury need not concur with the expert opinions expressed on this matter, but this Court will not deprive them of the opportunity to consider the testimony that will be offered and make whatever use of it they deem advisable.

. . . [P]laintiff's motion to bar admission of expert psychiatric testimony on the issue of coercion and general intent be, and . . . plaintiff's motion to strike the testimony of Dr. Louis J. West. . . is hereby denied.

LEGAL ANALYSIS AND WRITING 10.3

The following questions are based on the *How to Brief a Legal Case* format shown in the Appendix. Use this format to answer the following questions:

1. Summarize the facts in the previous case.
2. What is the legal issue?
3. What did the appellate court decide?
4. Why did the court decide this way?
5. Do you agree with the court's reasoning? Explain why or why not.

LEGAL RESEARCH USING THE INTERNET SKILLS 10.3

1. Use the Internet to see if you can find out more about the Patty Hearst kidnapping and subsequent trial. Did the expert witness testimony help? What was the final verdict?

OPINION ON ULTIMATE ISSUE

Ultimate Issue
The reason for or element of a legal action, usually pertaining to the guilt of a criminal action defendant or liability of a civil action defendant.

Most courts allow an expert to give an opinion without first testifying to the underlying data on which he bases his opinion (see Exhibit 10.5).

Testimony in the form of an opinion or inference otherwise admissible is generally not objectionable because it embraces an **ultimate issue** to be decided by the trier of fact (see Exhibit 10.5).[11] However, the federal courts, and some state courts, limit this to civil cases. In criminal cases, these courts do not allow an opinion on an ultimate issue when it involves the mental state or condition constituting an element of the crime or of a defense thereto.[12] Such ultimate issues would be matters for the trier of fact alone.

EXHIBIT 10.5   Opinion on Ultimate Issue

Federal Rules of Evidence
Rule 704. Opinion on Ultimate Issue

(a) Except as provided in subdivision (b), testimony in the form of an opinion or inference otherwise admissible is not objectionable because it embraces an ultimate issue to be decided by the trier of fact.

(b) No expert witness testifying with respect to the mental state or condition of a defendant in a criminal case may state an opinion or inference as to whether the defendant did or did not have the mental state or condition constituting an element of the crime charged or of a defense thereto. Such ultimate issues are matters for the trier of fact alone.

Rule 705. Disclosure of Facts or Data Underlying Expert Opinion
The expert may testify in terms of opinion or inference and give reasons therefor without first testifying to the underlying facts or data, unless the court requires otherwise. The expert may in any event be required to disclose the underlying facts or data on cross-examination.

COURT APPOINTED EXPERTS

Court Appointed Expert
An expert witness selected or appointed by the court to testify on a matter.

Generally, expert witnesses are called by one of the parties to the legal action. Sometimes, however, the trial court may step in and appoint an expert witness. This type of witness is often called a **court appointed expert.** This is often done when mental competency is at issue prior to trial or when an issue arises at trial that is too complicated for the jury to understand without the assistance of expert testimony. The federal courts, and most states, have a rule that sets out this process (see Exhibit 10.6). It provides that a trial court "may on its own motion or on the motion of any party enter an order to show cause why expert witnesses should not be appointed, and may request the parties to submit nominations."[13] It also provides that a court may appoint any expert witnesses agreed upon by the parties, or may appoint expert witnesses of its own selection, but only if the witness consents to testify. Most states authorize disclosure to the jury of the fact that the court appointed the expert witness. No matter who calls these expert witnesses, they are subject to cross-examination by either party.

EXHIBIT 10.6   Court Appointed Experts

Federal Rules of Evidence
Rule 706. Court Appointed Experts

   (a) Appointment. The court may on its own motion or on the motion of any party enter an order to show cause why expert witnesses should not be appointed, and may request the parties to submit nominations. The court may appoint any expert witnesses agreed upon by the parties, and may appoint expert witnesses of its own selection. An expert witness shall not be appointed by the court unless the witness consents to act. A witness so appointed shall be informed of the witness' duties by the court in writing, a copy of which shall be filed with the clerk, or at a conference in which the parties shall have opportunity to participate. A witness so appointed shall advise the parties of the witness' findings, if any; the witness' deposition may be taken by any party; and the witness may be called to testify by the court or any party. The witness shall be subject to cross-examination by each party, including a party calling the witness.

   (b) Compensation. Expert witnesses so appointed are entitled to reasonable compensation in whatever sum the court may allow. The compensation thus fixed is payable from funds which may be provided by law in criminal cases and civil actions and proceedings involving just compensation under the fifth amendment. In other civil actions and proceedings the compensation shall be paid by the parties in such proportion and at such time as the court directs, and thereafter charged in like manner as other costs.

   (c) Disclosure of appointment. In the exercise of its discretion, the court may authorize disclosure to the jury of the fact that the court appointed the expert witness.

   (d) Parties' experts of own selection. Nothing in this rule limits the parties in calling expert witnesses of their own selection.

CRITICAL THINKING QUESTIONS 10.3

1. Name the types of cases and various areas of law where the use of expert witnesses might be important and explain your reasoning for these conclusions.

2. What famous cases can you name that might have relied on expert witnesses?

LEGAL RESEARCH USING THE INTERNET SKILLS 10.4

1. Use the Internet to compare the rules pertaining to lay and expert opinion testimony in your state. What is the difference between the two? Do they follow the Federal Rules?

SUMMARY

As a general rule, witnesses must testify from personal knowledge. Sometimes it is easier for a witness to give an opinion rather than attempt to recount all of the specific facts that make up a particular set of perceptions or support a conclusion. For example, it may be easier on the jury to have a witness say it was "hot" outside rather than to establish what factors supported the conclusion about the temperature. Another example is the determination of age. Modern evidence law has allowed these opinions by lay witnesses if it is rationally based on personal knowledge and it helps the jury understand the evidence.

In addition to lay opinions, there are many issues presented at trial that involve special knowledge, or are so complicated or beyond the common knowledge of the jury that someone with special skills or education is required to help the jury understand the evidence or a matter in issue. An expert witness can testify if it can be shown that she has these special skills, knowledge, or experience. Her testimony must also be able to help the jury understand certain evidence or matters in issue.

KEY TERMS

Court Appointed Expert
Expert Witness

Lay Witness
Opinion

Opinion Testimony
Ultimate Issue

LEARNING OUTCOMES AND PRACTICE SKILLS CHECKLIST

☐ Learning Outcomes

After completing your reading, questions, and exercises, you should be able to demonstrate a better understanding of the learning concepts by answering the following questions:

1. Define *opinion testimony* and explain why we need rules to govern opinion testimony as evidence.
2. Distinguish between lay and expert witnesses.
3. Identify and assess the elements required in order to admit opinion testimony from a lay witness.
4. Describe the different types of opinion that a lay witness may be allowed to give.
5. Explain when opinion testimony by expert witnesses can be admitted.
6. Discuss the reasons for allowing opinions by expert witnesses.
7. Distinguish between the common law and modern rules for what an expert could base her opinion on.
8. Identify the additional requirements for testimony by experts added by the amendment to Federal Rule 702.
9. Explain whether an expert may give an opinion on an ultimate issue in a trial.
10. Define *court appointed expert* and describe how this occurs in a trial.

☐ Practice Skills

In addition to understanding the learning concepts, practice what you have learned through applications using critical thinking, legal analysis and writing, legal research, and advocacy skills, including:

Critical Thinking

1. Why do we have rules that govern opinion testimony by lay and expert witnesses?
2. Do you believe that these rules provide adequate safeguards for this testimony?
3. What public policy issues or considerations do you think might be behind these rules?
4. If it were up to you, would you keep these rules as they are, delete them, narrow them, or expand them? Explain your reasoning.
5. How do these rules influence the gathering of evidence or preparing of witnesses?

Legal Analysis and Writing

Analyze the following rules and cases by summarizing their holdings, explaining their significance, and assessing any issue that might arise in their application.

1. Rule 701.
2. Rule 702.
3. Rule 703.
4. *United States v. Yazzie.*
5. *United States v. Hearst.*

Legal Research Using the Internet

1. Find the annotated Federal Rules of Evidence on the Internet and assess the comments made in the proposing of the rules covered in this chapter.
2. Find your state's rules of evidence regarding relevance exceptions and concepts covered in this chapter. Compare and contrast with the federal and/or modern rules, and some of the state rules listed in this chapter.
3. Find out if your state appellate court posts their case decisions on the Internet. If so, find a case that illustrates an issue or rule discussed in this chapter. If your state decisions are not on the Internet, go instead to the web site for the U.S. Circuit Court of Appeals in your circuit, or search the U.S. Supreme Court decisions.

ADVOCACY AND COMMUNICATION SKILLS 10.1

Using the *Advocacy and Persuasive Arguments* format shown in the Appendix, form plaintiff and defense teams from small groups of no more than 3–4 each. Choose one of the following fact situations, prepare, and present an oral argument in support of why this testimony should or should not be admitted. Each side will have 3 minutes for their argument and 1 minute for rebuttal.

In a civil lawsuit for injury caused by a drunk driver, plaintiff wants to call the following witnesses to testify:

1. A lay witness who will testify that he was with defendant prior to the accident and that, in the opinion of the witness, defendant was drunk. Witness, however, comes from a non-drinking family and has never drank alcoholic beverages himself.
2. A police officer as an expert witness, based on her 5 years of experience working traffic patrol and arresting drunk drivers. As an expert witness, officer will testify that, in her opinion, defendant was extremely intoxicated and beyond the legal limit for drinking and driving. Even though

the defendant never took any blood or breath test, the officer bases her opinion on the skid marks that defendant's vehicle left in the road, and the results of the field sobriety test that the officer administered to the defendant after the accident.

PRACTICE APPLICATION 10.1

Use the format shown in the Appendix for the *IRAC Method of Legal Analysis* and the evidentiary rules discussed in this chapter to analyze the above *Advocacy* witness testimony and determine whether the testimony in each example should be admitted. Using the IRAC method, write a memo to your legal team giving your analysis and conclusions.

WEB SITES

Federal Rules of Evidence
http://www.law.cornell.edu/rules/fre/overview.html
FindLaw
http://www.findlaw.com
http://guide.lp.findlaw.com/casecode/
List of State Laws from Legal Information Institute of Cornell Law School
http://www.law.cornell.edu/states/listing.html

National Center for State Courts—State and Federal Court Web Sites
http://www.ncsconline.org/D_kis/info_court_web_sites.html#federal
U.S. Courts Site with Links to All Circuit Courts of Appeal
http://www.uscourts.gov/links.html

ENDNOTES

1. *McNaught v. New York Life Insurance Co.*, 143 Neb. 213 (1943).
2. *Central R.R. v. Monahan*, 11 F.2d 212 (2d Cir. 1926).
3. *United States v. Carlock*, 806 F.2d 535 (5th Cir. 1986).
4. Fed. R. Evid. 701, as amended through Dec 1, 2000.
5. *Asplund Mfg. v. Benton Harbor Engineering*, 57 F.3d 1190 (3rd Cir. 1995).
6. *Bowling v. Commonwealth*, 926 S.W.2d 667 (Ky. 1996).
7. *Wyoming Rules of Evidence*, Rule 702.
8. *Daubert v. Merrell Dow Pharmaceuticals, Inc.*, 509 U.S. 579 (1993).
9. Fed. R. Evid. 702, as amended through Dec 1, 2000.
10. *Texas Rules of Evidence*, Rule 703. Bases of Opinion Testimony by Experts.
11. *North Carolina Rules of Evidence*, Rule 704. Opinion on Ultimate Issue.
12. Fed. R. Evid. 704(b). Opinion on Ultimate Issue.
13. *North Carolina Rules of Evidence*, Rule 706. Court Appointed Experts.

SCIENTIFIC EVIDENCE AND TESTING

"When the question involved does not lie within the range of common experience or common knowledge, but requires special experience or special knowledge, then the opinions of witnesses skilled in that particular science, art, or trade to which the question relates are admissible in evidence."

—*Frye v. United States,*
293 F.1013 (D.C. Cir. 1923)

LEARNING OUTCOMES

In this chapter, you will learn about the following legal concepts:

- Admissibility of Scientific Evidence and Testing
- General Acceptance Test
- Relevancy Test
- The *Daubert* Standard
- Effect of the *Daubert* Decision

- Applying the *Daubert* Standard
- Experts Who Are Not Scientists
- Judge as Gatekeeper
- Abuse of Discretion

INTRODUCTION

Earlier, we examined the differences between a lay and expert witness, looked at what opinion evidence is, and discussed when opinion evidence can be given. In this chapter, we will look at the issues surrounding the expert witness providing opinions when complex scientific tests and procedures are used. We will examine why we need a standard for qualifying an expert opinion or procedure when these scientific tests are performed. We will also look at what the standard is, where it came from, and how it is applied today.

ADMISSIBILITY OF SCIENTIFIC EVIDENCE AND TESTING

Scientific Evidence and Testing
Evidence that has a scientific or highly technical basis, which requires an expert witness with specialized knowledge to assist the trier of fact to understand it.

One of the historical areas of controversy surrounding expert witnesses has been in the introduction of **scientific evidence and testing,** and its foundational expert witness testimony. Scientific evidence has a highly technical basis that requires an expert witness with specialized knowledge to assist the trier of fact to better understand it. This has been especially so when new or novel scientific testing, procedures, or evidence are being introduced. Tests scientifically determine the level of intoxication through a person's breath, blood, or urine. Tests analyze blood grouping, drug interactions, tire stress, fingerprints, and DNA. There are polygraph examinations, ballistics comparisons, radar and speed detection readings, voice identification, and hypnosis. These are all examples of scientific testing and evidence that have undergone challenges to both the validity of the testing and the results. These challenges are directed toward the expert witness who testifies in an attempt to establish a foundation and validity of the testing and results.

Practice Tip 11.1

Reference Manual on Scientific Evidence
Check out this valuable reference manual on scientific evidence at the Federal Judicial Center, Publications Page-Evidence: Reference Manual on Scientific Evidence: http://www.fjc.gov/

General Acceptance Test
Scientific evidence is admissible only if the principle upon which it is based is "sufficiently established to have general acceptance in the field to which it belongs."

GENERAL ACCEPTANCE TEST

For over 70 years, the accepted standard for this scientific evidence and testing was called the *Frye* test, or **"general acceptance" test.** This test was based on the following 1923 landmark case where a federal circuit court held that the results of a "scientific test" could be admitted if the test had "gained general acceptance in the particular field in which it belongs."

CASE

Frye v. United States
293 F.1013 (D.C. Cir. 1923).

VAN ORSDEL, Associate Justice.

Appellant, defendant below, was convicted of the crime of murder in the second degree, and from the judgment prosecutes this appeal. A sin-

gle assignment of error is presented for our consideration. In the course of the trial, counsel for defendant offered an expert witness to testify to the result of a deception test made upon defendant. The test is described as the systolic blood pressure deception test. It is asserted that blood pressure is influenced by change in the emotions of the witness, and that the systolic blood pressure rises are brought about by nervous impulses sent to the sympathetic branch of the autonomic nervous system. Scientific experiments, it is claimed, have demonstrated that fear, rage, and pain always produce a rise of systolic blood pressure, and that conscious deception or falsehood, concealment of facts, or guilt of crime, accompanied by fear of detection when the person is under examination, raises the systolic blood pressure in a curve, which corresponds exactly to the struggle going on in the subject's mind, between fear and attempted control of that fear, as the examination touches the vital points in respect of which he is attempting to deceive the examiner.

In other words, the theory seems to be that truth is spontaneous, and comes without conscious effort, while the utterance of a falsehood requires a conscious effort, which is reflected in the blood pressure. The rise thus produced is easily detected and distinguished from the rise produced by mere fear of the examination itself. In the former instance, the pressure rises higher than in the latter, and is more pronounced as the examination proceeds, while in the latter case, if the subject is telling the truth, the pressure registers highest at the beginning of the examination, and gradually diminishes as the examination proceeds. Prior to the trial defendant was subjected to this deception test, and counsel offered the scientist who conducted the test as an expert to testify to the results obtained. The offer was objected to by counsel for the government, and the court sustained the objection. Counsel for defendant then offered to have the proffered witness conduct a test in the presence of the jury. This also was denied. Counsel for defendant, in their able presentation of the novel question involved, correctly state in their brief that no cases directly in point have been found. The broad ground, however, upon which they plant their case is succinctly stated in their brief as follows:

> The rule is that the opinions of experts or skilled witnesses are admissible in evidence in those cases in which the matter of inquiry is such that inexperienced persons are unlikely to prove capable of forming a correct judgment upon it, for the reason that the subject-matter so far partakes of a science, art, or trade as to require a previous habit or experience or study in it, in order to acquire a knowledge of it. When the question involved does not lie within the range of common experience or common knowledge, but requires special experience or special knowledge, then the opinions of witnesses skilled in that particular science, art, or trade to which the question relates are admissible in evidence.

Numerous cases are cited in support of this rule. Just when a scientific principle or discovery crosses the line between the experimental and demonstrable stages is difficult to define. Somewhere in this twilight zone the evidential force of the principle must be recognized, and while courts will go a long way in admitting expert testimony deduced from a well-recognized scientific principle or discovery, the thing from which the deduction is made must be sufficiently established to have gained general acceptance in the particular field in which it belongs. We think the systolic blood pressure deception test has not yet gained such standing and scientific recognition among physiological and psychological authorities as would justify the courts in admitting expert testimony deduced from the discovery, development, and experiments thus far made. The judgment is affirmed.

LEGAL ANALYSIS AND WRITING 11.1

The following questions are based on the *How to Brief a Legal Case* format shown in the Appendix. Use this format to answer the following questions:

1. Summarize the facts in the previous case.
2. What is the legal issue?
3. What did the appellate court decide?
4. Why did the court decide this way?
5. Do you agree with the court's reasoning? Explain why or why not.

Frye Sets Precedent

Precedent
A rule of law established by a court decision that sets a principle or is later followed by other courts.

The 1923 *Frye* decision established a **precedent** that expert opinion based on a scientific technique was inadmissible unless the technique was "generally accepted" as reliable in the relevant scientific community. This required that "the thing from which the deduction is made must be sufficiently established to have gained general acceptance in the particular field in which it belongs."[1] The "general acceptance" test was the standard for determining admissibility of novel scientific evidence at trial for over 70 years, and is still followed by a handful of states.

CRITICAL THINKING QUESTIONS 11.1

1. Why do you think the *Frye* "general acceptance" test was the dominant standard for so many years?
2. What were the strengths and weaknesses of this "general acceptance" test?
3. Do you think this test can ever be totally replaced? Why or why not?

LEGAL RESEARCH USING THE INTERNET SKILLS 11.1

Using one of the following web sites as a resource, find out if your state rules of evidence use the *Frye* "general acceptance" test:

1. Legal Information Institute (LII), Cornell Law School (http://www.law.cornell.edu/states/listing.html)
2. FindLaw (http://guide.lp.findlaw.com/casecode/)

RELEVANCY TEST

Relevancy Test
Determines admissibility of scientific evidence and testing by weighing probative value and reliability of scientific testing against the test's potential for prejudice.

After the Federal Rules of Evidence were adopted, many courts began to refine the *Frye* "general acceptance" test to also ensure that the scientific testing was reliable and that the results were relevant. This new federal standard was called the **relevancy test.** Along with this new test for determining scientific evidence, there was a growing controversy as to what effect Federal Rule 702 had on the *Frye* principle. At the time, this Rule provided that a witness could testify and provide an opinion as an expert if qualified by "knowledge, skill, experience, training, or education," and "if scientific, technical, or other specialized knowledge will assist the trier of fact to understand the evidence (see Exhibit 11.1)."[2]

Exhibit 11.1   Examples of Rules for Admitting Expert Testimony on Scientific Evidence

New Jersey Rules of Evidence
Rule 702. Testimony by Experts.
If scientific, technical, or other specialized knowledge will assist the trier of fact to understand the evidence or to determine a fact in issue, a witness qualified as an expert by knowledge, skill, experience, training, or education may testify thereto in the form of an opinion or otherwise.

(Continued)

Exhibit 11.1   Examples of Rules for Admitting Expert Testimony on Scientific Evidence *Continued*

California Evidence Code
Section 720(a). A person is qualified to testify as an expert if he has special knowledge, skill, experience, training, or education sufficient to qualify him as an expert on the subject to which his testimony relates. Against the objection of a party, such special knowledge, skill, experience, training, or education must be shown before the witness may testify as an expert.

(b) A witness' special knowledge, skill, experience, training, or education may be shown by any otherwise admissible evidence, including his own testimony.

Increased Use of the Relevancy Test

The relevancy test, which was increasingly being used by federal courts in the late 1980s and early 1990s, weighed the **probative** value of scientific testing against the test's potential for prejudice. In a 1985 Third Circuit case that laid the groundwork for this new test, the court stated that the admission of scientific evidence requires an examination of:

Probative
That which tends to prove something.

(1) the soundness and reliability of the process or technique used.
(2) whether admitting the evidence would overwhelm, confuse, or mislead the jury.
(3) the proffered connection between the scientific research or test result to be presented and particular disputed factual issues in the case.[3]

In reaching this determination, the court looked to the rule requiring evidence to be relevant[4] evidence and weighed it against the rule that even relevant evidence may be excluded if its probative value is substantially outweighed by the danger of unfair prejudice or confusion to the jury.[5]

Another example of the newer relevancy test being used in federal courts was a 1990 decision involving the introduction of DNA evidence. In this case, a court rejected a strict application of *Frye* in favor of the flexible approach afforded by the relevancy test. The court concluded that the "appropriate considerations for the admission of novel scientific evidence were the same as those used to determine the admissibility of other evidence." The court went on to say that this test is "inherently a balancing one that weighs the probativeness, materiality, and reliability of the evidence against the tendency to mislead or confuse the jury, or unfairly prejudice the defendant." The court proceeded to outline factors to be considered when assessing whether a particular scientific technique is reliable:

(1) the potential rate of error,
(2) the existence and maintenance of standards,
(3) the care with which the scientific technique has been employed and whether it is susceptible to abuse,
(4) whether there are analogous relationships with other types of scientific techniques that are routinely admitted into evidence, and
(5) the presence of failsafe characteristics.

The court reasoned that one of the important characteristics of the relevancy test was that it provided a "flexible standard that adapts to the exigencies of a particular scientific technique and case. Thus, when a scientific technique is more likely to mislead or confuse the jury, the test requires that a proportionally stronger showing of reliability must be made. . . . "[6]

In 1990, another federal court looked even further for a proper foundation for any scientific testing to be admitted into evidence. The court adopted the following requirements:

1. Whether the . . . evidence is generally accepted by the scientific community.
2. Whether the testing procedures used are generally accepted if performed properly.
3. Whether the testing was performed properly.
4. Whether the evidence is more prejudicial than probative.
5. Whether the statistics used to determine probability of someone having the same genetic characteristics is more probative than prejudicial.[7]

Daubert Standard
An adaptation of the relevancy test of determining the admissibility of scientific evidence by weighing probative value of scientific testing and its reliability against the test's potential for prejudice.

THE *DAUBERT* STANDARD

By the early 1990s, the federal courts and the states that followed the Federal Rules had drawn battle lines over which test to use, the *Frye* precedent or the newer relevancy test. Finally, in a landmark 1993 decision, the U.S. Supreme Court unanimously rejected the *Frye* test as a basis for determining the admissibility of scientific expert testimony. The Court established a new standard based on the relevancy test and Federal Rule 702, which became known as the **Daubert standard.**

CASE

Daubert v. Merrell Dow Pharmaceuticals, Inc.

509 U.S. 579 (1993).

United States Supreme Court.

Justice Blackmun delivered the opinion of the Court.

In this case we are called upon to determine the standard for admitting expert scientific testimony in a federal trial.

I

Petitioners Jason Daubert and Eric Schuller are minor children born with serious birth defects. They and their parents sued respondent in California state court, alleging that the birth defects had been caused by the mothers' ingestion of Bendectin, a prescription anti-nausea drug marketed by respondent. Respondent removed the suits to federal court on diversity grounds. After extensive discovery, respondent moved for summary judgment, contending that Bendectin does not cause birth defects in humans and that petitioners would be unable to come forward with any admissible evidence that it does. In support of its motion, respondent submitted an affidavit of Steven H. Lamm, physician and epidemiologist, who is a well-credentialed expert on the risks from exposure to various chemical substances. Doctor Lamm stated that he had reviewed all the literature on

Bendectin and human birth defects—more than 30 published studies involving over 130,000 patients. No study had found Bendectin to be a human teratogen (i.e., a substance capable of causing malformations in fetuses).

On the basis of this review, Doctor Lamm concluded that maternal use of Bendectin during the first trimester of pregnancy has not been shown to be a risk factor for human birth defects. Petitioners did not (and do not) contest this characterization of the published record regarding Bendectin. Instead, they responded to respondent's motion with the testimony of eight experts of their own, each of whom also possessed impressive credentials. These experts had concluded that Bendectin can cause birth defects. Their conclusions were based upon in vitro (test tube) and in vivo (live) animal studies that found a link between Bendectin and malformations; pharmacological studies of the chemical structure of Bendectin that purported to show similarities between the structure of the drug and that of other substances known to cause birth defects; and the reanalysis of previously published epidemiological (human statistical) studies.

The District Court granted respondent's motion for summary judgment. The court stated that scientific evidence is admissible only if the principle upon which it is based is "sufficiently established to have general acceptance in the field to which it belongs." The court concluded that petitioners' evidence did not meet this standard. . . . Citing *Frye v. United States*, 54 App. D.C. 46, 293 F.1013 (1923), the court stated that expert opinion based on a scientific technique is inadmissible unless the technique is "generally accepted" as reliable in the relevant scientific community. . . . We granted certiorari, in light of sharp divisions among the courts regarding the proper standard for the admission of expert testimony.

In the 70 years since its formulation in the *Frye* case, the "general acceptance" test has been the dominant standard for determining the admissibility of novel scientific evidence at trial. Although under increasing attack of late, the rule continues to be followed by a majority of courts, including the Ninth Circuit. The *Frye* test has its origin in a short and citation-free 1923 decision concerning the admissibility of evidence derived from a systolic blood pressure deception test, a crude precursor to the polygraph machine. In what has become a famous (perhaps infamous) passage, the then Court of Appeals for the District of Columbia described the device and its operation and declared:

> Just when a scientific principle or discovery crosses the line between the experimental and demonstrable stages is difficult to define. Somewhere in this twilight zone the evidential force of the principle must be recognized, and while courts will go a long way in admitting expert testimony deduced from a well-recognized scientific principle or discovery, the thing from which the deduction is made must be sufficiently established to have gained general acceptance in the particular field in which it belongs. 54 App. D.C., at 47, 293 F., at 1014.

Because the deception test had "not yet gained such standing and scientific recognition among physiological and psychological authorities as would justify the courts in admitting expert testimony deduced from the discovery, development, and experiments thus far made," evidence of its results was ruled inadmissible.

The merits of the *Frye* test have been much debated, and scholarship on its proper scope and application is legion. Petitioners' primary attack, however, is not on the content, but on the continuing authority, of the rule. They contend that the *Frye* test was superseded by the adoption of the Federal Rules of Evidence. We agree. We interpret the legislatively enacted Federal Rules of Evidence as we would any statute. Rule 402 provides the baseline:

> All relevant evidence is admissible, except as otherwise provided by the Constitution of the United States, by Act of Congress, by these rules, or by other rules prescribed by the Supreme Court pursuant to statutory authority. Evidence which is not relevant is not admissible.

"Relevant evidence" is defined as that which has "any tendency to make the existence of any fact that is of consequence to the determination of the action more probable or less probable than it would be without the evidence." Rule 401. The Rule's basic standard of relevance thus is a liberal one. Rule 702, governing expert testimony, provides:

> If scientific, technical, or other specialized knowledge will assist the trier of fact to understand the evidence or to determine a fact in issue, a witness qualified as an expert by knowledge, skill, experience, training, or education, may testify thereto in the form of an opinion or otherwise.

Nothing in the text of this Rule establishes "general acceptance" as an absolute prerequisite to admissibility. Nor does respondent present any clear indication that Rule 702 or the Rules as a whole were intended to incorporate a "general acceptance" standard. The drafting history makes no mention of *Frye*, and a rigid "general acceptance" requirement would be at odds with the "liberal thrust" of the Federal Rules and their "general approach of relaxing the traditional barriers to 'opinion' testimony." *Beech Aircraft Corp. v. Rainey*, 488 U.S., at 169 (citing Rules 701 to 705).

. . . Rule 702. . . requires that the evidence or testimony "assist the trier of fact to understand the evidence or to determine a fact in issue." This condition goes primarily to relevance. "Expert testimony which does not relate to any issue in the case is not relevant and, ergo, nonhelpful." ("An additional consideration under Rule 702" and another aspect of relevancy "is whether expert testimony proffered in the case is sufficiently tied to the facts of the case that it will aid the jury in resolving a factual dispute"). The consideration has been aptly described. . . as one of "fit." "Fit" is not always obvious, and scientific validity for one purpose is not necessarily scientific validity for other, unrelated purposes.

C

. . . Faced with a proffer of expert scientific testimony, then, the trial judge must determine at the outset, pursuant to Rule 104(a), whether the expert is proposing to testify to (1) scientific knowledge that (2) will assist the trier of fact to understand or determine a fact in issue. This entails a preliminary assessment of whether the reasoning or methodology underlying the testimony is scientifically valid and of whether that reasoning or methodology properly can be applied to the facts in issue. We are confident that federal judges possess the capacity to undertake this review. Many factors will bear on the inquiry, and we do not presume to set out a definitive checklist or test. But some general observations are appropriate.

Ordinarily, a key question to be answered in determining whether a theory or technique is scientific knowledge that will assist the trier of fact will be whether it can be (and has been) tested. "Scientific methodology today is based on generating hypotheses and testing them to see if they can be falsified; indeed, this methodology is what distinguishes science from other fields of human inquiry. . . . Another pertinent consideration is whether the theory or technique has been subjected to peer review and publication. . . . Some propositions, moreover, are too particular, too new, or of too limited interest to be published. But submission to the scrutiny of the scientific community is a component of "good science," in part because it increases the likelihood that substantive flaws in methodology will be detected.

. . . The fact of publication (or lack thereof) in a peer-reviewed journal thus will be a relevant, though not dispositive, consideration in assessing the scientific validity of a particular technique or methodology on which an opinion is premised. Additionally, in the case of a particular scientific technique, the court ordinarily should consider the known or potential rate of error, and the existence and maintenance of standards controlling the technique's operation.

Finally, "general acceptance" can yet have a bearing on the inquiry. A "reliability assessment does not require, although it does permit, explicit identification of a relevant scientific community and an express determination of a particular degree of acceptance within that community." Widespread acceptance can be an important factor in ruling particular evidence admissible, and "a known technique that has been able to attract only minimal support within the community," may properly be viewed with skepticism.

The inquiry envisioned by Rule 702 is, we emphasize, a flexible one. Its overarching subject is the scientific validity "and thus the evidentiary relevance and reliability" of the principles that underlie a proposed submission. The focus, of course, must be solely on principles and methodology, not on the conclusions that they generate. Throughout, a judge assessing a proffer of expert scientific testimony under Rule 702 should also be mindful of other applicable rules. Rule 703 provides that expert opinions based on otherwise inadmissible hearsay are to be admitted only if the facts or data are "of a type reasonably relied upon by experts in the particular field in forming opinions or inferences upon the subject." Rule 706 allows the court at its discretion to procure the assistance of an expert of its own choosing. Finally, Rule 403 permits the exclusion of relevant evidence "if its probative value is substantially outweighed by the danger of unfair prejudice, confusion of the issues, or misleading the jury. . . ."

III

We conclude by briefly addressing what appear to be two underlying concerns of the parties and amici in this case. Respondent expresses apprehension that abandonment of "general acceptance" as the exclusive requirement for admission will result in a "free-for-all" in which befuddled juries are confounded by absurd and irrational pseudoscientific assertions. In this regard respondent seems to us to be overly pessimistic about the capabilities of the jury, and of the adversary system generally. Vigorous cross-examination, presentation of contrary evidence, and careful instruction on the burden of proof are the traditional and appropriate means of attacking shaky but admissible evidence. Additionally, in the event the trial court concludes that the scintilla of evidence presented supporting a position is insufficient to allow a reasonable juror to conclude that the position more likely than not is true, the court remains free to direct a judgment, Fed. Rule Civ. Proc. 50(a), and likewise to grant summary judgment, Fed. Rule Civ. Proc. 56. . . . These conventional devices, rather than wholesale exclusion under an uncompromising "general acceptance" test, are the appropriate safeguards where the basis of scientific testimony meets the standards of Rule 702.

Petitioners and, to a greater extent, their amici exhibit a different concern. They suggest that recognition of a screening role for the judge that allows for the exclusion of "invalid" evidence will sanction a stifling and repressive scientific orthodoxy, and will be inimical to the search for truth. It is true that open debate is an essential part of both legal and scientific analyses. Yet there are important differences between the quest for truth in the court room and the quest for truth in the laboratory. Scientific conclusions are subject to perpetual revision. Law, on the other hand, must resolve disputes finally and quickly. The scientific project is advanced by broad and wide ranging consideration of a multitude of hypotheses, for those that are incorrect will eventually be shown to be so, and that in itself is an advance. Conjectures that are probably wrong are of little use, however, in the project of reaching a quick, final, and binding legal judgment "often of great consequence" about a particular set of events in the past. We recognize that in practice, a gatekeeping role for the judge, no matter how flexible, inevitably on occasion will prevent the jury from learning of authentic insights and innovations. That, nevertheless, is the balance that is struck by Rules of Evidence designed not for the exhaustive search for cosmic understanding but for the particularized resolution of legal disputes.

IV

To summarize: "general acceptance" is not a necessary precondition to the admissibility of scientific evidence under the Federal Rules of Evidence, but the Rules of Evidence, especially Rule 702, do assign to the trial judge the task of ensuring that an expert's testimony both rests on a reliable foundation and is relevant to the task at hand. Pertinent evidence based on scientifically valid principles will satisfy those demands. The inquiries of the District Court and the Court of Appeals focused almost exclusively on "general acceptance," as gauged by publication and the decisions of other courts. Accordingly, the judgment of the Court of Appeals is vacated and the case is remanded for further proceedings consistent with this opinion.

LEGAL ANALYSIS AND WRITING 11.2

The following questions are based on the *How to Brief a Legal Case* format shown in the Appendix. Use this format to answer the following questions:

1. Summarize the facts in the previous case.
2. What is the legal issue?
3. What did the appellate court decide?
4. Why did the court decide this way?
5. Do you agree with the court's reasoning? Explain why or why not.

LEGAL RESEARCH USING THE INTERNET SKILLS 11.2

Find and read this landmark Supreme Court case online! Check out one of the legal research web sites below and use their "Search" feature to find this case. In the "Search" field, enter the case name.

1. FindLaw U.S. Supreme Court Decisions (http://www.findlaw.com/casecode/supreme.html)
2. U.S. Supreme Court (http://www.supremecourtus.gov/)
3. Supreme Court Collection of Cornell Law School (http://supct.law.cornell.edu/supct/)

EFFECT OF THE *DAUBERT* DECISION

The Court in *Daubert* believed that the *Frye* test was outdated because of its exclusion of otherwise relevant expert scientific testimony. The Court also believed that *Frye* might allow some questionable evidence as scientific—like astrology—if it were based on general acceptance among astrologers. The *Daubert* court wanted to focus more on the reliability of the testing and data. Relying on reliability and relevance as baseline measures, the Court went beyond the mere rejection of the *Frye* "general acceptance" test and set new standards for determining the admissibility of expert testimony in scientific evidence. The Court held that the trial judge was to act as a "gatekeeper" with the responsibility of "ensuring that an expert's testimony both rests on a reliable foundation and is relevant to the task at hand." Whenever this expert testimony is proffered, the trial judge must determine if it is based on scientific or technical knowledge and whether it will assist the trier of fact to understand or determine a fact in issue.

To determine if it is based on scientific or technical knowledge, the trial judge needs to first conduct a "preliminary assessment of whether the reasoning or methodology underlying the testimony is scientifically valid" and then "whether that reasoning or methodology properly can be applied to the facts in issue." To help with this, the Court listed five "considerations" that might be examined, including:

1. Whether it can be and has been tested.
2. Whether the theory or technique has been subjected to peer review and publication.
3. Known or potential rate of error.
4. Existence and maintenance of standards controlling the technique's operation.
5. Degree of general acceptance within the relevant scientific community.

Of these five factors, testing is essential. This is "what distinguishes science from other fields of human inquiry." The court indicated that the other factors, although "pertinent," were more "flexible" in their "consideration."

Although the *Daubert* court rejected the *Frye* "general acceptance" as the exclusive test for admitting scientific evidence, it can still be an important part of the process, especially in determining admissibility of new theories and technology that have not been generally accepted within the relevant scientific community. As the court stated in a 1985 case relied upon in *Daubert*:

> In many cases . . . the acceptance factor may well be decisive, or nearly so. Thus, we expect that a technique that satisfies the *Frye* test usually will be found to be reliable as well. On the other hand, a known technique which has been able to attract only minimal support within the community is likely to be found unreliable.[8]

EVIDENTIARY CHECKLIST 11.1

Factors to Consider in Admitting Scientific Evidence

☐ Does the matter at issue require scientific, technical, or other specialized knowledge?

☐ Will the scientific evidence or expert witness assist the trier of fact to better understand the evidence?

☐ Is the witness providing testimony about the scientific evidence or testing qualified as an expert by knowledge, skill, experience, training, or education?

☐ Is the testimony based upon sufficient facts or data?

☐ Is the testimony the product of reliable principles and methods?

☐ Does the expert witness apply these principles and methods reliably to the facts of the case?

As "gatekeeper," it will be the responsibility of the trial judge to determine this reliability and to assess the validity of the proffered expert testimony.

APPLYING THE *DAUBERT* STANDARD

The *Daubert* decision changed the law for determining scientific evidence in not only all of the federal courts, but many of the state courts as well (see Exhibit 11.2). The following case was the first major decision to apply the *Daubert* standard. The court required experts to tie their assessment of data to known scientific conclusions, based on research or studies. If they cannot, the court reasoned that there would be no comparison for the jury to assess and the experts' testimony would not be helpful to the jury.

Group 2 Case #11

♦ ───

CASE

Porter v. Whitehall Labs., Inc.

9 F.3d 607 (7th Cir. 1993)

Ripple, Circuit Judge.

Manual Porter instituted this action under our diversity jurisdiction seeking recovery from the defendants on a variety of theories for injuries sustained by ingesting ibuprofen. The defendant Whitehall Laboratories is a subsidiary of American Home Products Corporation (collectively "the Whitehall defendants") and manufactures Advil, a pain reliever containing ibuprofen. The Upjohn Company makes a prescription strength drug, Motrin, which contains ibuprofen. The district court granted summary judgment in favor of the defendants. Mr. Porter appealed. We now affirm the judgment of the district court.

. . . .

On October 3, 1986, Manual Porter fractured his left great toe at work. He sought treatment first from Dr. Diane Wells, an internist, who referred Mr. Porter to Bloomington Hospital. At the hospital, Mr. Porter was treated by Dr. Jones. Dr. Jones set a surgery date of October 10, 1993 to reset Mr. Porter's toe. Dr. Jones also prescribed Tylenol No. 3, a pain reliever, until the surgery. Because of his continuing pain, Mr. Porter called Dr. Wells on October 4, 1993. Dr. Wells' nurse practitioner gave Mr. Porter samples of Motrin, a prescription form of ibuprofen, and Vicoden, an acetaminophen. . . . Mr. Porter took fourteen Motrin tablets between October 13, 1986 and November 7, 1986. Mr. Porter took approximately fifteen Advil tablets between November 7 and November 18, 1986. Other than his injured toe, Mr. Porter had no significant health problems prior to November 19, 1986. On that day, he returned to Dr. Wells' office

with complaints of headache, vomiting, and blurred vision. Dr. Wells examined Mr. Porter and found that he was suffering from high blood pressure, significant papilledema (swelling of the fundi of the eyes), and puffiness of the face.

Based on these symptoms, Dr. Wells had Mr. Porter transferred by ambulance to Bloomington Hospital for treatment by Dr. Richard Combs, a nephrologist. Dr. Combs conducted a series of tests which revealed that Mr. Porter was experiencing kidney failure from which he would not recover. Dr. Combs' diagnosis of Mr. Porter's condition at that time was acute tubular necrosis secondary to ibuprofen; specifically, upon Mr. Porter's discharge on December 5, Dr. Combs wrote: "The patient's . . . ibuprofen reactions have both an interstitial and glomerular reaction and I believe this can explain all of his problems."

. . . .

In January 1987, Mr. Porter was readmitted to Bloomington Hospital for a renal biopsy. That biopsy revealed rapidly progressive glomerulonephritis ("RPGN"). Glomerulonephritis is an inflammation and disease of the filtering unit in the kidney that causes decreased renal function. . . . RPGN is a rare and serious disease which leads to end-stage renal failure in a significant number of cases without any ibuprofen or other drug use. Mr. Porter suffered from the types of RPGN known as anti-glomerular basement membrane glomerulonephritis ("anti-GBM") and membranoproliferative glomerulonephritis ("MPGN"). Ibuprofen is not known to be a cause of these or any other types of RPGN.

. . . .

In their motion for summary judgment, defendants contended that the record failed to establish a genuine issue of fact that ibuprofen is capable of causing anti-GBM, MPGN, or any other type of RPGN, or that ibuprofen caused Mr. Porter's RPGN. Furthermore, they argued that the record failed to establish that a genuine issue of fact existed with regard to ibuprofen causing a change from interstitial nephritis to RPGN.

. . .

In its analysis . . . the district court first noted that Mr. Porter must establish a causal nexus between ibuprofen and his acute renal failure to prevail on any of his counts. . . .

The district court next determined that expert testimony was necessary to assist the jury in determining causation. It concluded that "whether Mr. Porter's acute renal failure was an iatrogenic reaction to ibuprofen is a fact outside the understanding of lay jurors." Furthermore, because an expert opinion must be admissible to be considered in the determination of a motion for summary judgment, the district court next evaluated the admissibility of the expert testimony offered by Mr. Porter. In undertaking this task, the district court employed an analysis grounded in the Federal Rules of Evidence. An expert must clear three independent steps (or tests) before the expert's testimony is admissible. First, the person must be "qualified as an expert by knowledge, skill, experience, training, or education." Fed. R. Evid. 702. Second, the court must find that "scientific, technical, or other specialized knowledge will assist the trier of fact to understand the evidence or to determine a fact in issue." Third, the particular instant facts or data upon which an expert bases an opinion or inference must be "of a type reasonably relied upon by experts in the particular field informing opinions or inferences upon the subject." Fed. R. Evid. 703.

. . . .

The district court posited that the expert must be able to compare the data at hand with a known scientific conclusion or relationship. If experts cannot tie their assessment of data to known scientific conclusions, based on research or studies, then there is no comparison for the jury to evaluate and the experts' testimony is not helpful to the jury. . . .

The district court, applying this theme, determined that the plaintiff's expert testimony was not derived from the scientific method and therefore did not meet the requirements of Rule 702. . . . The testimony of Dr. Diane Wells does not meet *Daubert*'s standards. Dr. Wells testified: "What I'm giving you now is kind of a curb side opinion. If . . . you were asking me to give you an analytical, scientific opinion, then, I would have to research it, and I have neither the time nor the inclination to do that." However, a "scientific" opinion is just what Rule 702, as interpreted in *Daubert*, requires. Moreover, Dr. Wells stated frankly that she had no scientific support for her opinion that ibuprofen caused Mr. Porter's renal condition, and further that she had no evidence that ibuprofen leads to RPGN. Thus, Dr. Wells' testimony was properly excluded. Dr. Richard Combs described Mr. Porter's injuries as "acute renal failure, secondary to ibuprofen." However, after receiving the pathology report, Dr. Combs reevaluated his diagnosis and admitted that he could not state to a reasonable degree of scientific certainty that ibuprofen caused the RPGN. Like Dr. Wells, he could not point to studies, records, or data on which he based his opinion. The district court properly excluded this evidence because it was not well-grounded in the scientific method.

Dr. Francesco Del Greco testified that he believed ingestion of ibuprofen led to interstitial nephritis which in turn caused anti-GBM, the type of RPGN that, according to his diagnosis, Mr. Porter had. However, Dr. Del Greco agreed that his opinion in this case was a "hypothesis, the proof of which remains to be made." He also admitted that if his personal hypothesis turned out to be correct, it would be the first case in history in which ibuprofen caused RPGN. Because this testimony was based on subjective belief alone, it was properly excluded under *Daubert*. . . . Finally, Dr. Benjamin also theorized a progression whereby ibuprofen caused a kidney condition which progressed to RPGN. However, he admitted that such a conclusion was outside his area of expertise. Because Dr. Benjamin did not possess the requisite scientific knowledge for his testimony to be helpful to the jury, his testimony was properly excluded. Thus, the district court properly applied the first directive the Court gave in *Daubert* to all of the relevant experts.

. . . Clearly, the statements offered by the plaintiff's experts could be verified scientifically; however, none of them had been tested.

. . . The district court made the inquiries required by *Daubert* and applied them in a way consistent with the Court's direction. We find no error in the analysis of the district court and therefore affirm its judgment.

Affirmed.

The following questions are based on the *How to Brief a Legal Case* format shown in the Appendix. Use this format to answer the following questions:

1. Summarize the facts in the previous case.
2. What is the legal issue?
3. How did the appellate court decide?
4. Why did the court decide this way?
5. Do you agree with the court's reasoning? Explain why or why not.

Try to find and read the above case online! Check out one of the legal research web sites below and use their "Search" feature to find this case. In the "Search" field, enter the cite or case name.

1. U.S. Courts Site with Links to All Circuit Courts of Appeal (http://www.uscourts.gov/links.html)
2. National Center for State Courts—State and Federal Court Web Sites (http://www.ncsconline.org/D_kis/info_court_web_sites.html#federal)
3. FindLaw (http://guide.lp.findlaw.com/casecode/)

1. Name the types of cases and various areas of law where the use of scientific evidence or testing might be important and explain your reasoning for these conclusions.
2. In some cases (the O. J. Simpson murder trial, for example), the jury finds for the defendant despite convincing scientific evidence and expert witnesses that point to the guilt or liability of the defendant. What are some of the factors that might account for this?
3. What other cases can you name that might have relied on scientific evidence and expert witnesses?

EXHIBIT 11.2   Examples of Post-*Daubert* Rules for Scientific Evidence Testimony by Experts

Federal Rules of Evidence
Rule 702. Testimony by Experts.

   If scientific, technical, or other specialized knowledge will assist the trier of fact to understand the evidence or to determine a fact in issue, a witness qualified as an expert by knowledge, skill, experience, training, or education, may testify thereto in the form of an opinion or otherwise, if (1) the testimony is based upon sufficient facts or data, (2) the testimony is the product of reliable principles and methods, and (3) the witness has applied the principles and methods reliably to the facts of the case. (Amended Dec. 1, 2000)

(Continued)

EXHIBIT 11.2   Examples of Post-*Daubert* Rules for Scientific Evidence Testimony by Experts
Continued

Ohio Rules of Evidence
Rule 702. Testimony by Experts.
   A witness may testify as an expert if all of the following apply:

   (A) The witness's testimony either relates to matters beyond the knowledge or experience possessed by lay persons or dispels a misconception common among lay persons;

   (B) The witness is qualified as an expert by specialized knowledge, skill, experience, training, or education regarding the subject matter of the testimony;

   (C) The witness's testimony is based on reliable scientific, technical, or other specialized information. To the extent that the testimony reports the result of a procedure, test, or experiment, the testimony is reliable only if all of the following apply:

   (1) The theory upon which the procedure, test, or experiment is based is objectively verifiable or is validly derived from widely accepted knowledge, facts, or principles;

   (2) The design of the procedure, test, or experiment reliably implements the theory;

   (3) The particular procedure, test, or experiment was conducted in a way that will yield an accurate result.

EVIDENTIARY CHECKLIST 11.2

Scientific Evidence and Testing Checklist

±   Is it science?
±   Can it be tested?
±   Is it relevant?

EXPERTS WHO ARE NOT SCIENTISTS

One of the unanswered questions left by the *Daubert* decision was how far the new standard extended. Clearly, it pertained to scientific evidence and testing. Did it also apply to other "experts" who were not scientists, but whose expertise or testing involved technical or specialized knowledge? In 1999, the U.S. Supreme Court addressed this by looking at what ". . . technical, or other specialized knowledge" under Rule 701 as used in *Daubert* covered.

CASE

Kumho Tire Co. v. Carmichael
526 U.S. 137 (1999).
United States Supreme Court.

Justice Breyer delivered the opinion of the Court.

In *Daubert v. Merrell Dow Pharmaceuticals, Inc.*, 509 U.S. 579 (1993), this Court focused upon the admissibility of scientific expert testimony. It pointed out that such testimony is admissible only if it is both relevant and reliable. And it held that the Federal Rules of Evidence "assign to the trial judge the task of ensuring that an expert's testimony both rests on a reliable foundation and is relevant to the task at hand."

. . . This case requires us to decide how *Daubert* applies to the testimony of engineers and other experts who are not scientists. We conclude that *Daubert*'s general holding—setting forth the trial judge's general "gatekeeping" obligation—applies not only to testimony based on "scientific" knowledge, but also to testimony based on "technical" and "other specialized" knowledge. We also conclude that a trial court may consider one or more of the more specific factors that *Daubert* mentioned when doing so will help determine that testimony's reliability. But, as the Court stated in *Daubert*, the test of reliability is "flexible," and *Daubert*'s list of specific factors neither necessarily nor exclusively applies to all experts or in every case.

Rather, the law grants a district court the same broad latitude when it decides how to determine reliability as it enjoys in respect to its ultimate reliability determination. See *General Electric Co. v. Joiner*, 522 U.S. 136, 143 (1997) (courts of appeals are to apply "abuse of discretion" standard when reviewing District Court's reliability determination). Applying these standards, we determine that the District Court's decision in this case—not to admit certain expert testimony—was within its discretion and therefore lawful.

I

On July 6, 1993, the right rear tire of a minivan driven by Patrick Carmichael blew out. In the accident that followed, one of the passengers died, and others were severely injured. In October 1993, the Carmichaels brought this diversity suit against the tire's maker and its distributor, whom we refer to collectively as Kumho Tire, claiming that the tire was defective. The plaintiffs rested their case in significant part upon deposition testimony provided by an expert in tire failure analysis, Dennis Carlson, Jr., who intended to testify in support of their conclusion.

Carlson's depositions relied upon certain features of tire technology that are not in dispute. A steel-belted radial tire like the Carmichaels' is made up of a "carcass" containing many layers of flexible cords, called "plies," along which (between the cords and the outer tread) are laid steel strips called "belts." Steel wire loops, called "beads," hold the cords together at the plies' bottom edges. An outer layer, called the "tread," encases the carcass, and the entire tire is bound together in rubber, through the application of heat and various chemicals. . . .

Carlson's testimony also accepted certain background facts about the tire in question. He assumed that before the blowout the tire had traveled far. (The tire was made in 1988 and had been installed some time before the Carmichaels bought the used minivan in March 1993; the Carmichaels had driven the van approximately 7,000 additional miles in the two months they had owned it.)

Carlson noted that the tire's tread depth, which was 11/32 of an inch when new, had been worn down to depths that ranged from 3/32 of an inch along some parts of the tire, to nothing at all along others. He conceded that the tire tread had at least two punctures which had been inadequately repaired.

Despite the tire's age and history, Carlson concluded that a defect in its manufacture or design caused the blowout. . . . Carlson said that if a separation is not caused by a certain kind of tire misuse called "overdeflection" (which consists of underinflating the tire or causing it to carry too much weight, thereby generating heat that can undo the chemical tread/carcass bond), then, ordinarily, its cause is a tire defect. Second, he said that if a tire has been subject to sufficient overdeflection to cause a separation, it should reveal certain physical symptoms. These symptoms include (a) tread wear on the tire's shoulder that is greater than the tread wear along the tire's center, (b) signs of a "bead groove," where the beads have been pushed too hard against the bead seat on the inside of the tire's rim; (c) sidewalls of the tire with physical signs of deterioration, such as discoloration; and/or (d) marks on the tire's rim flange. Third, Carlson said that where he does not find at least two of the four physical signs just mentioned (and presumably where there is no reason to suspect a less common cause of separation), he concludes that a manufacturing or design defect caused the separation.

Carlson added that he had inspected the tire in question. He conceded that the tire to a limited degree showed greater wear on the shoulder than in the center, some signs of "bead groove," some discoloration, a few marks on the rim flange, and inadequately filled puncture holes (which can also cause heat that might lead to separation). . . . But, in each instance, he testified that the symptoms were not significant, and . . . Carlson concluded that the tire did not bear at least two of the four overdeflection symptoms, nor was there any less obvious cause of separation; and since neither overdeflection nor the punctures caused the blowout, a defect must have done so.

Kumho Tire moved the District Court to exclude Carlson's testimony on the ground that his methodology failed Rule 702's reliability requirement. The court agreed with Kumho that it should act as a *Daubert*-type reliability "gatekeeper," even though one might consider Carlson's testimony as "technical," rather than "scientific." The court then examined Carlson's methodology in light of the reliability-related factors that *Daubert* mentioned, such as a theory's testability, whether it "has been a subject of peer review or publication," the "known or potential rate of error," and the "degree of acceptance . . . within the relevant scientific community." The District Court found that all those factors argued against the reliability of Carlson's methods, and it granted the motion to exclude the testimony (as well as the defendants' accompanying motion for summary judgment).

. . . .

The Eleventh Circuit reversed. It "review[ed] . . ." the "district court's legal decision to apply *Daubert*." It noted that "the Supreme Court in *Daubert* explicitly limited its holding to cover only the 'scientific context,'" adding that "a *Daubert* analysis" applies only where an expert relies "on the application of scientific principles," rather than "on skill- or experience-based observation." It concluded that Carlson's testimony, which it viewed as relying on experience, "falls outside the scope of *Daubert*," that "the district court erred as a matter of law by applying *Daubert* in this case. . . ."

Kumho Tire petitioned for certiorari, asking us to determine whether a trial court "may" consider *Daubert*'s specific "factors" when determining the "admissibility of an engineering expert's testimony." We granted certiorari in light of uncertainty among the lower courts about whether, or how, *Daubert* applies to expert testimony that might be characterized as based not upon "scientific" knowledge, but rather upon "technical" or "other specialized" knowledge.

II

In *Daubert*, this Court held that Federal Rule of Evidence 702 imposes a special obligation upon a trial judge to "ensure that any and all scientific testimony . . . is not only relevant, but reliable." The initial question before us is whether this basic gatekeeping obligation applies only to "scientific" testimony or to all expert testimony. We . . . believe

that it applies to all expert testimony. For one thing, Rule 702 itself says:

> If scientific, technical, or other specialized knowledge will assist the trier of fact to understand the evidence or to determine a fact in issue, a witness qualified as an expert by knowledge, skill, experience, training, or education, may testify thereto in the form of an opinion or otherwise.

This language makes no relevant distinction between "scientific" knowledge and "technical" or "other specialized" knowledge. It makes clear that any such knowledge might become the subject of expert testimony. In *Daubert*, the Court specified that it is the Rule's word "knowledge," not the words (like "scientific") that modify that word, that "establishes a standard of evidentiary reliability." Hence, as a matter of language, the Rule applies its reliability standard to all "scientific," "technical," or "other specialized" matters within its scope.

. . . Finally, it would prove difficult, if not impossible, for judges to administer evidentiary rules under which a gatekeeping obligation depended upon a distinction between "scientific" knowledge and "technical" or "other specialized" knowledge. There is no clear line that divides the one from the others. Disciplines such as engineering rest upon scientific knowledge. Pure scientific theory itself may depend for its development upon observation and properly engineered machinery. And conceptual efforts to distinguish the two are unlikely to produce clear legal lines capable of application in particular cases. . . . And whether the specific expert testimony focuses upon specialized observations, the specialized translation of those observations into theory, a specialized theory itself, or the application of such a theory in a particular case, the expert's testimony often will rest "upon an experience confessedly foreign in kind to [the jury's] own." The trial judge's effort to assure that the specialized testimony is reliable and relevant can help the jury evaluate that foreign experience, whether the testimony reflects scientific, technical, or other specialized knowledge.

We conclude that *Daubert*'s general principles apply to the expert matters described in Rule 702. The Rule, in respect to all such matters, "establishes a standard of evidentiary reliability." It "requires a valid . . . connection to the pertinent inquiry as a precondition to admissibility." And where such testimony's factual basis, data, principles, methods, or their application are called sufficiently into question, the trial judge must determine whether the testimony has "a reliable basis in the knowledge and experience of [the relevant] discipline."

. . . .

Engineering testimony rests upon scientific foundations, the reliability of which will be at issue in some cases. In other cases, the relevant reliability concerns may focus upon personal knowledge or experience. As the Solicitor General points out, there are many different kinds of experts, and many different kinds of expertise. See Brief for United States (citing cases involving experts in drug terms, handwriting analysis, criminal modus operandi, land valuation, agricultural practices, railroad procedures, attorney's fee valuation, and others). . . . *Daubert* makes clear that the factors it mentions do not constitute a "definitive checklist or test." And *Daubert* adds that the gatekeeping inquiry must be " 'tied to the facts' " of a particular "case. . . ."

III

The District Court did not doubt Carlson's qualifications. . . . Rather, it excluded the testimony because, despite those qualifications, it initially doubted, and then found unreliable, "the methodology employed by the expert in analyzing the data obtained in the visual inspection, and the scientific basis, if any, for such an analysis." In our view, the doubts that triggered the District Court's initial inquiry here were reasonable, as was the court's ultimate conclusion.

. . . The tire in question, the expert conceded, had traveled far enough so that some of the tread had been worn bald; it should have been taken out of service; it had been repaired (inadequately) for punctures; and it bore some of the very marks that the expert said indicated, not a defect, but abuse through overdeflection. . . . Carlson testified precisely that in the absence of at least two of four signs of abuse (proportionately greater tread wear on the shoulder; signs of grooves caused by the beads; discolored sidewalls; marks on the rim flange) he concludes that a defect caused the separation. And his analysis depended upon acceptance of a further implicit proposition, namely, that his visual and tactile inspection could determine that the tire before him had not been abused despite some evidence of the presence of the very signs for which he looked (and two punctures).

For another thing . . . the expert could not say whether the tire had traveled more than 10, or 20, or 30, or 40, or 50 thousand miles, adding that 6,000 miles was "about how far" he could "say

with any certainty." The court could reasonably have wondered about the reliability of a method of visual and tactile inspection sufficiently precise to ascertain with some certainty the abuse-related significance of minute shoulder/center relative tread wear differences, but insufficiently precise to tell "with any certainty" from the tread wear whether a tire had traveled less than 10,000 or more than 50,000 miles. And these concerns might have been augmented by Carlson's repeated reliance on the "subjective[ness]" of his mode of analysis in response to questions seeking specific information regarding how he could differentiate between a tire that actually had been overdeflected and a tire that merely looked as though it had been. They would have been further augmented by the fact that Carlson said he had inspected the tire itself for the first time the morning of his first deposition, and then only for a few hours.

. . . Finally, the court, after looking for a defense of Carlson's methodology as applied in these circumstances, found no convincing defense. Rather, it found (1) that "none" of the *Daubert* factors, including that of "general acceptance" in the relevant expert community, indicated that Carlson's testimony was reliable; (2) that its own analysis "revealed no countervailing factors operating in favor of admissibility which could outweigh those identified in *Daubert*," and (3) that the "parties identified no such factors in their briefs." For these three reasons taken together, it concluded that Carlson's testimony was unreliable.

Respondents . . . argue . . . that a method of tire failure analysis that employs a visual/tactile inspection is a reliable method, and they point both to its use by other experts and to Carlson's long experience working for Michelin as sufficient indication that that is so. But no one denies that an expert might draw a conclusion from a set of observations based on extensive and specialized experience. Nor does anyone deny that, as a general matter, tire abuse may often be identified by qualified experts through visual or tactile inspection of the tire. As we said before, the question before the trial court was . . . whether this particular expert had sufficient specialized knowledge to assist the jurors "in deciding the particular issues in the case."

The particular issue in this case concerned the use of Carlson's two-factor test and his related use of visual /tactile inspection to draw conclusions on the basis of what seemed small observational differences. We have found no indication in the record that other experts in the industry use Carlson's two-factor test or that tire experts such as Carlson normally make the very fine distinctions about, say, the symmetry of comparatively greater shoulder tread wear that were necessary, on Carlson's own theory, to support his conclusions. Nor, despite the prevalence of tire testing, does anyone refer to any articles or papers that validate Carlson's approach. . . .

In sum, Rule 702 grants the district judge the discretionary authority, reviewable for its abuse, to determine reliability in light of the particular facts and circumstances of the particular case. The District Court did not abuse its discretionary authority in this case. Hence, the judgment of the Court of Appeals is Reversed.

LEGAL ANALYSIS AND WRITING 11.4

The following questions are based on the *How to Brief a Legal Case* format shown in the Appendix. Use this format to answer the following questions:

1. Summarize the facts in the previous case.
2. What is the legal issue?
3. What did the appellate court decide?
4. Why did the court decide this way?
5. Do you agree with the court's reasoning? Explain why or why not.

LEGAL RESEARCH USING THE INTERNET SKILLS 11.4

Find and read this important Supreme Court case online! Check out one of the legal research web sites below and use their "Search" feature to find this case. In the "Search" field, enter the case name.

1. FindLaw U.S. Supreme Court Decisions (http://www.findlaw.com/casecode/supreme.html)
2. U.S. Supreme Court (http://www.supremecourtus.gov/)
3. Supreme Court Collection of Cornell Law School (http://supct.law.cornell.edu/supct/)

Effect of *Kumho* Decision

The *Kumho* decision examined the language in Rule 702 underlying the *Daubert* decision. The Court found that the wording made no distinction between "scientific" knowledge and "technical" or "other specialized" knowledge.[9] The Court concluded that any such "specialized" knowledge might then become the subject of expert testimony. The Court held that it is the word "knowledge" in the rule that is key, not words like "scientific."[10] Therefore, as a matter of language, the *Daubert* decision applies its reliability standard to all scientific, technical, or "other specialized" matters within its scope.

EVIDENTIARY CHECKLIST 11.3

When Expert Opinion Based on Scientific Knowledge Can Be Admitted

Under the *Frye* "General Acceptance" Test

☐ When the method of analysis from which the opinion is made is sufficiently established to have gained general acceptance in the particular field in which it belongs.

Under the "Relevancy Test"

☐ When scientific, technical, or other specialized knowledge will assist the trier of fact to understand the evidence or to determine a fact in issue.

☐ When the expert opinion is based on this scientific, technical, or other specialized knowledge.

☐ When the expert is qualified by knowledge, skill, experience, training, or education.

☐ When the basis for analysis and opinion rests on a reliable foundation and is relevant to the fact in issue.

Under the *Daubert* Standard and New Federal Rule 702

☐ When scientific, technical, or other specialized knowledge will assist the trier of fact to understand the evidence or to determine a fact in issue.

☐ When the expert opinion is based on this scientific, technical, or other specialized knowledge.

☐ When the expert is qualified by knowledge, skill, experience, training, or education.

☐ When the testimony of the expert is based upon sufficient facts or data.

☐ When the testimony is the product of reliable principles and methods.

☐ When the expert has applied the principles and methods reliably to the facts of the case.

EVIDENTIARY CHECKLIST 11.4

Factors for Determining "Scientific Knowledge" Under the *Daubert* Test

☐ Whether it can be (and has been) tested.

☐ Whether the theory or technique has been subjected to peer review and publication.

☐ What is its known or potential rate of error?

☐ Whether there is existence and maintenance of standards controlling the technique's operation.

☐ What is its degree of general acceptance within the relevant scientific community?

CRITICAL THINKING QUESTIONS 11.3

1. Why did *Daubert* replace the *Frye* "general acceptance" test?
2. What are the strengths and weaknesses of the *Daubert* "relevance" test?
3. Compare and contrast the *Daubert* test with the *Frye* test.
4. In what areas might *Daubert* allow scientific evidence where *Frye* did not?

YOU BE THE JUDGE 11.1

In a boundary dispute over the location of an underground spring, plaintiff calls a dowser to testify that he dowsed plaintiff's land and estimates a spring flowing approximately 500 feet beneath the surface.

1. Does this testimony constitute scientific knowledge?
2. Should it be admitted under the *Frye* test?
3. Should it be admitted under the *Daubert* test?

Explain your reasons.

LEGAL ANALYSIS AND WRITING 11.5

Use the format shown in the Appendix for the *IRAC Method of Legal Analysis* and the rules set forth in *Daubert* to determine if the above dowsing could be admitted as scientific evidence.

JUDGE AS GATEKEEPER

Gatekeeper
Role of the trial judge in ensuring relevance and reliability of scientific evidence.

In *Daubert*, the Court stated that the role of the trial judge in determining the admissibility of scientific evidence was to act as a **"gatekeeper."** In this role, the judge was responsible for "ensuring that an expert's testimony both rests on a reliable foundation and is relevant to the task at hand." In other words, is it science and is it relevant to assisting the trier of fact to understand or determine a fact in issue?

ABUSE OF DISCRETION

Abuse of Discretion
The standard of review that an appellate court should apply in reviewing a trial court's decision to admit or exclude expert testimony under *Daubert*.

After the *Daubert* decision, some federal courts wondered what standard of review would be applied by appellate courts in reviewing a trial court's decision to admit or exclude expert testimony. Prior to *Daubert*, **abuse of discretion** was the review standard. In 1997, this issue was resolved when the Supreme Court determined that this would remain the standard.

CASE

General Electric Company v. Joiner
522 U.S. 136 (1997).

Chief Justice Rehnquist delivered the opinion of the Court.

We granted certiorari in this case to determine what standard an appellate court should apply in reviewing a trial court's decision to admit or exclude expert testimony under *Daubert v. Merrell Dow Pharmaceuticals, Inc.*, 509 U.S. 579 (1993). We hold that abuse of discretion is the appropriate standard.

... We have held that abuse of discretion is the proper standard of review of a district court's evidentiary rulings. The Court of Appeals suggested that *Daubert* somehow altered this general rule in the context of a district court's decision to exclude scientific evidence. But *Daubert* did not address the standard of appellate review for evidentiary rulings at all. It did hold that the "austere" *Frye* standard of "general acceptance" had not been carried over into the Federal Rules of Evidence. Thus, while the Federal Rules of Evidence allow district courts to admit a somewhat broader range of scientific testimony than would have been admissible under *Frye*, they leave in place the "gatekeeper" role of the trial judge in screening such evidence. But the question of admissibility of expert testimony is not such an issue of fact, and is reviewable under the abuse of discretion standard.

. . .

We hold, therefore, that abuse of discretion is the proper standard by which to review a district court's decision to admit or exclude scientific evidence.

LEGAL ANALYSIS AND WRITING 11.6

The following questions are based on the *How to Brief a Legal Case* format shown in the Appendix. Use this format to answer the following questions:

1. What is the legal issue in the previous case?
2. What did the Court decide?
3. Why did the Court decide this way?
4. Do you agree with the court's reasoning? Explain why or why not.

LEGAL RESEARCH USING THE INTERNET SKILLS 11.5

Find and read the full decision of this Supreme Court case online! Check out one of the legal research web sites below and use their "Search" feature to find this case. In the "Search" field, enter the case name.

1. FindLaw U.S. Supreme Court Decisions (http://www.findlaw.com/casecode/supreme.html)
2. U.S. Supreme Court (http://www.supremecourtus.gov/)
3. Supreme Court Collection of Cornell Law School (http://supct.law.cornell.edu/supct/)

CRITICAL THINKING QUESTIONS 11.4

1. What does the judge as "gatekeeper" mean?
2. Assess the strengths and weaknesses of this gatekeeper role.
3. What is the standard of review for an appellate court to determine if the trial judge made an error in admitting or not admitting scientific evidence?
4. Do you think this standard of review is adequate to ensure the reliability of scientific evidence? Explain your reasoning.
5. If it were up to you, would you keep the rules governing expert opinion testimony as they are, delete them, narrow them, or expand them? Explain your reasoning.

SUMMARY

There are many issues presented at trial that involve scientific knowledge, or are so complicated or beyond the common knowledge of the jury that someone with special skills or education is required to help the jury understand the evidence or a matter in issue. An expert witness can testify if it can be shown that she has these special skills, knowledge, or experience, and that her testimony can help the jury understand certain evidence or matters in issue. If the testimony pertained to scientific evidence or testing, the "general acceptance" test established by *Frye* was dominant in the courts for many years. This test required that the method of analysis from which the opinion about scientific evidence is made must be sufficiently established to have gained general acceptance in the particular field in which it belongs.

In 1993, a major decision by the U.S. Supreme Court in *Daubert* recognized a new test in the federal courts. This test evolved from the *relevancy test*, based on Federal Rule 702 and the newer standards set forth in *Daubert*. The test requires that the scientific evidence or testimony be able to assist the trier of fact to understand the evidence or to determine a fact in issue. In addition, the expert testimony must consist of scientific or technical knowledge or experience supported by appropriate validation. This "knowledge" can be determined by considering five factors, including whether it can be (and has been) tested, whether the theory or technique has been subjected to peer review and publication, its known or potential rate of error, the existence and maintenance of standards controlling the technique's operation, and the *Frye* standard for degree of general acceptance within the relevant scientific community.

Under the relevancy or *Daubert* test, the judge serves as the gatekeeper with abuse of discretion as the standard of review. The *Daubert* test is now used in all of the federal courts, as well as in many state courts. However, many state courts have yet to adopt the *Daubert* standard. The *Frye* test is still used in some state courts, and is one of the five factors in determining admissibility under the *Daubert* standards. As such, the *Frye* test remains an important element in assessing the reliability of scientific evidence.

KEY TERMS

Abuse of Discretion	General Acceptance Test	Relevancy Test
Daubert Standard	Precedent	Scientific Evidence and Testing
Gatekeeper	Probative	

LEARNING OUTCOMES AND PRACTICE SKILLS CHECKLIST

☐ Learning Outcomes

After completing your reading, questions, and exercises, you should be able to demonstrate a better understanding of the learning concepts by answering the following questions:

1. Define the general acceptance test and discuss its significance to scientific evidence and testing.
2. Compare and contrast the Frye and relevance tests for admitting scientific evidence.
3. Distinguish the relevance test from the standard set in Daubert.
4. Assess the five factors for determining "scientific knowledge" under the Daubert test.
5. Explain the significance of the Kumho Tire decision and how it affected the Daubert test.
6. Distinguish the newer Federal Rule 702 from the rule in other states governing testimony by experts.
7. Describe the role of the trial judge as "gatekeeper."
8. Identify the standard of review used by an appellate court when reviewing a trial judge's decision to admit scientific evidence.

☐ Practice Skills

In addition to understanding the learning concepts, practice what you have learned through applications using critical thinking, legal analysis and writing, legal research, and advocacy skills, including:

Critical Thinking

1. Why do we have rules that govern the admissibility of scientific evidence and testing?
2. Do you believe that the current rules provide adequate safeguards for this process?
3. What public policy issues or considerations do you think might be behind these rules?
4. Why do you think that many state courts have not adopted the Daubert standard?
5. If it were up to you, would you keep these rules as they are, delete them, narrow them, or expand them? Explain your reasoning.
6. How do these rules influence the gathering of evidence or preparing of witnesses?

Legal Analysis and Writing

Analyze the following rules and cases by summarizing their holdings, explaining their significance, and assessing any issue that might arise in their application.

1. Rule 702.
2. *Frye v. United States.*
3. *Daubert v. Merrell Dow.*
4. *Porter v. Whitehall Labs.*
5. *Kumho Tire v. Carmichael.*
6. *General Electric v. Joiner.*

Legal Research Using the Internet

1. Find the annotated Federal Rules of Evidence on the Internet and assess the comments made in the proposing of the rules covered in this chapter.
2. Find your state's rules of evidence regarding relevance exceptions and concepts covered in this chapter. Compare and contrast with the federal and/or modern rules, and some of the state rules listed in this chapter.
3. Find out if your state appellate court posts their case decisions on the Internet. If so, find a case that illustrates an issue or rule discussed in this chapter. If your state decisions are not on the Internet, go instead to the web site for the U.S. Circuit Court of Appeals in your circuit, or search the U.S. Supreme Court decisions.

ADVOCACY AND COMMUNICATION SKILLS 11.1

Using the *Advocacy and Persuasive Arguments* format shown in the Appendix, form prosecution and defense teams from small groups of no more than 3–4 each. Choose one of the following fact situations, research the issues, prepare, and present an oral argument in support of why this testimony should or should not be admitted. Each side will have 3 minutes for their argument and 1 minute for rebuttal.

In a criminal prosecution of a defendant for sending an Anthrax-laced letter through the mail, the prosecution wants to call the following witnesses to testify:

1. A handwriting expert who will testify to the reliability of a handwriting analysis as scientific evidence and that a handwriting analysis in this case revealed that the block-style printing on a letter and envelope were written by the defendant.
2. An expert in hypnosis who will testify to the reliability of hypnotically refreshed memory as scientific evidence and that a witness who was placed under hypnosis remembered the description of a person mailing a letter at a certain mail box over 1 month before.

The defense wants to call the following witness:

1. A polygraph expert who will testify to the reliability of a lie detector test as scientific evidence. The expert will further testify that the defendant was administered this test and passed.

For each witness, both the prosecution and defense teams will present arguments as to why the testimony should or should not be allowed.

PRACTICE APPLICATION 11.1

Use the format shown in the Appendix for the *IRAC Method of Legal Analysis* and the rules and cases discussed in this chapter to analyze the above *Advocacy* scientific evidence problems and determine whether the scientific evidence in each example could be admitted. Using the IRAC method, write a memo to your legal team giving your analysis and conclusions.

PRACTICE APPLICATION 11.2

Use the Internet to find out which test your state follows in admitting expert testimony regarding scientific evidence.

WEB SITES

Federal Judicial Center, Publications page-Evidence: *Reference Manual on Scientific Evidence*
http://www.fjc.gov/

FindLaw
http://guide.lp.findlaw.com/casecode/

FindLaw U.S. Supreme Court Decisions
http://www. findlaw.com/casecode/supreme.html

Legal Information Institute (LII), Cornell Law School
http://www.law.cornell.edu/states/listing .html

National Center for State Courts—State and Federal Court Web Sites
http://www.ncsconline.org/ D_kis /info_court_web_sites.html#federal

Supreme Court Collection of Cornell Law School
http://supct.law.cornell.edu/supct/

U.S. Courts Site with Links to All Circuit Courts of Appeal
http://www.uscourts.gov/links.html

U.S. Supreme Court
http:// www.supremecourtus. gov/

ENDNOTES

1. *Frye v. United States*, 293 F.1013 (D.C. Cir. 1923).
2. Fed. R. Evid. 702.
3. *United States v. Downing*, 753 F.2d 1224 (3d Cir. 1985).
4. Fed. R. Evid. 401.
5. Fed. R. Evid. 403.
6. *U.S. v. Jakobetz*, 747 F. Supp. 250, (Vt 1990) quoting *United States v. Williams*, 583 F.2d 1194 (1990).
7. *U.S. v. Two Bulls*, 918 F.2d 56 (1990).
8. *United States v. Downing*, 753 F.2d 1224 (3d Cir. 1985).
9. Fed. R. Evid. 702.
10. *Kumho Tire Co. v. Carmichael*, 526 U.S. 137 (1999).

HEARSAY

"Perhaps no rule of law has so bedeviled lawyers and judges nor been so uniformly misunderstood by both."

—McKay, Circuit Judge, dissenting, U.S. v. Rodriguez-Pando,
841 F.2d 1014 (10th Cir. 1988)

"Then call them to our presence—face to face, and frowning brow to brow, ourselves will hear the accuser and the accused freely speak."

—William Shakespeare, Richard II

LEARNING OUTCOMES

In this chapter, you will learn about the following legal concepts:

- Hearsay Rule
- What Is Hearsay?
- Where the Hearsay Rule Comes From
- Reasons for the Hearsay Rule
- Defining Hearsay
- Nonverbal Conduct

- Test to Determine Hearsay
- Statements Which Are Not Hearsay
- Prior Statement by Witness
- Admission by a Party-Opponent
- Hearsay Within Hearsay
- Effect of Hearsay Objection

INTRODUCTION

There are many steps taken in the legal process to ensure that evidence is credible and trustworthy when presented to the trier of fact. Two of the important safeguards pertaining to witness testimony are personal knowledge and cross-examination. Evidence is viewed as more trustworthy when a witness can testify to what he saw or heard, and is available to be cross-examined as to the credibility and accuracy of his testimony. There are many times, however, when relevant information has not been perceived firsthand, but has been heard secondhand: "John told me that he saw . . . . " "I was told . . . . " When a witness testifies to information that is received secondhand, how do we ensure the reliability of this testimony, especially when the person making the statement is not in the courtroom to be observed and cross-examined? This chapter will examine the issues surrounding the admitting or exclusion of this secondhand information as evidence.

HEARSAY RULE

Hearsay Rule
A rule excluding hearsay as evidence at trial.

Hearsay
A statement made out-of-court and offered in court as evidence to prove the truth of the assertion made in the statement.

The **hearsay rule** simply states that **hearsay** is not admissible unless provided for by exceptions in the Rules of Evidence or prescribed by other laws (see Exhibit 12.1). However, as we will see in this chapter, the hearsay rule is not as simple in its definition and application. One judge said of the hearsay rule, as we noted in the chapter's opening quote, "Perhaps no rule of law has so bedeviled lawyers and judges nor been so uniformly misunderstood by both."[1] Originally part of the common law, the hearsay rule has been codified in most states and in the federal courts.[2] The rule itself does not define what hearsay is, how it is to be determined, or what exceptions apply to it. These must be found in other rules within the hearsay sections.

EXHIBIT 12.1   Hearsay Rule

Tennessee Rules of Evidence
   Rule 802. Hearsay is not admissible except as provided by these rules or otherwise by law.

WHAT IS HEARSAY?

Hearsay is generally secondhand information that is heard from another. Whenever a witness begins to respond on the stand by saying, "I was told . . . ," "I heard it said . . . ," "Joan told me that . . . ," or "She said . . . ," a red flag should go up to warn of a potential hearsay issue (see Exhibit 12.2).

EXHIBIT 12.2   Example of Hearsay

Plaintiff:	What were you told when you opened the door?
Defense:	Objection, hearsay.
Court:	Sustained.
Plaintiff:	I'll rephrase. What did you hear when you opened the door?
Witness:	I heard Joe tell Mary that . . . .
Defense:	Objection, move to strike. Hearsay.

Hearsay is information that we heard from someone else or a situation where we rely on someone else as the basis for our information. Hearsay can also include a witness's own prior **out-of-court statement**. It includes any **statement** other than one made by the **declarant** *while testifying at trial*. Sometimes, however, what appears to be a hearsay issue can be fixed by rephrasing the question asked of the witness.

Out-of-Court Statement
A statement made outside of the courtroom and not by the witness while testifying at trial.

Statement
Oral or written assertion, or nonverbal conduct of a person if it is intended by the person as an assertion.

Declarant
Person who makes a statement.

Practice Tip 12.1

Rephrasing Hearsay Questions

Your legal team can avoid hearsay objections by better preparing the questions asked of witnesses, or by rephrasing a question already asked and objected to. Here is an example:

Plaintiff:	*What happened at that time?*
Witness:	*I told my friend, Joan, that a man was breaking the car window.*
Defense:	*Move to strike. Hearsay.*
Court:	*Sustained. We'll strike that. You may rephrase.*
Plaintiff:	*I'll rephrase. What did you see at that time?*
Witness:	*I saw a man breaking the car window.*

In the above example, the question was rephrased to allow the witness to answer from her own first-hand knowledge while testifying. Therefore, it will not constitute hearsay. If a witness cannot remember what she said and has to read her statement from a prior recorded source, it would be hearsay.[3]

WHERE THE HEARSAY RULE COMES FROM

The hearsay rule developed in England along with the evolution of the jury system in the late 1600s. Up until that time, English courts routinely decided cases on the basis of what a witness had heard from others, or from an accuser who may not appear in court to testify. Two cases were instrumental in bringing about changes in this. In 1603, Sir Walter Raleigh was convicted of treason on the basis of hearsay evidence. This evidence was in the form of a hearsay statement made by a sailor who had been told of a plot against the king while visiting Portugal, and from accusations by a Lord Cobham, an alleged co-conspirator who was being held in confinement and did not appear as a witness in the trial. Raleigh responded at his trial by stating:

> [I]t is strange to see how you press me still with my Lord Cobham, and yet will not produce him; . . . he is in the house hard by, and may soon be brought hither; let him be produced, and if he will yet accuse me or avow this confession of his, it shall convict me and ease you of further proof.[4]

Raleigh was convicted of treason based on this hearsay evidence. Cobham later denied making the accusations. As a result of this trial, many people began to call for changes in the common law for confronting witnesses and the use of hearsay evidence.

By 1670, this clamoring for change culminated in a famous trial involving the use of hearsay evidence to prosecute William Penn for unlawful assembly. The jury disregarded the trial judge's instructions to only regard the prosecution's evidence, and acquitted Penn. The trial judge imprisoned the jury for disregarding his instructions, but the chief judge upheld the independence of the jury to decide issues of fact on the credibility of the evidence.[5]

After the Penn trial, changes were made in the common law to govern the use of hearsay evidence. These common-law rules were brought over to the American colonies and later codified by most states in evidence rules. Except for the definition of conduct as hearsay, the modern rule, Rule 801, restates that common law definition.

REASONS FOR THE HEARSAY RULE

One of the primary reasons for the hearsay rule is to protect the jury from hearing unreliable out-of-court statements as evidence. Secondhand or out-of-court statements are only relevant and probative if the declarant (or person making them) was telling the truth and could accurately recall and relate the assertion made in the statement. When the declarant is not in court to testify, there is little way for the trier of fact to determine the truthfulness of the statements made.

The Supreme Court said in one case decision that "[t]he hearsay rule, which has long been recognized and respected by virtually every State, is based on experience and grounded in the notion that untrustworthy evidence should not be presented to the triers of fact. Out-of-court statements are traditionally excluded because they lack the conventional indicia of reliability: they are usually not made under oath or other circumstances that impress the speaker with the solemnity of his statements; the declarant's word is not subject to cross-examination; and he is not available in order that his demeanor and credibility may be assessed by the jury."[6]

To ensure this reliability, the law wants witnesses who can testify from personal knowledge of a matter—not what they were told. The effect of the hearsay rule is to require the person who made the original statements to come into court, testify under oath, and have an opportunity for the opposite side to question and cross-examine him or her. This process allows the jury to observe the demeanor of the witness, which might help them to better evaluate the credibility of the witness, and assess how trustworthy and probative the witness's statement might be (see Exhibit 12.3).

EXHIBIT 12.3   Reasons for Hearsay Rule

This hypothetical example shows some of the reasons why we have a hearsay rule:

Witness:	Joan told me that she saw the red car hit the plaintiff.
Defense:	Where was Joan when she saw this?
Witness:	I don't know. She didn't say.
Defense:	Who else was around when this happened?
Witness:	I don't know. She didn't say.
Defense:	What else did Joan see?
Witness:	How should I know? I wasn't there.

Instead of a witness testifying that "Joan told me that she saw the accident," we want to see and hear Joan say it, and assess her veracity and credibility in relation to her statement and the questions asked of her in cross-examination.

```
┌─────────────────────────────────────────────────────────────┐
│              EVIDENTIARY CHECKLIST 12.1                        │
│   ─────────────────────────────────────────────────────       │
│   How the Hearsay Rule Protects the Jury                       │
│   ☐    Witness declarant is required to testify in person.     │
│   ☐    Witness is under oath.                                  │
│   ☐    Witness is subject to cross-examination.                │
│   ☐    Jury can observe witness's demeanor and assess for      │
│        credibility and trustworthiness.                        │
└─────────────────────────────────────────────────────────────┘
```

DEFINING HEARSAY

Most evidence rules contain a section that defines hearsay. Wyoming is representative of the most commonly accepted definition of hearsay. Wyoming Rule 801(c) defines hearsay as a "statement, other than one made by the declarant while testifying at the trial or hearing, offered in evidence to prove the **truth of the matter asserted**."[7] Another way of defining hearsay is a statement made out-of-court and offered in court as evidence to prove that what was asserted in the statement is true. The out-of-court statement is usually made by someone other than the witness who is testifying to the statement at trial.

Truth of Matter Asserted
Proving what was said is true.

Understanding Terms in Hearsay Definition

To help understand what hearsay is and how to determine it, evidentiary rules have also provided meanings of the key terms found in the definition of hearsay (see Exhibit 12.4). The two key terms defined in the rules are *declarant* and *statement*.

Declarant

North Dakota Rule 801(b) defines declarant as "a person who makes a statement."[8] A declarant is the person who made the original statement now being testified to at trial. In classic hearsay situations, the declarant is someone other than the witness testifying. This is the "he said . . . she said" or "Joan told me . . . " case of hearsay. Sometimes, however, the witness and declarant are the same person. For example, a witness may testify that "I told Joan that I heard . . . . " This still may be hearsay because the statement was made out of court.

Statement

The meaning of the word *statement* is essential to understanding hearsay, since the definition of hearsay centers around it. Alaska Rule 801(a) defines statement as an "oral or written assertion or **nonverbal conduct** of a person, if it is intended by the person as an **assertion**."[9] An *assertion* is an action that communicates a statement. An oral or written assertion would be the act of speaking or writing to make a statement.

Nonverbal Conduct
Actions that do not involve speaking or writing.

Assertion
Action that communicates a statement.

NONVERBAL CONDUCT

Nonverbal conduct includes actions that do not involve speaking or writing. In the hearsay definition, nonverbal conduct constitutes hearsay if it is intended as an assertion, like a nod of the head in agreement or shaking of the head in disagreement. If it is not intended as an assertion, it is not hearsay. For example, a person opening an umbrella is not necessarily making a statement about it raining outside. Suppose, however, that a person is asked if it is raining and, in response, the person opens her umbrella. This type of response would be nonverbal conduct that is intended as an assertion.

EXHIBIT 12.4   Definitions

Idaho Rules of Evidence
Rule 801. Definitions. The following definitions apply under this Article:

(a) Statement. A "statement" is (1) an oral or written assertion or (2) nonverbal conduct of a person, if it is intended by the person as an assertion.

(b) Declarant. A "declarant" is a person who makes a statement.

(c) Hearsay. "Hearsay" is a statement, other than one made by the declarant while testifying at the trial or hearing, offered in evidence to prove the truth of the matter asserted.

TEST TO DETERMINE HEARSAY

If a witness is testifying about a statement made out-of-court and this evidence is being offered in order to prove what is being asserted in the statement, it is hearsay. However, if the statement is being offered to prove something other than what is being asserted in the statement, it is not hearsay. As an upcoming case in this chapter points out, statements not offered as an assertion of a fact but, rather, as the fact of an assertion are not hearsay.[10] This is a two-prong test: Is it an out-of-court statement and is the statement offered to prove the truth of the matter asserted?

EVIDENTIARY CHECKLIST 12.2

Test to Determine Hearsay
☐   Was the statement made out-of-court?
☐   Is statement offered to prove the truth of the matter asserted?

Was the Statement Made Out-of-Court?

The statement in question must have been made out-of-court or other than one made by the declarant while testifying at the trial or hearing. Even a statement made by the witness out-of-court prior to trial falls under the hearsay rule. For example:

Plaintiff Attorney:	Ms. Jones, what did you say to your son after you looked up?
Witness:	I told him that I saw the green car go through the stop sign.
Defendant Attorney:	Objection, your Honor. Hearsay.
Court:	Objection sustained.

Ms. Jones' statement, since it was originally made out-of-court, would constitute hearsay. To be admissible, it would need to be phrased in this way:

Plaintiff Attorney: Ms. Jones, what did you see when you looked up?
Witness: I saw the green car go through the stop sign.

Is Statement Offered to Prove the Truth of the Matter Asserted?

The second prong of the hearsay test is whether the statement is being offered to prove the truth of the matter asserted in the statement.

Example: Witness testifies, "My neighbor told me that morning that he saw the defendant beat up his wife."

If this statement is offered to prove that the defendant did in fact beat up his wife, then it is hearsay and not admissible.

However, if that same statement is offered to prove something else, such as that the neighbor had talked to the witness that morning, then the statement is not hearsay and is admissible.

Example: Witness testifies that "On July 4th, the defendant said to me, 'Yesterday, I went to the City Center.'"

If this statement is offered to prove that the defendant was at the City Center on July 3rd, then it is hearsay. If, however, it is being offered to show that the defendant had spoken to the witness on July 4th, then it is not hearsay because it is not being offered to prove the truth of what the defendant said.

EVIDENTIARY CHECKLIST 12.3

Hearsay

Out-of-Court Statement–Offered in evidence to prove truth of what was asserted in statement

= Hearsay

YOU BE THE JUDGE 12.1

In a civil tort action for defamation, plaintiff wants to offer a witness who will testify that he heard defendant call plaintiff a "thief." Plaintiff offers this evidence to prove an element of the defamation. Defense raises a hearsay objection.
Would you admit this testimony? Why or why not?

Practice Tip 12.2

Witness Preparation Checklist for Hearsay
To help ensure a successful witness examination and avoid hearsay issues, develop your own set of witness preparation checklists, using some of the following tips:

☐   *Can witness testify from personal knowledge?*
☐   *Did witness perceive matter being testified about through one of witness's senses, (i.e., sight, hearing, touch, smell, feel)?*

(Continued)

> *Practice Tip 12.2* *Continued*
>
> ☐   *Is witness able to recall and accurately relate her perception?*
> ☐   *Did witness tell anyone else what she saw or heard? (If so, determine who, what, when, where, how, and why.)*
> ☐   *Did witness rely on what anyone else perceived for any part of her testimony? (If so, determine who, what, when, where, how, and why.)*
> ☐   *Will witness be relating anything in any part of her testimony that was told to her or that she heard from someone else? (If so, determine who, what, when, where, how, and why.)*
> ☐   *If witness is relying on what was told her by someone else, is that someone else (the declarant) available to testify? If not, why not?*
> ☐   *Has that declarant testified or given any statements in any prior proceedings?*
> ☐   *Is the statement being offered to prove that what the declarant said is true?*
> ☐   *Is witness relying on any writing or other document that was shown to her for any part of her testimony?*

Were the Tape-Recorded Statements in New Mexico Hearsay?

In the following case, the defendant made a tape-recorded statement to police claiming that he had been coerced into smuggling drugs. The court excluded this statement at trial as hearsay. Note how the majority and dissenting opinions both rely on the same case for different conclusions, and how the dissent applies the "two-step analysis" to determine hearsay. Pay particular attention to how the dissent frames the method for analyzing and determining hearsay.

CASE

United States v. Rodriguez-Pando
841 F.2d 1014 (10th Cir. 1988).

[Rodriguez-Pando was driving a pickup truck on a county road in southwestern New Mexico when he was stopped by a police officer for weaving erratically. The officer had been in the area looking for evidence of aircraft landings on a tip that narcotics were being transported to that vicinity. After the officer asked Pando for the vehicle registration, Pando began to pull a gun from a rag in the glove compartment. The officer drew his weapon and ordered Pando to drop the gun, after which the officer arrested Pando. Looking into the back of the pickup truck, the officer found 1,100 pounds of cocaine. At the police station, Pando made a tape-recorded statement to the New Mexico State Police claiming that he had been coerced into transporting the drugs and that both he and his family were threatened that morning with physical harm if he did not cooperate. At trial, the court excluded the statement as hearsay. Pando was convicted of drug smuggling and

appeals, arguing, among other issues, that the trial court erred in excluding his tape-recorded statement to police.]

Tacha, Circuit Judge, delivered the opinion of the appellate court.

. . . .

Tape Recording

. . . Pando argues that the tape recording was admissible because it was not offered to prove that someone was going to kill him and his family, but rather to show his state of mind. It is true that the tape was not offered to prove that someone was actually going to kill Pando. However, we agree with the district court's implicit determination that the matter asserted in the tape was that Pando had been threatened. Thus, the tape was offered to prove the truth of the matter asserted and was therefore hearsay. The trial judge did not abuse his discretion in so holding.

Here we do not have the defendant testifying about matters within his personal knowledge, the words of Mr. X. Rather, we have what amounts to an offer of proof that a third party heard the defendant describe the words of Mr. X. This certainly seems to be an attempt to establish by hearsay that those words were spoken. The issue in this case then is not whether Pando could testify as to the out-of-court statement of the person who threatened him. The question is whether the jury may hear a tape recording of Pando's out-of-court repetition of the threat.

United States v. Herrera, 600 F.2d 502 (5th Cir. 1979), upon which Pando relies, involved different facts. In that case, the Fifth Circuit held that the trial court erroneously excluded the defendant's in-court testimony regarding a threat she had received. In *Herrera*, the defendant's repetition of the threat would have been made under oath and in the presence of the jury. Furthermore, *Herrera* would have been subject to cross-examination. By contrast, Pando's repetition of the threat was not made under oath; indeed, it was made in circumstances which cast serious doubt on its credibility—a post-arrest interview with a police officer. Nor did Pando repeat the threat in the presence of the jury. Moreover, Pando was not available for cross-examination concerning his assertion that he had been threatened. *Herrera* and similar cases cited by the defendant are simply inapposite. There is a great difference between what the defendant would testify, and what the third party would testify that the defendant said out of court, in terms of fair opportunity to test the truth of defendant's declaration that someone actually uttered the threatening words.

. . . .

[T]he district court in this case was concerned not with the admissibility of the threat itself, but with the admissibility of evidence offered through a third party regarding Pando's out-of-court repetition of the threat. The district court did not err in ruling that the recording was hearsay.

. . . .

Affirmed.

McKay, Circuit Judge, dissenting.

I agree with all the majority has said except its treatment of the hearsay issue. Perhaps no rule of law has so bedeviled lawyers and judges nor been so uniformly misunderstood by both. Of course, it has been difficult for those of us educated in former times to accept the fact that hearsay is whatever Fed. R. Evid. 801 says it is.

The key part of that rule for present purposes is 801(c). It provides:

> (c) Hearsay. "Hearsay" is a statement, other than one made by the declarant while testifying at the trial or hearing, offered in evidence to prove the truth of the matter asserted.

It is clear from the text of the rule itself that a hearsay objection always involves a two-step analysis. The first step is to determine if it was an out-of-court statement. No one disputes that in this case. The second (and mandatory) step is to see if it was "offered" for the truth of the matter asserted. No one can really dispute that the "offer" in this case was to show state of mind, not the truth of the matter asserted. The majority suggests that the trial court made an "implicit determination" that the "offer" was to prove the truth of the matter asserted. It is not up to the trial judge to "implicitly determine" that it was offered for the truth of the matter asserted. The duty of the trial court is to consider the party's offer and determine whether it is admissible as offered. The trial court cannot change the offer. Here the trial court did not rule that state of mind was not at issue or that this offer did not show state of mind. If there was another basis for excluding the evidence, the trial court did not rely on it; and we may not rely on it either.

The same statement can be hearsay in one trial and nonhearsay in another because the purpose for which it is offered determines whether the statement is hearsay. A statement not offered to prove the truth of the matter asserted but rather to indirectly infer a party's state of mind or to show the effect of a statement on a party has long been recognized as nonhearsay. The subject matter of the assertion is not an express articulation of state of mind; instead the declarant's state of mind may be inferred from the fact that the assertion was made. Whether the actual subject matter of the assertion is true or not is irrelevant. For example, the defendant in *United States v. Herrera*, 600 F.2d 502 (5th Cir. 1979), was convicted of transporting illegal aliens. At trial, she mounted a duress defense, claiming that a Ms. Escamilla had threatened her with physical harm in a telephone conversation if she did not cooperate. The trial court refused to admit testimony regarding the contents of the telephone conversation on hearsay grounds. The Fifth Circuit reversed the trial court, holding that the conversation was not hearsay.

The threatening statements made by Escamilla during the conversation were not offered to prove that Escamilla would actually carry through the threats, but rather to show Herrera's state of mind in consequence of the statements. The trial court instructed the jury on the duress defense; therefore, the jury was entitled to consider Escamilla's statements and Herrera's reaction to them in resolving the issue of criminal intent.

. . . .

The statement in the present case is to the effect that Mr. Pando was threatened with physical harm on the morning of his arrest if he failed to cooperate and transport the contraband. At trial, Mr. Pando sought to introduce this evidence in support of his defense that he lacked criminal intent because he performed the acts for which he was charged under mental duress and coercion. The statement was not offered to prove the truth of the substance of what was told to him, i.e., that someone was going to kill both him and his family. Mr. Pando could have misconstrued what was told to him or even imagined the threats. Rather, just as in *Herrera*, the statement was offered to demonstrate that Mr. Pando believed he was threatened with bodily harm, acted because of the impact of this statement, and thus lacked the requisite criminal intent. The statement was offered to indirectly establish his state of mind, the essence of his coercion defense. Hearsay analysis thus dictates that because the statement was not offered to prove the truth of what was said, it is nonhearsay and admissible. . . . I would remand for retrial.

LEGAL ANALYSIS AND WRITING 12.1

The following questions are based on the *How to Brief a Legal Case* format shown in the Appendix. Use this format to answer the following questions:

1. Summarize the facts in the previous case.
2. What is the legal issue?
3. What did the appellate court decide?
4. Why did the court decide this way?
5. Do you agree with the court's reasoning? Explain why or why not.

LEGAL RESEARCH USING THE INTERNET SKILLS 12.1

Try to find this case or another one that refers to it online! Check out one of the legal research web sites below, go to the federal circuit for this court decision, and use their "Search" feature to find this case or another case that refers to it. In the "Search" field, enter the cite or case name. If you have access to Westlaw or Lexis, try to find this case using one of these legal search sites.

1. U.S. Courts Site with Links to All Circuit Courts of Appeal (http://www.uscourts.gov/links.html)
2. National Center for State Courts—State and Federal Court Web Sites (http://www.ncsconline.org/D_kis/info_court_web_sites.html#federal)
3. FindLaw (http://guide.lp.findlaw.com/casecode/)

The "Godfather" of Salem, New Hampshire

In the following extortion case, the court examines comments by the drafters of the Federal Rules of Evidence that "if the significance of an offered statement lies solely in the fact that it was made, no issue is raised as to the truth of anything asserted, and the statement is not hearsay."

Group 2 Case #12

CASE

United States v. Hicks
848 F.2d 1 (1st Cir. 1988).

Coffin, Circuit Judge.

Appellant William Hicks was convicted in the United States District Court for the District of New Hampshire of attempted extortion under the Hobbs Act, 18 U.S.C. § 1951. The gist of the government's case was that defendant attempted to obtain between $5,000 and $10,000 from one James R. Proko in exchange for a guarantee that he would secure the approval by the Salem Town Planning Board of Proko's application for a Honda car dealership. Following a five-day trial, the jury returned a verdict of guilty. We affirm the conviction.

I.

James Proko and members of his family have owned and operated an automobile dealership in Nashua, New Hampshire for over thirty years. In late 1984, the Prokos received permission from Honda to establish a Honda dealership in Salem. They planned to build the dealership on land they had purchased several years earlier. The Prokos' plan for the property was filed with the Salem planning director, and a preliminary hearing was scheduled for May 14, 1985. At that meeting, the Planning Board raised several minor issues and scheduled a final hearing on the plan for May 28th.

The day of the final hearing, Hicks made the first in a series of contacts with James Proko, following a telephone call to James' brother Peter. Peter Proko testified that Hicks described himself as the "Godfather of Salem," and had conveyed that things were done differently in Salem than in Nashua. . . . Proko went to Hicks' house later that day, where, according to Proko, Hicks bragged that he "controlled" votes on the Planning Board. Proko was advised to make an "investment" of $10,000 to see that the plan would be approved. Hicks explained, as he would repeatedly over the next two weeks, that there were many ways in which members of the board could, if Proko refused to play by the local rules, delay and obstruct approval of the plan indefinitely. Proko told Hicks that he would get back to him on the offer. Minutes after Proko left Hicks' residence, a call was made from Hicks' phone to. . . where one Charles T. McMahon worked. McMahon was a Salem Planning Board member, as well as Hicks' close friend and former employee.

Proko then went to the police, and subsequently the FBI, with the story of the alleged extortion attempt. Under immediate time constraints, Proko requested that the Board postpone the hearing. It was rescheduled for June 11, 1985. The following day, Proko agreed to cooperate with the FBI. Numerous conversations between him and Hicks in the weeks and months that followed were secretly recorded and introduced at trial. Negotiations between Hicks and Proko took place frequently during the following two weeks. . . . Proko continued to resist Hicks' overtures, frequently yet unsuccessfully requesting a meeting with those board members with whom Hicks was allegedly in cahoots. On various occasions during this period, Hicks and McMahon had telephone conversations, often immediately preceding or following Hicks' talks with Proko. . . . This was followed by several more calls between Hicks and McMahon during the next day and a half preceding the board meeting.

About twenty or thirty minutes before the board meeting, the members met informally for coffee. Ross Moldoff, the town Planning Director, testified that he overheard McMahon asking a fellow board member, George Salisbury, to obstruct approval of Proko's plan:

> I heard Mr. McMahon say to Mr. Salisbury that he wanted to not take action on this plan tonight. He wanted George to help him find something or help him stop the approval of the plan that evening. He didn't want the plan approved that evening.

Another board member testified that at the meeting he oversaw a note passed from McMahon to Salisbury that said: "I need your help in stopping the Proko plan. I believe it's within two thousand feet of another used car lot." Just prior to the vote on the plan, McMahon raised the issue of a town ordinance barring the placement of used car lots within 2,000 feet of one another. There was another used car lot less than 2,000 feet from Proko's property, but outside the city line. After discussion, the Board decided to seek a formal ruling on the ordinance from town counsel. McMahon then moved for approval conditioned on a favorable ruling from counsel. This motion was unanimously approved.

The next day, Hicks once again contacted McMahon by phone, and McMahon was observed leaving Hicks' house later that afternoon. Three days later, the town counsel issued a formal ruling that the ordinance was inapplicable. Proko's plan was approved. Defendant was convicted of attempted extortion. Neither side called McMahon or Salisbury as a witness at trial.

II.

Appellant's primary complaint is that Moldoff should not have been able to testify regarding McMahon's alleged entreaty to Salisbury, because such testimony constituted hearsay. But this argument is groundless, because there is no hearsay problem here at all. McMahon's statement was not admitted for the truth of anything asserted. Indeed, there could be no "truth" or falsity in a request for assistance. The statement thus was not hearsay under Federal Rule of Evidence 801(c).

As the drafters of the Rules noted, "if the significance of an offered statement lies solely in the fact that it was made, no issue is raised as to the truth of anything asserted, and the statement is not hearsay." McMahon's statement was offered not to show what he wanted (although it did include an assertion to that effect), but solely to show that he had solicited help in stopping the plan; this in turn would be probative of whether the defendant had enlisted McMahon in an attempt to make good on the extortion threat. As such, the statement was a verbal act, and not hearsay at all. We have elsewhere noted that statements made incident to planning board meetings indicating hostility to approval of a plan may be offered to demonstrate that the proscribed behavior actually occurred, and therefore are not subject to hearsay treatment. Here, there is no need to evaluate McMahon's credibility. The only issue was whether McMahon actually said what he did, and as to that, Moldoff was available for cross-examination.

. . . .

V.

Having considered and rejected each of appellant's contentions, the judgment of conviction is affirmed.

LEGAL ANALYSIS AND WRITING 12.2

The following questions are based on the *How to Brief a Legal Case* format shown in the Appendix. Use this format to answer the following questions:

1. Summarize the facts in the previous case.
2. What is the legal issue?
3. What did the appellate court decide?
4. Why did the court decide this way?
5. Do you agree with the court's reasoning? Explain why or why not.

LEGAL RESEARCH USING THE INTERNET SKILLS 12.2

This case originated in New Hampshire and the appeal was heard by the United States Court of Appeals for the First Circuit. Check out one of the legal research web sites below and use their "Search" feature to find a reference to this case, or to explore other case decisions in the First Circuit or the New Hampshire state court. In the "Search" field, enter the cite or case name. If you have access to Westlaw or Lexis, try to find this case using one of these legal search sites.

1. U.S. Courts Site with Links to All Circuit Courts of Appeal (http://www.uscourts.gov/links.html)
2. National Center for State Courts—State and Federal Court Web Sites (http://www.ncsconline.org/D_kis/info_court_web_sites.html#federal)
3. FindLaw (http://guide.lp.findlaw.com/casecode/)
4. State of New Hampshire Laws and Court Decisions (http://www.state.nh.us/government/laws.html)

CRITICAL THINKING QUESTIONS 12.1

1. Why do we have rules that exclude hearsay?
2. In what specific types of cases might the admission of hearsay statements be important?
3. In *Rodriguez-Pando*, how did the court majority and dissenting opinion arrive at different conclusions while relying on the same previous *Herrera* case decision?
4. In the *Hicks* case, at what point in the Moldoff testimony would you have shouted an objection for hearsay?

The Case from Texas about a Prison Nickname

What is a "statement" for the purpose of determining hearsay? This case looks again to the drafters of the Federal Rules of Evidence, this time examining the comment that the "'key' to the definition of 'statement' is that 'nothing is an assertion unless intended to be one.'"

CASE

United States v. Weeks

919 F.2d 248 (5th Cir. 1990).

Appeal from the United States District Court for the Southern District of Texas.

Jones, Circuit Judge.

Defendant-appellant Danny Michael Weeks was convicted after a jury trial of two counts of kidnapping, two counts of interstate transportation of a stolen vehicle, and one count each of carrying a firearm during a crime of violence and possessing a firearm as a convicted felon. The district court sentenced Weeks to prison for two consecutive life terms followed by 17 years, plus a fine of $1,250,000. On appeal, Weeks alleges numerous errors by the trial court and the prosecutors. We affirm.

. . .

II.

HEARSAY

Weeks... claims that the district court erred in allowing an assistant warden of the Angola penitentiary to testify that Weeks' nickname in prison was "Gato." Because kidnap victims Linda Mayeaux and Karyn Laccheo both testified that their abductors used the names "Jimmy" and "Gato," this testimony helped to establish the identity of Weeks as one of the two abductors of the women. Weeks argues that the court should have excluded the warden's testimony as hearsay not falling within any exception. See Fed. R. Evid. 802. Hearsay is defined as "a statement, other than one made by the declarant while testifying at the trial or hearing, offered in evidence to prove the truth of the matter asserted;" a statement is "an oral or written assertion." Id. 801(a) and (c). We conclude that the warden's testimony reported non-assertive oral conduct and was therefore not hearsay.

The following exchanges took place between the witness and defense counsel Meyers and prosecutor Woodward (emphasis added):

BY MS. MEYERS:

Q: Have you ever heard, personally heard anyone call Danny Michael Weeks by a nickname?

A: I have heard other inmates. That's my personal knowledge of the inmates, and other security people call him by a nickname.

Q: Personally on the yard or have you heard them use it or just told you that was his name?

A: I've heard an officer before call him by that name.

. . . . .

Q: So the officer told you that name but didn't call Mr. Weeks that name and have him answer to that name?

A: Didn't have him answer to it.

. . . . .

Q: And the only way you have heard this name Gato is some guards used that name with reference to Mr. Weeks; is that correct?

A: I've heard a guard use it.

. . . . .

BY MR. WOODWARD:

Q: The guard is not the only person you've heard the name Gato from in regard to Danny Michael Weeks; isn't that true?

A: I have heard other inmates use it.

Had the interrogation ceased after the third question and answer ("So the officer told you . . . ?"), it is likely that the jury, in order to believe that Weeks' nickname was Gato, would have had to accept as true the out-of-court assertion of an unidentified "officer." The questioning continued, however, and the warden elaborated on his previously vague answer. He stated that he had heard both a guard and other inmates "use" the nickname. The jury could infer that the warden had personal knowledge of the nickname, knowledge acquired as people often acquire knowledge of names—by hearing other people "use" them in a non-assertive manner. We review a district court's evidentiary rulings for abuse of discretion. In the present context, this review is focused on the question whether the reported oral conduct of a guard and other inmates conveyed assertions. According to the drafters of the Federal Rules of Evidence, the "key" to the definition of "statement" is that "nothing is an assertion unless intended to be one." Moreover, "the rule is so worded as to place the burden upon the party claiming that the intention existed; ambiguous and doubtful cases will be resolved against him and in favor of admissibility." Fed. R. Evid. 801(a) Advisory Committee's Note. The district court implicitly ruled that Weeks did not meet his burden. Given our analysis above, the court did not abuse its discretion by admitting the testimony.

For the foregoing reasons, we affirm the judgment of the district court and sustain Weeks' convictions. Affirmed.

LEGAL ANALYSIS AND WRITING 12.3

The following questions are based on the *How to Brief a Legal Case* format shown in the Appendix. Use this format to answer the following questions:

1. Summarize the facts in the previous case.
2. What is the legal issue?
3. What did the appellate court decide?
4. Why did the court decide this way?
5. Do you agree with the court's reasoning? Explain why or why not.

LEGAL RESEARCH USING THE INTERNET SKILLS 12.3

Try to find and read this case online! Check out one of the legal research web sites below, go to the federal circuit for this court decision, and use their "Search" feature to find this case. In the "Search" field, enter the cite or case name. If you have access to Westlaw or Lexis, try to find this case using one of these legal search sites.

1. U.S. Courts Site with Links to All Circuit Courts of Appeal (http://www.uscourts.gov/links.html)
2. National Center for State Courts—State and Federal Court Web Sites (http://www.ncsconline.org/D_kis/info_court_web_sites.html#federal)
3. FindLaw (http://guide.lp.findlaw.com/casecode/)

Entrapment in Mexico?

In the following case from Texas, the defendant says that he was entrapped and wants to offer statements by a government informant as evidence of his inducement by the government to commit a crime. The appellate court says that statements not offered as an assertion of a fact but, rather, as the fact of an assertion are not hearsay. Does this make sense? Read on to find out more about what statements are or are not hearsay.

CASE

United States v. Cantu

876 F.2d 1134 (5th Cir. 1989).

Appeal from the United States District Court for the Southern District of Texas.

[Jose Cantu was convicted of importing heroin and possession of heroin with intent to distribute. He appeals, arguing that the trial court erred by excluding statements made to him by a government informant which Cantu proposed to offer in support of his defense of entrapment.

Government's Case:

Raul Santander and Juan Renteria worked with the Drug Enforcement Administration (DEA) as paid confidential informants. Renteria testified as a government witness at Cantu's trial. Santander was not called to testify because he was incarcerated in Mexico at the time of trial. Renteria testified that he met Cantu in Reynosa, Mexico in early December of 1987. Renteria and Santander were driving their car down the street when Cantu signaled them that their engine was smoking. Cantu offered to supply Renteria with 12 ounces of heroin. After this meeting Renteria met DEA agent Mario Alvarez at an apartment in McAllen, Texas, where it was decided that Renteria would arrange a buy with Cantu. Later, Renteria returned to Mexico to secure a sample of heroin from Cantu and arrange a buy. Cantu suggested that the sale take place in McAllen, Texas at a stereo store owned by his brother. The price of the heroin sample was agreed to at $250–$300. The meeting took place on December 14, 1987 at the stereo store in McAllen. Renteria introduced agents Alvarez and Leo Silva to Cantu. The agents posed as drug buyers. Cantu gave Alvarez a packet containing what tested to be 1.54 grams of 18 percent heroin and received $300. On December 17, 1987 Renteria accompanied Cantu to Monterrey, Mexico and discussed a transaction involving 50 kilograms of cocaine and 5 kilograms

of heroin. On the morning of December 22, 1987 Cantu called and advised that the heroin was available. A short time later agent Silva, posing as a drug buyer, arrived at the stereo store. Negotiations took place in Renteria's vehicle. Silva asked Cantu if he had the heroin. Cantu responded affirmatively and produced a packet of heroin and a knife to cut a sample. The price was agreed to and the arrest signal was given. The packet contained 164.9 grams of 20 percent heroin.

Defendant's Contention:

Cantu intended to testify and offer a defense of entrapment. He made the following proffer for the record: He met Santander in Reynosa when his car broke down and Santander offered him a ride home; they went to a restaurant where Santander offered to sell him cocaine and marihuana; Cantu demurred and Santander asked Cantu to locate a "client" for him. Santander made similar repeated requests over the telephone. Santander introduced Cantu to Renteria who also tried to get Cantu to make contact with customers. Santander wanted Cantu's help because "Christmas was coming and he [Santander] didn't want to spend it without money." A woman named Juanita, frequently present with Santander, provided the sample Cantu sold to agent Alvarez.

Trial Court:

On the second day of trial the government filed a motion in limine asking the trial court "to prohibit all defense counsel and all defense witnesses from making any statements or arguments regarding, or raising any questions regarding, or behavior which might be attributed to Santander, an individual who has not testified in this action, and who will not be called as a witness by the United States." The court granted this motion over Cantu's objection. At trial Cantu testified at length, including some of the statements contained in his proffer, but he could not testify about Santander's alleged persistence in trying to get him to secure customers for his illicit drug activities. That testimony was disallowed as hearsay. The trial court reasoned:

> [In] order to show [Cantu's] state of mind you have to prove the truth that all these statements were being made. And whether they were being made is really important—whether they were being truthfully made is really important . . . . [Whether] he was really being harassed, and all these other things is important. And it does become important to test their veracity and whether they were actually made, and there's no way to test that. And there's a big incentive on the part of the defendant to make these statements, and to say that these things were said, and there's no way to test that. So, the trustworthiness bothers this Court.]

Politz, Circuit Judge, delivered the opinion of the appellate court.

. . . .

1. Hearsay

The Federal Rules of Evidence define hearsay as "a statement, other than one made by the declarant while testifying at trial or hearing, offered in evidence to prove the truth of the matter asserted." Fed. R. Evid. 801(c). If the significance of a statement "lies solely in the fact that it was made," rather than in the veracity of the out-of-court declarant's assertion, the statement is not hearsay because it is not offered to prove the truth of the matter asserted.

Cantu, claiming an entrapment defense, offered Santander's statements as evidence of his inducement by the government to commit a crime. The defense of entrapment requires evidence of government inducement to act criminally and a lack of predisposition to engage in criminal conduct prior to contact with the government's agents.

Santander's statements were offered as evidence of Cantu's state of mind, bearing directly on his entrapment defense. Thus, the significance of the statements lies solely in the fact that they were made; the truth of the statements is irrelevant for that purpose. The trial court erred in concluding that the proffered statements were hearsay.

As we understand the proffer and Cantu's explanation, he sought to testify about Santander's persistence and his efforts to resist Santander's blandishments. The statements Santander allegedly made were not offered to prove that Santander really wanted Cantu to get drug customers but, rather, to prove that he made the statements. The statements were not offered as an assertion of a fact but, rather, as the fact of an assertion. As such the statements were not hearsay.

The trial court's concern over the trustworthiness of Cantu's testimony was misplaced. Cantu's credibility, like the testimony of any witness, was subject to the crucible of cross-examination and was within the exclusive province of the jury. The veracity of a claim that certain statements were made was subject to evaluation like any other testimony presented at trial. That evaluation was for the jury.

The trial court's erroneous exclusion of statements made by Santander deprived Cantu of a critical element of his entrapment defense. Cantu was unable to offer his explanation to the jury, for whatever credit the jury might have assessed that Santander initiated the subject of drugs during their first encounter and persistently harassed him to find buyers thereafter. Moreover, the restriction on Cantu's testimony arguably caused it to lack coherence and continuity. The error was not harmless.

The convictions are Reversed and the matter is Remanded for retrial.

LEGAL ANALYSIS AND WRITING 12.4

The following questions are based on the *How to Brief a Legal Case* format shown in the Appendix. Use this format to answer the following questions:

1. Summarize the facts in the previous case.
2. What is the legal issue?
3. What did the appellate court decide?
4. Why did the court decide this way?
5. Do you agree with the court's reasoning? Explain why or why not.

LEGAL RESEARCH USING THE INTERNET SKILLS 12.4

Try to find this case or a reference to it online! Check out one of the legal research web sites below, go to the federal circuit for this court decision, and use their "Search" feature to find this case or cases that refer to it. In the "Search" field, enter the cite or case name. If you have access to Westlaw or Lexis, try to find this case using one of these legal search sites.

1. U.S. Courts Site with Links to All Circuit Courts of Appeal (http://www.uscourts.gov/links.html)
2. National Center for State Courts—State and Federal Court Web Sites (http://www.ncsconline.org/D_kis/info_court_web_sites.html#federal)
3. FindLaw (http://guide.lp.findlaw.com/casecode/)

CRITICAL THINKING QUESTIONS 12.2

1. What are the reasons for the hearsay rule?
2. Do you think that the factors to ensure these safeguards are adequate? Why or why not?
3. Assess the strengths and weaknesses of the hearsay rule.
4. What does it mean when it is said, as in *Cantu*, that "statements were not offered as an assertion of a fact, but, rather, as the fact of an assertion?"

STATEMENTS WHICH ARE NOT HEARSAY

There are two areas of statements which, when offered under certain circumstances, do not constitute hearsay when offered in evidence at trial: **prior statement by witness** and **admission by a party-opponent**.

PRIOR STATEMENT BY WITNESS

Under Rule 801(d)(1), a prior statement by a witness will not be hearsay if the declarant testifies at the trial or hearing and is subject to cross-examination concerning the prior statement and any one of three other factors are present:

A. The prior statement was given under oath and subject to penalty of perjury at a trial, hearing, or other proceeding, or in a deposition, and is inconsistent with the declarant's testimony.

An example of this would be when a witness changes his story on the stand from what he testified to previously or from a statement given before under oath, such as at a deposition. The other side may then cross-examine the witness, offering their prior conflicting statement as evidence.

B. The prior statement is consistent with the declarant's testimony but is offered to rebut a charge against the declarant of recent fabrication or improper influence or motive.

If, under cross-examination, an allegation or suggestion is made that the declarant is lying or has an ulterior motive for providing his statement, the side that called the declarant as a witness may offer the declarant's prior statement to rebut the allegation.

Prior Statement by Witness
A statement made by a witness prior to testifying in court.

Admission by a Party-Opponent
A prior statement made by an opposing party to the legal action, or that party's agent or co-conspirator.

C. The prior statement is used for the identification of a person made after perceiving the person.

These prior statements may be from what the witness had said during a lineup being viewed, or comments made after recognizing someone (see Exhibit 12.5).

EXHIBIT 12.5   Prior Statement by Witness Not Hearsay

Wyoming Rules of Evidence
Rule 801(d) Statements Which Are Not Hearsay.—A statement is not hearsay if:

(1) Prior Statement by Witness.—The declarant testifies at the trial or hearing and is subject to cross-examination concerning the statement, and the statement is

(A) inconsistent with his testimony, and, if offered in a criminal proceeding, was given under oath subject to the penalty of perjury at a trial, hearing, or other proceeding, or in a deposition, or

(B) consistent with his testimony and is offered to rebut an express or implied charge against him of recent fabrication or improper influence or motive, or (C) one of identification of a person made after perceiving him . . . .

Are Out-Of-Court Statements by a Four-Year-Old Hearsay?

For over a hundred years, the prevailing common-law rule was that a prior consistent statement introduced to rebut a charge of recent fabrication or motive was admissible if the statement had been made before the alleged fabrication or motive came into being, but inadmissible if made afterward. In the following case, the U.S. Supreme Court decides whether Rule 801(d)(1)(B) adheres to that common-law requirement.

CASE

Tome v. United States
513 U.S. 150 (1995).
[Petitioner Tome was charged with sexually abusing his daughter A. T. when she was four years old. The Government theorized that he committed the assault while A. T. was in his custody and that the crime was disclosed while she was spending vacation time with her mother. The defense countered that the allegations were concocted so A. T. would not be returned to her father, who had primary physical custody. A. T. testified at the trial, and, in order to rebut the implicit charge that her testimony was motivated by a desire to live with her mother, the Government presented six witnesses who recounted out-of-court statements that A. T. made about the alleged assault while she was living with her mother. A. T.'s babysitter recited A. T.'s statement to her on August 22, 1990, that she did not want to return to her father because he "gets drunk and he thinks I'm his wife"; the

babysitter related further details given by A. T. on August 27, 1990, while A. T.'s mother stood outside the room and listened after the mother had been unsuccessful in questioning A. T. herself; the mother recounted what she had heard A. T. tell the babysitter; a social worker recounted details A. T. told her on August 29, 1990 about the assaults; and three pediatricians, Drs. Kuper, Reich, and Spiegel, related A. T.'s statements to them describing how and where she had been touched by Tome. All but A. T.'s statement to Dr. Spiegel implicated Tome.

The District Court admitted the statements under, inter alia, Federal Rule of Evidence 801(d)(1)(B), which provides that prior statements of a witness are not hearsay if they are consistent with the witness's testimony and offered to rebut a charge against the witness of "recent fabrication or improper influence or motive." Tome was convicted, and the Court of Appeals affirmed, adopting the Government's argument that A. T.'s statements were admissible even though they had been made after her alleged motive to fabricate arose. Reasoning that the premotive requirement is a function of relevancy, not the hearsay rules, the court balanced A. T.'s motive to lie against the probative value of one of the statements and determined that the District Court had not erred in admitting the statements.]

Justice Kennedy delivered the opinion of the Court.

Various federal Courts of Appeals are divided over the evidence question presented by this case. At issue is the interpretation of a provision in the Federal Rules of Evidence bearing upon the admissibility of statements, made by a declarant who testifies as a witness, that are consistent with the testimony and are offered to rebut a charge of a "recent fabrication or improper influence or motive." Fed. Rule Evid. 801(d)(1)(B). The question is whether out-of-court consistent statements made after the alleged fabrication, or after the alleged improper influence or motive arose, are admissible under the Rule.

. . . .

II

The prevailing common-law rule for more than a century before adoption of the Federal Rules of Evidence was that a prior consistent statement introduced to rebut a charge of recent fabrication or improper influence or motive was admissible if the statement had been made before the alleged fabrication, influence, or motive came into being, but it was inadmissible if made afterwards. . . . The question is whether Rule 801(d)(1)(B) embodies this temporal requirement. We hold that it does.

A

Rule 801 provides:

(d) Statements Which Are Not Hearsay.—A statement is not hearsay if—

(1) Prior Statement by Witness.—The declarant testifies at the trial or hearing and is subject to cross-examination concerning the statement, and the statement is. . .

(B) consistent with the declarant's testimony and is offered to rebut an express or implied charge against the declarant of recent fabrication or improper influence or motive.

Rule 801 defines prior consistent statements as nonhearsay only if they are offered to rebut a charge

of "recent fabrication or improper influence or motive." Noting the "troublesome" logic of treating a witness's prior consistent statements as hearsay at all (because the declarant is present in court and subject to cross-examination), the Advisory Committee decided to treat those consistent statements, once the preconditions of the Rule were satisfied, as nonhearsay and admissible as substantive evidence, not just to rebut an attack on the witness's credibility. . . .

. . . Prior consistent statements may not be admitted to counter all forms of impeachment or to bolster the witness merely because she has been discredited. In the present context, the question is whether A. T.'s out-of-court statements rebutted the alleged link between her desire to be with her mother and her testimony, not whether they suggested that A. T.'s in-court testimony was true. The Rule speaks of a party rebutting an alleged motive, not bolstering the veracity of the story told. . . . Impeachment by charging that the testimony is a recent fabrication or results from an improper influence or motive is, as a general matter, capable of direct and forceful refutation through introduction of out-of-court consistent statements that predate the alleged fabrication, influence or motive. A consistent statement that predates the motive is a square rebuttal of the charge that the testimony was contrived as a consequence of that motive. By contrast, prior consistent statements carry little rebuttal force when most other types of impeachment are involved.

. . . The underlying theory of the Government's position is that an out-of-court consistent statement, whenever it was made, tends to bolster the testimony of a witness and so tends also to rebut an express or implied charge that the testimony has been the product of an improper influence. Congress could have adopted that rule with ease, providing, for instance, that "a witness's prior consistent statements are admissible whenever relevant to assess the witness's truthfulness or accuracy." The theory would be that, in a broad sense, any prior statement by a witness concerning the disputed issues at trial would have some relevance in assessing the accuracy or truthfulness of the witness's in-court testimony on the same subject. The narrow Rule enacted by Congress, however, cannot be understood to incorporate the Government's theory. . . .

. . . .

D

The case before us illustrates some of the important considerations supporting the Rule as we interpret it, especially in criminal cases. If the Rule were to permit the introduction of prior statements as substantive evidence to rebut every implicit charge that a witness' in-court testimony results from recent fabrication or improper influence or motive, the whole emphasis of the trial could shift to the out-of-court statements, not the in-court ones. The present case illustrates the point. In response to a rather weak charge that A. T.'s testimony was a fabrication created so the child could remain with her mother, the Government was permitted to present a parade of sympathetic and credible witnesses who did no more than recount A. T.'s detailed out-of-court statements to them. Although those statements might have been probative on the question whether the alleged conduct had occurred, they shed but minimal light on whether A. T. had the charged motive to fabricate. At closing argument before the jury, the Government placed great reliance on the prior statements for substantive purposes but did not once seek to use them to rebut the impact of the alleged motive.

We are aware that in some cases it may be difficult to ascertain when a particular fabrication, influence, or motive arose. Yet, as the Government concedes, a majority of common-law courts were performing this task for well over a century, and the Government has presented us with no evidence that those courts, or the judicial circuits that adhere to the rule today, have been unable to make the determination. Even under the Government's hypothesis, moreover, the thing to be rebutted must be identified, so the date of its origin cannot be that much more difficult to ascertain. . . .

III

Courts must be sensitive to the difficulties attendant upon the prosecution of alleged child abusers. In almost all cases a youth is the prosecution's only eyewitness. But "this Court cannot alter evidentiary rules merely because litigants might prefer different rules in a particular class of cases." *United States v. Salerno*, 505 U.S. 317, (1992). When a party seeks to introduce out-of-court statements that contain strong circumstantial indicia of reliability, that are highly probative on the material questions at trial, and that are better than other evidence otherwise available, there is no need to distort the requirements of Rule 801(d)(1)(B). If its requirements are met, Rule 803(24) exists for that eventuality. We intimate no view, however, concerning the admissibility of any of A. T.'s out-of-court statements under that section, or any other evidentiary principle. These matters, and others, are for the Court of Appeals to decide in the first instance.

Our holding is confined to the requirements for admission under Rule 801(d)(1)(B). The Rule permits the introduction of a declarant's consistent out-of-court statements to rebut a charge of recent fabrication or improper influence or motive only when those statements were made before the charged recent fabrication or improper influence or motive. These conditions of admissibility were not established here.

The judgment of the Court of Appeals for the Tenth Circuit is reversed, and the case is remanded for further proceedings consistent with this opinion. It is so ordered.

LEGAL ANALYSIS AND WRITING 12.5

The following questions are based on the *How to Brief a Legal Case* format shown in the Appendix. Use this format to answer the following questions:

1. Summarize the facts in the previous case.
2. What is the legal issue?
3. What did the appellate court decide?
4. Why did the court decide this way?
5. Do you agree with the court's reasoning? Explain why or why not.

LEGAL RESEARCH USING THE INTERNET SKILLS 12.5

Find and read this Supreme Court case online! Was there a dissenting opinion? Concurring opinion? How many justices joined the majority for this decision?

Check out one of the legal research web sites below and use their "Search" feature to find this case. In the "Search" field, enter the cite or case name.

1. FindLaw U.S. Supreme Court Decisions (http://www.findlaw.com/casecode/supreme.html)
2. U.S. Supreme Court (http:/ /www.supremecourtus.gov/)
3. Supreme Court Collection of Cornell Law School (http://supct.law.cornell.edu/supct/)

EVIDENTIARY CHECKLIST 12.4

Prior Statement by Witness

A prior statement by a witness is not hearsay if:

☐ Declarant testifies at trial and is subject to cross-examination AND the statement is one of the following:

☐ Inconsistent with declarant's testimony and given under oath in a deposition or at other legal proceeding, or

☐ Consistent with declarant's testimony and offered to rebut charge of recent fabrication or improper influence or motive, or

☐ One of identification of a person after perceiving the person.

ADMISSION BY A PARTY-OPPONENT

The other area of statements which do not constitute hearsay involves statements made by a party to a legal action, or his agent, and used against that party at trial. It is essentially using statements made by a party against that party at trial under the rationale that said, it should satisfy the trustworthiness concern, because the party can explain it if he chooses (see Exhibit 12.6). To be allowed as an admission by a party-opponent, the statement must be offered against a party in the trial and any one of the following conditions must be met:

1. The prior statement is the party's own statement in either an individual or representative capacity and is being used against that party.

2. The prior statement must be one in which the party has manifested an adoption or belief in its truth.

3. The prior statement was made by a person authorized by the party to make a statement concerning the subject.

4. The prior statement was made by the party's agent concerning a matter within the scope of the agency or employment and made during the existence of the relationship.

5. The prior statement was made by a co-conspirator of a party during the course and in furtherance of the conspiracy.

A common example of an admission by party-opponent is a confession made by a defendant in a criminal action. Generally, any statement or admission made by a party to a civil or criminal action and offered against that party is admissible as long as the witness testifying to the statement is the one to whom the statement or admission was made. For instance, in order to admit an admission or confession made by a defendant to a police officer, it would be necessary to have that police officer testify to the statement made.

The prior statement does not need to have been made by the specific party to the lawsuit (for example, the plaintiff or defendant). It can also be made vicariously, by a partner, agent, or co-conspirator. It is sufficient if the prior statement was made by an agent or employee of the party, as long as that person was either authorized by the party to make the statement, or the statement was made by the agent or employee acting within the scope of the agency or employment. For example, statements of a real estate agent selling land on behalf of the owner to a prospective buyer may be admitted if the owner of the land is a party to a subsequent lawsuit.

EXHIBIT 12.6   Admissions by Party-Opponent Not Hearsay

Utah Rules of Evidence

Rule 801(d) Statements Which Are Not Hearsay.—A statement is not hearsay if:

(2) Admission by Party-Opponent. The statement is offered against a party and is

(A) the party's own statement, in either an individual or a representative capacity, or

(B) a statement of which the party has manifested an adoption or belief in its truth, or

(C) a statement by a person authorized by the party to make a statement concerning the subject, or

(D) a statement by the party's agent or servant concerning a matter within the scope of the agency or employment, made during the existence of the relationship, or

(E) a statement by a co-conspirator of a party during the course and in furtherance of the conspiracy.

Hearsay and Scope of Employment in a Mississippi Accident

A statement is not hearsay if it is offered against a party and was made by the party's agent concerning a matter within the scope of employment. In the following case, the court looks at a statement made by a Burger King employee after a car accident. In the statement, the employee stated that he was on his way to deliver something to his work when the accident occurred. Hearsay or not?

Case Brief #13

CASE

Corley v. Burger King Corp.

56 F.3d 709 (5th Cir. 1995).

Appeal from the United States District Court for the Southern District of Mississippi. D.C.

Per Curiam.

Jerry Smith and Reid Corley filed suit against the Burger King Corporation, alleging that while John LeBlanc, manager of the Bay St. Louis Burger King, was acting within the course and scope of his employment, he was involved in a car wreck with Smith and Corley. The district court found that Smith and Corley could not rely on hearsay to establish that LeBlanc was acting within the course and scope of his employment at the time of the accident. Finding no other evidence suggesting that LeBlanc's actions could be imputed to Burger King, the court granted Burger King's motion for summary judgment. Smith and Corley filed this appeal, and we reverse.

I.

In July 1991, Smith and Corley were traveling on U.S. Highway 90 in Hancock County, Mississippi. Their car was stopped at a red light when it was struck from behind by a car driven by John LeBlanc. Both Smith and Corley testified by affidavit that LeBlanc "stated that he had been at home watching a golf game on television when he got a call that the store he managed needed some CO_2 for their drink machine. He had gotten it and was headed to the store when the wreck happened." LeBlanc also told Smith and Corley that he had looked away from the road in order to look at a McDonald's that was on fire. When he looked back, it was too late.

II.

In order to impute LeBlanc's actions to Burger King, Smith and Corley must show that at the time of the accident, LeBlanc was acting within the scope of his employment. The district court held that "out of court statements made to third parties by employees cannot be used to establish agency under Mississippi law." We find that LeBlanc's statement is not hearsay and,

accordingly, is admissible to defeat Burger King's motion for summary judgment.

> A statement is not hearsay if . . . the statement is offered against a party and is . . . a statement by the party's agent or servant concerning a matter within the scope of the agency or employment, made during the existence of the relationship. Fed. R. Evid. 801(d)(2)(D).

Smith and Corley's testimony regarding LeBlanc's statements at the scene of the accident fall squarely within Rule 801(d)(2)(D). It is undisputed that at the time of the accident LeBlanc was the manager of the Bay St. Louis Burger King. LeBlanc's alleged statement that he was delivering CO_2 to the restaurant concerned "a matter within the scope of the agency or employment." See *Nekolny v. Painter*, 653 F.2d 1164 (7th Cir.1981) ("After the fact of the agency is established, Rule 801(d)(2)(D) requires only that the statement 'concern a matter within the scope of the agency or employment.' ").

III.

For the foregoing reasons, the decision of the district court is Reversed and the case is Remanded for further proceedings.

LEGAL ANALYSIS AND WRITING 12.6

The following questions are based on the *How to Brief a Legal Case* format shown in the Appendix. Use this format to answer the following questions:

1. Summarize the facts in the previous case.

2. What is the legal issue?

3. What did the appellate court decide?

4. Why did the court decide this way?

5. Do you agree with the court's reasoning? Explain why or why not.

LEGAL RESEARCH USING THE INTERNET SKILLS 12.6

Try to find this case or a reference to it online! Check out one of the legal research web sites below, go to the federal circuit for this court decision, and use their "Search" feature to find this case or cases that refer to it. In the "Search" field, enter the cite or case name. If you have access to Westlaw or Lexis, try to find this case using one of these legal search sites.

1. U.S. Courts Site with Links to All Circuit Courts of Appeal (http://www.uscourts.gov/links.html)

2. National Center for State Courts—State and Federal Court Web Sites (http://www.ncsconline.org/D_kis/info_court_web_sites.html#federal)

3. FindLaw (http://guide.lp.findlaw.com/casecode/)

Is a Statement by a Co-Conspirator Hearsay?

A statement is not hearsay if offered against a party and made by a co-conspirator during the course and in furtherance of the conspiracy. In the following case, the U.S. Supreme Court examines two important points. First, are out-of-court statements only presumed unreliable and, if so, can they be rebutted by appropriate proof? Second, must a court look only at the individual pieces of evidence to support a finding of conspiracy, or can a court look at the totality of the evidence?

CASE

Bourjaily v. United States
483 U.S. 171 (1987).

Chief Justice Rehnquist delivered the opinion of the Court.

Federal Rule of Evidence 801(d)(2)(E) provides: "A statement is not hearsay if. . . the statement is offered against a party and is. . . a statement by a co-conspirator of a party during the course and in furtherance of the conspiracy." We granted certiorari to answer. . . questions regarding the admission of statements under Rule 801(d)(2)(E): . . . whether the court must determine by independent evidence that the conspiracy existed and that the defendant and the declarant were members of this conspiracy. . . and. . . whether a court must in each case examine the circumstances of such a statement to determine its reliability.

In May 1984, Clarence Greathouse, an informant working for the Federal Bureau of Investigation (FBI), arranged to sell a kilogram of cocaine to Angelo Lonardo. Lonardo agreed that he would find individuals to distribute the drug. When the sale became imminent, Lonardo stated in a tape-recorded telephone conversation that he had a "gentleman friend" who had some questions to ask about the cocaine. In a subsequent telephone call, Greathouse spoke to the "friend" about the quality of the drug and the price. Greathouse then spoke again with Lonardo, and the two arranged the details of the purchase. They agreed that the sale would take place in a designated hotel parking lot, and Lonardo would transfer the drug from Greathouse's car to the "friend," who would be waiting in the parking lot in his own car. Greathouse proceeded with the transaction as planned, and FBI agents arrested Lonardo and petitioner immediately after Lonardo placed a kilogram of cocaine into petitioner's car in the hotel parking lot. In petitioner's car, the agents found over $20,000 in cash.

Petitioner was charged with conspiring to distribute cocaine, in violation of 21 U.S.C. § 846, and possession of cocaine with intent to distribute, a violation of 21 U.S.C. § 841(a)(1). The Government introduced, over petitioner's objection, Angelo Lonardo's telephone statements regarding the participation of the "friend" in the transaction. The District Court found that, considering the events in the parking lot and Lonardo's statements over the telephone, the Government had established by a preponderance of the evidence that a conspiracy involving Lonardo and petitioner existed, and that Lonardo's statements over the telephone had been made in the course of and in furtherance of the conspiracy. Accordingly, the trial court held that Lonardo's out-of-court statements satisfied Rule 801(d)(2)(E) and were not hearsay. Petitioner was convicted on both counts and sentenced to 15 years. The United States Court of Appeals for the Sixth Circuit affirmed. . . . We affirm.

Before admitting a co-conspirator's statement over an objection that it does not qualify under Rule 801(d)(2)(E), a court must be satisfied that the statement actually falls within the definition of the Rule. There must be evidence that there was a conspiracy involving the declarant and the nonoffering party, and that the statement was made "during the course and in furtherance of the conspiracy."

. . . [P]etitioner. . . challenges the admission of Lonardo's statements. Petitioner argues that in determining whether a conspiracy exists and whether the defendant was a member of it, the court must look only to independent evidence—that is, evidence other than the statements sought to be admitted. . . . Petitioner starts with the proposition that co-conspirators' out-of-court statements are deemed unreliable and are inadmissible, at least until a conspiracy is shown. Since these statements are unreliable, petitioner contends that they should not form any part of the basis for establishing a conspiracy, the very antecedent that renders them admissible.

Petitioner's theory ignores two simple facts of evidentiary life. First, out-of-court statements are only presumed unreliable. The presumption may be rebutted by appropriate proof. Second, individual pieces of evidence, insufficient in themselves to prove a point, may in cumulation prove it. The sum of an evidentiary presentation may well be greater than its constituent parts. Taken together, these two propositions demonstrate that a piece of evidence, unreliable in isolation, may become quite probative when corroborated by other evidence . . . . Even if out-of-court declarations by co-conspirators are presumptively unreliable, trial courts must be permitted to evaluate these statements for their evidentiary worth as revealed by the particular circumstances of the case. Courts often act as factfinders, and there is no reason to believe that courts are any less able to properly recognize the probative value of evidence in this particular area. The party opposing admission has an adequate incentive to point out the shortcomings in such evidence before the trial court finds the preliminary facts. If the opposing party is unsuccessful in keeping the evidence from the factfinder, he still has the opportunity to attack the probative value of the evidence as it relates to the substantive issue in the case.

We think that there is little doubt that a co-conspirator's statements could themselves be probative of the existence of a conspiracy and the participation of both the defendant and the declarant in the conspiracy. Petitioner's case presents a paradigm. The out-of-co of Lonardo indicated that Lonardo v a conspiracy with a "friend." The st cated that the friend had agreed wi buy a kilogram of cocaine and to dis statements also revealed that the friend would be at the hotel parking lot, in his car, and would accept the cocaine from Greathouse's car after Greathouse gave Lonardo the keys. Each one of Lonardo's statements may itself be unreliable, but taken as a whole, the entire conversation between Lonardo and Greathouse was corroborated by independent evidence. The friend, who turned out to be petitioner, showed up at the prearranged spot at the prearranged time. He picked up the cocaine, and a significant sum of money was found in his car. On these facts, the trial court concluded, in our view correctly, that the Government had established the existence of a conspiracy and petitioner's participation in it.

We need not decide in this case whether the courts below could have relied solely upon Lonardo's hearsay statements to determine that a conspiracy had been established by a preponderance of the evidence. . . . It is sufficient for today to hold that a court, in making a preliminary factual determination under Rule 801(d)(2)(E), may examine the hearsay statements sought to be admitted. . . . The courts below properly considered the statements of Lonardo and the subsequent events in finding that the Government had established by a preponderance of the evidence that Lonardo was involved in a conspiracy with petitioner. . . . We hold that Lonardo's out-of-court statements were properly admitted against petitioner.

. . . .

The judgment of the Court of Appeals is Affirmed.

LEGAL ANALYSIS AND WRITING 12.7

The following questions are based on the *How to Brief a Legal Case* format shown in the Appendix. Use this format to answer the following questions:

1. Summarize the facts in the previous case.
2. What is the legal issue?
3. What did the appellate court decide?
4. Why did the court decide this way?
5. Do you agree with the court's reasoning? Explain why or why not.

LEGAL RESEARCH USING THE INTERNET SKILLS 12.7

Find and read this Supreme Court case online! Check out one of the legal research web sites below and use their "Search" feature to find this case. In the "Search" field, enter the cite or case name.

1. FindLaw U.S. Supreme Court Decisions (http://www.findlaw.com/casecode/supreme.html)
2. U.S. Supreme Court (http://www.supremecourtus.gov/)
3. Supreme Court Collection of Cornell Law School (http://supct.law.cornell.edu/supct/)

EVIDENTIARY CHECKLIST 12.5

Admission of a Party-Opponent

An admission of a party-opponent is not hearsay if:

☐ The statement is offered against the party, AND is:
☐ The party's own statement, or
☐ A statement the party has adopted as true, or
☐ A statement by a person authorized by the party to make a statement concerning the subject, or
☐ A statement by the party's agent or servant concerning a matter within the scope of the agency or employment, or
☐ A statement by a co-conspirator of a party during the course and in furtherance of the conspiracy.

Hearsay Within Hearsay
Multiple hearsay; where there are two or more parts to a declarant's statement, each must be examined separately to determine if it falls within the hearsay rule or one of its exceptions.

HEARSAY WITHIN HEARSAY

Mississippi Rule of Evidence 805 reflects the rule governing the admissibility of multiple hearsay, or what is called **hearsay within hearsay**. This is when there are more than two parts to declarant's statement, each of which must be examined separately to determine if it falls within the hearsay rule or one of its exceptions (see Exhibit 12.7). Multiple hearsay is not excluded under the hearsay rule if each part of the combined statements conforms with an exception to the hearsay rule provided in these rules.[11]

EXHIBIT 12.7   Hearsay Within Hearsay

Ohio Rules of Evidence
Rule 805. Hearsay Within Hearsay.
   Hearsay included within hearsay is not excluded under the hearsay rule if each part of the combined statements conforms with an exception to the hearsay rule provided in these rules.

EFFECT OF HEARSAY OBJECTION

A hearsay objection must be specific and timely. An objection may be to the form of the question, as in "What did Harry say to you?" It may also be presented after the witness begins to answer: "Joe told me that . . . . " When the answer of the witness contains any of the damaging hearsay, the opposing party may "move to strike" the answer from the trial record.

Failure to Object

Failure to object to hearsay testimony results in the admission of the hearsay evidence.

CRITICAL THINKING QUESTIONS 12.3

1. When can prior statements of a witness be used and why do the rules allow this?

2. In the *Tome* case, the Court said that prior statements could be admitted only when made *before* the charged "recent fabrication or improper influence or motive." How would a trial court go about determining this?

3. What is the reasoning behind allowing statements by a party-opponent?

4. In what types of cases would statements or admissions by a party-opponent be important? Be specific in naming the type of case, area of law, and why the opinion might be important.

5. In the *Corley* case, why would it be hearsay if Corley heard LeBlanc make the statement, and Corley was available to testify in court under cross-examination that "I heard LeBlanc say . . . ?"

SUMMARY

Hearsay is a statement made out-of-court and offered in court as evidence to prove the truth of the assertion made in the statement: "He said . . . she said." The hearsay rule states that hearsay is not admissible unless provided by exceptions in the Rules of Evidence. The reason for a hearsay rule is primarily to protect the jury from hearing unreliable evidence. Secondhand or out-of-court statements are more relevant and probative if the person making them was telling the truth and could accurately recall and relate the assertion made in the statement. When the declarant is not in court to testify, there is little way for the trier of fact to determine the truthfulness of the statements made.

Hearsay can come in various forms, including oral statements, writings, and assertive conduct, such as someone who testifies that he or she saw another "nod his head in the affirmative." The test for determining hearsay is whether a statement was made out-of-court and is being offered in order to prove what is being asserted in the statement. If so, it is hearsay. However, if the statement is being offered to prove something other than what is being asserted in the statement, it is not hearsay. This is a two-prong test: Is it an out-of-court statement and is the statement offered to prove the truth of the matter asserted? There are two areas of statements made out-of-court that do not constitute hearsay when offered into evidence at trial: prior statement by witness and admission by party-opponent.

Admission by a Party- Opponent	Hearsay	Out-of-Court Statement
	Hearsay Rule	Prior Statement by Witness
Assertion	Hearsay Within Hearsay	Statement
Declarant	Nonverbal Conduct	Truth of Matter Asserted

LEARNING OUTCOMES AND PRACTICE SKILLS CHECKLIST

☐ Learning Outcomes

After completing your reading, questions, and exercises, you should be able to demonstrate a better understanding of the learning concepts by answering the following questions:

1. Explain the hearsay rule.
2. Describe the reasons or purpose behind the hearsay rule.
3. Identify the two historical cases that influenced the development of hearsay rules.
4. Define hearsay.
5. Discuss the meaning of *statement* within the definition of hearsay.
6. Distinguish the meaning of *oral or written assertion* with *nonverbal conduct* and give examples of how each would be used to communicate a statement.
7. Explain who a declarant is and distinguish from a witness giving testimony on the stand.
8. Describe the two-prong test for determining hearsay and give examples.
9. Define *truth of the matter asserted* and discuss how this is used in determining hearsay.
10. Identify the two classifications of statements which are not hearsay.
11. Describe the three situations when a prior statement by a witness would not constitute hearsay. Give examples.
12. Explain what an admission by a party-opponent is and when this type of statement would not constitute hearsay. Give examples.

☐ Practice Skills

In addition to understanding the learning concepts, practice what you have learned through applications using critical thinking, legal analysis and writing, legal research, and advocacy skills, including:

Critical Thinking

1. Why do we have rules that govern hearsay?
2. Do you believe that the current rules provide adequate safeguards for this process?
3. What public policy issues or considerations do you think might be behind these rules?
4. If it were up to you, would you keep the rules governing hearsay as they are, delete them, narrow them, or expand them? Explain your reasoning.
5. How do these rules influence the gathering of evidence or preparing of witnesses?

Legal Analysis and Writing

Analyze the following rules and cases by summarizing their holdings, explaining their significance, and assessing any issue that might arise in their application.

1. Rule 801(a).
2. Rule 801(c).
3. Rule 801(d)(1).
4. Rule 801(d)(2).
5. Rule 802.
6. *Tome v. United States.*
7. *Corley v. Burger King Corp.*
8. *Bourjaily v. United States.*

Legal Research Using the Internet

1. Find the drafters' comments to the Federal Rules of Evidence on the Internet and see if any issues were raised in the proposing of the rules covered in this chapter.
2. Find your state's rules of evidence regarding hearsay and the concepts covered in this chapter. Compare and contrast with the federal and/or modern rules, and some of the state rules listed in this chapter.
3. Find out if your state appellate court posts their case decisions on the Internet. If so, find a case that illustrates an issue or rule discussed in this chapter. If your state decisions are not on the Internet, go instead to the web site for the U.S. Circuit Court of Appeals in your circuit, or search the U.S. Supreme Court decisions.

PRACTICE APPLICATION 12.1

Defendant is charged with falsely spreading a bomb scare at his school. At trial,

1. Prosecution offers a witness, Marge, who testifies that she was standing in the school hallway when she heard a student walking by say that a bomb had been planted and it would go off at noon.
2. When prosecution asks Marge on the stand if the person who made that statement is in the courtroom, she nods her head and points to defendant.
3. Defense offers a prior statement given by Marge to police officers at the school that she did not clearly see who made the statement in the hallway about the bomb being planted.
4. Defense offers a witness, Sam, who testifies that he was in the school hallway when Marge turned to him and said that she had just heard a student say a bomb had been planted in the school.
5. Sam further testifies that when he asked Marge which student made the statement, Marge just "stared blankly, her jaw dropped, and she shook her head."

Use the format shown in the Appendix for the *IRAC Method of Legal Analysis* and the readings, rules, and cases discussed in this chapter to analyze the above case problems and determine whether the evidence in each example is hearsay. Write a memo giving your analysis, reasoning, and conclusions.

ADVOCACY AND COMMUNICATION SKILLS 12.1

Form teams from small groups of no more than 3–4 each. Prepare a set of questions to ask the witnesses in the above *Practice Application* and conduct a direct, cross, redirect, or recross-examination of the witness. During each line of questioning, the opposing team should be prepared to object, if needed, using objections from earlier readings. Use a different team member for each examination:

1. Plaintiff team will conduct a direct exam of no more than 5 minutes.
2. Defense team will conduct a cross-exam of no more than 5 minutes.
3. Plaintiff will have 3 minutes to redirect.
4. Defense will have 3 minutes to recross.

WEB SITES

Federal Rules of Evidence
http://www.law.cornell.edu/rules/fre/overview.html
FindLaw
http://www.findlaw.com
FindLaw
http://guide.lp.findlaw.com/casecode/
FindLaw U.S. Supreme Court Decisions
http://www.findlaw.com/casecode/supreme.html
Guide to State Rules of Evidence
http://expertpages.com/state_rules_of_evidence.htm
List of State Laws from Legal Information Institute of Cornell Law School

http://www.law.cornell.edu/states/listing.html
National Center for State Courts—State and Federal Court Web Sites
http://www.ncsconline.org/D_kis/info_court_web_sites.html#federal
Supreme Court Collection of Cornell Law School
http://supct.law.cornell.edu/supct/
U.S. Courts Site with Links to All Circuit Courts of Appeal
http://www.uscourts.gov/links.html
U.S. Supreme Court
http://www.supremecourtus.gov/

ENDNOTES

1. *United States v. Rodriguez-Pando*, 841 F.2d 1014 (10th Cir. 1988). McKay, Circuit Judge, dissenting.
2. See, for example, Fed. R. Evid. 802.
3. See, for example, *Utah Rules of Evidence*, URE 803(5). Recorded Recollection.
4. *1 Jardine's Crim. Trials 418* (1832).
5. *Bushel's Case*, 1670.
6. *California v. Green*, 399 U.S. 149, 158 (1970).
7. *Wyoming Rules of Evidence*, W.R.E. 801(c).
8. N.D.R.Ev. 801(b). Declarant.
9. Alaska R. Evid. 801(a). Statement.
10. *United States v. Cantu*, 876 F.2d 1134 (5th Cir. 1989).
11. See *Mississippi Rules of Evidence*, M.R.E. 805.

EXCEPTIONS TO THE HEARSAY RULE

"Reliability can be inferred without more in a case where the evidence falls within a firmly rooted hearsay exception. In other cases, the evidence must be excluded, at least absent a showing of particularized guarantees of trustworthiness."

— *Ohio v. Roberts, 448. U.S. 56 (1980)*

LEARNING OUTCOMES

In this chapter, you will learn about the following legal concepts:

- Exceptions to the Hearsay Rule

- Exceptions to the Hearsay Rule When Availability of Declarant Is Immaterial

- Declarant Unavailable to Testify

- Exceptions to the Hearsay Rule When Declarant Unavailable

- Catch-All Exception

INTRODUCTION

Hearsay is excluded from evidence because of the problems in establishing veracity and reliability. When a statement is made out of court or the person who originally made the statement is not testifying, the trier of fact is unable to assess the credibility and trustworthiness of the evidence. Sometimes, the nature of a statement or circumstances surrounding secondhand information is sufficient to meet the reliability standard. These instances make up the many exceptions of the hearsay rule. In this chapter, we will examine those exceptions and the issues surrounding them.

EXCEPTIONS TO THE HEARSAY RULE

As we discussed earlier, one of the primary reasons for the hearsay rule is to protect the jury from hearing unreliable out-of-court statements as evidence. There are, however, exceptions that the courts, over the years, have found to be as reliable as any in-court testimony offered directly by the declarant as a witness. Courts will allow these exceptions if the circumstances surrounding the out-of-court statements are sufficiently trustworthy to overcome the presumption of unreliability.

Exceptions Classified by Availability of Declarant

Declarant
Person who makes a statement.

These exceptions are divided into two categories according to their degree of reliability: when *availability of the declarant is immaterial* and when the *declarant is unavailable* to testify. Under the modern and Federal Rules of Evidence, Rules 803 and 804 are usually designated to contain these categories of exceptions to the hearsay rule. Rule 803 sets forth exceptions that are reliable enough on their own to justify admission of the statement as evidence even if the **declarant** is available to testify. Rule 804 contains exceptions reliable enough to be admitted, but only when declarant's direct testimony is unavailable. Commenting on why these exceptions are divided into the availability or unavailability of declarant, a New York court stated:

> A fundamental precept of the law of hearsay is that certain exceptions require that the proponent of the evidence prove the declarant's unavailability as a witness at trial, while other exceptions treat availability as immaterial.... Neither this Court nor courts of other jurisdictions have fashioned a doctrinal distinction to classify which exceptions to the hearsay rule should require the declarant's unavailability as a condition for admissibility. Rather, that factor and the particular exceptions to which it adheres have developed on the typical case-by-case basis. The drafters of the Federal Rules of Evidence, for example, placed exceptions into the "unavailability-needed" category when, in their judgment, the character of the hearsay was not sufficiently or inherently trustworthy to otherwise receive the evidence. As to the alternative "availability-immaterial" category, Professor McCormick suggests that some exceptions are placed into that grouping because those hearsay statements are by their nature at least as trustworthy as live testimony.[1]

Even With Exception, Hearsay May Not Be Admitted

It is important to remember that an exception to the hearsay rule does not by itself guarantee that the statement will be admitted. It must still satisfy the other evidentiary limitations and exclusionary rules, including relevance, authentication, opinion, privilege, and the best evidence rule, to name a few. In criminal actions, hearsay must also pass Fourth Amendment protections against unreasonable search and seizure, Fifth Amendment limitations on self-incrimination, and the Sixth Amendment right to confrontation and due process.

EXCEPTIONS TO THE HEARSAY RULE WHEN AVAILABILITY OF DECLARANT IS IMMATERIAL

The first major group of exceptions to the hearsay rule occurs when the availability of the declarant is not important. Rule 803 lists 23 such exceptions (see Exhibit 13.1).

EXHIBIT 13.1   Hearsay Exceptions—Availability of Declarant Immaterial

Rule 803. The following are not excluded by the hearsay rule, even though the declarant is available as a witness:

(1) Present Sense Impression

(2) Excited Utterance

(3) Then Existing Mental, Emotional, or Physical Condition

(4) Statements for Purposes of Medical Diagnosis or Treatment

(5) Recorded Recollection

(6) Records of Regularly Conducted Activity

(7) Absence of Entry in Records Kept in Accordance with the Provisions of Paragraph (6)

(8) Public Records and Reports

(9) Records of Vital Statistics

(10) Absence of Public Record or Entry

(11) Records of Religious Organizations

(12) Marriage, Baptismal, and Similar Certificates

(13) Family Records

(14) Records of Documents Affecting an Interest in Property

(15) Statements in Documents Affecting an Interest in Property

(16) Statements in Ancient Documents

(17) Market Reports, Commercial Publications

(18) Learned Treatises

(19) Reputation Concerning Personal or Family History

(20) Reputation Concerning Boundaries or General History

(21) Reputation as to Character

(22) Judgment of Previous Conviction

(23) Judgment as to Personal, Family, or General History, or Boundaries

---

These exceptions can be grouped into four general areas:

A. STATEMENTS

B. RECORDS AND REPORTS

C. REPUTATION

D. JUDGMENTS

Res Gestae
From the Latin, meaning "things done." Looks at a statement made in relation to the surrounding circumstances and the spontaneity involved.

State of Mind
Any range of thoughts, emotions, motives, or mental condition underlying a statement made.

A. Statement Exceptions

Rule 803(1)–(4) deals with out-of-court statements made under circumstances that provide the necessary elements of reliability and trustworthiness (see Exhibit 13.2). These were referred to as **res gestae** at common law. Res gestae, which means "things done," looked at the statement made in relation to the surrounding circumstances and the spontaneity involved. The rationale was that the more spontaneous the statement in relation to the event perceived, the more trustworthy it would be. Generally, the statements dealt with the declarant's **state of mind** at the time of the statement.

EXHIBIT 13.2   Statement Exceptions to the Hearsay Rule

The following are not excluded by the hearsay rule, even though the declarant is available as a witness:

Rule 803. Hearsay Exceptions—Availability of Declarant Immaterial.

(1) Present Sense Impression

(2) Excited Utterance

(3) Then Existing Mental, Emotional, or Physical Condition

(4) Statements for Purposes of Medical Diagnosis or Treatment

---

Present Sense Impression

Present Sense Impression
Statement describing or explaining an event or condition made while the declarant was perceiving the event or condition, or immediately thereafter.

Contemporaneous Declarations
Also referred to as a *present sense impression*, a statement describing or explaining an event or condition made while the declarant was perceiving the event or condition, or immediately thereafter.

Alaska Rule 803(1) reflects the modern definition of a **present sense impression** as a statement describing or explaining an event or condition made while the declarant was perceiving the event or condition, or immediately thereafter. This exception is founded on the theory that if a comment or statement is made at the same time as perceiving an event, there is less chance of a more considered and calculating response. The reliability of the statement is in the nature of its spontaneity.[2]

Present sense impression is also called **contemporaneous declarations**, and was referred to as one of the res gestae statements at common law. Dee testifying that she heard Bob say, "Look, that blue car ran the stop sign!" is a present sense impression. Another example would be a person who calls the police and says, "I see someone breaking into a car."

How Presented In Court.   The person who heard the declaration testifies to statements pertaining to present sense impressions or res gestae. For example, Dee testifies that she heard Bob say, "I feel really bad today."

Spontaneous
An immediate action or reaction without time for reflection.

Reflective Thought
Time taken for careful and considered thinking.

Spontaneous Statements versus Time for Reflection.   Whenever state of mind exceptions arise, one important question will be whether the statement was really **spontaneous** or whether there was time for **reflective thought**. State of mind and spontaneous statements must have been made while declarant was perceiving the event or immediately thereafter (see Exhibit 13.3). The reasoning is that there is little time for reflection and therefore fabrication if a statement is given spontaneously or at the time an

---

Practice Tip 13.1

Spontaneity versus Reflective Thought

When preparing a case to establish whether a statement qualifies as a present sense impression exception to the hearsay rule, determine the time lag between when the event occurred and when the statement was made. The key to qualifying under this exception is that the statement was made during or immediately after declarant perceived the event.

General Rule: *As time lag increases, spontaneity decreases, allowing more time for reflection and possible fabrication or memory lapse.*

EXHIBIT 13.3   Comparison of Rules for State of Mind Exceptions

New Jersey Rules of Evidence

Rule 803(c)(1). Present Sense Impression. A statement of observation, description or explanation of an event or condition made while or immediately after the declarant was perceiving the event or condition and without opportunity to deliberate or fabricate.

Louisiana Code of Evidence

Art. 801.D.(4). Things Said or Done. The statements are events speaking for themselves under the immediate pressure of the occurrence, through the instructive, impulsive and spontaneous words and acts of the participants, and not the words of the participants when narrating the events, and which are necessary incidents of the criminal act, or immediate concomitants of it, or form in conjunction with it one continuous transaction.

Kansas Statutes

Section 60-460(d). Contemporaneous Statements and Statements Admissible on Ground of Necessity Generally.

A statement which the judge finds was made (1) while the declarant was perceiving the event or condition which the statement narrates, describes or explains, (2) while the declarant was under the stress of a nervous excitement caused by such perception or (3) if the declarant is unavailable as a witness, by the declarant at a time when the matter had been recently perceived by the declarant and while the declarant's recollection was clear and was made in good faith prior to the commencement of the action and with no incentive to falsify or to distort.

---

event is perceived. The general rule is that as time lag increases, spontaneity decreases and there is more time for reflection and possible fabrication or memory lapse.

Excited Utterance

A favorite exception to the hearsay rule, especially in accident and criminal cases, is the **excited utterance** (see Exhibit 13.4). Oklahoma defines an excited utterance as a statement relating to a startling event or condition made while declarant was under the stress of excitement caused by the event or condition.[3] To be admitted, most courts require a showing that "at the time of the statement the declarant was under the stress of excitement caused by an external event sufficient to still her reflective faculties and had no opportunity for deliberation."[4]

This exception is also referred to in some states as a **spontaneous declaration** or res gestae statement.

Excited Utterance

Spontaneous Declaration A statement relating to a startling event or condition made while declarant was under the stress of excitement caused by the event or condition.

EXHIBIT 13.4   Exited Utterance Exception to Hearsay Rule

North Dakota Rules of Evidence
Rule 803(2). Excited Utterance. A statement relating to a startling event or condition made while the declarant was under the stress of excitement caused by the event or condition.

CASE

Tyrrell v. Wal-Mart Stores Inc.
97 N.Y. 2d 650 (2001).

While shopping with her husband in a Wal-Mart store, plaintiff slipped and fell on a white, jelly-like liquid. She commenced this personal injury action against Wal-Mart. At trial, her husband sought to testify that immediately after the fall, an unidentified Wal-Mart employee stated, "I told somebody to clean this mess up." Defendant argued that the statement was hearsay and that plaintiff failed to establish the applicability of an exception to the hearsay rule. Plaintiff countered the statement was admissible both because the employee was authorized to direct clean-up of the spill and as part of the res gestae. Supreme Court allowed the testimony, concluding that the statement was an admission that could be used against the employer because it related to a spill and all Wal-Mart employees were authorized to clean up spills. The court further noted the statement was admissible "as part of the res gestae."

On appeal, the Appellate Division held that because "plaintiff failed to establish that the alleged employee had the authority to speak on behalf of defendant," Supreme Court had erred in admitting the statement as an admission against Wal-Mart. However, since the record contained "no evidence to suggest that the statement was anything other than a spontaneous declaration," the Appellate Division—one Justice dissenting—concluded that Supreme Court had properly allowed the testimony. We now reverse.

In the proceedings below, plaintiff did not contest that the statement was hearsay, and argued that hearsay-rule exceptions applied. Accordingly, we assume without deciding that the statement was hearsay. Our law is well settled. The proponent of hearsay evidence must establish the applicability of a hearsay-rule exception. The Appellate Division correctly concluded that plaintiff failed to establish that the unidentified employee was authorized to make the alleged statement; thus, the statement did not constitute an admission binding on the employer. The Appellate Division erred, however, in concluding that the testimony was admissible because there was "no evidence to suggest that the statement was anything other than a spontaneous declaration." That conclusion improperly shifted the burden of establishing the exception to the hearsay rule. Because in this case plaintiff failed to show that at the time of the statement the declarant was under the stress of excitement caused by an external event sufficient to still her reflective faculties and had no opportunity for deliberation, the statement should not have been admitted as a spontaneous declaration.

Order reversed, with costs, and a new trial ordered, in a memorandum.

LEGAL ANALYSIS AND WRITING 13.1

The following questions are based on the *How to Brief a Legal Case* format shown in the Appendix. Use this format to answer the following questions:

1. Summarize the facts in the previous case.
2. What is the legal issue?
3. What did the appellate court decide?
4. Why did the court decide this way?
5. Do you agree with the court's reasoning? Explain why or why not.

Reason for Admitting Excited Utterances.   It is believed that there is little time for reflection and therefore fabrication if a statement is given spontaneously or at the time an event is perceived. In an excited utterance, the emotional state of the declarant plus the spontaneity of his or her statement prevents fabrication and ensures trustworthiness. As the Supreme Court noted, "A statement that has been offered in a moment of excitement—without the opportunity to reflect on the consequences of one's exclamation—may justifiably carry more weight with a trier of fact than a similar statement offered in the relative calm of the courtroom."[5]

To be admitted as an exception, it must be shown that the event was sufficiently startling to produce shock and excitement to a reasonable person, and that the declarant was under the stress of the excitement caused by the event or condition. An example of an excited utterance would be a declarant saying, "I was hit by a rock." Automobile accidents can provide excited utterances. An example would be declarant yelling, "Watch out! That red car is out of control!" Another common example is a victim or witness who makes a statement during a crime in progress. Examples of this might include:

"Oh my God, it's a holdup!"

"Help me, that man just took my purse!"

"I killed him. I didn't mean to."

In one case, a police officer testified that a robbery victim screamed, "That's him," when she saw the juvenile in police custody. The court held this was admissible as an excited utterance.[6] In another case, the declarant, while on the witness stand as an eyewitness to a murder, testified that moments after the shooting, she exclaimed, "Burnis shot Earl!" Even though the witness was also testifying to what she saw, her out-of-court statement was also admitted as an excited utterance.[7]

Spontaneity Requirement.   Under the common law, an excited utterance had to be spontaneous with the "startling event." The modern rules do not require this level of spontaneity, as long as the declarant was still under the "stress of excitement caused by the event" when she made the statement. Often, this will vary depending on the nature of the event. In criminal actions, for example, a statement by a child victim of sexual abuse may be allowed even though it was made some time after the abuse.

Hearsay and the Confrontation Clause

The **Confrontation Clause** is a constitutional protection based on the Sixth Amendment right of a defendant in a criminal proceeding "to be confronted with the witnesses against him."[8] In any criminal case where hearsay exceptions are offered in evidence, especially when the hearsay involves an incriminating statement, a Confrontation Clause issue might be confronted. Courts have long noted that "hearsay rules and the Confrontation Clause are generally designed to protect similar values,"[9] and "stem from the same roots."[10]

In a line of case decisions dating back to 1980,[11] the U.S. Supreme Court has held that "incriminating statements admissible under an exception to the hearsay rule are not admissible under the Confrontation Clause unless the prosecution produces, or demonstrates the unavailability of, the

Confrontation Clause
A constitutional protection based on the Sixth Amendment that provides a defendant the right "to be confronted with the witnesses against him. . ." in a criminal proceeding.

declarant whose statement it wishes to use and unless the statement bears adequate indicia of reliability." The Court has gone on to hold that the "reliability requirement can be met where the statement either falls within a firmly rooted hearsay exception or is supported by a showing of 'particularized guarantees of trustworthiness'."[12] These are established on a case-by-case basis.

In the following Supreme Court case, the statements of a 4-year-old child given hours after being abused are challenged under both the hearsay rule and the Confrontation Clause. In its opinion, the Court upholds the precedent that "where proffered hearsay has sufficient guarantees of reliability to come within a firmly rooted exception to the hearsay rule, the Confrontation Clause is satisfied."[13] The Court also addresses the question of whether, in admitting this evidence, the prosecution must either produce the declarant at trial or the trial court must find that the declarant is unavailable.

CASE

White v. Illinois

502 U.S. 346 (1992).

Chief Justice Rehnquist delivered the opinion of the Court.

In this case, we consider whether the Confrontation Clause of the Sixth Amendment requires that, before a trial court admits testimony under the "spontaneous declaration" and "medical examination" exceptions to the hearsay rule, the prosecution must either produce the declarant at trial or the trial court must find that the declarant is unavailable. The Illinois Appellate Court concluded that such procedures are not constitutionally required. We agree with that conclusion.

Petitioner was convicted by a jury of aggravated criminal sexual assault, residential burglary, and unlawful restraint. The events giving rise to the charges related to the sexual assault of S.G., then four years old. Testimony at the trial established that, in the early morning hours of April 16, 1988, S.G.'s babysitter, Tony DeVore, was awakened by S.G.'s scream. DeVore went to S.G.'s bedroom and witnessed petitioner leaving the room, and petitioner then left the house. DeVore knew petitioner, because petitioner was a friend of S.G.'s mother, Tammy Grigsby. DeVore asked S.G. what had happened. According to DeVore's trial testimony, S.G. stated that petitioner had put his hand over her mouth, choked her, threatened to whip her if she screamed, and had "touch[ed] her in the wrong places." Asked by DeVore to point to where

she had been touched, S.G. identified the vaginal area. Tammy Grigsby, S.G.'s mother, returned home about 30 minutes later. Grigsby testified that her daughter appeared "scared," and a "little hyper." Grigsby proceeded to question her daughter about what had happened. At trial, Grigsby testified that S.G. repeated her claims that petitioner choked and threatened her. Grigsby also testified that S.G. stated that petitioner "put his mouth on her front part." Grigsby also noticed that S.G. had bruises and red marks on her neck that had not been there previously. Grigsby called the police.

Officer Terry Lewis arrived a few minutes later, roughly 45 minutes after S.G.'s scream had first awakened DeVore. Lewis questioned S.G. alone in the kitchen. At trial, Lewis' summary of S.G.'s statement indicated that she had offered essentially the same story as she had first reported to DeVore and to Grigsby, including a statement that petitioner had "used his tongue on her in her private parts." After Lewis concluded his investigation, and approximately four hours after DeVore first heard S.G.'s scream, S.G. was taken to the hospital. She was examined first by Cheryl Reents, an emergency room nurse, and then by Dr. Michael Meinzen. Each testified at trial, and their testimony indicated that, in response to questioning, S.G. again provided an account of events that was essentially identical to the one she had given to DeVore, Grigsby, and Lewis. S.G. never testified at petitioner's trial. The State attempted on two occasions to call her as a witness, but she apparently experienced emotional difficulty on being brought to the courtroom, and in each instance left without testifying. The defense made no attempt to call S.G. as a witness, and the trial court neither made nor was it asked to make a finding that S.G. was unavailable to testify.

Petitioner objected on hearsay grounds to DeVore, Grigsby, Lewis, Reents, and Meinzen being permitted to testify regarding S.G.'s statements describing the assault. The trial court overruled each objection. With respect to DeVore, Grigsby, and Lewis the trial court concluded that the testimony could be permitted pursuant to an Illinois hearsay exception for spontaneous declarations. Petitioner's objections to Reents' and Meinzen's testimony was similarly overruled, based on both the spontaneous declaration exception and an exception for statements made in the course of securing medical treatment.

. . . .

. . . We note first that the evidentiary rationale for permitting hearsay testimony regarding spontaneous declarations and statements made in the course of receiving medical care is that such out-of-court declarations are made in contexts that provide substantial guarantees of their trustworthiness. But those same factors that contribute to the statements' reliability cannot be recaptured even by later in-court testimony. A statement that has been offered in a moment of excitement—without the opportunity to reflect on the consequences of one's exclamation—may justifiably carry more weight with a trier of fact than a similar statement offered in the relative calm of the courtroom. Similarly, a statement made in the course of procuring medical services, where the declarant knows that a false statement may cause misdiagnosis or mistreatment, carries special guarantees of credibility that a trier of fact may not think replicated by courtroom testimony.

. . . [C]ourts have adopted the general rule prohibiting the receipt of hearsay evidence. But where proffered hearsay has sufficient guarantees of reliability to come within a firmly rooted exception to the hearsay rule, the Confrontation Clause is satisfied. We therefore think it clear that the out-of-court statements admitted in this case had substantial probative value, value that could not be duplicated simply by the declarant's later testifying in court. And as we have also noted, a statement that qualifies for admission under a "firmly rooted" hearsay exception is so trustworthy that adversarial testing can be expected to add little to its reliability. . . . We therefore see no basis. . . for excluding from trial, under the aegis of the Confrontation Clause, evidence embraced within such exceptions to the hearsay rule as those for spontaneous declarations and statements made for medical treatment.

. . . .

For the foregoing reasons, the judgment of the Illinois Appellate Court is Affirmed.

LEGAL ANALYSIS AND WRITING 13.2

The following questions are based on the *How to Brief a Legal Case* format shown in the Appendix. Use this format to answer the following questions:

1. Summarize the facts in the previous case.
2. What is the legal issue?
3. What did the appellate court decide?
4. Why did the court decide this way?
5. Do you agree with the court's reasoning? Explain why or why not.

Then Existing Mental, Emotional, or Physical Condition

This exception involves a statement of the declarant's then existing state of mind, emotion, mental, or physical condition. To be admissible, a statement must pertain to a current or "then existing" state of mind. As one court noted, it must "face forward, rather than backward."[14]

LEGAL RESEARCH USING THE INTERNET SKILLS 13.1

Find and read the previous Supreme Court case online! Check out one of the legal research web sites below and use their "Search" feature to find this case. In the "Search" field, enter the cite or case name.

1. FindLaw U.S. Supreme Court Decisions (http://www.findlaw.com/casecode/supreme.html)
2. U.S. Supreme Court (http://www.supremecourtus.gov/)
3. Supreme Court Collection of Cornell Law School (http://supct.law.cornell.edu/supct/)

The reasoning behind the state of mind exception depends on the "contemporaneity of the statement and the unlikelihood of deliberate or conscious misrepresentation."[15] Statements of future intent might also be allowed. In an 1892 case, the Supreme Court held that a trier of fact could conclude from evidence of declarant's state of mind that the declarant or any other person described in the statement acted in conformity with the statement.[16]

An example of this is a witness who testifies that "Joan told me that she was on her way to a meeting with John to settle an argument." This statement would be admissible to show Joan's intent to meet with John and to settle an argument. It could also be offered to show that John intended to meet with Joan.

State of mind may include intent, plan, motive, design, mental feeling, pain, and bodily health. For example, a witness testifies that she heard the declarant say, "I am the son of Sam, and Sam is the devil!" If this statement is being offered to prove declarant's mental condition, it would be admissible. Another example is a witness who testifies that she heard the declarant say, "I'll take this shotgun and kill both of us if you leave me." This statement may not be admissible to prove the possession of the shotgun but may be admissible to prove the declarant's state of mind regarding motive or intent.

The exception does not include a statement of memory or belief to prove the fact remembered or believed. As one court put it, the state of mind exception ". . . does not permit the witness to relate any of the declarant's statements as to why he held the particular state of mind, or what he might have believed that would have induced the state of mind. If the reservation in the text of the rule is to have any effect, it must be understood to narrowly limit those admissible statements to declarations of condition—"I'm scared"—and not belief—"I'm scared because. . . ."[17]

Statements of memory or belief to prove a fact remembered or believed may be admitted if it relates to matters pertaining to declarant's will.

Statements for Purposes of Medical Diagnosis or Treatment

This exception includes statements made for purposes of medical diagnosis or treatment and includes the describing of medical history, or past or present symptoms, pain, or sensations. It usually involves statements made to medical personnel, but can be statements made to anyone. In prior cases, the U.S. Supreme Court has noted that "statements made in the course of receiving medical care . . . are made in contexts that provide substantial guarantees of their trustworthiness."[18] The exception is founded on the theory that reliability will emanate from a patient's desire to receive proper medical diagnosis and treatment. Patients understand that this may not occur unless the patient provides truthful information. As the Court noted in another case, "a statement made in the course of procuring medical services, where the declarant knows that a false statement may cause misdiagnosis or mistreatment, carries special guarantees of credibility that a trier of fact may not think replicated by courtroom testimony."[19]

An example of this exception is an emergency room worker who testifies that declarant stated he was injured after falling from a ladder at work. Another example might be a witness who testifies that "Joe told me that he was going to the doctor because his arm hurt him." Statements by victims of violent crime or domestic violence are often offered as evidence as part of this exception. In the following case, a doctor treats a victim of rape who makes statements to the doctor identifying the assailant and expressing fear for her future safety. In its decision, the court assesses whether statements of "identity" are "reasonably pertinent to diagnosis or treatment" to be admissible.

CASE

United States v. Joe

8 F.3d 1488 (10th Cir. 1993).
Appeal from the United States District Court for the District Of New Mexico.

Tacha, Circuit Judge.

. . . .

Melvin Joe and Julia Joe were married in November 1980. Ms. Joe filed a petition for divorce in August 1991 and the couple separated . . . . On February 23, 1992, Melvin and his brother, Wallace Joe, drank beer continually throughout the morning and afternoon and Melvin passed out in Wallace's truck at approximately two o'clock. Sometime after six o'clock, Melvin drove a Chevrolet blazer belonging to his mother, Edith Joe, to his wife's residence. He knocked on the front door. When no one answered, he kicked open the door and entered the home brandishing an unloaded .22 caliber rifle. Melvin and Julia Joe fought and Melvin became physically abusive. Eventually, with the help of a neighbor, Matilda Washburn, Julia was able to get Melvin to leave the house.

Fearful that Melvin would return, Julia, Ms. Washburn, and one of the Joe children decided to leave the house and go to Ms. Washburn's

home. As they exited, they noticed that Melvin had returned to the Blazer and was circling Julia's house. They stood next to the house for protection. The child, Jessica Joe, eventually ran to Ms. Washburn's house without interference. When Julia and Ms. Washburn tried to run, however, Melvin altered his circular pattern and drove straight at the fleeing Ms. Joe, striking her with the truck. Ms. Washburn went to the aid of the injured and screaming Julia Joe, helping her to the anticipated shelter of a nearby truck bed located in the field between the two houses. The truck bed, which had been completely removed from its frame, rested on four short wooden stumps. Melvin apparently was undeterred by this new obstacle. He turned the Blazer in the direction of the truck bed, and, from a distance of approximately fifty feet, accelerated toward the truck bed, ramming the end of it opposite where the two women were standing. Upon impact, Melvin continued to accelerate, knocking the truck bed off the wooden stumps and pushing it over and onto Julia and Ms. Washburn. Still accelerating, Melvin pushed the truck bed forward another fifty feet, running over the two women.

Julia Joe and Ms. Washburn both died of multiple internal and external injuries caused by blunt force. After kicking Julia's body several times, Melvin put it in the Blazer and drove to a hilly area three miles from the crime scene. Officers later recovered the abandoned Blazer with the keys in the ignition and Julia's body still inside. Two days later, on February 25, 1992, Melvin Joe turned himself in. Joe was indicted for two counts of first-degree murder.

B. Dr. Smoker's testimony

At trial, defense counsel conceded that Melvin Joe had killed the two women. Mr. Joe's defense was that at the time of the killings he was intoxicated and enraged over the pending divorce, thus negating the requisite specific intent to sustain a conviction for first-degree murder. With respect to Joe's intent, the government presented two types of evidence: the circumstances surrounding the murders and the testimony of Dr. Brett Smoker regarding statements made to him by Julia Joe. Dr. Smoker, an Indian Health Service family physician, testified that, eight days before Ms. Joe was killed, he treated her for an alleged rape and that she had identified her assailant as the defendant, Mr. Joe. (We will refer to Ms. Joe's comments regarding the alleged rape and her assailant as the "rape statement.") Dr. Smoker further testified that Ms. Joe stated she was "afraid sometimes" because Mr. Joe suspected her of having an extramarital affair and had threatened to kill her if he caught her with another man. (We will refer to Ms. Joe's comments regarding her fear and the basis for her fear as the "threat statement.")

The trial court admitted Dr. Smoker's testimony over defense counsel's timely objection. . . . The court. . . ruled that the threat and rape statements were admissible under the hearsay exception contained in Fed. R. Evid. 803(3)1, rather than the Rule 803(4) exception proffered by the government. . . . After hearing the evidence, including the testimony of Dr. Smoker, the jury convicted Joe of first-degree murder for killing his wife and second-degree murder for killing Ms. Washburn.

C. Grounds for this appeal

On appeal, Joe asserts the following errors: (1) Dr. Smoker's testimony that Melvin had previously raped and threatened Ms. Joe was inadmissible hearsay evidence. . . .

A. Rule 803(3)

We first address whether the district court properly admitted Dr. Smoker's testimony under Rule 803(3), which excepts from the hearsay rule "[a] statement of the declarant's then existing state of mind, emotion, sensation, or physical condition (such as intent, plan, motive, design, mental feeling, pain, and bodily health), but not including a statement of memory or belief to prove the fact remembered or believed." Fed. R. Evid. 803(3). The court ruled that both the rape statement and the threat statement fell within the Rule 803(3) exception to the hearsay rule.

Rule 803(3) clearly sanctions the admission of a declarant's out-of-court statement concerning her then existing state of mind. With respect to the threat statement, Rule 803(3) therefore would extend to Ms. Joe's statement that she was "afraid sometimes." We disagree with the district court's ruling, however, because Ms. Joe's statement to Dr. Smoker, though indicating her state of mind, also included an assertion of why she was afraid (i.e., because she thought her husband might kill her). This portion of Ms. Joe's statement is clearly a "statement of memory or belief" expressly excluded by the Rule 803(3) exception. This situation is identical to that in *United States v. Cohen*, 631 F.2d 1223 (5th Cir. 1980). In that case, a defendant charged with impersonating a federal officer contended that he lacked the requisite intent because he acted under duress. As evidence of duress, he sought to introduce out-of-court statements he had made relating alleged threats by Galkin, a co-conspirator. In admitting Cohen's out-of-court statement that he was scared but excluding the alleged basis for his fear under Rule 803(3), the Fifth Circuit explained:

> . . . The state-of-mind exception does not permit the witness to relate any of the declarant's statements as to why he held the particular state of mind, or what he might have believed that would have induced the state of mind. If the reservation in the text of the rule is to have any effect, it must be understood to narrowly limit those admissible statements to declarations of condition—"I'm scared"—and not belief—"I'm scared because Galkin threatened me."

Here, Dr. Smoker testified that Ms. Joe said she was afraid of her husband because he had threatened her. Ms. Joe's statement that she was afraid of her husband was admissible under Rule 803(3). The testimony relating Ms. Joe's belief underlying her fear, however, was not admissible under Rule 803(3). Further, we see no grounds for admitting the rape statement under Rule 803(3).

B. Alternative Grounds for Ruling on Dr. Smoker's Testimony

. . . The government argues that, because the rape and threat statements were made by Ms. Joe in the course of her treatment by Dr. Smoker, they are admissible under the exception to the hearsay rule contained in Fed. R. Evid. 803(4). Joe contends, however, that the statements were unrelated to diagnosis and treatment of her rape injuries and therefore not within the ambit of the Rule 803(4) exception. . . .

1. The rape statement

a. Rule 803(4)

Rule 803(4) excepts from the hearsay bar "statements made for purposes of medical diagnosis or treatment and describing medical history, or past or present symptoms, pain, or sensations, or the inception or general character of the cause or external source thereof insofar as reasonably pertinent to diagnosis or treatment." Fed. R. Evid. 803(4). The Rule 803(4) exception to the hearsay rule is founded on a theory of reliability that emanates from the patient's own selfish motive— [to receive effective treatment requires reliable information provided by patient]. The Supreme Court has noted that "statements made in the course of receiving medical care . . . are made in contexts that provide substantial guarantees of their trustworthiness." *White v. Illinois*, 112 S. Ct. 736 (1992). While this guaranty of trustworthiness extends to statements of causation, it does not ordinarily extend to statements regarding fault. Thus, a declarant's statement relating the identity of the person allegedly responsible for her injuries is not ordinarily admissible under Rule 803(4) because statements of identity are not normally thought necessary to promote effective treatment.

Nevertheless, the Fourth, Eighth and Ninth Circuits have held that statements made by a child to a physician which identify the sexual abuser as a member of the family or household are "reason-ably pertinent to diagnosis or treatment" and may therefore be admissible . . . . Unlike the victims in the cases cited above, Ms. Joe was not a child but rather the estranged wife of the alleged sexual abuser. However, the identity of the abuser is reasonably pertinent to treatment in virtually every domestic sexual assault case, even those not involving children. All victims of domestic sexual abuse suffer emotional and psychological injuries, the exact nature and extent of which depend on the identity of the abuser. The physician generally must know who the abuser was in order to render proper treatment because the physician's treatment will necessarily differ when the abuser is a member of the victim's family or household. In the domestic sexual abuse case, for example, the treating physician may recommend special therapy or counseling and instruct the victim to remove herself from the dangerous environment by leaving the home and seeking shelter elsewhere. In short, the domestic sexual abuser's identity is admissible under Rule 803(4) where the abuser has such an intimate relationship with the victim that the abuser's identity becomes "reasonably pertinent" to the victim's proper treatment.

The facts of this case underscore the point. After performing a rape kit test on Ms. Joe, Dr. Smoker asked her several questions relating to her injuries. In answering these questions, Ms. Joe identified her husband, Melvin Joe, as her sexual abuser. Dr. Smoker testified that the identity of the sexual assailant was important for his recommendation regarding Ms. Joe's after-care, including appropriate counseling. Moreover, after discovering her assailant's identity, Dr. Smoker specifically recommended that Ms. Joe seek protection, offering her the number of the Navajo Police Department and referring her to the women's shelter in Shiprock, New Mexico. It is abundantly clear that the statement made by Ms. Joe revealing the identity of her alleged abuser was "reasonably pertinent" to her proper treatment by Dr. Smoker. Thus, we conclude that Dr. Smoker's testimony regarding Ms. Joe's rape statement, which identified Mr. Joe as her assailant, is admissible under Fed. R. Evid. 803(4).

. . . .

We Affirm Joe's conviction. . . .

LEGAL ANALYSIS AND WRITING 13.3

The following questions are based on the *How to Brief a Legal Case* format shown in the Appendix. Use this format to answer the following questions:

1. Summarize the facts in the previous case.
2. What is the legal issue?
3. What did the appellate court decide?
4. Why did the court decide this way?
5. Do you agree with the court's reasoning? Explain why or why not.

LEGAL RESEARCH USING THE INTERNET SKILLS 13.2

Try to find this case or another one that refers to it online! Check out one of the legal research web sites below, go to the federal circuit for this court decision, and use their "Search" feature to find this case or another case that refers to it. In the "Search" field, enter the cite or case name. If you have access to Westlaw or Lexis, try to find this case using one of these legal search sites.

1. U.S. Courts Site with Links to All Circuit Courts of Appeal (http://www.uscourts.gov/links.html)
2. National Center for State Courts—State and Federal Court Web Sites (http://www.ncsconline.org/D_kis/info_court_web_sites.html#federal)
3. FindLaw (http://guide.lp.findlaw.com/casecode/)

CRITICAL THINKING QUESTIONS 13.1

1. What are some reasons for allowing these statement exceptions to the hearsay rule?
2. In what specific types of cases might the admission of these hearsay exceptions be important?
3. Assess the strengths and weaknesses of the statement exceptions to the hearsay rule.
4. In the *Tyrrell v. Wal-Mart Stores* case, the court held that the statement did not qualify as a spontaneous declaration. Would it have been admitted as a present sense impression? Explain why or why not.
5. When might one of the statement exceptions violate the Confrontation Clause, and what can be done in collecting evidence or preparing witnesses to prevent this?

B. Records and Reports Exceptions

The areas of exceptions under records and reports include documents that are regularly kept as part of the normal transaction of business (see Exhibit 13.5). These records may be admitted as proof of the information they contain. The range of exceptions includes not only business records, but records kept and maintained by public officials who have a duty to keep the records. These officials are usually called the "custodians" of the records. Records and reports exceptions are founded on the level of trustworthiness expected as a regular basis for keeping records. For public records, the trustworthiness is intrinsic to the official duty of a declarant to make and keep records in his or her public capacity. These exceptions may be challenged on the basis of lacking this essential trustworthiness element.

EXHIBIT 13.5 Records and Reports Exceptions to the Hearsay Rule

Rule 803. Hearsay Exceptions—Availability of Declarant Immaterial.

- (5) Recorded Recollection
- (6) Records of Regularly Conducted Activity
- (7) Absence of Entry in Records Kept in Accordance with the Provisions of Paragraph(6)
- (8) Public Records and Reports
- (9) Records of Vital Statistics
- (10) Absence of Public Record or Entry
- (11) Records of Religious Organizations
- (12) Marriage, Baptismal, and Similar Certificates
- (13) Family Records
- (14) Records of Documents Affecting an Interest in Property
- (15) Statements in Documents Affecting an Interest in Property
- (16) Statements in Ancient Documents
- (17) Market Reports, Commercial Publications
- (18) Learned Treatises

Recorded Recollection

More commonly referred to as **past recollection recorded**, the **recorded recollection** exception pertains to a writing or record that was made when fresh in the mind of a witness who later cannot recall what was said in order to testify about it (see Exhibit 13.6). The record or document must be shown to have been made or adopted by the witness when the matter was fresh in the witness's memory and to reflect that knowledge correctly. If the witness cannot independently recall the statement without using the record, the record may be read into evidence. However, the witness cannot be cross-examined as to what he remembers. The actual writing will not be received as an exhibit unless offered by an adverse party.

Past Recollection Recorded

Recorded Recollection
Writing or other record made at a time when fresh in the mind of a witness who is later unable to recall what was written when testifying.

EXHIBIT 13.6 Recorded Recollection

Florida Evidence Code
Section 90.803(5). Recorded Recollection. A memorandum or record concerning a matter about which a witness once had knowledge, but now has insufficient recollection to enable the witness to testify fully and accurately, shown to have been made by the witness when the matter was fresh in the witness's memory and to reflect that knowledge correctly. A party may read into evidence a memorandum or record when it is admitted, but no such memorandum or record is admissible as an exhibit unless offered by an adverse party.

An example of this is when a police officer is called to the stand and asked questions about an accident that the officer investigated several years before. If the officer cannot recall anything about the accident, but wrote a report on it at the time, the report may be admitted into evidence and the officer asked to read from it. In order to do this, the party calling the officer must first lay a foundation showing that the officer has no current recollection and the officer's memory is not jogged by seeing the writing. Next, it must be shown that the officer can authenticate the writing as one made or adopted while fresh in the memory of the officer. It also must be shown that the writing reflects the officer's personal knowledge at the time.

Business Records

Records of Regularly Conducted Activity
Any form of records, documents, or data compilation kept in the course of regularly conducted business activities.

This exception deals with **records of regularly conducted activity**. Often called the "**business records exception**," it extends to regularly kept records of all types, even though the person who originally entered the information cannot be identified or found. Requirements include that it was a regularly conducted business activity and the record was the regular practice of the business as shown by the **custodian of the records** or another qualified witness. The term "business" as used in this exception is applied very broadly and includes businesses, organizations, associations, and occupations of every kind, profit or nonprofit.

Business Records Exception
A hearsay exception that allows evidence of regularly kept business records.

Regularly Kept Records.   Regularly kept records can include any form of documents or data compilation that record the activities of a business. Examples of this might include memos, notes or reports kept of business meetings, time sheets, payroll, membership lists, and agendas. A business may take minutes of their regularly scheduled meetings, for example. A time clock or entry log may record when employees come and go at work. To qualify for this exception, the record must be kept in the course of regularly conducted business activities (see Exhibit 13.7).

Custodian of the Records
Someone officially designated at a business or public agency to oversee and maintain records.

What Is Not Admissible?   Records that are made for a special purpose, like pending litigation, would be considered "self-serving" and are not admissible under this exception. Another example of what would not be admitted is a statement given to a police officer and put in the officer's report.

Foundation Needed.   A party offering evidence of business records must first lay a foundation showing that the records were prepared in a timely manner and that the person making or transmitting the information had personal knowledge of the activities recorded. Next, it must show that the record was made in the course of regularly conducted business activity. Finally, it must show that it was the regular practice of that business to record this activity.

EXHIBIT 13.7   Records of Regularly Conducted Activities

Idaho Rules of Evidence
Rule 803(6). Records of Regularly Conducted Activity. A memorandum, report, record, or data compilation, in any form, of acts, events, conditions, opinions, or diagnoses, made at or near the time by, or from information transmitted by, a person with knowledge, if kept in the course of a regularly

(Continued)

EXHIBIT 13.7 Records of Regularly Conducted Activities *Continued*

conducted business activity, and if it was the regular practice of that business activity to make the memorandum, report, record, or data compilation, all as shown by the testimony of the custodian or other qualified witness, unless the source of information or the method or circumstances or preparation indicate lack of trustworthiness. The term "business" as used in this paragraph includes business, institution, association, profession, occupation, and calling of every kind, whether or not conducted for profit.

Practice Tip 13.2

Laying a Foundation for Business Records

Here is an example of questions that might be asked of a witness in laying a foundation to admit business records:

1. *I show you a record of a business meeting dated April 1, 2002 that has been marked as Exhibit #10 in identification.*

2. *Was this record made in the course of your company's regularly conducted business activity?*

3. *Was it the regular practice of your company to make this record?*

4. *Was the record made at or near the time of the meeting?*

5. *Was the record made from information supplied by a person who had personal knowledge of what transpired at the meeting?*

Absence of Entry in Records

This exception is just the opposite side of the business records exception. It provides that when business records are regularly kept, evidence that some business activity is not kept may also be admissible to prove that something did not exist or occur. For example, a business keeps a time clock or log that records when employees are at work. Evidence that there is no record in these records of a certain employee being at work on a particular day would be admissible to prove this. Another example might be the introduction of minutes taken at meetings to show that no meeting was held on a particular date or that someone was not present. A receipt book might show the payment or nonpayment of a bill on a particular date.

Public Records and Reports

This exception includes records prepared by a public official in the performance of his or her official duties (see Exhibit 13.8). Court documents and town or city clerk records are examples. The document is introduced in court as a certified copy of the original document and can be brought by the official custodian or keeper of the record, although his or her presence is not required. Investigative reports by police or other agencies are not included in this.

EXHIBIT 13.8 Public Records and Reports

Wyoming Rules of Evidence
Rule 803(8). Public Records and Reports. Records, reports, statements, or data compilations, in any form, of public offices or agencies, setting forth (A) the activities of the office or agency, or (B) matters observed pursuant to duty imposed by law as to which matters there was a duty to report, excluding,

(Continued)

EXHIBIT 13.8   Public Records and Reports   *Continued*

however, in criminal cases matters observed by police officers and other law enforcement personnel, or (C) in civil actions and proceedings and against the Government in criminal cases, factual findings resulting from an investigation made pursuant to authority granted by law, unless the sources of information or other circumstances indicate lack of trustworthiness.

Records of Vital Statistics

Records of vital statistics are data compilations, in any form, of births, fetal deaths, deaths, or marriages, if the report thereof was made to a public office pursuant to the requirements of law (see Exhibit 13.9).

EXHIBIT 13.9   Absence of Public Record or Entry

Rule 803(10). What Is Allowed. To prove the absence of a record, report, statement, or data compilation, in any form, or the nonoccurrence or nonexistence of a matter of which a record, report, statement, or data compilation, in any form, was regularly made and preserved by a public office or agency, evidence in the form of a certification in accordance with Rule 902, or testimony, that diligent search failed to disclose the record, report, statement, or data compilation, or entry.

YOU BE THE JUDGE 13.1

A Navy training flight took the lives of both pilots on board. The surviving spouses brought a civil action against the airplane manufacturer for negligence. At trial, the defense wants to introduce an investigative report that was conducted after the plane crash by the Navy's Judge Advocate General's office (JAG). The defense also wants to introduce opinions contained in the report by the JAG officer conducting the investigation. These opinions conclude that the cause of the plane crash was pilot error. The plaintiff objects to the introduction of both the report and the opinions on the basis of hearsay.
Would you allow this statement? Why or why not?

LEGAL RESEARCH USING THE INTERNET SKILLS 13.3

Find out how the court ruled on the above *You Be the Judge* problem by reading the Supreme Court decision online! The citation for it is:
   Beech Aircraft Corp. v. Rainey, 488 U.S. 153 (1988).
   Check out one of the legal research web sites below and use their "Search" feature to find this case. In the "Search" field, enter the cite or case name.

1. FindLaw U.S. Supreme Court Decisions (http://www.findlaw.com/casecode/supreme.html)
2. U.S. Supreme Court (http://www.supremecourtus.gov/)
3. Supreme Court Collection of Cornell Law School (http://supct.law.cornell.edu/supct/)

Family and Religious Records

There are several exceptions to the hearsay rule that pertain to family and religious records (see Exhibit 13.10). Records of religious organizations are allowed when they have been regularly kept and relate to personal or family history.[20] Examples of this may include records of births, deaths, marriages, or ancestry kept by religious organizations. Marriage, baptismal, and similar certificates are allowed. These may be from a member of the clergy, public official, or any other person authorized by law or a religious organization to perform the act that was certified.

EXHIBIT 13.10   Family and Religious Records

Rule 803(11). Records of Religious Organizations.

What Is Allowed. Records of births, marriages, divorces, deaths, legitimacy, ancestry, relationship by blood or marriage, or other similar facts of personal or family history, contained in a regularly kept record of a religious organization.

Rule 803(12). Marriage, Baptismal, and Similar Certificates.

What Is Allowed. Statements of fact contained in a certificate that the maker performed a marriage or other ceremony or administered a sacrament, made by a clergyman, public official, or other person authorized by the rules or practices of a religious organization or by law to perform the act certified, and purporting to have been issued at the time of the act or within a reasonable time thereafter.

Rule 803(13). Family Records.

What Is Allowed. Records and statements of fact concerning personal or family history contained in family Bibles, genealogies, charts, engravings on rings, inscriptions on family portraits, engravings on urns, crypts, or tombstones, or the like.

Property Records

Property records are allowed as exceptions to the hearsay rule when they deal with an interest in the property. Examples of this include deeds recorded in a town or county clerk's office, and wills that convey or affect property interest. The difference between Rule (14) and (15) is that one requires an official record that has been filed in accordance with state or local laws, and the other pertains to statements that establish or affect a property interest (see Exhibit 13.11). The "statements" rule is broader in its application. For example, a written will that was not recorded with any government agency may have provisions pertaining to the granting of property. Statements contained in this might be admitted under Rule 803(15).

EXHIBIT 13.11   Property Records

Rule 803(14). Records of Documents Affecting an Interest in Property.

What Is Allowed. The record of a document purporting to establish or affect an interest in property, as proof of the content of the original recorded document and its execution and delivery by each person by whom it purports to have been executed, if the record is a record of a public office and an applicable statute authorizes the recording of documents of that kind in that office.

Rule 803(15). Statements in Documents Affecting an Interest in Property.

What Is Allowed. A statement contained in a document purporting to establish or affect an interest in property if the matter stated was relevant to the purpose of the document, unless dealings with the property since the document was made have been inconsistent with the truth of the statement or the purport of the document.

Ancient Documents Rule

Ancient Documents Rule
A hearsay exception that allows statements in a document which has been in existence 20 years or more, and the authenticity of which is established.

Often called the **ancient documents rule**, this exception allows statements in a document which has been in existence 20 years or more, and the authenticity of which is established. This might include old land records, titles, contracts, property maps, or even such documents as articles or letters.

Commercial Reports

Stock market reports, as well as commercial reports and publications, are excepted from the hearsay rule if they are used and relied upon by the public or the users of that particular data (see Exhibit 13.12). Examples include stock quotes and other financial market data, city directories, and telephone books. A telephone directory could be offered to prove a phone number under this exception.

EXHIBIT 13.12   Market Reports, Commercial Publications

Rule 803(17).
   What Is Allowed. Market quotations, tabulations, lists, directories, or other published compilations, generally used and relied upon by the public or by persons in particular occupations.

Learned Treatises

Learned Treatises
A scholarly publication, report, or periodical.

In an earlier chapter, we discussed how an expert witness might base her opinion on facts or research that has been "reasonably relied upon by experts in the particular field.... "[21] The **learned treatises** exception to the hearsay rule allows statements contained in scholarly publications if relied upon by the expert witness during direct examination or called to the expert's attention during cross-examination (see Exhibit 13.13). In order to be admitted, a foundation must first be established that the publication is a reliable authority. The publication itself cannot be admitted as an exhibit. It can only be read into evidence.

EXHIBIT 13.13   Learned Treatises

Rule 803(18).
   What Is Allowed. To the extent called to the attention of an expert witness upon cross-examination or relied upon by the expert witness in direct examination, statements contained in published treatises, periodicals, or pamphlets on a subject of history, medicine, or other science or art, established as a reliable authority by the testimony or admission of the witness or by other expert testimony or by judicial notice. If admitted, the statements may be read into evidence but may not be received as exhibits.

C. Reputation Exceptions

Reputation exceptions rely on the trustworthiness and veracity of family and members of the community about such things as family or personal history, land boundaries, and even character (see Exhibit 13.14). These exceptions are founded on the theory that these relatives and close associates will have knowledge of and be able to provide reliable information about certain reputation facts. To be admitted, it must be established that the witness is a family or community member and can testify to the reputation in question.

EXHIBIT 13.14   Hearsay Exceptions—Availability of Declarant Immaterial

Rule 803. The following are not excluded by the hearsay rule, even though the declarant is available as a witness:

(19) Reputation Concerning Personal or Family History

(20) Reputation Concerning Boundaries or General History

(21) Reputation as to Character

Reputation May Still Be Excluded Under Other Rules

These exceptions only allow this reputation evidence as hearsay (see Exhibit 13.15). Reputation evidence must still clear other hurdles, including Rules 404, 405, and 608.

EXHIBIT 13.15   Reputation Exceptions

Rule 803(19). Reputation Concerning Personal or Family History.
   What Is Allowed. Reputation among members of a person's family by blood, adoption, or marriage, or among a person's associates, or in the community, concerning a person's birth, adoption, marriage, divorce, death, legitimacy, relationship by blood, adoption, or marriage, ancestry, or other similar fact of personal or family history.

Rule 803(20). Reputation Concerning Boundaries or General History.
   What Is Allowed. Reputation in a community, arising before the controversy, as to boundaries of or customs affecting lands in the community, and reputation as to events of general history important to the community or State or nation in which located is covered.

Rule 803(21). Reputation as to Character.
   What Is Allowed. Reputation evidence of a person's character among their associates in the community.

D. Judgment Exceptions

A **judgment** is a judicial decision or determination in a civil or criminal case. Hearsay exceptions allow for the admitting of judgments under certain circumstances (see Exhibit 13.16). Judgments of previous convictions are allowed for guilty verdicts and pleas, but not for the plea of **nolo contendere**, or "no contest." The reasoning behind this exception is that the reliability of the facts surrounding the judgment has already been tested by a court of law (see Exhibit 13.17). In the "no contest" plea, though, the defendant has not admitted or denied the facts. Therefore, its reliability is still untested. To be allowed under this exception, it must be shown that the conviction was for a crime punishable by death or imprisonment for more than a year. Like reputation evidence, a judgment may be admissible as a hearsay exception, but excluded under other rules of evidence.[22]

Judgment
A judicial decision or determination in a civil or criminal case.

Nolo Contendere
A plea of "no contest" to a criminal charge. It subjects defendant to the same punishment as pleading guilty, but allows defendant to neither admit or deny facts alleged.

EXHIBIT 13.16   Hearsay Exceptions—Availability of Declarant Immaterial

Rule 803. The following are not excluded by the hearsay rule, even though the declarant is available as a witness:

(22) Judgment of Previous Conviction

(23) Judgment as to Personal, Family, or General History, or Boundaries

EXHIBIT 13.17   Judgment Exceptions

Rule 803(22). Judgment of Previous Conviction.

What Is Allowed. This exception allows the admission of evidence of a final judgment, entered after a trial or upon a plea of guilty, but not upon a plea of nolo contendere, adjudging a person guilty of a crime punishable by death or imprisonment in excess of one year, to prove any fact essential to sustain the judgment, but not including, when offered by the Government in a criminal prosecution for purposes other than impeachment, judgments against persons other than the accused. The pendency of an appeal may be shown but does not affect admissibility.

Rule 803(23). Judgment as to Personal, Family or General History, or Boundaries.

What Is Allowed. Judgments as proof of matters of personal, family or general history, or boundaries, essential to the judgment, are admissible as exceptions to the hearsay rule if the same would be provable by evidence of reputation.

CRITICAL THINKING QUESTIONS 13.2

1. What are some reasons for allowing records and reports exceptions to the hearsay rule?
2. In what specific types of cases might the admission of these hearsay exceptions be important?
3. What type of records would not be allowed under these exceptions?
4. Why are investigative reports by law enforcement agencies not a part of these exceptions? Can these reports or the information in them be admitted under other rules or exceptions?
5. How do the reputation exceptions differ from other evidentiary rules governing the admitting of reputation evidence?
6. Of the exceptions discussed to this point, which do you think are the most important? Why? Which do you think are the least important? Why?
7. What changes would you make?

DECLARANT UNAVAILABLE TO TESTIFY

The second major section of exceptions to the hearsay rule applies to situations when the declarant is unavailable to testify. In some cases, this may be due to the declarant being physically unavailable. A declarant may have died or be too sick to appear in court. Sometimes, a declarant has moved and efforts to find him have failed. In many cases, the declarant may be physically available, but his testimony cannot be obtained. For example, a declarant may refuse to testify, or not be able to recall information.

Definition of Unavailability

As spelled out in Rule 804, a witness is "unavailable" when any of the following occurs regarding the subject matter of the declarant's statement (see Exhibit 13.18):

1. Declarant does not have to testify because of a *privilege*, such as marital privilege, attorney-client privilege, and so on.
2. Declarant *refuses to testify* despite an order of the court to do so.
3. Declarant testifies to a *lack of memory* of the subject matter.
4. Declarant is unable to be present or to testify because of *death, or physical or mental illness.*
5. Declarant is *absent* from the hearing and the proponent of a statement has been unable to procure the declarant's attendance by process or other reasonable means.

Not Unavailable if Wrongdoing

A declarant that is wrongfully kept from testifying by a party to the legal action is not unavailable as a witness. An example of this is a party who pays or threatens a witness not to testify.

EXHIBIT 13.18   Definition of Unavailability for Declarant

Utah Rules of Evidence
Rule 804(a). Definition of Unavailability. "Unavailability as a witness" includes situations in which the declarant:

(1) is exempted by ruling of the court on the ground of privilege from testifying concerning the subject matter of the declarant's statement; or

(2) persists in refusing to testify concerning the subject matter of the declarant's statement despite an order of the court to do so; or

(3) testifies to a lack of memory of the subject matter of the declarant's statement; or

(4) is unable to be present or to testify at the hearing because of death or then existing physical or mental illness or infirmity; or

(5) is absent from the hearing and the proponent of the declarant's statement has been unable to procure the declarant's attendance by process or other reasonable means.

A declarant is not unavailable as a witness if the exemption, refusal, claim of lack of memory, inability, or absence is due to the procurement or wrongdoing of the proponent of the declarant's statement for the purpose of preventing the witness from attending or testifying.

EXCEPTIONS TO HEARSAY RULE WHERE DECLARANT UNAVAILABLE

There are five types of exceptions when statements are not excluded by the hearsay rule if the declarant is unavailable as a witness: former testimony, statements under belief of impending death, statements against interest, statements of personal or family history, and forfeiture by wrongdoing (see Figure 13.19). These types of out-of-court statements are considered less reliable than under Rule 803, so a court will only allow them if a declarant is not available to testify.

EXHIBIT 13.19   Hearsay Exceptions—Declarant Unavailable

Rule 804(b). The following are not excluded by the hearsay rule if the declarant is unavailable as a witness:

(1) Former Testimony
(2) Statement Under Belief of Impending Death
(3) Statement Against Interest
(4) Statement of Personal or Family History
(5) [Transferred to Rule 807]
(6) Forfeiture by Wrongdoing

Former Testimony

If the declarant is unavailable as a witness, then declarant's prior testimony may be admitted as an exception to the hearsay rule if the party against whom the testimony is now being offered had an opportunity to examine or cross-examine the original testimony (see Exhibit 13.20). The key here is the protection of a party's opportunity to examine any testimony presented against that party. If that opportunity was provided when declarant previously testified, then it may be admitted at the later proceeding. An example of this is when a witness testifies under oath and subject to cross-examination at a deposition in a civil case or at a preliminary hearing in a criminal case. If that witness is unable to appear in a subsequent trial or court proceeding, the earlier testimony may be admitted under this exception.

EXHIBIT 13.20   Former Testimony Exception When Declarant Unavailable

Alaska Rules of Evidence
Rule 804(b)(1). Former Testimony. Testimony given as a witness at another hearing of the same or a different proceeding, or in a deposition taken in compliance with law in the course of another proceeding, if the party against whom the testimony is now offered, or, in a civil action or proceeding a predecessor in interest, had an opportunity and similar motive to develop the testimony by direct, cross, or redirect examination.

Grand Jury Testimony and the Fifth Amendment

In the following case, the U.S. Supreme Court looks at whether former testimony given at a grand jury proceeding may be used at trial when the declarants refuse to testify by invoking their Fifth Amendment rights.

CASE

United States v. Salerno

505 U.S. 317 (1992).

Justice Thomas delivered the opinion of the Court.

The seven respondents. . . allegedly took part in the activities of a criminal organization known as the Genovese Family of La Cosa Nostra (Family) in New York City. In 1987, a federal grand jury in the Southern District of New York indicted the respondents and four others on the basis of these activities. The indictment charged the respondents with a variety of federal offenses, including 41 acts constituting a "pattern of illegal activity" in violation of the Racketeer Influenced and Corrupt Organizations Act (RICO), 18 U.S.C. § 1962(b).

Sixteen of the alleged acts involved fraud in the New York construction industry in the 1980s. According to the indictment and evidence later admitted at trial, the Family used its influence over labor unions and its control over the supply of concrete to rig bidding on large construction projects in Manhattan. The Family purportedly allocated contracts for these projects among a so called "Club" of six concrete companies in exchange for a share of the proceeds. Much of the case concerned the affairs of the Cedar Park Concrete Construction Corporation (Cedar Park). Two of the owners of this firm, Frederick DeMatteis and Pasquale Bruno, testified before the grand jury under a grant of immunity. In response to questions by the United States, they repeatedly stated that neither they nor Cedar Park had participated in the Club. At trial, however, the United States attempted to show that Cedar Park, in fact, had belonged to the Club by calling two contractors who had taken part in the scheme and by presenting intercepted conversations among the respondents. The United States also introduced documents indicating that the Family had an ownership interest in Cedar Park.

To counter the United States' evidence, the respondents subpoenaed DeMatteis and Bruno as witnesses in the hope that they would provide the same exculpatory testimony that they had presented to the grand jury. When both witnesses invoked their Fifth Amendment privilege against self-incrimination and refused to testify, the respondents asked the District Court to admit the transcripts of their grand jury testimony. Although this testimony constituted hearsay, see Rule 801(c), the respondents argued that it fell within the hearsay exception in Rule 804(b)(1) for former testimony of unavailable witnesses. The District Court refused to admit the grand jury testimony. It observed that Rule 804(b)(1) permits admission of former testimony against a party at trial only when that party had a "similar motive to develop the testimony by direct, cross, or redirect examination." The District Court held that the United States did not have this motive, stating that the "motive of a prosecutor in questioning a witness before the grand jury in the investigatory stages of a case is far different from the motive of a prosecutor in conducting the trial." A jury subsequently convicted the respon-

dents of the RICO counts and other federal offenses.

The United States Court of Appeals for the Second Circuit reversed, holding that the District Court had erred in excluding DeMatteis and Bruno's grand jury testimony. Although the Court of Appeals recognized that "the government may have had no motive. . . to impeach. . . Bruno or DeMatteis" before the grand jury, it concluded that "the government's motive in examining the witnesses. . . was irrelevant." The Court of Appeals decided that, in order to maintain "adversarial fairness," Rule 804(b)(1)'s similar motive element should "evaporat[e]" when the government obtains immunized testimony in a grand jury proceeding from a witness who refuses to testify at trial. We granted certiorari, and now reverse and remand.

The hearsay rule prohibits admission of certain statements made by a declarant other than while testifying at trial. See Rule 801(c) (hearsay definition), 802 (hearsay rule). The parties acknowledge that the hearsay rule, standing by itself, would have blocked introduction at trial of DeMatteis and Bruno's grand jury testimony. Rule 804(b)(1), however, establishes an exception to the hearsay rule for former testimony. This exception provides: "The following are not excluded by the hearsay rule if the declarant is unavailable as a witness:

(1) Former Testimony. "Testimony given as a witness at another hearing. . . if the party against whom the testimony is now offered. . . had an opportunity and similar motive to develop the testimony by direct, cross, or redirect examination."

. . . .

The parties agree that DeMatteis and Bruno were "unavailable" to the defense as witnesses, provided that they properly invoked the Fifth Amendment privilege and refused to testify. See Rule 804(a)(1). They also agree that DeMatteis and Bruno's grand jury testimony constituted "testimony given as. . . witness[es] at another hearing." They disagree, however, about whether the "similar motive" requirement in the final clause of Rule 804(b)(1) should have prevented admission of the testimony in this case.

Nothing in the language of Rule 804(b)(1) suggests that a court may admit former testimony absent satisfaction of each of the Rule's elements. The United States thus asserts that, unless it had a "similar motive," we must conclude that the District Court properly excluded DeMatteis and

Bruno's testimony as hearsay. The respondents, in contrast, urge us not to read Rule 804(b)(1) in a "slavishly literal fashion." They contend that "adversarial fairness" prevents the United States from relying on the similar motive requirement in this case. We agree with the United States. When Congress enacted the prohibition against admission of hearsay in Rule 802, it placed 24 exceptions in Rule 803 and 5 additional exceptions in Rule 804. Congress thus presumably made a careful judgment as to what hearsay may come into evidence and what may not. To respect its determination, we must enforce the words that it enacted. The respondents, as a result, had no right to introduce DeMatteis and Bruno's former testimony under Rule 804(b)(1) without showing a "similar motive." This Court cannot alter evidentiary rules merely because litigants might prefer different rules in a particular class of cases.

LEGAL ANALYSIS AND WRITING 13.4

The following questions are based on the *How to Brief a Legal Case* format shown in the Appendix. Use this format to answer the following questions:

1. Summarize the facts in the previous case.
2. What is the legal issue?
3. What did the appellate court decide?
4. Why did the court decide this way?
5. Do you agree with the court's reasoning? Explain why or why not.

LEGAL RESEARCH USING THE INTERNET SKILLS 13.4

Find and read this Supreme Court case online! Check out one of the legal research web sites below and use their "Search" feature to find this case. In the "Search" field, enter the cite or case name.

1. FindLaw U.S. Supreme Court Decisions (http://www.findlaw.com/casecode/supreme.html)
2. U.S. Supreme Court (http://www.supremecourtus.gov/)
3. Supreme Court Collection of Cornell Law School (http://supct.law.cornell.edu/supct/)

Statement Under Belief of Impending Death—Dying Declaration

Another exception to the hearsay rule when the declarant is unavailable as a witness is the **statement under belief of impending death**, commonly referred to as a **dying declaration**. The "dying declaration" was carried over from early in the common law and codified in state and federal rules. It is generally used in criminal actions for homicide where the victim made a statement before dying. It may also be used in civil actions. It requires that the statement be made by a declarant while believing that his or her death is imminent and concerning the cause or circumstances of the impending death. The rationale behind admission of dying declarations is that a person about to meet her maker will not lie.

Statement Under Belief of Impending Death

Dying Declaration
Generally referred to as a *dying declaration*—a statement by a person who believes that her death is imminent.

Requirements for Admitting Dying Declaration

In order to be admitted under the dying declaration exception, the declarant must believe that his death is imminent and has thus given up all hope (see Exhibit 13.21). The declaration must concern the cause of declarant's death. The declarant must express the statement from his personal knowledge, not an opinion. For example, the statement, "I think the defendant shot me" would constitute an opinion and not be admissible. At common law, the declarant had to die before the declaration could be used. If the declarant is not dead, then declarant is "available" as a witness and can testify. Even when declarant does not die, however, the statement can still be used according to the Federal Rules as long as the court finds the declarant unavailable (see Exhibit 13.22).

EVIDENTIARY CHECKLIST 13.1

Elements Needed to Establish Dying Declaration Exception

- ☐ Declarant makes statement while believing that his death was imminent.
- ☐ Statement must concern the cause or circumstances of what declarant believes is his impending death.
- ☐ Declarant is making statement from personal knowledge, not an opinion.

How Presented in Court

A dying declaration or statement under belief of impending death may be testified to by any witness who heard or saw it. No particular form is required as to the statement. Most are oral, but it could also be written or by conduct, such as a nod of the head.

EXHIBIT 13.21   Comparison of Dying Declaration Rules

Wisconsin Statutes
Section 908.045(3). Statement Under Belief of Impending Death.
    A statement made by a declarant while believing that the declarant's death was imminent, concerning the cause or circumstances of what the declarant believed to be the declarant's impending death.

California Evidence Code
Section 1242. Evidence of a statement made by a dying person respecting the cause and circumstances of his death is not made inadmissible by the hearsay rule if the statement was made upon his personal knowledge and under a sense of immediately impending death.

Kansas Statutes
Section 60-460(e). Dying Declarations. A statement by a person unavailable as a witness because of the person's death if the judge finds that it was made (1) voluntarily and in good faith and (2) while the declarant was conscious of the declarant's impending death and believed that there was no hope of recovery.

EXHIBIT 13.22 Dying Declaration

Common Law	**Modern Rules**
May only be used in homicide cases	May be used in civil and criminal cases
Declarant must die	Declarant must be unavailable, but need not be dead

---

Dr. Shepard Has Poisoned Me

In the following case, distinguished Supreme Court Justice Cardozo examined whether a "dying declaration" statement was actually given under the circumstances of impending death.

CASE

Shepard v. United States

290 U.S. 96 (1933).

Justice Cardozo delivered the opinion of the Court.

The petitioner, Charles A. Shepard, a major in the medical corps of the United States army, has been convicted of the murder of his wife, Zenana Shepard, at Fort Riley, Kansas, a United States military reservation. . . . The crime is charged to have been committed by poisoning the victim with bichloride of mercury. The defendant was in love with another woman, and wished to make her his wife. There is circumstantial evidence to sustain a finding by the jury that to win himself his freedom he turned to poison and murder. Even so, guilt was contested and conflicting inferences are possible. The defendant asks us to hold that by the acceptance of incompetent evidence the scales were weighted to his prejudice and in the end to his undoing.

. . . On May 22, 1929, there was a conversation in the absence of the defendant between Mrs. Shepard, then ill in bed, and Clara Brown, her nurse. The patient asked the nurse to go to the closet in the defendant's room and bring a bottle of whisky that would be found upon a shelf. When the bottle was produced, she said that this was the liquor she had taken just before collapsing. She asked whether enough was left to make a test for the presence of poison, insisting that the smell and taste were strange. And then she added the words, "Dr. Shepard has poisoned me." . . . [T]he nurse having then testified to statements by Mrs. Shepard as to the prospect of recovery. "She said she was not going to get well; she was going to die.". . . There was a timely challenge of the ruling.

She said, "Dr. Shepard has poisoned me." The admission of this declaration, if erroneous, was more than unsubstantial error. As to that the parties are agreed. The voice of the dead wife was heard in accusation of her husband, and the accusation was accepted as evidence of guilt. If the evidence was incompetent, the verdict may not stand. Upon the hearing in this court the Government finds its main prop in the position that what was said by Mrs. Shepard was admissible as a dying declaration. This is manifestly the theory upon which it was offered and received. The prop, however, is a broken reed. To make out a dying declaration the declarant must have spoken without hope of recovery and in the shadow of impending death. The record furnishes no proof of that indispensable condition.

. . . We have said that the declarant was not shown to have spoken without hope of recovery and in the shadow of impending death. Her illness began on May 20. She was found in a state of collapse, delirious, in pain, the pupils of her eyes dilated, and the retina suffused with blood. The conversation with the nurse occurred two days later. At that time her mind had cleared up, and her speech was rational and orderly. There was as yet no thought by any of her physicians that she was dangerously ill, still less that her case was hopeless. To all seeming she had greatly improved, and was moving forward to recovery. There had been no diagnosis of poison as the cause of her distress. Not till about a week afterwards was there a relapse, accompanied by an infection of the mouth, renewed congestion of the eyes, and later hemorrhages of the bowels. Death followed on June 15.

Nothing in the condition of the patient on May 22 gives fair support to the conclusion that hope had then been lost. She may have thought she was going to die and have said so to her nurse, but this was consistent with hope, which could not have been put aside without more to quench it. Indeed, a fortnight later, she said to one of her physicians, though her condition was then grave, "You will get me well, won't you?" Fear or even belief that illness will end in death will not avail of itself to make a dying declaration. There must be "a settled hopeless expectation" that death is near at hand, and what is said must have been spoken in the hush of its impending presence. . . .

The petitioner insists that the form of the declaration exhibits other defects that call for its exclusion, apart from the objection that death was not imminent and that hope was still alive. Homicide may not be imputed to a defendant on the basis of mere suspicions, though they are the suspicions of the dying. To let the declaration in, the inference must be permissible that there was knowledge or the opportunity for knowledge as to the acts that are declared. . . . The form is not decisive, though it be that of a conclusion, a statement of the result with the antecedent steps omitted. "He murdered me" does not cease to be competent as a dying declaration because in the statement of the act there is also an appraisal of the crime. One does not hold the dying to the observance of all the niceties of speech to which conformity is exacted from a witness on the stand. What is decisive is something deeper and more fundamental than any difference of form. The declaration is kept out if the setting of the occasion satisfies the judge, or in reason ought to satisfy him, that the speaker is giving expression to suspicion or conjecture, and not to known facts. The difficulty is not so much in respect of the governing principle as in its application to varying and equivocal conditions. In this case, the ruling that there was a failure to make out the imminence of death and the abandonment of hope relieves us of the duty of determining whether it is a legitimate inference that there was the opportunity for knowledge. We leave that question open. . . .

LEGAL ANALYSIS AND WRITING 13.5

The following questions are based on the *How to Brief a Legal Case* format shown in the Appendix. Use this format to answer the following questions:

1. Summarize the facts in the previous case.
2. What is the legal issue?
3. What did the appellate court decide?
4. Why did the court decide this way?
5. Do you agree with the court's reasoning? Explain why or why not.

LEGAL RESEARCH USING THE INTERNET SKILLS 13.5

Find and read this Supreme Court case online! Check out one of the legal research web sites below and use their "Search" feature to find this case. In the "Search" field, enter the cite or case name.

1. FindLaw U.S. Supreme Court Decisions (http://www.findlaw.com/casecode/supreme.html)
2. U.S. Supreme Court (http://www.supremecourtus.gov/)
3. Supreme Court Collection of Cornell Law School (http://supct.law.cornell.edu/supct/)

Declaration or Statement Against Interest

Declaration Against Interest
Statement made which is contrary to declarant's property, monetary, or liberty interests.

A **declaration** or statement **against interest** is another hearsay exception where the declarant must be shown to be unavailable as a witness (see Exhibit 13.23). To be admitted, the statement must, at the time of its making, be so contrary to the declarant's pecuniary or proprietary interest, or so tending to subject the declarant to civil or criminal liability, that a reasonable person in the declarant's position would not have made the statement unless she believed it to be true. The reliability of this exception is founded on the theory that a person would not have said something like that if it weren't true. For example, Joan states "To pay Fran back for what she loaned me, I will owe her my whole paycheck for this month." A reasonable person might believe that Joan would not have made this statement unless it were true. Therefore, it would be admissible as a declaration against interest.

EXHIBIT 13.23   Statement Against Interest Exception When Declarant Unavailable

Ohio Rules of Evidence
Rule 804(B)(3). A statement that was at the time of its making so far contrary to the declarant's pecuniary or proprietary interest, or so far tended to subject the declarant to civil or criminal liability, or to render invalid a claim by the declarant against another, that a reasonable person in the declarant's position would not have made the statement unless the declarant believed it to be true. A statement tending to expose the declarant to criminal liability, whether offered to exculpate or inculpate the accused, is not admissible unless corroborating circumstances clearly indicate the trustworthiness of the statement.

Exculpate
Evidence which tends to clear a person of guilt.

Corroborating Evidence
Evidence that supports or strengthens other evidence.

This exception has limitations when used in criminal cases. If this statement tends to expose the declarant to criminal liability and is offered to **exculpate** the accused, then it is not admissible unless **corroborating evidence** clearly indicates the trustworthiness of the statement. The reasoning behind this is to prevent perjury and fabrication. For example, a declarant who is in prison on another charge makes a statement confessing to a crime for which his friend is being prosecuted.

Different than Admission by a Party-Opponent

The hearsay exception for the declaration against interest differs from the nonhearsay admission by a party-opponent in Rule 801(d)(2). Under the declaration against interest, it must be shown that the declarant is unavailable and that the statement is against the declarant's own interest. The admission by party-opponent does not require that the declarant be unavailable and the statement does not have to be against the declarant's interest (see Exhibit 13.24).

Statement of Personal or Family History

Sometimes called a statement of "pedigree," this exception allows the admission of statements concerning the declarant's personal or family history, including declarant's:

- Birth
- Adoption

EXHIBIT 13.24   Statement Against Interest versus Admission by Party-Opponent

Statement Against Interest	Admission by Party-Opponent
1. Declarant does not have to be party.	1. Declarant has to be a party.
2. Declarant is unavailable as a witness.	2. Declarant does not have to be unavailable as witness.
3. Statement is clearly against declarant's pecuniary, proprietary, or penal interest.	3. Statement does not have to be against declarant's interest.
4. Theory: "You would not have said something like that if it weren't true."	4. Theory: "You said it. You can explain it."

- Marriage
- Divorce
- Legitimacy
- Relationship by blood, adoption, or marriage

This exclusion also allows for a statement concerning the above matters, or death, of another person if the declarant was related to the other by blood, adoption, or marriage, or was so intimately associated with the other's family as to be likely to have accurate information concerning the matter declared. For example, a statement by a declarant that he had been adopted, or that his parents were unmarried when he was born, would be admitted under this exception. For the statement to be admitted, however, it still must be shown that the declarant is unavailable to testify.

Forfeiture by Wrongdoing

The final exception under the hearsay rules when a declarant is unavailable is **forfeiture by wrongdoing**. Also known as **waiver by wrongdoing**, this exception provides for the admitting of a statement against a party who engaged in wrongdoing intended to keep the declarant from testifying. In essence, the wrongdoer has waived or forfeited his right to object to a statement based on hearsay. An example is a defendant in a criminal case who murders a potential witness for the prosecution. In one case, the court found that "it is sufficient in this regard to show that the evildoer was motivated in part by a desire to silence the witness; the intent to deprive the prosecution of testimony need not be the actor's sole motivation."[23] This only applies to actions taken after the event to prevent a witness from testifying. Therefore, a statement by the victim of a murder would not fall under this exception. (It may, however, be admitted under the dying declaration exception.) The wrongdoing does not have to be from a criminal act or relate to a criminal trial. It may also be used in a civil case. The rule applies to all parties, including the government.

Forfeiture by Wrongdoing

Waiver by Wrongdoing
A hearsay exception that admits an out-of-court statement against a party who engaged in wrongdoing intended to keep the declarant from testifying.

Special Issues—Statements of Child Victims of Crimes

Although not provided for under the Federal Rules, many states have developed special hearsay exceptions to protect young children who are victims of crimes and abuse (see Exhibit 13.25). Generally, these exceptions are

LEGAL RESEARCH USING THE INTERNET SKILLS 13.6

1. Use one of the following web sites to find out whether your state rules of evidence are patterned after the Federal Rules or the Uniform Rules.

List of State Laws from Legal Information Institute of Cornell Law School (http://www.law.cornell.edu/states/listing.html)

FindLaw (http://www.findlaw.com)

Federal Rules of Evidence (http://www.law.cornell.edu/rules/fre/overview.html)

limited to crimes involving sexual abuse. These exceptions allow statements by the child if the statements concern the crime, and the circumstances surrounding the statement provide sufficient guarantees of trustworthiness. Many courts also permit two-way closed circuit televised testimony upon a finding that testimony will present substantial risk of trauma to a child under 12 years. In these cases, the defendant's right to confrontation is maintained by being allowed to observe and hear the testimony of the child and to confer with attorney and cross-examine the witness. In most of these cases, the witness can also hear and see the defendant. However, the court may not allow this if the judge believes this would present a risk of trauma that would substantially impair the ability of the child to testify.

EVIDENTIARY CHECKLIST 13.2

Elements for Allowing Statements of Child Victims

The following elements should be established in order to offer statements by children who are victims of sexual abuse:

- ☐ Statements are offered in cases where the child is a victim of sexual assault, lewd conduct, or incest.
- ☐ Statements concern the crime.
- ☐ Time, content, and circumstances of the statement provide sufficient guarantees of trustworthiness.
- ☐ Statements were not taken in preparation for a legal proceeding.
- ☐ Statements were made prior to defendant's initial appearance.

EXHIBIT 13.25   Example of Rule Allowing Statement of Child Victim

North Dakota Rules of Evidence
Rule 803(24). Child's Statement About Sexual Abuse.

An out-of-court statement by a child under the age of 12 years about sexual abuse of that child or witnessed by that child is admissible as evidence (when not otherwise admissible under another hearsay exception) if:

(Continued)

EXHIBIT 13.25   Example of Rule Allowing Statement of Child Victim   *Continued*

(a) The trial court finds, after hearing upon notice in advance of the trial of the sexual abuse issue, that the time, content, and circumstances of the statement provide sufficient guarantees of trustworthiness; and

(b) The child either:

    (i) Testifies at the proceedings; or

    (ii) Is unavailable as a witness and there is corroborative evidence of the act which is the subject of the statement.

CATCH-ALL EXCEPTION

Under a newer "catch-all" rule, called the **residual exception**, a statement not specifically covered by Rules 803 or 804, but having equivalent circumstantial guarantees of trustworthiness, is not excluded by the hearsay rule. This "catch-all" exception did not exist at common law. To be admitted, a statement must be shown to be material, more probative than any other evidence that might be obtained, and serve the interests of justice by its admission (see Exhibit 13.26 and Exhibit 13.27).

Residual Exception
A left-over or catch-all hearsay exception for those out-of-court statements that are not covered by Rules 803 or 804, but are found to have equivalent guarantees of trustworthiness.

EXHIBIT 13.26   "Catch-All" Hearsay Exception

North Dakota Rules of Evidence
Rule 807. Residual Exception. A statement not specifically covered by Rule 803 or 804 but having equivalent circumstantial guarantees of trustworthiness, is not excluded by the hearsay rule, if the court determines (A) the statement is offered as evidence of a material fact; (B) the statement is more probative on the point for which it is offered than any other evidence which the proponent can procure through reasonable efforts; and (C) the general purposes of these rules and the interests of justice will best be served by admission of the statement into evidence. However, a statement may not be admitted under this exception unless the proponent of it makes known to the adverse party and to the court in writing sufficiently in advance of its offer in evidence to provide the adverse party with a fair opportunity to prepare to meet it, the proponent's intention to offer the statement and the particulars of it, including the name and address of the declarant.

CRITICAL THINKING QUESTIONS 13.3

1. Why are the hearsay exceptions listed under Rule 804, Declarant unavailable, considered less reliable than those in Rule 803?
2. Of the exceptions discussed to this point, which do you think are the most important? Why? Which do you think are the least important? Why?
3. What changes would you make?
4. Why did the common law, and some courts today, require a declarant to die before his or her statement could be admitted under the dying declaration exception?

(Continued)

CRITICAL THINKING QUESTIONS 13.3   *Continued*

5. What are the reasons for the *forfeiture by wrongdoing* exception? Do you think these reasons are valid? Why or why not?

6. How can Confrontation Clause issues be avoided when providing some of the newer hearsay exceptions to children who are victims of sexual abuse?

7. Do we need a "catch-all" hearsay exception? Explain your answer and include examples of when this residual exception might be used.

EVIDENTIARY CHECKLIST 13.3

Approach to Hearsay Problems

☐   Is the evidence being offered a "statement" as defined by Rule 801?

☐   Was the statement made out-of-court?

☐   Is the statement being offered to prove the truth of the matter asserted?

☐   Is the statement nonhearsay because it is a prior statement by a witness or an admission by a party-opponent?

☐   If the statement is hearsay and the availability of the declarant is immaterial, can it be admitted under one of the exceptions listed in Rule 803?

☐   If the statement is hearsay and the declarant is unavailable, can it be admitted under one of the exceptions listed in Rule 804?

☐   If the statement is hearsay and it cannot be admitted under Rule 803 or 804, can another reason be found to admit it under Rule 807?

EXHIBIT 13.27   Hearsay Chart

What Is Not Hearsay

- Nonassertive conduct
- Statements not offered to prove the truth of the matter asserted
- Prior inconsistent statements made under oath
- Prior consistent statements offered to rebut charge of recent fabrication
- Prior statement of identification made after perceiving a person
- Admission of party-opponent

(Continued)

EXHIBIT 13.27 Hearsay Chart *Continued*

What Is Hearsay but Allowed Under Exception to Hearsay Rule

Hearsay Exceptions—Availability of Declarant Immaterial
Rule 803. The following are not excluded by the hearsay rule, even though the declarant is available as a witness:

(1) Present Sense Impression

(2) Excited Utterance

(3) Then Existing Mental, Emotional, or Physical Condition

(4) Statements for Purposes of Medical Diagnosis or Treatment

(5) Recorded Recollection

(6) Records of Regularly Conducted Activity

(7) Absence of Entry in Records Kept in Accordance With the Provisions of Paragraph (6)

(8) Public Records and Reports

(9) Records of Vital Statistics

(10) Absence of Public Record or Entry

(11) Records of Religious Organizations

(12) Marriage, Baptismal, and Similar Certificates

(13) Family Records

(14) Records of Documents Affecting Interest in Property

(15) Statements in Documents Affecting Interest in Property

(16) Statements in Ancient Documents

(17) Market Reports, Commercial Publications

(18) Learned Treatises

(19) Reputation Concerning Personal or Family History

(20) Reputation Concerning Boundaries or General History

(21) Reputation as to Character

(22) Judgment of Previous Conviction

(23) Judgment as to Personal, Family, or General History, or Boundaries

Hearsay Exceptions—Declarant Unavailable
Rule 804. The following are not excluded by the hearsay rule if the declarant is unavailable as a witness:

(1) Former Testimony

(2) Statement Under Belief of Impending Death

(3) Statement Against Interest

(4) Statement of Personal or Family History

(5) [Transferred to Rule 807]

(6) Forfeiture by Wrongdoing

SUMMARY

The hearsay rule protects the jury from hearing unreliable out-of-court statements as evidence. Exceptions have developed over the years when the circumstances surrounding an out-of-court statement are sufficiently trustworthy to overcome the presumption of unreliability. Hearsay exceptions are divided into two categories according to their degree of reliability: when *availability of the declarant is immaterial* and when the *declarant is unavailable* to testify.

The first major group of exceptions to the hearsay rule occurs when the availability of the declarant is not important. Rule 803 lists 23 such exceptions. These exceptions can be grouped into four general areas: statements, records and reports, reputation, and judgments. Out-of-court statements look at the statements made in relation to the surrounding circumstances and the spontaneity involved. The rationale was that the more spontaneous the statement in relation to the event perceived, the more trustworthy it would be. Generally, the statements dealt with the declarant's state of mind at the time of the statement. Records and reports exceptions include documents that are regularly kept as part of the normal transaction of business. The range of exceptions includes not only business records, but records kept and maintained by public officials who have a duty to keep the records. These exceptions are founded on the level of trustworthiness expected as a regular basis for keeping records. These exceptions may be challenged on the basis of lacking this essential trustworthiness element. Reputation exceptions rely on the trustworthiness and veracity of family and members of the community about such things as family or personal history, land boundaries, and even character. These exceptions are founded on the theory that these relatives and close associates will have knowledge of and be able to provide reliable information about certain reputation facts. Judgments of previous convictions are allowed for guilty verdicts and pleas, since the reliability of the facts surrounding the judgment has already been tested by a court of law.

The second major section of exceptions to the hearsay rule applies to situations when the declarant is unavailable to testify. In some cases, this may be due to the declarant being physically unavailable. A declarant may have died or be too sick to appear in court. Sometimes, a declarant has moved and efforts to find him have failed. In many cases, the declarant may be physically available, but her testimony cannot be obtained. For example, a declarant may refuse to testify, or not be able to recall information. A declarant that is wrongfully kept from testifying by a party to the legal action is not unavailable as a witness. An example of this is a party who pays or threatens a witness not to testify. There are five types of exceptions when statements are not excluded by the hearsay rule if the declarant is unavailable as a witness: former testimony, statements under belief of impending death, statements against interest, statements of personal or family history, and forfeiture by wrongdoing. These types of out-of-court statements are considered less reliable than under Rule 803, so a court will only allow them if a declarant is not available to testify.

An exception to the hearsay rule does not by itself guarantee that the statement will be admitted. It must still satisfy the other evidentiary limitations and exclusionary rules, including relevance, authentication, opinion, privilege, and the best evidence rule, to name a few. In criminal actions, hearsay must also pass Fourth Amendment protections against unreasonable search and seizure, Fifth Amendment limitations on self-incrimination, and the Sixth Amendment right to confrontation and due process.

KEY TERMS

Ancient Documents Rule
Business Records Exception
Confrontation Clause
Contemporaneous Declarations
Corroborating Evidence
Custodian of the Records
Declarant
Declaration Against Interest
Dying Declaration
Excited Utterance

Exculpate
Forfeiture by Wrongdoing
Judgment
Learned Treatises
Nolo Contendere
Past Recollection Recorded
Present Sense Impression
Recorded Recollection
Records of Regularly
    Conducted Activity

Reflective Thought
Res Gestae
Residual Exception
Spontaneous
Spontaneous Declaration
State of Mind
Statement Under Belief of
    Impending Death
Waiver by Wrongdoing

LEARNING OUTCOMES AND PRACTICE SKILLS CHECKLIST

☐ Learning Outcomes

After completing your reading, questions, and exercises, you should be able to demonstrate a better understanding of the learning concepts by answering the following questions:

1. Distinguish between the Rule 803 and 804 exceptions discussed in this chapter.
2. Explain why the rules divide these exceptions by availability of declarant. In your explanation, discuss which set of exceptions are considered more reliable, and why.
3. Define *res gestae* and describe how it is used in the hearsay exceptions.
4. Define the following terms and identify the essential elements that must be established to admit evidence under them as hearsay exceptions. Give examples of each.
   a) Excited Utterance
   b) Present Sense Impression
   c) State of Mind
   d) Recorded Recollection
   e) Business Records
   f) Public Records
   g) Ancient Documents
   h) Learned Treatise
   i) Judgment of Previous Conviction
   j) Former Testimony
   k) Statement Against Interest
   l) Forfeiture by Wrongdoing
   m) Dying Declaration
5. Distinguish *statement against interest* with *admission by party-opponent* in Rule 801(d)(2).
6. Define *Confrontation Clause* and describe how it pertains to hearsay exceptions.
7. Describe what is meant by a *residual exception* and what elements need to be established in order to admit statements under this exception.
8. Identify some other evidentiary rules that might still exclude evidence even when admissible as a hearsay exception.

☐ Practice Skills

In addition to understanding the learning concepts, practice what you have learned through applications using critical thinking, legal analysis and writing, legal research, and advocacy skills, including:

Critical Thinking

1. Why do we have the exceptions to the hearsay rule described in this chapter?
2. Do you believe that the current exceptions discussed in this chapter provide adequate safeguards?
3. What public policy issues or considerations do you think might be behind these rules?
4. If it were up to you, would you keep the exceptions to the hearsay rules as they are, delete them, narrow them, or expand them? Explain your reasoning.
5. How do these rules influence the gathering of evidence or preparing of witnesses?

Legal Analysis and Writing

Analyze the following rules and cases by summarizing their holdings, explaining their significance, and assessing any issue that might arise in their application.

1. Rule 803.
2. Rule 804.
3. *White v. Illinois.*
4. *United States v. Joe.*
5. *Shepard v. United States.*

Legal Research Using the Internet

1. Find the annotated Federal Rules of Evidence on the Internet and assess the comments made in the proposing of the rules covered in this chapter.
2. Find your state's rules of evidence regarding hearsay exceptions and concepts covered in this chapter. Compare and contrast with the federal and/or modern rules, and some of the state rules listed in this chapter.
3. Find out if your state appellate court posts their case decisions on the Internet. If so, find a case that illustrates an issue or rule discussed in this chapter. If your state decisions are not on the Internet, go instead to the web site for the U.S. Circuit Court of Appeals in your circuit, or search the U.S. Supreme Court decisions.

PRACTICE APPLICATION 13.1

The police receive an unidentified 911 emergency call stating, "I hear screams coming from Apartment B at 123 Main Street. I think Fred is beating his wife again." When police respond to the apartment, the defendant, named Fred, opens the door and states "Help me. Hurry. I pushed my wife and she fell and hit her head." The police call for paramedics. When the paramedics arrive, they find the wife on the floor, dazed and in a state of shock. They ask the wife how and where she had been injured. The wife responds by stating "My head hurts. My husband hit me in the head with a hammer because he thought I was cheating on him." While being worked on in the emergency room, the wife begins to lose consciousness. Before she dies, she grabs the arm of a nurse and states, "I'm dying. I can feel it. Tell my son that Fred did this to me." The wife survives and recovers, but loses all memory about what happened to her. Fred is charged with attempted murder. At the trial, the prosecution wants to introduce the following statements:

1. 911 call
2. Fred's statement to police
3. Wife's statement to paramedics
4. Wife's statement to nurse

Use the format shown in the Appendix for the *IRAC Method of Legal Analysis* and the readings, rules, and cases discussed in this chapter to analyze the above case problems and determine whether the evidence in each example can be admitted as an exception to the hearsay rule. Write a memo giving your analysis, reasoning, and conclusions.

ADVOCACY AND COMMUNICATION SKILLS 13.1

Form teams from small groups of no more than 3–4 each. Prepare a set of questions to ask the witnesses in the above *Practice Application* and conduct a direct, cross, redirect, or recross-examination of the witness. During each line of questioning, the opposing team should be prepared to object, if needed, using objections from earlier readings. Use a different team member for each examination:

1. Plaintiff team will conduct a direct exam of no more than 5 minutes.
2. Defense team will conduct a cross-exam of no more than 5 minutes.
3. Plaintiff will have 3 minutes to redirect.
4. Defense will have 3 minutes to recross.

WEB SITES

Federal Rules of Evidence
http://www.law.cornell.edu/rules/fre/overview.html
FindLaw
http://www.findlaw.com
FindLaw
http://guide.lp.findlaw.com/casecode/
FindLaw U.S. Supreme Court Decisions
http://www.findlaw.com/casecode/supreme.html
List of State Laws from Legal Information Institute of Cornell Law School
http://www.law.cornell.edu/states/listing.html

National Center for State Courts—State and Federal Court Web Sites
http://www.ncsconline.org/D_kis/info_court_web_sites.html#federal
Supreme Court Collection of Cornell Law School
http://supct.law.cornell.edu/supct/
U.S. Courts Site with Links to all Circuit Courts of Appeal
http://www.uscourts.gov/links.html
U.S. Supreme Court
http://www.supremecourtus.gov/

ENDNOTES

1. *People v. Buie*, 86 N.Y.2d 501 (1995).
2. Alaska R. Evid. 803(1). Present Sense Impression.
3. *Oklahoma Statutes*, Section 12-2803.
4. *Tyrrell v. Wal-Mart Stores Inc.*, 97 N.Y.2d 650 (2001).
5. *White v. Illinois*, 502 U.S. 346 (1992).

6. *See People v. Trowbridge,* 305 NY 471.
7. *People v. Caviness,* 38 N.Y.2d 227.
8. *Sixth Amendment to the U.S. Constitution.*
9. *California v. Green,* 399 U.S. 149 (1970).
10. *Dutton v. Evans,* 400 U.S. 74, 86 (1970).
11. See *Ohio v. Roberts,* 448 U.S. 56, 63 (1980).
12. *Idaho v. Wright,* 497 U.S. 805 (1990).
13. *White v. Illinois,* 502 U.S. 346 (1992).
14. *United States v. DiMaria,* 727 F.2d 265 (2d Cir. 1984).
15. *United States v. Harwood,* 998 F.2d 91 (2d Cir. 1993).
16. *Mutual Life Insurance Co. v. Hillmon,* 145 U.S. 285 (1892).
17. *United States v. Cohen,* 631 F.2d 1223 (5th Cir. 1980).
18. *White v. Illinois,* 502 U.S. 346 (1992).
19. Ibid.
20. See, for example, Fed. R. Evid. 803 (11).
21. See Fed. R. Evid. 703.
22. See, for example, Rules 410, 609.
23. *United States v. Houlihan,* 92 F.3d 1271 (1st Cir. 1996).

PRIVILEGES

"[P]rivileges are rooted in the imperative need for confidence and trust."
—*Trammel v. United States, 445 U.S. 40 (1980)*

LEARNING OUTCOMES

In this chapter, you will learn about the following legal concepts:

- What Is a Privilege?
- Why Grant Privileges?
- History of Privileges
- Modern Use of Privileges
- Forms of Privileges

- Statutory Privileges
- Constitutional Privileges
- Common Law Privileges
- Newer Privileges

INTRODUCTION

We have seen how rules of evidence promote the search for truth in a trial by determining what is relevant and admissible. In that search, courts have agreed that "the pertinent general principle, responding to the deepest needs of society, is that society is entitled to every man's evidence. As an underlying aim of judicial inquiry is ascertainable truth, everything rationally related to ascertaining the truth is presumptively admissible. Limitations are properly placed upon the operation of this general principle only to the very limited extent that permitting a refusal to testify or excluding relevant evidence has a public good transcending the normally predominant principle of utilizing all rational means for ascertaining truth."[1] The court underscored this principle during the Watergate era when it stated that "exceptions to the demand for every man's evidence are not lightly created nor expansively construed, for they are in derogation of the search for truth."[2]

In earlier chapters, we examined some of these limitations and exceptions. We looked at how relevant evidence can still be excluded if it is considered unreliable as hearsay or if it might tend to prejudice or confuse the jury. This chapter will look at another area that limits the admissibility of evidence—privileges and privileged communications. Since 16th-century England, beginning with the emergence of the attorney-client privilege, our common law has recognized that the interests of society were better served when certain special relationships are fostered and protected. The special nature of these relationships was considered to require trust, honesty, and confidentiality of communication as essential to their existence. Because public policy valued these relationships, legal privileges were allowed to protect their confidential nature, even at the expense of excluding relevant evidence at trial. Let's examine what these privileges are and how they are used.

WHAT IS A PRIVILEGE?

Privilege
A rule of law that allows a witness to refuse to give testimony or allows the holder of the privilege the right to prevent someone else from testifying on the same matter.

A **privilege** is a rule of law that either allows a witness to refuse to give testimony or allows a person the right to prevent someone else from testifying on the same matter. The person being granted a privilege is called the **holder of the privilege**.

General Elements of a Privilege

Holder of the Privilege
The person for whom the law intended the privilege to protect. For example, in the attorney-client privilege, the client is the holder. In the physician-patient privilege, the patient is the holder.

There are four general elements that need to be considered in determining whether a privilege at law exists.

1. Rooted in the Need for Confidence and Trust

The relationship sought to be protected must be a special one with a recognized need for confidential communication that serves the best interests of society. It must be "rooted in the imperative need for confidence and trust"[3] and one in which the community seeks to foster.

2. In Furtherance of Special Relationship

The need for confidentiality must be essential to the furtherance of this special relationship. The privilege must "serve public ends" and "encourage full and frank communication . . . and thereby promote broader public interests in the observance of law and administration of justice."[4]

3. Confidential Communication

The communication made during this relationship must be intended in confidence, that it will not be disclosed.

4. Interests Outweigh Need for Evidence

The privilege "promotes sufficiently important interests to outweigh the need for probative evidence. . . ."[5] The harm to the relationship that would be caused by the disclosure of the communications must be greater than the benefit gained by the evidence sought.

Able to Predict with Certainty

One of the primary reasons for the creation of privileges is to ensure that the public feels secure in these special relationships and can be assured that their conversations will be treated as confidential. The court has held that "if the purpose of the privilege is to be served, the participants in the confidential conversation must be able to predict with some degree of certainty whether particular discussions will be protected. An uncertain privilege, or one which purports to be certain but results in widely varying applications by the courts, is little better than no privilege at all."[6]

WHY GRANT PRIVILEGES?

We grant privileges as a matter of law out of public policy considerations. Confidential communication privileges are recognized by the courts "to protect those interpersonal relationships which are highly valued by society and peculiarly vulnerable to deterioration should their necessary component of privacy be continually disregarded by courts of law."[7] These relationships must promote "sufficiently important interests to outweigh the need for probative evidence."[8] The public need to foster these relationships and the confidence in them is viewed as more important than the testimony that might be given or relevant evidence that might be obtained.

HISTORY OF PRIVILEGES

Privileges have "ancient roots."[9] Perhaps the oldest is the attorney-client privilege. This privilege can be traced back to Roman law, when lawyers could refuse to be witnesses against their clients, and Roman slaves were not allowed to divulge communication made by their masters. The clergy privilege originated from the early historical practice of priests in the Catholic Church upholding a strict vow of confidentiality surrounding the confessional. Because the priests would not break this confidence, English courts rarely attempted to force their testimony. The marital privilege also "has ancient roots." Writing in 1628, Lord Coke observed that "it hath been resolved by the Justices that a wife cannot be produced either against or for her husband. This spousal disqualification sprang from two canons of medieval jurisprudence: first, the rule that an accused was not permitted to testify in his own behalf because of his interest in the proceeding; second, the concept that husband and wife were one . . . . From those two now long-abandoned doctrines, it followed that what was inadmissible from the lips of the defendant-husband was also inadmissible from his wife."[10] In 1637, the trial of Puritan dissident, John Lilburne, brought attention to a need for a privilege against self-incrimination, when he claimed this privilege in refusing to answer questions before the **Star Chamber**.

Star Chamber
An English court that conducted trials in secret during the 15th–17th century, employing harsh and brutal methods to force testimony and confessions from witnesses.

These early forms of privileges for attorney-client, husband-wife, and clergy were brought over from England and incorporated into our common law. They were subsequently codified by most states, although many were changed to fit the state's statutory needs. The privilege against self-incrimination was adopted, through the Fifth Amendment, into our Constitution and now stands as a fundamental right throughout our laws.

MODERN USE OF PRIVILEGES

Modern use of privileges can best be examined by comparing their adoption and use in the state and federal courts.

Privileges in State Courts

Most states have codified the common law privileges, and many have added a few new ones. However, privileges are not consistently applied from state to state, and their scope can vary greatly. There may be differences in the extent of each privilege, or who may claim it. In the patient's privilege, for example, some states only allow the privilege for confidential communications made to physicians who are licensed to practice medicine. Other states extend this privilege to psychologists, social workers, and others engaged in the diagnosis or treatment of a mental or emotional condition.[11] Some states allow the patient's privilege in both civil and criminal cases, while other states do not allow it to be used in a criminal proceeding. Several states do not recognize any type of patient's privilege. Under some state laws, privileged communications are presumed confidential and the party opposing the privilege has the burden of showing that the communication was not confidential. In other states, and under federal law, however, the proponent of a privilege may have this burden. In some states, adverse inference may not be drawn from the use of a privilege.[12] In other states, and in federal courts, such an adverse inference may be drawn in a civil case.[13]

Privileges in Federal Courts

When the U.S. Supreme Court submitted its proposed draft of the new Federal Rules of Evidence to Congress in 1972, its article on privileges provided 13 rules that contained nine privileges (see Exhibit 14.2). The privileges recommended in that draft included lawyer-client, psychotherapist-patient, husband-wife, clergy, political vote, trade secrets, identity of informer, certain statutory reports, and secrets of state. After much debate, with intense lobbying from special interest groups at all sides of the proposals, Congress decided to reject the proposed specific rules and, instead, adopt only one general provision which would pertain to privileges in the new Federal Rules of Evidence. This provision became Rule 501 (see Exhibit 14.1).

"In the Light of Reason and Experience"

Rule 501 provides that privileges in the federal courts are to be governed by common law principles as interpreted "in the light of reason and experience." This general provision governing privileges has led to considerable disagreement among the federal courts as to the scope of common law privileges and how they should be interpreted. There is also disagreement as to whether privileges in general should be narrowed or expanded. Many

---

EXHIBIT 14.1   Privileges in Federal Rules of Evidence

Federal Rules of Evidence
Rule 501. General Rule.

Except as otherwise required by the Constitution of the United States or provided by Act of Congress or in rules prescribed by the Supreme Court pursuant to statutory authority, the privilege of a witness, person, government, State, or political subdivision thereof shall be governed by the principles of the common law as they may be interpreted by the courts of the United States in the light of reason and experience. However, in civil actions and proceedings, with respect to an element of a claim or defense as to which State law supplies the rule of decision, the privilege of a witness, person, government, State, or political subdivision thereof shall be determined in accordance with State law.

EXHIBIT 14.2   Original Privilege Rules, Proposed by U.S. Supreme Court in 1972—Rejected by Congress

Rule 502	Required Reports Privileged by Statute
Rule 503	Lawyer-Client Privilege
Rule 504	Psychotherapist-Patient Privilege
Rule 505	Husband-Wife Privilege
Rule 506	Communications to Clergy Privilege
Rule 507	Political Vote Privilege
Rule 508	Trade Secrets Privilege
Rule 509	Secrets of State and Other Official Information Privilege
Rule 510	Identity of Informer Privilege

---

federal courts, for example, disagreed over recognizing any type of physician or psychotherapist-patient privilege. One court quoted Rule 501 in soundly rejecting the privilege, stating "the psychotherapist-patient privilege has developed by state statutory enactment. It does not exist at common law."[14]

However, it is believed by many that Rule 501 has opened the door for the refinement of existing privileges and the recognition of new privileges through its own wording. The U.S. Supreme Court addressed this in a 1980 decision, stating

> The Federal Rules of Evidence acknowledge the authority of the federal courts
> to continue the evolutionary development of testimonial privileges in federal
> criminal trials "governed by the principles of the common law as they may
> be interpreted . . . in the light of reason and experience."[15]

As you continue your reading, watch how this reasoning is used in the *Trammel* decision to narrow an existing common law privilege, and the *Jaffee* decision to recognize a new common law privilege.

LEGAL RESEARCH USING THE INTERNET SKILLS 14.1

Use the Internet to find Federal Rule 501. Check out the "Notes" under it and look through the legislative commentary to learn some of the reasons why these rules were rejected.

Cornell's LII web site is the site most used for this (http://www.law.cornell.edu/rules/fre).

FORMS OF PRIVILEGE

There are four forms of privilege granted by our legal system: right of holder to be exempt from testifying; right of holder to be exempt as to testifying about the privileged matter, even though testifying about all else; right of holder to be exempt from producing any object or writing; and right of holder to prevent another from testifying or producing any object or writing.

1. Right of holder to be exempt from testifying

This form of privilege protects someone from having to take the witness stand to testify. Most privileges allow for this, rather than the possible prejudice to a case if the holder is called to the witness stand and then is forced to invoke a legal privilege. Another example is the right not to testify under the Fifth Amendment.

2. Right of holder to be exempt as to testifying about the privileged matter, even though testifying about all else

Sometimes, a holder may testify as to other matters, but not have to testify as to privileged communications. Examples of this include the confidential communications portion of the marital privilege, and pleading Fifth Amendment rights against self-incrimination in refusing to answer specific questions.

3. Right of holder to be exempt from producing any object or writing

A holder may have the right to refuse to produce certain documents or recorded information. An example of this would be the work products in an attorney-client privilege.

4. Right of holder to prevent another from testifying or producing any object or writing

Finally, a holder may be able to prevent another from testifying. Most privileges provide for this. A patient may prevent her doctor from testifying. A penitent may prevent his clergy from offering any testimony.

Holder versus Who May Claim Privilege

In examining a privilege issue, it is important to both identify the *holder of the privilege* and those who may be able to claim the privilege. In an attorney-client privilege, for example, the client is the holder of the privilege. The attorney may also claim the privilege, but only on behalf of her client. In this same situation, if there is a guardian for the client, that person may also be able to claim the privilege on behalf of the client. The same is true for an administrator of the estate of the client. In a doctor-patient relationship, the patient is the holder, but the doctor may also claim the privilege on behalf of the patient.

Waiver of Privilege

Waiver
A voluntary relinquishment of a right or privilege.

Privileges can be waived. This **waiver** may take effect in several ways. The most common of these are failure to claim and voluntary disclosure or consent.

1. Failure to claim

If a witness fails to claim a privilege, it constitutes a waiver except where there has been no reasonable opportunity to claim the privilege or the privilege was claimed but the disclosure was still compelled.

2. Voluntary disclosure or consent

If a holder of a privilege voluntarily discloses any significant part of a privileged communication or consents to disclosure by anyone else, he or she waives the right to the privilege.

No Privilege Unless Recognized by Law

No privilege will be allowed in a legal proceeding unless the court has recognized it (see Exhibit 14.3). As previously discussed, Rule 501 provides that privileges in federal courts will be governed by common law, unless required by Constitution or statutory law. In most state courts, privileges are governed by statute. Many states have provisions that specifically prohibit the use of privileges unless recognized by law.

EXHIBIT 14.3   No Privilege Unless Provided by Law

California Evidence Code
Section 911. Except as otherwise provided by statute:
   (a) No person has a privilege to refuse to be a witness.
   (b) No person has a privilege to refuse to disclose any matter or to refuse to produce any writing, object, or other thing.
   (c) No person has a privilege that another shall not be a witness or shall not disclose any matter or shall not produce any writing, object, or other thing.

STATUTORY PRIVILEGES

There are some privileges granted through **statutory law** to protect confidential communication gathered in the course of doing government business or in the government's providing for the health, safety, and welfare of its citizens (see Exhibit 14.4). For example, grand jury hearings are confidential while in session. Certain information required to be reported to a government agency might be confidential. Examples of this might include information reported to a department of mental health, public health, or for unemployment insurance. Employees of legislature and the courts may have some type of privilege for certain communications carried out in the course of their employment. Information disclosed to arbitrators or mediators during a labor dispute or negotiation is often privileged. How we vote in an election is considered to be confidential information. We would not have to disclose this unless the court finds some type of voting fraud or illegal voting activity involved.

Statutory Law
Laws passed by legislature.

EXHIBIT 14.4   Example of Statutory Privilege

Texas Rules of Evidence
Rule 502. Required Reports Privileged by Statute.
   A person, corporation, association, or other organization or entity, either public or private, making a return or report required by law to be made has a privilege to refuse to disclose and to prevent any other person from disclosing the return or report, if the law requiring it to be made so provides. A public officer or agency to whom a return or report is required by law to be made has a privilege to refuse to disclose the return or report if the law requiring it to be made so provides. No privilege exists under this rule in actions involving perjury, false statements, fraud in the return or report, or other failure to comply with the law in question.

Some statutory reporting provisions are mandatory and may overcome any privilege asserted. Most states, for example, require medical personnel to report gunshots or suspected child abuse. Asserting a physician-patient privilege could not negate this.

CONSTITUTIONAL PRIVILEGES

Privilege against Self-Incrimination

A privilege based on the Fifth Amendment to the U.S. Constitution, which protects an individual against being compelled in any criminal case to be a witness against herself or testifying to anything that might incriminate her.

One of the most important privileges is set forth in the Fifth Amendment to the U.S. Constitution—the **privilege against self-incrimination**. Felix Frankfurter, a noted Supreme Court jurist, once said of this privilege, "Too many, even those who should be better advised, view this privilege [against self-incrimination] as a shelter for wrongdoers. They too readily assume that those who invoke it are either guilty of a crime or commit perjury in claiming the privilege. Such a view does scant honor to the patriots who sponsored the Bill of Rights as a condition to acceptance of the Constitution."[16]

Privilege against Self-Incrimination

The privilege against self-incrimination is found in the Fifth Amendment to the U.S. Constitution (see Exhibit 14.5), which reads, in part, that no person shall "be compelled in any criminal case to be a witness against himself...."

EXHIBIT 14.5   Constitutional Basis for Privilege against Self-Incrimination

[N]or shall any person ... be compelled in any criminal case to be a witness against himself ... —Fifth Amendment to the U.S. Constitution.

Historical Basis for Privilege

The historical basis for the Fifth Amendment privilege was eloquently stated by Chief Justice Earl Warren in his opinion from the landmark case of *Miranda v. Arizona*:

> We sometimes forget how long it has taken to establish the privilege against self-incrimination, the sources from which it came and the fervor with which it was defended. Its roots go back into ancient times, the critical historical event shedding light on its origins and evolution was the trial of one John Lilburn, a vocal anti-Stuart Leveller, who was made to take the Star Chamber Oath in 1637. The oath would have bound him to answer to all questions posed to him on any subject.

> He resisted the oath and declaimed the proceedings, stating:

> "Another fundamental right I then contended for, was, that no man's conscience ought to be racked by oaths imposed, to answer to questions concerning himself in matters criminal, or pretended to be so."

> On account of the Lilburn Trial, Parliament abolished the inquisitorial Court of Star Chamber. . . . The lofty principles to which Lilburn had appealed during his trial gained popular acceptance in England. These sentiments worked their way over to the Colonies and were implanted after great struggle into the Bill of Rights. . . . The privilege was elevated to constitutional status and has always been "as broad as the mischief against which it seeks to guard." *Counselman v. Hitchcock*, 142 U.S. 547, 562 (1892).

As a "noble principle often transcends its origins," the privilege has come rightfully to be recognized in part as an individual's substantive right, a "right to a private enclave where he may lead a private life. That right is the hallmark of our democracy."[17]

Two Parts to Privilege

There are two parts to this self-incrimination privilege: a *privilege asserted by a witness against compulsory self-incrimination*, and the *right of a criminal defendant not to testify*.

Privilege by Witness against Compulsory Self-Incrimination—"Taking the Fifth"

Witnesses who attend any legal proceeding by compulsory process and who are expected to answer questions or provide testimony that may incriminate them in a subsequent criminal action may "plead the fifth"; that is, invoke the Fifth Amendment privilege. This privilege may be used in any legal proceeding. Examples of this use can be seen in grand jury hearings where a suspect is called to the stand, in congressional hearings, at trial, or in pretrial proceedings. The standard form of invoking this privilege has been to state, "I refuse to answer on the grounds that the answer may tend to incriminate me." This privilege is used on a question-by-question basis only. It does not exempt the person from being called as a witness or from being asked any questions.

Miranda Rule

An offshoot of this privilege is found in criminal investigations where a suspect, in custody and being interrogated by law enforcement officers, may choose to "remain silent" and not answer any questions. This is called the **Miranda Rule**. According to the landmark case of *Miranda v. Arizona*, "The privilege against self-incrimination, which has had a long and expansive historical development, is the essential mainstay of our adversary system and guarantees to the individual the 'right to remain silent unless he chooses to speak in the unfettered exercise of his own will,' during a period of custodial interrogation as well as in the courts or during the course of other official investigations."[18]

Miranda Rule
Landmark U.S. Supreme Court case providing a suspect in a criminal case the right to remain silent during custodial interrogation.

Government Can Grant Immunity

Sometimes the government will have such a need for the witness testimony or statements that some type of **immunity** will be offered. Immunity protects the witness from subsequent prosecution or some form of liability from any testimony given. There are two types of immunity: *transactional* and *derivative use* immunity. Transactional immunity protects the witness from prosecution for anything relating to the transaction being testified about. Derivative use immunity protects the witness from having anything said being used against him and from having anything testified about being used to derive other evidence.

Immunity
A legal protection from matters testified to at trial. *Transactional* immunity protects the witness from anything testified to regarding the whole transaction; *derivative use* immunity protects from anything being used from the testimony to obtain further evidence.

Privilege of a Criminal Defendant Not to Testify

Under our system of justice, there is an absolute privilege for a criminal defendant not to testify at trial. This privilege cannot be waived unless the defendant chooses to testify (see Exhibit 14.6). Even if the defendant testified at an earlier legal proceeding, such as at the grand jury hearing or during a pretrial motion, the privilege not to testify at trial is intact.

EXHIBIT 14.6   Privilege against Self-Incrimination

Privilege by Witness against Compulsory Self-Incrimination
or
Privilege of a Criminal Defendant Not to Testify.

No Comment Rule

If a criminal defendant chooses not to testify, the prosecutor cannot mention or make any comment about this refusal. This is called the **no comment rule**. Further, the judge will usually instruct the jury about the defendant's privilege and admonish them not to weigh this in their consideration of the evidence.

COMMON LAW PRIVILEGES

As discussed at the beginning of this chapter, most privileges in evidence law stem from the common law. Except for constitutional protections and a few statutory ones, the federal courts will only accept privileges that are based in common law. States, however, have not only accepted (and codified to a great extent) these same common law privileges but have added newer ones. For example, the psychoanalyst-patient privilege is one that had been long accepted by most states, but not by the majority of the federal courts, until decided upon by the U.S. Supreme Court in 1996. We'll look at this important case later in this chapter. Other privileges that have been argued include those involving journalist-source, scholar's privilege, social worker, and mental health worker-client, accountant-client, and parent-child.

What Is the Privilege and Who May Claim?

Remember that it is most important in privilege issues to identify not only the holder of the privilege, but also who might be able to claim the privilege on behalf of the holder, even if the holder is not present. The holder usually has the privilege to refuse to testify or disclose a confidential communication and to prevent another from either testifying or disclosing a confidential communication. This privilege of the holder is presumed to pass to other parties to be used on behalf of the holder.

Attorney-Client Privilege

The U.S. Supreme Court described the attorney-client privilege as "the oldest of the privileges for confidential communications known to the common law."[19] Another court noted that "[i]n the eighteenth century, when the desire for truth overcame the wish to protect the honor of witnesses and several testimonial privileges disappeared, the attorney-client privilege was retained, on the new theory that it was necessary to

No Comment Rule
If a criminal defendant chooses not to testify, the prosecutor cannot mention or make any comment about this refusal.

encourage clients to make the fullest disclosures to their attorneys, to enable the latter to properly advise the clients. This is the basis of the privilege today."[20]

A client has a privilege to refuse to disclose and to prevent another person, usually the attorney, from disclosing confidential communications made to the attorney in the course of the attorney's providing of legal services. The purpose of the privilege is to encourage clients to be honest with and provide full disclosure to their attorney, free from worry about the consequences of disclosure. The attorney-client privilege can also extend to the attorney's representatives: paralegals, investigators, and legal secretaries (see Exhibit 14.7).

EXHIBIT 14.7   Example of Lawyer-Client Privilege Rule

Florida Evidence Code
Sec. 90.502. Lawyer-Client Privilege.

(1) For purposes of this section:

    (a) A "lawyer" is a person authorized, or reasonably believed by the client to be authorized, to practice law in any state or nation.

    (b) A "client" is any person, public officer, corporation, association, or other organization or entity, either public or private, who consults a lawyer with the purpose of obtaining legal services or who is rendered legal services by a lawyer.

    (c) A communication between lawyer and client is "confidential" if it is not intended to be disclosed to third persons other than:

        1. Those to whom disclosure is in furtherance of the rendition of legal services to the client.

        2. Those reasonably necessary for the transmission of the communication.

(2) A client has a privilege to refuse to disclose, and to prevent any other person from disclosing, the contents of confidential communications when such other person learned of the communications because they were made in the rendition of legal services to the client.

(3) The privilege may be claimed by:

    (a) The client.

    (b) A guardian or conservator of the client.

    (c) The personal representative of a deceased client.

    (d) A successor, assignee, trustee in dissolution, or any similar representative of an organization, corporation, or association or other entity, either public or private, whether or not in existence.

    (e) The lawyer, but only on behalf of the client. The lawyer's authority to claim the privilege is presumed in the absence of contrary evidence.

Elements of Attorney-Client Privilege

In a 1995 decision, the United States Court of Appeals for the Second Circuit clarified the elements of the attorney-client privilege. Emphasizing that "[t]he attorney-client privilege is designed to promote unfettered communication between attorneys and their clients so that the attorney may give fully informed legal advice . . . " the court held that the privilege is applied:

(1) Where legal advice of any kind is sought;

(2) from a professional legal adviser in his capacity as such;

(3) the communications relating to that purpose;

(4) made in confidence;

(5) by the client;

(6) are at his instance permanently protected;

(7) from disclosure by himself or the legal adviser;

(8) except the protection be waived . . .[21]

EVIDENTIARY CHECKLIST 14.1

Attorney-Client Privilege

Holder of Privilege

☐ Client

Who May Claim Privilege

☐ Client or Attorney on behalf of client

Other Elements Required to Establish Privilege

☐ Communication must be intended as confidential.

☐ Communication must be to facilitate professional legal advice.

☐ Confidentiality must be essential to furtherance of relationship.

Who May Claim Privilege?

The client holds this privilege and may, if challenged, have the burden of proving that the communication made falls within the scope of the privilege. In addition to the client, the client's guardian or estate may also claim this privilege on behalf of the client. The attorney is presumed to have authority to claim this privilege on behalf of the client, as well.

Attorney Work Products

Work Products
Materials prepared by attorneys in anticipation of trial or litigation.

Attorney **work products** are all written and recorded information and materials collected by the attorney for use in providing legal services to a client. Examples may include notes, investigation reports, interviews, and memoranda. The protection given to attorney work product serves a purpose "to avoid chilling attorneys in developing materials to aid them in giving legal advice and in preparing a case for trial."[22]

Test for Work Product Privilege. The legal test for the work product privilege is "whether, in light of the nature of the document and the factual situation in the particular case, the document can fairly be said to have been prepared or obtained because of the prospect of litigation." For a document to meet this standard, the lawyer must at least have had a subjective belief that litigation was a real possibility, and that belief must have been objectively reasonable.[23]

Exceptions

Not all work undertaken by lawyers finds protection in the work product privilege. Generally, the privilege will not apply to documents prepared by lawyers in the ordinary course of business or for other purposes not connected to the "prospect of litigation." A bill prepared by a lawyer's office, or a letter instructing a client about a court appearance, would not be privileged. Records that pre-existed the relationship are generally not privileged. Observations made by the attorney, like a fresh cut on the client's face or a client's drunken behavior, are generally not privileged.

YOU BE THE JUDGE 14.1

A retailer suspected its distributor of violation of price discrimination laws, and searched the distributor's trash dumpster for evidence. In the trash, the retailer found several handwritten drafts of letters that were intended to be confidential communications to the distributor's attorney. The distributor asserted attorney-client privilege with respect to these papers. How would you decide? Explain your reasons.

In Furtherance of a Crime or Fraud

There is no privilege when the communication made was in the furtherance of a crime or fraud, or where the services of the attorney were sought to enable or aid anyone to commit or plan to commit a crime or fraud (see Exhibit 14.8). This applies only to *future* wrongdoing, not to past misconduct or confessions.

EXHIBIT 14.8   Client Dangerousness Exception

California Evidence Code
     Section 956.6. There is no privilege under this article if the lawyer reasonably believes that disclosure of any confidential communication relating to representation of a client is necessary to prevent the client from committing a criminal act that the lawyer believes is likely to result in death or substantial bodily harm.

Malpractice Claims.   Another exception is when the communication is relevant to a dispute between the client and attorney over a breach of duty or malpractice by the attorney (see Exhibit 14.9).

"I Have Never Had A Sexual Relationship With the President"

In the following case, the Office of Independent Counsel had attempted to subpoena documents from Monica Lewinsky's attorney. Lewinsky responded, arguing that these documents were protected from disclosure by the attorney-client privilege, the work product privilege, and Lewinsky's Fifth Amendment privilege against self-incrimination (see Exhibit 14.10).

EXHIBIT 14.9   Sample of Motion Opposing Work Products Protective Order

UNITED STATES DISTRICT COURT
FOR THE SOUTHERN DISTRICT OF FLORIDA

UNITED STATES OF AMERICA	)
	)
v.	)
	) Criminal No. 12345
JOHN DOE,	)
	)
Defendant	)

UNITED STATES' RESPONSE OPPOSING
DEFENDANT'S MOTION FOR A PROTECTIVE ORDER

Counsel for the defendant has moved, pursuant to Fed. R. Crim. P. 16(d), for an order to protect what he refers to as his work product. . . . [T]he disclosure of the defendant's request to a third party for documents is not covered by the work product doctrine. The defendant's motion for a protective order is without standing or merit and should be denied.

In June 2002, the United States and ABC entered into a plea agreement which provided, among other things, that ABC would plead guilty to rigging bids. A copy of the plea agreement is attached. In exchange for ABC's agreement to cooperate with the United States in the investigation and litigation of cases involving these bids, the United States agreed not to bring any additional charges against ABC. . . .

As part of its cooperation, counsel for ABC agreed to inform the United States of any requests for documents made to ABC counsel by the defendant. Defendant did make these requests to ABC counsel and they informed the United States. The defendant's claim that the disclosure of his request to ABC counsel is protected as work product is without merit. The work product doctrine is a qualified privilege for certain materials and the mental processes of an attorney in anticipation of litigation or for trial. _United States v. Nobles_, 422 U.S. 225 (1975). This is a qualified privilege which may be waived. The defendant's communications with ABC counsel and the subsequent disclosure by ABC to the United States of defendant's request for documents is not protected by the work product doctrine when it was done so voluntarily by ABC.

For these reasons, the defendant's motion should be denied.

Respectfully submitted,

_____

Attorneys

CASE

In re Sealed Case

162 F. 3d 670 (1998)

United States Court of Appeals for the District Of Columbia Circuit.

. . . In 1997, Monica S. Lewinsky, a former White House intern, received a subpoena to produce items and to testify in _Paula Jones v. William Jefferson Clinton_, a civil matter then pending in the United States District Court for the Eastern District of Arkansas. The subpoena requested, among other things, documents relating to an alleged relation-ship between President Clinton and Lewinsky and any gifts the President may have given her. Lewinsky retained Francis D. Carter, Esq., to represent her regarding the subpoena. Carter drafted an affidavit for Lewinsky, which she signed under penalty of perjury. The affidavit, submitted to the Arkansas district court as an exhibit to Lewinsky's motion to quash the subpoena, states in relevant part:

> I have never had a sexual relationship with the President, [and] he did not propose that we have a sexual relationship. . . . The occasions that I saw the President after I left my employment at the

White House in April, 1996, were official receptions, formal functions or events related to the U.S. Department of Defense, where I was working at the time. There were other people present on those occasions.

On January 16, 1998. . . the Office of Independent Counsel investigate[d]. . . whether Monica Lewinsky. . . suborned perjury, obstructed justice. . . or otherwise violated federal law. . . concerning the civil case *Jones v. Clinton.* [A]s part of that investigation, a grand jury issued subpoenas to Carter, the first for documents and other items, the second for his testimony. Carter moved to quash the subpoenas, contending, inter alia, that the documents, testimony, and other items sought were protected from disclosure by the attorney-client privilege, the work product privilege, and Lewinsky's Fifth Amendment privilege against self-incrimination. Lewinsky, as the real-party-in-interest, filed a response in support of Carter's motion. The United States opposed the motion, arguing among other things that the crime-fraud exception vitiated any claims of attorney-client or work product privilege and that the Fifth Amendment did not bar production of the requested materials. The district court ordered Carter to comply with the two grand jury subpoenas except to the extent that compliance would "call for him to disclose materials in his possession that may not be revealed without violating Monica S. Lewinsky's Fifth Amendment rights."

. . . The district court held that the crime-fraud exception to the attorney-client privilege applied. After reviewing the government's in camera submission, the court found that "Ms. Lewinsky consulted Mr. Carter for the purpose of committing perjury and obstructing justice and used the material he prepared for her for the purpose of committing perjury and obstructing

justice.". . . [The district court did not find, nor did the Independent Counsel suggest, any impropriety by Carter.]

. . . Our review of the **in camera** materials on which the district court based its decision convinces us that the government sufficiently established the elements of a violation . . . . That is, the government offered "evidence that if believed by the trier of fact would establish the elements of" the crime of obstruction of justice. . . .

Lewinsky. . . maintains that the Tripp tapes were not "lawfully obtained" and therefore should not have been considered in camera. But the government satisfied its burden wholly apart from the Tripp tapes. Other government evidence—consisting of grand jury testimony and documents—established that the crime-fraud exception applied. Because that other evidence, if believed by the trier of fact, combined with the circumstances under which Lewinsky retained Carter, would establish the elements of the crime-fraud exception, there is no reason for us to consider her arguments about the tapes.

The district court [also] ruled that compelling Carter to produce materials his client gave him would violate Lewinsky's Fifth Amendment privilege because it would compel her to admit the materials exist and had been in her possession. The Supreme Court foreclosed that line of reasoning in *Fisher v. United States,* 425 U.S. 391 (1976). Documents transferred from the accused to his attorney are "obtainable without personal compulsion on the accused," and hence the accused's "Fifth Amendment privilege is. . . not violated by enforcement of the [subpoena] directed toward [his] attorneys. This is true whether or not the Amendment would have barred a subpoena directing the [accused] to produce the documents while they were in his hands."

CRITICAL THINKING QUESTIONS 14.1

1. Suppose a client goes to an attorney who advertises a free half-hour consultation and during this time admits to a crime, then decides not to hire the attorney. Should the attorney still be bound under the privilege? Why or why not?

2. How about the paralegal who first interviewed this client? The legal secretary who took notes during the interview? Explain your answer.

In Camera
In judge's chambers. Evidence that is viewed *in camera* is examined privately by a judge in chambers.

EXHIBIT 14.10 Exceptions to Lawyer-Client Privilege

Texas Rules of Evidence
Rule 503. Lawyer-Client Privilege.

. . .

(d) Exceptions. There is no privilege under this rule:

    (1) *Furtherance of crime or fraud.* If the services of the lawyer were sought or obtained to enable or aid anyone to commit or plan to commit what the client knew or reasonably should have known to be a crime or fraud;

    (2) *Claimants through same deceased client.* As to a communication relevant to an issue between parties who claim through the same deceased client, regardless of whether the claims are by testate or intestate succession or by *inter vivos* transactions;

    (3) *Breach of duty by a lawyer or client.* As to a communication relevant to an issue of breach of duty by a lawyer to the client or by a client to the lawyer;

    (4) *Document attested by a lawyer.* As to a communication relevant to an issue concerning an attested document to which the lawyer is an attesting witness; or

    (5) *Joint clients.* As to a communication relevant to a matter of common interest between or among two or more clients if the communication was made by any of them to a lawyer retained or consulted in common, when offered in an action between or among any of the clients.

LEGAL ANALYSIS AND WRITING 14.1

Using the *IRAC Method of Legal Analysis* (found in the Appendix), write a short memo analyzing the following case problems and deciding whether there is a privilege for each:

1. Client has been released on bail with condition that she submit daily to a blood alcohol test. She tells her attorney that she has been drinking and asks the attorney to make an excuse so that she can get out of taking the test. At a hearing to rescind bail, prosecutor wants the attorney to testify about this conversation. Attorney claims privilege.

2. Attorney's receptionist calls clients to remind them of their court date. One client fails to show and the court wants the attorney to divulge as to whether this client had knowledge of the court date. Attorney claims privilege.

3. A private attorney calls a public defender who is representing a defendant being tried with murder. The private attorney tells the public defender in confidence that her client has confessed to her about the murder that the defendant is being tried for. The public defender wants to call both the attorney and her client to testify. Both claim privilege.

LEGAL RESEARCH USING THE INTERNET SKILLS 14.2

Do attorneys' work products apply to IRS summonses? A corporation learned that one of its subsidiaries had made questionable payments to foreign government officials in order to secure government business. The corporation ordered its General Counsel to initiate an internal investigation. The General Counsel sent a questionnaire to all foreign managers seeking detailed information concerning such payments, and the responses were returned to the General Counsel. The General Counsel and outside counsel also interviewed the recipients of the questionnaire and other company officers and employees.

(Continued)

LEGAL RESEARCH USING THE INTERNET SKILLS 14.2 *Continued*

The Internal Revenue Service (IRS) began an investigation to determine the tax consequences of such payments and issued a summons demanding production of the questionnaires and the memoranda and notes of the interviews. Petitioner refused to produce the documents on the grounds that they were protected from disclosure by the attorney-client privilege and constituted the work product of attorneys prepared in anticipation of litigation.

How would you rule in this case? Look up this case on the Internet and compare what the court decided with your own decision. The citation for this U.S. Supreme Court case is:

Upjohn v. United States, 449 U.S. 383 (1981).

CRITICAL THINKING QUESTIONS 14.2

1. Where do we draw the line between legitimate confidential communications between a corporate attorney and the officers of the corporation, intended to help the attorney provide legal services . . . and communication that is couched under the work product in order to simply protect the corporation's image or profits? Isn't it the duty of the attorneys to protect the corporation?

2. Where do we draw the line between an attorney violating the law and upholding the legal code of ethics?

Marital Privilege

Long used at common law and recognized in some form in both federal and state courts is the *husband–wife* or *marital privilege*. There are two forms to this privilege: *testimonial* and *confidential communications* privileges.

Testimonial Privilege

Designed to promote accord and prevent disruption in the marital relationship, the **testimonial privilege** prohibits one spouse from testifying against another in a criminal case where the other spouse is the defendant. This privilege generally provides that a spouse may not be called as a witness nor be compelled to testify against the spouse in any criminal proceeding. The exception to this rule is when one of the spouses is charged with a crime or alleged to have committed a tort against the other spouse or a child of either.

Testimonial Privilege
A form of marital privilege that prohibits one spouse from testifying against another in a criminal case where the other spouse is the defendant.

No Testimonial Privilege in Federal Courts When Spouse Voluntarily Testifies.

In federal courts, there is no testimonial privilege if a spouse voluntarily takes the stand to become a witness and testify against the other spouse. In a major case decision, the Supreme Court reasoned that when a spouse is "willing to testify against the other in a criminal proceeding—whatever the motivation—their relationship is almost certainly in disrepair; there is probably little in the way of marital harmony for the privilege to preserve." This case overturned the long-standing precedent that a criminal defendant could prevent the voluntary testimony of a spouse.

CASE

Trammel v. United States

445 U.S. 40 (1980).

Chief Justice Burger delivered the opinion of the Court.

We granted certiorari to consider whether an accused may invoke the privilege against adverse spousal testimony so as to exclude the voluntary testimony of his wife. This calls for a re-examination of *Hawkins v. United States*, 358 U.S. 74 (1958).

I

On March 10, 1976, petitioner Otis Trammel was indicted... for importing heroin into the United States from Thailand and the Philippine Islands and for conspiracy to import heroin.... The indictment also named six unindicted co-conspirators, including petitioner's wife Elizabeth Ann Trammel.

Prior to trial on this indictment, petitioner... advised the court that the Government intended to call his wife as an adverse witness and asserted his claim to a privilege to prevent her from testifying against him. At a hearing on the motion, Mrs. Trammel was called as a Government witness under a grant of use immunity. She testified that she and petitioner were married in May 1975 and that they remained married. She explained that her cooperation with the Government was based on assurances that she would be given lenient treatment. She then described, in considerable detail, her role and that of her husband in the heroin distribution conspiracy.

After hearing this testimony, the District Court ruled that Mrs. Trammel could testify in support of the Government's case to any act she observed during the marriage and to any communication "made in the presence of a third person"; however, confidential communications between petitioner and his wife were held to be privileged and inadmissible....

At trial, Elizabeth Trammel testified within the limits of the court's pretrial ruling; her testimony, as the Government concedes, constituted virtually its entire case against petitioner. He was found guilty on both the substantive and conspiracy charges and sentenced to an indeterminate term of years pursuant to the Federal Youth Corrections Act.

. . . .

II

The privilege claimed by petitioner has ancient roots. Writing in 1628, Lord Coke observed that "it hath been resolved by the Justices that a wife cannot be produced either against or for her husband." 1 E. Coke, A Commentary upon Littleton 6b (1628). This spousal disqualification sprang from two canons of medieval jurisprudence: first, the rule that an accused was not permitted to testify in his own behalf because of his interest in the proceeding; second, the concept that husband and wife were one, and that since the woman had no recognized separate legal existence, the husband was that one. From those two now long-abandoned doctrines, it followed that what was inadmissible from the lips of the defendant-husband was also inadmissible from his wife.

Despite its medieval origins, this rule of spousal disqualification remained intact in most common-law jurisdictions well into the 19th century.... Indeed, it was not until 1933, in *Funk v. United States*, 290 U.S. 371, that this Court abolished the testimonial disqualification in the federal courts, so as to permit the spouse of a defendant to testify in the defendant's behalf. *Funk*, however, left undisturbed the rule that either spouse could prevent the other from giving adverse testimony. The rule thus evolved into one of privilege rather than one of absolute disqualification.

The modern justification for this privilege against adverse spousal testimony is its perceived role in fostering the harmony and sanctity of the marriage relationship. Notwithstanding this benign purpose, the rule was sharply criticized. These criticisms influenced the American Law Institute, which, in its 1942 Model Code of Evidence, advocated a privilege for marital confidences, but expressly rejected a rule vesting in the defendant the right to exclude all adverse testimony of his spouse. In 1953 the Uniform Rules of Evidence, drafted by the National Conference of Commissioners on Uniform State Laws, followed a similar course; it limited the privilege to confidential communications and "[abolished] the rule, still existing in some states, and largely a sentimental relic, of not requiring one spouse to testify against the other in a criminal action." Several state legislatures enacted similarly patterned provisions into law.

....

A

The Federal Rules of Evidence acknowledge the authority of the federal courts to continue the evolutionary development of testimonial privileges in federal criminal trials "governed by the principles of the common law as they may be interpreted... in the light of reason and experience." Fed. Rule Evid. 501....

B

Since 1958... support for the privilege against adverse spousal testimony has been eroded further. Thirty-one jurisdictions, including Alaska and Hawaii, then allowed an accused a privilege to prevent adverse spousal testimony. The number has now declined to 24.9.... The trend in state law toward divesting the accused of the privilege to bar adverse spousal testimony has special relevance because the laws of marriage and domestic relations are concerns traditionally reserved to the states.

C

Testimonial exclusionary rules and privileges contravene the fundamental principle that "the public ... has a right to every man's evidence." *United States v. Bryan*, 339 U.S. 323 (1950). As such, they must be strictly construed and accepted "only to the very limited extent that permitting a refusal to testify or excluding relevant evidence has a public good transcending the normally predominant principle of utilizing all rational means for ascertaining truth." *Elkins v. United States*, 364 U.S. 206 (1960) (Frankfurter, J., dissenting). Here we must decide whether the privilege against adverse spousal testimony promotes sufficiently important interests to outweigh the need for probative evidence in the administration of criminal justice.

It is essential to remember that the... privilege is not needed to protect information privately disclosed between husband and wife in the confidence of the marital relationship—once described by this Court as "the best solace of human existence." *Stein v. Bowman*, 13 Pet., at 223. Those confidences are privileged under the independent rule protecting confidential marital communications. The... privilege is invoked, not to exclude private marital communications, but rather to exclude evidence of criminal acts and of communications made in the presence of third persons. No other testimonial privilege sweeps so broadly. The privileges between priest and penitent, attorney and client, and physician and patient limit protection to private communications. These privileges are rooted in the imperative need for confidence and trust. The priest-penitent privilege recognizes the human need to disclose to a spiritual counselor, in total and absolute confidence, what are believed to be flawed acts or thoughts and to receive priestly consolation and guidance in return. The lawyer-client privilege rests on the need for the advocate and counselor to know all that relates to the client's reasons for seeking representation if the professional mission is to be carried out. Similarly, the physician must know all that a patient can articulate in order to identify and to treat disease; barriers to full disclosure would impair diagnosis and treatment.

The [testimonial] rule stands in marked contrast to these three privileges. Its protection is not limited to confidential communications; rather it permits an accused to exclude all adverse spousal testimony....

The contemporary justification for affording an accused such a privilege is also unpersuasive. When one spouse is willing to testify against the other in a criminal proceeding—whatever the motivation—their relationship is almost certainly in disrepair; there is probably little in the way of marital harmony for the privilege to preserve. In these circumstances, a rule of evidence that permits an accused to prevent adverse spousal testimony seems far more likely to frustrate justice than to foster family peace. Indeed, there is reason to believe that vesting the privilege in the accused could actually undermine the marital relationship....

IV

Our consideration of the foundations for the privilege and its history satisfy us that "reason and experience" no longer justify so sweeping a rule.... Accordingly, we conclude that the existing rule should be modified so that the witness-spouse alone has a privilege to refuse to testify adversely; the witness may be neither compelled to testify nor foreclosed from testifying. This modification—vesting the privilege in the witness-spouse—furthers the important public interest in marital harmony without unduly burdening legitimate law enforcement needs.

Here, petitioner's spouse chose to testify against him. That she did so after a grant of immunity and assurances of lenient treatment does not render her testimony involuntary.

Affirmed.

LEGAL ANALYSIS AND WRITING 14.2

1. What were the facts in this case?

2. What was the issue before the court?

3. What did the court decide?

4. Why did the court decide the way it did? What was the court's reasoning? Include relevant quotes from the case decision to illustrate and support your answer.

5. Do you agree with the court's decision? Why or why not?

LEGAL RESEARCH USING THE INTERNET SKILLS 14.3

Find and read this Supreme Court case online! Was there a dissenting opinion? Concurring opinion? How many justices joined the majority for this decision?

Effect of Trammel. The *Trammel* decision changed the common law rule in the federal courts regarding the marital testimony privilege. It made the witness-spouse the *holder* of this privilege and provided that this spouse could choose whether or not to testify against the other spouse. If the witness-spouse chose to testify, her testimony could not be prevented. This federal rule has also been adopted in many of the states.

Confidential Marital Communications Privilege

Confidential Communication
A form of marital privilege that prevents a spouse from testifying to or disclosing confidential communications made during the marriage.

The other type of marital privilege gives a spouse the privilege to refuse to disclose or to prevent the other spouse from disclosing a **confidential communication** made between the spouses while married (see Exhibit 14.11 to Exhibit 14.13). The purpose of this privilege is to protect the intimacy of the marital relationship and to encourage trust and open communications between the spouses.

Difference between Testimonial and Communications Privilege. The difference between the two marital privileges is that the confidential communications privilege can prevent a spouse from testifying to or disclosing confidential communications made during the marriage, even if that spouse would voluntarily testify. Where a spouse agrees to testify, that spouse could still testify about acts or non-confidential communications made during the marriage, but not about confidential communications. The communications privilege continues after the marriage as to confidential communications made during the marriage. The testimonial privilege may only be used during the marriage, but applies to acts or communication made prior to marriage.

Criminal Partnership Exception. The marital privilege cannot be used in cases where the spouses are partners or participants together in criminal activity.

Exception for Crime by Spouse against Other Spouse or Children. There is generally no marital privilege allowed when crimes are committed by one spouse against the other spouse or children. Some states, however, limit this exception to cases involving violence.

EVIDENTIARY CHECKLIST 14.2

Elements Required to Establish Marital Privilege

Holder of Privilege

- ☐ In testimonial privilege, holder is usually the testifying spouse (in some states, the other spouse is the holder)
- ☐ In confidential communication privilege, either spouse is the holder in most states

Who May Claim Privilege?

- ☐ In either privilege, testifying spouse is presumed capable of claiming

Other Elements Required to Establish Privilege

- ☐ Must be valid marriage
- ☐ Communication must be intended as confidential
- ☐ Confidentiality must be essential to furtherance of relationship

Specific Elements Required for Testimonial Privilege

- ☐ Usually only allowed in criminal cases
- ☐ Applies to acts or communication, including those made before the marriage (but only if still married at the time of trial)

Specific Elements Required for Confidential Communication Privilege

- ☐ Can be used in criminal or civil cases
- ☐ Applies only to communication made during marriage, but still applies after the marriage ends for those communications made during the marriage

---

EXHIBIT 14.11 Marital Privilege Rule in Texas

Texas Rules of Evidence
Rule 504. Husband-Wife Privileges.

  (a) Confidential Communication Privilege.

    (1) *Definition.* A communication is confidential if it is made privately by any person to the person's spouse and it is not intended for disclosure to any other person.

    (2) *Rule of privilege.* A person, whether or not a party, or the guardian or representative of an incompetent or deceased person, has a privilege during marriage and afterwards to refuse to disclose and to prevent another from disclosing a confidential communication made to the person's spouse while they were married.

(Continued)

EXHIBIT 14.11 Marital Privilege Rule in Texas *Continued*

(3) *Who may claim the privilege.* The confidential communication privilege may be claimed by the person or the person's guardian or representative, or by the spouse on the person's behalf. The authority of the spouse to do so is presumed.

(4) *Exceptions.* There is no confidential communication privilege:

   (A) *Furtherance of crime or fraud.* If the communication was made, in whole or in part, to enable or aid anyone to commit or plan to commit a crime or fraud.

   (B) *Proceeding between spouses in civil cases.*

   (C) *Crime against spouse or minor child.* In a proceeding in which the party is accused of conduct which, if proved, is a crime against the person of the spouse, any minor child, or any member of the household of either spouse.

   (D) *Commitment or similar proceeding.* In a proceeding to commit either spouse or otherwise to place that person or that person's property, or both, under the control of another because of an alleged mental or physical condition.

   (E) *Proceeding to establish competence.* In a proceeding brought by or on behalf of either spouse to establish competence.

EXHIBIT 14.12 Marital Privilege Rule in California

California Evidence Code

Section 970. Except as otherwise provided by statute, a married person has a privilege not to testify against his spouse in any proceeding.

Section 971. Except as otherwise provided by statute, a married person whose spouse is a party to a proceeding has a privilege not to be called as a witness by an adverse party to that proceeding without the prior express consent of the spouse having the privilege under this section unless the party calling the spouse does so in good faith without knowledge of the marital relationship.

. . .

Section 973(a). Unless erroneously compelled to do so, a married person who testifies in a proceeding to which his spouse is a party, or who testifies against his spouse in any proceeding, does not have a privilege under this article in the proceeding in which such testimony is given.

. . .

Section 980. Subject to Section 912 and except as otherwise provided in this article, a spouse (or his guardian or conservator when he has a guardian or conservator), whether or not a party, has a privilege during the marital relationship and afterwards to refuse to disclose, and to prevent another from disclosing, a communication if he claims the privilege and the communication was made in confidence between him and the other spouse while they were husband and wife.

Section 981. There is no privilege under this article if the communication was made, in whole or in part, to enable or aid anyone to commit or plan to commit a crime or a fraud.

EXHIBIT 14.13 Marital Privilege Rule in Utah

Utah Rules of Evidence
Rule 502. Husband-Wife.

   (a) Criminal proceedings. In a criminal proceeding, a wife shall not be compelled to testify against her husband, nor a husband against his wife.

   (b) Communications.

(Continued)

EXHIBIT 14.13   Marital Privilege Rule in Utah   *Continued*

(1) Definition. A communication is confidential if it is made privately by any person to his or her spouse and is not intended for disclosure to any other person.

(2) General rule of privilege. An individual has a privilege during the person's life to refuse to testify or to prevent his or her spouse or former spouse from testifying as to any confidential communication made by the individual to the spouse during their marriage and to prevent another from disclosing any such confidential communication.

(3) Who may claim the privilege. The privilege may be claimed by the person who made the confidential communication, or by the person's guardian or conservator. The non-communicating spouse to whom the confidential communication was made is presumed to be authorized, during the life of the communicating spouse, to claim the privilege on behalf of the person who made the confidential communication.

"Marital Communications Privilege Must Be Narrowly Construed."   In the following California case, the court cautions that the marital communications privilege must be narrowly construed "because it obstructs the truth seeking process."

CASE

United States v. White

974 F.2d 1135 (9th Cir. 1992).
Appeal from the United States District Court for the Northern District of California.

Choy, Circuit Judge.

Joseph Lamont White was convicted on one count of involuntary manslaughter. . . of causing the death of his two-year-old stepdaughter, Jasmine Jones. Jasmine died from severe head injuries she incurred while she was in White's care at a military personnel residence at Fort Ord, California. White's wife Jayne was serving in the Army and stationed at Fort Ord. White was responsible for caring for Ms. White's two children.

In January 1990, White expressed some frustration to Ms. White over his role as caretaker of the children. This frustration allegedly escalated into a threat to kill Jasmine and Ms. White should he have to continue to care for the children. Just over a week after the threat, White called his wife while she was on duty and told her that Jasmine was "breathing funny" and suffering from convulsions. Ms. White rushed home to find Jasmine unconscious. The Whites rushed Jasmine to the

hospital where medical examinations revealed that Jasmine suffered a massive subdural hematoma. . . and she died shortly thereafter. White was indicted for voluntary manslaughter. . . . Before trial, White filed a motion in limine to exclude the statements he made to his wife that conveyed a threat to kill her and her daughter. After the hearing, the district court denied the motion. The trial that began in January 1991 culminated in a guilty verdict on the lesser included offense of involuntary manslaughter.

. . . .

A. Marital Communications Privilege

White objects to the introduction of the following testimony of Ms. White:

Q: What did Joe say about hurting Jasmine or hurting you?

A: He told me that he was tired of keeping her and if I left him with her again, he would kill her and then he would have to kill me, too.

White argues that this testimony should have been excluded under Federal Rule of Evidence 501.1 The common law recognizes two separate marital privileges: (1) the "anti-marital facts" privilege which prohibits one spouse from testifying against another during the length of the marriage, and (2) the "marital communications" privilege which bars testimony concerning statements privately communicated between spouses. It is the latter privilege that is at issue here.

This court has counseled that the marital communications privilege must be narrowly construed "because it obstructs the truth seeking process. Use of the privilege in criminal proceedings requires a particularly narrow construction because of society's strong interest in the administration of justice." *United States v. Marashi*, 913 F.2d 724 (9th Cir. 1990). The public policy interests in protecting the integrity of marriages and ensuring that spouses freely communicate with one another underlie the marital communications privilege. When balancing these interests we find that threats against spouses and a spouse's children do not further the purposes of the privilege and that the public interest in the administration of justice outweighs any possible purpose the privilege serves in such a case.

The court held in *Marashi* that when the allegedly confidential communications relate to present or future crimes that involve both spouses, the privilege does not apply. 913 F.2d at 730. The court reasoned that "greater public good will result from permitting the spouse of an accused to testify willingly concerning their joint criminal activities than would have come from permitting the accused to erect a roadblock against the search for truth." Similarly, the marital communications privilege should not apply to statements relating to a crime where a spouse or a spouse's children are the victims.

. . . Protecting threats against a spouse or the spouse's children is inconsistent with the purposes of the marital communications privilege: promoting confidential communications between spouses in order to foster marital harmony.

. . . .

Affirmed.

Can a Partner in a "Common Law" Marriage use the Marital Communication Privilege? In the following North Carolina case, the defendant, Acker, was indicted for bank robbery. Her "common law" husband of 25 years agreed to testify against her at trial. Acker objected, claiming marital privilege. How would you decide the outcome?

CASE

United States v. Acker

52 F.3d 509 (1995). United States Court of Appeals for the Fourth Circuit.

Appeal from the United States District Court for the Western District of North Carolina, at Charlotte.

[Catherine Yvonne Acker was indicted for four bank robberies and conspiracy to rob a bank with her "common law" husband, Samuel Holly. Acker and Samuel Holly lived together for approximately 25 years, but never married. Prior to trial, Holly entered into a plea agreement in which he agreed to enter a plea of guilty to aiding and abetting one of the robberies and to testify for the prosecution in exchange for the dismissal of the conspiracy count and a recommendation for a probationary sentence. Acker objected to Holly testifying against her, claiming that all confidential conversations between them were privileged under spousal immunity or the marital communications privilege. This motion was denied by the trial judge, and Holly testified for the prosecution. Holly testified that appellant told him that she robbed three banks. She brought large amounts of money home after each of the robberies, and over time she explained to him various details of the robberies.]

Chapman, Senior Circuit Judge.

. . . .

Catherine Acker and Samuel Holly lived together as man and wife for a period of approximately 25 years, during which time they lived in either

New York or North Carolina. Neither of these states recognizes common law marriage. Appellant concedes that generally the claim of spousal privilege, whether it be the "adverse spousal testimony privilege" or the "marital communication privilege," must be supported by a valid marriage. However, she argues that under Fed. R. Evid. 501 and the Equal Protection Clause of the Fourteenth Amendment, we should recognize her relationship with Holly as a valid marriage and thereby extend to her the same rights and privileges that are extended to married individuals in federal courts.

There are two types of marital privilege: the privilege against adverse spousal testimony and the privilege of protecting confidential marital communications. The adverse spousal privilege is vested in the witness-spouse, who may neither be compelled to testify nor foreclosed from testifying. See *Trammel v. United States*, 445 U.S. 40, 53 (1980). In this case, Holly was the alleged witness-spouse, and he elected to testify against Acker in order to fulfill his obligation under his plea agreement with the government.

The "marital communication privilege," if applicable and properly raised, is with the defendant and prevents a spouse from testifying against the defendant regarding confidential communications between the spouses. Acker argues that almost all of Holly's testimony consisted of confidential communications between the two of them, rather than observations that Holly made at the time and place of the alleged crimes, and that when she made these statements to Holly, she intended for them to remain confidential. "The party asserting an evidentiary privilege, such as the marital communications privilege, bears the burden of establishing all of the essential elements involved." See *United States v. White*, 950 F.2d 426 (7th Cir. 1991). The first essential element that defendant must prove when claiming confidential marital communications privilege is the existence of a valid marriage between herself and the testifying witness. This she has failed to do. The marital communications privilege is in derogation of the truth, as are other evidentiary privileges; and therefore the "valid marriage" requirement must be interpreted strictly.

We do not interpret the language "in the light of reason and experience" contained in Rule 501 nor do we find anything in the Equal Protection Clause of the Fourteenth Amendment that will lead us away from the "bright line" rule that "marital communication privilege" must rest upon the foundation of a valid marriage. The light of present day experience may indicate that more couples are living together without the benefit of marriage, but reason dictates that before the courts extend a marital privilege to benefit a defendant, the defendant must have assumed both the privileges and the responsibilities of a valid marriage under the law of the state in which the privilege is asserted. The district court did not abuse its discretion in permitting Holly to testify against the defendant.

. . . .

[This case was reversed and remanded on other grounds.]

LEGAL RESEARCH USING THE INTERNET SKILLS 14.4

Try to find the entire *Acker* case decision or a reference to it online! Check out one of the federal court web sites, go to the federal circuit for this court decision, and use their "Search" feature to find this case or cases that refer to it. In the "Search" field, enter the cite or case name. If you have access to Westlaw or Lexis, try to find this case using one of these legal search sites.

1. U.S. Courts Site: (http://www.uscourts.gov/links.html)
2. Findlaw: (http://guide.lp.findlaw.com/casecode/)

Use the *IRAC Legal Analysis Method* shown in the Appendix and the above decision in *United States v. Acker* to resolve the following case problem:

Al and Ima lived together in California for 10 years as "common law" man and wife, but never legally married. For purposes of spousal support and community property settlements, California recognizes common law marriages. During this time, Ima ran for and was elected to public office, and Al managed Ima's political campaign and contributions. Al is now being investigated by the local prosecutor's office for embezzling money from Ima's political contributions during that campaign. Just before the prosecutor convened a grand jury and issued a subpoena for Ima to appear and testify, Al and Ima were legally married. Ima notifies the prosecutor that she is invoking the marital privilege not to testify against her husband.

1. What's the issue(s) here?
2. What legal rule(s) from *United States v. Acker* can be used to resolve the issue?
3. Analyze and apply the rule(s) to the facts in this case problem involving Ima and Al in order to reach your conclusion as to whether Ima can use the marital privilege to avoid testifying before the grand jury.
4. What distinguishes this case problem from the one in *Acker*?

Patient's Privilege

Most courts recognize some type of patient's privilege to refuse to disclose and to prevent any other person from disclosing confidential communications made to his or her doctor for the purpose of diagnosing or treating a physical or emotional condition (see Exhibit 14.14). States, however, differ on the extent of this privilege. Some restrict it to use in civil proceedings. Some allow the privilege in both civil and criminal actions. Some states restrict the privilege to a doctor licensed to practice medicine. Other states may extend the privilege to a wide range of health care providers, including nurses, dentists, substance abuse counselors, and mental health workers. A few states have statutory laws that prohibit the disclosure of any information required in attending a patient.

EXHIBIT 14.14   Comparison of Patient's Privilege—Texas and Vermont

Texas Rules of Evidence
Rule 509. Physician-Patient Privilege.

   (b) Limited Privilege in Criminal Proceedings.

   There is no physician-patient privilege in criminal proceedings. However, a communication to any person involved in the treatment or examination of alcohol or drug abuse by a person being treated voluntarily or being examined for admission to treatment for alcohol or drug abuse is not admissible in a criminal proceeding.

   (c) General Rule of Privilege in Civil Proceedings. In a civil proceeding:

   (1) Confidential communications between a physician and a patient, relative to or in connection with any professional services rendered by a physician to the patient, are privileged and may not be disclosed.

   (2) Records of the identity, diagnosis, evaluation, or treatment of a patient by a physician that are created or maintained by a physician are confidential and privileged and may not be disclosed.

(Continued)

EXHIBIT 14.14   Comparison of Patient's Privilege—Texas and Vermont   *Continued*

Vermont Rules of Evidence
Rule 503. Patient's Privilege.

> (b) General rule of privilege. A patient has a privilege to refuse to disclose and to prevent any other person, including a person present to further the interest of the patient in the consultation, examination or interview, from disclosing confidential communications made for the purpose of diagnosis or treatment of his physical, mental, dental, or emotional condition, including alcohol or drug addiction, among himself, his physician, dentist, nurse, or mental health professional, and persons who are participating in diagnosis or treatment under the direction of a physician, dentist, nurse, or mental health professional, including members of the patient's family.

Who May Claim Privilege?

The patient or his or her guardian may claim the patient's privilege. The personal representative of a deceased patient may also claim it. The doctor is presumed to have authority to claim the privilege on behalf of the patient (see Exhibit 14.15).

Exceptions

Most states require that physicians and medical professionals report certain types of incidents or crimes. There is usually mandatory reporting required when physicians treat incidents of suspected child abuse and any gunshot wounds. There is no privilege extended to these reportings. In addition, there may be an exception when a court orders a medical or psychiatric examination. Also, no exception extends when the medical condition treated is an element of the claim or defense.

EVIDENTIARY CHECKLIST 14.3

Patient's Privilege Checklist

Holder of Privilege

☐   Patient

Who May Claim Privilege?

☐   Patient or Physician/Psychotherapist on behalf of patient

Other Elements Required to Establish Privilege

☐   Communication must be intended as confidential.
☐   Communication must facilitate professional medical care.
☐   Confidentiality must be essential to furtherance of relationship.

EXHIBIT 14.15   What Information Is Privileged?

New York Civil Practice Law and Rules
CPLR Sec. 4504. Physician, Dentist, Podiatrist, Chiropractor and Nurse.

    (a) Confidential information privileged. Unless the patient waives the privilege, a person authorized to practice medicine, registered professional nursing, licensed practical nursing, dentistry, podiatry or chiropractic shall not be allowed to disclose any information which he acquired in attending a patient in a professional capacity, and which was necessary to enable him to act in that capacity.

Is There a Psychotherapist Privilege?

In the following important case, the U.S. Supreme Court recognized the psychotherapist-patient privilege, ending a long conflict between lower courts about the application of any patient's privilege. This case is being presented in a more complete version, to help you better understand what the Court bases their decision on, how they arrive at their decision after examining prior cases and other state statutes, and what their reasoning is for adopting such a major rule. Equally important is the dissenting opinion and the issues raised, questioning not only the rationale in the majority opinion, but the possible dangers that this decision might bring.

CASE

Jaffee v. Redmond
518 U.S. 1 (1996).

Justice Stevens delivered the opinion of the Court.

After a traumatic incident in which she shot and killed a man, a police officer received extensive counseling from a licensed clinical social worker. The question we address is whether statements the officer made to her therapist during the counseling sessions are protected from compelled disclosure in a federal civil action brought by the family of the deceased. Stated otherwise, the question is whether it is appropriate for federal courts to recognize a "psychotherapist privilege" under Rule 501 of the Federal Rules of Evidence.

I

Petitioner is the administrator of the estate of Ricky Allen. Respondents are Mary Lu Redmond, a former police officer, and the Village of Hoffman Estates, Illinois, her employer during the time that she served on the police force. Petitioner commenced this action against respondents after Redmond shot and killed Allen while on patrol duty.

On June 27, 1991, Redmond was the first officer to respond to a "fight in progress" call at an apartment complex. As she arrived at the scene, two of Allen's sisters ran toward her squad car, waving their arms and shouting that there had been a stabbing in one of the apartments. Redmond testified at trial that she relayed this information to her dispatcher and requested an ambulance. She then exited her car and walked toward the apartment building. Before Redmond reached the building, several men ran out, one waving a pipe. When the men ignored her order to get on the ground, Redmond drew her service revolver. Two other men then burst out of the building, one, Ricky Allen, chasing the other. According to Redmond, Allen was brandishing a butcher knife and disregarded her repeated commands to drop the weapon. Redmond shot Allen when she believed he was about to stab the man he was chasing. Allen died at the scene.

. . . Petitioner filed suit in Federal District Court alleging that Redmond had violated Allen's constitutional rights by using excessive force during the encounter at the apartment complex. . . . At trial, petitioner presented testimony from members of Allen's family that conflicted with Redmond's version of the incident in several important respects. They testified, for example, that Redmond drew her gun before exiting her squad car and that Allen was unarmed when he emerged from the apartment building.

During pretrial discovery petitioner learned that after the shooting Redmond had participated in about 50 counseling sessions with Karen Beyer, a clinical social worker licensed by the State of Illinois and employed at that time by the Village of Hoffman Estates. Petitioner sought access to Beyer's notes concerning the sessions for use in cross-examining Redmond. Respondents vigorously resisted the discovery. They asserted that the contents of the conversations between Beyer and Redmond were protected against involuntary disclosure by a psychotherapist-patient privilege. The district judge rejected this argument. Neither Beyer nor Redmond, however, complied with his order to disclose the contents of Beyer's notes. At depositions and on the witness stand both either refused to answer certain questions or professed an inability to recall details of their conversations.

In his instructions at the end of the trial, the judge advised the jury that the refusal to turn over Beyer's notes had no "legal justification" and that the jury could therefore presume that the contents of the notes would have been unfavorable to respondents. The jury awarded petitioner $45,000 on the federal claim and $500,000 on her state-law claim. The Court of Appeals for the Seventh Circuit reversed and remanded for a new trial. Addressing the issue for the first time, the court concluded that "reason and experience," the touchstones for acceptance of a privilege under Rule 501 of the Federal Rules of Evidence, compelled recognition of a psychotherapist-patient privilege. "Reason tells us that psychotherapists and patients share a unique relationship, in which the ability to communicate freely without the fear of public disclosure is the key to successful treatment." As to experience, the court observed that all 50 States have adopted some form of the psychotherapist-patient privilege. The court attached particular significance to the fact that Illinois law expressly extends such a privilege to social workers like Karen Beyer. The court also noted that, with one exception, the federal decisions rejecting the privilege were more than five years old and that the "need and demand for counseling services has skyrocketed during the past several years."

The Court of Appeals qualified its recognition of the privilege by stating that it would not apply if "in the interests of justice, the evidentiary need for the disclosure of the contents of a patient's counseling sessions outweighs that patient's privacy interests." Balancing those conflicting interests, the court observed, on the one hand, that the evidentiary need for the contents of the confidential conversations was diminished in this case because there were numerous eyewitnesses to the shooting, and, on the other hand, that Officer Redmond's privacy interests were substantial. Based on this assessment, the court concluded that the trial court had erred by refusing to afford protection to the confidential communications between Redmond and Beyer. The United States courts of appeals do not uniformly agree that the federal courts should recognize a psychotherapist privilege under Rule 501. Because of the conflict among the courts of appeals and the importance of the question, we granted certiorari. We affirm.

II

Rule 501 of the Federal Rules of Evidence authorizes federal courts to define new privileges by interpreting "common law principles. . . in the light of reason and experience." The authors of the Rule borrowed this phrase from our opinion in *Wolfle v. United States*, 291 U.S. 7 (1934), which in turn referred to the oft-repeated observation that "the common law is not immutable but flexible, and by its own principles adapts itself to varying conditions." *Funk v. United States*, 290 U.S. 371. The Senate Report accompanying the 1975 adoption of the Rules indicates that Rule 501 "should be understood as reflecting the view that the recognition of a privilege based on a confidential relationship. . . should be determined on a case-by-case basis." S. Rep. No. 93-1277, p. 13 (1974). The Rule thus did not freeze the law governing the privileges of witnesses in federal trials at a particular point in our history, but rather directed federal courts to "continue the evolutionary development of testimonial privileges." *Trammel v. United States*, 445 U.S. 40 (1980); see also *University of Pennsylvania v. EEOC*, 493 U.S. 182 (1990).

The common-law principles underlying the recognition of testimonial privileges can be stated simply. "'For more than three centuries it has now been recognized as a fundamental maxim that the public. . . has a right to every man's evidence. . . . Exceptions from the general rule disfavoring testimonial privileges may be justified, however, by a "public good transcending the normally predominant principle of utilizing all rational means for ascertaining the truth." *Trammel*, 445 U.S. at 50, quoting *Elkins v. United States*, 364 U.S. 206 (1960) (Frankfurter, J., dissenting). Guided by these principles, the question we address today is whether a privilege protecting confidential communications between a psychotherapist and her patient "promotes sufficiently important interests to outweigh the need for probative evidence. . . ." Both "reason and experience" persuade us that it does.

III

Like the spousal and attorney-client privileges, the psychotherapist-patient privilege is "rooted in the imperative need for confidence and trust." Treatment by a physician for physical ailments can often proceed successfully on the basis of a physical examination, objective information supplied by the patient, and the results of diagnostic tests. Effective psychotherapy, by contrast, depends upon an atmosphere of confidence and trust in which the patient is willing to make a frank and complete disclosure of facts, emotions, memories, and fears. Because of the sensitive nature of the problems for which individuals consult psychotherapists, disclosure of confidential communications made during counseling sessions may cause embarrassment or disgrace. For this reason, the mere possibility of disclosure may impede development of the confidential relationship necessary for successful treatment. As the Judicial Conference Advisory Committee observed in 1972 when it recommended that Congress recognize a psychotherapist privilege as part of the Proposed Federal Rules of Evidence, a psychiatrist's ability to help her patients "is completely dependent upon [the patients'] willingness and ability to talk freely. . . ." Advisory Committee's Notes to Proposed Rules, 56 F.R.D. 183 (1972). By protecting confidential communications between a psychotherapist and her patient from involuntary disclosure, the proposed privilege thus serves important private interests.

Our cases make clear that an asserted privilege must also "serve public ends." *Upjohn Co. v. United States*, 449 U.S. 383 (1981). Thus, the purpose of the attorney-client privilege is to "encourage full and frank communication between attorneys and their clients and thereby promote broader public interests in the observance of law and administration of justice." And the spousal privilege, as modified in *Trammel*, is justified because it "furthers the important public interest in marital harmony," 445 U.S. at 53. The psychotherapist privilege serves the public interest by facilitating the provision of appropriate treatment for individuals suffering the effects of a mental or emotional problem. The

mental health of our citizenry, no less than its physical health, is a public good of transcendent importance.

In contrast to the significant public and private interests supporting recognition of the privilege, the likely evidentiary benefit that would result from the denial of the privilege is modest. If the privilege were rejected, confidential conversations between psychotherapists and their patients would surely be chilled, particularly when it is obvious that the circumstances that give rise to the need for treatment will probably result in litigation. Without a privilege, much of the desirable evidence to which litigants such as petitioner seek access—for example, admissions against interest by a party—is unlikely to come into being. This unspoken "evidence" will therefore serve no greater truth-seeking function than if it had been spoken and privileged.

That it is appropriate for the federal courts to recognize a psychotherapist privilege under Rule 501 is confirmed by the fact that all 50 States and the District of Columbia have enacted into law some form of psychotherapist privilege. We have previously observed that the policy decisions of the States bear on the question whether federal courts should recognize a new privilege or amend the coverage of an existing one. Because state legislatures are fully aware of the need to protect the integrity of the factfinding functions of their courts, the existence of a consensus among the States indicates that "reason and experience" support recognition of the privilege. In addition, given the importance of the patient's understanding that her communications with her therapist will not be publicly disclosed, any State's promise of confidentiality would have little value if the patient were aware that the privilege would not be honored in a federal court. Denial of the federal privilege therefore would frustrate the purposes of the state legislation that was enacted to foster these confidential communications.

It is of no consequence that recognition of the privilege in the vast majority of States is the product of legislative action rather than judicial decision. Although common-law rulings may once have been the primary source of new developments in federal privilege law, that is no longer the case. In *Funk v. United States*, 290 U.S. 371 (1933), we recognized that it is appropriate to treat a consistent body of policy determinations by state legislatures as reflecting both "reason" and "experience." That rule is properly respectful of the States and at the same time reflects the fact that once a state legislature has enacted a privilege there is no longer an opportunity for common-law creation of the protection. The history of the psychotherapist privilege illustrates the latter point. In 1972 the members of the Judicial Conference Advisory Committee noted that the common law "had indicated a disposition to recognize a psychotherapist-patient privilege when legislatures began moving into the field." Proposed Rules, 56 F.R.D. at 242. The present unanimous acceptance of the privilege shows that the state lawmakers moved quickly. That the privilege may have developed faster legislatively than it would have in the courts demonstrates only that the States rapidly recognized the wisdom of the rule as the field of psychotherapy developed.

[FOOTNOTE: Petitioner acknowledges that all 50 state legislatures favor a psychotherapist privilege. She nevertheless discounts the relevance of the state privilege statutes by pointing to divergence among the States concerning the types of therapy relationships protected and the exceptions recognized. A small number of state statutes, for example, grant the privilege only to psychiatrists and psychologists, while most apply the protection more broadly. Compare Haw. Rules Evid. 504, 504.1 and N.D. Rule Evid. 503 (privilege extends to physicians and psychotherapists), with Ariz. Rev. Stat. Ann. § 32-3283 (1992) (privilege covers "behavioral health professionals"); Tex. Rule Civ. Evid. 510(a)(1) (privilege extends to persons "licensed or certified by the State of Texas in the diagnosis, evaluation or treatment of any mental or emotional disorder" or "involved in the treatment or examination of drug abusers"); Utah Rule Evid. 506 (privilege protects confidential communications made to marriage and family therapists, professional counselors, and psychiatric mental health nurse specialists). The range of exceptions recognized by the States is similarly varied. These variations in the scope of the protection are too limited to undermine the force of the States' unanimous judgment that some form of psychotherapist privilege is appropriate.]

The uniform judgment of the States is reinforced by the fact that a psychotherapist privilege was among the nine specific privileges recommended by the Advisory Committee in its proposed privilege rules. In *United States v. Gillock*, 445 U.S. 360 (1980), our holding that Rule 501 did not include a state legislative privilege relied, in part, on the fact that no such privilege was included in the Advisory Committee's draft. The reasoning in Gillock thus supports the opposite conclusion in this case. In rejecting the proposed draft that had specifically identified each privilege rule and substituting the present more open-ended Rule 501, the Senate Judiciary Committee explicitly stated that its action "should not be understood as disapproving any recognition of a psychiatrist-patient... privilege contained in the [proposed] rules." S. Rep. No. 93-1277, at 13. Because we agree with the judgment of the state legislatures and the Advisory Committee that a psychotherapist-patient privilege will serve a "public good transcending the normally predominant principle of utilizing all rational means for ascertaining truth," *Trammel*, 445 U.S. at 50, we hold that confidential communications between a licensed psychotherapist and her patients in the course of diagnosis or treatment are protected from compelled disclosure under Rule 501 of the Federal Rules of Evidence.

IV

All agree that a psychotherapist privilege covers confidential communications made to licensed psychiatrists and psychologists. We have no hesitation in concluding in this case that the federal privilege should also extend to confidential communications made to licensed social workers in the course of psychotherapy. The reasons for recognizing a privilege for treatment by psychiatrists and psychologists apply with equal force to treatment by a clinical social worker such as Karen Beyer. Today, social workers provide a significant amount of mental health treatment. Their clients often include the poor and those of modest means who could not afford the assistance of a psychiatrist or psychologist, but whose counseling sessions serve the same public goals. Perhaps in recognition of these circumstances, the vast majority of States explicitly extend a testimonial privilege to licensed social workers. We therefore agree with the Court of Appeals that "drawing a distinction between the counseling provided by costly psychotherapists and the counseling provided by more readily accessible social workers serves no discernible public purpose."

We part company with the Court of Appeals on a separate point. We reject the balancing component of the privilege implemented by that court and a small number of States. Making the promise of confidentiality contingent upon a trial judge's later evaluation of the relative importance of the patient's interest in privacy and the evidentiary need for disclosure would eviscerate the effectiveness of the privilege. As we explained in *Upjohn*, if the purpose of the privilege is to be served, the participants in the confidential conversation "must be able to predict with some degree of certainty whether particular discussions will be protected. An uncertain privilege, or one which purports to be certain but results in widely varying applications by the courts, is little better than no privilege at all."

These considerations are all that is necessary for decision of this case. A rule that authorizes the recognition of new privileges on a case-by-case basis makes it appropriate to define the details of new privileges in a like manner. Because this is the first case in which we have recognized a psychotherapist privilege, it is neither necessary nor feasible to delineate its full contours in a way that would "govern all conceivable future questions in this area."

V

The conversations between Officer Redmond and Karen Beyer and the notes taken during their counseling sessions are protected from compelled disclosure under Rule 501 of the Federal Rules of Evidence. The judgment of the Court of Appeals is affirmed. It is so ordered.

Justice Scalia, with whom The Chief Justice joins as to Part III, dissenting.

The Court has discussed at some length the benefit that will be purchased by creation of the evidentiary privilege in this case: the encouragement of psychoanalytic counseling. It has not mentioned the purchase price: occasional injustice. That is the cost of every rule which excludes reliable and probative evidence—or at least every one categorical enough to achieve its announced policy objective . . . .

. . .

I

The case before us involves confidential communications made by a police officer to a state-licensed clinical social worker in the course of psychotherapeutic counseling. Before proceeding to a legal analysis of the case, I must observe that the Court makes its task deceptively simple by the manner in which it proceeds. It begins by characterizing the

issue as "whether it is appropriate for federal courts to recognize a 'psychotherapist privilege,'" and devotes almost all of its opinion to that question. Having answered that question (to its satisfaction) in the affirmative, it then devotes less than a page of text to answering in the affirmative the small remaining question whether "the federal privilege should also extend to confidential communications made to licensed social workers in the course of psychotherapy."

Of course the prototypical evidentiary privilege analogous to the one asserted here—the lawyer-client privilege—is not identified by the broad area of advice-giving practiced by the person to whom the privileged communication is given, but rather by the professional status of that person. Hence, it seems a long step from a lawyer-client privilege to a tax advisor-client or accountant-client privilege. But if one recharacterizes it as a "legal advisor" privilege, the extension seems like the most natural thing in the world. That is the illusion the Court has produced here: It first frames an overly general question ("Should there be a psychotherapist privilege?") that can be answered in the negative only by excluding from protection office consultations with professional psychiatrists (i.e., doctors) and clinical psychologists. And then, having answered that in the affirmative, it comes to the only question that the facts of this case present ("Should there be a social worker-client privilege with regard to psychotherapeutic counseling?") with the answer seemingly a foregone conclusion. At that point, to conclude against the privilege one must subscribe to the difficult proposition, "Yes, there is a psychotherapist privilege, but not if the psychotherapist is a social worker."

Relegating the question actually posed by this case to an afterthought makes the impossible possible in a number of wonderful ways. For example, it enables the Court to treat the Proposed Federal Rules of Evidence developed in 1972 by the Judicial Conference Advisory Committee as strong support for its holding, whereas they in fact counsel clearly and directly against it. The Committee did indeed recommend a "psychotherapist privilege" of sorts; but more precisely, and more relevantly, it recommended a privilege for psychotherapy conducted by "a person authorized to practice medicine" or "a person licensed or certified as a psychologist." Proposed Rule of Evidence 504, 56 F.R.D. 183

(1972), which is to say that it recommended against the privilege at issue here. . . .

II

. . . When is it, one must wonder, that the psychotherapist came to play such an indispensable role in the maintenance of the citizenry's mental health? For most of history, men and women have worked out their difficulties by talking to, inter alios, parents, siblings, best friends and bartenders—none of whom was awarded a privilege against testifying in court. Ask the average citizen: Would your mental health be more significantly impaired by preventing you from seeing a psychotherapist, or by preventing you from getting advice from your mom? I have little doubt what the answer would be. Yet there is no mother-child privilege.

How likely is it that a person will be deterred from seeking psychological counseling, or from being completely truthful in the course of such counseling, because of fear of later disclosure in litigation?

. . . .

The Court confidently asserts that not much truth-finding capacity would be destroyed by the privilege anyway, since "without a privilege, much of the desirable evidence to which litigants such as petitioner seek access . . . is unlikely to come into being." If that is so, how come psychotherapy got to be a thriving practice before the "psychotherapist privilege" was invented? Were the patients paying money to lie to their analysts all those years? Of course the evidence-generating effect of the privilege (if any) depends entirely upon its scope, which the Court steadfastly declines to consider. And even if one assumes that scope to be the broadest possible, is it really true that most, or even many, of those who seek psychological counseling have the worry of litigation in the back of their minds? I doubt that, and the Court provides no evidence to support it.

The Court suggests one last policy justification: since psychotherapist privilege statutes exist in all the States, the failure to recognize a privilege in federal courts "would frustrate the purposes of the state legislation that was enacted to foster these confidential communications." This is a novel argument indeed. A sort of inverse pre-emption: the truth-seeking functions of federal courts must be adjusted so as not to conflict with the policies of the States. This reasoning cannot be squared

with *Gillock*, which declined to recognize an evidentiary privilege for Tennessee legislators in federal prosecutions, even though the Tennessee Constitution guaranteed it in state criminal proceedings. *Gillock*, 445 U.S. at 368. Moreover . . . state policies regarding the psychotherapist privilege vary considerably from State to State, no uniform federal policy can possibly honor most of them. If furtherance of state policies is the name of the game, rules of privilege in federal courts should vary from State to State, a la *Erie*.

The Court concedes that there is "divergence among the States concerning the types of therapy relationships protected and the exceptions recognized." To rest a newly announced federal common-law psychotherapist privilege, assertable from this day forward in all federal courts, upon "the States' unanimous judgment that some form of psychotherapist privilege is appropriate," is rather like announcing a new, immediately applicable, federal common law of torts, based upon the States' "unanimous judgment" that some form of tort law is appropriate. In the one case as in the other, the state laws vary to such a degree that the parties and lower federal judges confronted by the new "common law" have barely a clue as to what its content might be.

III

Turning from the general question that was not involved in this case to the specific one that is: The Court's conclusion that a social-worker psychotherapeutic privilege deserves recognition is even less persuasive. In approaching this question, the fact that five of the state legislatures that have seen fit to enact "some form" of psychotherapist privilege have elected not to extend any form of privilege to social workers, ought to give one pause. . . .

Second, the Court does not reveal the enormous degree of disagreement among the States as to the scope of the privilege. It concedes that the laws of four States are subject to such gaping exceptions that they are "little better than no privilege at all," so that they should more appropriately be categorized with the five States whose laws contradict the action taken today. I would add another State to those whose privilege is illusory. See Wash. Rev. Code §18.19.180 (1994) (disclosure of information required "in response to a subpoena from a court of law"). In adopting any sort of a social worker privilege, then, the Court can at most claim that it is following the legislative "experience" of 40 States, and contradicting the "experience" of 10.

But turning to those States that do have an appreciable privilege of some sort, the diversity is vast. In Illinois and Wisconsin, the social-worker privilege does not apply when the confidential information pertains to homicide, and in the District of Columbia when it pertains to any crime "inflicting injuries" upon persons. In Missouri, the privilege is suspended as to information that pertains to a criminal act, and in Texas when the information is sought in any criminal prosecution. In Kansas and Oklahoma, the privilege yields when the information pertains to "violations of any law," in Indiana, when it reveals a "serious harmful act," and in Delaware and Idaho, when it pertains to any "harmful act." In Oregon, a state-employed social worker like Karen Beyer loses the privilege where her supervisor determines that her testimony "is necessary in the performance of the duty of the social worker as a public employee." In South Carolina, a social worker is forced to disclose confidences "when required by statutory law or by court order for good cause shown to the extent that the patient's care and treatment or the nature and extent of his mental illness or emotional condition are reasonably at issue in a proceeding." The majority of social-worker-privilege States declare the privilege inapplicable to information relating to child abuse. And the States that do not fall into any of the above categories provide exceptions for commitment proceedings, for proceedings in which the patient relies on his mental or emotional condition as an element of his claim or defense, or for communications made in the course of a court-ordered examination of the mental or emotional condition of the patient.

Thus, although the Court is technically correct that "the vast majority of States explicitly extend a testimonial privilege to licensed social workers," that uniformity exists only at the most superficial level. No State has adopted the privilege without restriction; the nature of the restrictions varies enormously from jurisdiction to jurisdiction; and 10 States, I reiterate, effectively reject the privilege entirely. It is fair to say that there is scant national consensus even as to the propriety of a social-worker psychotherapist privilege, and none whatever as to its appropriate scope. In other words, the state laws to which the Court appeals for support demonstrate most convincingly that adoption of a social-worker psychotherapist privilege is a job for Congress.

The question before us today is not whether there should be an evidentiary privilege for social workers providing therapeutic services. Perhaps there should. But the question before us is whether (1) the need for that privilege is so clear, and (2) the desirable contours of that privilege are so evident, that it is appropriate for this Court to craft it in common-law fashion, under Rule 501. Even if we were writing on a clean slate, I think the answer to that question would be clear. But given our extensive precedent to the effect that new privileges "in derogation of the search for truth" "are not lightly created," the answer the Court gives today is inexplicable.

. . . I respectfully dissent.

LEGAL ANALYSIS AND WRITING 14.4

1. What were the facts in this case?
2. What was the issue before the court?
3. What did the court decide?
4. Why did the court decide the way it did? What was its reasoning? Include relevant quotes from the case decision to illustrate and support your answer.
5. What was the argument of the dissenting opinion?
6. Do you agree with the court's decision or the dissent? Why or why not?

LEGAL RESEARCH USING THE INTERNET SKILLS 14.5

Find and read the entire decision of this important Supreme Court case online! Were there any other dissenting opinions? Any concurring opinions? How many justices joined the majority for this decision? What other issues were raised by the dissent?

CRITICAL THINKING QUESTIONS 14.3

1. What effect, if any, does the U.S. Supreme Court decision in *Jaffee* have on state laws pertaining to patient privilege?
2. Does this rule extend this privilege to social workers who are working as psychotherapists?

Does Patient Privilege Extend to Pharmacy Records?

In the following Vermont case, the court decides whether the patient privilege extends to pharmacy records.

CASE

State v. Welch

160 Vt. 70. (1992).
Vermont Supreme Court.

GIBSON, J.

. . . Defendant argues that her right to privacy was violated by a warrantless inspection of her prescription records at. . . area pharmacies. . . . Defendant argues that she has a legitimate expectation of privacy in her pharmacy records because they are medical records and society recognizes the confidentiality of medical records. The State contends that there is no legitimate expectation of privacy in prescription records that must be kept readily available, pursuant to. . . law, for inspection by authorized officials.

. . . [W]e reject defendant's claim that her privacy interest in the pharmacy records is predicated upon doctor-patient confidentiality. Neither the statute. . . nor the evidentiary rule includes pharmacists among the professionals covered by the patient's privilege. The reason may be that the communications involved in pharmacy records are between a prescriber and a pharmacist, not between a prescriber and patient. But even if pharmacists were included, the rules of evidence exempt from privilege any report of a medical condition "required to be made by statute." V.R.E. 503(d)(6).

. . . [I]t is the duty of every doctor and hospital to report promptly to the board of health all cases wherein a person has been or is being treated for drug abuse. We are satisfied that there is no patient's privilege available to defendant herein with respect to her pharmaceutical records.

JOHNSON, J, dissenting.

Today, the majority rules that the police have unlimited access to the prescription records of every pharmacist in the state. . . and may, without warrant or probable cause, search those records in hopes of finding violations of law, not by pharmacists, but by patients.

. . . I do not understand the majority's reasoning. The patient's privilege is very broad. Our law prohibits physicians from disclosing "any information acquired in attending a patient in a professional capacity, and which was necessary to enable the provider to act in that capacity." See *State v. Raymond*, 139 Vt. 464 (1981) (privilege prevented nurse from testifying that the defendant had alcohol on his breath); see also V.R.E. 503(b) (privileged information includes "confidential communications made for the purpose of diagnosis or treatment of [the patient's] physical, mental, dental, or emotional condition"). Certainly the information disclosed in this case meets these definitions . . . .

Around midnight, Miller called the state mental hospital and told the receptionist on duty that he had just murdered someone. Miller had no history of being a patient at the hospital. The receptionist called the police, and then gave the call to the on-duty physician, a licensed psychiatrist. While waiting for the police to apprehend Miller, the psychiatrist kept Miller on the phone, assuring him of confidentiality and questioning him using a standard clinical interview technique. During this time, Miller confessed to the psychiatrist. Subsequently, the police arrested Miller and charged him with murder.

Can Miller invoke the patient's privilege to prevent the psychiatrist from testifying against him?

CRITICAL THINKING QUESTIONS 14.4

1. Should a "psychotherapist privilege" cover a child who talks to the school nurse? School counselor?
2. What about a patient who confesses to a crime while under "laughing gas" at the dentist's office?

Clergy or Religious Privilege

Called the *clergy-penitent* or *religious privilege*, this privilege provides that a person may refuse to disclose or to prevent another from disclosing a confidential communication by the person to a member of the clergy acting in his or her role as spiritual adviser. This privilege has its roots in the confidentiality of the confessional, dating back hundreds of years for priest-penitent.

The privilege applies only to communications made to a clergyperson in his or her spiritual and professional capacity and with a reasonable expectation of confidentiality. As is the case with the attorney-client privilege, the presence of third parties, if essential to and in furtherance of the communication, should not void the privilege.

Seldom used for clergy in providing actual religious counseling, this privilege does come under attack when it involves non-religious counseling. In one case, the court refused to grant the defendant a clergy privilege over a statement made to a Reverend, where the defendant was really looking for advice about avoiding his income taxes.[24] Citing *Trammel*, the Court said that the "clergy-penitent privilege is limited to private communications rooted in confidence and trust. The privilege 'recognizes the human need to disclose to a spiritual counselor, in total and absolute confidence, what are believed to be flawed acts or thoughts and to receive priestly consolation and guidance in return.' If, however, one seeks out the clergy only for income tax avoidance, we see no more need for a protective privilege than if the taxpayer had consulted his butcher or barber. The taxpayer is not a penitent seeking spiritual relief from his sins, only a citizen seeking relief from his obligation to pay taxes."[25]

Who May Claim Privilege?

The person who made the confidential communication to a member of the clergy may claim the clergy or religious privilege (see Exhibit 14.16 to Exhibit 14.18). The member of the clergy is also presumed to have the authority to claim the privilege, but only on behalf of the communicant.

EXHIBIT 14.16   Example of Clergy Privilege

California Evidence Code
Section 1032. As used in this article, "penitential communication" means a communication made in confidence, in the presence of no third person so far as the penitent is aware, to a clergyman who, in the course of the discipline or practice of his church, denomination, or organization, is authorized or accustomed to hear such communications and, under the discipline or tenets of his church, denomination, or organization, has a duty to keep such communications secret.

Section 1033. Subject to Section 912, a penitent, whether or not a party, has a privilege to refuse to disclose, and to prevent another from disclosing, a penitential communication if he claims the privilege.

Section 1034. Subject to Section 912, a clergyman, whether or not a party, has a privilege to refuse to disclose a penitential communication if he claims the privilege.

EXHIBIT 14.17   Example of Clergy Privilege

Vermont Rules of Evidence
Rule 505. Religious Privilege.

   (a) Definitions. As used in this rule:

   (1) A "clergyman" is a minister, priest, rabbi, accredited Christian Science Practitioner, or other similar functionary of a religious organization, or an individual reasonably believed so to be by the person consulting him.

   (2) A communication is "confidential" if made privately and not intended for further disclosure except to other persons present in furtherance of the purpose of the communication.

   (b) General rule of privilege. A person has a privilege to refuse to disclose and to prevent another from disclosing a confidential communication by the person to a clergyman in his professional character as spiritual adviser.

   (c) Who may claim the privilege. The privilege may be claimed by the person, by his guardian or conservator, or by his personal representative if he is deceased. The person who was the clergyman at the time of the communication is presumed to have authority to claim the privilege, but only on behalf of the communicant.

EXHIBIT 14.18   Example of Clergy Privilege

New Jersey Rules of Evidence
Rule 511. Cleric-Penitent Privilege.

Any communication made in confidence to a cleric in the cleric's professional character, or as a spiritual adviser in the course of the discipline or practice of the religious body to which the cleric belongs or of the religion which the cleric professes, shall be privileged. Privileged communications shall include confessions and other communications made in confidence between and among the cleric and individuals, couples, families or groups in the exercise of the cleric's professional or spiritual counseling role. As used in this section, "cleric" means a priest, rabbi, minister or other person or practitioner authorized to perform similar functions of any religion.

The privilege accorded to communications under this rule shall belong to both the cleric and the person or persons making the communication and shall be subject to waiver only under the following circumstances:

   (1) both the person or persons making the communication and the cleric consent to the waiver of the privilege; or

   (2) the privileged communication pertains to a future criminal act, in which case, the cleric alone may, but is not required to, waive the privilege.

EVIDENTIARY CHECKLIST 14.4

Clergy Privilege

Holder of Privilege

☐   Parishioner

Who May Claim Privilege?

☐   Parishioner or Clergy on behalf of parishioner

Other Elements Required to Establish Privilege

☐   Communication must be intended as confidential.

☐   Communication must be to facilitate legitimate religious purposes.

☐   Confidentiality must be essential to furtherance of relationship.

YOU BE THE JUDGE 14.2

Priests from the Boston area have asked the court to rule on the following issue. Under Massachusetts law, clergy, including priests, are among those professionals who are required to report any suspected child abuse to state authorities. The priests are claiming that when they learn of the abuse through a confession, it should invoke the priest-penitent privilege.

How would you decide this? Explain your reasoning for your conclusions and include references from the readings to support and illustrate your answer.

Identity of Informant Privilege

In this privilege, the government has the privilege to refuse to disclose the identity of a person who has furnished confidential information to law enforcement. This privilege is subject to defendant's constitutional right to prepare her defense and to confront witnesses against her.

Who May Claim?

A representative of the government agency to which the confidential information was given may claim this privilege. However, the informant in question is not given the privilege or the right to claim it.

Exceptions

The exceptions to this privilege include an informant who is called to testify for the government, and in certain cases when an informant is found able to give testimony relevant to any issue in a criminal case or when identity is material to the issue of guilt or innocence. The judge makes this decision.

State Secrets Privilege

The rationale behind the **state secrets** privilege is in the need to keep some documents and communications secret and confidential in the operation of the government. The U.S. Supreme Court has held that "the privilege which protects military and state secrets has been limited in this country. . . . The privilege belongs to the Government and must be asserted by it; it can neither be claimed nor waived by a private party. It is not to be lightly invoked. There must be a formal claim of privilege, lodged by the head of the department that has control over the matter. . . . The court itself must determine whether the circumstances are appropriate for the claim of privilege, and yet do so without forcing a disclosure of the very thing the privilege is designed to protect. . . . Where there is a strong showing of necessity, the claim of privilege should not be lightly accepted, but even the most compelling necessity cannot overcome the claim of privilege if the court is ultimately satisfied that military secrets are at stake."[26]

The state secrets privilege was at center stage in 1974, when President Nixon tried to assert an **executive privilege** against turning over the Watergate tapes. The U.S. Supreme Court ruled that this privilege must be examined on a case-by-case basis, by weighing the public interests and need for the evidence against the executive's interest in keeping the information secret.[27]

To determine whether the public's interest in and need for the evidence outweighs the government's interest in secrecy, many courts apply a 1979 federal court decision, balancing the following factors:

1. The relevance of the evidence sought to be protected
2. The availability of other evidence
3. The "seriousness" of the litigation and the issues involved
4. The role of the government in the litigation; and
5. The possibility of future timidity by government employees who will be forced to recognize that their secrets are violable.[28]

A central point in this balancing test is that the Court must assess the need for the information by the party seeking it (including its availability through reasonable alternatives), and whether the deliberative process will in fact be "chilled" in the future by disclosure today.

State Secrets
Documents and communications that need to be kept secret and confidential in the operation of government.

Executive Privilege
The right of the president or a governor to be exempt from the disclosure of confidential documents or communications necessary to the discharge of the executive office or duties.

Is There a Secret Service "Protective Function" Privilege?

The following case examines whether the Secret Service can refuse to answer questions about the President based on a "protective function" privilege.

CASE

In re Sealed Case

United States Court of Appeals for the District of Columbia Circuit.

No. 98-3069 (1998).

[During depositions conducted by Kenneth Starr's Office of Independent Counsel as part of grand jury proceedings investigating President Clinton,

agents of the United States Secret Service refused to answer certain questions on the ground that the information sought was protected from disclosure by a "protective function privilege." The district court issued an order compelling the Secret Service agents to testify and the U.S. Court of Appeals affirmed this in a decision that read, in part,]

...

Recalling the Supreme Court's caution that privileges "are not lightly created nor expansively construed," *Nixon*, 418 U.S. at 710, we are constrained not to recognize any new privilege the need for which is less than "clear and convincing." Here the need is fairly disputed, and "[i]n an area where empirical information would be useful, it is scant and inconclusive." In these circumstances we cannot say that the proposed protective function privilege clearly "promotes sufficiently important interests to outweigh the need for probative evidence" in a criminal investigation. *Jaffee*, 518 U.S. at 9-10.

IV. Conclusion

The Secret Service has failed to carry its heavy burden under Rule 501 of establishing the need for the protective function privilege it sought to assert in this case. Consequently, we leave to Congress the question whether a protective function privilege is appropriate in order to ensure the safety of the President and, if so, what the contours of that privilege should be. The order of the district court compelling testimony of Secret Service officers is therefore affirmed.

NEWER PRIVILEGES

In the past 30 years, there have been numerous attempts to have some type of relationship or communication protected as a privilege. We have seen how some, like the psychotherapist privilege, have proven successful, while others, like the pharmacy records and secret service protection, have failed. Two of the most controversial have been arguments for a parent-child privilege, and the push by news organizations for a reporter privilege.

Parent-Child Privilege

As a general rule, there is no parent-child privilege. Only a few courts have extended similar protections regarding confidential communications in the marital privilege to those between parent and child. In a 1983 Nevada case, *In re Agosto*, the court quashed a grand jury subpoena that would have required a son to give testimony against his father. The *Agosto* court concluded that the "expansive approach toward federal interpretation of testimonial privileges" under Rule 501 justified "affording the same protection to the parent-child relationship as is afforded the marriage relationship itself." The court held that there can be "little doubt that the confidence and privacy inherent in the parent-child relationship must be protected and sedulously fostered by the courts. . . . Agosto may claim the parent-child privilege not only for confidential communications which transpired between his father and himself, but he may likewise claim the privilege for protection against being compelled to be a witness and testify adversely against his father in any criminal proceeding." The reasoning behind extending this privilege is that the "Constitution protects the sanctity of the family precisely because the institution of the family is deeply rooted in this Nation's history and tradition."[29]

A later case expressed views that reflect the majority of jurisdictions. In this case, a Seventh Circuit court rejected the parent-child privilege, saying that "generalized claims regarding the well-recognized sanctity of family life must give way to the overriding needs of the truth seeking process. Moreover, every federal court, other than *Agosto*, that has considered the claim for a privilege based solely on the parent-child relationship has rejected the claim.

The Fourth, Fifth, Ninth, and Eleventh Circuits have expressly rejected the parent-child privilege." The court went on to point out that "past substantive due process cases based on 'family' interests all have involved systematic regulation of the interest, and not isolated incidents of 'intrusion' into family privacy." They found no "legal basis, constitutional or other," to support the "parent-child privilege in criminal cases."[30]

CRITICAL THINKING QUESTIONS 14.5

1. Do you think there should be a parent-child privilege? Explain your answer.

2. How can we justify a marital privilege between husband and wife based on the need to protect a significant family relationship, but not extend it to a child that trusts and confides in a parent?

3. What about a child who tells a parent in confidence about her best friend who is using drugs and the parent is asked to testify to this conversation? What if the child told the parent in confidence about her own drug problem? Must the parent divulge this information?

YOU BE THE JUDGE 14.3

A 13-year-old observed her parents using illegal drugs and repeatedly begged them to quit. When they continued their drug use, the child turned in her parents to the police. Will the child have to testify against her parents? Why or why not?

Journalist–Source Privilege

Although some states have enacted statutory laws protecting reporter's confidential sources, most courts have still not expanded the interpretation of the First Amendment right to freedom of press to this area. Most courts feel that the public has a right to know and that this outweighs the private interest of newspersons not to reveal their source. However, this is changing (see Exhibit 14.19). In a 1995 Ninth Circuit case, the court found that "all but one of the federal circuits to address the issue have interpreted *Branzburg v. Hayes*[31] as establishing a qualified privilege for journalists against compelled disclosure of information gathered in the course of their work. . . . Rooted in the First Amendment, the privilege is a recognition that society's interest in protecting the integrity of the newsgathering process, and in ensuring the free flow of information to the public, is an interest of sufficient social importance to justify some incidental sacrifice of sources of facts needed in the administration of justice."[32]

The journalist's privilege, when upheld by courts, is a qualified one. Once a reporter invokes the privilege, the burden shifts to the other side to show a compelling need for the journalist's materials sufficient to overcome the privilege. In cases where libel is alleged, however, the privilege is likely to be denied by the court. To do otherwise might provide the journalist or news organization with a form of immunity from a lawsuit.

Exhibit 14.19   Journalist Privilege

California Evidence Code
    Section 1070(a). A publisher, editor, reporter, or other person connected with or employed upon a newspaper, magazine, or other periodical publication, or by a press association or wire service, or any person who has been so connected or employed, cannot be adjudged in contempt by a judicial, legislative, administrative body, or any other body having the power to issue subpoenas, for refusing to disclose, in any proceeding as defined in Section 901, the source of any information procured while so connected or employed for publication in a newspaper, magazine or other periodical publication, or for refusing to disclose any unpublished information obtained or prepared in gathering, receiving or processing of information for communication to the public.

YOU BE THE JUDGE 14.4

Are a college's "tenure" files protected under an academic freedom privilege? An associate professor, denied tenure by a university, filed charges alleging discrimination with the EEOC. The EEOC issued a subpoena seeking the professor's tenure file and the tenure files of five other faculty members alleged to have received more favorable treatment. The university refused to produce the tenure-review files, stating that they were "confidential peer review information" and privileged under First Amendment principles of academic freedom.

LEGAL RESEARCH USING THE INTERNET SKILLS 14.6

Find the answer to the above *You Be the Judge* problem by researching and reading this case decision on the Internet. Compare what the court held with your conclusions. The citation for this case is:

University of Pennsylvania v. Equal Employment Opportunity Commission, 493 U.S. 182 (1990).

Is There an Accountant Privilege?

Although recognized in some states, there is no accountant privilege in federal courts or in the majority of state courts. In 1973, the U.S. Supreme Court ruled that there is no constitutional basis for an accountant privilege.[33]

Is There a Stenographer Privilege?

In the following Oregon case, the court looks at whether a stenographer privilege exists.

CASE

United States v. Schoenheinz

548 F.2d 1389 (9th Cir. 1977).

Appeal from the United States District Court, District of Oregon.

Appellant appeals from an order of the district court enforcing an Internal Revenue Service summons directing the appellant to testify and to produce documents relating to taxpayers Johnson, Linder, and National Inventory Control Systems, a corporation. Appellant contends that the district court erred in holding that the employer-stenographer privilege, secured by Oregon's statutory law, could not be asserted in this proceeding to enforce an IRS summons. Appellant performed secretarial services for the taxpayers and related business entities during the period under investigation. She appeared in response to the summonses, answering some questions and declining to answer others, on the ground that those communications were protected by the Oregon statute. The taxpayers intervened, filed an answer, and moved to dismiss the petition, asserting the employer-stenographer privilege.

Federal common law controls the application of privilege in this case. (Rule 501, Fed. Rules of Evidence.) There is no federally recognized employer-stenographer privilege, and we decline to create one. We perceive no reason to expand derivative privileges in the federal court system. The relationship between the stenographer and the taxpayers in this case consists solely of an ordinary relationship between a corporation and a corporate employee, or individual employer-businessman and his stenographer.

AFFIRMED.

Political Vote Privilege

The political vote privilege allows a person to refuse to disclose the nature or results of his or her vote at a political election. (see Exhibit 14.20)

Exhibit 14.20 Political Vote Privilege

Texas Rules of Evidence
Rule 506. Political Vote.
    Every person has a privilege to refuse to disclose the tenor of the person's vote at a political election conducted by secret ballot unless the vote was cast illegally.

SUMMARY

In this chapter, you have examined the laws of privileges as they have developed in both state and federal courts. The historical roots and rationale for privileges can be traced back hundreds of years in our common law. Privileges are, in the words of the court, "rooted in the imperative need for confidence and trust." They were created by the courts to "protect those interpersonal relationships which are highly valued by society and peculiarly vulnerable to deterioration should their necessary component of privacy be continually disregarded by courts of law. They must "serve public ends" and "encourage full and frank communication . . . and thereby promote broader public interests in the observance of law and administration of justice." Finally, privileges must promote "sufficiently important interests to outweigh the need for probative evidence." Today, privileges in the state courts have been codified in some form, with new privileges added in some states. In the federal courts, privileges remain governed by the common law. However, these common law privileges continue to evolve. The U.S. Supreme Court has used Rule 501 to "acknowledge the authority of the federal courts to continue the evolutionary development of testimonial privileges in federal criminal trials governed by the principles of the common law as they may be interpreted . . . in the light of reason and experience." In *Trammel*, this justified a narrowing of a privilege no longer deemed necessary. In *Jaffee*, it justified an expansion to adopt a new privilege not formally recognized by the common law. That the Court relied on state laws to reach their decision in both of these cases signifies the interdependent nature of the federal and state laws on privileges.

KEY TERMS

Confidential Communications	No Comment Rule	Statutory Laws
Executive Privilege	Privilege	Testimonial Privilege
Holder of the Privilege	Privilege Against Self-	Waiver
Immunity	Incrimination	Work Products
In Camera	Star Chamber	
Miranda Rule	State Secrets	

LEARNING OUTCOMES AND PRACTICE SKILLS CHECKLIST

☐ Learning Outcomes

After completing your reading, questions, and exercises, you should be able to demonstrate a better understanding of the learning concepts by answering the following questions:

1. Define a legal privilege and explain why we protect some communication as privileged.
2. Explain why the Federal Rules of Evidence do not include specific privileges and discuss how the Federal Rules treat this.
3. Distinguish between the holder of a privilege and who may claim it.
4. Identify the four forms of privileges.
5. Differentiate statutory, constitutional, and common-law privileges.
6. Identify the constitutional basis for self-incrimination and explain the two different parts to this privilege.
7. Describe the general elements required to establish a privilege.
8. Assess the specific elements and exceptions to the following privileges:
   a. Attorney-Client Privilege
   b. Patient's Privilege
   c. Religious Privilege
   d. Marital Privilege
9. Distinguish between the informant and the state secret privilege, including the reasoning behind both.
10. Identify and discuss two of the newer privileges.

☐ Practice Skills

In addition to understanding the learning concepts, practice what you have learned through applications using critical thinking, legal analysis and writing, legal research, and advocacy skills, including:

Critical Thinking

1. Why do we have rules that protect privileged communication and exclude it from evidence?
2. Do you believe that the current rules provide adequate safeguards for this process?
3. What public policy issues or considerations do you think might be behind these rules?
4. If it were up to you, would you keep the rules governing privileges as they are, delete them, narrow them, or expand them? Explain your reasoning.
5. Are there other relationships that you feel should be privileged? Explain your answer.
6. Rules of privileges are not consistently applied in state and federal courts. Would you change this? Why or why not?
7. How do these rules influence the gathering of evidence or preparing of witnesses?

Legal Analysis and Writing

Analyze the following rules and cases by summarizing their holdings, explaining their significance, and assessing any issue that might arise in their application.

1. Rule 501.
2. Proposed Federal Rules 503–510 (Only need to analyze significance of these rules being proposed).
3. *Trammel v. United States.*
4. *United States v. Acker.*
5. *Jaffee v. Redmond.*
6. *State v. Welch.*

Legal Research Using the Internet

1. Find your state's rules of evidence regarding privileges and the concepts covered in this chapter. Compare and contrast with the federal and/or modern rules, and some of the other state rules listed in this chapter. What privileges are recognized in your state rules?
2. Does your state recognize any of the newer privileges—parent-child, accountant, journalist, or mental health counselor?
3. Find out if your state appellate court posts their case decisions on the Internet. If so, find a case that illustrates a privilege issue or rule discussed in this chapter. If your state decisions are not on the Internet, go instead to the web site for the U.S. Circuit Court of Appeals in your circuit, or search the U.S. Supreme Court decisions.

PRACTICE APPLICATION 14.1

A defendant being tried for murder told his attorneys that he had committed three other murders. One of the attorneys decided to check out his client's story. In doing so, the attorney located the body of one of the young women that his client had admitted killing. The attorney did not report his discovery to the authorities, even though laws existed that required this disclosure. When, to establish an insanity defense, the defendant later admitted to the additional murders, the attorney's knowledge of the body's location became public. The attorney argues that "a confidential, privileged communication existed between him and his client, which should excuse the attorney from making full disclosure to the authorities."

Is the attorney correct? Should the attorney be sanctioned or punished for not disclosing this information? Why or why not? Write a short memo stating your analysis and conclusions, using rules, readings, and cases from this chapter to support your answer.

LEGAL RESEARCH USING THE INTERNET 14.7

The above problem is from a 1975 New York case that may be difficult to find, but if you want to find out what happened, try searching for it or a more recent case that refers to it on the Internet. The citation for the case is:

People v. Belge, 372 N.Y.S.2d 798 (1975).

ADVOCACY AND COMMUNICATION SKILLS 14.1

Using the *Advocacy and Persuasive Arguments* format shown in the Appendix, select one of the following topics, inform your instructor whether you will argue for or against the issue, prepare, and deliver an oral persuasive argument: Are you *for* or *against* the placing of limitations on:

1. Attorney-client privilege?
2. Marital privilege?
3. Patient's privilege?
4. Clergy privilege?
5. Identity of informant privilege?
6. Secrets of State or executive privilege?

Are you *for* or *against* the recognition of:

1. Journalist privilege?
2. Parent-child privilege?
3. Accountant privilege?
4. Crisis counselor's privilege?

You will have 3 minutes to state your position and support it. After the other side presents her arguments, you will have an additional minute to rebut her position.

WEB SITES

Courts.Net Directory of State and Federal Courts
http://www.courts.net/
Federal Rules of Evidence
http://www.law.cornell.edu/rules/fre/overview.html
FindLaw Search for Federal Courts of Appeal Decisions
http://www.findlaw.com/10fedgov/judicial/ appeals_courts.html
FindLaw U.S. Supreme Court Decisions
http://www.findlaw.com/casecode/supreme.html
Listing of State Laws from Legal Information Institute of Cornell Law School
http://www.law.cornell.edu/states/listing.html

National Center for State Courts
http://www.ncsconline.org/
Supreme Court Collection of Cornell Law School
http://supct.law.cornell.edu/supct/
Uniform Rules of Evidence proposed by the National Conference of Commissioners on Uniform State Laws
http://www.law.upenn.edu/bll/ulc/ulc_frame.html
U.S. Supreme Court
http://www.supremecourtus.gov/
Villanova Law School State and Federal Court Search
http://vls.law.vill.edu/compass/

ENDNOTES

1. *Elkins v. United States*, 364 U.S. 206 (1960) (Frankfurter dissenting).
2. *United States v. Nixon*, 418 U.S. 683 (1974).
3. *Trammel v. United States*, 445 U.S. 40 (1980).
4. *Upjohn Co. v. United States*, 449 U.S. 383 (1981).
5. Ibid.
6. Ibid.
7. *United States v. Byrd*, 750 F.2d at 589.
8. *University of Pennsylvania v. EEOC*, 493 U.S. 182 (1990).
9. *Trammel v. United States*.
10. Ibid.
11. Compare Section 90.503, Florida Evidence Code, with Rule 509, Texas Rules of Evidence.
12. See, for example, Cal. Evid. Code, § 913.
13. *Baxter v. Palmigiano*, 425 U.S. 308 (1976).
14. *In re Grand Jury Proceedings*, 867 F.2d 562 (9th Cir. 1989).
15. *Trammel v. United States*.
16. Felix Frankfurter, *Ullman v. United States*, 350 U.S. 422 (1956).
17. *Miranda v. Arizona*, 384 U.S. 436 (1966).
18. Ibid.
19. *Upjohn Co. v. United States*, 449 U.S. 383 (1981).
20. *In re Colton*, 201 F. Supp. 13 (S.D.N.Y. 1961).
21. *In re Richard Roe, Inc.*, 68 F.3d 38 (2d Cir. 1995).
22. *Moore v. City of East Cleveland*, 431 U.S. 494 (1977).
23. Ibid.
24. *United States v. Dube*, 820 F.2d 886 (7th Cir. 1987).
25. Ibid.
26. *United States v. Reynolds*, 345 U.S. 1 (1953).
27. *United States v. Nixon*, 418 U.S. 683 (1974).
28. *In re Franklin National Bank Securities Litigation*, 478 F. Supp. 577 (E.D.N.Y. 1979).
29. *In re Agosto*, 553 F. Supp. 1298 (D. Nev. 1983).
30. *United States v. Davies*, 768 F.2d 893 (7th Cir. 1985).
31. *408 U.S. 665 (1972)*.
32. *Mark v. Shoen*, 48 F.3d 412 (1995).
33. *Couch v. United States*, 409 U.S. 322 (1973).

CLOSING ARGUMENTS— FUTURE OF EVIDENCE LAW

"One cannot understand where a nation and its laws are and where they are headed without a good understanding of what has gone on before. The future is inexorably linked to the past."

—Savigny, Of the Vocation of Our Age
for Legislation and Jurisprudence (1814)

LEARNING OUTCOMES

In this chapter, you will learn about the following legal concepts:

- "What has Gone on Before . . . "
  —The Development of Evidence Law

- "What it is" Today . . . The Role and Purpose of Evidence Law

- The Role of Judge as Gatekeeper

- "What it tends to Become . . . "
  —The Future of Evidence Law

- Technology and Evidence Law

- Scientific Evidence

INTRODUCTION

As we noted at the beginning of this book and again in this final chapter's quote, Savigny wrote that "One cannot understand where a nation and its laws are and where they are headed without a good understanding of what has gone on before. The future is inexorably linked to the past."[1] Oliver Wendell Holmes, noted Supreme Court jurist, said that the "life of the law has not been logic: it has been experience.... In order to know what it is, we must know what it has been, and what it tends to become."[2]

As we close this text, let's reflect briefly at "what has gone on before" in the laws of evidence and think about "what it is" today and "what it tends to become" in the future.

"WHAT HAS GONE ON BEFORE. . . "
—THE DEVELOPMENT OF EVIDENCE LAW

Societies have long struggled to develop effective methods and procedures to resolve legal disputes. In common law countries, these methods have evolved into an adversary system where opponents engage in a "controlled battle or contest" under the belief that out of this contest "truth will emerge." Under this adversarial process, the judge has assumed the role of referee, governing the contest and ruling on questions of law. The jury system evolved from a partisan, investigating body to citizens selected to impartially hear and decide the facts of a case. To protect the jury from hearing information that might mislead or confuse them, evidence rules were developed by the courts and promulgated in the form of common law. These common law rules were later codified and expanded into statutory provisions in most states. In 1975, after several years of study, the U.S. Supreme Court proposed, and the Congress enacted, the Federal Rules of Evidence. These rules became the model for the majority of the state evidence codes.

The U.S. Supreme Court stated that the "basic purpose of a trial is the determination of truth."[3] Throughout this book, we have examined how these rules promote the search for truth in a trial by determining what is relevant and admissible. As one state rule declares, the "object of all legal investigation is the discovery of truth. The rules of evidence are framed with a view to this prominent end, seeking always for pure sources and the highest evidence."[4] In that "discovery of truth," courts have agreed that "the pertinent general principle, responding to the deepest needs of society, is that society is entitled to every man's evidence. As an underlying aim of judicial inquiry is ascertainable truth, everything rationally related to ascertaining the truth is presumptively admissible. Limitations are properly placed upon the operation of this general principle only to the very limited extent that permitting a refusal to testify or excluding relevant evidence has a public good transcending the normally predominant principle of utilizing all rational means for ascertaining truth."[5]

"WHAT IT IS" TODAY. . . THE ROLE AND PURPOSE
OF EVIDENCE LAW

Today, the role of evidence law continues to serve the purposes for which it has developed over the years (see Exhibit 15.1). It provides a framework of guidelines and safeguards to protect the jury and help to ensure an orderly, efficient legal process. It governs the "controlled" nature of the contest between adversarial parties by establishing rules and procedures for proving a legal action. Finally, it seeks to promote social and public policies for ensuring fairness and a just determination of the proceedings in the ascertainment of truth. The U.S. Supreme Court addressed the overriding goal of fairness by holding that the "law does not require that a defendant receive a perfect trial, only a fair one."[6] Many of the evidence rules are designed to provide safeguards to ensure this fairness.

EXHIBIT 15.1   Role and Purpose of Evidence Law

☐   Provide a framework of guidelines and safeguards to protect the jury and help to ensure an orderly, efficient legal process

☐   Govern the "controlled" nature of the contest between adversarial parties by establishing rules and procedures for proving a legal action

☐   Promote social and public policies for ensuring fairness and a just determination of the proceedings in the ascertainment of truth

---

THE ROLE OF JUDGE AS GATEKEEPER

Evidence law places much of the responsibility for ensuring fairness and efficiency in the hands of the trial judge. The trial judge serves as a referee and a "gatekeeper," interpreting the evidence rules and deciding what evidence will be admissible and what evidence must be excluded. The judge also helps to ensure the "control" in the "controlled contest" by governing the trial proceedings and assuring proper conduct between the adversaries. As the Supreme Court noted about this role, the "line separating acceptable from improper advocacy is not easily drawn; there is often a gray zone. . . . the trial judge has the responsibility to maintain decorum in keeping with the nature of the proceeding; "the judge is not a mere moderator, but is the governor of the trial for the purpose of assuring its proper conduct." The judge "must meet situations as they arise and [be able] to cope with. . . the contingencies inherent in the adversary process."[7]

CRITICAL THINKING QUESTIONS 15.1

1. What did Oliver Wendell Holmes mean when he wrote that the "life of the law has not been logic: it has been experience. . . ?" How does this apply to evidence law?

2. What did he mean when he said "in order to know what it is, we must know what it has been, and what it tends to become. . . ?"

3. Do you think that our adversarial system of resolving legal disputes through a "controlled contest" works adequately? Why or why not?

4. How can we justify a goal for evidence law as the "ascertainment of truth" when some important evidence may be excluded at trial simply because it misleads or confuses the jury?

5. What does the Court mean in their holding that the "law does not require that a defendant receive a perfect trial, only a fair one?" Give some examples of this.

6. Are we placing too much responsibility on the judge as "gatekeeper," "referee," and "governor" of legal proceedings and the admissibility of evidence? Why or why not?

7. What safeguards do you think are in place or should be in place to help the judge with these responsibilities?

"WHAT IT TENDS TO BECOME . . . " —THE FUTURE OF EVIDENCE LAW

Evidence law, like most law, is both dynamic and static. It changes slowly through legislative changes and refinements, and through interpretation of its wording by the courts. Nonetheless, it remains stable. Not much has really changed in evidence law over the past several hundred years. It still has the same purposes and goals. It still has most of the same rules that require relevance and competency, and excludes irrelevant evidence or evidence that violates rules of hearsay or privileged communication.

Often, modifications of evidence law reflect changes in society, or the influence of public policy. The *original document* rule has changed over the years to reflect the growing reliance on copies of writings and recordings. Rules governing character evidence have changed to reflect society's concerns for victims of sexual assault, and rules excluding evidence of prior crimes have been modified in some courts when the evidence concerns sex offense or child molestation cases.

Many areas of our evidence law still warrant scrutiny and change. The character evidence rules are still assailed as unfair. Critics complain that the hearsay rule is rendered ineffective by its voluminous exceptions. Witness rules are too restrictive. Privileges are out of date. And, nobody uses an original document anymore. Even legal scholars are worried that our legal process is losing the ability to "see the forest for the trees"—to "ascertain the truth" because of the proliferation of evidence rules, many of which are confusing and ambiguous. They point to other legal systems, like the civil code countries, that have few evidentiary rules. Even England, the origin of our own laws and procedures, has reduced the number of evidence rules in their legal process. Critics also point to the emphasis on and perpetuation of the adversarial nature of our trial process. In a court system where over 95 percent of our legal actions are settled or resolved before trial, the future trend may be toward more **appropriate dispute resolution** mandated before adversarial proceedings can be initiated. Appropriate dispute resolution includes exploring alternative means of settling or resolving a legal dispute. Parties to a legal action may be referred for informal counseling, **mediation**, or **arbitration** in an attempt to resolve a legal dispute or action before it has to go to trial.

There are, however, recent developments that may also portend of significant future changes in evidence law. Two of these are technological advances and the changes in how scientific evidence is viewed.

TECHNOLOGY AND EVIDENCE LAW

The technology revolution has exploded with new advances over the past few years. It is expected to advance even more dramatically over the next 10 years. Computers and wireless devices that can connect to the Internet lead this revolution. The effect on trials can be seen by the increase in courtrooms with computers, the number of courts that now allow for electronic filings, e-mail correspondence, posting of case opinions, and real-time court transcriptions being displayed on computer screens. With the advent of miniaturization and wireless connectivity, it is expected that, in the near future, courtrooms will have flat screen computers or monitors for all of the players in the trial process. The courtroom of the

Appropriate Dispute Resolution
Alternative means of resolving legal disputes, ranging from informal counseling to mediation to a full-scale adversarial trial.

Mediation
A dispute resolution process where a neutral third party attempts to bring about a settlement or compromise between two disputing parties.

Arbitration
A dispute resolution process where parties to a legal action agree to have their dispute referred to and settled by an impartial third party or group outside of the trial process.

future will allow the judge and each of the parties to a legal action to have a computer in front of them. They will be able to use their computer to access and retrieve information, conduct legal research, communicate with others, and instantaneously pull up records of depositions, hearings, and transcripts of previous testimony. As the court reporter records testimony, it will be displayed real-time on the computer monitors, allowing a party to instantly compare the witness's testimony to statements made earlier in the trial or at previous hearings or depositions. Witnesses may no longer always have to appear "live" in the courtroom to testify. Video conferencing may allow a witness to testify "live" from any location throughout the world.

Evidence will be able to be viewed through the individual monitors and on a big screen computer projection. Gone will be the time-consuming routine of handing exhibits of evidence around for viewing, or passing out photos one by one, or of a witness trying to set up and write on a board to illustrate something, or point something out of a sketch from an accident or crime scene. Instead, the presenting counsel will simply click a button and the item of evidence will pop up on the big screen computer projection, while simultaneously being shown on the small monitor in front of each juror. Using a **specialized legal software** program for exhibiting evidence, or one of the presentation software applications, the witness will utilize computer animation and graphics to illustrate or explain the evidence or matter at issue.

Computer Animation as Evidence

Computer animation evidence is already being used in many courtrooms. In the following California case, the court wrestled with what may be the portentous concern of the future—the role of computer animation as evidence.

Specialized Legal Software
A computer program specially designed to be used in some aspect of law or legal practice, like the animated presentation of evidence, organizing evidence exhibits, or case management.

Computer Animation Evidence
A newer form of demonstrative evidence that utilizes sophisticated computer-generated graphics and animation to illustrate and reconstruct evidence or scenes.

CASE

People v. Hood

53 Cal. App. 4th 965 (1997).

Ramirez, P. J.

After his first trial resulted in a hung jury, James Newman Hood was convicted, following a second trial, of first-degree murder, during which he used a handgun. He was sentenced to prison for four years, plus twenty-five years to life, and appeals, claiming evidence was improperly admitted, the prosecutor committed misconduct during argument to the jury, and his new trial motion should have been granted. We reject his contentions and affirm.

FACTS

Hood and his business partner owned and managed, inter alia, an office complex in Bloomington. The victim had worked for Hood as a construction worker and foreperson. During his employment, the victim had been charged with killing Hood's wife in Tulare County. He was tried for the crime and acquitted in 1990. In January 1992, the victim and a cohort burglarized two of the offices at the complex, taking valuable construction equipment. They then attempted to extract money from Hood and his partner for the return of the equipment. The cohort was eventually arrested for his participation in the offense, and the police were eager to speak to the victim about his activities. On March 2, 1992, the victim, after having spoken by phone with Hood, entered the management office at the complex, greeted Hood's secretary and entered Hood's private office. Within a very short period of time, Hood fired seven bullets into the victim, killing him. The prosecutor contended that the killing was deliberate and premeditated; the defense contended that the victim had threatened Hood beforehand and was in the process of pulling out a gun when Hood shot him in self-defense.

ISSUES AND DISCUSSION

1. Admission of Evidence

a. The Prosecution's Computer Animation

Before the first trial, the prosecution moved to be permitted to introduce a computer animation of the shooting, based upon information supplied by Hood's secretary and the detective who did measurements at the scene and on the reports and opinions of the pathologist who performed the autopsy on the victim and prosecution ballistics and gunshot residue experts. Hood opposed admission of the animation, claiming, inter alia, that, under the *Kelly* [*People v. Kelly*, 17 Cal. 3d 24 (1976)] formulation. . . computer animation had not gained the scientific acceptance necessary for admissibility. The trial court ruled that the animation was illustrative, similar to an expert who draws on a board, and was not being introduced as evidence in and of itself, but only to illustrate the testimony of various prosecution experts.

Both the prosecution and the defense introduced computer animations of the shooting at the first trial. However, the defense later concluded that its animation was not as accurate as it could be and, therefore, it prepared a new one for the second trial. Before the second trial began, Hood again objected to the prosecution's animation on the basis of foundation; however, the trial court overruled the objection, finding that both the prosecution's and the defense's animations had adequate foundations.

Before the prosecution's computer animation was played for the jury, the trial court gave the jury the following instruction: ". . . [Y]ou're reminded that. . . this is an animation based on a compilation of a lot of different experts' opinions. And there are what we call crime scene reconstruction experts who could, without using a computer, get on the stand and testify that based on this piece of evidence and this piece of evidence that they've concluded that the crime occurred in a certain manner. And then they can describe to you the manner in which it occurred. And they can sometimes use charts or diagrams or re-create photographs to demonstrate that. And the computer animation that we have here is nothing more than that kind of an expert opinion being demonstrated or illustrated by the computer animation, as opposed to charts and diagrams." While Hood was on the stand, the trial court further instructed the jury as to the computer animations presented by the prosecution and defense: "I. . . again remind you that all of the animated video reenactments or re-creations are only designed to be an aid to testimony or reconstruction, the same as if an expert testified and drew certain diagrams on the board. They are not intended to be a film of what actually occurred or an exact re-creation. And, therefore, there may be things in each of the videos—in fact, you've heard from some of the witnesses that in each of the videos. . . there are things that are not exactly accurate or not exactly as they occurred, but reasonably close, and it's important to keep that in mind with regard to all of the animated videos, that they are not actual films of what occurred nor are they intended to be exact, detailed replications of every detail or every event or every movement. They are only an aid to giving an overall view of a particular version of the events, based on particular viewpoints or particular interpretations of the evidence."

Hood here begins his attack on the admission of the prosecution's computer animation, reiterating the point he made before the first trial that it did not meet the requirements of the *Kelly* formulation. We agree with the trial court that it did not need to do so. The *Kelly* formulation applies to "new scientific procedures" (*People v. Bury*, 41 Cal. App. 4th 1194 (1996)) or "a new scientific technique. . . [or] . . . novel method of proof" (*People v. Kelly*, supra, 17 Cal. 3d at p. 30). The *Kelly* formula exists to prevent "[l]ay jurors [from] tend[ing] to give considerable weight to 'scientific' evidence when presented by 'experts' with impressive credentials. We have acknowledged the existence of a '. . . misleading aura of certainty which often envelops a new scientific process, obscuring its currently experimental nature.'. . . '[S]cientific proof may in some instances assume a posture of mystic infallibility in the eyes of a jury. . . .'"

The scientific procedures and techniques envisioned in *Kelly* and the dangers addressed therein were not involved here. The prosecution and defense computer animations were tantamount to drawings by the experts from both sides to illustrate their testimony. We view them as a mechanized version of what a human animator does when he or she draws each frame of activity, based upon information supplied by experts, then fans through the frames, making the characters drawn appear to be moving. If the animations here had been done by hand, rather than by a computer, there would have been no *Kelly* issue as to the work done by the animators. By the same token, there was no *Kelly* issue as to the functioning of the computer in creating the animations. Given the nature of the testimony at trial as to how the prosecution's animation had been prepared, the introduction of the defense's contradictory animation and the instructions given the jury concerning both animations, there was no danger that the jury was swept away by the presentation of a new scientific technique which it could not understand and, therefore, would not challenge. As the People correctly point out, Hood cites no authority for applying the *Kelly* formula to computer animation.

Next, Hood contends that the prosecution's animation was based on "a number of factors, including the reactions and stats [sic] of mind of two people under conditions of extreme stress, for which there simply was no clear evidence. [The computer expert who prepared the prosecution's animation] cumulated assumptions (styled as 'expert' inferences) together to create an overall scenario that became remote from the necessary evidentiary foundation. Even the prosecution witnesses admitted other explanations of the proven facts were possible. . . . This re-enactment was also based on inadmissible speculation regarding the position and posture of [the victim] at the time of the shots. . . . [T]he resulting construct improperly sought to demonstrate [Hood]'s purported intent by portraying his actions in conformity with the prosecution's mental state theory." Unfortunately, Hood asserted none of these grounds below, and, therefore, waived them. (Evid. Code, § 353.)

Hood contends that admission of the prosecution's animation invaded the province of the jury in that it constituted an expert statement of how the killing occurred, which was for the jury to determine. As with Hood's objections just discussed, he failed to object below on this ground and is therefore prohibited from doing so now. Moreover, the defense's animation was no less an expert statement of how the killing occurred.

Next, Hood faults the prosecutor for certain remarks he made concerning the People's computer animation. First, he points out that the prosecutor solicited testimony from the computer expert who prepared the animation that besides showing it to a detective who had taken measurements at the scene and certain prosecution experts, all of whom later testified at trial, he also showed it to "[p]eople in the detective's bureau at the sheriff's department. . . to determine whether it was accurate in their opinion. . . . " However, Hood failed to object to this testimony; therefore he cannot now complain about it. (Evid. Code, § 353.)

Hood also cries foul over the following colloquy between the prosecutor and his computer expert:

Q: [BY THE PROSECUTOR]: And I specifically asked you not to put in[to the animation] any figures about Mr. Hood, didn't I?

A: [BY THE COMPUTER EXPERT]: That's true.

Q: [BY THE PROSECUTOR]: I just wanted to show what we know from the evidence about [the victim's] actions, but I did not ask you to put in anybody—

Defense counsel unsuccessfully objected below to the prosecutor's reference to "what we know" on the basis that what the prosecution knew did not include Hood's version of the shooting. This is not adequate to preserve Hood's current objection on the ground that the prosecutor was personally vouching for the animation.

Finally, Hood contends that the trial court abused its discretion in determining that the probative value of the prosecution's computer animation outweighed its prejudicial impact. Aside from reiterating the points made and rejected below, Hood asserts that the animation was emotionally charged and preyed on the emotions of the jury. We disagree. The animation was clinical and emotionless. This, combined with the instruction given the jurors about how they were to utilize both animations, persuades us that the trial court did not abuse its discretion in this regard.

The judgment is affirmed.

The following questions are based on the *How to Brief a Legal Case* format shown in the Appendix. Use this format to answer the following questions:

1. Summarize the facts in the previous case.
2. What is the legal issue?
3. What did the appellate court decide?
4. Why did the court decide this way?
5. Do you agree with the court's reasoning? Explain why or why not.

Try to find this case or another one with a similar issue online! Check out one of the legal research web sites below, go to the federal circuit for this court decision, and use their "Search" feature to find this case or another case that refers to it. In the "Search" field, enter the cite or case name. If you have access to Westlaw or Lexis, try to find this case using one of these legal search sites.

1. U.S. Courts Site with Links to All Circuit Courts of Appeal (http://www.uscourts.gov/links.html)
2. National Center for State Courts—State and Federal Court Web Sites (http://www.ncsconline.org/D_kis/info_court_web_sites.html#federal)
3. FindLaw (http://guide.lp.findlaw.com/casecode/)

In the *Hood* case, the California court found that the computer animation was "clinical and emotionless." The trial court had cautioned the jury that the animation was "only designed to be an aid to testimony or reconstruction, the same as if an expert testified and drew certain diagrams on the board. They are not intended to be a film of what actually occurred or an exact re-creation." While this may be sufficient for this particular case, it raises concerns for how jurors perceive this form of evidence in the future, as it improves in quality and realism. One only needs to see a movie today with its action or crowd scene done with computer animation to realize the dramatic and visual impact that this form of computer-generated graphics can produce on the viewer.

Scientific Evidence

Another area of current change and the subject of significant future uncertainty is how scientific evidence is viewed by different courts. As we have seen in our readings, for over 70 years in this country, the accepted test for scientific evidence and testing was called the *Frye* standard, or *"general acceptance" test*. This standard was based on a 1923 case where a federal circuit court held that the results of a "scientific test" could be admitted if the test had "gained general acceptance in the particular field in which it belongs."

In 1993, a major decision by the U.S. Supreme Court in *Daubert* recognized a new test in the federal courts. This test was based on Federal Rule 702 and required that the scientific evidence or testimony be able to assist the trier of fact to understand the evidence or to determine a fact in issue.

In addition, the expert testimony had to consist of scientific or technical knowledge or experience supported by appropriate validation. This "knowledge" can be determined by considering five factors, including whether it can be (and has been) tested, whether the theory or technique has been subjected to peer review and publication, its known or potential rate of error, the existence and maintenance of standards controlling the technique's operation, and the *Frye* standard for degree of general acceptance within the relevant scientific community.

The problem was that many state courts refused to adopt the new standard. In addition, subsequent federal circuit and Supreme Court decisions modified the *Daubert* standard to an extent that most courts had difficulty figuring out how the standard could be applied. This confusion does not appear to be getting better. The following case shows how this standard might, in the future, change many of the long-accepted areas of scientific evidence. In this 2002 case out of a Pennsylvania federal district court, the judge deals with a request from defendants to exclude fingerprint identification evidence. The defendants claim that this evidence, which has been accepted as reliable scientific evidence for almost a hundred years, fails to meet the newer *Daubert* standard of testing and scientific knowledge.

CASE

United States v. Plaza

179 F.Supp. 2d 492 (2002).
United States District Court for the Eastern District of Pennsylvania.

Pollak, J.

Currently before the court is defendants' Motion to Preclude the United States from Introducing Latent Fingerprint Identification Evidence, in which defendants contend that evidence relating to fingerprints fails to conform to the standard for admitting expert testimony under Federal Rule of Evidence 702, as interpreted by the United States Supreme Court in *Daubert v. Merrell Dow*, 509 U.S. 579 (1993) and *Kumho Tire v. Carmichael*, 526 U.S. 137 (1999). . . .

IV. Admission of Expert Testimony

For several decades, the standard for admission of expert testimony was the "general acceptance" standard that was established in *Frye v. United States*, 293 F.1013 (D.C. Cir. 1923): "[W]hile courts will go a long way in admitting expert testimony deduced from a well-recognized scientific principle or discovery, the thing from which the deduction is made must be sufficiently established to have gained general acceptance in the particular field in which it belongs." In articulating the "general acceptance" standard, the *Frye* court addressed only the admissibility of novel scientific evidence. Other courts subsequently extended "general acceptance" as a test of admissibility for all scientific evidence. Some fifty years after *Frye*'s articulation of the "general acceptance" standard, Congress adopted Federal Rule of Evidence 702. . . .

Rule 702 did not mention "general acceptance," much less adopt this as the test for admission of expert testimony. Nevertheless, many courts continued to use the "general acceptance" standard until the Supreme Court clarified, in 1993, that *Frye*'s "general acceptance" standard had been superseded by Federal Rule of Evidence 702. *Daubert*, 509 U.S. at 587. *Daubert* emphasized that the basic standard of relevance under the Rules is "a liberal one," but that a "trial judge must ensure that any and all scientific testimony or evidence admitted is not only relevant, but reliable." That is, trial judges are called on to play a "gatekeeping role" with respect to scientific testimony. . . . In applying Rule 702 to the admission of scientific testimony, the Court emphasized that, for evidence to be considered "reliable," the proposed expert's opinion must actually be based on what Rule 702 terms "scientific knowledge."

. . . [I]n order to qualify as "scientific knowledge," an inference or assertion must be derived by the scientific method. . . . In short, the requirement that an expert's testimony pertain to "scientific knowledge" establishes a standard of evidentiary reliability. In further delineating what trial judges should be looking for in scientific testimony, Justice Blackmun presented four "general observations," which are commonly referred to as the "*Daubert* factors": (1) whether the technique "can be (and has been) tested," (2) whether the technique has been "subjected to peer review and publication," (3) "the known or potential rate of error... and the existence and maintenance of standards controlling the technique's operation," and (4) "general acceptance." In *Kumho Tire*, the Court held that *Daubert's* interpretation of Rule 702 applies with equal force to proposed expert testimony based on technical or other specialized knowledge. The Court also emphasized that the four *Daubert* factors are flexible and that the "list of specific factors neither necessarily nor exclusively applies to all experts or in every case." In an effort to bring Rule 702 into closer verbal harmony with *Daubert* and *Kumho Tire*, Congress amended Federal Rule of Evidence 702:

> If scientific, technical, or other specialized knowledge will assist the trier of fact to understand the evidence or to determine a fact in issue, a witness qualified as an expert by knowledge, skill, experience, training, or education, may testify thereto in the form of an opinion or otherwise, if (1) the testimony is based upon sufficient facts or data, (2) the testimony is the product of reliable principles and methods, and (3) the witness has applied the principles and methods reliably to the facts of the case. Fed. R. Evid. 702. This newly amended Rule 702 took effect on December 1, 2000 and is thus applicable to the case at hand.

V. Fingerprint Identifications

The primary question that the parties dispute is whether fingerprint identifications are scientifically reliable and thus admissible under Federal Rule of Evidence 702, as construed by the Supreme Court in *Daubert* and *Kumho Tire*. . . .

A. Testing

1. Definition of "Testing"

The first *Daubert* factor is "whether a theory or technique. . . can be (and has been) tested." According to the government, "[t]he ACE-V process and the experts' conclusions have been tested empirically over a period of 100 years and in any particular case they can be tested by examination of the evidence by another expert." The second clause of this sentence seems to be arguing that, following testimony by one fingerprint examiner that a particular latent print corresponds with a particular known print, testimony by a second examiner constitutes a form of "testing." However, this is not "testing" of the "theory" or the "technique" of fingerprint identification in the *Daubert* sense. With respect to "theory," the fact that a second examiner, following the same "technique" as a prior examiner, reaches the same (or, indeed, a different) result, would not seem to shed any light on the validity of the "theory" underlying that "technique. . . . " Some courts that have addressed the admissibility of fingerprint testimony have also equated the use of fingerprint identifications in court with "testing." In *Havvard*, for example, the court stated, "The methods of latent print identification. . . have been tested for roughly 100 years. They have been tested in adversarial proceedings with the highest possible stakes—liberty and sometimes life." 117 F. Supp. 2d at 854. "[A]dversarial" testing in court is not, however, what the Supreme Court meant when it discussed testing as an admissibility factor. . . . If "adversarial" testing were the benchmark—that is if the validity of a technique were submitted to the jury in each instance—then the preliminary role of the judge in determining the scientific validity of a technique would never come into play. Thus, even 100 years of "adversarial" testing in court cannot substitute for scientific testing when the proposed expert testimony is presented as scientific in nature.

Absence of Testing of Fingerprint Techniques

[T]he government had little success in identifying scientific testing that tended to establish the reliability of fingerprint identifications. By contrast, defense testimony strongly suggested that fingerprint identification techniques have not been tested in a manner that could be properly characterized as scientific. Particularly pointed was the testimony of forensic scientist David Stoney, the Director of the McCrone Research Institute in Chicago. According to Dr. Stoney:

> The determination that a fingerprint examiner makes. . . when comparing a latent fingerprint with a known fingerprint, specifically the determination that there is sufficient basis for an absolute identification is not a scientific determination. It is a subjective determination standard. It is a subjective determination without objective standards to it.

. . . .

Dr. Stoney's point that "[t]he determination that a fingerprint examiner makes. . . when comparing a latent fingerprint with a known fingerprint. . . is a subjective determination," was fully confirmed by the testimony presented by government witnesses Ashbaugh and Meagher. After describing the "analysis" ingredient of ACE-V, Sergeant Ashbaugh proceeded to discuss "comparison" and "evaluation" in the following terms:

> Once the comparison is complete, and we recommend that the whole print be compared, the next thing that we would do is then evaluate what we saw during comparison as far as agreement of the various ridge formations. And I break it down into actually two separate areas. The first area is, do I have agreement? If you say yes to that, if you form the opinion you have agreement, then you have to ask yourself, is there sufficient unique detail present to individualize? That final decision is a subjective decision. It's based on your knowledge and experience and your ability. And that, if you say yes, I feel there's enough to individualize, then you formed an opinion of identification.

FBI supervisory fingerprint specialist Meagher gave very similar testimony:

A: The analysis and comparison process is a very objective process. The evaluation process is the subjective opinion of that examiner that he has reached the conclusion that it's ident, non-ident.

Q: The evaluation, the ultimate determination is a subjective one, is it not, sir?

A: Yes.

The significance of the fact that the determinations are "subjective" was explained by the further testimony of Dr. Stoney:

> Now, by subjective I mean that it [a fingerprint identification determination] is one that is dependent on the individual's expertise, training, and the consensus of their agreement of other individuals in the field. By not scientific, I mean that there is not an objective standard that has been tested; nor is there a subjective process that has been objectively tested. It is the essential feature of a scientific process that there be something to test, that when that something is tested the test is capable of showing it to be false.

B. Peer Review and Publication

The second *Daubert* factor is "whether the theory or technique has been subjected to peer review and publication." As with the testing factor, the purpose of the inquiry into peer review and publication is to gauge the scientific reliability of the proposed testimony. . . . Thus, formal peer review is an "integral part of the scientific publication process. . . . " The government maintains that "[t]he fingerprint field and its theories and techniques have been published and peer reviewed during a period of over 100 years." It is the case that there are numerous writings that discuss the fingerprint identification techniques employed by fingerprint examiners. But it is not apparent that their publication constitutes "submission to the scrutiny of the scientific community" in the *Daubert* sense. Even those who stand at the top of the fingerprint identification field—people like David Ashbaugh and Stephen Meagher—tend to be skilled professionals who have learned their craft on the job and without any concomitant advanced academic training. It would thus be a misnomer to call fingerprint examiners a "scientific community" in the *Daubert* sense. . . .

C. Rate of Error and Controlling Standards

The third *Daubert* factor is that trial judges "consider the known or potential rate of error. . . and the existence and maintenance of standards controlling the technique's operation." The government divides the "rate of error" question into two parts—"methodology error" and "practitioner error."

. . .

Mr. Meagher's testimony with respect to error rate. . . is as follows:

Q: Now—Your Honor, if I could just have a moment here. Let's move on into error rate, if we can, please, sir? I want to address error rate as we have—you've heard testimony about ACE-V, about the comparative process, all right? Have you had an opportunity to discuss and read about error rate?

A: Yes.

Q: Are you familiar with that concept when you talk about methodologies?

A: Sure.

Q: And where does that familiarity come from, what kind of experience?

A: Well, when you're dealing with a scientific methodology such as we have for ever since I've been trained, there are distinctions—there's two parts of errors that can occur. One is the methodological error, and the other one is a practitioner error. If the scientific method is followed, adhered to in your process, then the error in the analysis and comparative process will be zero. It only becomes the subjective opinion of the examiner involved at the evaluation phase. And that would become the error rate of the practitioner.

Q: And when you're talking about this, you're referring to friction ridge analysis, correct?

A: That is correct. It's my understanding of that regardless of friction ridge analysis. The analysis comparative evaluation and verification process is pretty much the standard scientific methodology and a lot of other disciplines besides—

Q: And that may be so. Are you an expert or familiar with other scientific areas of methodologies?

A: No, I'm not an expert, but I do know that some of those do adhere to the same methodology as we do.

Q: Are you an expert on their error rate?

A: No.

Q: Based on the uniqueness of fingerprints, friction ridge, etceteras, do you have an opinion as to what the error rate is for the work that you do, latent print examinations?

A: As applied to the scientific methodology, it's zero.

This court accepts... Mr. Meagher's response to the question whether "you have an opinion as to what the error rate is for the work that you do, latent print examinations": "As applied to the scientific methodology, it's zero." Assuming, for the purposes of the motions now at issue before this court, that fingerprint "methodology error" is "zero," it is this court's view that the error rate of principal legal consequence is that which relates to "practitioner error." As Dr. Stoney explained at the *Mitchell* hearing:

> You can't have a fingerprint examination without a fingerprint examiner. If you attempt to say errors that individuals make don't count, then you wouldn't have a scientific process that is being tested anymore. The individual is an inherent part of getting to the opinion in this process. And, errors that individuals make are a very important part of evaluating whether or not it works.

It is the practitioner error rate that affects, for better or worse, the reliability of the fingerprint identification testimony on which the government seeks to have the jury base some aspects of its verdicts. Accordingly, the next *Daubert* ingredient to be considered is practitioner error.

B. "Practitioner Error"

After having opined, in his *Mitchell* testimony, that the error for "scientific methodology" is "zero," Mr. Meagher was questioned by government counsel about "practitioner error":

Q: How would one correct the practitioner error that you talked about? Sir, you do not deny that there's practitioner error, correct?

A: Yes, there is.

Q: Practitioners make mistakes?

A: Sure, we're human.

Q: And how would one, like myself, if I was charged with a crime and part of that evidence had to do with fingerprint analysis and fingerprint opinion, how would I be able to see if there was practitioner error?

A: Well, the images exist. You haven't done anything. They can simply be—the corrected action can simply be given to another qualified examiner for review.

Q: So what you used to—as an examiner used to come to an opinion, any other practitioner could pick up, do ACE-V and come to whatever opinion they are going to come to?

A: That is correct.

As previously noted, Mr. Meagher had conducted a survey in which he sent Byron Mitchell's ten-print card and alleged latent fingerprints to state agencies. The ten-print card was to be compared with the state fingerprint records: the result—that only Pennsylvania, the state in which Mitchell had been incarcerated, reported a "hit"—was significant confirmation of the uniqueness of fingerprints. The other aspect of the Meagher survey—a request that state agencies determine whether the latent prints matched the known Mitchell prints—offered scant support for the accuracy of fingerprint identification. Nine of the thirty-four responding agencies did not make an identification in the first instance. In his testimony, Mr. Meagher offered a variety of explanations: the examiner did not know that the survey was related to a *Daubert* hearing; the photos of the ten-print card or latent prints were insufficiently clear; three of the examiners "just screwed up;" insufficient time; the examiner "attitude toward the survey was not as serious as it should have been;" and "[i]t was late in the day and [the examiner] was probably tired." While the survey results fall far short of establishing a "scientific" rate of error, they are (modestly) suggestive of a discernible level of practitioner error.

. . .

Government and defense witnesses agreed that the actual identification of a latent fingerprint—that is, the decision that the ridges of the two prints that are being compared are sufficiently "identical" to be considered an "absolutely him" match—is a subjective determination. Sergeant Ashbaugh testified for the government:

> The opinion of individualization or identification is subjective. It is an opinion formed by the friction ridge identification specialist based on the friction ridge formations found in agreement during comparison. The validity of the opinion is coupled with an ability to defend that position and both are found in one's personal knowledge, ability and experience.

Likewise, Mr. Meagher testified for the government that the evaluation phase is characterized by "the subjective opinion of the examiner." Dr. Stoney, testifying for the defense, agreed:

> The determination that a fingerprint examiner makes or that an examiner makes when comparing a latent fingerprint with a known fingerprint, specifically the determination that there is sufficient basis for an absolute identification is not a scientific determination. It is a subjective determination standard. It is a subjective determination without objective standards to it.

With such a high degree of subjectivity, it is difficult to see how fingerprint identification—the matching of a latent print to a known fingerprint—is controlled by any clearly describable set of standards to which most examiners subscribe.

C. Examiner Qualifications

... There are no mandatory qualification standards for individuals to become fingerprint examiners, nor is there a uniform certification process. Mr. Meagher, for example, testified that while some FBI fingerprint examiners are certified by the International Association for Identification (IAI), he is not certified by the IAI, but by the FBI.

D. General Acceptance

In *Daubert*, the Supreme Court noted that "general acceptance"—the major ingredient of the *Frye* legacy—can still lend support to a trial judge's finding that a technique is scientifically reliable. The government points out that fingerprint identifications have been used for over 100 years. In addition, Mr. Meagher testified that he sent a survey to state law enforcement agencies, with a striking result: "Unanimously, all states responded, the fact that they do use fingerprints as a means to individualize and they all believe in the two basic principles to our discipline, that is, fingerprints are unique and permanent." It is apparent that law enforcement officials uniformly

place strong reliance on the fingerprint examiner community's acceptance, and utilization, of ACE-V and its kindred identification processes. General acceptance by the fingerprint examiner community does not, however, meet the standard set by Rule 702. First, there is the difficulty that fingerprint examiners, while respected professionals, do not constitute a "scientific community" in the *Daubert* sense. Second, the Court cautioned in *Kumho Tire* that general acceptance does not "help show that an expert's testimony is reliable where the discipline itself lacks reliability." The failure of fingerprint identifications fully to satisfy the first three *Daubert* factors militates against heavy reliance on the general acceptance factor. Thus, while fingerprint examinations conducted under the general ACE-V rubric are generally accepted as reliable by fingerprint examiners, this by itself cannot sustain the government's burden in making the case for the admissibility of fingerprint testimony under Federal Rule of Evidence 702.

VI. Admission of Fingerprint Testimony

Pursuant to the foregoing discussion, it is the court's view that the ACE-V fingerprint identification regime is hard to square with *Daubert*. The one *Daubert* factor that ACE-V satisfies in significant fashion is the fourth factor: ACE-V has attained general acceptance within the American fingerprint examiner community. But the caveat must be added that, in the court's view, the domain of knowledge occupied by fingerprint examiners should be described, in Rule 702 terms, by the word "technical," rather than by the word "scientific," the word the government deploys. Given that *Kumho Tire* establishes that the *Daubert* analysis is applicable to "technical" as well as "scientific" knowledge, it may be thought that this court's characterization of the knowledge base of fingerprint examiners as "technical" rather than "scientific" is a semantic distinction which is of no practical consequence. However, as discussed above, the court finds that ACE-V does not adequately satisfy the "scientific" criterion of testing (the first *Daubert* factor) or the "scientific" criterion of peer review (the second *Daubert* factor). Further, the court finds that the information of record is unpersuasive, one way or another, as to ACE-V's "scientific" rate of error (the first aspect of *Daubert*'s third factor), and that, at the critical evaluation stage, ACE-V does not operate under uniformly accepted "scientific" standards (the second aspect of *Daubert*'s third factor).

Since the court finds that ACE-V does not meet *Daubert*'s testing, peer review, and standards criteria, and that information as to ACE-V's rate of error is in limbo, the expected conclusion would be that the government should be precluded from presenting any fingerprint testimony. But that conclusion—apparently putting at naught a century of judicial acquiescence in fingerprint identification processes—would be unwarrantably heavy-handed. The *Daubert* difficulty with the ACE-V process is by no means total. The difficulty comes into play at the stage at which, as experienced fingerprint specialists Ashbaugh and Meagher themselves acknowledge, the ACE-V process becomes "subjective"—namely, the evaluation stage. By contrast, the antecedent analysis and comparison stages are, according to the testimony, "objective": analysis of the rolled and latent prints and comparison of what the examiner has observed in the two prints. Up to the evaluation stage, the ACE-V fingerprint examiner's testimony is descriptive, not judgmental. Accordingly, this court will permit the government to present testimony by fingerprint examiners who, suitably qualified as "expert" examiners by virtue of training and experience, may (1) describe how the rolled and latent fingerprints at issue in this case were obtained, (2) identify and place before the jury the fingerprints and such magnifications thereof as may be required to show minute details, and (3) point out observed similarities (and differences) between any latent print and any rolled print the government contends are attributable to the same person. What such expert witnesses will not be permitted to do is to present "evaluation" testimony as to their "opinion" (Rule 702) that a particular latent print is in fact the print of a particular person. The defendants will be permitted to present their own fingerprint experts to counter the government's fingerprint testimony, but defense experts will also be precluded from presenting "evaluation" testimony. Government counsel and defense counsel will, in closing arguments, be free to argue to the jury that, on the basis of the jury's observation of a particular latent print and a particular rolled print, the jury may find the existence, or the non-existence, of a match between the prints. . . .

VII. Conclusion

For the foregoing reasons:

A. This court will take judicial notice of the uniqueness and permanence of fingerprints.

B. The parties will be able to present expert fingerprint testimony (1) describing how any latent and rolled prints at issue in this case were obtained, (2) identifying, and placing before the jury, such fingerprints and any necessary magnifications, and (3) pointing out any observed similarities and differences between a particular latent print and a particular rolled print alleged by the government to be attributable to the same persons.

But the parties will not be permitted to present testimony expressing an opinion of an expert witness that a particular latent print matches, or does not match, the rolled print of a particular person and hence is, or is not, the fingerprint of that person.

LEGAL ANALYSIS AND WRITING 15.2

The following questions are based on the *How to Brief a Legal Case* format shown in the Appendix. Use this format to answer the following questions:

1. Summarize the facts in the previous case.
2. What is the legal issue?
3. What did the appellate court decide?
4. Why did the court decide this way?
5. Do you agree with the court's reasoning? Explain why or why not.

LEGAL RESEARCH USING THE INTERNET SKILLS 15.2

Try to find this case or another one with a similar issue online! Check out one of the legal research web sites below, go to the federal circuit for this court decision, and use their "Search" feature to find this case or another case that refers to it. In the "Search" field, enter the cite or case name. If you have access to Westlaw or Lexis, try to find this case using one of these legal search sites.

1. U.S. Courts Site with Links to All Circuit Courts of Appeal (http://www.uscourts.gov/links.html)
2. National Center for State Courts—State and Federal Court Web Sites (http://www.ncsconline.org/D_kis/info_court_web_sites.html#federal)
3. FindLaw (http://guide.lp.findlaw.com/casecode/)

The *Plaza* case illustrates the current problems in interpreting *Daubert* and provides a glimpse into probable future issues involving scientific evidence and expert testimony. A related future concern is whether our legal professionals and judges will be adequately grounded in "scientific knowledge" in order to meet the challenges in proving the new standard. If the standard is no longer what is "generally accepted" in the scientific community and instead requires an understanding of different scientific methodologies and procedures, how will the lawyers and judges of the future prepare for this?

In a recent Wisconsin case, the prosecution in a criminal case obtained an arrest warrant based on a suspect's DNA code without knowing the identity of the suspect. The suspect was later identified and arrested when his DNA was obtained and matched in a different matter. Science and technology are changing the nature of our society and have had a significant impact on our legal process as well. The children of today are learning computers at a very early age. They are growing up around wireless technology, the Internet, and computer graphics and animation much like we grew up around the technological revolution of our age—color television and the cordless phone! These children will become the legal professionals of the future—how will that affect the gathering and presentation of evidence?

CRITICAL THINKING QUESTIONS 15.2

1. What do you think is meant by the concern that our legal process is losing the ability to "see the forest for the trees?"
2. How can this be prevented or remedied?
3. Assess what you think might be the strengths and weaknesses in using computer animation for the presentation of evidence.
4. Would the result in the *Hood* case have been different if the defendant had been indigent and could not afford to present an opposing computer animation?
5. Do you think the *Plaza* decision will be overturned on appeal? Why or why not?

SUMMARY

Our evidence law has endured and evolved over the past several hundred years. Developed to help protect the jury, govern proceedings, and ensure fairness in our adversarial process, evidence law has adapted to changing social and public concerns. Although evidentiary rules will face many challenges as we continue to move toward a more technologically advanced legal system, the fundamental basis upon which evidence law rests should remain stable. What Supreme Court Justice Sutherland wrote in 1933 should prove equally relevant in 2033:

> The fundamental basis upon which all rules of evidence must rest—if they are to rest upon reason—is their adaptation to the successful development of the truth. And, since experience is of all teachers the most dependable, and since experience also is a continuous process, it follows that a rule of evidence at one time thought necessary to the ascertainment of the truth should yield to the experience of a succeeding generation whenever that experience has clearly demonstrated the fallacy or unwisdom of the old rule.[8]

KEY TERMS

Appropriate Dispute
  Resolution
Arbitration

Computer Animation
  Evidence
Mediation

Specialized Legal
  Software

LEARNING OUTCOMES AND PRACTICE SKILLS CHECKLIST

☐ Learning Outcomes

After completing your reading, questions, and exercises, you should be able to demonstrate a better understanding of the learning concepts by answering the following questions:

1. Explain the role and purpose of evidence rules in the legal process.
2. Describe how the role of evidence law continues to serve the purposes for which it has developed over the years.
3. Assess what is meant by the judge as "gatekeeper."
4. Identify some of the changes in evidence rules over recent years.
5. Explain how computer animation is used as evidence and what guidelines are in place to ensure that it is not utilized improperly.
6. Assess some of the challenges faced by courts in interpreting and applying the *Daubert* standard to scientific evidence and expert testimony.

☐ Practice Skills

In addition to understanding the learning concepts, practice what you have learned through applications using critical thinking, legal analysis and writing, legal research, and advocacy skills, including:

Critical Thinking

1. Why are the primary purposes of the evidence rules to ensure fairness to the ends that the truth be ascertained and proceedings justly determined?

2. Are these goals really compatible? Why or why not?
3. How can we balance these goals in a way that ensures fairness yet ascertains the truth?
4. Do you believe that our present rules of evidence provide adequate safeguards for the parties to a legal action?
5. If it were up to you, what changes would you make to the rules of evidence, and why?
6. Name the changes that you think will take place in evidence law in future years as a result of technology.

Legal Analysis and Writing

Analyze the following cases by summarizing their holdings, explaining their significance, and assessing any issue that might arise in their application.

1. *People v. Hood.*
2. *United States v. Plaza.*

Legal Research Using the Internet

1. Find your state's rules of evidence regarding concepts covered in this chapter. Identify any evidence rules that are new or have been changed in recent years.
2. Visit the web sites listed in the *Practice Tip* 15.1 section. Find and assess recommendations for future changes to the Federal Rules of Evidence. Do you agree with these proposed changes?
3. Find out if your state appellate court posts their case decisions on the Internet. If so, find a case that illustrates an issue or potential future change for evidence law discussed in this chapter. If your state decisions are not on the Internet, go instead to the web site for the U.S. Circuit Court of Appeals in your circuit, or search the U.S. Supreme Court decisions.

PRACTICE APPLICATION 15.1

In a criminal action, prosecution wants to use computer animation as evidence to prove that defendant intentionally drove her car into a crowd of pedestrians, killing two people. The defendant is indigent and cannot afford to hire a computer expert to either produce an opposing animation or to contest the animation introduced by the prosecution.

Should the prosecution be allowed to introduce computer animation as evidence in this case? Use the format shown in the Appendix for the *IRAC Method of Legal Analysis* and the readings, rules, and cases discussed in this chapter to analyze this question. Write a short memo giving your analysis, reasoning, and conclusions.

ADVOCACY AND COMMUNICATION SKILLS 15.1

Using the *Advocacy and Persuasive Arguments* format shown in the Appendix, select one of the following topics, inform your instructor whether you will argue for or against the issue, prepare, and deliver an oral persuasive argument:

1. Do our present rules of evidence live up to their goals of ensuring fairness and just proceedings in the ascertainment of truth?

2. Should we keep the advocacy system or place more emphasis on appropriate dispute resolution?

3. Should we allow computer-generated graphics to be used as evidence?

You will have 3 minutes to state your position and support it. After the other side presents his arguments, you will have an additional minute to rebut his position.

Practice Tip 15.1

Resources for Future Directions in Evidence Law

Here are some interesting Internet resources for keeping track of new changes in evidence law, as well as future recommendations and trends:

Evidence Cases, News, and Materials at Legal Information Institute (LII)

(http://www.law.cornell.edu/topics/evidence.html)

The Evidence Site, written and edited by members of the Evidence Section of the Association of American Law Schools with support from the University of Michigan School of Law

(http://www.law.umich.edu/thayer/)

The Evidence Project, Proposed Revisions to the Federal Rules of Evidence

(http://www.wcl.american.edu/pub/journals/evidence/toc.html)

WEB SITES

Evidence Cases, News, and Materials at Legal Information Institute (LII)

http://www.law.cornell.edu/topics/evidence.html

FindLaw

http://guide.lp.findlaw.com/casecode/

National Center for State Courts—State and Federal Court Web Sites

http://www.ncsconline.org/D_icis/info_court_web_sites.html#federal

The Evidence Project, Proposed Revisions to the Federal Rules of Evidence

http://www.wcl.american.edu/pub/journals/evidence/toc.html

The Evidence Site, written and edited by members of the Evidence Section of the Association of American Law Schools with support from the University of Michigan School of Law

http://www.law.umich.edu/thayer/

U.S. Courts Site with Links to All Circuit Courts of Appeal

http://www.uscourts.gov/links.html

ENDNOTES

1. Savigny, *Of the Vocation of Our Age for Legislation and Jurisprudence* (1814).
2. Oliver Wendell Holmes, *The Common Law*, 1909.
3. *Tehan v. Shott*, 382 U.S. 406 (1966).
4. Ga. Code, Section 24-1-2.
5. *Elkins v. United States*, 364 U.S. 206, 234 (1960) (Frankfurter dissenting).
6. *Michigan v. Tucker*, 417 U.S. 433 (1974).
7. *United States v. Young*, 470 U.S. 1 (1985).
8. *Funk v. United States*, 290 U.S. 371 (1933).

APPENDIX A

Thinking Law

THINKING LAW

The law, unlike other topics, is dynamic and can change. In order to understand it, you must learn to **think law**; in other words, to "**think like a lawyer.**" That means thinking about what the purpose behind each rule of evidence is and who or what it is trying to protect.

Because most of our rules wind up being reviewed and refined further by an appellate court, we need to pay attention to legal decisions which may uphold, change, or affect the rules of evidence: What did the court decide and how did they interpret the rule of evidence or individual right in issue? How many and which justices decided for the majority? Which justices disagreed and filed a "minority" opinion? Which argument do you agree with? Why?

CASE METHOD

Legal cases are essential to evidence law, because they interpret and refine the existing rules of evidence, help us to learn the underlying rationale for each rule, and lay the groundwork for future rules.

We should not limit ourselves to **what** decision the court made, but **how** and **why** they arrived at that decision! To do this, you must **read** each case carefully in order to understand the legal reasoning process that guided the decision.

When you read the cases, think about the individual judges and justices deciding the case. Who are they? What walk of life do they come from? What biases or philosophy do they bring to the job? What did they do for or to the court? How will their opinion or legal philosophy shape the laws of evidence for the future?

Question: Can you name any Supreme Court justices whose personal beliefs or philosophy may have affected legal issues in our country?

READING LEGAL CASES

To understand the law, you must read it, not merely read *about* it. Reading and briefing cases helps you to understand how a particular court **thinks law** and uses legal reasoning in order to arrive at a decision regarding an issue.

To properly learn the rules of evidence, you have to learn to identify the **issues** which the court had to resolve and the **reasoning** that the court used to decide how to interpret the rules.

Important to Read Cases Thoroughly

Before you can identify these case issues and the reasoning behind them, you must first read the case thoroughly. It's important to really read it, not just look it over. Make notes to yourself, and go over it several times. Look up definitions that you do not know. Ask yourself what the court is trying to say or do. In fact, you should try to read the case at least three times.

Read Cases Three Times!

On the first read, **skim** through the material to get an idea of what the case is all about. Ask yourself who the parties are and what the court is trying to decide. (A helpful hint is to follow the **bold** headings in your text giving the title of that particular section of study.)

Next, read the case a second time and try to **organize** it into a Case Brief Format, identifying the facts and holding of the court.

A third, **thorough** reading should help you to identify the legal issues presented, why the court arrived at its decision, and the principle of law referenced.

Dissenting Opinions Are Important, Too!

Remember to read the dissenting opinion, if given. Today's dissenting opinion by the minority members of the court may be tomorrow's majority opinion.

In a 1928 case, a defendant was convicted of importing liquor from evidence gathered by tapping the telephone line between his home and office. The Court said that as long as there was no illegal, **physical trespass**, the evidence was admissible.

Justice Brandeis wrote a dissent in which he argued that the Fourth and Fifth Amendments to the U.S. Constitution "conferred, as against the government, the **right to be let alone** . . . [and] to protect that right, **every unjustifiable intrusion** by the government upon the privacy of the individual, **whatever the means** employed, must be deemed a violation of the Fourth Amendment." *Olmstead v. United States*, 277 U.S. 438 (1928).

Almost 40 years later, the Court overturned *Olmstead* and, in a 1969 case, the Court overturned a defendant's conviction for possession of obscene movies in his own home, without proof of sales, distribution, or showing them for profit.

Writing for the **majority**, Justice Thurgood Marshall relied on Justice Brandeis' dissent in *Olmstead* that the Constitution protects people's "right to receive information and ideas . . . regardless of their social worth"; that people have a "right to be free, except in very limited circumstances, from unwanted governmental intrusions into one's privacy . . . **the right to be let alone**." *Stanley v. Georgia*, 394 U.S. 557 (1969).

Although it took over 40 years, the Court slowly changed its membership and thinking, gradually accepting what had been the dissenting **minority** opinion and elevating this dissent into the basis for a new rule and **precedent** of law.

Writing Case Briefs

Case briefs are a way of cutting through a lot of the **obiter dictum**, or verbiage which accompanies many court decisions, and effectively summarizing the essential facts and relevant issues of law. It helps you to organize your thinking and gets you into the habit of writing concisely. Understanding how case briefs are written is an important part of **thinking law**.

Six Parts to Writing Case Briefs

There are basically six parts to writing a case brief: citation, factual summary, issue of law before the court, holding of court, reasoning for holding, rule of law, and dissenting opinion. The format that you should use for a case brief is described below.

Full Citation

The citation is at the top of the case brief, usually centered on the page. The full citation includes the name of the case, where it can be found in a law library, and the date that it was decided.

Name of Case
The case name should be underlined or in italics (e.g., *Cruzan v. Director, Missouri Department of Health*).
"Citation" (Year decided)
A citation tells where the case can be found. It is written in the following form: **497 U.S. 261** (Number Abbreviation Number)

49   U.S.   261
      / | \
Volume #   Book   Page #

If you saw a citation for *Cruzan* v. *Director, Missouri Department of Health*, 497 U.S. 261 (1990), and you wanted to look up the entire case, you would go to a law library and find Volume 497 of the reporter or book entitled "United States Reports" (these are all abbreviated; the full abbreviations can be found in any law library), then turn to page 261. The case would be printed in its entirety. Often, you will find two numbers at the end (e.g., 497 U.S. 261, 263). This means that although the case begins on page 261, the issue you are reading about can also be found on page 263.

APPENDIX B

How to Brief a Legal Case

HOW TO BRIEF A LEGAL CASE

Format of a Case Brief

Name of Case
Citation (Year Decided)

Facts: *Briefly* give the facts of the case. Who did what to whom, when, how, and sometimes, why? Include the parties, trial court's decision, and the *procedural history* (i.e., how the case got to the appellate level).

Issue: This is the legal issue raised on appeal or before the court. Phrase it in the form of a question, (e.g., "May a wife be forced to testify against her husband in a criminal trial in which the husband is the defendant?")

Holding: This is *what* the appellate court decided, usually answered "yes" or "no" in response to the issue in question, and followed by what the court did to the lower court's judgment: affirmed, reversed, or remanded.

Reasoning: This is *why* the court decided the way that they did, often tracing the history of this particular law or issue, exploring legislative intent, and citing precedent—the court uses legal analysis to apply the rule of law or their interpretation of a rule to the facts in this particular case in order to support their conclusion.

Rule of Law: This is a rule or principle of law that will affirm present laws or establish a new precedent and law.

Dissent: Briefly discuss the dissenting opinion, if given and if relevant.

In briefing cases, remember to read the cases thoroughly before writing your brief and to keep your written briefs concise. The facts should be no more than one or two paragraphs. The issue is stated in the form of a question, which is then answered by the holding of the court. The reasoning is usually a brief review of the precedents examined by the court in order to reach their decision. Your briefs should be typed or printed in the same format as shown, with the headings flush along the left margin of your paper.

Sample Case Brief:

The following is an example of a case brief format for the *Larmay* court opinion found in Chapter 2.

Larmay v. Vanetten
129 Vt. 368 (1971)

Facts: Plaintiff was in a vehicle travelling north on a highway. Defendant was travelling south. Defendant's car veered into northbound traffic lane and collided with plaintiff. Plaintiff sued defendant for negligence. At a jury trial, after evidence was presented, plaintiff moved for a directed verdict on the basis that defendant was guilty of negligence as a matter of law. In support of this, plaintiff cited Vermont Statutes that state "operators of vehicles must exercise due care and not pass to the left of center unless the way ahead is clear and unobstructed." Plaintiff asserted that since these rules of the road were violated, it made out a legal presumption of negligence against defendant which then must be rebutted. Since defendant "offered no countervailing evidence to the presumption" a directed verdict must be granted. Defendant argued that plaintiff did not have to produce any evidence to rebut the presumption because plaintiff could not "establish, through evidence, that it was an act of the defendant which caused defendant's vehicle to cross the center line." The court agreed with the plaintiff and granted a directed verdict. Defendant appeals, again arguing that even though she didn't produce evidence, there was a "reasonable inference" from the evidence presented that defendant's crossing the center line could be from "mechanical failure or dangerous road conditions."

Issue: Does a defendant have a duty to produce evidence to rebut a presumption of negligence that has been duly raised by plaintiff?

Held: Yes. Once a presumption has been raised, it "shifts to the party against whom it operates the burden of evidence."

Reasoning: The court found that the "burden of showing that the defendant was guilty of some negligent act. . . that proximately caused the accident was. . . on the plaintiff." This was done by plaintiff's introduction of evidence which created a prima facie presumption of negligence. Once this presumption was created, "it shifts to the party against whom it operated the burden of evidence. And the prima facie case would become the established case, if nothing further appears" from the defendant. The court said that "if the defendant desired to overcome the effect of the presumption, it was her duty to present evidence to rebut it." The defendant offered none. This, the court said, "left the presumption of negligence standing unchallenged."

Rule of Law: Once a presumption has been raised, it "shifts to the party against whom it operates the burden of evidence."

APPENDIX C

IRAC Method of Legal Analysis

IRAC METHOD OF LEGAL ANALYSIS

Legal analysis involves applying a rule of law to a set of facts in order to reach a conclusion that resolves a particular legal issue. One way to apply legal analysis is called the *IRAC method*, an acronym for determining the **Issue** involved in a legal problem, finding the **Rule** of law that governs that specific area of law, and then **Analyzing** and **Applying** the rule to the facts in order to arrive at a legal **Conclusion**. You will use the IRAC method in paragraph form, using a format similar to the following:

> The issue here is whether. . . The rule of law that covers this area is. . . . In this case, if. . . then [this is your analysis and application of the rule to the facts]; Therefore, this is the conclusion.

For example, a witness wants to testify about an incident that she was not present for, but that she heard other people discuss later. Would you allow this witness to testify? If you were answering this using the IRAC method in paragraph form, it might look something like this:

> The issue here is whether a witness can testify about an incident that she was not present for, but heard other people discuss later. The rule of law that covers this area is Rule 602. This rule states that a witness may not testify to a matter unless evidence is introduced sufficient to support a finding that the witness has *personal knowledge* of the matter. In this case, the witness does not have personal knowledge of the incident and can only testify to what others have

said. Therefore, lacking personal knowledge, the witness cannot testify.

Often, in a legal setting, IRAC is part of an inter-office memorandum regarding some case problem or issue the legal team faces. An example of this format for the previous problem would be:

To:	Attorney
From:	Paralegal
Date:	[Today's date]
Re:	*Jones v. Smith*, Case #1234
Issue(s):	Whether a witness can testify to an incident that she was not present for, but heard other people discuss later.
Short Answer:	No
Analysis:	The rule of law that covers this area is Rule 602. This rule states that a witness may not testify to a matter unless evidence is introduced sufficient to support a finding that the witness has *personal knowledge* of the matter. In this case, the witness does not have personal knowledge of the incident and can only testify to what others have said. Therefore, lacking personal knowledge, the court would uphold any objection to the witness testifying.
Conclusion:	The witness will not be allowed to testify.

APPENDIX D

Advocacy and Persuasive Arguments

ADVOCACY AND PERSUASIVE ARGUMENTS

One of the basic tasks of a legal or criminal justice professional is being an advocate. Advocacy includes using a form of oral argument to support, prove, or convince others about a matter. The form of argument used is called a *persuasive argument*. It is the process of persuading someone to your point of view by offering facts and reasoning; or, when advocating a legal issue, citing legal points and authorities, like statutory laws and court decisions, to support your argument.

To be an effective advocate requires strong communication skills. Each chapter in this text includes an *Advocacy and Communication Skills* exercise designed to help you to strengthen these skills. As you prepare and deliver these oral arguments, concentrate on the following areas:

Posture:	Stand straight. Do not slouch. Keep your hands out of your pocket.
Eye Contact:	Make and maintain eye contact with your audience.
Delivery:	Speak clearly and in a persuasive manner. Do not talk in a monotone. Adjust or modulate your voice to emphasize the points being made. Do not simply read from a speech.
Argument Style:	An effective argument is one that is based primarily on the law and the logical presentation of the facts involved. An appeal to emotion can also be a means of supporting your argument, especially when dealing with eviden-

tiary issues that may be relevant but prejudicial.

Substance of Argument:	The substance of an argument is its basis. What are you basing your argument on and how have you supported this basis? The substance should be based on legal points and authorities, like specific evidentiary laws and rules, and court decisions.
Legal Resources Used:	Be prepared to cite the legal resources used in your argument.

Generally, the basic format of an argument or a presentation is the following:

1. Introduction
2. Body
3. Conclusion

However, an oral argument over a legal issue may require the use of legal analysis in covering the necessary points and law. When preparing for a legal issue, review the *IRAC Method of Legal Analysis* as a guide in presenting your argument.

Supporting Memo

When you present an oral argument, you should first submit a brief supporting memo (one or two paragraphs only) to the instructor. This memo should identify the issue you plan to argue and include a *road map* paragraph in which you briefly provide an overview of what you will be arguing and your position on the issue. This memo should also include a list of citations or outside research sources and references used to support your argument.

APPENDIX E

Federal Rules of Evidence

FEDERAL RULES OF EVIDENCE

Effective July 1, 1975, as amended to December 1, 2000.

ARTICLE I. GENERAL PROVISIONS

Rule 101. Scope.

These rules govern proceedings in the courts of the United States and before the United States bankruptcy judges and United States magistrate judges, to the extent and with the exceptions stated in rule 1101.

Rule 102. Purpose and Construction.

These rules shall be construed to secure fairness in administration, elimination of unjustifiable expense and delay, and promotion of growth and development of the law of evidence to the end that the truth may be ascertained and proceedings justly determined.

Rule 103. Rulings on Evidence.

(a) Effect of erroneous ruling. Error may not be predicated upon a ruling which admits or excludes evidence unless a substantial right of the party is affected, and

  (1) Objection. In case the ruling is one admitting evidence, a timely objection or motion to strike appears of record, stating the specific ground of objection, if the specific ground was not apparent from the context; or

  (2) Offer of proof. In case the ruling is one excluding evidence, the substance of the evidence was made known to the court by offer or was apparent from the context within which questions were asked. Once the court makes a definitive ruling on the record admitting or excluding evidence, either at or before trial, a party need not renew an objection or offer of proof to preserve a claim of error for appeal.

(b) Record of offer and ruling. The court may add any other or further statement which shows the character of the evidence, the form in which it was offered, the objection made, and the ruling thereon. It may direct the making of an offer in question and answer form.

(c) Hearing of jury. In jury cases, proceedings shall be conducted, to the extent practicable, so as to prevent inadmissible evidence from being suggested to the jury by any means, such as making statements or offers of proof or asking questions in the hearing of the jury.

(d) Plain error. Nothing in this rule precludes taking notice of plain errors affecting substantial rights although they were not brought to the attention of the court.

(Amended effective Dec. 1, 2000.)

Rule 104. Preliminary Questions.

(a) Questions of admissibility generally. Preliminary questions concerning the qualification of a person to be a witness, the existence of a privilege, or the admissibility of evidence shall be determined by the court, subject to the provisions of subdivision (b). In making its determination it is not bound by the rules of evidence except those with respect to privileges.

(b) Relevancy conditioned on fact. When the relevancy of evidence depends upon the fulfillment of a condition of fact, the court shall admit it upon, or subject to, the introduction of evidence sufficient to support a finding of the fulfillment of the condition.

(c) Hearing of jury. Hearings on the admissibility of confessions shall in all cases be conducted out of the hearing of the jury. Hearings on other preliminary matters shall be so conducted when the interests of justice require, or when an accused is a witness and so requests.

(d) Testimony by accused. The accused does not, by testifying upon a preliminary matter, become subject to cross-examination as to other issues in the case.

(e) Weight and credibility. This rule does not limit the right of a party to introduce before the jury evidence relevant to weight or credibility.

Rule 105. Limited Admissibility.

When evidence which is admissible as to one party or for one purpose but not admissible as to another party or for another purpose is admitted, the court, upon request, shall restrict the evidence to its proper scope and instruct the jury accordingly.

Rule 106. Remainder of or Related Writings or Recorded Statements.

When a writing or recorded statement or part thereof is introduced by a party, an adverse party may require the introduction at that time of any other part or any other writing or recorded statement which ought in fairness to be considered contemporaneously with it.

ARTICLE II. JUDICIAL NOTICE

Rule 201. Judicial Notice of Adjudicative Facts.

(a) Scope of rule. This rule governs only judicial notice of adjudicative facts.

(b) Kinds of facts. A judicially noticed fact must be one not subject to reasonable dispute in that it is either (1) generally known within the territorial jurisdiction of the trial court or (2) capable of accurate and ready determination by resort to sources whose accuracy cannot reasonably be questioned.

(c) When discretionary. A court may take judicial notice, whether requested or not.

(d) When mandatory. A court shall take judicial notice if requested by a party and supplied with the necessary information.

(e) Opportunity to be heard. A party is entitled upon timely request to an opportunity to be heard as to the propriety of taking judicial notice and the tenor of the matter noticed. In the absence of prior notification, the request may be made after judicial notice has been taken.

(f) Time of taking notice. Judicial notice may be taken at any stage of the proceeding.

(g) Instructing jury. In a civil action or proceeding, the court shall instruct the jury to accept as conclusive any fact judicially noticed. In a criminal case, the court shall instruct the jury that it may, but is not required to, accept as conclusive any fact judicially noticed.

ARTICLE III. PRESUMPTIONS IN CIVIL ACTIONS AND PROCEEDINGS

Rule 301. Presumptions in General in Civil Actions and Proceedings.

In all civil actions and proceedings not otherwise provided for by Act of Congress or by these rules, a presumption imposes on the party against whom it is directed the burden of going forward with evidence to rebut or meet the presumption, but does not shift to such party the burden of proof in the sense of the risk of non persuasion, which remains throughout the trial upon the party on whom it was originally cast.

Rule 302. Applicability of State Law in Civil Actions and Proceedings.

In civil actions and proceedings, the effect of a presumption respecting a fact which is an element of a claim or defense as to which State law supplies the rule of decision is determined in accordance with State law.

ARTICLE IV. RELEVANCY AND ITS LIMITS

Rule 401. Definition of "Relevant Evidence."

"Relevant evidence" means evidence having any tendency to make the existence of any fact that is of consequence to the determination of the action more probable or less probable than it would be without the evidence.

Rule 402. Relevant Evidence Generally Admissible; Irrelevant Evidence Inadmissible.

All relevant evidence is admissible, except as otherwise provided by the Constitution of the United States, by Act of Congress, by these rules, or by other rules prescribed by the Supreme Court pursuant to statutory authority. Evidence which is not relevant is not admissible.

Rule 403. Exclusion of Relevant Evidence on Grounds of Prejudice, Confusion, or Waste of Time.

Although relevant, evidence may be excluded if its probative value is substantially outweighed by the danger of unfair prejudice, confusion of the issues, or misleading the jury, or by considerations of undue delay, waste of time, or needless presentation of cumulative evidence.

Rule 404. Character Evidence Not Admissible to Prove Conduct; Exceptions; Other Crimes.

(a) **Character evidence generally**. Evidence of a person's character or a trait of character is not admissible for the purpose of proving action in conformity therewith on a particular occasion, except:

(1) **Character of accused**. Evidence of a pertinent trait of character offered by an accused, or by the prosecution to rebut the same, or if evidence of a trait of character of the alleged victim of the crime is offered by an accused and admitted under Rule 404(a)(2), evidence of the same trait of character of the accused offered by the prosecution;

(2) **Character of alleged victim**. Evidence of a pertinent trait of character of the alleged victim of the crime offered by an accused, or by the prosecution to rebut the same, or evidence of a character trait of peacefulness of the alleged victim offered by the prosecution in a homicide case to rebut evidence that the alleged victim was the first aggressor;

(3) **Character of witness**. Evidence of the character of a witness, as provided in rules 607, 608, and 609.

(b) **Other crimes, wrongs, or acts**. Evidence of other crimes, wrongs, or acts is not admissible to prove the character of a person in order to show action in conformity therewith. It may, however, be admissible for other purposes, such as proof of motive, opportunity, intent, preparation, plan, knowledge, identity, or absence of mistake or accident, provided that upon request by the accused, the prosecution in a criminal case shall provide reasonable notice in advance of trial, or during trial if the court excuses pretrial notice on good cause shown, of the general nature of any such evidence it intends to introduce at trial.

(Amended effective Dec. 1, 2000.)

Rule 405. Methods of Proving Character.

(a) **Reputation or opinion**. In all cases in which evidence of character or a trait of character of a person is admissible, proof may be made by testimony as to reputation or by testimony in the form of an opinion. On cross-examination, inquiry is allowable into relevant specific instances of conduct.

(b) **Specific instances of conduct**. In cases in which character or a trait of character of a person is an essential element of a charge, claim, or defense, proof may also be made of specific instances of that person's conduct.

Rule 406. Habit; Routine Practice.

Evidence of the habit of a person or of the routine practice of an organization, whether corroborated or not and regardless of the presence of eyewitnesses, is relevant to prove that the conduct of the person or organization on a particular occasion was in conformity with the habit or routine practice.

Rule 407. Subsequent Remedial Measures.

When, after an injury or harm allegedly caused by an event, measures are taken that, if taken previously, would have made the injury or harm less likely to occur, evidence of the subsequent measures is not admissible to prove negligence, culpable conduct, a defect in a product, a defect in a product's design, or a need for a warning or instruction. This rule does not require the exclusion of evidence of subsequent measures when offered for another purpose, such as proving ownership, control, or feasibility of precautionary measures, if controverted, or impeachment.

Rule 408. Compromise and Offers to Compromise.

Evidence of (1) furnishing or offering or promising to furnish, or (2) accepting or offering or promising to accept, a valuable consideration in compromising or attempting to compromise a claim which was disputed as to either validity or amount, is not admissible to prove liability for or invalidity of the claim or its amount.

Evidence of conduct or statements made in compromise negotiations is likewise not admissible. This rule does not require the exclusion of any evidence otherwise discoverable merely because it is presented in the course of compromise negotiations. This rule also does not require exclusion when the evidence is offered for another purpose, such as proving bias or prejudice of a witness, negativing a contention of undue delay, or proving an effort to obstruct a criminal investigation or prosecution.

Rule 409. Payment of Medical and Similar Expenses.

Evidence of furnishing or offering or promising to pay medical, hospital, or similar expenses occasioned by an injury is not admissible to prove liability for the injury.

Rule 410. Inadmissibility of Pleas, Plea Discussions, and Related Statements.

Except as otherwise provided in this rule, evidence of the following is not, in any civil or criminal proceeding, admissible against the defendant who made the plea or was a participant in the plea discussions:

(1) a plea of guilty which was later withdrawn;
(2) a plea of nolo contendere;
(3) any statement made in the course of any proceedings under Rule 11 of the Federal Rules of Criminal Procedure or comparable state procedure regarding either of the foregoing pleas; or

(4) any statement made in the course of plea discussions with an attorney for the prosecuting authority which do not result in a plea of guilty or which result in a plea of guilty later withdrawn.

However, such a statement is admissible (i) in any proceeding wherein another statement made in the course of the same plea or plea discussions has been introduced and the statement ought in fairness be considered contemporaneously with it, or (ii) in a criminal proceeding for perjury or false statement if the statement was made by the defendant under oath, on the record and in the presence of counsel.

Rule 411. Liability Insurance.

Evidence that a person was or was not insured against liability is not admissible upon the issue whether the person acted negligently or otherwise wrongfully. This rule does not require the exclusion of evidence of insurance against liability when offered for another purpose, such as proof of agency, ownership, or control, or bias or prejudice of a witness.

Rule 412. Sex Offense Cases; Relevance of Alleged Victim's Past Sexual Behavior or Alleged Sexual Predisposition.

(a) **Evidence generally inadmissible**. The following evidence is not admissible in any civil or criminal proceeding involving alleged sexual misconduct except as provided in subdivisions (b) and (c):

(1) Evidence offered to prove that any alleged victim engaged in other sexual behavior.
(2) Evidence offered to prove any alleged victim's sexual predisposition.

(b) **Exceptions**.

(1) In a criminal case, the following evidence is admissible, if otherwise admissible under these rules:

(A) evidence of specific instances of sexual behavior by the alleged victim offered to prove that a person other than the accused was the source of semen, injury or other physical evidence;
(B) evidence of specific instances of sexual behavior by the alleged victim with respect to the person accused of

the sexual misconduct offered by the accused to prove consent or by the prosecution; and

(C) evidence the exclusion of which would violate the constitutional rights of the defendant.

(2) In a civil case, evidence offered to prove the sexual behavior or sexual predisposition of any alleged victim is admissible if it is otherwise admissible under these rules and its probative value substantially outweighs the danger of harm to any victim and of unfair prejudice to any party. Evidence of an alleged victim's reputation is admissible only if it has been placed in controversy by the alleged victim.

(c) Procedure to determine admissibility.

(1) A party intending to offer evidence under subdivision (b) must

(A) file a written motion at least 14 days before trial specifically describing the evidence and stating the purpose for which it is offered unless the court, for good cause requires a different time for filing or permits filing during trial; and (B) serve the motion on all parties and notify the alleged victim or, when appropriate, the alleged victim's guardian or representative.

(2) Before admitting evidence under this rule the court must conduct a hearing in camera and afford the victim and parties a right to attend and be heard. The motion, related papers, and the record of the hearing must be sealed and remain under seal unless the court orders otherwise.

Rule 413. Evidence of Similar Crimes in Sexual Assault Cases.

(a) In a criminal case in which the defendant is accused of an offense of sexual assault, evidence of the defendant's commission of another offense or offenses of sexual assault is admissible, and may be considered for its bearing on any matter to which it is relevant.

(b) In a case in which the Government intends to offer evidence under this rule, the attorney for the Government shall disclose the evidence to the defendant,

including statements of witnesses or a summary of the substance of any testimony that is expected to be offered, at least 15 days before the scheduled date of trial or at such later time as the court may allow for good cause.

(c) This rule shall not be construed to limit the admission or consideration of evidence under any other rule.

(d) For purposes of this rule and Rule 415, "offense of sexual assault" means a crime under Federal law or the law of a State (as defined in section 513 of title 18, United States Code) that involved

(1) any conduct proscribed by chapter 109A of title 18, United States Code;

(2) contact, without consent, between any part of the defendant's body or an object and the genitals or anus of another person;

(3) contact, without consent, between the genitals or anus of the defendant and any part of another person's body;

(4) deriving sexual pleasure or gratification from the infliction of death, bodily injury, or physical pain on another person; or

(5) an attempt or conspiracy to engage in conduct described in paragraphs (1)–(4).

Rule 414. Evidence of Similar Crimes in Child Molestation Cases.

(a) In a criminal case in which the defendant is accused of an offense of child molestation, evidence of the defendant's commission of another offense or offenses of child molestation is admissible, and may be considered for its bearing on any matter to which it is relevant.

(b) In a case in which the Government intends to offer evidence under this rule, the attorney for the Government shall disclose the evidence to the defendant, including statements of witnesses or a summary of the substance of any testimony that is expected to be offered, at least 15 days before the scheduled date of trial or at such later time as the court may allow for good cause.

(c) This rule shall not be construed to limit the admission or consideration of evidence under any other rule.

(d) For purposes of this rule and Rule 415, "child" means a person below the age of 14, and "offense of child molestation" means a crime under Federal law or the law of a State (as defined in section 513 of title 18, United States Code) that involved

(1) any conduct proscribed by chapter 109A of title 18, United States Code, that was committed in relation to a child;

(2) any conduct proscribed by chapter 110 of title 18, United States Code;

(3) contact between any part of the defendant's body or an object and the genitals or anus of a child;

(4) contact between the genitals or anus of the defendant and any part of the body of a child;

(5) deriving sexual pleasure or gratification from the infliction of death, bodily injury, or physical pain on a child; or

(6) an attempt or conspiracy to engage in conduct described in paragraphs (1)–(5).

Rule 415. Evidence of Similar Acts in Civil Cases Concerning Sexual Assault or Child Molestation.

(a) In a civil case in which a claim for damages or other relief is predicated on a party's alleged commission of conduct constituting an offense of sexual assault or child molestation, evidence of that party's commission of another offense or offenses of sexual assault or child molestation is admissible and may be considered as provided in Rule 413 and Rule 414 of these rules.

(b) A party who intends to offer evidence under this Rule shall disclose the evidence to the party against whom it will be offered, including statements of witnesses or a summary of the substance of any testimony that is expected to be offered, at least 15 days before the scheduled date of trial or at such later time as the court may allow for good cause.

(c) This rule shall not be construed to limit the admission or consideration of evidence under any other rule.

ARTICLE V. PRIVILEGES

Rule 501. General Rule.

Except as otherwise required by the Constitution of the United States or provided by Act of Congress or in rules prescribed by the Supreme Court pursuant to statutory authority, the privilege of a witness, person, government, State, or political subdivision thereof shall be governed by the principles of the common law as they may be interpreted by the courts of the United States in the light of reason and experience. However, in civil actions and proceedings, with respect to an element of a claim or defense as to which State law supplies the rule of decision, the privilege of a witness, person, government, State, or political subdivision there of shall be determined in accordance with State law.

ARTICLE VI. WITNESSES

Rule 601. General Rule of Competency.

Every person is competent to be a witness except as otherwise provided in these rules. However, in civil actions and proceedings, with respect to an element of a claim or defense as to which State law supplies the rule of decision, the competency of a witness shall be determined in accordance with State law.

Rule 602. Lack of Personal Knowledge.

A witness may not testify to a matter unless evidence is introduced sufficient to support a finding that the witness has personal knowledge of the matter. Evidence to prove personal knowledge may, but need not, consist of the witness's own testimony. This rule is subject to the provisions of rule 703, relating to opinion testimony by expert witnesses.

Rule 603. Oath or Affirmation.

Before testifying, every witness shall be required to declare that the witness will testify truthfully, by oath or affirmation administered in a form calculated to awaken the witness's conscience and impress the witness's mind with the duty to do so.

Rule 604. Interpreters.

An interpreter is subject to the provisions of these rules relating to qualification as an expert and the administration of an oath or affirmation to make a true translation.

Rule 605. Competency of Judge as Witness.

The judge presiding at the trial may not testify in that trial as a witness. No objection need be made in order to preserve the point.

Rule 606. Competency of Juror as Witness.

(a) **At the trial**. A member of the jury may not testify as a witness before that jury in the trial of the case in which the juror is sitting. If the juror is called so to testify, the opposing party shall be afforded an opportunity to object out of the presence of the jury.

(b) **Inquiry into validity of verdict or indictment**. Upon an inquiry into the validity of a verdict or indictment, a juror may not testify as to any matter or statement occurring during the course of the jury's deliberations or to the effect of anything upon that or any other juror's mind or emotions as influencing the juror to assent to or dissent from the verdict or indictment or concerning the juror's mental processes in connection therewith, except that a juror may testify on the question whether extraneous prejudicial information was improperly brought to the jury's attention or whether any outside influence was improperly brought to bear upon any juror. Nor may a juror's affidavit or evidence of any statement by the juror concerning a matter about which the juror would be precluded from testifying be received for these purposes.

Rule 607. Who May Impeach.

The credibility of a witness may be attacked by any party, including the party calling the witness.

Rule 608. Evidence of Character and Conduct of Witness.

(a) **Opinion and reputation evidence of character**. The credibility of a witness may be attacked or supported by evidence in the form of opinion or reputation, but subject to these limitations:

(1) the evidence may refer only to character for truthfulness or untruthfulness, and

(2) evidence of truthful character is admissible only after the character of the witness for truthfulness has been attacked by opinion or reputation evidence or otherwise.

(b) **Specific instances of conduct**. Specific instances of the conduct of a witness, for the purpose of attacking or supporting the witness's credibility, other than conviction of crime as provided in rule 609, may not be proved by extrinsic evidence. They may, however, in the discretion of the court, if probative of truthfulness or untruthfulness, be inquired into on cross-examination of the witness (1) concerning the witness's character for truthfulness or untruthfulness, or (2) concerning the character for truthfulness or untruthfulness of another witness as to which character the witness being cross-examined has testified.

The giving of testimony, whether by an accused or by any other witness, does not operate as a waiver of the accused's or the witness's privilege against self-incrimination when examined with respect to matters which relate only to credibility.

Rule 609. Impeachment by Evidence of Conviction of Crime.

(a) **General rule**. For the purpose of attacking the credibility of a witness,

(1) evidence that a witness other than an accused has been convicted of a crime shall be admitted, subject to Rule 403, if the crime was punishable by death or imprisonment in excess of one year under the law under which the witness was convicted, and evidence that an accused has been convicted of such a crime shall be admitted if the court determines that the probative value of admitting this evidence outweighs its prejudicial effect to the accused; and

(2) evidence that any witness has been convicted of a crime shall be admitted if it involved dishonesty or false statement, regardless of the punishment.

(b) Time limit. Evidence of a conviction under this rule is not admissible if a period of more than 10 years has elapsed since the date of the conviction or of the release of the witness from the confinement imposed for that conviction, whichever is the later date, unless the court determines, in the interests of justice, that the probative value of the conviction supported by specific facts and circumstances substantially outweighs its prejudicial effect. However, evidence of a conviction more than 10 years old as calculated herein, is not admissible unless the proponent gives to the adverse party sufficient advance written notice of intent to use such evidence to provide the adverse party with a fair opportunity to contest the use of such evidence.

(c) Effect of pardon, annulment, or certificate of rehabilitation. Evidence of a conviction is not admissible under this rule if (1) the conviction has been the subject of a pardon, annulment, certificate of rehabilitation, or other equivalent procedure based on a finding of the rehabilitation of the person convicted, and that person has not been convicted of a subsequent crime which was punishable by death or imprisonment in excess of one year, or (2) the conviction has been the subject of a pardon, annulment, or other equivalent procedure based on a finding of innocence.

(d) Juvenile adjudications. Evidence of juvenile adjudications is generally not admissible under this rule. The court may, however, in a criminal case allow evidence of a juvenile adjudication of a witness other than the accused if conviction of the offense would be admissible to attack the credibility of an adult and the court is satisfied that admission in evidence is necessary for a fair determination of the issue of guilt or innocence.

(e) Pendency of appeal. The pendency of an appeal therefrom does not render evidence of a conviction inadmissible. Evidence of the pendency of an appeal is admissible.

Rule 610. Religious Beliefs or Opinions.

Evidence of the beliefs or opinions of a witness on matters of religion is not admissible for the purpose of showing that by reason of their nature the witness' credibility is impaired or enhanced.

Rule 611. Mode and Order of Interrogation and Presentation.

(a) Control by court. The court shall exercise reasonable control over the mode and order of interrogating witnesses and presenting evidence so as to (1) make the interrogation and presentation effective for the ascertainment of the truth, (2) avoid needless consumption of time, and (3) protect witnesses from harassment or undue embarrassment.

(b) Scope of cross-examination. Cross-examination should be limited to the subject matter of the direct examination and matters affecting the credibility of the witness. The court may, in the exercise of discretion, permit inquiry into additional matters as if on direct examination.

(c) Leading questions. Leading questions should not be used on the direct examination of a witness except as may be necessary to develop the witness' testimony. Ordinarily leading questions should be permitted on cross-examination. When a party calls a hostile witness, an adverse party, or a witness identified with an adverse party, interrogation may be by leading questions.

Rule 612. Writing Used to Refresh Memory.

Except as otherwise provided in criminal proceedings by section 3500 of title 18, United States Code, if a witness uses a writing to refresh memory for the purpose of testifying, either

(1) while testifying, or
(2) before testifying, if the court in its discretion determines it is necessary in the interests of justice, an adverse party is entitled to have the writing produced at the hearing, to inspect it, to cross-examine the witness thereon, and to introduce in evidence those portions which relate to the testimony of the witness. If it is claimed that the writing contains matters not related to the subject matter of the testimony the court shall examine the writing in camera, excise any portions not

so related, and order delivery of the remainder to the party entitled thereto. Any portion withheld over objections shall be preserved and made available to the appellate court in the event of an appeal. If a writing is not produced or delivered pursuant to order under this rule, the court shall make any order justice requires, except that in criminal cases when the prosecution elects not to comply, the order shall be one striking the testimony or, if the court in its discretion determines that the interests of justice so require, declaring a mistrial.

Rule 613. Prior Statements of Witnesses.

(a) **Examining witness concerning prior statement**. In examining a witness concerning a prior statement made by the witness, whether written or not, the statement need not be shown nor its contents disclosed to the witness at that time, but on request the same shall be shown or disclosed to opposing counsel.

(b) **Extrinsic evidence of prior inconsistent statement of witness**. Extrinsic evidence of a prior inconsistent statement by a witness is not admissible unless the witness is afforded an opportunity to explain or deny the same and the opposite party is afforded an opportunity to interrogate the witness thereon, or the interests of justice otherwise require. This provision does not apply to admissions of a party-opponent as defined in rule 801(d)(2).

Rule 614. Calling and Interrogation of Witnesses by Court.

(a) **Calling by court**. The court may, on its own motion or at the suggestion of a party, call witnesses, and all parties are entitled to cross-examine witnesses thus called.

(b) **Interrogation by court**. The court may interrogate witnesses, whether called by itself or by a party.

(c) **Objections**. Objections to the calling of witnesses by the court or to interrogation by it may be made at the time or at the next available opportunity when the jury is not present.

Rule 615. Exclusion of Witnesses.

At the request of a party the court shall order witnesses excluded so that they cannot hear the testimony of other witnesses, and it may make the order of its own motion. This rule does not authorize exclusion of

(1) a party who is a natural person, or
(2) an officer or employee of a party which is not a natural person designated as its representative by its attorney, or
(3) a person whose presence is shown by a party to be essential to the presentation of the party's cause, or
(4) a person authorized by statute to be present.

ARTICLE VII. OPINIONS AND EXPERT TESTIMONY

Rule 701. Opinion Testimony by Lay Witnesses.

If the witness is not testifying as an expert, the witness' testimony in the form of opinions or inferences is limited to those opinions or inferences which are (a) rationally based on the perception of the witness, and (b) helpful to a clear understanding of the witness' testimony or the determination of a fact in issue, and (c) not based on scientific, technical, or other specialized knowledge within the scope of Rule 702. (Amended effective Dec. 1, 2000.)

Rule 702. Testimony by Experts.

If scientific, technical, or other specialized knowledge will assist the trier of fact to understand the evidence or to determine a fact in issue, a witness qualified as an expert by knowledge, skill, experience, training, or education, may testify thereto in the form of an opinion or otherwise, if (1) the testimony is based upon sufficient facts or data, (2) the testimony is the product of reliable principles and methods, and (3) the witness has applied the principles and methods reliably to the facts of the case. (Amended effective Dec. 1, 2000.)

Rule 703. Bases of Opinion Testimony by Experts.

The facts or data in the particular case upon which an expert bases an opinion or inference may be those perceived by or made known to the expert at or before the hearing. If of a type reasonably relied upon by experts in the particular field in forming opinions or inferences upon the subject, the facts or data need not be admissible in evidence in order for the opinion or inference to be admitted. Facts or data that are otherwise inadmissible shall not be disclosed to the jury by the proponent of the opinion or inference unless the court determines that their probative value in assisting the jury to evaluate the expert's opinion substantially outweighs their prejudicial effect. (Amended effective Dec. 1, 2000.)

Rule 704. Opinion on Ultimate Issue.

(a) Except as provided in subdivision (b), testimony in the form of an opinion or inference otherwise admissible is not objectionable because it embraces an ultimate issue to be decided by the trier of fact.

(b) No expert witness testifying with respect to the mental state or condition of a defendant in a criminal case may state an opinion or inference as to whether the defendant did or did not have the mental state or condition constituting an element of the crime charged or of a defense thereto. Such ultimate issues are matters for the trier of fact alone.

Rule 705. Disclosure of Facts or Data Underlying Expert Opinion.

The expert may testify in terms of opinion or inference and give reasons therefor without first testifying to the underlying facts or data, unless the court requires otherwise. The expert may in any event be required to disclose the underlying facts or data on cross-examination.

Rule 706. Court Appointed Experts.

(a) **Appointment**. The court may on its own motion or on the motion of any party enter an order to show cause why expert witnesses should not be appointed, and may request the parties to submit nominations. The court may appoint any expert witnesses agreed upon by the parties, and may appoint expert witnesses of its own selection. An expert witness shall not be appointed by the court unless the witness consents to act. A witness so appointed shall be informed of the witness's duties by the court in writing, a copy of which shall be filed with the clerk, or at a conference in which the parties shall have opportunity to participate. A witness so appointed shall advise the parties of the witness's findings, if any; the witness's deposition may be taken by any party; and the witness may be called to testify by the court or any party. The witness shall be subject to cross-examination by each party, including a party calling the witness.

(b) **Compensation**. Expert witnesses so appointed are entitled to reasonable compensation in whatever sum the court may allow. The compensation thus fixed is payable from funds which may be provided by law in criminal cases and civil actions and proceedings involving just compensation under the fifth amendment. In other civil actions and proceedings the compensation shall be paid by the parties in such proportion and at such time as the court directs, and thereafter charged in like manner as other costs.

(c) **Disclosure of appointment**. In the exercise of its discretion, the court may authorize disclosure to the jury of the fact that the court appointed the expert witness.

(d) **Parties' experts of own selection**. Nothing in this rule limits the parties in calling expert witnesses of their own selection.

ARTICLE VIII. HEARSAY
Rule 801. Definitions.

The following definitions apply under this article:

(a) **Statement**. A "statement" is (1) an oral or written assertion or (2) nonverbal conduct of a person, if it is intended by the person as an assertion.

(b) **Declarant**. A "declarant" is a person who makes a statement.

(c) **Hearsay**. "Hearsay" is a statement, other than one made by the declarant while testifying at the trial or hearing, offered in evidence to prove the truth of the matter asserted.

(d) **Statements which are not hearsay**. A statement is not hearsay if

(1) **Prior statement by witness**. The declarant testifies at the trial or hearing and is subject to cross-examination concerning the statement, and the statement is (A) inconsistent with the declarant's testimony, and was given under oath subject to the penalty of perjury at a trial, hearing, or other proceeding, or in a deposition, or (B) consistent with the declarant's testimony and is offered to rebut an express or implied charge against the declarant of recent fabrication or improper influence or motive, or (C) one of identification of a person made after perceiving the person; or

(2) **Admission by party-opponent**. The statement is offered against a party and is (A) the party's own statement, in either an individual or a representative capacity or (B) a statement of which the party has manifested an adoption or belief in its truth, or (C) a statement by a person authorized by the party to make a statement concerning the subject, or (D) a statement by the party's agent or servant concerning a matter within the scope of the agency or employment, made during the existence of the relationship, or (E) a statement by a coconspirator of a party during the course and in furtherance of the conspiracy. The contents of the statement shall be considered but are not alone sufficient to establish the declarant's authority under subdivision (C), the agency or employment relationship and scope thereof under subdivision (D), or the existence of the conspiracy and the participation therein of the declarant and the party against whom the statement is offered under subdivision (E).

Rule 802. Hearsay Rule.

Hearsay is not admissible except as provided by these rules or by other rules prescribed by the Supreme Court pursuant to statutory authority or by Act of Congress.

Rule 803. Hearsay Exceptions; Availability of Declarant Immaterial.

The following are not excluded by the hearsay rule, even though the declarant is available as a witness:

(1) **Present sense impression**. A statement describing or explaining an event or condition made while the declarant was perceiving the event or condition, or immediately thereafter.

(2) **Excited utterance**. A statement relating to a startling event or condition made while the declarant was under the stress of excitement caused by the event or condition.

(3) **Then existing mental, emotional, or physical condition**. A statement of the declarant's then existing state of mind, emotion, sensation, or physical condition (such as intent, plan, motive, design, mental feeling, pain, and bodily health), but not including a statement of memory or belief to prove the fact remembered or believed unless it relates to the execution, revocation, identification, or terms of declarant's will.

(4) **Statements for purposes of medical diagnosis or treatment**. Statements made for purposes of medical diagnosis or treatment and describing medical history, or past or present symptoms, pain, or sensations, or the inception or general character of the cause or external source thereof insofar as reasonably pertinent to diagnosis or treatment.

(5) **Recorded recollection**. A memorandum or record concerning a matter about which a witness once had knowledge but now has insufficient recollection to enable the witness to testify fully and accurately, shown to have been made or adopted by the witness when the matter was fresh in the witness's memory and to reflect that knowledge correctly. If admitted, the memorandum or record may be read into evidence but may not itself be received as an exhibit unless offered by an adverse party.

(6) **Records of regularly conducted activity**. A memorandum, report, record, or data compilation, in any form, of acts, events, conditions, opinions, or diagnoses, made at or near the time by, or from information transmitted by, a person with knowledge, if kept in the course of a regularly conducted business activity, and if it was the regular practice of that business activity to

make the memorandum, report, record or data compilation, all as shown by the testimony of the custodian or other qualified witness, or by certification that complies with Rule 902(11), Rule 902(12), or a statute permitting certification, unless the source of information or the method or circumstances of preparation indicate lack of trustworthiness. The term "business" as used in this paragraph includes business, institution, association, profession, occupation, and calling of every kind, whether or not conducted for profit.

(7) **Absence of entry in records kept in accordance with the provisions of paragraph (6).** Evidence that a matter is not included in the memoranda reports, records, or data compilations, in any form, kept in accordance with the provisions of paragraph (6), to prove the nonoccurrence or nonexistence of the matter, if the matter was of a kind of which a memorandum, report, record, or data compilation was regularly made and preserved, unless the sources of information or other circumstances indicate lack of trustworthiness.

(8) **Public records and reports.** Records, reports, statements, or data compilations, in any form, of public offices or agencies, setting forth (A) the activities of the office or agency, or (B) matters observed pursuant to duty imposed by law as to which matters there was a duty to report, excluding, however, in criminal cases matters observed by police officers and other law enforcement personnel, or (C) in civil actions and proceedings and against the Government in criminal cases, factual findings resulting from an investigation made pursuant to authority granted by law, unless the sources of information or other circumstances indicate lack of trustworthiness.

(9) **Records of vital statistics.** Records or data compilations, in any form, of births, fetal deaths, deaths, or marriages, if the report thereof was made to a public office pursuant to requirements of law.

(10) **Absence of public record or entry.** To prove the absence of a record, report, statement, or data compilation, in any form, or the nonoccurrence or nonexistence of a matter of which a record, report, statement, or data compilation, in any form, was regularly made and preserved by a public office or agency, evidence in the form of a certification in accordance with rule 902, or testimony, that diligent search failed to disclose the record, report, statement, or data compilation, or entry.

(11) **Records of religious organizations.** Statements of births, marriages, divorces, deaths, legitimacy, ancestry, relationship by blood or marriage, or other similar facts of personal or family history, contained in a regularly kept record of a religious organization.

(12) **Marriage, baptismal, and similar certificates.** Statements of fact contained in a certificate that the maker performed a marriage or other ceremony or administered a sacrament, made by a clergyman, public official, or other person authorized by the rules or practices of a religious organization or by law to perform the act certified, and purporting to have been issued at the time of the act or within a reasonable time thereafter.

(13) **Family records.** Statements of fact concerning personal or family history contained in family Bibles, genealogies, charts, engravings on rings, inscriptions on family portraits, engravings on urns, crypts, or tombstones, or the like.

(14) **Records of documents affecting an interest in property.** The record of a document purporting to establish or affect an interest in property, as proof of the content of the original recorded document and its execution and delivery by each person by whom it purports to have been executed, if the record is a record of a public office and an applicable statute authorizes the recording of documents of that kind in that office.

(15) **Statements in documents affecting an interest in property.** A statement contained in a document purporting to establish or affect an interest in property if the matter stated was relevant to the purpose of the document, unless dealings with the property since the document was made have been inconsistent with

the truth of the statement or the purport of the document.

(16) Statements in ancient documents. Statements in a document in existence 20 years or more the authenticity of which is established.

(17) Market reports, commercial publications. Market quotations, tabulations, lists, directories, or other published compilations, generally used and relied upon by the public or by persons in particular occupations.

(18) Learned treatises. To the extent called to the attention of an expert witness upon cross-examination or relied upon by the expert witness in direct examination, statements contained in published treatises, periodicals, or pamphlets on a subject of history, medicine, or other science or art, established as a reliable authority by the testimony or admission of the witness or by other expert testimony or by judicial notice. If admitted, the statements may be read into evidence but may not be received as exhibits.

(19) Reputation concerning personal or family history. Reputation among members of a person's family by blood, adoption, or marriage, or among a person's associates, or in the community, concerning a person's birth, adoption, marriage, divorce, death, legitimacy, relationship by blood, adoption, or marriage, ancestry, or other similar fact of personal or family history.

(20) Reputation concerning boundaries or general history. Reputation in a community, arising before the controversy, as to boundaries of or customs affecting lands in the community, and reputation as to events of general history important to the community or State or nation in which located.

(21) Reputation as to character. Reputation of a person's character among associates or in the community.

(22) Judgment of previous conviction. Evidence of a final judgment, entered after a trial or upon a plea of guilty (but not upon a plea of nolo contendere), adjudging a person guilty of a crime punishable by death or imprisonment in excess of one year, to prove any fact essential to sustain the judgment, but not including, when offered by the Government in a criminal prosecution for purposes other than impeachment, judgments against persons other than the accused. The pendency of an appeal may be shown but does not affect admissibility.

(23) Judgment as to personal, family, or general history, or boundaries. Judgments as proof of matters of personal, family or general history, or boundaries, essential to the judgment, if the same would be provable by evidence of reputation.

(24) [Other exceptions.] [Transferred to Rule 807]

(Amended effective Dec. 1, 2000.)

Rule 804. Hearsay Exceptions; Declarant Unavailable.

(a) Definition of unavailability. "Unavailability as a witness" includes situations in which the declarant

(1) is exempted by ruling of the court on the ground of privilege from testifying concerning the subject matter of the declarant's statement; or

(2) persists in refusing to testify concerning the subject matter of the declarant's statement despite an order of the court to do so; or

(3) testifies to a lack of memory of the subject matter of the declarant's statement; or

(4) is unable to be present or to testify at the hearing because of death or then existing physical or mental illness or infirmity; or

(5) is absent from the hearing and the proponent of a statement has been unable to procure the declarant's attendance (or in the case of a hearsay exception under subdivision (b)(2), (3), or (4), the declarant's attendance or testimony) by process or other reasonable means. A declarant is not unavailable as a witness if exemption, refusal, claim of lack of memory, inability, or absence is due to the procurement or wrongdoing of the proponent of a statement for the purpose of preventing the witness from attending or testifying.

(b) Hearsay exceptions. The following are not excluded by the hearsay rule if the declarant is unavailable as a witness:

(1) **Former testimony.** Testimony given as a witness at another hearing of the same or a different proceeding, or in a deposition taken in compliance with law in the course of the same or another proceeding, if the party against whom the testimony is now offered, or, in a civil action or proceeding, a predecessor in interest, had an opportunity and similar motive to develop the testimony by direct, cross, or redirect examination.

(2) **Statement under belief of impending death**. In a prosecution for homicide or in a civil action or proceeding, a statement made by a declarant while believing that the declarant's death was imminent, concerning the cause or circumstances of what the declarant believed to be impending death.

(3) **Statement against interest**. A statement which was at the time of its making so far contrary to the declarant's pecuniary or proprietary interest, or so far tended to subject the declarant to civil or criminal liability, or to render invalid a claim by the declarant against another, that a reasonable person in the declarant's position would not have made the statement unless believing it to be true. A statement tending to expose the declarant to criminal liability and offered to exculpate the accused is not admissible unless corroborating circumstances clearly indicate the trustworthiness of the statement.

(4) **Statement of personal or family history**. (A) A statement concerning the declarant's own birth, adoption, marriage, divorce, legitimacy, relationship by blood, adoption, or marriage, ancestry, or other similar fact of personal or family history, even though declarant had no means of acquiring personal knowledge of the matter stated; or (B) a statement concerning the foregoing matters, and death also, of another person, if the declarant was related to the other by blood, adoption, or marriage or was so intimately associated with the other's family as to be likely to have accurate information concerning the matter declared.

(5) [Other exceptions.] [Transferred to Rule 807]

(6) **Forfeiture by wrongdoing**. A statement offered against a party that has engaged or acquiesced in wrongdoing that was intended to, and did, procure the unavailability of the declarant as a witness.

Rule 805. Hearsay Within Hearsay.

Hearsay included within hearsay is not excluded under the hearsay rule if each part of the combined statements conforms with an exception to the hearsay rule provided in these rules.

Rule 806. Attacking and Supporting Credibility of Declarant.

When a hearsay statement, or a statement defined in Rule 801(d)(2)(C), (D), or (E), has been admitted in evidence, the credibility of the declarant may be attacked, and if attacked may be supported, by any evidence which would be admissible for those purposes if declarant had testified as a witness. Evidence of a statement or conduct by the declarant at any time, inconsistent with the declarant's hearsay statement, is not subject to any requirement that the declarant may have been afforded an opportunity to deny or explain. If the party against whom a hearsay statement has been admitted calls the declarant as a witness, the party is entitled to examine the declarant on the statement as if under cross-examination.

Rule 807. Residual Exception.

A statement not specifically covered by Rule 803 or 804 but having equivalent circumstantial guarantees of trustworthiness, is not excluded by the hearsay rule, if the court determines that (A) the statement is offered as evidence of a material fact; (B) the statement is more probative on the point for which it is offered than any other evidence which the proponent can procure through reasonable efforts; and (C) the general purposes of these rules and the interests of justice will best be served by admission of the statement into evidence. However, a statement may not be admitted under this exception unless the proponent of it makes known to the adverse party sufficiently in advance of the trial or hearing to provide the adverse party with a fair opportunity to prepare to meet it, the proponent's intention to offer the statement and the particulars of it, including the name and address of the declarant.

ARTICLE IX. AUTHENTICATION AND IDENTIFICATION

Rule 901. Requirement of Authentication or Identification.

(a) General provision. The requirement of authentication or identification as a condition precedent to admissibility is satisfied by evidence sufficient to support a finding that the matter in question is what its proponent claims.

(b) Illustrations. By way of illustration only, and not by way of limitation, the following are examples of authentication or identification conforming with the requirements of this rule:

(1) Testimony of witness with knowledge. Testimony that a matter is what it is claimed to be.

(2) Nonexpert opinion on handwriting. Nonexpert opinion as to the genuineness of handwriting, based upon familiarity not acquired for purposes of the litigation.

(3) Comparison by trier or expert witness. Comparison by the trier of fact or by expert witnesses with specimens which have been authenticated.

(4) Distinctive characteristics and the like. Appearance, contents, substance, internal patterns, or other distinctive characteristics, taken in conjunction with circumstances.

(5) Voice identification. Identification of a voice, whether heard firsthand or through mechanical or electronic transmission or recording, by opinion based upon hearing the voice at any time under circumstances connecting it with the alleged speaker.

(6) Telephone conversations. Telephone conversations, by evidence that a call was made to the number assigned at the time by the telephone company to a particular person or business, if (A) in the case of a person, circumstances, including self-identification, show the person answering to be the one called, or (B) in the case of a business, the call was made to a place of business and the conversation related to business reasonably transacted over the telephone.

(7) Public records or reports. Evidence that a writing authorized by law to be recorded or filed and in fact recorded or filed in a public office, or a purported public record, report, statement, or data compilation, in any form, is from the public office where items of this nature are kept.

(8) Ancient documents or data compilation. Evidence that a document or data compilation, in any form, (A) is in such condition as to create no suspicion concerning its authenticity, (B) was in a place where it, if authentic, would likely be, and (C) has been in existence 20 years or more at the time it is offered.

(9) Process or system. Evidence describing a process or system used to produce a result and showing that the process or system produces an accurate result.

(10) Methods provided by statute or rule. Any method of authentication or identification provided by Act of Congress or by other rules prescribed by the Supreme Court pursuant to statutory authority.

Rule 902. Self-authentication.

Extrinsic evidence of authenticity as a condition precedent to admissibility is not required with respect to the following:

(1) Domestic public documents under seal. A document bearing a seal purporting to be that of the United States, or of any State, district, Commonwealth, territory, or insular possession thereof, or the Panama Canal Zone, or the Trust Territory of the Pacific Islands, or of a political subdivision, department, officer, or agency thereof, and a signature purporting to be an attestation or execution.

(2) **Domestic public documents not under seal**. A document purporting to bear the signature in the official capacity of an officer or employee of any entity included in paragraph (1) hereof, having no seal, if a public officer having a seal and having official duties in the district or political subdivision of the officer or employee certifies under seal that the signer has the official capacity and that the signature is genuine.

(3) **Foreign public documents**. A document purporting to be executed or attested in an official capacity by a person authorized by the laws of a foreign country to make the execution or attestation, and accompanied by a final certification as to the genuineness of the signature and official position (A) of the executing or attesting person, or (B) of any foreign official whose certificate of genuineness of signature and official position relates to the execution or attestation or is in a chain of certificates of genuineness of signature and official position relating to the execution or attestation. A final certification may be made by a secretary of an embassy or legation, consul general, consul, vice consul, or consular agent of the United States, or a diplomatic or consular official of the foreign country assigned or accredited to the United States. If reasonable opportunity has been given to all parties to investigate the authenticity and accuracy of official documents, the court may, for good cause shown, order that they be treated as presumptively authentic without final certification or permit them to be evidenced by an attested summary with or without final certification.

(4) **Certified copies of public records**. A copy of an official record or report or entry therein, or of a document authorized by law to be recorded or filed and actually recorded or filed in a public office, including data compilations in any form, certified as correct by the custodian or other person authorized to make the certification, by certificate complying with paragraph (1), (2), or (3) of this rule or complying with any Act of Congress or rule prescribed by the Supreme Court pursuant to statutory authority.

(5) **Official publications**. Books, pamphlets, or other publications purporting to be issued by public authority.

(6) **Newspapers and periodicals**. Printed materials purporting to be newspapers or periodicals.

(7) **Trade inscriptions and the like**. Inscriptions, signs, tags, or labels purporting to have been affixed in the course of business and indicating ownership, control, or origin.

(8) **Acknowledged documents**. Documents accompanied by a certificate of acknowledgment executed in the manner provided by law by a notary public or other officer authorized by law to take acknowledgments.

(9) **Commercial paper and related documents**. Commercial paper, signatures thereon, and documents relating thereto to the extent provided by general commercial law.

(10) **Presumptions under Acts of Congress**. Any signature, document, or other matter declared by Act of Congress to be presumptively or prima facie genuine or authentic.

(11) **Certified domestic records of regularly conducted activity**. The original or a duplicate of a domestic record of regularly conducted activity that would be admissible under Rule 803(6) if accompanied by a written declaration of its custodian or other qualified person, in a manner complying with any Act of Congress or rule prescribed by the Supreme Court pursuant to statutory authority, certifying that the record

(A) was made at or near the time of the occurrence of the matters set forth by, or from information transmitted by, a person with knowledge of those matters;

(B) was kept in the course of the regularly conducted activity; and

(C) was made by the regularly conducted activity as a regular practice.

A party intending to offer a record into evidence under this paragraph must provide written notice of that intention to all adverse parties, and must make the record and declaration available for inspection sufficiently in advance of their offer into evidence to provide an adverse party with a fair opportunity to challenge them.

> **(12) Certified foreign records of regularly conducted activity.** In a civil case, the original or a duplicate of a foreign record of regularly conducted activity that would be admissible under Rule 803(6) if accompanied by a written declaration by its custodian or other qualified person certifying that the record
>
> > (A) was made at or near the time of the occurrence of the matters set forth by, or from information transmitted by, a person with knowledge of those matters;
> >
> > (B) was kept in the course of the regularly conducted activity; and
> >
> > (C) was made by the regularly conducted activity as a regular practice.

The declaration must be signed in a manner that, if falsely made, would subject the maker to criminal penalty under the laws of the country where the declaration is signed. A party intending to offer a record into evidence under this paragraph must provide written notice of that intention to all adverse parties, and must make the record and declaration available for inspection sufficiently in advance of their offer into evidence to provide an adverse party with a fair opportunity to challenge them.
(Amended effective Dec. 1, 2000.)

Rule 903. Subscribing Witness' Testimony Unnecessary.

The testimony of a subscribing witness is not necessary to authenticate a writing unless required by the laws of the jurisdiction whose laws govern the validity of the writing.

ARTICLE X. CONTENTS OF WRITINGS, RECORDINGS, AND PHOTOGRAPHS

Rule 1001. Definitions.

For purposes of this article the following definitions are applicable:

> **(1) Writings and recordings.** "Writings" and "recordings" consist of letters, words, or numbers, or their equivalent, set down by handwriting, typewriting, printing, photostating, photographing, magnetic impulse, mechanical or electronic recording, or other form of data compilation.
>
> **(2) Photographs.** "Photographs" include still photographs, X-ray films, video tapes, and motion pictures.
>
> **(3) Original.** An "original" of a writing or recording is the writing or recording itself or any counterpart intended to have the same effect by a person executing or issuing it. An "original" of a photograph includes the negative or any print therefrom. If data are stored in a computer or similar device, any printout or other output readable by sight, shown to reflect the data accurately, is an "original."
>
> **(4) Duplicate.** A "duplicate" is a counterpart produced by the same impression as the original, or from the same matrix, or by means of photography, including enlargements and miniatures, or by mechanical or electronic re-recording, or by chemical reproduction, or by other equivalent techniques which accurately reproduces the original.

Rule 1002. Requirement of Original.

To prove the content of a writing, recording, or photograph, the original writing, recording, or photograph is required, except as otherwise provided in these rules or by Act of Congress.

Rule 1003. Admissibility of Duplicates.

A duplicate is admissible to the same extent as an original unless (1) a genuine question is raised as to the authenticity of the original or (2) in the circumstances it would be unfair to admit the duplicate in lieu of the original.

Rule 1004. Admissibility of Other Evidence of Contents.

The original is not required, and other evidence of the contents of a writing, recording, or photograph is admissible if

> **(1) Originals lost or destroyed.** All originals are lost or have been destroyed, unless the proponent lost or destroyed them in bad faith; or

(2) Original not obtainable. No original can be obtained by any available judicial process or procedure; or

(3) Original in possession of opponent. At a time when an original was under the control of the party against whom offered, that party was put on notice, by the pleadings or otherwise, that the contents would be a subject of proof at the hearing, and that party does not produce the original at the hearing; or

(4) Collateral matters. The writing, recording, or photograph is not closely related to a controlling issue.

Rule 1005. Public Records.

The contents of an official record, or of a document authorized to be recorded or filed and actually recorded or filed, including data compilations in any form, if otherwise admissible, may be proved by copy, certified as correct in accordance with rule 902 or testified to be correct by a witness who has compared it with the original. If a copy which complies with the foregoing cannot be obtained by the exercise of reasonable diligence, then other evidence of the contents may be given.

Rule 1006. Summaries.

The contents of voluminous writings, recordings, or photographs which cannot conveniently be examined in court may be presented in the form of a chart, summary, or calculation. The originals, or duplicates, shall be made available for examination or copying, or both, by other parties at reasonable time and place. The court may order that they be produced in court.

Rule 1007. Testimony or Written Admission of Party.

Contents of writings, recordings, or photographs may be proved by the testimony or deposition of the party against whom offered or by that party's written admission, without accounting for the nonproduction of the original.

Rule 1008. Functions of Court and Jury.

When the admissibility of other evidence of contents of writings, recordings, or photographs under these rules depends upon the fulfillment of a condition of fact, the question whether the condition has been fulfilled is ordinarily for the court to determine in accordance with the provisions of rule 104. However, when an issue is raised (a) whether the asserted writing ever existed, or (b) whether another writing, recording, or photograph produced at the trial is the original, or (c) whether other evidence of contents correctly reflects the contents, the issue is for the trier of fact to determine as in the case of other issues of fact.

ARTICLE XI. MISCELLANEOUS RULES

Rule 1101. Applicability of Rules.

(a) Courts and judges. These rules apply to the United States district courts, the District Court of Guam, the District Court of the Virgin Islands, the District Court for the Northern Mariana Islands, the United States courts of appeals, the United States Claims Court, and to United States bankruptcy judges and United States magistrate judges, in the actions, cases, and proceedings and to the extent hereinafter set forth. The terms "judge" and "court" in these rules include United States bankruptcy judges and United States magistrate judges.

(b) Proceedings generally. These rules apply generally to civil actions and proceedings, including admiralty and maritime cases, to criminal cases and proceedings, to contempt proceedings except those in which the court may act summarily, and to proceedings and cases under title 11, United States Code.

(c) Rule of privilege. The rule with respect to privileges applies at all stages of all actions, cases, and proceedings.

(d) Rules inapplicable. The rules (other than with respect to privileges) do not apply in the following situations:

(1) Preliminary questions of fact. The determination of questions of fact preliminary to admissibility of evidence when the issue is to be determined by the court under rule 104.

(2) Grand jury. Proceedings before grand juries.

(3) Miscellaneous proceedings. Proceedings for extradition or rendition; preliminary examinations in criminal cases; sentencing, or granting or revoking probation; issuance of warrants for arrest, criminal summonses, and search warrants; and proceedings with respect to release on bail or otherwise.

(e) Rules applicable in part. In the following proceedings these rules apply to the extent that matters of evidence are not provided for in the statutes which govern procedure therein or in other rules prescribed by the Supreme Court pursuant to statutory authority: the trial of misdemeanors and other petty offenses before United States magistrate judges; review of agency actions when the facts are subject to trial de novo under section 706(2)(F) of title 5, United States Code; review of orders of the Secretary of Agriculture under section 2 of the Act entitled "An Act to authorize association of producers of agricultural products" approved February 18, 1922 (7 U.S.C. 292), and under sections 6 and 7(c) of the Perishable Agricultural Commodities Act, 1930 (7 U.S.C. 499f, 499g(c)); naturalization and revocation of naturalization under sections 310-318 of the Immigration and Nationality Act (8 U.S.C. 1421-1429); prize proceedings in admiralty under sections 7651-7681 of title 10, United States Code; review of orders of the Secretary of the Interior under section 2 of the Act entitled "An Act authorizing associations of producers of aquatic products" approved June 25, 1934 (15 U.S.C. 522); review of orders of petroleum control boards under section 5 of the Act entitled "An Act to regulate interstate and foreign commerce in petroleum and its products by prohibiting the shipment in such commerce of petroleum and its products produced in violation of State law, and for other purposes," approved February 22, 1935 (15 U.S.C. 715d); actions for fines, penalties, or forfeitures under part V of title IV of the Tariff Act of 1930 (19 U.S.C. 1581-1624), or under the Anti-Smuggling Act (19 U.S.C. 1701-1711); criminal libel for condemnation, exclusion of imports, or other proceedings under the Federal Food, Drug, and Cosmetic Act (21 U.S.C. 301-392); disputes between seamen under sections 4079, 4080, and 4081 of the Revised Statutes (22 U.S.C. 256-258); habeas corpus under sections 2241-2254 of title 28, United States Code; motions to vacate, set aside or correct sentence under section 2255 of title 28, United States Code; actions for penalties for refusal to transport destitute seamen under section 4578 of the Revised Statutes (46 U.S.C. 679); actions against the United States under the Act entitled "An Act authorizing suits against the United States in admiralty for damage caused by and salvage service rendered to public vessels belonging to the United States, and for other purposes," approved March 3, 1925 (46 U.S.C. 781-790), as implemented by section 7730 of title 10, United States Code.

Rule 1102. Amendments.

Amendments to the Federal Rules of Evidence may be made as provided in section 2072 of title 28 of the United States Code.

Rule 1103. Title.

These rules may be known and cited as the Federal Rules of Evidence.

GLOSSARY

Abuse of Discretion The standard of review that an appellate court should apply in reviewing a trial court's decision to admit or exclude expert testimony under *Daubert*.

Admissible Evidence that would be allowed at trial.

Admission by a Party-Opponent A prior statement made by an opposing party to the legal action, or that party's agent or co-conspirator.

Adversary System Legal system where parties to a legal dispute face off against each other and contest all issues before a court of law, under the legal maxim that *out of controlled battle would the truth emerge.*

Ancient Documents Rule A hearsay exception that allows statements in a document which has been in existence 20 years or more, and the authenticity of which is established.

Appeal A formal request made of a higher court to review the findings of a lower court for error.

Appropriate Dispute Resolution Alternative means of resolving legal disputes, ranging from informal counseling to mediation to a full-scale adversarial trial.

Arbitration A dispute resolution process where parties to a legal action agree to have their dispute referred to and settled by an impartial third party or group outside of the trial process.

Assertion Action that communicates a statement.

Authentication Part of laying a foundation, where a witness testifies that evidence is what it purports to be.

Balancing Test Test which weighs the probative value of evidence against its prejudicial effect.

Beyond a Reasonable Doubt Burden of proof in a criminal action. It requires the trier of fact to believe something to be "almost certainly true" without leaving any reasonable doubt.

Beyond the Scope Questioning of a witness that goes beyond what was covered in the previous line of questions.

Bolstering Evidence Evidence used to support or fortify a case or witness.

Brady Motion A motion to dismiss a case because evidence favorable to the accused has been suppressed by the State, either willfully or inadvertently, resulting in prejudice to the defendant.

Burden of Going Forward When a matter is at issue, a party must present evidence to address the issue.

Burden of Persuasion To present enough evidence to convince or persuade the trier of fact.

Burden of Production To introduce evidence on an issue sufficient enough to avoid an adverse ruling by the court.

Burden of Proof The duty to meet a certain standard or establish the requisite degree of belief in the mind of the trier of fact regarding the evidence submitted.

Business Records Exception A hearsay exception that allows evidence of regularly kept business records.

Capable of Communicating A witness must be able to express himself or herself and communicate so as to be reasonably understood by the judge or jury.

Case Law Judge-made law based on court decisions; term is used today interchangeably with common law.

Cause of Action The basis for a lawsuit.

Chain of Custody Means for verifying the authenticity and integrity of evidence by establishing where the evidence has been and who handled it prior to trial.

Character Evidence Personal qualities and traits that describe a person and how he or she would act under a particular set of circumstances.

Circuit Court From "riding the circuit," a judge that travels around holding court sessions in different areas.

Circumstantial Evidence Evidence which proves a disputed fact indirectly by first proving another fact. From this other fact an inference may be drawn as to the original disputed fact.

Civil Law The world's leading legal system, based on Roman law and Napoleonic Code; relies on the judge or magistrate to conduct an investigation, gather evidence, question witnesses, and determine facts.

Clear and Convincing Evidence Burden of proof in certain types of civil actions. Requires trier of fact to reasonably believe that there is a high probability that a fact is true.

Common Law Case law; a uniform set of laws for a state or country based on court decisions.

Competency Being legally fit to testify as a witness.

Computer Animation Evidence A newer form of demonstrative evidence that utilizes sophisticated computer-generated graphics and animation to illustrate and reconstruct evidence or scenes.

Conclusive Presumption A rule of law that proof of certain facts establishes a specific legal right or legal status. A conclusive presumption cannot be contradicted and no evidence can be admitted to the contrary.

Conditional Relevance An admissibility standard when presenting certain evidence, when the relevancy of that evidence depends upon the fulfillment of a condition of fact.

Confidential Marital Communication Type of marital privilege that gives a spouse the privilege to refuse to disclose or to prevent the other spouse from disclosing a confidential communication made between the spouses while married.

Confrontation Clause A constitutional protection based on the Sixth Amendment that provides a defendant in a criminal proceeding the right "to be confronted with the witnesses against him . . . " in a criminal proceeding.

Contemporaneous Declarations Also referred to as a *present sense impression*, a statement describing or explaining an event or condition made while the declarant was perceiving the event or condition, or immediately thereafter.

Corroborating Evidence Evidence that supports or strengthens other evidence.

Court Appointed Expert An expert witness selected or appointed by the court to testify on a matter.

Credibility Believability and trustworthiness of a witness.

Cross-Examination Questioning of a witness by the opposing party on matters within the scope of the direct examination, usually to discredit the testimony of the witness or to develop facts that may help the cross-examiner's case.

Custodian of the Records Someone officially designated at a business or public agency to oversee and maintain records.

***Daubert* Standard** An adaptation of the relevancy test of determining the admissibility of scientific evidence by weighing the probative value of scientific testing and its reliability against the test's potential for prejudice.

Declarant Person who makes a statement.

Declaration Against Interest Statement made which is contrary to the declarant's property, monetary, or liberty interests.

Defendant The party defending against a civil or criminal action.

Demonstrative Evidence Evidence that "demonstrates," illustrates, or recreates evidence that has already been presented.

Deposition A discovery device where information about a legal action is gathered by questioning witnesses or parties outside of the courtroom, but under oath and with a court reporter present to record the testimony.

Direct Evidence Evidence that proves a disputed fact directly, through an eyewitness, for example.

Direct Examination Initial questioning of a witness by the party that called the witness to the stand.

Discovery A pretrial device where parties to a legal action attempt to learn more about their opponent's case and evidence.

Doctrine of Scintilla Rule Where there is any evidence, however slight, tending to support a material issue, it must be left up to the jury to decide.

Documentary Evidence A writing or record, including letters, typewriting, wills, contracts, deeds, notes, printings, pictures, sketches, or recordings.

Due Process Fundamental principle in our legal system holding that a person has a right to reasonable notice of a charge against him, and an opportunity to be heard in his defense, which includes the right to call witnesses on his behalf and to confront those witnesses against him.

Duty to Tell the Truth Legal obligation of a witness to testify truthfully under the penalty of perjury.

Dying Declaration A statement by a person who believes that his or her death is imminent.

Evidence Anything that tends to prove or disprove a fact at issue in a legal action.

Evidence of Character When used to describe a witness, character includes those personal qualities and traits pertaining to truthfulness. Evidence of character would be facts or information used to attack or support a witness's qualities for truthfulness.

Excited Utterance A statement relating to a startling event or condition made while declarant was under the stress of excitement caused by the event or condition.

Exclusionary Rule A legal rule, established by case law, that prohibits the admission of illegally obtained evidence in a criminal action.

Exculpate Evidence which tends to clear a person of guilt.

Exculpatory Clause A portion of a writing or contract that clears a party of an otherwise harmful act or holds a party harmless from default.

Exculpatory Evidence Evidence that tends to clear a party of blame or guilt.

Executive Privilege The right of the president or a governor to be exempt from disclosure of confidential documents or communications necessary to the discharge of the executive office or duties.

Exhibit An item offered in evidence that is properly marked for later identification.

Expert Witness A witness qualified by specialized skills or knowledge whose testimony or opinion can assist the trier of fact to better understand evidence in issue.

Extrinsic Evidence Evidence obtained from outside the courtroom. An example of extrinsic evidence might be an employment application that a witness had falsified.

Federal Rules of Evidence Statutory evidentiary rules used in all federal courts and as a model for most states.

Felony A crime punishable by death or imprisonment, generally in excess of one year.

Forfeiture by Wrongdoing A hearsay exception that admits an out-of-court statement against a party who engaged in wrongdoing intended to keep the declarant from testifying.

Gatekeeper Role of the trial judge in ensuring relevance and reliability of scientific evidence.

General Acceptance Test Scientific evidence is admissible only if the principle upon which it is based is "sufficiently established to have general acceptance in the field to which it belongs."

Grand Jury A body of community members responsible for determining whether probable cause exists to bind an accused over for criminal prosecution.

Habit A person's customary practice or pattern of behavior when repeatedly engaging in particular actions or situations.

Hammurabi Code One of the earliest known set of formal laws, established around 1750 B.C. by Hammurabi, prince of Babylonia.

Harmless Error A properly objected to mistake made during trial that is found by an appellate court not to affect substantial rights and therefore does not constitute grounds for reversal.

Hearsay A statement made out-of-court and offered in court as evidence to prove the truth of the assertion made in the statement.

Hearsay Rule A rule excluding hearsay as evidence at trial.

Hearsay Within Hearsay Multiple hearsay; where there are two or more parts to a declarant's statement, each must be examined separately to determine if it falls within the hearsay rule or one of its exceptions.

Holder of Privilege A person the law intends a privilege to protect. For example, in the attorney-client privilege, the client is the holder. In the physician-patient privilege, the patient is the holder.

Identification Part of laying a foundation, where a witness testifies that he or she can recognize a piece of evidence and identify it.

Immunity A legal protection from matters testified to at trial. *Transactional* immunity protects the witness from anything testified to regarding the whole transaction; *derivative use* immunity protects from anything being used from the testimony to obtain further evidence.

Impeachment Attacking the credibility of a witness in order to convince the jury that the testimony given is not truthful or that the witness is unreliable.

In Absentia A trial held when defendant is not present.

In Camera   In judge's chambers. Evidence that is viewed *in camera* is examined privately by a judge in chambers.

Inadmissible   Evidence that would not be allowed at trial.

Inference   A deduction of fact that may logically be drawn from another fact.

Interrogatories   A series of written questions, answered under oath, sent to a witness or party by an opposing party, to help facilitate the gathering of information and evidence in preparation for a case.

Judgment   A judicial decision or determination in a civil or criminal case.

Judicial Notice   When a judge recognizes and accepts a certain fact that is commonly known in the community or capable of accurate and ready determination.

Juvenile Adjudication   A final determination in a juvenile delinquency proceeding, similar to a verdict in an adult prosecution.

Lay Witness   An ordinary (non-expert) witness with no special training or expertise in the matter testified about and who is providing testimony from personal knowledge.

Laying a Foundation   Presenting evidence that sets the groundwork for other evidence, authenticating and identifying the evidence.

Leading Question   Question that contains or suggests the answer to a witness.

Learned Treatises   A scholarly publication, report, or periodical.

Legal Capacity   Being legally fit or qualified.

Legal Integrity of Evidence   The principle that evidence must not be tampered with, altered, substituted, or falsified.

Legal Relevance   Premise that, even when relevant, evidence is not admissible if it violates any other evidence rule or law.

Logical Relevance   When evidence tends to prove or disprove a fact in issue.

Make the Record   Making the record means entering something in the transcript or official documents compiled in a trial so that the appellate court will be able to see it in case of an appeal. The "record" consists of all of these documents.

Material   Evidence being offered must have a bearing on or relate to the issue in dispute.

Mediation   A dispute resolution process where a neutral third party attempts to bring about a settlement or compromise between two disputing parties.

Miranda Rule   Landmark U.S. Supreme Court case providing a suspect in a criminal case the right to remain silent during custodial interrogation.

Mistrial   A mistrial can be found by the trial judge when a prejudicial error occurs during trial causing harm that the judge does not believe can be undone without a new trial.

Motion for Directed Verdict   A request to the trial judge by a party to a legal action, asking the judge to direct a verdict for that party because the opposing party failed to meet his or her burden of production.

Motion in Limine   Similar to *motion to exclude*, except that it may be raised either before or during trial.

Motion to Compel   A formal request for a trial judge to order the production of documents or other evidence.

Motion to Exclude   A request made by a party to a legal action asking the judge to prevent certain evidence from being admitted at trial because it violates a law or rule of evidence.

Motion to Strike   An objection to a statement made by a witness with a request to the judge to have the statement stricken from the trial record.

Motion to Suppress   Similar to *motion to exclude*, with its primary use in criminal actions and generally based on constitutional grounds.

No Comment Rule   If a criminal defendant chooses not to testify, the prosecutor cannot mention or make any comment about this refusal.

Nolo Contendere   A plea of "no contest" to a criminal charge. It subjects defendant to the same punishment as pleading guilty, but allows defendant to neither admit or deny the facts alleged.

Nonverbal Conduct   Actions that do not involve speaking or writing.

Object   To challenge evidence or testimony introduced at trial.

Objection   A challenge to the admissibility of evidence, usually done as or just before evidence is offered.

Objection to Form   When an opposing party challenges the form of a question asked of a witness.

Objection to Substance When an opposing party challenges the substantive evidence being offered or the answer being called for in a question to a witness.

Offer of Proof Condition where a party having evidence excluded offers an explanation to the trial judge as to why the evidence is important and admissible.

Onus Probandi Burden of proof.

Opinion Judgment or conclusion made based on impressions, perceptions, or, in the case of experts, special skills and knowledge.

Opinion and Reputation Evidence Evidence used to attack or support a witness's character for truthfulness.

Opinion Testimony When a witness offers judgment or conclusion in the form of his or her view about what certain evidence means.

Out-of-Court Statement A statement made outside of the courtroom and not by the witness while testifying at trial.

Overruled To decide against or disallow. When a judge overrules an objection, the evidence objected to is allowed.

Pardon Official forgiveness or exemption from penalties or punishment of criminal conviction, usually given by a governor or president.

Past Recollection Recorded When a witness is unable to refresh his or her memory by reviewing notes or writing, the witness may not testify, but the document may be read from into evidence.

Personal Knowledge A witness must be able to testify from a firsthand perception of having seen, heard, felt, touched, or smelled something.

Physical Evidence Something that can be tangibly perceived; objects or materials that can be seen, touched, or felt.

Plain Error A mistake that was not properly objected to at trial, but on appeal is found to affect substantial rights in such a fundamental way that it would cause a party to be deprived of a fair trial if not rectified.

Plain Error Doctrine Appellate courts may, of their own motion, notice errors to which no exception has been taken, if the errors are obvious, or if they otherwise seriously affect the fairness, integrity, or public reputation of judicial proceedings.

Plaintiff The party bringing a civil legal action.

Precedent A court decision that serves as a rule of law or standard to be looked at in deciding subsequent cases.

Prejudicial Error A properly objected to mistake made during trial that is found by an appellate court to affect substantial rights constituting grounds for reversal.

Preponderance of Evidence The burden of proof in a civil action. Plaintiff must produce sufficient evidence to persuade the trier of fact that what plaintiff claims is more likely true than not.

Present Memory Refreshed Situation when witness is permitted to refer to his or her writings or notes in order to jog his or her memory.

Present Sense Impression Statement describing or explaining an event or condition made while the declarant was perceiving the event or condition, or immediately thereafter.

Presumption An assumption of fact that the law requires to be made from another fact.

Presumption of Innocence In a criminal case, an accused is presumed innocent until proven guilty.

Pretrial Motion An official request made of the judge prior to a trial, with an opportunity for the opposing party to challenge the request. A pretrial motion usually asks the court to order admission or exclusion of certain evidence.

Privilege A rule of law that allows a witness to refuse to give testimony or allows the holder of the privilege the right to prevent someone else from testifying on the same matter.

Privileged Communication A confidential communication that is in the best interests of society to protect. An evidentiary privilege allows a witness to refuse to give testimony or the right to prevent someone else from testifying on the same matter.

Prima Facie Translates to "at first sight" and means that, at first sight, all of the elements for a particular legal action have been established.

Prior Statement by Witness A statement made by a witness prior to testifying in court.

Probable Cause Standard of proof required for search warrants and arrests in criminal actions. Requires that evidence be considered "more probable than not" in proving what is alleged.

Probative Tends to prove something.

Procedural Law Rules that set forth the legal process and tell us how to enforce the law.

Production of Documents A discovery device requesting certain written records and documentary evidence.

Prosecutor A government attorney who represents society in prosecuting a criminal action.

Public Policy The influence of public opinion in the context of particular times and events on the shaping of laws.

Rape Shield Laws Laws designed to protect the privacy of victims of sexual assaults when they testify in court.

Reasonable Person Test Sufficient admissible evidence must be submitted to allow a reasonable person to find that a fact exists.

Reasonable Suspicion Standard of proof required for a law enforcement officer to stop and question a person, based on the officer's reasonable suspicion that the person has committed a crime, is committing a crime, or is about to commit a crime.

Rebuttable Presumption A presumption that the jury must make unless evidence to the contrary is introduced.

Record Papers, pleadings, complaints, motions, briefs, orders, jury instructions, and the like that go into a lawsuit or court proceeding.

Records of Regularly Conducted Activity Any form of records, documents, or data compilation kept in the course of regularly conducted business activities.

Recross-Examination After redirect examination, another round of witness questioning by the opposing party on matters within the scope of the redirect examination.

Redirect Examination After a witness has been cross-examined by the opposing party, the original party that called the witness to the stand may conduct a reexamination.

Reflective Thought Time taken for careful and considered thinking.

Rehabilitation Restoring the credibility of a witness after his or her credibility has been attacked on the stand.

Relevancy A basic requirement for the admissibility of evidence is that it tends to prove or disprove a fact in issue.

Relevancy Test Test which determines the admissibility of scientific evidence and testing by weighing the probative value and reliability of scientific testing against the test's potential for prejudice.

Relevant Evidence is relevant when it tends to prove or disprove a fact in issue.

Reputation How a person's character is generally viewed or estimated by others in that person's community.

Res Gestae From the Latin, meaning "things done." Looks at a statement made in relation to the surrounding circumstances and the spontaneity involved.

Residual Exception A left-over or catch-all hearsay exception for those out-of-court statements that are not covered by Federal Rules 803 or 804, but are found to have equivalent guarantees of trustworthiness.

Routine Practice A regular course of conduct of a group of persons or an organization in response to repeated specific situations.

Scientific Evidence and Testing Evidence that has a scientific or highly technical basis, which requires an expert witness with specialized knowledge to assist the trier of fact to understand it.

Self-Authenticating When the presenting of a document itself is sufficient to establish authentication, without any need for outside evidence.

Self-Incrimination A privilege based on the Fifth Amendment to the U.S. Constitution, which protects an individual against being compelled in any criminal case to be a witness against herself or testifying to anything that might incriminate her.

Sidebar A conference between the judge and attorneys, usually held in front or to the side of the judge's bench and out of hearing from the jury.

Social Policy The influence of societal norms, values, traditions, and longer-term goals on the shaping of laws.

Specialized Legal Software A computer program specially designed to be used in some aspect of law or legal practice, like the animated presentation of evidence, organizing evidence exhibits, or case management.

Spontaneous An immediate action or reaction without time for reflection.

Spontaneous Declaration Also referred to as an *excited utterance*, a statement relating to a startling event or condition made while the declarant was under the stress of excitement caused by the event or condition.

Standard of Probability Evidence is relevant if what it tends to show would be more probable than it would be without the evidence.

Star Chamber An English court that conducted trials in secret during the 15th–17th century, employing harsh and brutal methods to force testimony and confessions from witnesses.

Stare Decisis "Let the decision stand." A legal doctrine holding that a court should apply a principle which has already been decided to all later cases with similar facts.

State of Mind Any range of thoughts, emotions, motives, or mental condition underlying a statement made.

Statement Oral or written assertion, or non-verbal conduct of a person if it is intended by the person as an assertion.

Statement under Belief of Impending Death Generally referred to as a *dying declaration*—a statement by a person who believes that her death is imminent.

Statutory Law Laws passed by legislature.

Stipulation An agreement between parties to a legal action, where one party admits to or agrees not to contest the offering of a certain fact, relieving the other party from the burden of proving it.

Subpoena Duces Tecum An order of a court, at the request of a party to a legal action, requiring another party to produce certain documents or records.

Subsequent Remedial Measures Measures taken after an event to repair or ensure that an unsafe condition does not happen again.

Substantive Law Defines the law, providing elements and sanctions.

Sustained To decide for or affirm. When a judge sustains an objection, the evidence objected to is excluded.

Syllabus A summary of a court's opinion, which covers each primary point of law decided.

Testimonial Evidence Oral or "spoken" evidence presented by witnesses who come into court to give their testimony under oath.

Testimonial Privilege Type of marital privilege that prohibits one spouse from testifying against another in a criminal case where the other spouse is the defendant.

Timely and Specific An objection must be made prior to or when the challenged evidence is being offered. It must be specific as to the form and grounds for the objection.

Transcript Formal record, taken by a court reporter, of what is said and done at trial, including any "on-the-record" conversations or offers of proof.

Trial by Battle Legal disputes resolved through a contest or fight between the opposing parties. The victor won the case.

Trial by Ordeal Earliest known form of trial, where defendant was cast into a holy river while tied down by rocks. Sinking usually meant guilt. Other variations of ordeal included being boiled in oil or burned at the stake.

Truth of Matter Asserted Proving what was said is true.

Ultimate Issue The reason for or element of a legal action, usually pertaining to the guilt of a criminal action defendant or liability of a civil action defendant.

Uniform Rules of Evidence Evidence code modeled after the Federal Rules and published by the National Conference of Commissioners on Uniform State Laws.

Voucher Rule Old common law rule that the party calling a witness "vouched" for that witness's credibility. Replaced in most states by a modern rule that allows the credibility of a witness to be attacked by any party.

Wager of Law When witness or one submitting proof of a matter takes an oath pledging its truth.

Waiver A voluntary relinquishment of a right or privilege.

Waiver by Wrongdoing A hearsay exception that admits an out-of-court statement against a party who engaged in wrongdoing intended to keep the declarant from testifying.

Witness A person who testifies at trial, generally from firsthand knowledge about a fact at issue.

Witness Bias Prejudice, special interest, or some motive that may influence a witness's testimony.

Work Products Materials prepared by attorneys in anticipation of trial or litigation.

Writ Written order by a court, instructing someone to either do or cease doing something.

Writ of Habeas Corpus Meaning, "You have the body," this writ is used to order a person detaining another to produce the person detained and explain why that person is being detained.

Writ of Novel Disseisin Administrative order issued by a king to dispossess a subject of property or to settle a dispute over land and taxes.

INDEX